Romantic Women Poets

$\mathcal{B}$LACKWELL $\mathcal{A}$NTHOLOGIES

Editorial Advisers

Blackwell Anthologies are a series of extensive and comprehensive volumes designed to address the numerous issues raised by recent debates regarding the literary canon, value, text, context, gender, genre and period. While providing the reader with key canonical writings in their entirety, the series is also ambitious in its coverage of hitherto marginalized texts, and flexible in the overall variety of its approaches to periods and movements. Each volume has been thoroughly researched to meet the current needs of teachers and students.

ROMANTIC WOMEN POETS

AN ANTHOLOGY

EDITED BY **DUNCAN WU**

BLACKWELL
Publishers

Copyright © Blackwell Publishers Ltd, 1997
Introduction, selection, apparatus and arrangement copyright © Duncan Wu, 1998

First published 1997

2 4 6 8 10 9 7 5 3 1

Blackwell Publishers Ltd
108 Cowley Road
Oxford OX4 1JF
UK

Blackwell Publishers Inc.
350 Main Street
Malden, Massachusetts 02148
USA

British Library Cataloguing in Publication Data
A CIP catalogue record for this book is available from the British Library.

Library of Congress Cataloging-in-Publication Data

ISBN 0–631–20329–X (hbk.); ISBN 0–631–20330–3 (pbk.)

Typeset in $9\frac{1}{2}$ on 11 pt M Garamond
by Graphicraft Typesetters Ltd., Hong Kong
Printed in Great Britain by T.J. International, Cornwall.

This book is printed on acid-free paper

Contents

Selected Contents by Subject

Alphabetical List of Authors

Introduction

I

Writing to John Murray, publisher of the *Quarterly Review*, in February 1818, Byron teased him for the vicious notice of Sydney Owenson, Lady Morgan's *France* by that doberman of reviewers, John Wilson Croker: 'what cruel work you make with Lady Morgan – you should recollect that she is a woman – though to be sure they are now and then very provoking – still as authoresses they can do no great harm'.[1] It would be hard to invent a remark that encapsulates so succinctly the condescension by which the attitude of male romantics to their female contemporaries is characterized. And yet in this case Byron is sticking up for a woman writer against one of the most notoriously bad reviews of the period. With the exception of Felicia Hemans, Croker seems to have nursed a grudge against every woman whose work he covered; his attack on Anna Laetitia Barbauld's *Eighteen Hundred and Eleven* had effectively put an end to her career in 1812, even discouraging her from a long-meditated collected works, and the essay on *France* was intended to have the same effect on Morgan. Her biographer wrote that it was 'almost proverbial for its virulence and bitterness',[2] and even today it retains its power to shock. Croker assembled his arguments under the headings of 'bad taste – bombast and nonsense – blunders – ignorance of the French language and manners – general ignorance – Jacobinism – falsehood – licentiousness and impiety'.[3] What follows is a catalogue of insult and misrepresentation – not least, under 'general ignorance', the accusation that Lady Morgan 'is more ignorant than a boarding-school girl'.[4]

But the truth is that Croker's animus is roused only indirectly by Owenson's sex; her crime was to profess support for Irish nationalism and French Jacobinism. To declare such affiliations was bad enough; the fact that she was a woman compounded the impropriety. Throughout the period covered by this volume, the whiff of disrepute enveloped political writing by female authors. The critical demolition of Mary Wollstonecraft

---

[1] Marchand vi 12–13.
[2] *Sydney Owenson, Lady Morgan's Memoirs: Autobiography, Diaries and Correspondence* (2 vols, London, 1862), i 57.
[3] *Quarterly Review* 17 (April 1817) 260–86, p. 264.
[4] Ibid., p. 267.

both before and after her death stood as an example to any woman rash enough to follow in her footsteps.[5] It would always be safer to deal only obliquely with political matters, and in a way that left conservatives unthreatened, as Felicia Hemans managed to do – though, even then, she was criticized for her Welsh nationalism. In short, reviewers of the day had distinct expectations and aesthetic standards when assessing the work of women.

This was not quite as gratuitous as it may sound; it would not be hard to argue that they were a special case. For one thing, Wollstonecraft was right about the inadequacy of formal education for girls, and the literature of the eighteenth, and early nineteenth centuries is littered with the testimonies of those who suffered the consequences. Writing to Gilbert Burnet in 1710, Lady Mary Wortley Montagu complained that 'We are permitted no books but such as tend to the weakening and effeminating [of] the mind, our natural defects are every way indulged, and tis looked upon as in a degree criminal to improve our reason, or fancy we have any. We are taught to place all our art in adorning our outward forms, and permitted, without reproach, to carry that custom even to extravagancy, while our minds are entirely neglected, and by disuse of reflections, filled with nothing but the trifling objects our eyes are daily entertained with.'[6] Over a decade later, in his A Letter to a Young Lady (1723), Swift commented that 'It is a little hard that not one gentleman's daughter in a thousand should be brought to read, or understand her own natural tongue, or be judge of the easiest books that are written in it; as anyone may find, who can have the patience to hear them, when they are disposed to mangle a play or novel, where the least word out of the common road is sure to disconcert them; and it is no wonder, when they are not so much as taught to spell in their childhood, nor can ever attain to it in their whole lives.'[7] Swift and Montagu, it should be remembered, were of the progressive class; women in the lower orders found it harder still to get educated, and most received no schooling at all. None of those in this volume received anything like the education enjoyed by Byron at Harrow or Shelley at Eton. Susanna Blamire was fortunate indeed in attending her village school, Sydney Owenson in being taught by Madame Terson at Clontarf, and Mary Robinson in being a pupil at the Chelsea academy of the alcoholic Meribah Lorington. They were in a minority: most of the writers here were taught at home by unusually enlightened mothers. Theodosia Tighe, Elizabeth Batten, Catherine Grant, Felicity Hemans, Amelia Alderson: these are the women whose work this volume commemorates, for had they not educated their daughters, the likelihood is that none of their daughters' poetry could have been written. At the extreme end of the scale, the orphaned Isabella Lickbarrow was an autodidact; the preface to her final volume announces that she was 'indebted to herself only, for what little knowledge she may possess'. It is scant consolation to discover that, by the 1820s, opinions had begun to shift, such that one reviewer of Felicia Hemans's The Siege of Valencia (1823) could begin with a variation on the ubi sunt: 'Formerly there were two styles of female education,

---

5   To take just one example, the reviewer of Godwin's Memoirs of Mary Wollstonecraft (1798) in the European Magazine commented: 'It will be read with disgust by every female who has any pretensions to delicacy; with detestation by everyone attached to the interests of religion and morality; and with indignation by anyone who might feel any regard for the unhappy woman whose frailties should have been buried in oblivion. Licentious as the times are, we trust it will obtain no imitators of the heroine in this country' (European Magazine 33 (1798) 246–51, p. 251).
6   The Complete Letters of Lady Mary Wortley Montagu ed. Robert Halsband (3 vols, Oxford, 1965), i 44–5.
7   Jonathan Swift, Irish Tracts 1720–1723 and Sermons ed. Louis Landa (Oxford, 1948), pp. 91–2.

and consequently two styles of women; the really learned, and the really simple; the first nurtured in classic lore and disciplined in scholastic exercises; the second taught to sow neatly and read the English Bible distinctly; the one skilful in drawing conclusions, the other in drawing pancakes.'[8] The reviewer's sympathies did not lie with those fortunate enough to have escaped this pedagogical apartheid – a development he blames on the bluestockings: 'a bluestocking is the most odious character in society; nature, sense, and hilarity fly at her approach; affectation, absurdity, and peevishness follow in her train; she sinks, wherever she is placed, like the yolk of an egg, to the bottom, and carries the filth and the lees with her.'[9]

No doubt such commentators were in the minority, but they serve to underline how threatening the very existence of women writers must have seemed to those who preferred to think of them making pancakes than composing octosyllabics on the French Revolution. By the time Princess Victoria became Queen, in 1837, women writers were so numerous and popular that one observer could remark: 'There have been as famous statesmen, warriors, philosophers, poets, painters, in other times as there are now; but never were the beauty and power of feminine intellect felt as they are at present.'[10] For the likes of Felicia Hemans and Letitia Landon, this was both liberating and imprisoning. It was, no doubt, a relief not to have to assume the freakish status accorded Phillis Wheatley and Ann Yearsley in the late 1700s, but acceptance into the literary market-place all too often meant brutal exploitation, low rates of pay, endless working hours, over-production, and artistic bankruptcy. In Hemans's case the pressure led to premature death at the age of forty-two. By the early nineteenth century, publishing had become a highly lucrative business; technological developments had enabled books and periodicals to be cheaply produced, literacy was more widespread than ever, and such fads as the gothic had led to an increasing sensationalization of subject-matter (it can be no coincidence that at least three of the writers in this volume were best known as novelists – Ann Radcliffe, Charlotte Dacre, and Sydney Owenson). And there was one other factor – a growing constituency of reader who, thanks to the spread of education and the growth of circulating libraries,[11] was making their demands known to publishers: women. Thus, from being a distinct oddity in the 1770s, such that Hannah More had needed a letter of recommendation, in the form of a rave review, from a senior male author, John Langhorne, to admit her to the select, and predominantly male, fraternity of publishing authors, women had by 1837 become integral to the prosperity of the publishing industry, both as supplier and consumer.

Even so, such poets as Hemans and Landon remained subject to critical judgements determined to some extent by extra-literary factors. Prejudices about the inherent attributes of the feminine, though blown apart by the incendiary rhetoric and vigour of Wollstonecraft's *Vindication of the Rights of Woman*, continued to circulate for 150 years, generating rigid expectations of what women ought to write. Novels were their ideal province, it was believed, because fiction was thought to entail none of the skills demanded for poetry – metrical competence, the ability to rhyme, and so forth. And when women did compose poetry, they were expected to stick to subjects that left conventional notions of femininity unchallenged – love poetry, paraphrases of the Scriptures, hymns, didactic blank verse treatises, pastorals, and odes to personified virtues. In other

---

[8] *British Critic* 20 (1823) 50–61, pp. 50–1.
[9] Ibid., p. 51.
[10] *Literary Gazette* 485 (6 May 1826) 275–6, p. 275.

[11] By 1821 there were 6,500 libraries in England, serving more than 30,000 families.

words, readers of the period had a gender-specific view of women's writing which was a crucial determinant of critical response; take, for instance, Francis Jeffrey's 1829 review of Hemans's *Records of Woman* and *The Forest Sanctuary*:

> Women, we fear, cannot do everything; nor even everything they attempt. But what they can do, they do, for the most part, excellently – and much more frequently with an absolute and perfect success, than the aspirants of our rougher and more ambitious sex. They cannot, we think, represent naturally the fierce and sullen passions of men – nor their coarser vices – nor even scenes of actual business or contention – and the mixed motives, and strong and faulty characters, by which affairs of moment are usually conducted in the great theatre of the world. For much of this they are disqualified by the delicacy of their training and habits, and the still more disabling delicacy which pervades their conceptions and feelings; and from much they are excluded by their actual inexperience of the realities they might wish to describe – by their substantial and incurable ignorance of business – of the way in which serious affairs are actually managed – and the true nature of the agents and impulses that give movement and direction to the stronger currents of ordinary life.[12]

You have to remind yourself that there's nothing hostile about this. Hemans was friendly with its author, and he goes on to portray her as an exemplar of the woman writer. But it would be hard to concoct a statement more insensitive to Hemans's artistic project. Bar *The Switzer's Wife*, all the heroines of *Records of Woman* are in states of extreme emotional anguish, and each poem concludes with the death of either her or her lover. In fact, 'the true nature of the agents and impulses that give movement and direction to the stronger currents of ordinary life' accurately describes one of the central preoccupations of Hemans's volume. But Jeffrey can justify Hemans only as a *female* writer, and in order to do this he has no choice but to ignore the controlling logic of the volume, commending it as 'infinitely sweet, elegant, and tender'.[13] It was when women openly flouted these gender-driven expectations that they landed themselves in hot water. By the time it became generally known that Helen Maria Williams was living with the divorced John Hurford Stone, her radicalism had removed her beyond the pale of literary London; for her Jacobinism, as much as anything else, she was to remain an exile in that well-known den of iniquity, Paris, for the rest of her life. And to the best of my knowledge, no reviewer ever faced up to Owenson's Irish republicanism. There are exceptions, as in the case of Mary Scott, whose feminist *The Female Advocate* attracted surprisingly favourable notices, but these are few and far between. More typically, reviewers such as John Wilson Croker condemned such works as Anna Laetitia Barbauld's *Eighteen Hundred and Eleven* not just because their radical sentiments were unacceptable, but because it was mildly indecent that a woman should express them at all; political satire is simply not a feminine mode, he argues, trotting out the injunction that women should stick to writing childrens' books, hymns, and the like:

> Mrs Barbauld's former works have been of some utility; her *Lessons for Children*, her *Hymns in Prose*, her *Selections from the Spectator*, *et id genus omne*, though they display not much of either taste or talents, are yet something better than harmless: but

---

[12] *Edinburgh Review* 50 (1829) 32–47, p. 32.　　[13] Ibid., p. 34.

we must take the liberty of warning her to desist from satire, which indeed is satire on herself alone; and of entreating, with great earnestness, that she will not, for the sake of this ungrateful generation, put herself to the trouble of writing any more party pamphlets in verse.[14]

Keats was the poet commonly thought to have been killed by a review (another of Croker's, as it happens[15]) – a myth propagated by Shelley for his own purposes;[16] in fact, the poet Croker really dispatched was Barbauld, and her fate remains one of the tragedies of romantic literature.[17] It might be argued that she should have been more resilient, like Lady Morgan, but Lucy Aikin's comments suggest that friends and family may have helped bring about her retirement from the fray: 'Who indeed, that knew and loved her, could have wished her to expose again that honoured head to the scorns of the unmanly, the malignant, and the base?'[18]

The silencing of Barbauld tells us a good deal more than that certain male reviewers of the time sharpened their axes when they saw a new poem by a female writer. It may seem odd to regard Croker as a proto-feminist – but that, at least in theoretical terms, is what he was. In applying the argument that, as a woman, Barbauld was best equipped to write about 'female' subjects, he took precisely the same line as some modern-day gender critics. Anne K. Mellor for one argues that it is possible to distinguish male and female romanticisms, the former epitomized by the sublime excursions of Wordsworth, the latter associated with reason, practicality, and such concepts as duty and domestic affection; as she puts it, 'the tension created by gender difference remains central to the structure, the content and the production of Romantic literary texts'.[19] In both cases the argument is for a kind of separatism based on the idea that literature is qualified by gender. Mellor's most important 'female romantic' is probably Felicia Hemans, whom she portrays in terms of a 'domestic ideology'[20] – a concept that cannot accommodate such important aspects of her poetic identity as her Welsh nationalism and serious interest in world history.

Contemporary reviewers had exactly the same trouble: one critic of Hemans's *Siege of Valencia* – a war poem, no less – wrote that its author 'is especially excellent in painting the strength and the weaknesses of her own lovely sex, and there is a womanly nature throughout all her thoughts and her aspirations, which is new and inexpressibly touching. A mother *only* could have poured forth the deep and passionate strain of eloquence which follows.'[21] The modern line, articulated by Mellor, is remarkably similar; she says that Hemans 'constructed her self and poetry as the icon of female domesticity, the embodiment of the "cult of true womanhood"'.[22] Only the jargon has changed; the substance remains the same. It is a line that both relegates the feminine to a second division category (*à la* Croker), and distorts our understanding of what women writers were trying to achieve.

Part of the problem is that romanticism itself is something of a red herring, and in recent years has been more elusive than ever. No longer sought after, it is positively

---

[14] *Quarterly Review* 7 (1812) 309–13, p. 313.

[15] *Quarterly Review* 19 (1818) 204–8.

[16] See James A. W. Heffernan, '*Adonais*: Shelley's Consumption of Keats', *Romanticism: A Critical Reader* 173–91.

[17] See, among other sources, William Keach, 'A Regency Prophecy and the End of Anna Barbauld's Career', *SIR* 33 (1994) 569–77.

[18] *The Works of Anna Laetitia Barbauld. With a Memoir by Lucy Aikin* (2 vols, 1825), i. lii.

[19] *Romanticism and Gender* (London 1993), p. 209.

[20] Ibid., pp. 123–43.

[21] *British Critic* 20 (1823) 50–61, p. 52.

[22] *Romanticism and Gender* (1993), p. 123.

shunned; all the certainties of the last decades are gone, and the very act of problematizing it comprises the big critical project of the 1990s. Such widespread agnosticism bespeaks an anxiety, to which the concept of the 'long eighteenth century' – the fatuous idea that the romantic period is a logical extension of the preceding century – is no more than a panacea. The fact is that literature does not evolve in straight lines. It does not exist even as a single entity, and to talk of 'discursive formations' universally recognized by all writers at any given historical moment is to devise fictions just as likely to self-deconstruct as those it is meant to replace.[23] No doubt the romantic movement *per se* was never much of a reality, but I wonder in what sense it might have been. Who would talk of British poets today as constituting a single movement? It would be inadvisable, to say the least, but it might be argued that most are aware of the work of their contemporaries, and that they regard themselves as part of a community. There is a good deal of evidence to indicate that most of the women in this book saw themselves in much the same way – as participants in a shared culture. They composed poems about their sister poets and artists, and identified, at some point or other, with certain common aims. One thinks of Seward's injunctions against the Jacobinism of Williams and Smith; More's patronage of Yearsley; Wollstonecraft's promotion of Ann Batten Cristall. Barbauld, in particular, exemplifies the life of a woman of letters; she was at the centre of literary life in London and the provinces for many years, wrote and edited prolifically, and was one of the main poetry reviewers for the *Monthly Review*. She is also one of those whose career spans almost the entirety of this volume; originally a bluestocking, she encouraged Isabella Lickbarrow (whom she reviewed in the *Monthly*), and may have helped promote Ann Batten Cristall (to whose *Poetical Sketches* she subscribed). Like Charlotte Smith and Helen Maria Williams, she was an early and potent influence on others. Wordsworth and Coleridge were fervent admirers of all three at school and university: it was they whom Wordsworth sought out when first he visited London, Brighton, and Paris, and it was to Barbauld (and Georgiana Cavendish, Duchess of Devonshire) that he and Coleridge sent a first edition of *Lyrical Ballads* (1800).

Contact was not purely literary: Georgiana Cavendish helped bring up Lady Caroline Lamb; Lamb and Cavendish were friends of Sydney Owenson;[24] and Owenson was a friend of Mary Tighe, whose work she read in manuscript. They moved in a shared world, read each others' work, and often alluded to it. None of this took place, it should be emphasized, in isolation from male writers. Joanna Baillie and Felicia Hemans were both admirers of Wordsworth, and met the poet at various times. And it's impossible to read Letitia Landon without hearing the tones and rhythms of Scott and Byron in the background. But the influence was not all one way. Felicia Hemans was described as a 'tyger' by the young Shelley, on the basis of her 1808 *Poems* and an account of a meeting with Medwin;[25] Tighe exerted a strong and formative influence on Keats; Charlotte Dacre's *Zofloya* set the tone for Shelley's *Zastrozzi*. No one failed to read Ann Radcliffe. In short, the community of contributors to literary life during the romantic period is comprised of distinguished female, as well as male, writers. The point is not whether this amounted to a movement (it didn't), but that the richness of that fifty-year mini-renaissance reflected a vitality to which writers of both sexes contributed. Against

---

[23] Such is the central strategy of Robert J. Griffin, *Wordsworth's Pope: A Study of Literary Historiography* (Cambridge, 1995).

[24] 'The Duchess of Devonshire is unceasing in her attentions to me; not only is her house open to us,

but she calls and takes me out to show me what is best to be seen', *Sydney Owenson, Lady Morgan's Memoirs: Autobiography, Diaries and Correspondence*, ii 128–9.

[25] See p. 489, below.

any doubt as to that period of reinvigoration, we should remind ourselves that, had it not existed, Jeffrey might not have ranted against the Lake Poets, and Lockhart might been more appreciative of Keats.[26] Nebulous it may be, but that inferred awareness of the new is probably just enough to carry the 'r' word in safety – any more intellectual ballast and it buckles under the strain.

Not, of course, that the romantics might not also be distinguished by their pre-occupations: sensibility, slavery, Jacobinism (for and against), imagination, Sappho, the city, the gothic, the French Revolution, America, and the Lake District all recur through-out this volume (see Selected Contents by Subject). But none were the preserve of 'the feminine'. If, however, as Stuart Curran has argued, women of the time 'tended to see differently from men',[27] it may be that their approach to these subjects was distinctive in some way. This line of thought is developed in Curran's introduction to his admirable edition of Charlotte Smith's poetry, where he argues that Smith's *Beachy Head* volume of 1807, 'with its variety of natural treatments – from the opening meditative reminiscence through fable to allegory to didactive moralism and religious exemplum, all attended by an array of botanical, geological, and ornithological learning – testifies to an alternate Romanticism that seeks not to transcend or to absorb nature but to contemplate and honor its irreducible alterity.'[28] How, in contemplating and honouring the irreducible alterity of the natural world, does Smith's poetry differ from Bloomfield's *The Farmer's Boy* or any number of works by Clare – *The Badger*, say, or *The Shepherd's Calendar*? No one would seek to deny that Smith has a distinctive style and voice, but whether that distinct-iveness is entirely gender-determined is questionable. It is more likely to be the product of a combination of factors of which gender may be one. Artistic process is rarely reducible to single factors.

Perhaps without fully knowing what they do, modern critics play into the hands of those who would like to regard women writers as limited by their sex; in fact, the poetry presented here offers ample proof (were any needed) that the best of them – Hemans, Smith, Barbauld, Williams, Lickbarrow, and Robinson – could write as persuas-ively as their male contemporaries, whether addressing the political situation, evoking the Wordsworthian sublime, or, as they and their male contemporaries sometimes did, discussing filial or parental affection. Reviewers of the day wanted to argue that women wrote only about certain subjects in a certain way, irrespective of the truth; curiously, modern critics make the same case in arguing for their distinctiveness. Either way, it blinds us to the richness and diversity of the literature. This is (though not in so many words) the conclusion of Anna Laetitia Barbauld's most recent editors, William McCarthy and Elizabeth Kraft, who, in their introduction, point out that 'She wrote what might be considered "typical" women's verse – celebrations of domestic life and character, nature poetry, hymns and prayers – but she also wrote biting satire, riddles, odes, and poems in the mock-heroic style. Her sensibility can be called neither masculine nor feminine; they are not categories that enlighten a reading of her verse, which must be taken on its own terms.'[29] These are some of the wisest and (from a critical perspective) liberating comments on any women writer in recent years. If one of the most basic

---

[26] See *Romanticism* 599–601, 1005–8.
[27] 'The I Altered', *Romanticism and Feminism* ed. Anne K. Mellor (Bloomington, 1988), pp. 185–207, p. 195.
[28] *The Poems of Charlotte Smith* ed. Stuart Curran (New York, 1993), pp. xxvii–xxviii.

[29] *The Poems of Anna Laetitia Barbauld* ed. William McCarthy and Elizabeth Kraft (Athens, Georgia, 1994), p. xxiii.

critical reflexes is to categorize, it should be resisted when reading poetry, or words lose their power to surprise.

When I began work on this volume the task I set myself was to reflect, as far as possible, something of how the writers concerned saw themselves. After all is said and done, I would not claim that there were not times when, partly from a certain defensiveness, women writers of the romantic period found solidarity in groups. The most obvious example is that of the bluestockings. But they were never separatist in aim; Johnson, Burke, Reynolds and Walpole were all, at one time or another, part of the circle – and they cannot have been unaware of its empowering effect on their female counterparts. Although initially a social grouping, it espoused what were effectively feminist principles, and functioned partly as the intellectual body – a sort of alternative academe – that More celebrated in *Sensibility* and *Bas Bleu*.[30] It is that assumption of their centrality within the cultural life of society that distinguishes so many of these writers – whether Anna Seward in Lichfield society, Georgiana Cavendish (active in her role as patroness of other women writers), or Mary Robinson, who first found her public through association with the Della Cruscans. It is not, in other words, as 'women writers' that most of these poets saw themselves, but as operators in the cultural mainstream. You have to possess such certainty to declare your inner convictions in the way that Anna Laetitia Barbauld did in *Eighteen Hundred and Eleven*, that Helen Maria Williams, Ann Yearsley and Hannah More did in their 1788 slavery poems, and that Charlotte Smith does in *The Emigrants*. And no doubt it was that confidence that so inflamed male reviewers. Revealingly, when attacking Lady Morgan's *France*, one of Croker's headings was 'ignorance' of her subject – she 'is more ignorant than a boarding-school girl'. Why? Because one of his greatest anxieties was that she might have known more about the subject than he did.[31] And when demolishing Barbauld, it is on the grounds that she is not up to political debate on an intellectual level, and should stick to what she does best: 'her *Lessons for Children*, her *Hymns in Prose*, her *Selections from the Spectator, et id genus omne*'. To accept a gendered view of art is to marginalize yourself, and none of the writers here were prepared to do that. They presumed to comment on politics and morality alongside their male contemporaries in the cockpit of literary and political debate, and were, for that reason, often embattled, reminded at every turn of the prejudices that made their aspirations unacceptable to so many male contemporaries. Who, after all, would want, like Helen Maria Williams and Lady Morgan, to hear the anticipated *tut-tut* of patrician contempt every time they wrote about politics? It would be wrong to argue that such a sense of embattlement *defined* them, but no woman of the time could publish her work without being sensitive to it.

To an extent, therefore, this volume is about a group of writers defined by their resistance to the prescriptions of those who told them what they ought to be writing about, and how they should to go about it. More positively, it is about those in the engine-room of cultural change. Poets like Mary Robinson, Felicia Hemans, and Letitia Landon understood, with the publication of *Lyrical Ballads*, that something new was happening in literature, and sought both to embody and extend that sense of newness.

---

[30] See especially Sylvia Harcstark Myers, *The Bluestocking Circle: Women, Friendship, and the Life of the Mind in Eighteenth-Century England* (Oxford, 1990).
[31] In this respect Byron's graciousness in his views on Lady Morgan's sequel, *Italy*, merits acknowledgement. On 24 August 1821 he told Thomas Moore, a

mutual friend, that 'Her work is fearless and excellent on the subject of Italy – pray tell her so – and I know the country. I wish she had fallen in with *me*, I could have told her a thing or two that would have confirmed her positions' (Marchand viii 189).

And, in their different ways, such writers as Mary Tighe in *Psyche*, Ann Batten Cristall in *Poetical Sketches*, and, less conspicuously, Isabella Lickbarrow in *Poetical Effusions*, created a verse that departed from the post-Popean norm. All were implicated in a change of course detectable throughout the literature of the period; for that reason alone it would be mistaken to detach them from it. In devoting a volume exculsively to them, I am uneasily aware that I may seem to be doing precisely that. But if their work is ever to be valued for its inherent worth as literature, it must be within their own cultural and historical context. They were not a race apart, but participants in the intellectual cut-and-thrust, engaged with the same artistic issues and dilemmas as male contemporaries, and in finding solutions no less artful, unpredictable, and original.

II

It is a misconception to believe that canons do not change, or that the canon of 'romantic' poetry has been revised only in the last decade. In fact, the term is a scriptural one, and refers to the books of the Bible deemed to have been inspired by God; you don't need to be a theologian to be aware that debate on the subject has been raging as long as the Bible itself. The fact is that canons have always been infinitely mutable, shifting, and subject to a perpetual remaking by successive generations. When Wordsworth read *The Floure and the Leafe* in 1805 it was in the belief that it was by Chaucer; that is not the commonly held view today. More strikingly, perhaps, more new Wordsworth poems have been published since 1974 than in the first thirty years of his life. What does this tell us? That the canon does not stop renewing itself just because the author is dead. That the concept of a final or definitive canon is a bogey invoked by those who wish to force the pace of change; it has never been anything but a fiction. In other words, the canon itself is nothing to be afraid of. Its inherent instability is a guarantee of perpetual openness, and that I find not just reassuring, but liberating. Every new edition or anthology is not a threat, but an opportunity for rediscovery. We should be suspicious only when critics argue that it is time the canon was set in concrete.

'Most of the material in this collection has not been reprinted since its original publication and will be unfamiliar to its readers. Without the usual precedents against which the anthologist's judgements and criteria can be tested, one must rely on one's own instinct and interests, which will inevitably mean prejudices and predispositions.'[32] This declaration by Roger Lonsdale in the introduction to his *Eighteenth-Century Women Poets* is about as disarming as you can get, and holds good, I suspect, for most anthologists, whatever their subject. My task throughout this volume has been to reflect, as far as possible, the variety and range of each writer's work at the time it was written. For that reason I have tended to use first editions except in special cases, which are explained in headnotes. The headnotes also provide basic biographical information and accounts of critical reception at the time of publication. It would not be right simply to reproduce the texts with original punctuation. Rules of punctuation varied so widely throughout the period, and are frequently so misleading or incorrect, even by standards of the time, that I have repunctuated throughout, according to the principles explained

---

[32] *Eighteenth-Century Women Poets* ed. Roger Lonsdale (Oxford, 1989), pp. xliii–iv.

below (pp. xxix–xxx). I began the task of anthologizing women romantics in *Romanticism: An Anthology* (Blackwell, 1994), and the present volume represents the logical conclusion to that work. Ideally, I hope that readers will use the two volumes together. For that reason, I have duplicated as little as possible from the earlier book; hence the absence of Dorothy Wordsworth and Elizabeth Barrett, and of Lady Caroline Lamb's *A New Canto*.

Editorial Principles

The following principles are formulated to ensure ease of reading for the modern reader, and are designed to preserve, as far as possible, the form in which each work was first published. The only exceptions to them are foreign language extracts, which are reproduced with the orthography and accidentals of the copy-text.

Capitalization

Late eighteenth- and early nineteenth-century poetry texts often contain more capital letters than would be expected today. They are retained only for evident personifications (as opposed to figurative usages); 'Heaven' is used only when it means 'God' (as opposed to 'sky'). In doubtful or dubious cases I have taken the view that, for the modern reader, capitalization can generate confusion and have preferred to decapitalize.

Orthography

Spellings are modernized throughout except where it materially affects pronunciation; for example, such archaisms as 'ribband' and 'corse', have been allowed to stand, while 'groupe' is emended to 'group', 'shew' to 'show', 'Shakspeare' to 'Shakespeare', 'cloaths' to 'clothes', 'prophane' to 'profane'. 'Tho' and 'thro' have been expanded to 'though' and 'through'. Elisions have been filled in except where they are required by the exigencies of metre; thus, 'fill'd' is emended to 'filled' and 'call'd' to called', but 'ling'ring', 'shelt'ring', and 'th' adjoining' are allowed to stand.

Punctuation

Punctuation in printed texts of the period is generally heavier than modern readers are used to, and is not always accurate. As a rule I have used the published texts as guides, lightening where possible.

Italics

Italics in the copy-text have generally been allowed to stand except where they are either unnecessary or obtrusive, in which case they have been silently eliminated. All italics in literary texts are those of the copy-text except where otherwise stated.

Manuscripts

In the case of manuscripts, the following procedures are followed, with the intention of presenting each draft as it stood on completion: deletions are accepted only when alternative readings are provided; where they are not, the original is retained. Alternative readings are accepted only when the original has been deleted; where they are not, the original is retained. Where the original reading is deleted but legible, and the alternative is either fragmentary, illegible, or inchoate, the original has been retained. I have silently corrected all scribal errors. Ampersands are expanded to 'and' throughout.

Annotation

I have glossed obscure or unusual usages, allusions and echoes, and have on occasion offered paraphrases in the notes of phrases or sentences that seemed to me difficult to construe. I have also supplied points of information, particularly on personages, in-jokes, volumes referred to, and so forth. It is my hope that the level of annotation supplied in headnotes and footnotes will be sufficient to provide most readers with the basic materials required to enjoy the poetry.

Acknowledgements

A volume such as this can be undertaken only with the support of librarians. First and foremost, I must thank the staff of the Bodleian Library, where much of the textual work on this edition was conducted, and in particular the staffs of the Upper and Lower Reading Rooms, who were, as always, unfailingly helpful and good-humoured. I acknowledge also the generous co-operation of Alan Sterenberg and the staff of the British Library; the staff of the Palaeography Room, Senate House, London; and Robert Bertholf and his staff at the Poetry Collection, SUNY at Buffalo.

My labours were mitigated by the kindness of numerous individuals, and it is a pleasure to thank them here. In particular, it was a stroke of good fortune to have coincided at the Bodleian with Antonia Forster, who kindly gave me the run of her forthcoming index of literary reviews 1775–1800, and provided me with many references I would not otherwise have found. For points of information, translations of foreign language texts, and help of various kinds, I thank Mary Wedd, Stephen Johnson, David Fairer, Susan Wolfson, Massimiliano Demata, David Chandler, Stuart Curran, Adriana Craciun, Janice Patten, Barry Juniper, Richard Parish, J. B. McLaughlin, Colin Thompson, Peter Dickson, L. G. Mitchell, Douglas Gifford, Dorothy A. Porter Macmillan, Donald Mackenzie, my typists – Abby Bidwell and Pat Wallace – and Constance Parrish.

I am grateful to the Master and Fellows of St Catherine's College, Oxford, who kindly elected me to a Visiting Fellowship that made work on this volume much less arduous than it would otherwise have been. My greatest debt must be to my colleagues at the University of Glasgow for granting me the study leave without which this book could not have been written, and particularly to Pat Reilly and Richard Cronin who as Heads of Department sanctioned it. I thank them all for tolerating my absence from the Department of English Literature with good grace.

I hope this volume will stand in some measure as a tribute to those editors and bibliographers who have preceded me, and from whose labours I have greatly benefitted, notably J. R. de J. Jackson, Roger Lonsdale, Jennifer Breen, Andrew Ashfield, Jonathan Wordsworth, Stuart Curran, Jerome J. McGann, William McCarthy and Elizabeth Kraft.

As always, Andrew McNeillie, my editor at Blackwell, has aided and abetted my research in ways too numerous fully to acknowledge here. I am grateful to him for continuing encouragement.

Glasgow, 1996

Manuscripts

For permission to edit from manuscripts in their possession I wish to thank the Bodleian Library, Paul F. Betz and the Librarian, SUNY at Buffalo.

Anna Seward, *Sonnet written from an Eastern Apartment in the Bishop's Palace at Lichfield, which commands a view of Stowe Valley. April 1771*: Bodleian MS. Pigott d. 12, a twelve-leaf MS entitled 'Unpublished Verses Written by Anna Seward'. It is not in Seward's hand, and may date from as late as 1800. Most of its contents, which include *Eyam* and *To Time Past*, were published.

Susanna Blamire, *A North Country Village*: Fair copy MS notebook, in Blamire's hand, with some corrections and notes in another hand (some initialled P.M.). In the possession of Paul F. Betz.

Lady Caroline Lamb, *By those eyes where sweet expression*: Fair copy MS, in Lamb's hand, consisting of a single sheet of paper. Goodyear Collection, SUNY at Buffalo, NY.

Felicia Dorothea Hemans, *The Spirit's Mysteries*: fair copy MS in Hemans's hand, single sheet folded in two. British Library Add MS 36,747.

Abbreviations

British Literature 1640–1789	*British Literature 1640–1789: An Anthology* ed. Robert DeMaria Jr (Oxford, 1996)
EHC	*The Poetical Works of Samuel Taylor Coleridge* ed. E. H. Coleridge (2 vols, Oxford, 1912)
ERR	*European Romantic Review*
Griggs	*The Collected Letters of Samuel Taylor Coleridge* ed. E. L. Griggs (6 vols, Oxford, 1956–71)
HLQ	*Huntington Library Quarterly*
Jackson	J. R. de J. Jackson, *Romantic Poetry by Women: A Bibliography 1770–1835* (Oxford, 1993)
Limits	*At the Limits of Romanticism* ed. Mary A. Favret and Nicola J. Watson (Bloomington, 1994)
Marchand	*Byron's Letters and Journals* ed. Leslie A. Marchand (12 vols, London, 1973–82)
MLQ	*Modern Language Quarterly*
Observations on the Lakes	William Gilpin, *Observations relative chiefly to Picturesque Beauty . . . in several parts of England; particularly the Mountains and Lakes of Cumberland and Westmorland* (2 vols, London, 1786)
Ovid, *Epistles*	*The Epistles of Ovid translated into English Prose* (1746)
PBSA	*Papers of the Bibliographical Society of America*
Romanticism	*Romanticism: An Anthology* ed. Duncan Wu (Oxford, 1994)
Romanticism: A Critical Reader	*Romanticism: A Critical Reader* ed. Duncan Wu (Oxford, 1995)
RR	*Re-Visioning Romanticism: British Women Writers, 1776–1837* ed. Carol Shiner Wilson and Joel Haefner (Philadelphia, 1994)
RWW	*Romantic Women Writers: Voices and Countervoices* ed. Paula R. Feldman and Theresa M. Kelley (Hanover, NH, 1995)
SIR	*Studies in Romanticism*
TWC	*The Wordsworth Circle*

Ann Yearsley (1756–1806) by Joseph Grozer after S. Sheills. Reproduced by courtesy of the National Portrait Gallery, London.

Anna Seward (1742–1809)

She was born in Eyam, Derbyshire, the daughter of Thomas Seward and Elizabeth Hunter, of Lichfield. Her father was headmaster of Lichfield Grammar School, and had taught Samuel Johnson. Under his tutelage she was reading Milton at two, and composing religious verse by the age of ten. An accident lamed her in childhood. In 1750 her father became Canon of Lichfield Cathedral, and from 1754 the family resided in the Bishop's Palace. Partly, no doubt, because her brother and two sisters died in infancy, Anna enjoyed an intensely close relationship with Honora Sneyd, adopted by the Sewards as a child; Honora's marriage to Richard Lovell Edgeworth in 1773 caused her profound unhappiness, and their affection is the subject of some of her finest verse.

Her literary reputation was established with the *Elegy on Captain Cook* (1780), which had entered its fourth edition by 1784. The hanging of Major André, a suitor of Honora Sneyd, in the American War, provided the occasion for her *Monody on Major André* (1781), a success both at home and in America. And her popularity was consolidated by *Poem to the Memory of Lady Miller* (1782) and *Louisa, a Poetical Novel, in Four Epistles* (1784). She was an habituée of literary circles, contributing to literary journals, most notably when she wrote a series of letters signed 'Benvolio' to the *Gentleman's Magazine* in 1786, intended to puncture what she regarded as Johnson's inflated posthumous reputation.

Unlike many other women writers of the time, she enjoyed financial security. After her father's death in 1790 she lived comfortably on £400 per annum. She supported the French Revolution at its outset, and her 'Sonnet to France on her present Exertions', published in the *Gentleman's Magazine*, makes no secret of her belief that, even if violence was necessary, it was a price worth paying for liberty. However, she later changed her mind, and admonished her former friend Helen Maria Williams for continuing radicalism (see p. 235, below).

The 'swan of Lichfield' was a formidable critic of other writers; besides Johnson, she criticized Hannah More and Charlotte Smith, and made clear her disdain for supporters of the French Revolution. Another sonnet in the *Gentleman's Magazine*, 'Advice to Mrs Smith', underlines her sense of importance as a judge of others' poetry. The third edition of Smith's *Elegiac Sonnets* had just been published to considerable acclaim, but Seward was convinced that the translations from Petrarch and particularly Goethe were morally degenerate in the 'Deceitful lustre' they bestowed on the subject of suicide. These are, in fact, some of the best sonnets in the volume, and Smith was wise to ignore Seward's advice (see pp. 81–3). By the time of her death, her own verse was attracting much criticism for its affected manner. Her executor, Walter Scott, edited her *Poetical Works* in three volumes after her death, but stayed clear of her *Letters* (6 vols, 1811), which had been substantially revised for print.

Her visit to Lady Eleanor Butler and Sarah Ponsonby, the Ladies of Llangollen, was the occasion for the title poem in *Llangollen Vale, with Other Poems* (1796). The volume was generally well received, most notably in the *Analytical Review*, which began: 'The public is no stranger to the enchanting power of Miss S's muse, and will not be displeased to be informed that she has resumed her lyre, and touches its strings with increasing strength and sweetness'.[1] 'To Time Past' is regarded so highly as to merit its being reprinted in full. Likewise, the *Critical Review* compliments the volume, observing that

---

[1] *Analytical Review* 23 (1796) 386–90, p. 386.

Seward 'ranks amongst the best poets of the present day'.[2] There were dissenters, however; a number of critics voiced anxiety about Seward's stilted diction. The *British Critic* observed that in the title poem 'there is sometimes a want of perspicuity, sometimes of sense, and more than one mark of affectation'.[3] And the *Monthly Review* commented:

> The name prefixed to this small assemblage of poems will be a sufficient warrant, with the lover of productions of this class, to expect the gratification resulting from elegant description, refined sentiment, copious imagery, and harmonious versification. If this copiousness and refinement have on some occasions run out into prolixity, and the perpetual study of uncommon and poetical expression have sometimes led to affectation and obscurity, these blemishes will not call forth severe criticism from one whose mind is more sensible to beauties than defects.[4]

These points are delivered with considerable tact, and are entirely justified. Nonetheless, they seem to have incensed Seward, who arranged for her cousin, Henry White, to write a letter to the *Gentleman's Magazine* in her defence, providing numerous examples from other writers of the words and constructions to which the reviewers had taken exception. This drew forth a riposte from one Stephen Brown, in the following issue, arguing that the reviews had been mild and inoffensive in their comments; he added, in a state of obvious exasperation: 'What a dickens! Cannot these fine lady-writers be satisfied with moderate praise? Must it be heaped up, and flowing over?'[5]

The selections here from *Llangollen Vale* show Seward at her best. 'To Time Past', composed in 1772, is one of her finest love poems to Honora Sneyd. Written in anticipation of Honora's impending marriage to Edgeworth, it brings Anna's anxiety at what the future may hold for herself into painfully sharp focus; besides an intense feeling of loss, she foresees not 'jocund spring', but the bare bleak fields of winter. Perhaps because *Eyam* is a poem about memory, it reminds us of *The Prelude*; like that work, it is confessional, and attempts to describe the emotional attachments of places the poet used to know. The result is an intensely personal work, and one that deals with a Wordsworthian topic in a distinctive, and yet quite un-Wordsworthian manner.

Further Reading

Margaret Eliza Ashmun, *The Singing Swan* (London, 1931)

G. S. Rousseau, 'Anna Seward to William Hayley: A Letter from the Swan of Lichfield', *Harvard Library Bulletin* 15 (1967) 273–80

J. P. F., 'Anna Seward and William Hayley: The Beginning of a Literary Friendship', *Bodleian Library Record* 9 (1977) 304–5

Daniel Robinson, 'Reviving the Sonnet: Women Romantic Poets and the Sonnet Claim', *ERR* 6 (1995) 98–127

---

[2]   *Critical Review* 17 (1796) 154–8, p. 155.
[3]   *British Critic* 7 (1796) 404–7, p. 405.
[4]   *Monthly Review* 20 (1796) 151–4, pp. 151–2.
[5]   See *Gentleman's Magazine* 66 (1796) 556–9, 633–4.

SONNET WRITTEN FROM AN EASTERN APARTMENT IN THE BISHOP'S PALACE
AT LICHFIELD, WHICH COMMANDS A VIEW OF STOWE VALLEY. APRIL 1771
(EDITED FROM MS)[1]

In this chill morning of a wintry spring
I look into the gloomed and rainy vale;
The sullen clouds, the whistling winds assail,
Lour on the fields, and with their ruffling wing
Disturb the lake. But love and memory cling   5
To their *known* scene in this cold influence pale;
Yet *prized*, as when it bloomed in summer's gale,
Tinged by his setting sun. And thus, when fling
The powers of sickness o'er some beauteous form
Their shadowy languors (form devoutly dear   10
As thine to me, Honora[2]), with more warm
And anxious gaze the eyes of Love sincere
Bend on the charms, dim in their tintless snow,
Than when with health's purpureal[3] grace they glow.

From Llangollen Vale, with Other Poems (1796)

TO TIME PAST. WRITTEN DEC. 1772

Return, blessed years, when not the jocund sprng,
Luxuriant summer, nor the amber hours
Calm autumn gives, my heart invoked to bring
Joys whose rich balm o'er all the bosom pours! –
When ne'er I wished might grace the closing day   5
One tint purpureal[1] or one golden ray;
When the loud storms that desolate the bowers
Found dearer welcome than favonian[2] gales,
And winter's bare bleak fields, than summer's flowery vales!

Yet not to deck pale hours with vain parade   10
Beneath the blaze of wide-illumined dome;
Not for the bounding dance; not to pervade
And charm the sense with music; nor, as roam
The mimic passions o'er theatric scene,

SONNET WRITTEN . . . AT LICHFIELD
[1] This sonnet is edited from a twelve-page manuscript in the Bodleian Library entitled 'Unpublished Verses Written by Anna Seward'. It is not in her hand, and may date from around 1800. Seward's own note to the poem runs as follows: 'The energetic spirit of Milton's sonnets, and the majestic grace of their varied pauses undulating through the lines, induced the author of these to adopt their model rather than the more facile measures of the modern sonnet, viz. three stanzas closing with a couplet.'
[2] Honora Sneyd, adopted as a child by Seward's parents, with whom Seward enjoyed a close attachment.
[3] *purpureal* presumably the purple colour that indicates good health.

TO TIME PAST
[1] *purpureal* purple.
[2] *favonian* of the west wind, and therefore favourable, gentle.

To laugh or weep – oh not for these, I ween,   15
But for delights that made the *heart* their home
Was the grey night-frost on the sounding plain
More than the sun invoked, that gilds the grassy lane.
Yes, for the joys that trivial joys excel,
My loved Honora,[3] did we hail the gloom   20
Of dim November's eve; and, as it fell,
And the bright fires shone cheerful round the room,
Dropped the warm curtains with no tardy hand,
And felt our spirits and our hearts expand,
Listening their steps, who still, where'er they come,   25
Make the keen stars that glaze the settled snows,
More than the sun invoked, when first he tints the rose.

Affection, friendship, sympathy – your throne
Is winter's glowing hearth, and ye were ours;
Thy smile, Honora, made them all our own.   30
Where are they *now*? Alas, their choicest powers
Faded at thy retreat, for thou art gone!
And many a dark long eve I sigh alone
In thrilled remembrance of the vanished hours,
When storms were dearer than the balmy gales,   35
And winter's bare bleak fields than green luxuriant vales.

From Gentleman's Magazine 56 (1786) 791

ADVICE TO MRS SMITH. A SONNET.[1]

Muse of the south, whose soul-enchanting shell
With mournful notes can melt the softened heart,
And to each breast of sympathy impart
The tender sorrow thou describ'st so well!
Ah, never let thy lyre superior dwell   5
On themes thy better judgement must disdain!
It ill befits that verse like thine should tell
Of Petrarch's love, or Werther's frantic pain![2]
Let not or foreign taste or tales enchain
The genuine freedom of thy flowing line;   10
Nor the dark dreams of suicide[3] obtain
Deceitful lustre from such tones as thine;

---

[3] Honora Sneyd, adopted as a child by Seward's parents, with whom Seward enjoyed a close attachment. Their separation at this moment was caused by Honora's impending marriage to Richard Lovell Edgeworth in 1773, an event that distressed Seward deeply.
ADVICE TO MRS SMITH
[1] This sonnet is written in response to the third edition of Charlotte Smith's *Elegiac Sonnets* (1786)

(included in its entirety, pp. 72–88, below), and appeared in the *Gentleman's Magazine* for September 1786.
[2] Smith's new edition contained four sonnets adapted from Petrarch, and five from Goethe's *Sorrows of Young Werther*.
[3] Goethe's hero, Werther, commits suicide.

But still, to nature and to virtue given,
Thy heavenly talent dedicate to heaven!

From Llangollen Vale, with Other Poems (1796)

EYAM[1] (COMPOSED AUGUST 1788)

For one short week I leave, with anxious heart,
Source of my filial cares, the FULL OF DAYS,
Lured by the promise of harmonic art
To breathe her Handel's[2] soul-exalting lays.
Pensive I trace the Derwent's amber wave,[3]   5
Foaming through sylvan banks, or view it lave
The soft, romantic vallies, high o'er-peered
By hills and rocks, in savage grandeur reared.
   Not two short miles from thee, can I refrain
Thy haunts, my native Eyam, long unseen?   10
Thou and thy loved inhabitants again
Shall meet my transient gaze. Thy rocky screen,
Thy airy cliffs, I mount, and seek thy shade,
Thy roofs that brow the steep, romantic glade;
But while on me the eyes of Friendship glow,   15
Swell my pained sighs, my tears spontaneous flow.
   In scenes paternal, not beheld through years,
Nor viewed till *now* but by a father's side,
Well might the tender, tributary tears
From keen regrets of duteous fondness glide!   20
Its pastor, to this human flock no more
Shall the long flight of future days restore;
Distant he droops, and that once-gladdening eye
Now languid gleams, e'en when his friends are nigh.[4]
   Through this known walk, where weedy gravel lies,   25
Rough and unsightly, by the long, coarse grass
Of the once smooth and vivid green, with sighs
To the deserted rectory I pass,
Stray through the darkened chamber's naked bound
Where childhood's earliest, liveliest bliss I found: 30
How changed since erst, the lightsome walls beneath,
The social joys did their warm comforts breathe!

EYAM
[1] 'This poem was written in August 1788, on a journey through Derbyshire, to a music meeting at Sheffield. The author's father was Rector of Eyam, an extensive village that runs along a mountainous terrace in one of the highest parts of the Peak. She was born there, and there passed the first seven years of her life, visiting the place often with her father in future periods. The middle part of this village is built on the edge of a deep dell, which has very picturesque and beautiful features' (Seward's note).
[2] Georg Friedrich Handel (1685–1759).
[3] 'From the peculiar nature of the clay on the mountains from which it descends, the River Derwent has a yellow tint, that well becomes the dark foliage on its banks, and the perpetual foam produced by a narrow, and rocky channel' (Seward's note).
[4] Thomas Seward (1708–90) was senile by the time this poem was composed.

Ere yet I go, who may return no more,
That sacred pile, mid yonder shadowy trees,
Let me revisit. Ancient, massy door,   35
Thou gratest hoarse! My vital spirits freeze,
Passing the vacant pulpit, to the space
Where humble rails the decent altar grace,
And where my infant sister's ashes sleep,[5]
Whose loss I left the childish sport to weep.   40
  Now the low beams, with paper garlands hung,[6]
In memory of some village youth or maid,
Draw the soft tear from thrilled remembrance sprung;
How oft my childhood marked that tribute paid.
The gloves, suspended by the garland's side,   45
White as its snowy flowers, with ribbands tied;
Dear village, long these wreaths funereal spread,
Simple memorials of thy early dead!
  But oh, thou blank and silent pulpit! – thou
That with a father's precepts, just and bland,   50
Didst win my ear, as reason's strength'ning glow
Showed their full value, now thou seemst to stand
Before my sad, suffused,[7] and trembling gaze,
The dreariest relic of departed days;
Of eloquence paternal, nervous, clear,   55
DIM APPARITION THOU – and bitter is my tear.

From Gentleman's Magazine 59 (1789) 743

SONNET TO FRANCE ON HER PRESENT EXERTIONS

Thou, that where Freedom's sacred fountains play,
  Which sprung effulgent, though with crimson stains,
  On transatlantic shores[1] and widening plains,
  Hast, in their living waters, washed away
Those cankering spots, shed by tyrannic sway   5
  On thy long drooping lilies; English veins
  Swell with the tide of exultation gay
  To see thee spurn thy deeply-galling chains.
Few of Britannia's free-born sons forbear
  To bless thy cause; cold is the heart that breathes   10
  No wish fraternal.[2] France, we bid thee share

---

[5] Seward's brother and two sisters died in infancy.

[6] 'The ancient custom of hanging a garland of white roses, made of writing paper, and a pair of white gloves, over the pew of the unmarried villagers, who die in the flower of their age, is observed to this day in the village of Eyam, and in most other villages and little towns in the Peak' (Seward's note).

[7] *suffused* tearful.

SONNET TO FRANCE ON HER PRESENT EXERTIONS
[1] *transatlantic shores* a reference to the American Revolution.
[2] *fraternal* an allusion to the French revolutionary ideal of 'fraternité'.

The blessings twining with our civic wreaths,
While Victory's trophies, permanent as fair,
Crown the bright sword that Liberty unsheathes.[3]

Anna Laetitia Barbauld (*née* Aikin) (1743–1825)

Born at Kibworth, Leicester, the elder child of Dr John Aikin, a schoolmaster, and
Jane Jennings. In 1758 her father became a teacher at the Warrington Academy for
Dissenters,[1] where one of his colleagues, Joseph Priestley (friend of Benjamin Franklin,
discoverer of oxygen, and founder of modern Unitarianism), encouraged her poetic
talents, one of her earliest works being *A Summer Evening's Meditation* (*Romanticism* 17–20).
Her brother John (1747–1822), a physician and accomplished author, worked with her,
and together they published *Miscellaneous Pieces in Prose* in 1773, the same year which saw
the publication of her *Poems*. The latter volume was a considerable success, running to a
fifth edition by 1777. In 1774, despite some well-founded doubts, she married Rochemont
Barbauld, a Dissenting minister who had been educated at the Warrington Academy;
together they ran a successful boys' school in Palgrave, Suffolk, until 1785. They had
no children, but in 1777 adopted her nephew, Charles Rochemont Aikin, for whom she
composed her popular *Lessons for Children* (1778) and *Hymns in Prose for Children* (1781).
Visits to London brought her into contact with the bluestockings, among whom she
is celebrated in More's *Sensibility* (see pp. 24–34). Despite the success of their school,
her husband felt increasingly pressured by his work, and it was closed in 1785, allowing
them to travel in France and Switzerland for a year. By this time, Mrs Barbauld had
become a figure of considerable note in the literary world; she was profiled in the
European Magazine in March 1786, which commended her work for revealing 'marks of
a refined and vigorous imagination, of cultivated genius, elegant manners, unbigoted
religion, and unenthusiastical devotion'.[2]

On returning to England, she and her husband settled in Hampstead, where she
devoted herself to pamphleteering, most notably in defence of Dissenters (1790), demo-
cratic government and popular education (1792), and an attack on the newly declared
war with France in 1793. Political concerns were never far from her mind, and her
Epistle to William Wilberforce (1791) (*Romanticism* 20–3) ranks as one of the most eloquent
anti-slavery poems of the day. From 1796 her brother took over editorship of the
Monthly Magazine, an important periodical published by the radical sympathizer, Joseph
Johnson, and read by Wordsworth and Coleridge, among others. She contributed a good
deal of poetry to it, including her poem *To Mr Coleridge* (1797) (*Romanticism* 24–5); in
1800 Wordsworth ordered his publisher to send her a complimentary copy of the
new two-volume *Lyrical Ballads*, and George Dyer included three of her poems in an
anthology of *Odes*.[3]

---

[3] The unsheathing of Liberty's sword must be read as
a condonement of violence in the revolutionary cause.
ANNA LAETITIA BARBAULD (*NÉE* AIKIN)
[1] Dissenters from the established Church of Eng-
land. Originally applied to Roman Catholics but here,
as elsewhere in this volume, applied to Protestant
Dissenters, especially Unitarians – as in the case of
Barbauld.
[2] *European Magazine* 9 (1786) 139–40, p. 140.
[3] *Odes* ed. George Dyer (Ludlow, 1800), includes her
poems *To Content*, *To Wisdom*, and *To Spring*.

In 1802 the Barbaulds moved to Stoke Newington; by this time her husband's mental health was increasingly fragile, and in 1808, after several fits of violence against her, he drowned himself. She was tremendously productive at this period, editing Akenside and Collins, the *Letters* of Richardson, *The British Novelists* (50 vols, 1810), and reviewing fiction for the *Monthly Review* (1809–15). She died in Stoke Newington in 1825.

She is represented here by one poem, in some ways her most important – *Eighteen Hundred and Eleven* (1812), a passionate, shrewd work about the disastrous state in which the country found itself. By the time it was composed in 1811 Britain and France had been at war for 17 of the previous 19 years. The war was waged not just in Europe but in the colonies with the result that civilian populations, at home and abroad, suffered the effects of scarcity and high prices. Britain's economy was near collapse – the monetary system was badly inflated, and a series of bankruptcies led to layoffs, labour revolts, and cuts in production. There was no sign that any of this would end. Barbauld viewed the crisis from a liberal perspective, and saw the argument for an end to the war as overwhelming. The poem argues that waste, ruination, and ultimate self-destruction can be the only result of its continuation.

For daring to versify such sentiments she exposed herself to the unbridled vituperation of the Tory reviewers. Writing anonymously in June 1812, John Wilson Croker of the *Quarterly Review* was responsible for the most decisive and withering attack, initiated with two sentences that set the tone for what was to come: 'Our old acquaintance Mrs Barbauld turned satirist! The last thing we should have expected, and, now that we have seen her satire, the last thing that we could have desired.'[4] His sarcasms continue with reference to her sex:

> We had hoped, indeed, that the empire might have been saved without the inter-
> vention of a lady-author: we even flattered ourselves that the interests of Europe
> and of humanity would in some degree have swayed our public councils, without
> the descent of (dea ex machina) Mrs Anna Laetitia Barbauld in a quarto, upon the
> theatre where the great European tragedy is now performing. Not such, however,
> is her opinion; an irresistible impulse of public duty – a confident sense of com-
> manding talents – have induced her to dash down her shagreen spectacles and her
> knitting needles, and to sally forth, hand in hand with her renowned compatriot,[5]
> in the magnanimous resolution of saving a sinking state, by the instrumentality of
> a pamphlet in prose and a pamphlet in verse.[6]

Croker concluded with comments that underline his political motivation:

> Mrs Barbauld's former works have been of some utility; her *Lessons for Children*,
> her *Hymns in Prose*, her *Selections from the Spectator*, *et id genus omne*, though they
> display not much of either taste or talents, are yet something better than harmless:
> but we must take the liberty of warning her to desist from satire, which indeed is
> satire on herself alone; and of entreating, with great earnestness, that she will not,
> for the sake of this ungrateful generation, put herself to the trouble of writing
> any more party pamphlets in verse.[7]

---

[4] *Quarterly Review* 7 (1812) 309–13, p. 309.
[5] William Roscoe, books by whom were reviewed in the same number of the *Quarterly*, and who is mentioned in the poem.

[6] Ibid.
[7] Ibid., p. 313.

As Croker's was the most influential of the hostile reviews, two of his specific criticisms are quoted in my notes. The anonymous reviewer in the *Eclectic* was openly hostile to the poem's liberalism:

> Disposed as we are to receive every performance of Mrs Barbauld with peculiar cordiality, yet her choice of a subject in this instance, as well as her manner of treating it, is so unfortunate, that we scarcely ever read a poem of equal merit with so little pleasure. It consists, in one word, of ingenious speculations on the utter ruin of England. The whole tone of it is in a most extraordinary degree unkindly and unpatriotic, – we had almost said unfilial. . . . It seems hardly possible that such a poem as this could have been produced, without the concurrence of a peculiarly frigid temperament, – with a system of speculative opinions which seems contrived to damp every glowing sentiment, – and the spirit of that political party, which cherishes no sympathy with the honour and happiness of England, but delights to magnify her faults, expose her weakness, and anticipate her disasters.[8]

The *British Critic* characterized the poem as presenting a 'most gloomy picture', and went on: 'All this may possibly be true, but where is the wisdom or where the Patriotism of exaggerating the present or of anticipating future or greater calamities? Let Britons persevere in their duty to themselves and their country, and these melancholy images may yet appear to exist only in the writer's gloomy imagination.'[9] She might have expected some support from the journal to which she contributed, the *Monthly Review*, but the anonymous reviewer avoids praising the poem, resorting to the same strategy deployed by the *British Critic*:

> We say that in the long revolution of ages this melancholy picture *may* be realized, and that so far the visions of this elegant author are not idle chimeras of the brain; yet we wish to persuade ourselves that we still have a long career of glory to run, and that the prophetic warnings of such writers as Mrs Barbauld, by operating on our good sense, may even defer the period of their completion.[10]

The onslaught was unmitigated by praise from any quarter, and even though she must have understood that much of it was politically motivated, it destroyed her confidence; as Lucy Aikin recalled in her memoir: 'Who indeed, that knew and loved her, could have wished her to expose again that honoured head to the scorns of the unmanly, the malignant, and the base? . . . She even laid aside the intention which she had entertained of preparing a new edition of her Poems, long out of print and often enquired for in vain'.[11] The ridicule that greeted one of her most important works effectively brought her literary career to an end; she published no further volumes of poetry during her lifetime.

Further Reading

Julie Ellison, 'The Politics of Fancy in the Age of Sensibility', *RR* 228–55
The Poems of Anna Laetitia Barbauld ed. William McCarthy and Elizabeth Kraft (Athens, Georgia, 1994)

---

[8] *Eclectic Review* 8 (1812) 474–8, pp. 474–5.
[9] *British Critic* 40 (1812) 408–9, p. 409.
[10] *Monthly Review* 67 (1812) 428–32, p. 428.

[11] *The Works of Anna Laetitia Barbauld. With a Memoir by Lucy Aikin* (2 vols, 1825), i. lii–liii.

William McCarthy, '"We hoped the Woman was Going to Appear": Repression, Desire, and Gender in Anna Laetitia Barbauld's Early Poems', *RWW* 113–37

William Keach, 'A Regency Prophecy and the End of Anna Barbauld's Career', *SIR* 33 (1994) 569–77

Eighteen Hundred and Eleven, A Poem (composed by 1 December 1811; published February 1812)

Still the loud death drum, thundering from afar,
O'er the vexed nations pours the storm of war:[1]
To the stern call still Britain bends her ear,
Feeds the fierce strife, the alternate hope and fear –
Bravely, though vainly, dares to strive with fate,   5
And seeks by turns to prop each sinking state.[2]
Colossal Power[3] with overwhelming force
Bears down each fort of Freedom in its course;
Prostrate she lies beneath the despot's sway,
While the hushed nations curse him – and obey.   10
   Bounteous in vain, with frantic man at strife,
Glad nature pours the means – the joys of life;
In vain with orange-blossoms scents the gale,
The hills with olives clothes, with corn the vale;
Man calls to Famine, nor invokes in vain,   15
Disease and Rapine follow in her train;
The tramp of marching hosts disturbs the plough,
The sword, not sickle, reaps the harvest now,
And where the soldier gleans the scant supply,
The helpless peasant but retires to die;[4]   20
No laws his hut from licensed outrage shield,
And war's least horror is the ensanguined field.
   Fruitful in vain, the matron counts with pride
The blooming youths that grace her honoured side;
No son returns to press her widowed hand,   25
Her fallen blossoms strew a foreign strand.
Fruitful in vain, she boasts her virgin race,
Whom cultured arts adorn and gentlest grace;
Defrauded of its homage, Beauty mourns,[5]
And the rose withers on its virgin thorns.   30
Frequent, some stream obscure, some uncouth name
By deeds of blood is lifted into fame;
Oft o'er the daily page some soft one bends
To learn the fate of husband, brothers, friends,

EIGHTEEN HUNDRED AND ELEVEN, A POEM
[1] Britain and France had been at war for seventeen of the previous nineteen years (see headnote).
[2] Britain had failed to prevent Russia (1807), Spain (1808) and Austria (1809) from surrendering to France.
[3] *Colossal Power* Napoleon.

[4] Famine was widespread throughout Europe thanks to the disruption of agriculture by armies (l. 17), and seizures of crops to feed them (l. 19).
[5] No young men survive to pay homage to the beautiful young women who mourn their deaths.

Or the spread map with anxious eye explores   35
Its dotted boundaries and pencilled shores,
Asks *where* the spot that wrecked her bliss is found,
And learns its name but to detest the sound.
    And think'st thou, Britain, still to sit at ease,
An island queen amidst thy subject seas,   40
While the vexed billows, in their distant roar,
But soothe thy slumbers, and but kiss thy shore?
To sport in wars, while danger keeps aloof,
Thy grassy turf unbruised by hostile hoof?
So sing thy flatterers – but, Britain, know,   45
Thou who hast shared the guilt must share the woe.[6]
Nor distant is the hour; low murmurs spread,
And whispered fears, creating what they dread;
Ruin, as with an earthquake shock, is here,
There, the heart-witherings of unuttered fear,   50
And that sad death, whence most affection bleeds,
Which sickness, only of the soul, precedes.
Thy baseless wealth dissolves in air away
Like mists that melt before the morning ray:
No more on crowded mart or busy street   55
Friends, meeting friends, with cheerful hurry greet;
Sad on the ground thy princely merchants bend
Their altered looks, and evil days portend,
And fold their arms, and watch with anxious breast
The tempest blackening in the distant west.[7]   60
    Yes, thou must droop; thy Midas dream is o'er;
The golden tide of commerce leaves thy shore,
Leaves thee to prove the alternate ills that haunt
Enfeebling Luxury and ghastly Want;
Leaves thee, perhaps, to visit distant lands,   65
And deal the gifts of Heaven with equal hands.
    Yet, oh my country – name beloved, revered,
By every tie that binds the soul endeared,
Whose image to my infant senses came
Mixed with Religion's light and Freedom's holy flame!   70
If prayers may not avert, if 'tis thy fate
To rank amongst the names that once were great,
Not like the dim, cold crescent shalt thou fade,
Thy debt to Science and the Muse unpaid;
Thine are the laws surrounding states revere,   75
Thine the full harvest of the mental year,
Thine the bright stars in glory's sky that shine,

---

[6] Nonetheless, Britain remained the only European country not to experience invasion.
    Lines 47–60 refer to the 'ruin' that followed hard on the heels of the financial disasters of 1810. Bankers had committed suicide, and a ruined merchant was to be responsible for the assassination of the Prime Minister, Spencer Percival, only months after this poem's publication. The 'tempest' in the west refers to impending conflict with the United States; war was declared in June 1812.

And arts that make it life to live are thine.
If westward streams the light that leaves thy shores,
Still from thy lamp the streaming radiance pours.   80
Wide spreads thy race from Ganges to the pole,
O'er half the western world thy accents roll;
Nations beyond the Appalachian hills
Thy hand has planted and thy spirit fills;
Soon as their gradual progress shall impart   85
The finer sense of morals and of art,
Thy stores of knowledge the new states shall know,
And think thy thoughts, and with thy fancy glow;
Thy Lockes, thy Paleys shall instruct their youth,
Thy leading star direct their search for truth;   90
Beneath the spreading Platan's tent-like shade,
Or by Missouri's rushing waters laid,
'Old father Thames' shall be the poet's theme,
Of Hagley's woods[8] the enamoured virgin dream,
And Milton's tones the raptured ear enthrall,   95
Mixed with the roar of Niagara's fall;
In Thomson's glass[9] the ingenuous youth shall learn
A fairer face of Nature to discern;
Nor of the bards that swept the British lyre
Shall fade one laurel, or one note expire.   100
Then, loved Joanna,[10] to admiring eyes
Thy storied groups in scenic pomp shall rise;
Their high-souled strains and Shakespeare's noble rage
Shall with alternate passion shake the stage.
Some youthful Basil from thy moral lay   105
With stricter hand his fond desires shall sway;
Some Ethwald, as the fleeting shadows pass,
Start at his likeness in the mystic glass;
The tragic Muse resume her just control,
With pity and with terror purge the soul,   110
While wide o'er transatlantic realms thy name
Shall live in light, and gather *all* its fame.
    Where wanders Fancy down the lapse of years,
Shedding o'er imaged woes untimely tears?
Fond moody power! As hopes, as fears prevail,   115
She longs, or dreads, to lift the awful veil;
On visions of delight now loves to dwell,
Now hears the shriek of woe or Freedom's knell.
Perhaps, she says, long ages past away,

---

[8] Hagley Park was the estate of George, Lord Lyttelton (1709–73), in Worcestershire, near present-day Birmingham; it is praised by James Thomson in *Spring* (1728) 904ff. In the 1740s Lyttelton turned it into one of the most admired, and renowned, landscape gardens of the eighteenth century.

[9] *Thomson's glass* his poem, *The Seasons* (1730).
[10] Joanna Baillie (1762–1851), whose *Plays on the Passions* (1798–1812) had met with considerable success (see pp. 226–7); Barbauld refers specifically to *Count Basil* and *Ethwald*.

And set in western waves our closing day,   120
Night, Gothic night, again may shade the plains
Where Power is seated and where Science reigns;
England, the seat of arts, be only known
By the grey ruin and the mouldering stone,
That Time may tear the garland from her brow,   125
And Europe sit in dust, as Asia now.
   Yet then the ingenuous youth whom Fancy fires
With pictured glories of illustrious sires,
With duteous zeal their pilgrimage shall take
From the Blue Mountains or Ontario's lake,   130
With fond adoring steps to press the sod
By statesmen, sages, poets, heroes trod;
On Isis'[11] banks to draw inspiring air,
From Runnymede[12] to send the patriot's prayer;
In pensive thought, where Cam's slow waters wind,[13]   135
To meet those shades that ruled the realms of mind;
In silent halls to sculptured marbles bow
And hang fresh wreaths round Newton's awful brow.[14]
Oft shall they seek some peasant's homely shed
Who toils unconscious of the mighty dead,   140
To ask where Avon's winding waters stray[15]
And thence a knot of wildflowers bear away;
Anxious enquire where Clarkson,[16] friend of man,
Or all-accomplished Jones[17] his race began;
If of the modest mansion aught remains   145
Where Heaven and nature prompted Cowper's strains;[18]
Where Roscoe,[19] to whose patriot breast belong
The Roman virtue and the Tuscan song,
Led Ceres to the black˙ and barren moor
Where Ceres never gained a wreath before[20] –   150

---

[11] *Isis* poetical name for the River Thames in Oxford.
[12] *Runnymede* King John signed the Magna Carta in Runnymede.
[13] The Cam rises in Hertfordshire, flows by Cambridge into the Isle of Ely, and there joins the Ouse.
[14] *Newton's awful brow* Sir Isaac Newton was a Fellow of Trinity College, Cambridge, and Lucasian Professor of Mathematics. He is commemorated by a statue in the antechapel of Trinity, mentioned by Wordsworth, *Thirteen-Book Prelude*, iii 58–9.
[15] Stratford, birthplace of Shakespeare, through which flows the River Avon.
[16] Thomas Clarkson (1760–1846), prominent campaigner for abolition of the slave trade.
[17] Sir William Jones (1746–94), linguist and orientalist.
[18] William Cowper (1731–1800), poet.
[19] William Roscoe (1753–1831), scholar, poet, and agriculturalist, author of *The Life and Pontificate of Leo the Tenth* (1805).

[20] 'The Historian of the age of Leo has brought into cultivation the extensive tract of Chatmoss' (Barbauld's note). A reference to Roscoe's experiments at Chat Moss in Lancashire in which he reclaimed moorland for the cultivation of high-quality crops. Croker in the *Quarterly* was particularly scathing about this; quoting lines 147–50, he comments: 'Or, in other words (as the note kindly informs us), to Mr Roscoe's farm in Derbyshire, where, less we apprehend, by the Roman virtue and the Tuscan song, than by the homely process of drainage and manuring, he has brought some hundred acres of Chatmoss into cultivation. O the unequal dispensations of this poetical providence! Chatham and Nelson empty names! Oxford and Cambridge in ruins! London a desert, and the Thames a sedgy brook! while Mr Roscoe's barns and piggeries are in excellent repair, and objects not only of curiosity but even of reverence and enthusiasm' (*Quarterly Review* 7 (1812) 311–12).

With curious search their pilgrim steps shall rove
By many a ruined tower and proud alcove,
Shall listen for those strains that soothed of yore
Thy rock, stern Skiddaw, and thy fall, Lodore;[21]
Feast with Dun Edin's[22] classic brow their sight,   155
And 'visit Melross by the pale moonlight'.[23]
   But who their mingled feelings shall pursue
When London's faded glories rise to view?
The mighty city, which by every road,
In floods of people poured itself abroad;   160
Ungirt by walls, irregularly great,
No jealous drawbridge, and no closing gate;
Whose merchants (such the state which commerce brings)
Sent forth their mandates to dependent kings;
Streets, where the turbaned Moslem, bearded Jew,   165
And woolly Afric, met the brown Hindu;
Where through each vein spontaneous plenty flowed,
Where Wealth enjoyed, and Charity bestowed.
Pensive and thoughtful shall the wanderers greet
Each splendid square, and still, untrodden street;   170
Or of some crumbling turret, mined by time,
The broken stair with perilous step shall climb,
Thence stretch their view the wide horizon round,
By scattered hamlets trace its ancient bound,
And, choked no more with fleets, fair Thames survey –   175
Through reeds and sedge pursue his idle way.
   With throbbing bosoms shall the wanderers tread
The hallowed mansions of the silent dead,
Shall enter the long aisle and vaulted dome[24]
Where Genius and where Valour find a home;   180
Awestruck, midst chill sepulchral marbles breathe,
Where all above is still as all beneath;
Bend at each antique shrine, and frequent turn
To clasp with fond delight some sculptured urn,
The ponderous mass of Johnson's form to greet,   185
Or breathe the prayer at Howard's sainted feet.[25]
   Perhaps some Briton, in whose musing mind
Those ages live which Time has cast behind,
To every spot shall lead his wondering guests
On whose known site the beam of glory rests: 190
Here Chatham's[26] eloquence in thunder broke,

[21] Skiddaw mountain and the Lodore falls in the Lake District were frequently mentioned by picturesque poets and prose writers of the day.

[22] *Dun Edin* poetical name for Edinburgh.

[23] An allusion to Scott's popular poem, *The Lay of the Last Minstrel* (1805), ii 1–2: 'If thou wouldst view fair Melrose aright, / Go visit it by the pale moonlight'. Melrose Abbey was then, as now, popular with tourists.

[24] i.e. of St Paul's cathedral.

[25] Statues of Samuel Johnson and John Howard (prison reformer) stand in the nave of St Paul's.

[26] *Chatham* William Pitt the elder, first Earl of Chatham (1708–78).

Here Fox persuaded, or here Garrick spoke;[27]
Shall boast how Nelson, fame and death in view,
To wonted victory led his ardent crew,
In England's name enforced, with loftiest tone,[28]   195
Their duty – and too well fulfilled his own;
How gallant Moore,[29] as ebbing life dissolved,
But hoped his country had his fame absolved;
Or call up sages whose capacious mind
Left in its course a track of light behind;   200
Point where mute crowds on Davy's lips reposed,
And Nature's coyest secrets were disclosed;[30]
Join with their Franklin, Priestley's injured name,[31]
Whom, then, each continent shall proudly claim.
    Oft shall the strangers turn their eager feet   205
The rich remains of ancient art to greet,
The pictured walls with critic eye explore,
And Reynolds be what Raphael was before.[32]
On spoils from every clime their eyes shall gaze,
Egyptian granites and the Etruscan vase;   210
And when midst fallen London, they survey
The stone where Alexander's ashes lay,[33]
Shall own with humbled pride the lesson just
By Time's slow finger written in the dust.
    There walks a spirit[34] o'er the peopled earth –   215
Secret his progress is, unknown his birth;
Moody and viewless as the changing wind,

---

[27] Charles James Fox (1749–1806), Whig leader, and a focus for liberal opinion, particularly during the Tory ministries of Pitt the younger (1783–1801, 1804–6); David Garrick (1717–79), actor-manager.
[28] 'Every reader will recollect the sublime telegraphic dispatch, "England expects every man to do his duty"' (Barbauld's note). Admiral Nelson issued this order prior to the Battle of Trafalgar (21 October 1805), in which he was killed, despite a British victory.
[29] '"I hope England will be satisfied", were the last words of General Moore' (Barbauld's note). General Sir John Moore led the army that failed to prevent Napoleon from taking Madrid. He evacuated his troops at the Battle of Corunna, but at the expense of his own life.
[30] Sir Humphry Davy (1778–1829) lectured on chemistry and physics at the Royal Institution.
[31] Benjamin Franklin and Joseph Priestley both carried out experiments with electricity in the 1790s. They were also political radicals, and Priestley was hounded out of England by a mob drummed up by Tory opponents, on account of his sympathies with the French Revolution. He emigrated to America in 1794.
[32] Sir Joshua Reynolds was the most distinguished and successful portrait painter of his day, and had been,

from 1768 to 1792, President of the Royal Academy. He published his *Discourses* from 1769 to 1791, and, in 1784, was made Painter-in-Ordinary to the King – an honour which, as he pointed out, brought him a stipend less than that of the King's rat-catcher.
[33] Barbauld has in mind the granite sarcophagus on display at the British Museum from 1802 onwards, believed to be that of Alexander the Great.
[34] *spirit* perhaps that of civilization, or at least the spirit that makes civilization possible. It has been observed that in this account of the rise and fall of civilizations Barbauld is probably inspired by Comte de Volney's *The Ruins, or A Survey of the Revolutions of Empires* (1792), which enjoyed considerable popularity in England at this period, being read by Shelley, among others. As might be expected, Croker in the *Quarterly* ridiculed the 'spirit'. Quoting lines 215–18, he commented: 'This extraordinary personage is prodigiously wise and potent, but withal a little fickle, and somewhat, we think, for so wise a being, unjust and partial. He has hitherto resided in this country, and chiefly in London; Mrs Barbauld, however, foresees that he is beginning to be tired of us, and is preparing to go out of town' (*Quarterly Review* 7 (1812) 312).

No force arrests his foot, no chains can bind;
Where'er he turns, the human brute awakes,
And, roused to better life, his sordid hut forsakes;   220
He thinks, he reasons, glows with purer fires,
Feels finer wants, and burns with new desires.
Obedient Nature follows where he leads –
The steaming marsh is changed to fruitful meads;
The beasts retire from man's asserted reign,   225
And prove his kingdom was not given in vain.
Then from its bed is drawn the ponderous ore,
Then Commerce pours her gifts on every shore,
Then Babel's towers and terraced gardens rise,
And pointed obelisks invade the skies;   230
The prince commands, in Tyrian purple[35] dressed,
And Egypt's virgins weave the linen vest.
Then spans the graceful arch the roaring tide,
And stricter bounds the cultured fields divide.
Then kindles Fancy, then expands the heart,   235
Then blow the flowers of Genius and of Art;
Saints, heroes, sages, who the land adorn,
Seem rather to descend than to be born;
Whilst History, midst the rolls consigned to fame,
With pen of adamant inscribes their name.   240
   The genius now forsakes the favoured shore,
And hates, capricious, what he loved before;
Then empires fall to dust, then arts decay,
And wasted realms enfeebled despots sway;
Even Nature's changed; without his fostering smile   245
Ophir[36] no gold, no plenty yields the Nile;
The thirsty sand absorbs the useless rill,
And spotted plagues from putrid fens distil.
In desert solitudes then Tadmor[37] sleeps,
Stern Marius then o'er fallen Carthage weeps;[38]   250
Then with enthusiast love the pilgrim roves
To seek his footsteps in forsaken groves,
Explores the fractured arch, the ruined tower,
Those limbs disjointed of gigantic power;
Still at each step he dreads the adder's sting,   255
The Arab's javelin, or the tiger's spring;
With doubtful caution treads the echoing ground,
And asks where Troy or Babylon is found.

---

[35]   Tyrian purple in ancient times, a purple or crimson
dye was made at Tyre from molluscs.
[36]   Ophir was the land from which in biblical times
Solomon's navy fetched gold; see I Kings 9:26–8
[37]   Tadmor a biblical name for the oasis of Palmyra
between Syria and Babylon.

[38]   Plutarch relates that, on being denied entry to
Carthage by its Roman governor, Sextilius, Caius Marius
remarked: 'Tell him, then, that thou hast seen Caius
Marius a fugitive, seated amid the ruins of Carthage'.

And now the vagrant Power no more detains
The Vale of Tempe, or Ausonian plains;[39]   260
Northward he throws the animating ray,
O'er Celtic nations bursts the mental day –
And, as some playful child the mirror turns,
Now here, now there, the moving lustre burns;
Now o'er his changeful fancy more prevail   265
Batavia's[40] dykes than Arno's purple vale,
And stinted suns, and rivers bound with frost,
Than Enna's plains or Baia's viny coast;[41]
Venice the Adriatic weds in vain,
And Death sits brooding o'er Campania's plain;   270
O'er Baltic shores and through Hercynian groves,[42]
Stirring the soul, the mighty impulse moves;
Art plies his tools, and Commerce spreads her sail,
And wealth is wafted in each shifting gale.
The sons of Odin[43] tread on Persian looms,   275
And Odin's daughters breathe distilled perfumes;
Loud minstrel bards, in Gothic halls, rehearse
The Runic rhyme, and 'build the lofty verse';[44]
The Muse, whose liquid notes were wont to swell
To the soft breathings of the Aeolian shell,   280
Submits, reluctant, to the harsher tone,
And scarce believes the altered voice her own.
And now, where Caesar saw with proud disdain
The wattled hut and skin of azure stain,[45]
Corinthian columns rear their graceful forms,   285
And light verandas brave the wintry storms,
While British tongues the fading fame prolong
Of Tully's eloquence and Maro's song.[46]
Where once Bonduca whirled the scythed car,[47]
And the fierce matrons raised the shriek of war,   290
Light forms beneath transparent muslins float,
And tutored voices swell the artful note.
Light-leaved acacias and the shady plane
And spreading cedar grace the woodland reign;
While crystal walls[48] the tenderer plants confine,   295
The fragrant orange and the nectared pine;[49]

---

[39] Tempe was a valley in Thessaly celebrated as a rural paradise. *Ausonian* Italian.
[40] *Batavia* Holland.
[41] *Enna's plains* Enna was a town in the middle of Sicily surrounded by a plain renowned as an earthly paradise. *Baia* Roman resort on the Bay of Naples famed for its hot springs.
[42] *Hercynian groves* the Black Forest in Germany.
[43] *sons of Odin* Vikings.

[44] *build the lofty verse* an allusion to Milton's *Lycidas*: 'Who would not sing for Lycidas? he knew / Himself to sing, and build the lofty rhyme' (ll. 10–11).
[45] *azure stain* Julius Caesar described how the Scots painted themselves with blue warpaint in his *Gallic Wars*.
[46] *Tully* Marcus Tullius Cicero; *Maro* Virgilius Maro.
[47] *scythed car* the Saxon queen, Boadicea, fixed knives to the axles of her chariot.
[48] *crystal walls* greenhouses.
[49] *pine* pineapple.

The Syrian grape there hangs her rich festoons,
Nor asks for purer air, or brighter noons;
Science and Art urge on the useful toil,
New mould a climate and create the soil,   300
Subdue the rigour of the northern bear,[50]
O'er polar climes shed aromatic air,
On yielding Nature urge their new demands,
And ask not gifts but tribute at her hands.
 London exults – on London Art bestows   305
Her summer ices and her winter rose;
Gems of the east her mural crown adorn,
And Plenty at her feet pours forth her horn;
While even the exiles her just laws disclaim,
People a continent, and build a name.[51]   310
August she sits, and with extended hands
Holds forth the Book of Life to distant lands.[52]
 But fairest flowers expand but to decay;
The worm is in thy core, thy glories pass away;
Arts, arms and wealth destroy the fruits they bring;   315
Commerce, like beauty, knows no second spring.
Crime walks thy streets, Fraud earns her unblessed bread,
O'er want and woe thy gorgeous robe is spread,
And angel charities in vain oppose:
With grandeur's growth the mass of misery grows.   320
For see, to other climes the genius soars,
He turns from Europe's desolated shores;
And lo! even now, midst mountains wrapped in storm,
On Andes' heights he shrouds his awful form;
On Chimborazo's[53] summits treads sublime,   325
Measuring in lofty thought the march of Time;
Sudden he calls, ''Tis now the hour!' he cries,
Spreads his broad hand, and bids the nations rise.
La Plata[54] hears amidst her torrents' roar;
Potosi[55] hears it, as she digs the ore: 330
Ardent, the genius fans the noble strife,
And pours through feeble souls a higher life,
Shouts to the mingled tribes from sea to sea,
And swears thy world, Columbus, shall be free.[56]

---

[50] *the northern bear* the constellation of the Bear, which contains the North Star.

[51] Those exiled and disowned by Britain's (un)just and oppressive laws leave for other countries – Australia or America.

[52] A reference to the work of the British and Foreign Bible Society (founded 1804), which distributed bibles at home and abroad.

[53] Chimborazo is the highest peak in the Andes, in present-day Ecuador. The first recorded climb was in June 1797.

[54] La Plata is a large river in South America, formed by the union of the great rivers Parana and Uruguay.

[55] St Luis de Potosi is a city in Mexico situated in the midst of rich gold mines.

[56] Barbauld's optimism about South America stems from news of independence movements among the Spanish colonies there.

Hannah More (1745–1833)

'Nearly all the contemporaries of Hannah More are forgotten', S. C. Hall wrote in 1871, 'their reputation was for a day; hers has stood the test of time'.[1] For Dr Johnson, she was 'the most powerful versificatrix in the English language'.[2] In purely financial terms, Hannah More was one of the most successful writers of her day, having made £30,000 from her publications by 1825.

She was born at Fishponds in the parish of Stapleton, near Bristol, 2 February 1745, the fourth of five daughters of Mary Grace and Jacob More (d. 1783), a teacher at the Free School, who was determined to ensure that his five daughters should be capable of making a useful independent living in the same profession. By the age of four Hannah had learnt to read so well as to astonish the local clergyman with her recital of the catechism. Her father was apparently 'frightened by his own success' at teaching her Latin and mathematics, but the entreaties of his family encouraged him to continue. Her eldest sister set up her own school in Bristol in 1757, and Hannah studied a wide range of subjects there, including Italian, Spanish and Latin.

An encounter with the poet John Langhorne in 1773 led her to publish *The Search After Happiness* later that year. This pastoral play, which celebrates women writers, won plaudits from him in the *Monthly Review*: 'The ingenious author of the poem before us in every respect merits our protection. Whether we consider the harmony of her verse, or the happiness of her sentiments, her strength of thought, or her purity of expression, it equally excites our admiration: for this pastoral drama was written at the age of EIGHTEEN!'[3] Her tragedy *The Inflexible Captive* was performed at Bristol the following year, with a prologue by Langhorne and an epilogue by Garrick. The meeting with Garrick in 1774 was another stroke of good fortune. He gave her enormous encouragement, and introduced her to some of the greatest minds of the day, including Burke, Johnson, Reynolds and, crucially, Elizabeth Montagu, queen of the bluestockings, who, with Mrs Vesey, was already bringing together the various participants of that important salon. Like many literary coteries, the bluestockings were never as close-knit and exclusive as they are assumed to have been. At various times they included Anna Laetitia Barbauld, Elizabeth Carter, Mrs Boscawen, the Duchess of Beaufort, Mrs Leveson, Mrs Walsingham, the Duchess of Portland, and occasionally entertained visits from Reynolds, Johnson, Walpole, and Lord Lyttelton. In a letter to her sister of 1781, Hannah described a typical bluestocking gathering: 'I never knew a great party turn out so pleasantly as the other night at the Pepys's. There was all the pride of London – every wit, and every wit-ess; though these, when they get into a cluster, I have sometimes found to be as dull as other people; but the spirit of the evening was kept up on the strength of a little lemonade, till past eleven, without cards, scandal, or politics'.[4] The bluestockings regarded cards, scandal and politics as improper.

On visits to London Hannah often stayed out of town with Garrick and his wife Eva Marie at their luxurious riverside villa in Hampton. It was on one of these visits that he encouraged her to work on a new tragedy, *Percy*, about a model heroine misjudged

---

[1] *A Book of Memories of Great Men and Women of the Age, from Personal Acquaintance* (1871), p. 72.
[2] Sir William Forbes, *An Account of the Life and Writings of James Beattie, LL.D.* (2 vols, Edinburgh, 1806), ii 147.

[3] *Monthly Review* 49 (1773) 202–4, p. 202.
[4] William Roberts, *Memoirs of the Life and Correspondence of Mrs Hannah More* (3rd edn, 4 vols, London, 1835), i 208.

and murdered by a jealous husband. It opened in London in 1777 to immediate acclaim and sold 4,000 copies in a fortnight. Mrs Siddons's performance reputedly reduced Charles James Fox, the Whig leader, to tears.[5] She stopped writing for the stage after Garrick's death in January 1779. There was a pious streak in Hannah, and no doubt the death of her mentor led her to reconsider the direction her writing had taken. Nonetheless, in the next few years she was to win much acclaim with the most celebrated of her poems about the bluestockings, 'Sensibility', which appeared in her 1782 volume, *Sacred Dramas*. Another, lighter poem about the blues, *Bas-bleu*, was published to equal acclaim in 1786. In the late 1780s she retired to a cottage in Cowslip Green, Somerset, and devoted herself to didactic and educational works: *Thoughts on the Importance of the Manners to the Great to General Society* (1788), *An Estimate of the Religion of the Fashionable World* (1791), and other such titles. They were tremendously successful, often running into numerous editions within a few years.

Of these, one of the most notable must be the Cheap Repository tracts. They seem to have been the idea of Hannah's friend Bishop Porteus, who noted the quality and popularity of the didactic titles which she had sold in large quantities to a largely middle-class audience. It was late 1791 or early 1792, and the revolutionary fervour that gripped working people made the likes of Hannah and her reactionary friends somewhat uneasy. Porteus suggested to her that she 'write some little thing tending to open their eyes under their present wild impressions of liberty and equality'.[6] The secret agenda of the Cheap Repository was always to reform the working class, and to teach them to be satisfied with their lot (it should be noted that despite being an enormous success, few copies were actually sold to working people; most were purchased by committees and given away in charity schools, workhouses, hospitals, and prisons). Everyone was aware of the political aims of the series; the reviewer of a collection of the ballads, published in 1797 in book form, restated them:

> Every enlightened friend of mankind must see the importance of communicating to the poor and ignorant the means of instruction, and must rejoice to find that a Society is instituted and liberally supported for the purpose of circulating, at a very cheap rate, small tracts of various kinds, but all tending to impress on the minds of the common people the sentiments of piety and virtue.[7]

In marketing terms the series attempted to bridge the gulf which separated Hannah's didactic books from bawdy ballads sung at alehouses and bought as broadsides and chap-books from travelling pedlars (or chapmen). To this end a number of moral tales and ballads, over fifty by Hannah herself, were decked out with rakish titles and woodcuts in the guise of the broadside ballad to which working people were accustomed. As Hannah commented, 'It is as vulgar as heart can wish, but it is only designed for the most vulgar class of readers.'[8] The first was published on 3 March 1795; over 300,000 copies were sold by 18 April, and two million within the first year. *The Story of Sinful Sally*, first published in February 1796, is typical: the text is interspersed by four woodcuts, each showing sinful Sally at a different stage in her journey to an unpleasant death from venereal disease.[9] *The Sorrows of Yamba*, another of the Cheap Repository tracts, embodies

5   Ibid., ii 54.
6   Ibid., ii 345.
7   *Monthly Review* 22 (1797) 357–9, pp. 357–8.
8   Ibid.

9   The original broadside is reproduced in facsimile by Jonathan Wordsworth and Stephen Hebron, *Romantic Women Writers* (Grasmere, 1994), p. 18.

Hannah's anti-slavery convictions (see *Romanticism* 27–31). The series stopped in about 1799, when, due to ill health, she was compelled to give it up.

The best of her poetry was composed at the beginning of her career. *Sensibility* and *Bas-Bleu* are, in style and content, distinctive products of the late eighteenth century, and it may seem odd to include them in an anthology dedicated to romantic women writers. But female romanticism is informed by the cult of sensibility, and Hannah's poems are seminal among the poems which it inspired. *Sensibility* is here edited from the earliest, and best, text of 1782. It had been circulating for at least a year in manuscript prior to publication; the printed version of 1782 is the most satisfactory. Later texts depersonalize its contents; it was always intended to be written for, and inspired by, a small coterie. It contains lots of in-jokes, as well as a moving tribute to Garrick that in later versions is toned down and, ultimately, eliminated. *Bas-bleu*, which has been described as the 'signature' poem of the bluestockings,[10] circulated in manuscript for years before publication. It was read by Johnson, who commented to Mrs Thrale: 'Miss Hannah More has written a poem called the *Bas-bleu*, which is in my opinion a very great performace; it wanders about in manuscript, and surely will soon find its way to Bath'.[11] Like *Sensibility*, it was intended for the amusement of the small group of people who inspired it, and is full of witticisms comprehensible only to them; for this reason, it too was revised, toned down, and made far less lively in subsequent editions. The general air of frivolity in both these poems is characteristically charming, and no doubt enshrines something of the good humour that made the bluestockings such an intriguing group of people. But it would be wrong to deduce that they aspired to no more than the occasional bunfight; as Hannah's annotations to both poems indicate, they were famous partly for the moral and religious works that several of their number (notably Hester Chapone and Catherine Macaulay) had published, and for campaigning on behalf of universal education. Moreover, as Sylvia Harcstark Myers has argued, Elizabeth Carter argued that it was 'unfair to women to keep them from rational conversation with men because it kept them from developing their intellectual capacities':[12] this is the feminist subtext that underlies More's portrayal of this group of unusually well-educated women who wished to rid society of card-playing in exhange for polite conversation.

In 1787 Hannah wrote to Elizabeth Carter to tell her of 'the great object I have so much at heart – the project to abolish the slave trade in Africa. This most important cause has very much occupied my thoughts this summer; the young gentleman who has embarked in it with the zeal of an apostle has been much with me, and engaged all my little interest, and all my affections in it. It is to be brought before parliament in the spring. Above one hundred members have promised their votes.'[13] The 'young gentleman' was William Wilberforce, then in his twenties; she was in her forties. Despite the age difference, and the fact that he was a liberal and she a conservative, they had much in common, and became firm friends. Both were disciples of the reformed slave trader John Newton, and that no doubt helped bring them together. At the age of twenty-eight, Wilberforce was already campaigning energetically in Parliament for measures

---

[10]   See Joel Haefner, 'The Romantic Scene(s) of Writing', *RR* 256–73, p. 261.

[11]   William Roberts, *Memoirs of the Life and Correspondence of Mrs Hannah More*, i 320 n. 1. The MS was in circulation by September 1783, when it was read by William Pepys; Johnson saw it in March 1784 (see *The*

Letters of Samuel Johnson ed. Bruce Redford (5 vols, Princeton, NJ, 1992–4), iv 297).

[12]   *The Bluestocking Circle: Women, Friendship, and the Life of the Mind in Eighteenth-Century England* (Oxford, 1990), p. 262.

[13]   William Roberts, *Memoirs of the Life and Correspondence of Mrs Hannah More*, ii 70–1.

to be taken to eliminate slavery at home and in the colonies. Hannah believed that slavery was an abomination, and was advising her friends to boycott the use of West Indian sugar in their tea. She even carried about with her Clarkson's[14] plan of an African slave ship, showing it to interested and horrified guests at dinner parties.

She was following events closely when, on 21 May 1788, Sir William Dolben proposed a Bill to the House of Commons that limited the number of slaves which could be transported from Africa to British colonies in the West Indies. It may sound like a comparatively small measure now, but it marked the beginning of the move towards abolition, and aroused considerable opposition from business interests. On 26 May merchants and inhabitants of Liverpool presented a petition to the House, saying that Dolben's Bill would cause them all financial ruin. Fortunately, the Bill was passed in both Houses. *Slavery: A Poem* was written in anticipation of the Bill, within two weeks ('too short and too much hurried', Hannah said[15]), and reveals Hannah's impatience with the caution of the measures proposed. The poem as a whole argues for complete abolition. Two other poems on the same subject, from much the same viewpoint, appeared in 1788, by Ann Yearsley and Helen Maria Williams (see pp. 158–67, 243–51, below). Hannah's poem and Yearsley's were published close together in time. Yearsley was of course a former protégée (see pp. 150–2); their public falling-out, and Yearsley's subsequent desire for 'revenge' (which Hannah later said had 'absolutely broken' the peace of her life) no doubt had a good deal to do with the simultaneous publication of these works. The two poems were often compared by the reviewers, frequently to Hannah's detriment. It must be admitted that she was beginning to take herself and her writing very seriously, and that its earnestness makes *Slavery* heavy going. Even contemporary reviewers found the poem's manner contrived; the *European Magazine* praised Hannah's intentions but deplored her syle: 'A very well-meant, but feebly executed, production, intended to second the present impulse in favour of the emancipation of negroes. The authoress is occasionally obscure. The first eighteen lines are metaphysically abstruse'.[16] The *Critical* was more charitable; it commended Hannah's support of the abolitionists, noting that she 'shows herself no despicable advocate in their favour, as the following passage, in which the sentiments are no less just than happily expressed, will sufficiently show'.[17] Most kindly of all, the *New Annual Register* remarked that 'The sentiments which she expresses are humane and just; her descriptions pathetic and affecting; and her indignation against those who degrade the sable race in the scale of being is delivered in language that is poetical and spirited'.[18]

On the whole, though, Hannah was fortunate with reviewers. John Langhorne's review of *The Search After Happiness* (see p. 19) did much to establish her reputation. By the time she published *Sacred Dramas* and *Florio* she was a popular literary figure about town, and unlikely to attract critical displeasure. In the main, reviews for *Sacred Dramas* were favourable; critics rightly discerned that the central point of *Sensibility* was its critique of debased forms of sentiment. The *Gentleman's Magazine* argued that she 'carries her theory, we think, a little too far. That tenderness and compassion for the animal creation are often affected, and may be carried to a ridiculous extravagance, like those of Lady Brumpton in *The Funeral*,[19] we allow; nevertheless, in a certain degree,

---

[14] Thomas Clarkson (1760–1846) had, since 1785, worked alongside William Wilberforce for the abolition of the slave trade.

[15] William Roberts, *Memoirs of the Life and Correspondence of Mrs Hannah More*, ii 99.

[16] *European Magazine* 13 (1788) 166–7, p. 166.

[17] *Critical Review* 65 (1788) 226.

[18] *New Annual Register* 9 (1788) 260.

[19] *The Funeral*, a popular comedy by Sir Richard Steele.

they may be compatible with, and are perhaps often characteristic of, true sensibility.'[20] The *Monthly Review* was less pedantic, approving of *Sensibility* for its moral content:

> In a book 'chiefly intended for young persons', it is not with impropriety that Miss More has introduced the concluding composition, *Sensibility*, there being nothing of which they are more apt to form mistaken ideas than of that sympathetic tenderness which is supposed to have its source in the amiable affections of the heart. From these mistaken ideas it is that so many, by giving way to the immoderate indulgence of sensibility, destroy their own peace, while a still greater number, by its affectation, render themselves disgusting.[21]

For similar reasons the *European Magazine* commended the poem: 'It displays a considerable portion of that quality which gives name to the poem, and shows the writer in a very amiable point of view, as an individual. Her candour, friendship, gratitude, and taste, are eminently conspicuous in several parts of the poem'.[22] Reviews for *Florio*, and its companion-piece, *Bas-bleu*, were similarly favourable. 'The language and versification are easy and correct', observed the *Gentleman's Magazine*, 'and the observations forcible, lively, and just. An account of a book which everyone reads, or an extract from it, is by no means necessary. It has received general and deserved applause; and we are happy in adding our testimony in its favour to that of the public'.[23] The *European Magazine* noted merely that 'The reputation of Miss More . . . will receive no inconsiderable increase from this publication, which abounds in keen yet delicate satire';[24] while the *Critical Review* commented: 'Though we certainly lose much from our ignorance of many characters and circumstances to which allusions are made, the perusal has given us great entertainment. Sound sense, and agreeable pleasantry, is everywhere visible'.[25]

In later years she continued to enjoy literary success with such works as *Coelebs in Search of a Wife* (1809) which, though published anonymously, went into eleven editions within the year. The enduring popularity of her work during the nineteenth century drew many pilgrims to her door, and she was compelled to reserve two days a week for visitors so that she could spend the remainder in peace. She died peacefully on 7 September 1833, at the age of 88, leaving her fortune to a range of charitable institutions and religious societies.

Further Reading

Jeremy and Margaret Collingwood, *Hannah More* (Oxford, 1990)

Sylvia Harcstark Myers, *The Bluestocking Circle: Women, Friendship, and the Life of the Mind in Eighteenth-Century England* (Oxford, 1990)

Elizabeth Kowaleski-Wallace, *Their Father's Daughters: Hannah More, Maria Edgeworth, and Patriarchal Complicity* (New York, 1991)

Julie Ellison, 'The Politics of Fancy in the Age of Sensibility', *RR* 228–55

Joel Haefner, 'The Romantic Scene(s) of Writing', *RR* 256–73

Selected Writings of Hannah More ed. Robert Hole (London, 1996)

G. H. Spinney, 'Cheap Repository Tracts: Hazard and Marshall Edition, *The Library* 4th Ser. 20 (1940) 295–340

---

[20] *Gentleman's Magazine* 52 (1782) 125–6, p. 126.

[21] *Monthly Review* 67 (1782) 31–5, p. 32.

[22] *European Magazine* 1 (1782) 205–6, p. 205.

[23] *Gentleman's Magazine* 56 (1786) 327.

[24] *European Magazine* 9 (1786) 109.

[25] *Critical Review* 61 (1786) 263–8, p. 267.

From Sacred Dramas: chiefly intended for young persons: the subjects taken from the Bible. To which is added, Sensibility, A Poem (1782)

SENSIBILITY: A POETICAL EPISTLE TO THE HON. MRS BOSCAWEN[1]

Spirits are not finely touched but to fine issues.[2]

Shakespeare

The following little poem was sent several years ago, as an epistle to the honoured friend to whom it is inscribed. It has since been enlarged, and several passages have been added, or altered, as circumstances required.[3]

Accept, Boscawen, these unpolished lays,
Nor blame too much the verse you cannot praise;
For you, far other bards have waked the string,
Far other bards for you were wont to sing.
Yet on the gale their parting music steals;   5
Yet your charmed ear the loved impression feels;
You heard the lyres of Lyttelton and Young,[4]
And this a grace, and that a seraph strung.
These are no more! But not with these decline
The Attic chasteness and the flame divine: 10
Still sad Elfrida's poet[5] shall complain,
And either Warton breathe his classic strain.[6]
Nor fear lest genuine poesy expire
While tuneful Beattie wakes old Spenser's lyre.[7]
His sympathetic lay his soul reveals,   15
And paints the perfect bard from what he feels.
Illustrious Lowth![8] For him the muses wove
The fairest garland from their greenest grove.
Though Latian[9] bards had gloried in his name,

SENSIBILITY

[1] Frances, daughter of William Evelyn Glanville, Esq., married Admiral Edward Boscawen, Viscount Falmouth, in 1742. He was a national hero, having thwarted a French invasion in an important battle in Lagos Bay in August 1759. He died of typhoid fever, 10 January 1761. In 1775, More told her sister that 'Mrs Boscawen's life has been a continued series of afflictions that may almost bear a parallel with those of the righteous man of Uz'.

[2] *Measure for Measure* I i 35–6.

[3] More continued to revise the poem through successive editions.

[4] *Lyttelton and Young* At the behest of Elizabeth Montagu and Elizabeth Carter, Edward Young (1683–1765) composed *Resignation* to console Mrs Boscawen for her husband's death. George, Lord Lyttelton (1709–73), was introduced to Mrs Boscawen by Mrs Montagu.

[5] *sad Elfrida's poet* 'Milton calls Euripedes "sad Electra's poet"' (More's note). More refers to Milton's *Sonnet VIII. When the assault was intended to the City* 13. 'Elfrida's poet' was William Mason (1725–97), author of *Elfrida: a dramatic poem* (1752).

[6] Joseph Warton (1722–1800) and his brother Thomas Warton the younger (1728–90) were distinguished classicists. Joseph translated and edited Virgil in 1753; Thomas composed a number of works in Latin.

[7] *The Minstrel* (1771–4) by James Beattie (1735–1803) was a popular poem, partly autobiographical, in Spenserian stanzas.

[8] Robert Lowth, Bishop of London (1710–87), renowned as a skilled Latinist and Hebrew scholar. His most famous work was *De Sacra Poesi Hebraeorum* (1753), translated by Gregory in 1787 as *Lectures on the Sacred Poetry of the Hebrews*.

[9] *Latian* Latin.

When in full brightness burnt the Latian flame,   20
Yet fired with nobler hopes than transient bays,
He scorned the meed of perishable praise,
Spurned the cheap wreath by human science won,
Borne on the wing sublime of Amos'[10] son;
He seized his mantle as the prophet flew,   25
And caught some portion of his spirit too.
   To snatch bright beauty from devouring fate
And bid it boast with him a deathless date;
To show how genius fires, how taste restrains,
While what both are, his pencil best explains,   30
Have we not Reynolds?[11] Lives not Jenyns yet,
To prove his lowest title was a wit?[12]
Though purer flames thy hallowed zeal inspire
Than ere were kindled at the muse's fire,
Thee, mitred Chester,[13] all the Nine[14] shall boast,   35
And is not Johnson theirs, himself an host?[15]
   Yes: still for you your gentle stars dispense
The charm of friendship and the feast of sense;
Yours is the bliss, and Heav'n no dearer sends
To call the wisest, brightest, best, your friends.   40
   With Carter trace the wit to Athens known,[16]
Or find in Montagu[17] that wit our own;
Or, pleased, attend Chapone's instructive page,[18]
Which charms her own, and forms the rising age;
Or boast in Walsingham[19] the various pow'r   45

[10] *Borne on the wing . . . spirit too* a reference to the Old Testament prophet Elijah (Amos' son) who was taken up into heaven by a chariot of fire. He was watched by Elisha, his successor, who, in Elijah's wake, picked up his cloak (mantle) with which he parted the waters of the River Jordan; see II Kings 2:11–14.
[11] 'See his Discourses to the Academy' (More's note). Sir Joshua Reynolds (1723–92), was the most renowned portrait-painter of the age, and a close friend of Angelica Kauffmann, a renowned bluestocking artist. His first discourse was delivered in 1769, and subsequent lectures became yearly fixtures at the Royal Academy. He first met More in 1775, when she described his most recent discourse as 'a masterpiece for matter as well as style'.
[12] Later editions of *Sensibility* carried the note: 'Mr Soame Jenyns had just published his work *On the Internal Evidence of the Christian Religion*.' Soame Jenyns (1704–87), poet and pamphleteer, was much admired by More; she claimed to know someone converted to Christianity by his *View of the Internal Evidence of the Christian Religion* (1776).
[13] 'See the Bishop's admirable Poem on Death' (More's note). Beilby Porteus, Bishop of Chester, and, later, London (1731–1808), first published the popular

Death: A Poetical Essay in 1759. His response to this allusion was an appreciative quatrain:

> How potent is thy Muse, oh More,
>   Whose vivifying breath
> Can do what Muse ne'er did before:
>   Give life and fame to – *death*!

[14] *Nine* the Muses.
[15] More was a friend of Dr Johnson, whom she met in 1774; as she wrote at the time: 'Abyssinia's Johnson! Dictionary Johnson! *Rambler*'s, *Idler*'s, and *Irene*'s Johnson!'
[16] Elizabeth Carter's translation, *All the Works of Epictetus which are now extant* (1758), was a considerable success in its day.
[17] Elizabeth Montagu, 'Queen of the Blue-stockings' (1720–1800). 'She is not only the finest genius, but the finest lady I ever saw', More wrote in 1775.
[18] Hester Chapone (1727–1801), friend and collaborator of Richardson, who called her 'a little spitfire'. Her best-known work, to which More refers here, was *Letters on the Improvement of the Mind* (1773), dedicated to Mrs Montagu. It was enormously popular, being reprinted sixteen times by the end of the century.
[19] Mrs Boyle Walsingham was a bluestocking and close friend of More's; she lived at Thames Ditton in Surrey.

To soothe the lonely, grace the lettered hour –
To polished life its highest charm she gives,
Whose song is music, and whose canvas lives.
Delany shines, in worth serenely bright,
Wisdom's strong ray, and virtue's milder light;   50
And she who blessed the friend, and graced the page
Of Swift, still lends her lustre to our age:[20]
Long, long protract thy light, oh star benign,
Whose setting beams with added brightness shine!
    Oh much-loved Barbauld,[21] shall my heart refuse   55
Its tribute to thy virtues and thy muse?
While round thy brow the poet's wreath I twine,
This humble merit shall at least be mine,
In all thy praise to take a gen'rous part,
Thy laurels bind thee closer to my heart.   60
My verse thy merits to the world shall teach,
And love the genius it despairs to reach.
    Yet what is wit, and what the poet's art?
Can genius shield the vulnerable heart?
Ah no, where bright imagination reigns,   65
The fine-wrought spirit feels acuter pains:
Where glow exalted sense, and taste refined,
There keener anguish rankles in the mind;
There feeling is diffused through every part,
Thrills in each nerve, and lives in all the heart;   70
And those whose gen'rous souls each tear would keep
From others' eyes, are born themselves to weep.
    Say, can the boasted pow'rs of wit and song
Of life one pang remove, one hour prolong?
Presumptuous hope, which daily truths deride –   75
For you, alas, have wept, and Garrick died![22]
Ne'er shall my heart his loved remembrance lose,
Guide, critic, guardian, glory of my muse!
Oh shades of Hampton,[23] witness, as I mourn,
Could wit or song elude *his* destined urn?   80
Though living virtue still your haunts endears,
Yet buried worth shall justify my tears.

[20]   Mary Delany (1700–88), bluestocking, had known
Pope and Swift in her youth. She met Swift in 1733,
and enjoyed a correspondence with him. In a letter
of 1788, Burke told Hannah that Mrs Delany 'was
almost the only person he ever saw who, at eight-
eight, blushed like a girl' (William Roberts, *Memoirs of
the Life and Correspondence of Mrs Hannah More*, ii 97).
[21]   In 1782 Anna Laetitia Barbauld was best known
for her first volume of poems, which included *Corsica*
(1773), of which Mrs Montagu was a keen admirer.
She had already been praised in verse by Mary Scott,
The Female Advocate; see pp. 134–5. An article in the

Westminster Magazine for June 1776, 'Observations on
Female Literature in General, including some Par-
ticulars Relating to Mrs Montagu and Mrs Barbauld',
complimented her both for her appearance and her
intellectual conversation.
[22]   David Garrick (1717–79), actor-manager, was
More's principal mentor; see headnote above.
[23]   Garrick's house, Hampton Villa in Middlesex,
housed a famous Temple to Shakespeare; More fre-
quently stayed with him and his wife on her visits to
London.

Garrick! Those pow'rs which form a friend were thine;
And let me add, with pride, that friend was mine –
With pride! At once the vain emotion's fled,   85
Far other thoughts are sacred to the dead.
Who now with spirit keen, yet judgement cool,
Th' unequal wand'rings of my muse shall rule?
Whose partial praise my worthless verse ensure?
For Candour smiled when Garrick would endure.   90
If harsher critics were compelled to blame,
I gained in friendship what I lost in fame;
And friendship's fost'ring smiles can well repay
What critic rigour justly takes away.
With keen acumen how his piercing eye   95
The fault concealed from vulgar view would spy!
While with a gen'rous warmth he strove to hide –
Nay, vindicate – the fault his judgement spied.
So pleased, could he detect a happy line,
That he would fancy merit ev'n in mine.   100
Oh gen'rous error, when by friendship bred!
His praises flattered me, but not misled.
No narrow views could bound his lib'ral mind;
His friend was man, his party humankind.
Agreed in this, opposing statesmen strove   105
Who most should gain his praise, or court his love.
His worth all hearts as to one centre drew;
Thus Tully's Atticus was Caesar's too.
His wit so keen, it never missed its end,
So blameless too, it never lost a friend;   110
So chaste, that modesty ne'er learned to fear,
So pure, religion might unwounded hear.
How his quick mind, strong pow'rs, and ardent heart,
Impoverished nature, and exhausted art,
A brighter bard records,[24] a deathless muse!   115
But I his talents in his virtues lose:
. Great parts are nature's gift; but that he shone
Wise, moral, good and virtuous, was his own.
Though Time his silent hand across has stole,
Soft'ning the tints of sorrow on the soul,   120
The deep impression long my heart shall fill,
And every mellowed trace be perfect still.
Forgive, Boscawen, if my sorrowing heart,
Intent on grief, forget the rules of art;
Forgive, if wounded recollection melt –   125
You best can pardon who have oft'nest felt.

---

[24] 'Mr Sheridan's Monody' (More's note). Richard
Brinsley Sheridan's *Verses to the Memory of Garrick,
spoken as a monody* was published in 1779.

You who for many a friend and hero mourn,
Who bend in anguish o'er the frequent urn;
You who have found how much the feeling heart
Shapes its own wound, and points itself the dart;   130
You who from tender sad experience feel
The wound such minds receive can never heal; .
That grief a thousand entrances can find,
Where parts superior dignify the mind;
Would you renounce the pangs those feelings give,   135
Secure in joyless apathy to live?
    For though in souls where taste and sense abound,
Pain through a thousand avenues can wound;
Yet the same avenues are open still,
To casual blessings as to casual ill.   140
Nor is the trembling temper more awake
To every wound which misery can make,
Than is the finely-fashioned nerve alive
To every transport pleasure has to give.
For if, when home-felt[25] joys the mind elate,   145
It mourns in secret for another's fate;
Yet when its own sad griefs invade the breast,
Abroad, in others' blessings, see it blessed!
Ev'n the soft sorrow of remembered woe,
A not unpleasing sadness may bestow.   150
    Let not the vulgar read this pensive strain,
Their jests the tender anguish would profane.
Yet these some deem the happiest of their kind,
Whose low enjoyments never reached the mind;
Who ne'er a pain but for themselves have known,   155
Nor ever felt a sorrow but their own;
Who call romantic every finer thought
Conceived by pity, or by friendship wrought.
Ah, wherefore happy? Where's the kindred mind?
Where the large soul that takes in humankind?   160
Where the best passions of the mortal breast?
Where the warm blessing when another's blessed?
Where the soft lenitives of others' pain,
The social sympathy, the sense humane,
The sigh of rapture and the tear of joy,   165
Anguish that charms, and transports that destroy?
For tender Sorrow has her pleasures too,
Pleasures which prosp'rous Dullness never knew.
She never knew, in all her coarser bliss,

---

[25] *Home-felt* experienced inwardly. The phrase derives
from Milton, *Comus* 262: 'a sacred, and *home-felt* de-
light'. It occurs also in Pope's *Essay on Man* ii 256,
and in Warton's translation of Virgil:

Yet calm content, secure from guilty cares,
Yet *home-felt pleasure*, peace, and rest, are
    theirs . . .

(Warton, *Georgics* ii 566–7)

The sacred rapture of a pain like this!   170
Nor think the cautious only are the just;
Who never was deceived I would not trust.
Then take, ye happy vulgar, take your part
Of sordid joy which never touched the heart.
Benevolence, which seldom stays to choose,   175
Lest pausing Prudence teach her to refuse;
Friendship which, once determined, never swerves,
Weighs ere it trusts, but weighs not ere it serves;
And soft-eyed Pity, and Forgiveness bland,
And melting Charity with open hand;   180
And artless Love, believing and believed,
And gen'rous Confidence which ne'er deceived;
And Mercy stretching out, ere Want can speak,
To wipe the tear from pale Affliction's cheek:
These ye have never known – then take your part   185
Of sordid joy, which never touched the heart.
   You who have melted in bright glory's flame
Or felt the spirit-stirring breath of fame;
Ye noble few, in whom her promised meed
Wakes the great thought, and makes the wish the deed;   190
Ye who have tasted the delight to give,
And, God's own agents, bid the wretched live;
Who the chill haunts of Desolation seek,
Raise the sunk heart, and flush the fading cheek;
Ye who with pensive Petrarch love to mourn,   195
Or weave fresh chaplets for Tibullus' urn;
Who cherish both in Hammond's plaintive lay,[26]
The Provence myrtle, and the Roman bay;
Ye who divide the joys, and share the pains
Which merit feels, or Heav'n-born Fancy feigns;   200
Would you renounce such joys, such pains as these,
For vulgar pleasures, or for selfish ease?
Would you, to 'scape the pain, the joy forego,
And miss the transport to avoid the woe?
Would you the sense of real sorrow lose,   205
Or cease to woo the melancholy muse?
No, Greville,[27] no! Thy song, though steeped in tears,
Though all thy soul in all thy strain appears,
Yet wouldst thou all thy well-sung anguish choose,
And all th' inglorious peace thou begg'st, refuse.   210

---

[26] James Hammond (1710–42), poet and politician, whose posthumously published *Love Elegies* (1743) were an instant success. They imitated Tibullus, and were damned by Johnson for their 'frigid pedantry'.
[27] 'Beautiful Ode to Indifference' (More's note). Frances Macartney (?1726–89), was the wife of Richard

Fulke Greville, godmother of Fanny Burney, and author of 'A Prayer for Indifference'. For more on this see Jerome J. McGann, *The Poetics of Sensibility* (1996), pp. 50–4.

Or you, Boscawen, when you fondly melt
In raptures none but mothers ever felt;
And view, enamoured, in your beauteous race,
All Leveson's sweetness, and all Beaufort's grace;[28]
Yet think what dangers each loved child may share,   215
The youth if valiant, and the maid if fair;
That perils multiply as blessings flow,
And constant sorrows on enjoyments grow;
You who have felt how fugitive is joy,
That while we clasp the phantom we destroy;   220
That life's bright sun is dimmed by clouded views,
And who most to love have most to lose;
Yet from these fair possessions would you part,
To shield from future pain your guarded heart?
Would your fond mind renounce its tender boast,   225
Or with their opening bloom of promise lost?
Yield the dear hopes which break upon your view,
For all the quiet Dullness ever knew?
Debase the objects of your tend'rest prayer
To save the dangers of a distant care?   230
Consent, to shun the anxious fears you prove,
They less should merit, or you less should love?
   Yet while I hail the sympathy divine,
Which makes, oh man, the wants of others thine;
I mourn heroic Justice, scarcely owned,   235
And principle for sentiment dethroned.
While Feeling boasts her ever-tearful eye,
Stern Truth, firm Faith, and manly Virtue fly.
   Sweet sensibility, thou soothing pow'r
Who shedd'st thy blessings on the natal hour   240
Like fairy favours! Art can never seize,
Nor affectation catch thy pow'r to please:
Thy subtle essence still eludes the chains
Of definition, and defeats her pains.
Sweet sensibility, thou keen delight!   245
Thou hasty moral, sudden sense of right!
Thou untaught goodness! Virtue's precious seed!
Thou sweet precursor of the gen'rous deed!
Beauty's quick relish! Reason's radiant morn,
Which dawns soft light before Reflection's born!   250
To those who know thee not, no words can paint,
And those who know thee, know all words are faint!
'Tis not to mourn because a sparrow dies,
To rave in artificial ecstasies;
'Tis not to melt in tender Otway's fires;   255

---

[28] Leveson and Beaufort are Mrs Boscawen's daughters. Frances married Admiral John Leveson-Gower in 1773; Elizabeth married Henry, 5th Duke of Beaufort, in 1766.

'Tis not to faint when injured Shore expires;
'Tis not because the ready eye o'erflows
At Clementina's or Clarissa's woes.[29]
    Forgive, oh Richardson, nor think I mean,
With cold contempt, to blast thy peerless scene;   260
If some faint love of virtue glow in me,
Pure spirit, I first caught that flame from thee.
    While soft Compassion silently relieves,
Loquacious Feeling hints how much she gives;
Laments how oft her wounded heart has bled,   265
And boasts of many a tear she never shed.
    As words are but th' external marks to tell
The fair ideas in the mind that dwell;
And only are of things the outward sign,
And not the things themselves they but define;   270
So exclamations, tender tones, fond tears,
And all the graceful drapery Pity wears;
These are not Pity's self, they but express
Her inward sufferings by their pictured dress;
And these fair marks, reluctant I relate,   275
These lovely symbols may be counterfeit.
Celestial Pity, why must I deplore
Thy sacred image stamped on basest ore?
There are, who fill with brilliant plaints the page,
If a poor linnet meet the gunner's rage;   280
There are, who for a dying fawn display
The tend'rest anguish in the sweetest lay;[30]
Who for a wounded animal deplore,
As if friend, parent, country, were no more;
Who boast quick rapture trembling in their eye,   285
If from the spider's snare they save a fly;
Whose well-sung sorrows every breast inflame,
And break all hearts but his from whom they came;
Yet scorning life's *dull* duties to attend,
Will persecute a wife, or wrong a friend;   290
Alive to every woe by fiction dressed,
The innocent he wronged, the wretch distressed,
May plead in vain; their suff'rings come not near,
Or he relieves them cheaply with a tear.[31]

---

[29] More refers to Catullus' poem in which Lesbia mourns her dead sparrow; Thomas Otway's *Venice Preserved* (1682); Nicholas Rowe's tragedy, *Jane Shore* (1714); Richardson's *Clarissa* (1747–8), and *Sir Charles Grandison* (1754), the heroine of which is called Clementina Porretta.

[30] More apparently disapproved of Marvell's *The Nymph Complaining for the Death of Her Faun*.

[31] More attacks a kind of sensibility that she and the other bluestockings regarded as debased. In 1782, shortly after *Sensibility* had been published, she told her sister: 'Mrs Montagu, Mrs Chapone, and Mrs Carter, are mightily pleased that I have attacked that mock feeling and sensibility which is at once the boast and disgrace of these times, and which is equally deficient in taste and truth' (William Roberts, *Memoirs of the Life and Correspondence of Mrs Hannah More*, i 236).

Not so the tender moralist of Tweed;   295
His Man of Feeling is a man indeed.[32]
    Oh blessed Compassion! Angel Charity!
More dear one genuine deed performed for thee
Than all the periods Feeling e'er can turn,
Than all thy soothing pages, polished Sterne![33]   300
    Not that by deeds alone this love's expressed,
If so, the affluent only were the blessed;
One silent wish, one prayer, one soothing word,
The precious page of Mercy shall record;
One soul-felt sigh by pow'rless Pity giv'n,   305
Accepted incense, shall ascend to heav'n!
    Since trifles make the sum of human things,
And half our mis'ry from our foibles springs;
Since life's best joys consist in peace and ease,
And few can save or serve, but all may please: 310
Oh let th' ungentle spirit learn from hence,
A small unkindness is a great offence.
Large bounties to bestow we wish in vain,
But all may shun the guilt of giving pain.
To bless mankind with tides of flowing wealth,   315
With pow'r to grace them or to crown with health
Our little lot denies; but Heav'n decrees
To all, the gift of minist'ring to ease.
The gentle offices of patient love,
Beyond all flatt'ry, and all price above;   320
The mild forbearance at another's fault,
The taunting word, suppressed as soon as thought;
On these Heav'n bade the bliss of life depend,
And crushed ill-fortune when he made a friend.
    A solitary blessing few can find,   325
Our joys with those we love are intertwined;
And he, whose helpful tenderness removes
Th' obstructing thorn which wounds the breast he loves,
Smooths not another's rugged path alone,
But scatters roses to adorn his own.   330
    The hint malevolent, the look oblique,
The obvious satire, or implied dislike;
The sneer equivocal, the harsh reply,
And all the cruel language of the eye;
The artful injury whose venomed dart   335
Scarce wounds the hearing while it stabs the heart;
The guarded phrase whose meaning kills, yet told,
The list'ner wonders how you thought it cold;
Small slights, contempt, neglect unmixed with hate,

---

[32] Henry Mackenzie (1745–1831), native of Edin-   [33] Later versions of the poem read 'perverted Sterne'.
burgh, published his sentimental novel, *The Man of
Feeling*, in 1771.

Make up in number what they want in weight.   340
These, and a thousand griefs minute as these,
Corrode our comfort and destroy our ease.
As this strong feeling tends to good or ill,
It gives fresh pow'r to vice or principle;
'Tis not peculiar to the wise and good;   345
'Tis passion's flame, the virtue of the blood.
But to divert it to its proper course,
There Wisdom's pow'r appears, there Reason's force;
If, ill-directed, it pursues the wrong,
It adds new strength to what before was strong;   350
Breaks out in wild irregular desires,
Disordered passions and illicit fires.
But if the virtuous bias rule the soul,
This lovely feeling then adorns the whole;
Sheds its sweet sunshine on the moral part,   355
Nor wastes on fancy what should warm the heart.
Cold and inert the mental pow'rs would lie
Without this quick'ning spark of deity.
To draw the rich materials from the mine,
To bid the mass of intellect refine,   360
To melt the firm, to animate the cold,
And Heav'n's own impress stamp on nature's gold;
To give immortal Mind its finest tone,
Oh sensibility, is all thy own!
This is th' ethereal flame which lights and warms,   365
In song transports us, and in action charms.
'Tis *this* that makes the pensive strains of Gray[34]
Win to the open heart their easy way;
Makes the touched spirit glow with kindred fire,
When sweet Serena's[35] poet wakes the lyre.   370
'Tis *this*, though nature's hidden treasures lie
Bare to the keen inspection of her eye,
Makes Portland's[36] face its brightest rapture wear,
When her large bounty smooths the bed of care;
'Tis *this* that breathes through Sévigné's sweet page,[37]   375
That nameless grace which soothes a second age;
'Tis *this* whose charms the soul resistless seize,
And gives Boscawen half her pow'r to please.

---

[34] 'This is meant of the *Elegy in a Country Churchyard*, of which exquisite poem *sensibility* is, perhaps, the characteristic beauty' (More's note).

[35] 'Triumphs of Temper' (More's note). Serena is the principal character in William Hayley's *The Triumphs of Temper* (1781), much admired by the bluestockings.

[36] Lady Margaret Cavendish Harley, 2nd Duchess of Portland, was prominent among the bluestockings. She died in 1785.

[37] Marie de Rabutin-Chantal, Marquise de Sévigné (1626–96); her letters are the only literary source of information on life under Louis XIV. Her equally remarkable, but more personal, letters to her daughter were first translated into English in 1727, and gained immediate popularity. These are the ones most admired by Hannah who, in a letter of 1786, commended their 'excess of maternal tenderness' (William Roberts, *Memoirs of the Life and Correspondence of Mrs Hannah More*, ii 36).

Yet why those terrors? Why that anxious care,
Since your last hope[38] the deathful war will dare?   380
Why dread that energy of soul which leads
To dang'rous glory by heroic deeds?
Why tremble lest his ardent soul aspire?
You fear the son because you knew the sire.
Hereditary valour you deplore   385
And dread, yet wish to find one hero more.

From Florio: A Tale, and The Bas-bleu; or, Conversation (1786)

THE BAS-BLEU; OR, CONVERSATION. ADDRESSED TO MRS VESEY.[1]

Advertisement

The following trifle owes its birth and name to the mistake of a foreigner of distinction,[2] who gave the literal appellation of the *Bas-bleu* to a small party of friends, who had been sometimes called, by way of pleasantry, the bluestockings. The slight performance occasioned by this little circumstance was never intended to appear in print: it is, in general, too local and too personal for publication, and was only written with a wish to amuse the amiable lady to whom it is addressed, and a few partial friends. But copies having been multiplied far beyond the intention of the author,[3] she has been advised to publish it, lest it should steal into the world in a state of still greater imperfection – though she is almost ashamed to take refuge in so hackneyed an apology, however true.

Vesey, of verse the judge and friend,
Awhile my idle strain attend!
Not with the days of early Greece
I mean to ope my slender piece –
The rare symposium[4] to proclaim   5
Which crowned th' Athenians' social name;
Or how Aspasia's[5] parties shone,
The first *bas-bleu* at Athens known.[6]

---

[38]   'Admiral Boscawen's only remaining son was then in America, and at the Battle of Lexington' (More's note). George Evelyn Boscawen, 3rd Viscount Falmouth, born in 1758, survived the American War, and died in 1808.

THE BAS-BLEU
[1]   Elizabeth Vesey (?1715–91), known to her friends as The Sylph. She met Elizabeth Montagu in 1749, and was famous for her London parties, 1770–84, with bluestocking gatherings every other Tuesday. More sent this poem to her when her sight was failing, partly to cheer her up.

[2]   The French Ambassadress, to be precise, according to Elizabeth Carter.
[3]   Numerous copies circulated in manuscript: Mrs Boscawen had one made for Mrs Delany; Mary Hamilton read it in manuscript; even King George wanted one in More's own hand.
[4]   *symposium* convivial meeting for conversation, from the title of one of Plato's dialogues.
[5]   Aspasia of Miletus, mistress of Pericles, said to have engaged in intellectual disputes with Socrates.
[6]   In later versions of the poem, More specifically mentions Socrates, Alcibiades and Pericles as early bluestockings.

Nor need I stop my tale to show
(At least to readers such as you)   10
How all that Rome eteemed polite
Supped with Lucullus[7] every night –
Lucullus who, from Pontus come,
Brought conquests, and brought cherries home.
Name but the suppers in th' Apollo,   15
What classic images will follow!
How wit flew round, while each might take
Conchylia[8] from the Lucrine lake;[9]
And Attic salt,[10] and garum sauce,[11]
And lettuce from the Isle of Cos   20
(The first and last from Greece transplanted,
Used here – because the rhyme I wanted);
How pheasants' heads, with cost collected,
And phenicopters[12] stood neglected,
To laugh at Scipio's lucky hit,   25
Pompey's *bon mot*, or Caesar's wit!
Intemperance, list'ning to the tale,
Forgot the mullet[13] growing stale,
And Admiration, balanced, hung
'Twixt peacocks' brains, and Tully's tongue.[14]   30
I shall not stop to dwell on these,
But be as epic as I please,
And plunge at once *in medias res.*[15]
To prove that privilege I plead,
I'll quote some Greek I cannot read;   35
Stunned by authority, you yield,
And I, not reason, keep the field.
    Long was society o'er-run
By whist, that desolating Hun;[16]
Long did quadrille[17] despotic sit,   40
That Vandal[18] of colloquial wit;

---

[7] Lucius Licinius Lucullus (114–57 BC) gave himself up to a hedonistic lifestyle that eventually drove him insane. He is famous for having introduced cherry trees to Italy.

[8] *Conchylia* shellfish.

[9] *Lucrine lake* former lake near Naples famed for its fish.

[10] *Attic salt* refined, delicate, poignant wit.

[11] *garum sauce* made from fermented fish, used by the Romans.

[12] *phenicopters* birds, the tongues of which were a fine delicacy among the Romans.

[13] 'Seneca says that in his time the Romans were arrived at such a pitch of luxury, that the mullet was reckoned stale which did not die in the hands of the guest' (More's note). Mullet is, of course, a fish;

Seneca the younger (4 BC–AD 65) was tutor and advisor to the Emperor Nero.

[14] Marcus Tullius Cicero, Roman orator.

[15] *in medias res* into the middle of the story.

[16] As young women, Elizabeth Montagu and the Duchess of Portland had objected to the amount of time taken up by cards. Hester Chapone (then Mulso) had written against card-playing in *The Rambler* No. 10 (see Samuel Johnson, *The Rambler* ed. W. J. Bate and Albrecht D. Strauss (3 vols, New Haven and London, 1969), i 50–6). Huns were a race of warlike nomads from Asia who invaded Europe under their famous king Attila in the middle of the fifth century.

[17] *quadrille* square dance performed by four couples.

[18] *Vandal* member of the Germanic tribe that invaded western Europe in the fourth and fifth centuries.

And conversation's setting light
Lay half-obscured in Gothic night,
Till Leo's triple crown to you,
Boscawen sage, bright Montagu,   45
Divided, fell – your cares in haste
Rescued the ravaged realms of taste;
And Lyttelton's accomplished name,[19]
And witty Pulteney[20] shared the fame;
The men, not bound by pedant rules,   50
Nor ladies *précieuses ridicules;*[21]
For polished Walpole[22] showed the way,
How wits may be both learned and gay;
And Carter taught the female train,
The deeply wise are never vain;   55
And she who Shakespeare's wrongs redressed,[23]
Proved that the brightest are the best.
    Oh, how unlike the wit that fell,
Rambouillet, at thy quaint Hotel![24]
Where point, and turn, and *equivoque,*[25]   60
Distorted every word they spoke!
All so intolerably bright,
Plain common sense was put to flight –
Each speaker, so ingenious ever,
'Twas tiresome to be quite so clever.   65
There twisted wit forgot to please,
And mood and figure[26] banished ease:
Poor exiled Nature houseless strayed,
Till Sévigné received the maid.
    Though here she comes to bless our isle,   70
Not universal is her smile.
Muse, snatch the lyre which Cambridge strung,
When he the *empty ballroom* sung!
'Tis tuned above thy pitch, I doubt,
And thou no music wouldst draw out;   75

---

[19] George, 1st Baron Lyttelton (1709–73), friend of Pope, Fielding, and Thomson, among many others.
[20] William Pulteney, Earl of Bath (1684–1764), statesman, and friend of Elizabeth Carter (on whom he settled an annuity of £100) and Elizabeth Montagu.
[21] Men were not bound by the pedantic rules of card-games, and women were not turned into ridiculous, precious fools. Moliere's *Les Précieuses ridicules* is a one-act farce, first performed 1659.
[22] Horace Walpole, 4th Earl of Orford (1717–97), author of *The Castle of Otranto* (1764), friend of More. One of his letters to her can be found in *British Literature 1640–1789* 980–3.

[23] Elizabeth Montagu published her *Essay on the Writings and Genius of Shakespeare* in 1769, defending him against the strictures of Voltaire.
[24] 'The society at the Hôtel de Rambouillet, though composed of polite and ingenious persons, was much tainted with affectation and false taste. See Voiture, Menage, etc.' (More's note). At the Hôtel de Rambouillet, Catherine de Vivonne de Savelli, Marquise de Rambouillet, presided over the first French salon, 1610–65. Vincent Voiture (1597–1648) was a leading light, as was Gilles Ménage (1613–92), the flirtatious 'professor' of Madame de Lafayette and Madame de Sévigné.
[25] *equivoque* play on words.
[26] *mood and figure* due logical form.

Yet, in a lower note, presume
To sing the full, dull drawing-room.
  Where the dire circle keeps its station,
Each common phrase is an oration;
And cracking fans and whisp'ring misses   80
Compose their conversation blisses.
The matron marks the goodly show,
While the tall daughter eyes the beau –
The frigid beau! Ah, luckless fair!
'Tis not for you that studied air;   85
Ah, not for you that sidelong glance,
And all that charming nonchalance;
Ah, not for you the three long hours
He worshipped the 'cosmetic powers' –
That finished head which breathes perfume,   90
And kills the nerves of half the room;
And all the murders meant to lie
In that large, languishing, grey eye.
Desist – less wild th' attempt would be
To warm the snows of Rhodope.[27]   95
Too cold to feel, too proud to feign,
For him you're wise and fair in vain.
  Chill shade of that affected Peer
Who dreaded mirth, come safely here!
For here no vulgar joy effaces   100
Thy rage for polish,[28] ton,[29] and graces.
Cold Ceremony's leaden hand
Waves o'er the room her poppy wand;
Arrives the stranger, every guest
Conspires to torture the distressed;   105
At once they rise, so have I seen –
You guess the simile I mean;
Take what comparison you please –
The crowded streets, the swarming bees,
The pebbles on the shores that lie,   110
The stars which form the galaxy –
This serves t' embellish what is said,
And shows, besides, that one has read –
At once they rise; th' astonished guest
Back in a corner slinks, distressed,   115
Scared at the many bowing round,
And shocked at her own voice's sound,
Forgot the thing she meant to say,
Her words, half-uttered, die away;
In sweet oblivion down she sinks,   120

---

[27] *Rhodope* mountain range in Thrace.   [29] *ton* fashionable society.
[28] *polish* refinement.

And of her ten appointments thinks,
While her loud neighbour on the right
Boasts what she has to do tonight –
So very much, you'd swear her pride is
To match the labours of Alcides.[30]   125
'Tis true, in hyperbolic measure,
She nobly calls her labours *pleasure*;
In this, unlike Alcmena's son,[31]
She never means they should be done;
Her fancy of no limits dreams,   130
No *ne plus ultra*[32] stops her schemes;
Fired at th' idea, out she flounces,
And a new martyr John announces.

   We pass the pleasures vast and various
Of routs not social, but gregarious;   135
And, pleased, to gentler scenes retreat,
Where Conversation holds her seat.

   Small were that art which would ensure
The circle's boasted quadrature![33]
See Vesey's plastic genius make   140
A circle every figure take;[34]
Nay, shapes and forms, which would defy
All science of geometry,
Isosceles, and parallel –
Names hard to speak, and hard to spell!   145
Th' enchantress waved her wand, and spoke!
Her potent wand the circle broke;
The social spirits hover round
And bless the liberated ground.
Ask you what charms this gift dispense?   150
'Tis the strong spell of common sense.
Away fell Ceremony flew,
And with her bore Detraction too.

   Nor only geometric art
Does this presiding power impart;   155
But chemists too, who want the essence
Which makes or mars all coalescence,
Of her the secret rare might get,
How different kinds amalgamate;
And he, who wilder studies chose,   160

---

[30] *Alcides* Alcides, or Heracles, had twelve labours imposed on him by Eurystheus, culminating in the descent into the underworld for Cerberus.
[31] *Alcmena's son* Heracles, whose father was Zeus.
[32] *ne plus ultra* prohibition of further progress.

[33] *quadrature* squaring the circle; the expression of an area bounded by a circle by means of an equivalent square.
[34] In later editions of the poem, More explained: 'This amiable lady was remarkable for her talent in breaking the formality of a circle by inviting her parties to form themselves into little separate groups'.

Find here a new metempsychose[35] –
How forms can other forms assume
Within her Pythagoric room;
Or be (and stranger is th' event)
The very things which nature meant;   165
Nor strive, by art and affectation,
To cross their genuine destination.
Here sober duchesses are seen,
Chaste wits, and critics void of spleen;
Physicians, fraught with real science,   170
And Whigs and Tories in alliance;
Poets fulfilling Christian duties,
Just lawyers, reasonable beauties;
Bishops who preach, and Peers who pay,
And Countesses who seldom play;   175
Learned antiquaries who, from college,
Reject the rust, and bring the knowledge;
And, hear it, age, believe it, youth,
Polemics,[36] really seeking truth;
And travellers of that rare tribe,   180
Who've *seen* the countries they describe;
Ladies who point[37] (nor think me partial)
An epigram as well as Martial;[38]
Yet in all female worth succeed
As well as those who cannot read.   185
  Right pleasant were the task, I ween,
To name the groups which fill the scene;
But rhyme's of such fastidious nature,
She proudly scorns all nomenclature,
Nor grace our northern names her lips,   190
Like Homer's catalogue of ships.
  Once, faithful memory, heave a sigh!
Here Roscius[39] gladdened every eye.
Why comes not Maro?[40] Far from town,
He rears the urn to Taste, and Brown;[41]   195
His English garden breathes perfume,
And promises perennial bloom.
Here rigid Cato,[42] awful sage,
Bold censor of a thoughtless age,
Once dealt his pointed moral round,   200

[35] *metempsychose* to transfer a soul from one body to another.
[36] *Polemics* controversialists, argumentative writers.
[37] *point* compose.
[38] Marcus Valerius Martial, Roman poet of the first century AD, known for satirical epigrams.
[39] *Roscius* Garrick.
[40] *Maro* William Mason (1725–97), famous for a long blank verse poem on landscape gardening, *The English Garden* (1771–81).
[41] *Brown* Lancelot 'Capability' Brown (1715–83), innovative and ambitious landscape gardener of the day; responsible for the epic landscaping at Kew and Blenheim.
[42] *Cato* Samuel Johnson.

And, not unheeded, fell the sound;
The muse his honoured memory weeps,
For Cato[43] now with Roscius sleeps!
Here once Hortensius[44] loved to sit,
Apostate now from social wit;   205
Ah, why in wrangling senates waste
The noblest parts, the happiest taste?
Why democratic thunders wield,
And quit the muse's calmer field?
Taste thou the gentler joys they give –   210
With Horace, and with Lelius live.[45]
    Hail Conversation, soothing power,
Sweet goddess of the social hour!
Not with more heartfelt warmth, at least,
Does Lelius bend, thy true High Priest,   215
Than I, the lowest of thy train,
These field-flowers bring to deck thy fane.
Who to thy shrine like him can haste
With warmer zeal or purer taste?
Oh may thy worship long prevail,   220
And thy true votaries never fail!
Long may thy polished altars blaze
With wax-lights' undiminished rays!
Still be thy nightly offerings paid,
Libations large of lemonade!   225
On silver vases, loaded rise
The biscuits' ample sacrifice!
Nor be the milk-white streams forgot
Of thirst-assuaging, cool orgeat;[46]
Rise, incense pure from fragrant tea,   230
Delicious incense, worthy thee!
    Hail, Conversation, heav'nly fair,
Thou bliss of life, and balm of care!
Call forth the long-forgotten knowledge
Of school, of travel, and of college!   235
For thee, best solace of his toil,
The sage consumes his midnight oil,
And keeps late vigils to produce
Materials for thy future use.
If none behold, ah! wherefore fair?   240
Ah, wherefore wise, if none must hear?

---

[43] Johnson died in 1784.

[44] *Hortensius* Edmund Burke (1729–97), statesman and writer. He and More had been friends, but his pro-American stance during the Revolution had alienated her. They enjoyed a rapprochement in 1786, shortly after publication of *Bas-Bleu*, though she was still able to comment, in a letter of April 1786, that 'business and politics have impaired his agreeableness' (William Roberts, *Memoirs of the Life and Correspondence of Mrs Hannah More*, ii 14).

[45] Horace and Lelius are Horace Walpole and Sir William Weller Pepys. Pepys was a lawyer and a close friend and correspondent of More.

[46] *orgeat* syrup or cooling drink made from barley.

Our intellectual ore must shine,
Not slumber idly in the mine.
Let Education's moral mint
The noblest images imprint;   245
Let Taste her curious touchstone hold,
To try if standard be the gold –
But 'tis thy commerce, Conversation
Must give it use by circulation;
That noblest commerce of mankind,   250
Whose precious merchandise is mind!
  What stoic traveller would try
A sterile soil and parching sky,
Or dare th' intemperate northern zone,
If what he saw must ne'er be known?   255
For this he bids his home farewell,
The joy of seeing is to tell.
Trust me, he never would have stirred
Were he forbid to speak a word;
And Curiosity would sleep,   260
If her own secrets she must keep:
The bliss of telling what is past
Becomes her rich reward at last.
Yet not from low desire to shine,
Does Genius toil in Learning's mine;   265
Not to indulge in idle vision,
But strike new light by strong collision.
  O'er books the mind inactive lies,
Books, the mind's food, not exercise!
Her vigorous wing she scarcely feels,   270
Till use the latent strength reveals;
Her slumbering energies called forth,
She rises, conscious of her worth;
And, at her new-found powers elated,
Thinks them not roused, but new-created.   275
  Enlightened spirits! you, who know
What charms from polished converse flow,
Speak, for you can, the pure delight
When kindred sympathies unite;
When correspondent tastes impart   280
Communion sweet from heart to heart;
You ne'er the cold gradations need
Which vulgar souls to union lead;
No dry discussion to unfold
The meaning, caught as soon as told: 285
But sparks electric only strike
On souls electrical alike;
The flash of intellect expires
Unless it meet congenial fires.

The language to th' elect alone   290
Is, like the mason's mystery, known;
In vain th' unerring sign is made
To him who is not of the *trade*.
What lively pleasure to divine
The thought implied, the hinted line,   295
To feel allusion's artful force,
And trace the image to its source!
Quick Memory blends her scattered rays
Till Fancy kindles at the blaze;
The works of ages start to view,   300
And· ancient wit elicits new.
    But wit and parts if thus we praise,
What nobler altars should we raise,
Those sacrifices could we see
Which wit, oh Virtue, makes to thee!   305
At once the rising thought to dash,
To quench at once the bursting flash!
The shining mischief to subdue,
And lose the praise and pleasure too!
This is high principle's control!   310
This is true continence of soul!
    Blush, heroes, at your cheap renown,
A vanquished realm, a plundered town!
Your conquests were to gain a name;
This conquest triumphs over fame: 315
So pure its essence, 'twere destroyed
If known and, if commended, void.
Amidst the brightest truths believed,
Amidst the fairest deeds achieved,
Shall stand recorded and admired,   320
That Virtue sunk what Wit inspired!
    But let the lettered and the fair,
And, chiefly, let the Wit beware;
You, whose warm spirits never fail,
Forgive the hint which ends my tale: 325
Though Science nursed you in her bow'rs,
Though Fancy crown your brow with flowers,
Each thought, though bright invention fill,
Though Attic bees each word distil;
Yet, if one gracious power refuse   330
Her gentle influence to infuse,
In vain shall listening crowds approve,
They'll praise you, but they will not love.
What is this power you're loath to mention,
This charm, this witchcraft? 'Tis Attention.   ·335
Mute angel, yes; thy looks dispense
The silence of intelligence;

Thy graceful form I well discern,
In act to listen and to learn;
'Tis thou for talents shalt obtain   340
That pardon Wit would hope in vain;
Thy wondrous power, thy secret charm
Shall Envy of her sting disarm;
Thy silent flattery soothes our spirit,
And we forgive eclipsing merit;   345
The sweet atonement screens the fault,
And love and praise are cheaply bought.
  With mild complacency to hear,
Though somewhat long the tale appear,
'Tis more than wit, 'tis moral beauty,   350
'Tis pleasure rising out of duty.

Slavery: A Poem (1788)

Oh great design!
Ye sons of mercy! Oh complete your work;
Wrench from Oppression's hand the iron rod,
And bid the cruel feel the pains they give.

Thomson's Liberty

If Heaven has into being deigned to call
Thy light, oh liberty, to shine on all,
Bright intellectual sun, why does thy ray
To earth distribute only partial day?
Since no resisting cause from spirit flows,   5
Thy penetrating essence to oppose;[1]
No obstacles by nature's hand impressed,
Thy subtle and ethereal beams arrest;
Nor motion's laws can speed thy active course,
Nor strong repulsion's pow'rs obstruct thy force –   10
Since there is no convexity in mind,
Why are thy genial beams to parts confined?
While the chill north with thy bright ray is blessed
Why should fell darkness half the south invest?
Was it decreed, fair Freedom, at thy birth,   15
That thou shouldst ne'er irradiate *all* the earth?
While Britain basks in thy full blaze of light,
Why lies sad Afric quenched in total night?
  Thee only, sober goddess, I attest,
In smiles chastised, and decent graces dressed;   20
Not that unlicensed monster of the crowd

SLAVERY

[1] The *European Magazine* found the first eighteen lines of the poem 'metaphysically abstruse', and asked:

'What is meant by a "resisting cause flowing from spirit to oppose a penetrating essence"?' (*European Magazine* 13 (1788) 166–7, p. 166).

Whose roar terrific bursts in peals so loud,
Deaf'ning the ear of Peace; fierce Faction's tool
Of rash Sedition born, and mad Misrule,
Whose stubborn mouth, rejecting Reason's rein,   25
No strength can govern, and no skill restrain;
Whose magic cries the frantic vulgar draw,
To spurn at order, and to outrage law;
To tread on grave Authority and Pow'r,
And shake the work of ages in an hour.   30
Convulsed her voice, and pestilent her breath,
She raves of mercy while she deals out death –
Each blast is fate; she darts from either hand
Red conflagration o'er th' astonished land;
Clamouring for peace, she rends the air with noise,   35
And to reform a part, the whole destroys.
    Oh plaintive Southerne,[2] whose impassioned strain
So oft has waked my languid muse in vain!
Now, when congenial themes her cares engage,
She burns to emulate thy glowing page;   40
Her failing efforts mock her fond desires,
She shares thy feelings, not partakes thy fires.
Strange pow'r of song – the strain that warms the heart
Seems the same inspiration to impart;
Touched by the kindling energy alone,   45
We think the flame which melts us is our own;
Deceived, for genius we mistake delight;
Charmed as we read, we fancy we can write.
    Though not to me, sweet bard, thy pow'rs belong,
Fair Truth, a hallowed guide, inspires my song!   50
Here art would weave her gayest flow'rs in vain,
For Truth the bright invention would disdain.
For no fictitious ills these numbers flow,
But living anguish and substantial woe;
No individual griefs my bosom melt,   55
For millions feel what Oroonoko felt:[3]
Fired by no single wrongs, the countless host
I mourn, by rapine dragged from Afric's coast.
    Perish th' illiberal thought which would debase
The native genius of the sable race!   60
Perish the proud philosophy which sought
To rob them of the pow'rs of equal thought!
Does then th' immortal principle within

---

[2] 'Author of the tragedy of Oroonoko' (More's note). Thomas Southerne's *Oroonoko* (1695–6) was enormously popular during the eighteenth century, being adapted three times by 1788. It was itself an adaptation of Aphra Behn's anti-slavery novel (1688).

[3] The story of Oroonoko is essentially tragic. The heir to an African king, he is taken as a slave to Surinam, an English colony.

Change with the casual colour of a skin?
Does matter govern spirit, or is mind   65
Degraded by the form to which 'tis joined?
    No; they have heads to think, and hearts to feel,
And souls to act, with firm though erring zeal;
For they have keen affections, kind desires,
Love strong as death, and active patriot fires;   70
All the rude energy, the fervid flame
Of high-souled passion and ingenuous shame –
Strong but luxuriant virtues boldly shoot
From the wild vigour of a savage root.
    Nor weak their sense of honour's proud control,   75
For pride is virtue in a pagan soul;
A sense of worth, a conscience of desert,
A high, unbroken haughtiness of heart;
That self-same stuff which erst proud empires swayed,
Of which the conquerors of the world were made.   80
Capricious fate of man! That very pride
In Afric scourged, in Rome was deified.
    No muse, oh Qua-shi,[4] shall thy deeds relate,
No statute snatch thee from oblivious fate!
For thou wast born where never gentle muse   85
On valour's grave the flow'rs of genius strews;
And thou wast born where no recording page
Plucks the fair deed from time's devouring rage.
Had fortune placed thee on some happier coast,
Where polished souls heroic virtue boast,   90
To thee, who sought'st a voluntary grave,
Th' uninjured honours of thy name to save,
Whose generous arm thy barbarous master spared,
Altars had smoked, and temples had been reared.
    Whene'er to Afric's shores I turn my eyes,   95
Horrors of deepest, deadliest guilt arise;
I see, by more than fancy's mirror shown,
The burning village and the blazing town,
See the dire victim torn from social life,
The shrieking babe, the agonizing wife!   100

---

4 "'It is a point of honour among negroes of a high spirit to die, rather than to suffer their glossy skin to bear the mark of the whip. Qua-shi had somehow offended his master, a young planter with whom he had been bred up in the endearing intimacy of a play-fellow. His services had been faithful; his attachment affectionate. The master resolved to punish him, and pursued him for that purpose. In trying to escape, Qua-shi stumbled and fell; the master fell upon him. They wrestled long with doubtful victory. At length, Qua-shi got uppermost, and being firmly seated on his master's breast, he secured his legs with one hand, and with the other drew a sharp knife; then said, 'Master, I have been bred up with you from a child; I have loved you as myself; in return, you have condemned me to a punishment, of which I must ever have borne the marks – thus only I can avoid them.' So saying, he drew the knife with all his strength across his own throat, and fell down dead, without a groan, on his master's body." Ramsay's *Essay on the Treatment of African Slaves* (More's note). More refers to James Ramsay (1733–89), *An Essay on the Treatment and Conversion of African Slaves in the British Sugar Colonies* (1784).

She, wretch forlorn, is dragged by hostile hands,
To distant tyrants sold, in distant lands!
Transmitted miseries and successive chains
The sole sad heritage her child obtains!
Ev'n this last wretched boon their foes deny: 105
To weep together, or together die.
By felon hands, by one relentless stroke,
See the fond links of feeling nature broke!
The fibres twisting round a parent's heart,
Torn from their grasp, and bleeding as they part.   110
   Hold, murderers, hold! Nor aggravate distress;
Respect the passions you yourselves possess!
Ev'n you, of ruffian heart and ruthless hand,
Love your own offspring, love your native land.
Ah, leave them holy freedom's cheering smile,   115
The Heav'n-taught fondness for the parent soil;
Revere affections mingled with our frame,
In every nature, every clime the same;
In all, these feelings equal sway maintain;
In all, the love of home and freedom reign –   120
And Tempe's vale[5] and parched Angola's sand
One equal fondness of their sons command.
Th' unconquered savage laughs at pain and toil,
Basking in freedom's beams which gild his native soil.
   Does thirst of empire, does desire of fame   125
(For these are specious crimes), our rage inflame?
No; sordid lust of gold their fate controls –
The basest appetite of basest souls;
Gold, better gained by what their ripening sky,
Their fertile fields, their arts[6] and mines supply.   130
   What wrongs, what injuries does Oppression plead,
To smooth the horror of th' unnatural deed?
What strange offence, what aggravated sin?
They stand convicted of a darker skin!
Barbarians, hold! Th' opprobrious commerce spare,   135
Respect His sacred image which they bear.
Though dark and savage, ignorant and blind,
They claim the common privilege of kind;
Let malice strip them of each other plea,
They still are men, and men should still be free.   140
Insulted reason loathes th' inverted trade –
Dire change! The agent is the purchase made!
Perplexed, the baffled muse involves the tale;
Nature confounded, well may language fail!

---

[5] *Tempe's vale* idyllic valley in Thessaly, praised by Virgil, *Georgics* ii 469.

[6] 'Besides many valuable productions of the soil, cloths and carpets of exquisite manufacture are brought from the coast of Guinea' (More's note).

The outraged goddess, with abhorrent eyes,   145
Sees man the traffic, souls the merchandise!
    Plead not, in reason's palpable abuse,
Their sense of feeling callous and obtuse;[7]
From heads to hearts lies nature's plain appeal –
Though few can reason, all mankind can feel.   150
Though wit may boast a livelier dread of shame,
A loftier sense of wrong, refinement claim;
Though polished manners may fresh wants invent,
And nice[8] distinctions nicer souls torment –
Though these on finer spirits heavier fall,   155
Yet natural evils are the same to all.
Though wounds there are which reason's force may heal,
There needs no logic sure to make us feel.
The nerve, howe'er untutored, can sustain
A sharp, unutterable sense of pain,   160
As exquisitely fashioned in a slave
As where unequal fate a sceptre gave.
Sense is as keen where Congo's sons preside
As where proud Tiber rolls his classic tide.
Rhetoric or verse may point the feeling line –   165
They do not whet sensation, but define.
Did ever slave less feel the galling chain,
When Zeno[9] proved there was no ill in pain?
Their miseries philosophic quirks[10] deride;
Slaves groan in pangs disowned by Stoic pride.   170
    When the fierce sun darts vertical his beams,
And thirst and hunger mix their wild extremes;
When the sharp iron wounds his inmost soul,[11]
And his strained eyes in burning anguish roll –
Will the parched negro find, ere he expire,   175
No pain in hunger, and no heat in fire?
    For him, when fate his tortured frame destroys,
What hope of present fame or future joys?
For this have heroes shortened nature's date;
For that have martyrs gladly met their fate;   180
But him, forlorn, no hero's pride sustains,
No martyr's blissful visions soothe his pains;
Sullen, he mingles with his kindred dust,

---

[7] 'Nothing is more frequent than this cruel and stupid argument, that they do not *feel* the miseries inflicted on them as Europeans would do' (More's note). This was one of the arguments of the merchants who claimed that regulation of the slave trade would put them out of business, when Sir William Dolben brought in a Bill to limit the number of slaves which could be transported in 1788 (see headnote).
[8] *nice* subtle.

[9] *Zeno* Zeno of Citium (*c*.335 BC–*c*.263), founded the Stoic school of philosophy.
[10] *quirks* quibbles, subtle or evasive arguments.
[11] 'This is not said figuratively. The writer of these lines has seen a complete set of chains, fitted to every separate limb of these unhappy, innocent men, together with instruments for wrenching open the jaws, contrived with such ingenious cruelty as would shock the humanity of an inquisitor' (More's notes).

For he has learned to dread the Christian's trust.
To him what mercy can that pow'r display,   185
Whose servants murder, and whose sons betray?
Savage, thy venial error I deplore –
They are *not* Christians who infest thy shore!
    Oh thou sad spirit, whose preposterous yoke
The great deliverer death at length has broke!   190
Released from misery, and escaped from care,
Go meet that mercy man denied thee here.
In thy dark home, sure refuge of th' oppressed,
The wicked vex not, and the weary rest.
And if some notions, vague and undefined,   195
Of future terrors have assailed thy mind;
If such thy masters have presumed to teach,
As terrors only they are prone to preach
(For should they paint eternal mercy's reign,
Where were th' oppressor's rod, the captive's chain?);   200
If, then, thy troubled soul has learned to dread
The dark unknown thy trembling footsteps tread –
On Him, who made thee what thou art, depend:
He, who withholds the means, accepts the end.
Not *thine* the reckoning dire of light abused,   205
Knowledge disgraced, and liberty misused;
On *thee* no awful judge incensed shall sit
For parts perverted, and dishonoured wit.
Where ignorance will be found the surest plea,
How many learned and wise shall envy *thee*!   210
    And thou, white savage, whether lust of gold
Or lust of conquest ruled thee uncontrolled –
Hero or robber – by whatever name
Thou plead thy impious claim to wealth or fame;
Whether inferior mischiefs be thy boast,   215
A petty tyrant rifling Gambia's coast;
Or bolder carnage track thy crimson way,
Kings dispossessed, and provinces thy prey,
Panting to tame wide earth's remotest bound,
All Cortez[12] murdered, all Columbus found;   220
O'er plundered realms to reign, detested lord,
Make millions wretched, and thyself abhorred;
In reason's eye, in wisdom's fair account,
Your sum of glory boasts a like amount;
The means may differ, but the end's the same: 225
Conquest is pillage with a nobler name.
Who makes the sum of human blessings less,

---

[12] Hernán Cortez (1485–1547), Spanish conquista-
dor, who overthrew the Aztec empire and won Mexico
for Spain.

Or sinks the stock of general happiness,
No solid fame shall grace, no true renown,
His life shall blazon, or his memory crown.   230
　　Had those advent'rous spirits who explore
Through ocean's trackless wastes the far-sought shore;
Whether of wealth insatiate, or of pow'r,
Conquerors who waste, or ruffians who devour –
Had these possessed, oh Cook,[13] thy gentle mind,   235
Thy love of arts, thy love of humankind;
Had these pursued thy mild and liberal plan,
Discoverers had not been a curse to man!
Then, blessed philanthropy, thy social hands
Had linked dissevered worlds in brothers' bands,   240
Careless if colour or if clime divide;
Then, loved and loving, man had lived and died.
　　The purest wreaths which hang on glory's shrine,
For empires founded, peaceful Penn,[14] are thine;
No bloodstained laurels crowned thy virtuous toil,   245
No slaughtered natives drenched thy fair-earned soil.
Still thy meek spirit in thy flock survives,[15]
Consistent still, *their* doctrines rule their lives;
Thy followers only have effaced the shame
Inscribed by Slavery on the Christian name.   250
　　Shall Britain, where the soul of Freedom reigns,
Forge chains for others she herself disdains?
Forbid it, Heaven! Oh let the nations know
The liberty she loves she will bestow;
Not to herself the glorious gift confined,   255
She spreads the blessing wide as huankind;
And, scorning narrow views of time and place,
Bids all be free in earth's extended space.
　　What page of human annals can record
A deed so bright as human rights restored?   260
Oh may that godlike deed, that shining page,
Redeem *our* fame, and consecrate *our* age!
　　And see, the cherub Mercy from above,
Descending softly, quits the sphere of love!
On feeling hearts she sheds celestial dew,   265
And breathes her spirit o'er th' enlightened few;
From soul to soul the spreading influence steals,
Till every breast the soft contagion feels.
She bears, exulting, to the burning shore,
The loveliest office angel ever bore: 270

---

[13] James Cook (1728–79) circumnavigated the world in the *Endeavour*, 1768–71.
[14] William Penn (1644–1718), Quaker and founder of Pennsylvania.

[15] 'The Quakers have emancipated all their slaves throughout America' (More's note).

To vindicate the pow'r in heaven adored;
To still the clank of chains, and sheathe the sword;
To cheer the mourner, and with soothing hands
From bursting hearts unbind th' oppressor's bands;
To raise the lustre of the Christian name,   275
And clear the foulest blot that dims its fame.
  As the mild spirit hovers o'er the coast,
A fresher hue the withered landscapes boast;
Her healing smiles the ruined scenes repair,
And blasted Nature wears a joyous air.   280
She spreads her blest commission from above,
Stamped with the sacred characters of love;
She tears the banner stained with blood and tears,
And, Liberty, thy shining standard rears!
As the bright ensign's glory she displays,   285
See pale Oppression faints beneath the blaze!
The giant dies, no more his frown appals;
The chain, untouched, drops off; the fetter falls.
Astonished Echo tells the vocal shore,
'Oppression's fall'n, and Slavery is no more!'   290
The dusky myriads crowd the sultry plain,
And hail that mercy long invoked in vain;
Victorious pow'r! She bursts their two-fold bands,
And Faith and Freedom spring from Mercy's hands.

Cheap Repository: The Story of Sinful Sally. Told by Herself. (1796)

Showing how, from being Sally of the Green, she was first led to become Sinful Sally, and afterwards Drunken Sal, and how at last she came to a most melancholy and almost hopeless end, being therein a warning to all young women both in town and country. Price one halfpenny.[1]

Come each maiden lend an ear,
  Country lass and London belle!
Come and drop a mournful tear
  O'er the tale that I shall tell!

I that ask your tender pity,   5
  Ruined now and all forlorn,
Once like you was young and pretty,
  And as cheerful as the morn.

THE STORY OF SINFUL SALLY
[1] As explained in the headnote above, this poem, and many others like it, were originally sold individually as broadsides; that is, printed on large pieces of paper which were sold by travelling pedlars ('chapmen').

In yon distant cottage sitting,
   Far away from London town,   10
Once you might have seen me knitting
   In my simple kersey² gown.

Where the little lambkins leap,
   Where the meadow looks so gay,
Where the drooping willows weep,   15
   Simple Sally used to stray.

Then I tasted many a blessing,
   Then I had an honest fame;
Father, mother, me caressing,
   Smiled and thought me free from blame.   20

Then amid my friends so dear,
   Life it speeded fast away;
Oh, it moves a tender tear
   To think how peaceful was the day!

From the villages surrounding,   25
   Ere I well had reached eighteen,
Came the modest youths abounding,
   All to Sally of the Green.

Courting days were thus beginning,
   And I soon had proved a wife;   30
Oh, if I had kept from sinning,
   Now how blessed had been my life!

Come each maiden, lend an ear,
   Country lass and London belle!
Come ye now and deign to hear   35
   How poor sinful Sally fell.

Where the hill begins inclining,
   Half a furlong from the road,
O'er the village white and shining
   Stands Sir William's great abode.   40

Near his meadow I was tripping,
   Vainly³ wishing to be seen,
When Sir William met me skipping,
   And he spoke me on the Green;

---

² *kersey* coarse cloth woven from wool.   ³ *Vainly* Sally's troubles begin with the sin of vanity.

Bid me quit my cloak of scarlet,[4]   45
  Blamed my simple kersey gown,
Eyed me then, so like a varlet
  Such as live in London town.

With his presents I was loaded,
  And bedecked in ribbons gay;   50
Thus my ruin was foreboded –
  Oh how crafty was his way!

Vanished now from cottage lowly,
  My poor parents' heart I break,
Enter on a state unholy,   55
  Turn a mistress to a rake.

Now no more by morning light
  Up to God my voice I raise;
Now no shadows of the night
  Call my thoughts to prayer and praise.   60

Hark! A well known sound I hear!
  'Tis the church's Sunday bell;
No, I dread to venture near;
  No, I'm now the child of hell.

Now I lay my Bible by,   65
  Choose that impious book so new;
Love the bold blaspheming lie,
  And that filthy novel too.

Next to London town I pass
  (Sinful Sally is my name),   70
There to gain a front of brass[5]
  And to glory in my shame.

Powdered well, and puffed, and painted,
  Rivals all I there outshine;
With skin so white and heart so tainted,   75
  Rolling in my chariot fine.

In the park I glitter daily,
  Then I dress me for the play,
Then to masquerade so gaily,
  All London hears me tear away.   80

---

[4] *scarlet* significantly, Sally is a scarlet woman even   [5] *brass* unblushing impudence.
before her sinful career begins. The obvious comparison
is with the whore of Babylon, Revelation 17:3–6.

When I meet some meaner[6] lass,
    Then I toss with proud disdain;
Laugh and giggle as I pass,
    As if I never knew a pain.

But amidst my peals of laughter   85
    Horror seizes oft my frame;
Pleasure now, damnation after,
    And a never-dying flame.[7]

'Save me, save me, Lord!' I cry,
    'Save my soul from Satan's chain!'   90
Now I see salvation nigh,
    Now I turn to sin again.

By a thousand ills o'ertaken
    See me now quite sinking down,
Till so lost and so forsaken   95
    Sal is cast upon the town.

At the dusk of evening grey,
    Forth I step from secret cell,
Roaming like a beast of prey
    Or some hateful imp of hell.   100

Ah, how many youths so blooming
    By my wanton looks I've won;
Then by vices all consuming
    Left them ruined and undone!

Thus the cruel spider stretches   105
    Wide his web for every fly;
Then each victim that he catches
    Straight he poisons till he die.

Now no more by conscience troubled,
    Deep I plunge in every sin;   110
True, my sorrows are redoubled,
    But I drown them all in gin.

See me next with front so daring
    Band of ruffian rogues among;
Fighting, cheating, drinking, swearing –   115
    And Sal's the vilest of the throng.

---

[6] *meaner* poorer.

[7] *a never-dying flame* a reference, presumably, to the flames of hell.

Mark that youngest of the thieves;
  Taught by Sal he ventures further;
What he filches Sal receives –
  'Tis for Sal he does the murder.   120

See me then attend my victim
  To the fatal gallows tree,
Pleased to think how I have nicked[8] him,
  Made him swing while I am free.

Jack I laughing see depart,   125
  While with Dick I drink and sing;
Soon again I'll fill the cart,
  Make this present lover swing.

But while thus with guilt surprising,
  Sal pursues her bold career,   130
See God's dreadful wrath arising
  And the day of vengeance near.

Fierce disease my body seizes,
  Racking pain afflicts my bones;[9]
Dread of death my spirit freezes,   135
  Deep and doleful are my groans.

Here with face so shrunk and spotted
  On the clay-cold ground I lie;
See how all my flesh is rotted –
  Stop, oh stranger, see me die!   140

Conscience, as my breath's departing,
  Plunges too his arrow deep,
With redoubled fury starting
  Like some giant from his sleep.

In this pit of ruin lying   145
  Once again before I die,
Fainting, trembling, weeping, sighing –
  Lord, to thee I'll lift mine eye.

Thou canst save the vilest harlot,
  Grace I've heard is free and full,   150
Sins that once were red as scarlet
  Thou canst make as white as wool.

---

[8] *nicked* tricked, cheated.   [9] Sally endures the symptoms of venereal disease.

Saviour, whom I've pierced so often,
    Deeper still my guilt imprint!
Let thy mighty spirit soften   155
    This my hardened heart of flint!

Vain, alas, is all my groaning,
    For I fear the die is cast;
True, thy blood is all atoning,
    But my day of grace is past.   160

Saviour, hear me or I perish!
    None who lives is quite undone;
Still a ray of hope I'll cherish
    Till eternity's begun.

Susanna Blamire (1747–1794)

Susanna was the youngest child of William Blamire and Isabella Simpson. Her mother died in 1754, and her father remarried the following year. After that, she, her sister, and two older brothers were brought up by their widowed aunt, Mary Simpson, on her farm at Thackwood, near Stokedalewath. She was educated at the village school at Raughton Head, where the fee was a shilling a quarter, and later was taught at home by ushers from Sebergham Grammar School. During these years she developed a love of reading and writing. As she grew up, she enjoyed composing poetry, but with no thought of publication; she wrote many lyrics to accompany herself on the guitar. This was discouraged by her brother William, and her Aunt Simpson, but she persisted, scribbling poems on the backs of old bills and letters. After her sister's marriage to Lieut.-Col. Graham, a soldier in the 42nd Highland Regiment, she lived with them in Gartmore, and later in Ireland and London. After Graham's death in 1773, she returned to Thackwood to live with her sister. On occasional visits to Carlisle they became friendly with the poet Catherine Gilpin (1738–1811), who lived at 10 Finkle Street, Carlisle, and with whom they sometimes wrote poems. Her health was delicate from the mid 1780s onwards, and she died in Carlisle in 1794.

She was utterly unknown as a writer during her lifetime, although scattered publications appeared in journals and newspapers, or as broadsides, from the 1780s. It was not until the 1830s, when Henry Lonsdale began assembling her manuscripts, that anyone valued her verse sufficiently to think it worth collecting. His edition, *The Poetical Works of Miss Susanna Blamire, 'The Muse of Cumberland'*, appeared in 1842. Her most impressive single work is that published by Lonsdale as *Stoklewath; or, the Cumbrian Village*, though entitled *A North Country Village* in the manuscript. It is highly unusual among her works in that it survives in fair copy; most of her poems were written on scraps of paper. Lonsdale did a fine job, but like many Victorian editors took what would now be regarded as unacceptable liberties with the copy-text, rewriting lines where he detected stylistic infelicities or solecisms. The poem is too long to present in its entirety, but this sizeable extract is edited directly from the manuscript by kind permission of the owner, Paul F. Betz.

Further Reading

Susanna Blamire, 'The Muse of Cumberland': A Tribute with Selections from her Work ed. Ted Relph (Carlisle, 1994)

Jonathan Wordsworth, Susanna Blamire: Poet of Friendship 1747–1794 (Privately published, 1995)

A NORTH COUNTRY VILLAGE (EXTRACT; EDITED FROM MANUSCRIPT)

In this gay village hangs a wondrous sign –
The Hounds and Hare are the immense design.
There hunters crack their whips, and seem to bound
O'er every hedge, not touch the mimic ground;   460
The huntsman winds his horn, his big cheeks swell,
And whippers-in[1] make lagging terriers yell;
The charmful[2] scene tempts many a wight to stay
As to the school he drags the weary way.
Around the front inviting benches wait,   465
Conscious of many a glass and sage debate;
The great man of the village[3] cracks his joke,
Reads o'er the news, and whiffs the curling smoke;
Tells tales of old, and nods, and heaves the can,[4]
Makes fixed decrees, and seems much more than man.   470
    'Come Jack, sit down. Thy father, man, and me,
Broke many a glass, and many a freak[5] had we.
'Twas when he sought thy mother, at Carl fair[6]
(I mind that corn[7] was very bad that year),
We met thy mother and my wife i' th' street,   475
And took them into Becks to get a treat;
Blind Joseph played, and I took out thy mother,
Thy father he was shy, he got another;
And when I took her back, as you may see,
I whipped her blushing on thy father's knee.   480
Then in came Robin Bell, who liked her too,
And bit his lip, and turned both red and blue,
Teased her to dance, as you may see, and then
Kept her himself, nor brought her back again.
I fired at this, while up thy father rose,   485

A NORTH COUNTRY VILLAGE
[1] whippers-in their job is to keep the hounds together during the hunt, using a whip.
[2] charmful delightful, charming.
[3] The great man of the village the lord of the manor.
[4] can containing beer.
[5] freak caper, lark.
[6] Carl fair Carlisle fair, held every 26 August, and so noted, as Robert Anderson wrote, 'for the number and choice of commodities, that there is hardly a villager within the circuit of ten miles who does not attend it, except perhaps two or three unhappy swains and nymphs, whom the authority of a morose parent, or a churlish master or mistress, confines at home. A Cumberland lad, when he meets his sweetheart at a fair, whether by appointment or accident, throws his arms round her waist in all the raptures of love, conducts her to a dancing-room, places her beside him on a bench, and treats her liberally with cake and punch. When a vacancy happens on the floor, he leads her out to dance a jig or reel' (Ballads in the Cumberland Dialect (Wigton, 1808), pp. 201–2).
[7] corn that is, the corn harvest.

Gave him a kick, and tweaked him by the nose.
They stripped to fight, as you may see, and I
In seeing fair play got a blackened eye;
I durst not show my face at home next day,
But bade my mother say I went away,   490
But kept my bed, i'fegs,[8] as you may see –
Who is it now fights for their lasses, eh?'
The blacksmith laughed, the cobbler gave a smile,
And the pleased tailor scratched his head the while.
    But hark, what mingled sounds of joy and woe   495
From yon poor cottage bursting seem to flow?
'Tis honest Sarah – sixpence-Harry's come,
And after all his toils got safely home.
'Welcome, old soldier, welcome from the wars!
Honour the man, my lads, seamed o'er with scars!   500
Come give's thy hand, and bring the t' other can,
And tell us all thou's done and seen, my man.'
    Now expectation stares in every eye,
The jaw falls down, and every soul draws nigh,
With ear turned up, and head held all awry.   505
    'Why sir, the papers tell you all that's done,
What battle's lost, and what is hardly won.
But when the eye looks into private woes,
And sees the grief that from one battle flows,
Small cause of triumph can the bravest feel,   510
For brave hearts never yet were made of steel.
    'It happened once, in storming of a town,
When our brave men had pushed the ramparts down,
We found them starving, the last loaf was gone,
Beef was exhausted, flour they had none;   515
Their springs we drain, to ditches yet they fly –
The stagnant ditch but treacherous supply,
For soon the putrid source their blood distains,[9]
And the quick fever[10] hastens through their veins.
In the same room the dying and the dead –   520
Nay sometimes, even in the self-same bed,
You saw the mother with her childern[11] lie,
None but the father to close either eye.
    'In a dark corner, once myself I found
A youth whose blood was pouring through the wound;   525
No sister's hand, or tender mother's eye
To stanch that wound was fondly watching by;
Famine had done her work, and low were laid
The loving mother and the blooming maid.

---

[8] *i'fegs* truly, in faith.
[9] *distains* poisons, contaminates.
[10] *the quick fever* typhoid fever.

[11] *childern* archaic form, normalized in Lonsdale's text
to 'children'.

He raised his eyes, and bade me strike the blow –   530
"I've nought to lose", he cried, "so fear no foe".
"No foe is near", I softly made reply;
"A soldier-friend would save and not destroy."
A drop of cordial in my flask I found –
And I myself am sovereign[12] for a wound;   535
I'll bleed you all, lads, if you should be ill,
And in the toothache I've no little skill!
Our drummer too, poor man, dealt much in horns,
And I've his very knack of cutting corns.
        'Well, as I dressed[13] the youth, I found 'twas he   540
That oft had charmed the sentinels and me;
From post to post like lightning he would fly,
And pour down thunder from his red-hot sky;
We praised him for't, so I my Captain told,
For well I knew he liked the foe that's bold;   545
So then the surgeon took him in his charge,
And Captain made him prisoner at large.'
        'Was he a Spanishman or Frenchman whether?
But it's no matter – they're all rogues together!'
        'You're much mistaken; goodness, I have found,   550
Springs like the grass that clothes the common ground;
Some more, some less, you know, grows everywhere;
Some soils are fertile, and some are but bare.
Nay, 'mongst the Indians I've found kindly cheer,
With as much pity as I could do here.   555
        'Once in their woods I strayed a length of way,
And thought I'd known the path that homeward lay;
We'd gone to forage – but I lost the rest,
Which, till quite out of hearing, never guessed.
I hollowed[14] loud, some voices made reply,   560
But not my comrades, nor one friend was nigh.
Some men appeared, their faces painted o'er,
The wampum-belt[15] and tomahawk they bore;
Their ears were hung with beads, that largely spread
A breadth of wing, and covered half the head.   565
I kissed the ground – one older than the rest
Stepped forth, and laid his hand upon my breast,
Then seized my arms, and signed that I should go
And learn with them to bend the sturdy bow.
I bowed and followed; sadly did I mourn,   570
And never more expected to return.'
Here Sarah sobbed, and stepped behind the door,
And with her apron hid the falling shower.

---

[12]   *sovereign* highly efficacious, useful.
[13]   *dressed* i.e. his wounds.
[14]   *hollowed* cried out, yelled.

[15]   *wampum-belt* belt containing cylindrical beads which
served as currency for north American Indians.

'We travelled on some days through woods alone,
At length we reached their happy silent home.   575
A few green acres did the plot compose,
Which woods surround, and fencing rocks enclose.
Skirting their banks, a river fond of play
Sometimes stood still – and sometimes ran away;
The branching deer would taste the limpid tide,   580
Cropping[16] the wild herbs on its flow'ry side,
Around the silent hut would sometimes stray,
Then, at the sight of man, bound swift away –
But all in vain; the hunter's flying dart
Springs from the bow and soon o'ertakes the heart.   585
  'A mother and four daughters here we found,
With shells encircled, and with feathers crowned,
Bright pebbles shone amidst the plaited hair,
While lesser shells surround the moon-like ear.
With screams at sight of me away they flew,   590
For fear or pleasure springs from what is new;
Then, to their brothers, screaming still they ran,
Thinking my clothes and me the self-same man;
When bolder grown, they ventured something near,
Light touched my coat, but started back with fear.   595
  'When time and use had chased their fears away,
And I had learnt some few short words to say,
They oft would tell me, would I but allow
The rampant lion to o'erhang my brow,
And on my cheek the spotted leopard wear,   600
Stretch out my ears, and let my arms go bare?'
'Oh mercy on us!' cried the listeners round,
Their gaping wonder bursting into sound.
  'Though different in their manners, yet their heart
Was equal mine in every better part.   605
Brave to a fault (if courage fault can be);
Kind to their fellows, doubly kind to me.
Some little arts my travelled judgment taught,
For which no gift to them seemed what it ought.
  'Needless with bows for me the woods to roam,   610
I therefore tried to do some good at home.
The birds, or deer, or boars, were all their food,
Save the swift sailors[17] of the silver flood;
And when long storms the wintry stores would drain,
Hunger would ask the stinted meal in vain.   615
  'Some goats I saw would browse the rocks among,
And oft I thought to trap their playful young;
But not till first a fencing hedge surrounds

---

[16] *Cropping* eating; cf. the lamb at Pope, *Essay on Man*   [17] *sailors* fish.
i 83: 'Pleased to the last, he crops the flow'ry food'.

Their future fields, and the enclosure bounds;
For many a father owns a hatchet here,   620
Which falls descending to his wealthy heir.
The playful kid we from the pitfall bring
(O'erspread with earth and many a specious thing,
Light lay the branches o'er the treacherous deep,
And favourite herbs amongst the long grass creep);[18]   625
The little prisoner soon is learnt to stand,
And crop[19] the food from the betrayer's hand.
A wintry store now rose up to their view,
And in another field the clover grew;
But without scythes or hooks, how could we lay   630
The ridgy swathe and turn it into hay?
At last, of stone we formed a sort of spade,
Broad at the end, and sharp, for cutting made;
We pushed along, the tender grass gave way,
And soon the sun turned every pile to hay.   635
It was not long before the flock increased,
And I first gave the unknown milky feast,
Save when the coconut her stores produce,
Her goblet flowing with the milky juice.
Some clay I found, and useful bowls I made,   640
Though I must own I marred the potter's trade;
Yet use is everything – they did the same
As if from China the smooth vessels came.
  'The curdling cheese I taught them next to press,
And twirled on strings the roasting meat to dress.   645
In all the woods the Indian corn was found,
Whose grains I scattered in the faithful ground;
The willing soil leaves little here to do,
Or asks the furrows of the searching plough;
Yet something like one with delight I made   650
(For tedious are the labours of the spade).
The coulter and the sock[20] were pointed stone,
The eager brothers drew the traces[21] on;
I stalked behind, and threw the faithful grain,
While wooden harrows closed the earth again.   655
Soon sprung the seed, and soon 'twas in the ear,[22]
Nor wait the golden sheaves the falling year;
In this vast clime two harvests load the field,
And fifty crops th' exhaustless soil can yield.
  'Some bricks I burnt, and now a house arose,   660
Finer than aught the Indian chieftain knows;

---

[18] The trap consisted of a pit covered over with branches, grasses, earth, and some tasty vegetation to decoy the prey.
[19] *crop* eat.
[20] *The coulter and the sock* parts of the plough.
[21] *traces* ropes connecting the horses to the plough.
[22] *in the ear* the corn was bearing ears.

A wicker door, with claylike plaster lined,
Served to exclude the roving wintry wind;
A horn-glazed window gave a scanty light,
Yet lamps cheered up the gloom of length'ning night;   665
The cotton shrub through all the woods had run,
And plenteous wicks our rocks and spindles spun.
   'Around their fields the yam I taught to grow,
With all the fruits they either love or know.
The bed I raised from the damp earth, and now   670
Some little comfort walked our dwelling through.
My fame was spread, the neighbouring Indians came,
Viewed all our works, and strove to do the same.
The wampum-belt my growing fame records,
That tells great actions without help of words.   675
I gained much honour, and each friend would bring
Of various presents many an high-prized thing.
And when, with many a prayer, I ask once more
To seek my friends, and wander to the shore,
They all consent – but drop a sorrowing tear,   680
And many a one his load of skins would bear.
Riches were mine, but fate not willed it so –
They grew the treasure of the Spanish foe;
My Indian friends threw down their fleecy load,
And, like the bounding elk, leapt back into the wood.   685
   'What, though a prisoner, countrymen I found,
Heard my own tongue, and blessed the cheerful sound;
It seemed to me as if my home was there,
And every dearest friend would soon appear.
   'At length a cartel[23] gave us back to share   690
The wounds and dangers of a bloody war.
Peace dawned at last, and now the sails were spread;
Some mount the ship alive, some few half-dead.
Not this afflicts the gallant soldier's mind –
What is't to him though limbs are left behind?   695
Chelsea[24] a crutch and bench will yet supply,
And be the veteran's dear lost limb and eye!
   'When English ground first struck the sailor's view,
"Huzza for England!" roared the jovial crew.
The waving crutch leapt up in every hand,   700
While one poor leg was left alone to stand;
The very name another limb bestows,
And through the artery the lost blood new flows.
   'We reached the shore and kissed the much-loved ground,
And fondly fancied friends would crowd around;   705

---

[23] *cartel* a ship engaged in exchanging prisoners.
[24] *Chelsea* The Chelsea Hospital for veteran soldiers was founded by Charles II, and its buildings designed by Christopher Wren. It was completed in 1692, and still stands today.

But few with wretchedness acquaintance claim,
And little pride is everywhere the same.
   'In coming down one night I lost my way,
And losing too the seeing eye of day,
Wherever a light dipped glimmering through the trees,   710
I thither urged my weary trembling knees,
Tapped at the door and begged in piteous tone –
They'd let a wandering soldier find his home.
They barred the door and bade me beg elsewhere,
They'd no spare beds for vagabonds to share.   715
This was the tale in every cot I sought,
And greater houses grew upon the fault:
The dog was loosed to keep me far at bay,
And saucy footmen bade me walk away,
Or else a constable should find a home   720
For wandering captains from the wars new-come.
Alas, thought I, is this the soldier's praise
For loss of health, of limb, of length of days?
And is this England – England, my delight,
For whom I thought it glory but to fight –   725
That has no covert for the soldier's night?
   'I turned half-fainting, led through all the gloom
By the faint glimmerings of the clouded moon.
One path I kept, that seemed at times to end,
And oft refused the guiding clue to lend;   730
The thread unhoped as oft again I found,
Till it forsook the open fields around;
By slow degrees to towering woods it crept,
As if beneath their shade it nightly slept.
I here had halted lest some beast of prey   735
By midnight theft had paced the treacherous way,
But that a twinkling light sometimes appeared,
Sometimes grew dim, and sometimes brightly cleared;
This could not be the lure of beast of prey –
They know no art of imitating day,   740
Much pleased I thought. The mazy path yet led
Through shrubby copse, by taller trees o'erspread;
A wimpling[25] rill ran out and wreathed its way
Through tufts of flowers that made its borders gay.
And now a rock the parting leaves unfold   745
On which a weathering oak had long grown old;
The curling ivy oft attempts to hide
Its sad decay with robes of verdant pride,
Yet through her leafy garb the eye can peer,
And see it buys the youthful dress too dear.   750
   'A hollow cavern now methought I spied,

---

[25] *wimpling* winding, meandering.

Where clustering grapes came wandering down its side,
Between whose leaves a ray of light would dart,
That both rejoiced and terrified my heart.
I ventured in, how soft my step and slow –   755
Nought save a taper my stretched eyeballs saw;
From a far cavern rushed a fuller light
That gave a holy hermit to my sight.
Himself and Piety seemed but the same,
And Wisdom for grey hairs another name;   760
Some traces yet of sorrow might be found
That o'er his features walked their pensive round;
Devotion seemed to bid them not to stray,
But human feelings gave the wanderers' way.
  'His eye he raised from the instructive page,   765
An eye more sunk by wearing grief than age;
Surprise a moment o'er his features spread,
And gave them back their once accustomed red.
  '"Welcome my son, a hermit's welcome share,
And let the welcome mend the scanty fare.   770
A soldier's toils the softest couch requires,
Most strength'ning food and renovating fires;
Not such the hermit's needy cell bestows,
Pampered alone by luxury of woes.
The falling tear bedews the crusty bread,   775
And the moss pillow props the weary head;
The limpid brook the heats of thirst allay,
And gathered fruits the toilsome search repay;
When hunger calls there are a feastful store,
And pressing Sorrow cares for nothing more;   780
Sufficient that her eye unseen can weep,
Stream while awake, and flow yet more in sleep.
  '"Tis now twelve years since Solitude first drew
Her closing curtain round my opening view,
Since first I left my once delightful home,   785
To deal with grief and her dark shades alone."
Much I expressed my wonder how a mind
So stored as his could herd from all mankind.
  '"You speak", he said, "like one whose soul is free,
Slave to no wish, nor chained to misery.   790
When ceaseless anguish clouds the summer's sky,
And fairest prospects tarnish in the eye;
When cheerful scenes spread every lure in vain,
And sweet society but adds to pain;
When weeping memory incessant brings   795
The sad reversion of all former things,
And show-like Fancy all her colouring lends,
To gild those views that opened with our friends;
When joyful days through the whole year would run,

And mirth set out and travel with the sun;   800
When Youth and Pleasure hand in hand would stray,
And every month was little less than May;
When changing Fortune shifts th' inconstant scene,
And only points to where our joys *have* been –
Is it a wonder from the world we run,   805
And all its fleeting empty pageants shun?
  "'There is a something in a well-known view
That seems to show our long-past pleasures through;
Sure in the eye a fairyland is found,
When former scenes bring former friends around.   810
Let but the woods, the rocks, the streams appear,
And every friend you see or think you hear;
Their words, their dress, their every look you find,
Swells to the sight, and bursts upon the mind.
Though many a spring has lent the blossom gay,   815
And many an autumn blown the leaf away,
Unchanged the lasting images remain
Which strong remembrance ever holds the same.
  "'E'en the mind's eye a glassy mirror shows,
And far too deeply her bold pencil draws;   820
The life-like pictures swim before the sight,
Glow through the day, and darken through the night.
Ah sure, e'en now my Ethelind appears,
Though dimly seen through this sad vale of tears:
That winning form, where elegance has wove   825
Th' thousand softnesses of gentlest love;
That meaning eye, that artless blushing cheek,
Which leaves so little for the tongue to speak;
The nameless graces of her polished mind;
That laughing wit, and serious sense refined;   830
That all together which no art can reach,
And which 'tis nature's very rare to teach;
That nameless something which pervades the soul
Wins not by halves, but captivates the whole;
Yet if one feature shone before the rest,   835
'Twas surely Pity by Religion dressed.
Have I not seen the softly stealing tear
Hang like a jewel in an Ethiop's ear?
That fine dark eye the glittering diamond shed
While from her cheek the frightened roses fled,   840
Ashamed that such a gem so brightly clear,
Aught, save the lily, should presume to wear.
  "'Sure there's a pleasure in recounting woes,
And some relief in every tear that flows.
Else why call back those days for ever flown   845
And with them every joy this heart can own?
Pleasure and pain is the sad mixture still;

Taste but the good, and you must taste the ill.
Dear Recollection is a sorceress fair
That brings up pleasures livelier than they were;   850
Delighted Fancy dwells upon the view,
Compares those scenes to what she meets with now;
The present hour grows dull, her charms decay,
And one by one drop silently away.
Neglect succeeds; neglect, the worst of foes   855
That married love or ardent friendship knows,
Whose torpid soul congealed in stupors lie,
Nor sees one charm, nor hears one smothering sigh;
Sees not the hourly load of comforts brought
By fond affection, watching every thought,   860
Nor the heart beating with the wish to please –
Cold, cold neglect beholds no charms like these.”'

From Ballads in the Cumberland Dialect, ed. Robert Anderson (Wigton, 1808)

JOE AND NED (TUNE: RANTING, ROARING WILLY)

JOE

Wey, Ned, man! thou luiks sae down-hearted,
   Yen wad swear aw thy kindred wer dead;
For a sixpence thy Jen and thee's parted,
   What then, man, ne'er bodder thy head!

There's lasses enew,[1] I'll upod te,   5
   And thou may be suin as weel matched;
There's ay as guid fish i' the river,
   As onie that ever wer catched.

NED

Oh, Joe! tou kens nought o' the matter,
   Sae let's ha'e nae mair o' thy jeer;[2]   10
Auld England's gown's worn till a tatter,
   And they'll nit new don[3] her, I fear.

True liberty never can flourish
   Till man in his reets is a king,
Till we tak a tithe-pig[4] frae the bishop,   15
   As he's duin frae us, is the thing.

JOE AND NED
[1] *enew* enough.
[2] *jeer* teasing.
[3] *don* dress.
[4] *tithe-pig* pig taken by the church as a tithe.

JOE

What, Ned! And is that aw that ails thee?
  Mess, lad, tou deserves maist to hang!
What, tek a bit lan frae its oaner?
  Is this then thy feyne *Reets o' Man?*[5]   20

Tou ploughs and tou sows and tou reaps, man,
  Tou gangs and tou comes where tou will;
Nowther king, lword or bishop dare touch thee,
  Sae lang as tou dis fwok nae ill.

NED

How can te say sae, Joe? Tou kens, now,   25
  If hares wer as plenty as hops,
I durstn't fell yen[6] for my life, man,
  Nor tekt out of auld Cwoley's[7] chops;

While girt[8] fwok they ride down my dikes[9] aw,
  And spang[10] o'er my fields o' new wheat,   30
Nought but ill words I get for the damage –
  Can onie yen tell me that's reet?

JOE

Aye, there I mun oan the shoe pinches,
  Just there to fin faut[11] is nae shame;
Ne'er ak![12] there's nae hard laws in England,   35
  Except that bit[13] thing about game.[14]

And wer we aw equal at mwornin,
  We cudn't remain sae till neet;
Some arms are far stranger than others,
  And some heads will tek in mair leet.[15]   40

Tou cudn't mend laws if tou wad, man,
  It's for otherguess[16] noddles than thine;
Lord help thee! sud beggars yence[17] rule us,
  They'd tek off beath thy cwoat and mine.

What is't then but law that stands by us,   45
  While we stand by country and king?
For as to bein parfet and parfet,
  I tell thee, there is nae sec thing.

---

[5] Paine's *The Rights of Man* (1791–2) was widely read by working people during the revolutionary period.
[6] *yen* one.
[7] *Cwoley* farmer's dog.
[8] *girt* great.
[9] *dikes* hedges.
[10] *spang* bound (on horseback).
[11] *fin faut* find fault.
[12] *Ne'er ak* Don't fret.
[13] *bit* small.
[14] *game* an understatement; the usual penalty for poaching game was hanging. As late as 1823 Sydney Smith described the game laws as 'carried to a pitch of oppression which is a disgrace to the country'.
[15] *leet* light.
[16] *otherguess* other kinds of.
[17] *yence* once.

Charlotte Smith (*née* Turner)   (1749–1806)

'Most sincerely do we lament the death of Mrs Charlotte Smith. We acknowledged in her a genuine child of genius, a most vivid fancy, refined taste, and extraordinary sensibility' – so wrote the reviewer of Charlotte Smith's last volume of poems, *Beachy Head, and Other Poems*, in the *British Critic*.[1] More recently, Stuart Curran, the most recent editor of her complete poetical works, has remarked that 'Charlotte Smith was the first poet in England whom in retrospect we would call Romantic'.[2] Her three most important poetical works, *Elegiac Sonnets*, *The Emigrants* and *Beachy Head* are included in this selection.

She was born in London, the elder daughter of Nicholas Turner of Stoke House, Guildford, and Bignor Park, Sussex, and Anna Towers. She and her sister were brought up by an aunt after their mother's death when she was three. After her father's second marriage in 1764, he arranged for her to marry Benjamin Smith, the son of a wealthy West Indian merchant and director of the East India Company. This might have seemed like a good idea at the time, but litigation over the will of Smith's father, and his own profligacy and extravagance, led to his imprisonment for seven months from December 1783. Some of this punishment Charlotte shared with him; by this time they had a large and growing family. She began to publish sonnets in the *European Magazine* in 1782, and published her *Elegiac Sonnets* for the first time in 1784. The volume was an immediate success. Wordsworth and Coleridge both read her sonnets as young men, and were profoundly influenced by them: Wordsworth footnoted an allusion to her work in his first published volume, *An Evening Walk* (1793), and Coleridge included her poems in his *Sonnets from Various Authors* (1796). She continued to add to the volume in successive editions. Such was its success that it became a two-volume work in 1797, with no less than 827 subscribers.

What made her sonnets so distinctive was the way in which the various hardships she had faced, though never explicitly outlined, coloured her close natural observations, producing an interesting blend of the confessional and the sentimental. It was a poetry that managed to be precise in its observations of the author's inner and outer worlds. The sonnet was at this period a very fashionable form in which to be writing, and Charlotte had a knack of exploiting popular taste, especially with translations of sonnets by Goethe's Werther, all the rage at that time. In doing so, she aroused the envious criticisms of Anna Seward, who accused Charlotte of promoting 'the dark dreams of suicide'.[3] For this anthology, I have edited *Elegiac Sonnets* from the third edition of 1786. Twenty of the sonnets were published here for the first time in book form, including those translated from Goethe's *Werther*. The complete contents of the volume are presented, as no justice is done by offering them piecemeal. By the time they were published the popularity of earlier editions ensured an appreciative reception from the reviewers; the *Critical Review* even reminded its readers that it had recognized Charlotte's qualities in the first place, and took the credit for her success: 'We received the first edition of these sonnets with the cheering smiles of approbation . . . The public confirmed our award by an extensive demand, and they are now arrived at the third edition'.[4] By this

---

[1]   *British Critic* 30 (1807) 170–4, p. 170.

[2]   *The Poems of Charlotte Smith* ed. Stuart Curran (New York, 1993), p. xix.

[3]   See p. 4, above.

[4]   *Critical Review* 61 (1786) 467–8, p. 467.

time, reviewers were keenly attuned to the melancholy tones behind the sonnets; this critic goes on: 'We are sorry to see the eye, which can shine with so much poetic fire, sullied with a tear, and we hope the soothings of the favoured muse may wipe it fom her cheek'.[5] The *Gentleman's Magazine* goes further: 'A very trifling compliment is paid to Mrs Smith when it is observed how much her sonnets exceed those of Shakespeare and Milton. She has undoubtedly conferred honour on a species of poetry which most of her predecessors in this country have disgraced'.[6] This is a particularly interesting review because it shows how the personal nature of the poetry was arousing interest and, in fact, concern, for Charlotte herself. The reviewer no doubt spoke for many when he said: 'We cannot, however, forbear expressing a hope that the misfortunes she so often hints at, are all imaginary. We must have perused her very tender and exquisite effusions with diminished pleasure, could we have supposed her sorrows to be real. It would be hard indeed if a lady, who has so much contributed to the delight of others, should feel any want of happiness herself.'[7] The *St James' Chronicle* was so impressed with the 1786 edition that it announced: 'the uncommon elegance of Mrs Charlotte Smith's *Elegiac Sonnets* has actually forced a second specimen of them into the *St James' Chronicle*'. It then reprinted Sonnets X, XXXII, and XXV.[8]

In the mid-1780s, after Smith's release from prison, the family went to France and rented a house near Dieppe, probably to avoid his creditors. This cannot have been easy, and helps account for Charlotte's sympathy for the exiles from revolutionary France whom she saw wandering Brighton beach several years later: 'I mourn your sorrows, for I too have known / Involuntary exile'.[9] The Smiths settled again in Sussex, now with nine children, but in 1788 Charlotte moved to Brighton and sought permanent separation from her husband. Her literary reputation was continuing to grow; by this time no one could publish a volume of sonnets without having their work compared with hers. The reviewer of William Lisle Bowles's *Fourteen Sonnets* (1789) in the *Critical* begins: 'The melancholy muse of Smith has decorated the shrine of poetry with many a beautiful wreath of this kind'.[10] In that year a fifth, enlarged edition of *Elegiac Sonnets* appeared, one of the subscribers to which was Wordsworth, then an undergraduate at St John's College, Cambridge. In 1791 he would visit her in Brighton on his way to Paris to obtain a letter of introduction to Helen Maria Williams. On this occasion he almost certainly saw a number of her manuscript works. Literary friends and patrons at this moment included the poets William Hayley and William Cowper, to the latter of whom she dedicated *The Emigrants*.

During the late 1780s, in dire need of money to support her large family, she wrote novels: *Emmeline* (1788), *Ethelinde* (1789), *Celestina* (1791), *Desmond* (1792), and *The Old Manor House* (1793). The composition of these lengthy works took a heavy toll on her health, and they never generated sufficient income for the needs of her family. Her literary reputation was assured by this time, as Andrew Bechet remarked in his review of *Ethelinde*: 'The character of Mrs Smith, both as a poet and as a novelist, is so firmly established, that our commendation at the present time may be thought unnecessary; but, of the work before us, as a new performance, some account must be given.'[11]

5   Ibid., pp. 467–8.
6   *Gentleman's Magazine* 56.1 (1786) 333–4, p. 334.
7   Ibid., p. 333.
8   *St James' Chronicle* 27–9 April 1786. It is worth noting that this elicited a tributary sonnet from 'D',

To Mrs Smith, on Reading her Sonnets, Lately Published, in the *St James' Chronicle* 15–17 June 1786.
9   *The Emigrants* 155–6.
10   *Critical Review* 67 (1789) 504–5, p. 504.
11   *Monthly Review* 2 (1791) 161.

Like the young Wordsworth, and many others of the time, she was an admirer of the Revolution. With the execution of Louis XVI in January 1793, and the resulting declaration of war on France by the British, radicals at home found themselves torn between the outrage inspired by events in Paris and feelings of patriotism. This ambivalence is evident in *The Emigrants*.

The Emigrants is in the first place a political work. For Charlotte, the point about the French clergy and nobility who have found safety from the horrors of the Revolution through exile in rural Sussex is that hard experience has revealed to them the injustice of both their former conduct towards the poor, and the assumptions on which it was based (i 244–95). This is important because the same injustices of which they were guilty are practised still in England (i 315–46). In the second part of the poem her radical indignation is displaced by horror at the execution of Louis and the uncertain fate of his family. The poem as a whole thus needs to be seen in the context of the shifts in radical thought, prompted by the violent turn taken by the Revolution.[12] Though provided both in her preface and the poem itself with an immediate historical and political context, *The Emigrants* is also a very personal work. Charlotte writes about the emigrant clergy of France partly because she feels an affinity with them in their suffering (see i 153–61); similarly, her rather surprising sympathy for Marie Antoinette derives largely from her identification with her as a 'mother, petrified with grief' (ii 152):

> Ah, who knows,
> From sad experience, more than I, to feel
> For thy desponding spirit, as it sinks
> Beneath procrastinated fears for those
> More dear to thee than life!
>
> (ii 169–73)

Charlotte's proficiency within the strict form of the sonnet stood her in good stead when it came to handling blank verse: she avoids monotony (the perennial pitfall of bad writing in this form) by constant variation of tone and rhythm, run-on-line, and stretching the rules of syntax to the limit (see for instance i 169–95). Her frequent use of personification should not blind us to the passion that underlies this remarkable poem, most notably in its culminating account of its author's own sufferings, making this a forthright and moving autobiographical work in blank verse, and a worthy precursor to *The Prelude*.

It is not easy, at such a distance, to realize what a risk Charlotte took in writing a poem about French emigrants when Britain was at war with France. More particularly, *The Emigrants* expresses some determined and emphatic views about the French clergy, and Catholicism in particular. This was a bone of contention with at least one reviewer. By 1793 her literary reputation was well established, and many of them, suspecting that *The Emigrants* would enjoy a reasonable sale whatever they said, made approving noises.[13] But others, no doubt feeling that Charlotte had enjoyed an easy ride for too long on the back of her sonnets, used them as a means to attack *The Emigrants*. The reviewer in the *British Critic* began, like most of them, by acknowledging the 'simplicity, perspicuity,

---

[12] See also Helen Maria Williams's *Letters Written in France* (1790) and *A Sketch of the Politics of France* (1795); *Romanticism* 139–43.

[13] See for instance the *Monthly Review* 12 (1793) 375–6 and the *Analytical Review* 17 (1793) 91–3.

elegance, and passion of her sonnets',[14] by way of observing that Charlotte's blank verse does not have 'any claim to particular commendation'.[15] More particularly, he goes on to criticize Charlotte's allusion to her own hardships before making plain the grounds on which his argument stands:

> As philanthropists, we feel compassion at the sad allusion to sorrows, which the writer, in her own person, tells us she has suffered: but as critics, we cannot approve of the egotism which occupies too large a portion of her present work. In sonnets, and elegy, the poet is allowed to pour forth his complaints, and may appear as the principal person: in a poem like the Emigrants, the writer should have brought forward a greater number of other characters, and have been herself more concealed.
>
> To genius we pay the most unbounded tribute of admiration and respect, when it is employed on subjects that become a good and great mind: but when fine talents descend to propagate popular cant against order, tending to excite discontent; or when they become the instruments by which 'to stab at once the morals of a land' (Cowper) . . . by treating with petulant and unseasonable scoffs the institutions of religion, we lament that the gifted powers of imagination should be so grossly perverted. . . . The virtuous and pious, no less than ingenious Cowper, is everywhere the advocate of the Christian religion and its sacred ordinances: and it is an indecency ill-becoming Mrs Smith to sneer at usages manifestly tending to public utility and general piety.[16]

The reviewer could not have known, but Charlotte had some cause for resenting some of the practices of Catholic clerics in France: while resident there during the 1780s, one of her children had been forcibly taken away in deep snow for baptism. In any case, the reviewer's defensive remarks underline how delicate were the matters discussed in the poem. The *Critical Review* concurred with the *British Critic* in taking exception to the personal nature of Charlotte's poetry which had, in the sonnets, been so appealing:

> We will not say that we are entirely disappointed: there is in this poem good scenery and well-discriminated groups of figures, but there is too much of mere reflection, verging towards humble prose, and the pathos is weakened by the author's adverting too often to perplexities in her own situation. . . . Herself, and not the French emigrant, fills the foreground; begins and ends the piece; and the pity we should naturally feel for those overwhelming and uncommon distresses she describes, is lessened by their being brought into parallel with the inconveniences of a narrow income or a protracted law-suit.[17]

Charlotte would have taken little heart from the review in the *European Magazine*, which commended the poem as a whole, but criticized it on the grounds that 'some of the

---

[14] *British Critic* 1 (1793) 403–6, p. 403.
[15] Ibid., p. 405. This tactic is deployed also by the *Critical Review*: 'The versification of this poem is, in general, tame. Blank verse requires a fuller cadence

and a larger sweep of harmony than the confined and elegant sonnet' (*Critical Review* 9 (1793) 299–302, p. 302).
[16] Ibid.
[17] *Critical Review* 9 (1793) 299–302, pp. 299–300.

expressions are very *hazardées*'.[18] A page was then taken up with enumerating some of the usages and constructions that offended the reviewer – Charlotte's use of 'innumerous' for 'innumerable' (line 5), for instance, and the elision of the particle in 'cause thy creatures [to] cease' (line 422).

Charlotte died in 1806 at Tilford near Farnham in Surrey, and was buried at Stoke Church in Guildford, close to her family home. She left behind a mass of manuscripts, many of which were unfortunately destroyed on the spot. Of those which survived, most seemed to have provided copy for *Beachy Head, and Other Poems* (1807). *Beachy Head* is in many respects an extraordinary work. Like so many other great poems of the time, it is unfinished, as its first editor states in the Advertisement: 'The poem entitled *Beachy Head* is not completed according to the original design. That the increasing debility of its author has been the cause of its being left in an imperfect state will, it is hoped, be a sufficient apology.'[19] There are some textual details that support the belief that the poem is unfinished: there is a hiatus in the manuscript at line 654 (which modern editors have preferred to fill), and its structure, particularly towards the end, seems to become increasingly fragmentary. Moreover, the punctuation of the first edition text is clearly editorial and needs, especially for the modern reader, to be emended and in some places corrected. It certainly cannot be left as it is. But what exemplifies *Beachy Head* as an important romantic work is what Stuart Curran calls its 'multitudinous, uncanny particularity'[20] – the sharp and sensitive detail with which Smith describes the natural world that surrounds her. That 'particularity' extends beyond a close knowledge of local flora and fauna to include an intense and pervasive awareness of the history of southeast England from prehistoric times onwards, local traditions and folklore, and notable inhabitants. It is an attempt to preserve in poetry the life and times of the region in a manner not dissimilar from Wordsworth's account of the Lakes in such poems as *Michael* and *The Brothers*.

Reviewers treated the poem kindly, often paying a final tribute to the deceased author in their account of the volume. The *British Critic*, so hostile fourteen years before, found *Beachy Head* 'distinguished by great vigour and, by what was the characteristic of the author's mind, a sweet and impressive tenderness of melancholy'.[21] The *Universal Magazine* found in the poem 'the quaint moralizing of Cowper, and the plaintive tenderness of Gray',[22] while the *Literary Panorama* commended her close observation of the natural world: 'the notes which accompany these poems are proofs of her general attention and accuracy'.[23] The *Monthly Review* most accurately summarized the critical consensus:

> The same tenderness and sensibility, the same strain of moral reflection, and the same enthusiastic love of nature, pervade all her effusions. It appears also as if the wounded feelings of Charlotte Smith had found relief and consolation, during her latter years, in an accurate observation not only of the beautiful *effect* produced by the endless diversity of natural objects that daily solicit our regard, but also in a careful study of their scientific arrangement, and their more minute variations.[24]

[18] *European Magazine* 24 (1793) 41–5, p. 42.
[19] *Beachy Head, and Other Poems* (1807), p. vii.
[20] *The Poems of Charlotte Smith* ed. Stuart Curran, p. xxvii.
[21] *British Critic* 30 (1807) 170–4, p. 171.
[22] *Universal Magazine* 7 (1807) 228–31, p. 229.
[23] *Literary Panorama* 2 (1807) 294–5, p. 294.
[24] *Monthly Review* 56 (1808) 99–101, p. 99.

Further Reading

The Poems of Charlotte Smith ed. Stuart Curran (New York, 1993)

Florence Anna May Hilbish, *Charlotte Smith, Poet and Novelist, 1749–1806* (Philadelphia, 1941)

Stuart Curran, 'The I Altered', *Romanticism and Feminism* ed. Anne K. Mellor (Bloomington, Indiana, 1988), pp. 185–207

Judith Pascoe, 'Female Botanists and the Poetry of Charlotte Smith', *RR* 193–209

Katharine M. Rogers, 'Romantic Aspirations, Restricted Possibilities: The Novels of Charlotte Smith', *RR* 72–88

Anon., 'Memoir of Mrs Charlotte Smith', *Monthly Mirror* 3 (1808), Supplementary Number

Matthew Bray, 'Removing the Anglo-Saxon Yoke: The Francocentric Vision of Charlotte Smith's Later Works', *TWC* 24 (1993) 155–8

Jacqueline Labbe, 'Selling One's Sorrows: Charlotte Smith, Mary Robinson, and the Marketing of Poetry, *TWC* 25 (1994) 68–71

Daniel Robinson, 'Reviving the Sonnet: Women Romantic Poets and the Sonnet Claim', *ERR* 6 (1995) 98–127

Elegiac Sonnets: the third edition. With twenty additional sonnets. (1786)

To WILLIAM HAYLEY, ESQ.[1]

Sir,

While I ask your protection for these essays, I cannot deny having myself some esteem for them. Yet permit me to say that did I not trust to your candour and sensibility, and hope they will plead for the errors your judgement must discover, I should never have availed myself of the liberty I have obtained – that of dedicating these simple effusions to the greatest modern master of that charming talent, in which I can never be more than a distant copyist.

I am,

Sir,

Your most obedient and obliged servant,

Charlotte Smith

PREFACE TO THE FIRST EDITIONS

The little poems which are here called sonnets have, I believe, no very just claim to that title, but they consist of fourteen lines, and appear to me no improper vehicle for a single sentiment. I am told, and I read it as the opinion of very good judges, that the legitimate sonnet is ill-calculated for our language. The specimens Mr Hayley has given, though they form a strong exception, prove no more than that the difficulties of the attempt vanish before uncommon powers.

Some very melancholy moments have been beguiled by expressing in verse the sensations those moments brought. Some of my friends, with partial indiscretion, have

---

To WILLIAM HAYLEY, ESQ

[1] William Hayley (1745–1820), poet, biographer, translator, friend of Blake, Anna Seward, Cowper, and others. To date his most successful poem, at least in commercial terms, was *The Triumphs of Temper*, to which Smith alludes in *Sonnet XIX*, below. Hayley and Smith were neighbours in Sussex, and Hayley was instrumental in helping her publish the *Elegiac Sonnets* in 1784.

multiplied the copies they procured of several of these attempts, till they found their way into the prints of the day in a mutilated state, which, concurring with other circumstances, determined me to put them into their present form. I can hope for readers only among the few who, to sensibility of heart, join simplicity of taste.

PREFACE TO THE THIRD EDITION

The reception given by the public, as well as my particular friends, to the two first editions of these small poems, has induced me to add to the present such other sonnets as I have written since, or have recovered from my acquaintance, to whom I had given them without thinking well enough of them at the time to preserve any copies myself. A few of those last written I have attempted on the Italian model, with what success I know not, but I am persuaded that to the generality of readers those which are less regular will be more pleasing.

As a few notes were necessary, I have added them at the end. I have there quoted such lines as I have borrowed, and, even where I am conscious the ideas were not my own, I have restored them to their original possessors.

Woolbeding,[2] 22 March 1786

SONNET I

The partial[1] muse has, from my earliest hours,
    Smiled on the rugged path I'm doomed to tread,
And still with sportive hand has snatched wildflowers
    To weave fantastic garlands for my head;
But far, far happier is the lot of those   5
    Who never learned her dear delusive art,
Which, while it decks the head with many a rose,
    Reserves the thorn to fester in the heart.[2]
For still she bids soft Pity's melting eye
    Stream o'er the ills she knows not to remove,   10
Points every pang, and deepens every sigh
    Of mourning friendship or unhappy love.
Ah then, how dear the muse's favours cost
If those paint sorrow best who feel it most![3]

SONNET II. WRITTEN AT THE CLOSE OF SPRING.

The garlands fade that spring so lately wove –
    Each simple flower, which she had nursed in dew;
Anemonies[1] that spangled every grove,
    The primrose wan, and harebell, mildly blue.

---

[2] *Woolbeding* small town in the South Downs in West Sussex.
SONNET I
[1] *partial* friendly, partial to the poet.
[2] Philomel was seduced, according to Ovid, by her brother-in-law, Tereus, King of Thrace. She was turned into a nightingale, and her sad song was said to be caused by a thorn in her breast.

[3] In her notes, Smith acknowledges an echo of Pope, *Eloisa to Abelard* 365–6: 'The well sung woes shall soothe my pensive ghost; / He best can paint them who shall feel them most'.
SONNET II
[1] '*Anemone nemorosa*: the wood-anemone' (Smith's note).

No more shall violets linger in the dell,   5
   Or purple orchis variegate the plain,
Till spring again shall call forth every bell,
   And dress with humid hands her wreaths again.
Ah, poor humanity! So frail, so fair
   Are the fond visions of thy early day,   10
Till tyrant passion and corrosive care
   Bid all thy fairy colours fade away!
Another May new buds and flowers shall bring;
Ah, why has happiness no second spring?

SONNET III. TO A NIGHTINGALE.[1]

Poor melancholy bird, that all night long
   Tell'st to the moon thy tale of tender woe;
   From what sad cause can such sweet sorrow flow,
And whence this mournful melody of song?

Thy poet's musing fancy would translate   5
   What mean the sounds that swell thy little breast,
   When still at dewy eve thou leav'st thy nest,
Thus to the listening night to sing thy fate.

Pale sorrow's victims wert thou once among,
   Though now released in woodlands wild to rove;   10
   Say, hast thou felt from friends some cruel wrong,
Or diedst thou – martyr of disastrous love?
Ah, songstress sad, that such my lot might be:
To sigh and sing at liberty, like thee!

SONNET IV. TO THE MOON.

Queen of the silver bow,[1] by thy pale beam,
   Alone and pensive, I delight to stray
And watch thy shadow trembling in the stream,
   Or mark the floating clouds that cross thy way.
And while I gaze, thy mild and placid light   5
   Sheds a soft calm upon my troubled breast;
And oft I think, fair planet of the night,
   That in thy orb the wretched may have rest.
The sufferers of the earth perhaps may go,
   Released by death, to thy benignant sphere,   10
And the sad children of despair and woe
   Forget in thee their cup of sorrow here.
Oh, that I soon may reach thy world serene,
Poor wearied pilgrim, in this toiling scene!

SONNET III
[1] 'The idea from the 43rd sonnet of Petrarch. Secondo
parte: *Quel rosignioul, che si soave piange*' (Smith's note).

SONNET IV
[1] *Queen of the silver bow* Diana the huntress, goddess
of the moon.

SONNET V. TO THE SOUTH DOWNS.

Ah, hills beloved! – where once, an happy child,
    Your beechen shades, 'your turf, your flowers among',[1]
I wove your bluebells into garlands wild,
    And woke your echoes with my artless song.
Ah, hills beloved! your turf, your flowers remain;   5
    But can they peace to this sad breast restore,
For one poor moment soothe the sense of pain,
    And teach a breaking heart to throb no more?
And you, Aruna,[2] in the vale below,
    As to the sea your limpid waves you bear,   10
Can you one kind Lethean[3] cup bestow
    To drink a long oblivion to my care?
Ah no! When all, e'en hope's last ray, is gone,
There's no oblivion but in death alone!

SONNET VI. TO HOPE.

Oh hope, thou soother sweet of human woes!
    How shall I lure thee to my haunts forlorn?
For me wilt thou renew the withered rose,
    And clear my painful path of pointed thorn?
Ah, come, sweet nymph, in smiles and softness dressed,   5
    Like the young hours that lead the tender year;
Enchantress come, and charm my cares to rest!
    Alas, the flatterer flies, and will not hear;
A prey to fear, anxiety, and pain,
    Must I a sad existence still deplore?   10
Lo! the flowers fade, but all the thorns remain,
    'For me the vernal garland blooms no more'.[1]
Come then, 'pale Misery's love',[2] be thou my cure,
And I will bless thee, who though slow art sure.

SONNET VII. ON THE DEPARTURE OF THE NIGHTINGALE.

Sweet poet of the woods, a long adieu!
    Farewell, soft minstrel of the early year!
Ah, 'twill be long ere thou shalt sing anew
    And pour thy music on the 'night's dull ear'.[1]

SONNET V

[1] Smith notes a borrowing from Gray's *Ode on a Distant Prospect of Eton College* 8: 'Whose turf, whose shades, whose flowers among'.

[2] 'The River Arun' (Smith's note).

[3] *Lethean* water from the River Lethe, river of forgetfulness in Hades, which enabled souls to forget their previous existence.

SONNET VI

[1] Smith notes the borrowing from Pope, *Imitation of the first Ode of the fourth Book of Horace* 32.

[2] This is, Smith notes, a borrowing from Shakespeare, *King John* III iv 35.

SONNET VII

[1] A borrowing, as Smith notes, from Shakespeare, *Henry V* Prologue 11.

Whether on spring thy wandering flights await,[2]   5
    Or whether silent in our groves you dwell,
The pensive muse shall own thee for her mate,[3]
    And still protect the song she loves so well.
With cautious step, the love-lorn youth shall glide
    Through the lone brake[4] that shades thy mossy nest;   10
And shepherd girls from eyes profane shall hide
    The gentle bird, who sings of pity best.
For still thy voice shall soft affections move,
And still be dear to sorrow and to love!

SONNET VIII. TO SPRING.

Again the wood, and long withdrawing vale,
    In many a tint of tender green are dressed,
Where the young leaves unfolding scarce conceal
    Beneath their early shade the half-formed nest
Of finch or woodlark; and the primrose pale   5
    And lavish cowslip, wildly scattered round,
Give their sweet spirits to the sighing gale.
    Ah, season of delight, could aught be found
    To soothe awhile the tortured bosom's pain,
Of sorrow's rankling shaft to cure the wound   10
    And bring life's first delusions once again,
'Twere surely met in thee! Thy prospect fair,
Thy sounds of harmony, thy balmy air,
Have power to cure all sadness but despair.[1]

SONNET IX

Blessed is yon shepherd on the turf reclined,
    Who on the varied clouds which float above
Lies idly gazing, while his vacant mind
    Pours out some tale antique of rural love!
Ah, *he* has never felt the pangs that move   5
    Th' indignant spirit when, with selfish pride,
Friends on whose faith the trusting heart relied
    Unkindly shun th' imploring eye of woe;
The ills they ought to soothe with taunts deride,
    And laugh at tears themselves have forced to flow!   10
Nor *his* rude bosom those fine feelings melt,
    Children of sentiment and knowledge born,
Through whom each shaft with cruel force is felt,
    Empoisoned by deceit or barbed with scorn.

---

[2] 'Alludes to the supposed migration of the nightingale' (Smith's note).
[3] Smith notes the allusion to Milton, *Sonnet I* 13–14: 'Whether the muse or love call thee his mate, / Both them I serve, and of their train am I'.

[4] *brake* thicket.
SONNET VIII
[1] *all sadness but despair* an allusion, as Smith notes, to *Paradise Lost* iv 155–6: 'Vernal delight and joy, able to drive / All sadness but despair'.

SONNET X. TO MRS G.

Ah, why will mem'ry with officious care
  The long lost visions of my days renew?
Why paint the vernal landscape green and fair
  When life's gay dawn was opening to my view?
Ah, wherefore bring those moments of delight,   5
  When with my Anna,[1] on the southern shore,
I thought the future, as the present, bright?
  Ye dear delusions, ye return no more!
Alas, how different does the truth appear
  From the warm picture youth's rash hand portrays!   10
How fades the scene, as we approach it near,
  And pain and sorrow strike how many ways!
Yet of that tender heart, ah, still retain
A share for me, and I will not complain!

SONNET XI. TO SLEEP.

Come, balmy sleep, tired nature's soft resort,
  On these sad temples all thy poppies shed,
And bid gay dreams from Morpheus'[1] airy court
  Float in light vision round my aching head![2]
Secure of all thy blessings, partial power,   5
  On his hard bed the peasant throws him down;
And the poor sea-boy, in the rudest hour,
  Enjoys thee more than he who wears a crown.[3]
Clasped in her faithful shepherd's guardian arms,
  Well may the village girl sweet slumbers prove;   10
And they, oh gentle sleep, still taste thy charms
  Who wake to labour, liberty, and love.
But still thy opiate aid dost thou deny
To calm the anxious breast, to close the streaming eye.

SONNET XII. WRITTEN ON THE SEASHORE. OCTOBER 1784.

On some rude fragment of the rocky shore,
  Where on the fractured cliff the billows break,
  Musing, my solitary seat I take,
And listen to the deep and solemn roar.

SONNET X
[1] *Anna* probably a reference to Catherine Anne Dorset, Smith's sister, who wrote charming childrens' stories of animals in human dress.
SONNET XI
[1] Morpheus was the Greek god of sleep.
[2] In later editions of *Elegiac Sonnets*, Smith noted the borrowing from William Mason, *Elegy V. On the Death of a Lady* 12: 'Float in light vision round the poet's head'.

[3] As she notes, Smith is recalling *2 Henry IV* III 1 18–20:

> Wilt thou upon the high and giddy mast
> Seal up the shipboy's eyes, and rock his brains
> In cradle of the rude impetuous surge?

O'er the dark waves the winds tempestuous howl;   5
   The screaming seabird quits the troubled sea,
   But the wild gloomy scene has charms for me,[1]
And suits the mournful temper of my soul.[2]

Already shipwrecked by the storms of fate,
   Like the poor mariner methinks I stand,   10
   Cast on a rock; who sees the distant land
From whence no succour comes – or comes too late;
Faint and more faint are heard his feeble cries,
Till in the rising tide th' exhausted sufferer dies.

SONNET XIII. FROM PETRARCH.[1]

Oh place me where the burning noon
   Forbids the withered flower to blow;
Or place me in the frigid zone
   On mountains of eternal snow;
Let me pursue the steps of fame,   5
   Or poverty's more tranquil road;
Let youth's warm tide my veins inflame,
   Or sixty winters chill my blood:
Though my fond soul to heaven were flown,
   Or though on earth 'tis doomed to pine,   10
Prisoner or free, obscure or known,
   My heart, oh Laura, still is thine.
Whate'er my destiny may be,
That faithful heart still burns for thee!

SONNET XIV. FROM PETRARCH.[1]

Loose to the wind her golden tresses streamed,
   Forming bright waves with amorous zephyr's sighs;
   And though averted now, her charming eyes
Then with warm love and melting pity beamed.
Was I deceived? Ah surely, nymph divine,   5
   That fine suffusion on thy cheek was love!
What wonder then those lovely tints should move,

SONNET XII
[1]   For echoes by Smith and Wordsworth see *Emigrants* i 157 and n., below.
[2]   'This line is not my own, but I know not where to look for it' (Smith's note). In later editions of the volume Smith replaced this with the annotation, 'Young'. As Curran notes, her source is in fact Edward Young's *The Revenge* (1721):

   Rage on, ye winds, burst clouds, and
     waters roar!

You bear a just resemblance of my
   fortune,
And suit the gloomy habit of my soul.
            (I i 5–7)

SONNET XIII
[1]   '*Pommi ove'l sol, occide i fiori e l'erba*. Petrarch, Sonnetto 112. Parte primo' (Smith's note).
SONNET XIV
[1]   '*Erano i capei d'oro all aura sparsi*. Sonnetto 69. Parte primo' (Smith's note).

Should fire this heart, this tender heart of mine?
Thy soft melodious voice, thy air, thy shape,
   Were of a goddess, not a mortal maid;   10
   Yet though thy charms, thy heavenly charms should fade,
My heart, my tender heart could not escape,
   Nor cure for me in time or change be found:
   The shaft extracted does not cure the wound.

SONNET XV. FROM PETRARCH.[1]

Where the green leaves exclude the summer beam,
   And softly bend as balmy breezes blow,
And where, with liquid lapse, the lucid stream
   Across the fretted rock is heard to flow,
Pensive I lay; when she whom earth conceals,   5
   As if still living, to my eyes appears,
And pitying Heaven her angel form reveals,
   To say, 'Unhappy Petrarch, dry your tears!
Ah why, sad lover, thus before your time,
   In grief and sadness should your life decay,   10
And like a blighted flower, your manly prime
   In vain and hopeless sorrow fade away?
Ah, wherefore should you mourn, that her you love,
Snatched from a world of woe, survives in bliss above!'

SONNET XVI. FROM PETRARCH.[1]

Ye vales and woods, fair scenes of happier hours!
   Ye feathered people, tenants of the grove!
And you, bright stream, befringed with shrubs and flowers,
   Behold my grief, ye witnesses of love!

For ye beheld my infant passion rise,   5
   And saw through years unchanged my faithful flame;
Now cold in dust, the beauteous object lies,
   And you, ye conscious scenes, are still the same!

While busy memory still delights to dwell
   On all the charms these bitter tears deplore,   10
And with a trembling hand describes too well
   The angel form I shall behold no more,
To heaven she's fled, and nought to me remains
But the pale ashes which her urn contains.

SONNET XV
[1] '*Se lamentar augelli o verde fronde.* Sonnetto 21. Parte secondo' (Smith's note).

SONNET XVI
[1] '*Valle che de lamenti miei se piena.* Sonnetto 33. Parte secondo' (Smith's note).

SONNET XVII. FROM THE THIRTEENTH CANTATA OF METASTASIO.[1]

On thy grey bark, in witness of my flame,
    I carve Miranda's cypher, beauteous tree;
Graced with the lovely letters of her name,
    Henceforth be sacred to my love and me!

Though the tall elm, the oak, and sombre pine,   5
    With broader arms may noon's fierce ardours break,
To shelter me and her I love, be thine;
    And thine to see her smile and hear her speak.

No bird, ill-omened, round thy graceful head
    Shall clamour harsh, or wave his heavy wing,   10
But fern and flowers arise beneath thy shade,
    Where the wild bees their lullabies shall sing;
And in thy boughs the murmuring ring-dove rest,
And there the nightingale shall build her nest.

SONNET XVIII. TO THE EARL OF EGREMONT.[1]

Wyndham, 'tis not thy blood, though pure it runs
    Through a long line of glorious ancestry,
Percys and Seymours, Britain's boasted sons,
    Who trust the honours of their race to thee;

'Tis not thy splendid domes, where science loves   5
    To touch the canvas, and the bust to raise;
Thy rich domains, fair fields, and spreading groves –
    'Tis not all these the muse delights to praise.

In birth and wealth and honours, great thou art,
    But nobler in thy independent mind;   10
And in that liberal hand and feeling heart
    Given thee by Heaven – a blessing to mankind!
Unworthy oft may titled fortune be;
A soul like thine is true nobility!

SONNET XIX. TO MR HAYLEY. ON RECEIVING SOME ELEGANT LINES FROM HIM.

For me the muse a simple band designed
    Of 'idle'[1] flowers that bloom the woods among,

SONNET XVII
[1] '*Scrivo in te l'amato nome / Di colei, per cui, mi moro.* I do not mean this as a translation; the original is much longer, and full of images which could not be introduced in a sonnet – and some of them, though very beautiful in the Italian, would I believe not appear to advantage in an English dress' (Smith's note).

SONNET XVIII
[1] Sir George O'Brien Wyndham, 3rd Earl of Egremont (1751–1837), Sussex philanthropist, liberal, and patron of the arts.
SONNET XIX
[1] *idle* the quotation marks are puzzling; possibly Charlotte is thinking of the sermon on the mount, Luke 12:27.

Which, with the cypress and the willow joined,
  A garland formed as artless as my song;
And little dared I hope its transient hours   5
  So long would last, composed of buds so brief,
Till Hayley's hand, among the vagrant flowers,
  Threw from his verdant crown a deathless leaf.
For high in fame's bright fane has judgement placed
  The laurel wreath Serena's poet[2] won,   10
Which, wov'n with myrtles by the hands of Taste,
  The muse decreed for this her favourite son.
And those immortal leaves his temples shade,
  Whose fair eternal verdure shall not fade!

SONNET XX. TO THE COUNTESS OF A——. WRITTEN ON THE ANNIVERSARY OF HER MARRIAGE.[1]

On this blessed day may no dark cloud or shower
  With envious shade the sun's bright influence hide;
But all his rays illume the favoured hour
  That saw thee, Mary, Henry's lovely bride!

With years revolving may it still arise,   5
  Blessed with each good approving Heaven can lend;
And still with ray serene, shall those blue eyes
  Enchant the husband, and attach the friend.

For you, fair friendship's amaranth[2] shall blow,[3]
  And love's own thornless roses bind your brow;   10
And when, long hence, to happier worlds you go,
  Your beauteous race shall be what you are now;
And future Nevills through long ages shine,
  With hearts as good, and forms as fair as thine.

SONNET XXI. SUPPOSED TO BE WRITTEN BY WERTHER.

Go, cruel tyrant of the human breast,
  To other hearts thy burning arrows bear!
Go where fond hope and fair illusion rest –
  Ah, why should love inhabit with despair?
Like the poor maniac[1] I linger here,   5
  Still haunt the scene where all my treasure lies,
Still seek for flowers where only thorns appear,

---

[2] *Serena's poet* Serena is the protagonist of William Hayley's *The Triumphs of Temper* (1781).
SONNET XX
[1] Mary, Lady Abergavenny (1760–96) married Henry Nevill, Earl of Abergavenny (1755–1843) on 3 October 1781. She was the daughter of Smith's brother-in-law.
[2] *amaranth* a mythical unfading flower.

[3] *blow* bloom.
SONNET XXI
[1] 'See the story of the lunatic: "Is this the destiny of man? Is he only happy before he possesses his reason, or after he has lost it? Full of hope you go to gather flowers in winter, and are grieved not to find any – and do not know why they cannot be found." *Sorrows of Werther*, Volume 2' (Smith's note).

And drink delicious poison from her eyes.[2]
Towards the deep gulf that opens on my sight
   I hurry forward, passion's helpless slave,   10
And, scorning reason's mild and sober light,
   Pursue the path that leads me to the grave:
So round the flame the giddy insect flies,
And courts the fatal fire by which it dies.

SONNET XXII. BY THE SAME. TO SOLITUDE.[1]

Oh solitude, to thy sequestered vale
   I come to hide my sorrow and my tears,
And to thy echoes tell the mournful tale
   Which scarce I trust to pitying friendship's ears.
Amidst thy wild woods and untrodden glades,   5
   No sounds but those of melancholy move;
And the low winds that die among thy shades
   Seem like soft pity's sighs for hopeless love.
And sure some story of despair and pain
   In yon deep copse thy murm'ring doves relate;   10
And hark, methinks in that long plaintive strain,
   Thine own sweet songstress[2] weeps my wayward fate;
Ah, nymph, that fate assist me to endure,
And bear awhile what death alone can cure!

SONNET XXIII. BY THE SAME. TO THE NORTH STAR.[1]

Towards thy bright beams I turn my swimming eyes,
   Fair, fav'rite planet, which in happier days
Saw my young hopes (ah, faithless hopes!) arise,
   And on my passion shed propitious rays;
Now nightly wandering mid the tempests drear   5
   That howl the woods and rocky steeps among,
I love to see thy sudden light appear
   Through the swift clouds driv'n by the wind along;
Or in the turbid water, rude and dark,
   O'er whose wild stream the gust of winter raves,   10
Thy trembling light with pleasure still I mark,
   Gleam in faint radiance on the foaming waves:

---

[2] In later editions Smith added a footnote acknowledging a borrowing from Pope, *Eloisa to Abelard*:

   Still on thy breast enamoured let me lie,
   Still drink delicious poison from thy eye,
   Pant on thy lip, and to thy heart be
      pressed.
                (ll. 121–3)

SONNET XXII
[1] "'I climb steep rocks, I break my way through copses, among thorns and briars, which tear me to pieces, and I feel a little relief." *Sorrows of Werther*, Volume 1' (Smith's note).

[2] *songstress* the nightingale.

SONNET XXIII
[1] "'The greater bear, favourite of all the constellations; for when I left you of an evening it used to shine opposite your window." *Sorrows of Werther*, Volume 2' (Smith's note).

So o'er my soul short rays of reason fly,
Then fade – and leave me to despair and die!

SONNET XXIV. BY THE SAME.[1]

Make there my tomb, beneath the lime-tree's shade,
  Where grass and flowers in wild luxuriance wave;
Let no memorial mark where I am laid,
  Or point to common eyes the lover's grave!
But oft at twilight morn, or closing day,   5
  The faithful friend with falt'ring step shall glide,
Tributes of fond regret by stealth to pay,
  And sigh o'er the unhappy suicide.
And sometimes, when the sun with parting rays
  Gilds the long grass that hides my silent bed,   10
The tear shall tremble in my Charlotte's eyes;
  Dear, precious drops – they shall embalm the dead.
Yes! Charlotte o'er the mournful spot shall weep,
Where her poor Werther and his sorrows sleep.

SONNET XXV. BY THE SAME. JUST BEFORE HIS DEATH.[1]

Why should I wish to hold[2] in this low sphere,
  'A frail and feverish being?' Wherefore try
Poorly, from day to day, to linger here,
  Against the powerful hand of destiny?
By those who know the force of hopeless care   5
  On the worn heart, I sure shall be forgiven;
If to elude dark guilt, and dire despair,
  I go uncalled to mercy and to heaven!
Oh thou, to save whose peace I now depart,
  Will thy soft mind thy poor lost friend deplore,   10
When worms shall feed on this devoted heart,
  Where even thy image shall be found no more?
Yet may thy pity mingle not with pain,
For then thy hapless lover dies in vain.

SONNET XXVI. TO THE RIVER ARUN.

On thy wild banks, by frequent torrents worn,
  No glittering fanes or marble domes appear,
Yet shall the mournful muse thy course adorn,
  And still to her thy rustic waves be dear.

SONNET XXIV
[1] "'At the corner of the churchyard which looks towards the fields, there are two lime-trees. It is there I wish to rest." *Sorrows of Werther*, Volume 2' (Smith's note).

SONNET XXV
[1] "'May my death remove every obstacle to your happiness. Be at peace, I entreat you; be at peace". *Sorrows of Werther*, Volume 2' (Smith's note).
[2] *hold* remain.

For with the infant Otway,[1] lingering here,   5
  Of early woes she bade her votary dream,
While thy low murmurs soothed his pensive ear,
  And still the poet consecrates the stream.
Beneath the oak and birch that fringe thy side,
  The first-born violets of the year shall spring,   10
And in thy hazels, bending o'er the tide,
  The earliest nightingale delight to sing,
While kindred spirits, pitying, shall relate
Thy Otway's sorrows, and lament his fate!

SONNET XXVII

Sighing I see yon little troop at play,
  By sorrow yet untouched, unhurt by care,
While free and sportive they enjoy today
  'Content and careless of tomorrow's fare!'[1]
Oh happy age, when hope's unclouded ray   5
  Lights their green path, and prompts their simple mirth,
Ere yet they feel the thorns that lurking lay
  To wound the wretched pilgrims of the earth,
Making them rue the hour that gave them birth,
  And threw them on a world so full of pain   10
Where prosperous folly treads on patient worth,
  And to deaf pride, misfortune pleads in vain.
Ah, for their future fate, how many fears
Oppress my heart and fill mine eyes with tears!

SONNET XXVIII. TO FRIENDSHIP.

Oh thou, whose name too often is profaned,
  Whose charms celestial few have hearts to feel!
Unknown to folly and by pride disdained,
  To thy soft solace may my sorrows steal!
Like the fair moon, thy mild and genuine ray   5
  Through life's long evening shall unclouded last;
While the frail summer friendship fleets away,
  As fades the rainbow from the northern blast.
'Tis thine, oh nymph, with 'balmy hands to bind'[1]
  The wounds inflicted in misfortune's storm,   10
    And blunt severe affliction's sharpest dart;

SONNET XXVI

[1] 'Otway was born at Trotten, a village in Sussex. Of Woolbeding, another village on the banks of the Arun (which runs through them both), his father was rector. Here it was, therefore, that he probably passed many of his early years. The Arun is here an inconsiderable stream, winding in a channel deeply worn, among meadow, heath and wood' (Smith's note). Thomas Otway (1652–85), dramatist, was known chiefly for his tragedy, *Venice Preserved* (1681). He died in poverty, and is said to have choked to death on a bread roll.

SONNET XXVII

[1] '[James] Thomson' (Smith's note); the borrowing is from *Autumn* 191.

SONNET XXVIII

[1] 'Collins' (Smith's note). The borrowing is from *Ode to Pity* 2. William Collins (1721–59), see also *Sonnet XXX* below.

'Tis thy pure spirit warms my Anna's mind,
    Beams through the pensive softness of her form,
    And holds its altar on her spotless heart.

SONNET XXIX. TO MISS C——. ON BEING DESIRED TO ATTEMPT WRITING A COMEDY.

Wouldst thou then have *me* tempt the comic scene
    Of laughing Thalia[1] – used so long to tread
    The gloomy paths of sorrow's cypress shade,
    And the lorn lay with sighs and tears to stain?
Alas, how much unfit her sprightly vein!   5
    Arduous to try and seek the sunny mead,
    And bowers of roses, where she loves to lead
The sportive subjects of her golden reign!
Enough for me if still, to soothe my days,
    Her fair and pensive sister[2] condescend   10
With tearful smile to bless my simple lays;
    Enough if her soft notes she sometimes lend,
To gain for me, of feeling hearts, the praise,
    And chiefly thine, my ever partial friend!

SONNET XXX. TO THE RIVER ARUN.

Be the proud Thames of trade the busy mart!
    Arun, to thee will other praise belong;
Dear to the lover's and the mourner's heart,
    And ever sacred to the sons of song!

Thy shadowy rocks unhappy love shall seek,   5
    Where mantling loose, the green clematis[1] flaunts,
And sorrow's drooping form and faded cheek
    Choose on thy willowed shore her lonely haunts.

Banks which inspired thy Otway's plaintive strain!
    Wilds whose lorn echoes learned the deeper tone   10
Of Collins' powerful shell![2] Yet once again

SONNET XXIX
[1] *Thalia* muse of comedy.
[2] *sister* Erato, muse of lyric poetry.
SONNET XXX
[1] 'Clematis: the plant bindwith, or virgin's bower, which towards the end of June begins to cover the hedges and sides of rocky hollows with its beautiful foliage, and flowers of a yellowish white and of an agreeable fragrance, which are succeeded by seed-pods, that bear some resemblance to feathers or hair, whence it is sometimes called Old Man's Beard' (Smith's note).
[2] 'Collins, as well as Otway, was a native of this country, and I should imagine at some period of his life an inhabitant of this neighbourhood, since, in his beautiful *Ode on the Death of Colonel Ross*, he says:

The muse shall still, with social aid,
    Her gentlest promise keep,
E'en humble Harting's cottaged vale
Shall learn the sad repeated tale
    And bid her shepherds weep.

And in the *Ode to Pity*:

Wild Arun too has heard thy strains,
And Echo, midst my native plains,
Been soothed with Pity's lute.'
                                    (Smith's note)

William Collins (1721–59) was a native of Sussex, in which county the village of Harting is to be found.

Another poet, Hayley, is thine own!
Thy classic stream anew shall hear a lay
Bright as its waves and various as its way!

SONNET XXXI. WRITTEN ON FARM WOOD, SOUTH DOWNS, IN MAY 1784.

Spring's dewy hand on this fair summit weaves
  The downy grass with tufts of Alpine flowers,[1]
And shades the beechen slopes with tender leaves,
  And leads the shepherd to his upland bowers,
Strewn with wild thyme; while slow-descending showers   5
  Feed the green ear, and nurse the future sheaves.
Ah, blessed the hind whom no sad thought bereaves
  Of the gay season's pleasures! All his hours
To wholesome labour given, or thoughtless mirth;
  No pangs of sorrow past or coming dread   10
Bend his unconscious spirit down to earth,
  Or chase calm slumbers from his careless head.
Ah, what to me can those dear days restore,
When scenes could charm that now I taste no more!

SONNET XXXII. TO MELANCHOLY. WRITTEN ON THE BANKS OF THE ARUN, OCTOBER 1785.

When latest autumn spreads her evening veil,
  And the grey mists from these dim waves arise,
  I love to listen to the hollow sighs
Through the half leafless wood that breathes the gale.
For at such hours the shadowy phantom, pale,   5
  Oft seems to fleet before the poet's eyes;
  Strange sounds are heard, and mournful melodies,
As of night-wanderers who their woes bewail;
Here, by his native stream, at such an hour,
  Pity's own Otway I methinks could meet,   10
  And hear his deep sighs swell the saddened wind.
Oh melancholy, such thy magic power,
  That to the soul these dreams are often sweet,
  And soothe the pensive visionary mind!

SONNET XXXIII. TO THE NAIAD OF THE ARUN.

Go, rural naiad, wind thy stream along
  Through woods and wilds, then seek the ocean caves
Where sea-nymphs meet their coral rocks among,
  To boast the various honours of their waves!

SONNET XXXI
[1] 'An infinite variety of plants are found on these hills, particularly about this spot. Many sorts of orchis and cistus of singular beauty, with several others with which I am but imperfectly acquainted' (Smith's note).

'Tis but a little, o'er thy shallow tide, 5
 That toiling trade her burdened vessel leads;
But laurels grow luxuriant on thy side,
 And letters live along thy classic meads.
Lo, where mid British bards[1] thy natives shine!
 And now another poet helps to raise 10
Thy glory high – the poet of *The Mine*[2] –
 Whose brilliant talents are his smallest praise:
And who, to all that genius can impart,
Adds the cool head and the unblemished heart!

SONNET XXXIV. TO A FRIEND.

Charmed by thy suffrage shall I yet aspire
 (All inauspicious as my fate appears,
 By troubles darkened, that increase with years)
To guide the crayon, or to touch the lyre?
Ah me! the sister muses still require 5
 A spirit free from all intrusive fears,
 Nor will they deign to wipe away the tears
Of vain regret that dim their sacred fire.
But when thy sanction crowns my simple lays,
 A ray of pleasure lights my languid mind, 10
For well I know the value of thy praise;
 And to how few the flattering meed[1] confined,
 That thou, their highly favoured brows to bind,
Wilt weave green myrtle and unfading bays!

SONNET XXXV. TO FORTITUDE.

Nymph of the rock, whose dauntless spirit braves
 The beating storm, and bitter winds that howl
Round thy cold breast; and hear'st the bursting waves
 And the deep thunder with unshaken soul;
Oh come and show how vain the cares that press 5
 On my weak bosom, and how little worth
Is the false fleeting meteor happiness,
 That still misleads the wanderers of the earth!
Strengthened by thee, this heart shall cease to melt
 O'er ills that poor humanity must bear; 10
Nor friends estranged, or ties dissolved be felt
To leave regret, and fruitless anguish there.
And when at length it heaves its latest sigh,
Thou and mild hope shall teach me how to die!

SONNET XXXIII
[1] *British bards* 'Otway, Collins, Hayley' (Smith's note).
[2] John Sargent, author of *The Mine* (1785).

SONNET XXXIV
[1] *meed* reward, tribute.

SONNET XXXVI

Should the lone wanderer, fainting on his way,
   Rest for a moment of the sultry hours,
And though his path through thorns and roughness lay,
   Pluck the wild rose, or woodbine's gadding flowers;
Weaving gay wreaths beneath some sheltering tree,   5
   The sense of sorrow he awhile may lose;
So have I sought thy flowers, fair poesy,
   So charmed my way with friendship and the muse!
But darker now grows life's unhappy day,
   Dark with new clouds of evil yet to come,   10
Her pencil sickening fancy throws away,
   And weary hope reclines upon the tomb;
And points my wishes to that tranquil shore
Where the pale spectre care pursues no more.

The Emigrants, A Poem, in Two Books (1793)

TO WILLIAM COWPER, ESQ.

Dear Sir,

There is, I hope, some propriety in my addressing a composition to you, which would never perhaps have existed had I not, amid the heavy pressure of many sorrows, derived infinite consolation from your poetry, and some degree of animation and of confidence from your esteem.[1]

The following performance is far from aspiring to be considered as an imitation of your inimitable poem, *The Task*; I am perfectly sensible that it belongs not to a feeble and feminine hand to draw the bow of Ulysses.[2]

The force, clearness, and sublimity of your admirable poem; the felicity, almost peculiar to your genius, of giving to the most familiar objects dignity and effect, I could never hope to reach – yet, having read *The Task* almost incessantly from its first publication[3] to the present time, I felt that kind of enchantment described by Milton when he says

        The angel ended, and in Adam's ear
        So charming left his voice, that he awhile
        Thought him still speaking.

                       (*Paradise Lost* viii 1–3)

And from the force of this impression, I was gradually led to attempt, in blank verse, a delineation of those interesting objects which happened to excite my attention, and which even pressed upon an heart that has learned, perhaps from its own sufferings, to feel with acute though unavailing compassion the calamity of others.

A dedication usually consists of praises and of apologies; *my* praise can add nothing to the unanimous and loud applause of your country. She regards you with pride as

---

To WILLIAM COWPER ESQ.

[1] Cowper praised Smith's abilities when introduced to her by William Hayley in early August 1792.

[2] Ulysses acquired, when young, a bow which he never used, valuing it so highly that he left it at home. The contest to draw its string and win the hand of Penelope forms the culmination of the homecoming which ends *The Odyssey*.

[3] *The Task* was first published in 1784.

one of the few who, at the present period, rescue her from the imputation of having degenerated in poetical talents; but in the form of apology I should have much to say, if I again dared to plead the pressure of evils, aggravated by their long continuance, as an excuse for the defects of this attempt.

Whatever may be the faults of its execution, let me vindicate myself from those that may be imputed to the design. In speaking of the emigrant clergy,[4] I beg to be understood as feeling the utmost respect for the integrity of their principles, and it is with pleasure I add my suffrage to that of those who have had a similar opportunity of witnessing the conduct of the emigrants of all descriptions during their exile in England – which has been such as does honour to *their* nation, and ought to secure to them in ours the esteem of every liberal mind.

Your philanthropy, dear sir, will induce you, I am persuaded, to join with me in hoping that this painful exile may finally lead to the extirpation of that reciprocal hatred so unworthy of great and enlightened nations; that it may tend to humanize both countries, by convincing each that good qualities exist in the other; and at length annihilate the prejudices that have so long existed to the injury of both.

Yet it is unfortunately but too true that with the body of the English, this national aversion has acquired new force by the dreadful scenes which have been acted in France during the last summer[5] – even those who are the victims of the Revolution have not escaped the odium which the undistinguishing multitude annex to all the natives of a country where such horrors have been acted. Nor is this the worst effect those events have had on the minds of the English: by confounding the original cause with the wretched catastrophes that have followed its ill management, the attempts of public virtue with the outrages that guilt and folly have committed in its disguise – the very name of liberty has not only lost the charm it used to have in British ears, but many who have written or spoken in its defence have been stigmatized as promoters of anarchy, and enemies to the prosperity of their country. Perhaps even the author of *The Task*, with all his goodness and tenderness of heart, is in the catalogue of those who are reckoned to have been too warm in a cause which it was once the glory of Englishmen to avow and defend. The exquisite poem, indeed, in which you have honoured liberty by a tribute highly gratifying to her sincerest friends, was published some years before the demolition of regal despotism in France – which, in the fifth Book, it seems to foretell.[6] All the truth and energy of the passage to which I allude must have been strongly felt when, in the Parliament of England, the greatest orator of our time quoted the sublimest of our poets – when the eloquence of Fox did justice to the genius of Cowper.

I am, dear sir,
    With the most perfect esteem,
        Your obliged and obedient servant,
        CHARLOTTE SMITH
           Brighthelmstone, 10 May 1793

---

[4] *the emigrant clergy* On 26 May 1792 the French government decided that priests who refused to join the Constitutional Church were effectively traitors, and should be deported. With the end of the monarchy on 10 August that decree became immediately effective, and led to the exile of many clergyman to England. The presence of three bishops and 220 priests among the victims of the September massacres underlined the dangers to the clergy at this moment.

[5] The storming of the Tuileries (10 August 1792) was followed by the imprisonment of the king and his family, and the September massacres of royalist and other prisoners in Paris (3–7 September).

[6] *Task* Book V includes a passage in praise of liberty (ll. 446 ff.), and one contrasting the monarchy in England and France (to the detriment of the latter) (ll. 331–62).

BOOK I

Scene: on the cliffs to the eastward of the town of Brighthelmstone in Sussex[7]

Time: a morning in November 1792

Slow in the wintry morn, the struggling light
Throws a faint gleam upon the troubled waves;
Their foaming tops, as they approach the shore,
And the broad surf that, never ceasing, breaks
On the innumerous[8] pebbles, catch the beams   5
Of the pale sun, that with reluctance gives
To this cold northern isle its shortened day.
Alas, how few the morning wakes to joy!
How many murmur at oblivious night
For leaving them so soon; for bearing thus   10
Their fancied bliss (the only bliss they taste!)
On her black wings away; changing the dreams
That soothed their sorrows, for calamities
(And every day brings its own sad proportion);
For doubts, diseases, abject dread of death,   15
And faithless friends, and fame and fortune lost,
Fancied or real wants, and wounded pride
That views the daystar but to curse his beams.
Yet He whose Spirit into being called
This wondrous world of waters; He who bids   20
The wild wind lift them till they dash the clouds,
And speaks to them in thunder; or whose breath,
Low murmuring o'er the gently heaving tides,
When the fair moon, in summer night serene,
Irradiates with long trembling lines of light   25
Their undulating surface; that great Power,
Who, governing the planets, also knows
If but a sea-mew falls,[9] whose nest is hid
In these incumbent cliffs; He surely means
To us, his reasoning creatures, whom He bids   30
Acknowledge and revere his awful hand,
Nothing but good. Yet man, misguided man,
Mars the fair work that he was bid enjoy,
And makes himself the evil he deplores.
How often, when my weary soul recoils   35
From proud oppression, and from legal crimes

---

[7] Smith lived in Brighton 1788–93.

[8] *innumerous* innumerable. A poeticized form, which at least one reviewer found objectionable; see headnote, above.

[9] *Matthew* 10:29: 'Are not two sparrows sold for a farthing? and one of them shall not fall on the ground without your Father.' The passage was recalled often by eighteenth-century writers, thanks perhaps to Pope's *Essay on Man*:

Who sees with equal eye, as God of all,
A hero perish, or a sparrow fall . . .
(i 87–8)

(For such are in this land, where the vain boast
Of equal law is mockery, while the cost
Of seeking for redress is sure to plunge
Th' already injured to more certain ruin,   40
And the wretch starves before his counsel pleads) –
How often do I half abjure society
And sigh for some lone cottage, deep embowered
In the green woods that these steep chalky hills
Guard from the strong south-west;[10] where round their base   45
The beech wide flourishes, and the light ash
With slender leaf half hides the thymy turf!
There do I wish to hide me, well content
If on the short grass, strewn with fairy flowers,
I might repose thus sheltered;[11] or, when eve   50
In orient crimson lingers in the west,
Gain the high mound, and mark these waves remote
(Lucid though distant), blushing with the rays
Of the far-flaming orb that sinks beneath them.
For I have thought that I should then behold   55
The beauteous works of God unspoiled by man
And less affected then by human woes
I witnessed not; might better learn to bear
Those that injustice and duplicity
And faithlessness and folly fix on me: 60
For never yet could I derive relief,
When my swoln heart was bursting with its sorrows,
From the sad thought that others like myself
Live but to swell affliction's countless tribes!
Tranquil seclusion I have vainly sought;   65
Peace, who delights in solitary shade,
No more will spread for me her downy wings,
But, like the fabled Danaïds or the wretch
Who ceaseless up the steep acclivity
Was doomed to heave the still rebounding rock,[12]   70
Onward I labour – as the baffled wave
Which yon rough beach repulses, that returns
With the next breath of wind, to fail again.
Ah, mourner, cease these wailings! Cease and learn
That not the cot sequestered where the briar   75
And woodbine wild embrace the mossy thatch
(Scarce seen amid the forest gloom obscure),

---

[10]   *the strong south-west* wind.
[11]   *I might repose thus sheltered* a reworking of Virgil's
famous topos: 'o quis me gelidis in vallibus Haemi /
Sistat, et ingenti ramorum protegat umbra!' (*Georgics* ii
488–9).
[12]   Lines 68–70 refer to the fifty daughters of Danaeus,
King of Argos, who ordered them to kill their fifty

husbands, who he suspected of plotting against him.
The daughters were punished by having eternally to
draw water into leaking pots in Hades. Sisyphus was
condemned in hell to roll uphill a huge stone which
perpetually rolled down again.

Or more substantial farm, well-fenced and warm,
Where the full barn and cattle foddered round
Speak rustic plenty; nor the statelier dome   80
By dark firs shaded, or the aspiring pine
Close by the village church (with care concealed
By verdant foliage, lest the poor man's grave
Should mar the smiling prospect of his lord);
Where offices well-ranged, or dovecote stocked,   85
Declare manorial residence – not these
Or any of the buildings new and trim,
With windows circling towards the restless sea,
Which, ranged in rows,[13] now terminate my walk,
Can shut out for an hour the spectre care   90
That, from the dawn of reason, follows still
Unhappy mortals, till the friendly grave
(Our sole secure asylum) 'ends the chase'.[14]
    Behold, in witness of this mournful truth
A group approach me, whose dejected looks   95
(Sad heralds of distress!) proclaim them men
Banished for ever and for conscience sake
From their distracted country, whence the name
Of freedom misapplied, and much abused
By lawless anarchy, has driven them far   100
To wander – with the prejudice they learned
From bigotry (the tut'ress of the blind)
Through the wide world unsheltered; their sole hope
That German spoilers through that pleasant land
May carry wide the desolating scourge   105
Of war and vengeance.[15] Yet unhappy men,
Whate'er your errors, I lament your fate;
And, as disconsolate and sad ye hang
Upon the barrier of the rock, and seem
To murmur your despondence, waiting long   110
Some fortunate reverse that never comes,
Methinks in each expressive face I see
Discriminated anguish. There droops[16] one
Who in a moping cloister long consumed
This life inactive, to obtain a better,[17]   115
And thought that meagre abstinence, to wake
From his hard pallet with the midnight bell,
To live on eleemosynary bread,[18]

---

[13] *ranged in rows* recently-built Georgian terraces, erected
during Brighton's heyday as a social centre.
[14] *ends the chase* 'I have a confused notion that this
expression, with nearly the same application, is to be
found in Young, but I cannot refer to it' (Smith's
note). Curran notes that the phrase is from Samuel
Pratt's 'Pro and Con' in Dodsley's *Miscellanies* (1785).

[15] *war and vengeance* many French emigrants had joined
the Prussian army on the borders, which had been
attempting to invade France since May 1792.
[16] *droops* the diction is Miltonic; cf. *Samson Agonistes*
594: 'So much I feel my genial spirits *droop*'.
[17] *a better* i.e. a better life.
[18] *eleemosynary bread* alms.

And to renounce God's works, would please that God.
And now the poor pale wretch receives, amazed,   120
The pity strangers give to his distress
(Because these strangers are, by his dark creed,
Condemned as heretics), and with sick heart
Regrets his pious prison and his beads.[19]
Another, of more haughty port, declines   125
The aid he needs not, while in mute despair
His high indignant thoughts go back to France,
Dwelling on all he lost – the Gothic[20] dome
That vied with splendid palaces,[21] the beds
Of silk and down, the silver chalices,   130
Vestments with gold enwrought for blazing altars,
Where, amid clouds of incense, he held forth
To kneeling crowds the imaginary bones[22]
Of saints supposed, in pearl and gold enchased,[23]
And still with more than living monarchs' pomp   135
Surrounded; was believed by mumbling bigots
To hold the keys of heaven, and to admit
Whom he thought good to share it. Now, alas,
He to whose daring soul and high ambition
The world seemed circumscribed – who, wont to dream   140
Of Fleuri, Richelieu, Alberoni,[24] men
Who trod on empire, and whose politics
Were not beyond the grasp of his vast mind –
Is, in a land once hostile, still profaned
By disbelief and rites unorthodox,   145
The object of compassion. At his side,
Lighter of heart than these, but heavier far[25]
Than he was wont, another victim comes –
An Abbé who with less contracted brow
Still smiles and flatters, and still talks of hope,   150
Which, sanguine as he is, he does not feel,
And so he cheats the sad and weighty pressure

---

[19] 'Lest the same attempts at misrepresentation should now be made, as have been made on former occasions, it is necessary to repeat that nothing is farther from my thoughts than to reflect invidiously on the emigrant clergy, whose steadiness of principle excites veneration, as much as their sufferings compassion. Adversity has now taught them the charity and humility they perhaps wanted when they made it a part of their faith that salvation could be obtained in no other religion than their own' (Smith's note).
[20] *Gothic* used here in the architectural sense, referring to a manner common in Western Europe between the twelfth and sixteenth centuries.
[21] 'Let it not be considered as an insult to men in fallen fortune, if these luxuries (undoubtedly inconsistent

with their profession) be here enumerated. France is not the only country where the splendour and indulgences of the higher, and the poverty and depression of the inferior clergy, have alike proved injurious to the cause of religion' (Smith's note).
[22] *imaginary bones* the reviewer in the *European Magazine* notes that this phrase 'is not only affected, but vicious; for the bones are certainly *real*, to whatever body they may have belonged' (24 (1793) 42).
[23] *enchased* set.
[24] *Fleuri, Richelieu, Alberoni* powerful cardinals.
[25] *heavier far* an echo of Michael's words to Adam and Eve, who are told that they shall 'possess / A paradise within thee, happier far' (*Paradise Lost* xii 586–7).

Of evils present. Still, as men misled
By early prejudice (so hard to break),
I mourn your sorrows, for I too have known   155
Involuntary exile[26] and, while yet
England had charms for me,[27] have felt how sad
It is to look across the dim cold sea
That melancholy rolls its refluent[28] tides
Between us and the dear regretted land   160
We call our own – as now ye pensive wait
On this bleak morning, gazing on the waves
That seem to leave your shore, from whence the wind
Is loaded to your ears with the deep groans
Of martyred saints and suffering royalty,[29]   165
While to your eyes the avenging power of Heaven
Appears in awful anger to prepare
The storm of vengeance, fraught with plagues and death.
Even he of milder heart, who was indeed
The simple shepherd in a rustic scene,   170
And mid the vine-clad hills of Languedoc
Taught to the barefoot peasant, whose hard hands
Produced the nectar he could seldom taste,[30]
Submission to the Lord for whom he toiled –
He, or his brethren, who to Neustria's sons[31]   175
Enforced religious patience, when, at times,
On their indignant hearts Power's iron hand
Too strongly struck, eliciting some sparks
Of the bold spirit of their native north –
Even these parochial priests, these humbled men   180
Whose lowly undistinguished cottages
Witnessed a life of purest piety,
While the meek tenants were, perhaps, unknown
Each to the haughty lord of his domain,
Who marked them not (the noble scorning still   185
The poor and pious priest, as with slow pace
He glided through the dim-arched avenue
Which to the castle led, hoping to cheer

---

[26] *Involuntary exile* Smith and her family were compelled to live near Dieppe, 1784–5, as a means of eluding her husband's creditors.

[27] *had charms for me* Smith echoes herself; cf. *Sonnet XII. Written on the Sea Shore* 7: 'But the wild gloomy scene has charms for me'. Cf. also Wordsworth, *Lines Left upon a Seat in a Yew-Tree* 21: 'Stranger! these gloomy boughs / Had charms for him'.

[28] *refluent* flowing back.

[29] *suffering royalty* After the storming of the Tuileries by the Paris mob on 10 August 1792 the royal family sought refuge at the Legislative Assembly; they were imprisoned at the Temple on 12 August.

[30] 'See the finely descriptive verses written at Montauban in France in 1750 by Dr Joseph Warton, printed in Dodsley's *Miscellanies* iv. 203' (Smith's note). Warton's *Verses written at Montauban in France, 1750* was published in Robert Dodsley's *Collection of Poems* vol. 4 (1755), pp. 207–8, and reprinted in the *London Magazine* 24 (1755) 183–4. The poem laments that the French peasants pick grapes without being able to afford to taste the wine they produce: 'No cups nectareous shall their toils repay' (l. 5).

[31] *Neustria's sons* inhabitants of Normandy.

The last sad hour of some laborious life
That hastened to its close) – even such a man   190
Becomes an exile, staying not to try
By temperate zeal to check his madd'ning flock,
Who at the novel sound of liberty
(Ah, most intoxicating sound to slaves!)
Start into licence. Lo! dejected now,   195
The wandering pastor mourns, with bleeding heart.
His erring people, weeps and prays for them,
And trembles for the account that he must give
To Heaven for souls entrusted to his care.
Where the cliff, hollowed by the wintry storm,   200
Affords a seat with matted seaweed strewn,
A softer form reclines; around her run,
On the rough shingles or the chalky bourn,
Her gay unconscious children, soon amused,
Who pick the fretted stone or glossy shell   205
Or crimson plant marine, or they contrive
The fairy vessel with its ribband sail
And gilded paper pennant; in the pool
Left by the salt wave on the yielding sands,
They launch the mimic navy. Happy age,   210
Unmindful of the miseries of man!
Alas, too long a victim to distress,
Their mother, lost in melancholy thought,
Lulled for a moment by the murmurs low
Of sullen billows, wearied by the task   215
Of having here, with swoln and aching eyes,
Fixed on the grey horizon, since the dawn
Solicitously watched the weekly sail
From her dear native land – now yields awhile
To kind forgetfulness, while fancy brings,   220
In waking dreams, that native land again!
Versailles appears, its painted galleries
And rooms of regal splendour, rich with gold,
Where, by long mirrors multiplied,[32] the crowd
Paid willing homage – and, united there,   225
Beauty gave charms to empire. Ah! too soon
From the gay visionary pageant roused,
See the sad mourner start, and, drooping, look
With tearful eyes and heaving bosom round
On drear reality, where dark'ning waves,   230
Urged by the rising wind, unheeded foam
Near her cold rugged seat. To call her thence
A fellow-sufferer comes: dejection deep

---

[32] *by long mirrors multiplied* the Palace of Versailles has
a long chamber lined with mirrors.

Checks, but conceals not quite, the martial air
And that high consciousness of noble blood   235
Which he has learned from infancy to think
Exalts him o'er the race of common men.
Nursed in the velvet lap of luxury
And fed by adulation, could *he* learn
That worth alone is true nobility,   240
And that *the peasant* who, 'amid the sons
Of Reason, Valour, Liberty, and Virtue,
Displays distinguished merit, is a noble
Of Nature's own creation'?[33] If even here,
If in this land of highly-vaunted freedom   245
Even Britons controvert the unwelcome truth,
Can it be relished by the sons of France –
Men who derive their boasted ancestry
From the fierce leaders of religious wars,
The first in chivalry's emblazoned page,   250
Who reckon Gueslin, Bayard or De Foix[34]
Among their brave progenitors? *Their* eyes,
Accustomed to regard the splendid trophies
Of heraldry (that with fantastic hand
Mingles, like images in feverish dreams,   255
'Gorgons and hydras and chimeras dire'[35]
With painted puns, and visionary shapes),
See not the simple dignity of virtue,
But hold all base, whom honours such as these
Exalt not from the crowd[36] – as one who long   260
Has dwelt amid the artificial scenes
Of populous city[37] deems that splendid shows,
The theatre, and pageant pomp of courts,
Are only worth regard; forgets all taste
For nature's genuine beauty; in the lapse   265
Of gushing waters hears no soothing sound,
Nor listens with delight to sighing winds
That on their fragrant pinions waft the notes
Of birds rejoicing in the tangled copse;
Nor gazes pleased on ocean's silver breast,   270

---

[33] 'These lines are Thomson's, and are among those sentiments which are now called (when used by living writers) not commonplace declamation but sentiments of dangerous tendency' (Smith's note). I am unable to trace a source in Thomson for these lines.

[34] *Gueslin, Bayard or De Foix* famous French warriors.

[35] *Gorgons and hydras and chimeras dire Paradise Lost* i 628.

[36] 'It has been said, and with great appearance of truth, that the contempt in which the nobility of France held the common people was remembered, and with all that vindictive asperity which long endurance of oppression naturally excites, when, by a wonderful concurrence of circumstances, the people acquired the power of retaliation. Yet let me here add what seems to be in some degree inconsistent with the former charge – that the French are good masters to their servants, and that in their treatment of their negro slaves they are allowed to be more mild and merciful than other Europeans' (Smith's note).

[37] *populous city* cf. Satan in *Paradise Lost*, 'As one who long in populous city pent' (ix 445).

While lightly o'er it sail the summer clouds
Reflected in the wave that, hardly heard,
Flows on the yellow sands: so to *his* mind
That long has lived where Despotism hides
His features harsh, beneath the diadem   275
Of worldly grandeur, abject slavery seems,
If by that power imposed, slavery no more.
For luxury wreathes with silk the iron bonds,
And hides the ugly rivets with her flowers,
Till the degenerate triflers, while they love   280
The glitter of the chains, forget their weight.
But more, the men whose ill-acquired wealth[38]
Was wrung from plundered myriads by the means
Too often legalised by power abused,
Feel all the horrors of the fatal change,   285
When their ephemeral greatness, marred at once
(As a vain toy that Fortune's childish hand
Equally joyed to fashion or to crush),
Leaves them exposed to universal scorn
For having nothing else, not even the claim   290
To honour, which respect for heroes past
Allows to ancient titles – men like these
Sink even beneath the level whence base arts
Alone had raised them, unlamented sink,
And know that they deserve the woes they feel.   295
    Poor wand'ring wretches, whosoe'er ye are
That hopeless, houseless, friendless, travel wide
O'er these bleak russet downs, where, dimly seen,
The solitary shepherd shiv'ring tends
His dun discoloured flock (shepherd unlike   300
Him whom in song the poet's fancy crowns
With garlands, and his crook with vi'lets binds) –
Poor vagrant wretches! Outcasts of the world
Whom no abode receives, no parish owns,
Roving, like nature's commoners, the land   305
That boasts such general plenty – if the sight
Of wide-extended misery softens yours
Awhile, suspend your murmurs, here behold
The strange vicissitudes of fate, while thus
The exiled nobles from their country driven,   310
Whose richest luxuries were theirs, must feel

---

[38] 'The financiers and *fermiers generaux* are here intended. In the present moment of clamour against all those who have spoken or written in favour of the first Revolution of France, the declaimers seem to have forgotten that under the reign of a mild and easy-tempered monarch, in the most voluptuous court in the world, the abuses by which men of this descrip-tion were enriched had arisen to such height that their prodigality exhausted the immense resources of France, and, unable to supply the exigencies of govern-ment, the ministry were compelled to call *le tiers etat* – a meeting that gave birth to the Revolution which has since been so ruinously conducted' (Smith's note).

More poignant anguish than the lowest poor,
Who, born to indigence, have learned to brave
Rigid Adversity's depressing breath!
Ah, rather Fortune's worthless favourites   315
Who feed on England's vitals – pensioners
Of base corruption, who, in quick ascent
To opulence unmerited, become
Giddy with pride, and as ye rise, forgetting
The dust ye lately left, with scorn look down   320
On those beneath ye (though your equals once
In fortune, and in worth superior still,
They view the eminence on which ye stand
With wonder, not with envy, for they know
The means by which ye reached it, have been such   325
As in all honest eyes degrade ye far
Beneath the poor dependent, whose sad heart
Reluctant pleads for what your pride denies) –
Ye venal, worthless hirelings of a court!
Ye pampered parasites whom Britons pay   330
For forging fetters for them! – rather here
Study a lesson that concerns ye much,
And, trembling, learn that if oppressed too long
The raging multitude, to madness stung,
Will turn on their oppressors and no more   335
By sounding titles and parading forms
Bound like tame victims, will redress themselves!
Then swept away by the resistless torrent
Not only all your pomp may disappear,
But in the tempest lost, fair Order sink   340
Her decent head, and lawless Anarchy
O'erturn celestial Freedom's radiant throne –
As now in Gallia, where Confusion, born
Of party rage and selfish love of rule,
Sully the noblest cause that ever warmed   345
The heart of patriot virtue.[39] There arise
The infernal passions: Vengeance, seeking blood,
And Avarice, and Envy's harpy fangs
Pollute the immortal shrine of Liberty,
Dismay her votaries, and disgrace her name.   350
Respect is due to principle, and they
Who suffer for their conscience have a claim,
Whate'er that principle may be, to praise.
These ill-starred exiles then who bound by ties
To them the bonds of honour, who resigned   355

---

[39] 'This sentiment will probably *renew* against me the
indignation of those who have an interest in asserting
that no such virtue anywhere exists' (Smith's note).

Their country to preserve them, and now seek
In England an asylum, well deserve
To find that (every prejudice forgot
Which pride and ignorance teaches) we for them
Feel as our brethren, and that English hearts   360
Of just compassion ever own the sway
As truly as our element, the deep,
Obeys the mild dominion of the moon.
This they *have* found, and may they find it still!
Thus mayst thou, Britain, triumph! May thy foes,   365
By Reason's gen'rous potency subdued,
Learn that the God thou worshippest delights
In acts of pure humanity! May thine
Be still such bloodless laurels, nobler far
Than those acquired at Cressy or Poictiers[40] –   370
Or of more recent growth, those well bestowed
On him[41] who stood on Calpe's blazing height
Amid the thunder of a warring world,
Illustrious rather from the crowds he saved
From flood and fire, than from the ranks who fell   375
Beneath his valour! Actions such as these,
Like incense rising to the throne of Heaven,
Far better justify the pride that swells
In British bosoms, than the deafening roar
Of victory from a thousand brazen throats,   380
That tell with what success wide-wasting war
Has by our brave compatriots thinned the world.

BOOK II

Quippe ubi fas versum atque nefas: tot bella per orbem
Tam multae scelerum facies; non ullus aratro
Dignus honos: squalent abductis arva colonis,
Et curvae rigidum falces conflantur in ensem.
Hinc movet Euphrates, illinc Germania bellum;
Vicinae ruptis inter se legibus urbes
Arma ferunt: saevit toto Mars impius orbe.

Virgil, *Georgics* i 505–11[1]

---

[40] *Cressy or Poictiers* two important battles fought by Edward III in his attempt to win the French throne.
[41] *him* George Augustus Eliott, 1st Baron Heathfield (1717–90), who maintained British rule of Gibraltar throughout a four-year siege, by sea and land, from the Spanish (1779–83).
BOOK II
[1] 'For here right and wrong are confounded: there are so many wars throughout the world: so many sorts of wickedness: the due honours are not paid to the plough: the husbandmen are carried away and the fields lie neglected, and the crooked sickles are beaten into cruel swords. Here Euphrates, and there Germany, makes war: the neighbouring cities break their leagues, and wage war with each other: impious Mars rages all over the globe' (Martyn's translation).

*Scene: on an eminence on one of those downs, which afford to the south a view of the sea;
to the north of the weald of Sussex*

Time: an afternoon in April 1793[2]

Long wintry months are past; the moon that now
Lights her pale crescent even at noon has made
Four times her revolution, since with step
Mournful and slow,[3] along the wave-worn cliff,
Pensive I took my solitary way   5
Lost in despondence, while contemplating
Not my own wayward destiny alone
(Hard as it is, and difficult to bear!),
But in beholding the unhappy lot
Of the lorn exiles who amid the storms   10
Of wild disastrous anarchy are thrown,
Like shipwrecked sufferers, on England's coast,
To see, perhaps, no more their native land
Where Desolation riots.[4] They, like me,
From fairer hopes and happier prospects driven,   15
Shrink from the future, and regret the past.
But on this upland scene, while April comes
With fragrant airs to fan my throbbing breast,
Fain would I snatch an interval from care
That weighs my wearied spirit down to earth,   20
Courting, once more, the influence of hope
(For 'Hope' still waits upon the flowery prime)[5]
As here I mark Spring's humid hand unfold
The early leaves that fear capricious winds,
While, even on sheltered banks, the timid flowers   25
Give, half-reluctantly, their warmer hues
To mingle with the primroses' pale stars.
No shade the leafless copses yet afford,
Nor hide the mossy labours of the thrush
That, startled, darts across the narrow path;   30
But quickly reassured, resumes his task,
Or adds his louder notes to those that rise
From yonder tufted brake, where the white buds
Of the first thorn are mingled with the leaves

---

[2] After the execution of Louis XVI, 21 January
1793, violence in Paris began to intensify. Robespierre
was to come to power in July. Britain declared war
on France in February.

[3] *step / Mournful and slow*

> With how sad steps and slow, ô Moone,
> thou climb'st the skies,
> How silently, and with how wanne a
> face...

(Sidney, *Astrophil and Stella*, sonnet 31, 1–2)

[4] *Where Desolation riots* counter-revolutionary distur-
bances had been going on in France for a long time;
the Vendée was particularly badly affected in March
1793.

[5] 'Shakespeare' (Smith's note). As Curran points out,
the allusion is not to Shakespeare but to Edmund
Waller, *To my young Lady Lucy Sidney* 13: 'Hope waits
upon the flowery prime'.

Of that which blossoms on the brow of May.[6]   35
    Ah, 'twill not be! so many years have passed
Since, on my native hills, I learned to gaze
On these delightful landscapes, and those years
Have taught me so much sorrow that my soul
Feels not the joy reviving nature brings,   40
But, in dark retrospect, dejected dwells
On human follies, and on human woes.
What is the promise of the infant year,
The lively verdure, or the bursting blooms,
To those who shrink from horrors such as war   45
Spreads o'er the affrighted world? With swimming eye,
Back on the past they throw their mournful looks,
And see the temple which they fondly hoped
Reason would raise to Liberty, destroyed
By ruffian hands; while, on the ruined mass,   50
Flushed with hot blood, the fiend of discord sits
In savage triumph, mocking every plea
Of policy and justice, as she shows
The headless corse of one whose only crime
Was being born a monarch.[7] Mercy turns   55
From spectacle so dire her swoln eyes,
And Liberty, with calm unruffled brow
Magnanimous, as conscious of her strength
In reason's panoply, scorns to distain[8]
Her righteous cause with carnage, and resigns   60
To fraud and anarchy the infuriate crowd.
    What is the promise of the infant year
To those who (while the poor but peaceful hind
Pens, unmolested, the increasing flock
Of his rich master in this sea-fenced isle)   65
Survey, in neighbouring countries, scenes that make
The sick heart shudder, and the man who thinks
Blush for his species? *There* the trumpet's voice
Drowns the soft warbling of the woodland choir;
And violets, lurking in their turfy beds   70
Beneath the flow'ring thorn, are stained with blood.
There fall, at once, the spoiler and the spoiled,
While war, wide-ravaging, annihilates
The hope of cultivation, gives to fiends,
The meagre, ghastly fiends of Want and Woe,   75
The blasted land. There, taunting in the van
Of vengeance-breathing armies, Insult stalks,

---

[6] Smith refers firstly to blackthorn, the buds of which appear before the leaves, and secondly to hawthorn (or may-tree), the leaves of which come first, in mid to late May.

[7] Louis XVI, executed 21 January 1793.
[8] *distain* stain, sully.

And, in the ranks, 'Famine, and Sword, and Fire,
Crouch for employment.'[9] Lo! the suffering world,
Torn by the fearful conflict, shrinks amazed   80
From Freedom's name, usurped and misapplied,
And, cow'ring to the purple tyrant's rod,
Deems *that* the lesser ill. Deluded men!
Ere ye profane her ever-glorious name,
Or catalogue the thousands that have bled   85
Resisting her, or those who greatly died
Martyrs to liberty, revert awhile
To the black scroll that tells of regal crimes
Committed to destroy her; rather count
The hecatombs of victims who have fallen   90
Beneath a single despot, or who gave
Their wasted lives for some disputed claim
Between anointed robbers – monsters both![10]
'Oh polished perturbation – golden care!'[11] –
So strangely coveted by feeble man   95
To lift him o'er his fellows – toy for which
Such showers of blood have drenched th' affrighted earth.
Unfortunate *his* lot, whose luckless head
Thy jewelled circlet, lined with thorns, has bound;
And who, by custom's laws, obtains from thee   100
Hereditary right to rule, unchecked,
Submissive myriads: for untempered power,
Like steel ill-formed, injures the hand
It promised to protect. Unhappy France!
If e'er thy lilies, trampled now in dust   105
And blood-bespotted, shall again revive
In silver splendour, may the wreath be wov'n
By voluntary hands,[12] and freemen, such
As England's self might boast, unite to place
The guarded diadem on *his* fair brow,   110
Where Loyalty may join with Liberty
To fix it firmly. In the rugged school
Of stern adversity so early trained,
His future life, perchance, may emulate
That of the brave Bernois,[13] so justly called   115
The darling of his people, who revered

---

[9] 'Shakespeare' (Smith's note). *Henry V*, Prologue 7–8. Wordsworth makes the same allusion in a similar passage of *Descriptive Sketches*, also published in 1793: 'Like lightnings eager for th' almighty word, / Look up for sign of havoc, Fire and Sword' (ll. 802–3).
[10] 'Such was the cause of quarrel between the Houses of York and Lancaster, and of too many others with which the page of history reproaches the reason of man' (Smith's note).

[11] 'Shakespeare' (Smith's note). *2 Henry IV* IV v 23.
[12] *If e'er thy lilies ... voluntary hands* If France ever again revives the monarchy, let it be voluntary.
[13] 'Henry the Fourth of France. It may be said of this monarch that, had all the French sovereigns resembled him, despotism would have lost its horrors; yet he had considerable failings, and his greatest virtues may be chiefly imputed to his education in the school of adversity' (Smith's note).

The warrior less than they adored the man!
But ne'er may party rage, perverse and blind,
And base venality, prevail to raise
To public trust a wretch[14] whose private vice   120
Makes even the wildest profligate recoil,
And who, with hireling ruffians leagued, has burst
The laws of nature and humanity,
Wading beneath the patriot's specious mask
And in equality's illusive name,   125
To empire through a stream of kindred blood!
Innocent prisoner, most unhappy heir
Of fatal greatness,[15] who art suffering now
For all the crimes and follies of thy race,
Better for thee, if o'er thy baby brow   130
The regal mischief never had been held –
Then, in an humble sphere, perhaps content,
Thou hadst been free and joyous on the heights
Of Pyrennean mountains shagged with woods
Of chestnut, pine and oak; as on these hills   135
Is yonder little thoughtless shepherd lad
Who, on the slope abrupt of downy turf
Reclined in playful indolence, sends off
The chalky ball, quick bounding far below,
While, half-forgetful of his simple task,   140
Hardly his length'ning shadow, or the bells'
Slow tinkling of his flock, that supping tend
To the brown fallows in the vale beneath,
Where nightly it is folded, from his sport
Recall the happy idler. While I gaze   145
On his gay vacant countenance, my thoughts
Compare with his obscure, laborious lot,
Thine, most unfortunate, imperial boy –
Who round thy sullen prison daily hear'st
The savage howl of Murder as it seeks   150
Thy unoffending life; while sad within
Thy wretched mother,[16] petrified with grief,
Views thee with stony eyes, and cannot weep!
Ah, much I mourn thy sorrows, hapless Queen,
And deem thy expiation made to Heaven   155
For every fault to which prosperity
Betrayed thee when it placed thee on a throne
Where boundless power was thine, and thou wert raised

---

[14] *wretch* almost certainly Marat, editor of *L'ami du peuple*, an energetically pro-revolutionary paper; assassinated by Charlotte Corday, 13 July 1793.
[15] *Innocent prisoner . . . greatness* the Dauphin Louis XVII, then seven years old, who is thought to have died in June 1795.

[16] *Thy wretched mother* Marie Antoinette, with whom Louis XVII was imprisoned. She was executed on 16 October 1793.

High (as it seemed) above the envious reach
Of destiny! Whate'er thy errors were, 160
Be they no more remembered, though the rage
Of party swelled them to such crimes as bade
Compassion stifle every sigh that rose
For thy disastrous lot. More than enough
Thou hast endured, and every English heart, 165
Ev'n those that highest beat in Freedom's cause,
Disclaim as base, and of that cause unworthy,
The vengeance or the fear that makes thee still
A miserable prisoner! Ah, who knows,
From sad experience, more than I, to feel 170
For thy desponding spirit, as it sinks
Beneath procrastinated fears for those
More dear to thee than life! But eminence
Of misery is thine, as once of joy;
And as we view the strange vicissitude 175
We ask anew where happiness is found.
Alas, in rural life, where youthful dreams
See the Arcadia that romance describes,
Not even content resides! In yon low hut
Of clay and thatch, where rises the grey smoke 180
Of smould'ring turf cut from the adjoining moor,
The labourer, its inhabitant, who toils
From the first dawn of twilight till the sun
Sinks in the rosy waters of the west,
Finds that with poverty it cannot dwell – 185
For bread, and scanty bread, is all he earns
For him and for his household. Should disease
Born of chill wintry rains arrest his arm,
Then, through his patched and straw-stuffed casement, peeps
The squalid figure of extremest Want, 190
And from the parish the reluctant dole,
Dealt by th' unfeeling farmer, hardly saves
The ling'ring spark of life from cold extinction;
Then the bright sun of spring, that smiling bids
All other animals rejoice, beholds, 195
Crept from his pallet, the emaciate wretch
Attempt with feeble effort to resume
Some heavy task above his wasted strength,
Turning his wistful looks (how much in vain!)
To the deserted mansion where no more 200
The owner (gone to gayer scenes) resides,
Who made even luxury virtue; while he gave
The scattered crumbs to honest Poverty.
But, though the landscape be too oft deformed
By figures such as these, yet peace is here, 205
And o'er our vallies, clothed with springing corn,
No hostile hoof shall trample, nor fierce flames

Wither the wood's young verdure, ere it form
Gradual the laughing May's luxuriant shade;
For by the rude sea guarded we are safe,   210
And feel not evils such as with deep sighs
The emigrants deplore, as they recall
The summer past, when nature seemed to lose
Her course in wild distemperature,[17] and aid,
With seasons all reversed, destructive war.   215
    Shuddering, I view the pictures they have drawn
Of desolated countries where the ground,
Stripped of its unripe produce, was thick strewn
With various death – the warhorse falling there
By famine, and his rider by the sword.   220
The moping clouds sailed heavy charged with rain,
And bursting o'er the mountain's misty brow
Deluged, as with an inland sea, the vales;[18]
Where through the sullen evening's lurid gloom,
Rising like columns of volcanic fire,   225
The flames of burning villages illumed
The waste of water; and the wind that howled
Along its troubled surface brought the groans
Of plundered peasants, and the frantic shrieks
Of mothers for their children; while the brave,   230
To pity still alive, listened aghast
To these dire echoes, hopeless to prevent
The evils they beheld, or check the rage
Which ever, as the people of one land
Meet in contention, fires the human heart   235
With savage thirst of kindred blood, and makes
Man lose his nature, rendering him more fierce
Than the gaunt monsters of the howling waste.
    Oft have I heard the melancholy tale
Which, all their native gaiety forgot,   240
These exiles tell – how hope impelled them on,
Reckless of tempest, hunger or the sword,
Till, ordered to retreat they knew not why
From all their flattering prospects, they became
The prey of dark suspicion and regret:[19]   245
Then in despondence sunk the unnerved arm

---

[17] *distemperature* inclemency; in this case, extreme heat.
[18] 'From the heavy and incessant rains during the last campaign, the armies were often compelled to march for many miles through marshes overflowed, suffering the extremities of cold and fatigue. The peasants frequently misled them and, after having passed these inundations at the hazard of their lives, they were sometimes under the necessity of crossing them a second and a third time. Their evening quarters after such a day of exertion were often in a wood without shelter, and their repast, instead of bread, unripe corn, without any other preparation than being mashed into a sort of paste' (Smith's note).
[19] 'It is remarkable that, notwithstanding the excessive hardships to which the army of the emigrants was exposed, very few in it suffered from disease till they began to retreat; then it was that despondence consigned to the most miserable death many brave men who deserved a better fate, and then despair impelled some to suicide, while others fell by mutual wounds, unable to survive disappointment and humiliation' (Smith's note).

Of gallant Loyalty. At every turn
Shame and Disgrace appeared, and seemed to mock
Their scattered squadrons – which the warlike youth,
Unable to endure, often implored,   250
As the last act of friendship, from the hand
Of some brave comrade, to receive the blow
That freed the indignant spirit from its pain.
  To a wild mountain, whose bare summit hides
Its broken eminence in clouds, whose steeps   255
Are dark with woods, where the receding rocks
Are worn by torrents of dissolving snow,
A wretched woman, pale and breathless, flies,
And gazing round her, listens to the sound
Of hostile footsteps. No, it dies away!   260
Nor noise remains but of the cataract,
Or surly breeze of night that mutters low
Among the thickets where she trembling seeks
A temporary shelter, clasping close
To her hard-heaving heart her sleeping child,   265
All she could rescue of the innocent group
That yesterday surrounded her. Escaped
Almost by miracle, fear, frantic fear,
Winged her weak feet! Yet half-repentant now
Her headlong haste, she wishes she had stayed   270
To die with those affrighted Fancy paints
The lawless soldier's victims. Hark, again
The driving tempest bears the cry of Death!
And with deep sudden thunder, the dread sound
Of cannon vibrates on the tremulous earth,   275
While, bursting in the air, the murderous bomb
Glares o'er her mansion. Where the splinters fall
Like scattered comets, its destructive path
Is marked by wreaths of flame! Then, overwhelmed
Beneath accumulated horror, sinks   280
The desolate mourner, yet in death itself,
True to maternal tenderness, she tries
To save the unconscious infant from the storm
In which she perishes, and to protect
This last dear object of her ruined hopes   285
From prowling monsters, that from other hills
More inaccessible, and wilder wastes,
Lured by the scent of slaughter, follow fierce
Contending hosts, and to polluted fields
Add dire increase of horrors. But, alas,   290
The mother and the infant perish both![20]

[20] Lines 254–91 rework a topos common in late eighteenth-century poetry; cf. Darwin, *The Loves of the Plants* (1789) iii 351–68; Wordsworth, *An Evening Walk* (1793) 279–300. For further discussion see Mary Jacobus, *Tradition and Experiment in Wordsworth's Lyrical Ballads (1798)* (Oxford, 1976), pp. 134–48.

The feudal chief whose Gothic battlements
Frown on the plain beneath, returning home
From distant lands, alone and in disguise,
Gains at the fall of night his castle walls,   295
But at the vacant gate no porter sits
To wait his lord's admittance. In the courts
All is drear silence. Guessing but too well
The fatal truth, he shudders as he goes
Through the mute hall where, by the blunted light   300
That the dim moon through painted casements lends,
He sees that devastation has been there.
Then, while each hideous image to his mind
Rises terrific, o'er a bleeding corse
Stumbling he falls; another interrupts   305
His staggering feet – all, all who used to rush
With joy to meet him, all his family
Lie murdered in his way! And the day dawns
On a wild raving maniac whom a fate
So sudden and calamitous has robbed   310
Of reason, and who round his vacant walls
Screams unregarded and reproaches Heaven!
Such are thy dreadful trophies, savage War,
And evils such as these, or yet more dire,
Which the pained mind recoils from – all are thine!   315
The purple pestilence that to the grave
Sends whom the sword has spared is thine, and thine
The widow's anguish and the orphan's tears!
Woes such as these does man inflict on man,
And by the closet murderers whom we style   320
Wise politicians are the schemes prepared
Which, to keep Europe's wavering balance even,
Depopulate her kingdoms, and consign
To tears and anguish half a bleeding world!
    Oh could the time return when thoughts like these   325
Spoiled not that gay delight which vernal suns
Illuminating hills, and woods, and fields,
Gave to my infant spirits! Memory come,
And from distracting cares that now deprive
Such scenes of all their beauty, kindly bear   330
My fancy to those hours of simple joy,
When, on the banks of Arun, which I see
Make its irriguous course through yonder meads,
I played, unconscious then of future ill!
There (where from hollows fringed with yellow broom,   335
The birch with silver rind, and fairy leaf,
Aslant the low stream trembles) I have stood
And meditated how to venture best
Into the shallow current, to procure
The willow-herb of glowing purple spikes,   340

Or flags[21] whose sword-like leaves concealed the tide,
Startling the timid reed-bird from her nest,
As with aquatic flowers I wove the wreath,
Such as, collected by the shepherd girls,
Deck in the villages the turfy shrine,   345
And mark the arrival of propitious May.
How little dreamed I then the time would come
When the bright sun of that delicious month
Should, from disturbed and artificial sleep,
Awaken me to never-ending toil,   350
To terror and to tears – attempting still
With feeble hands and cold desponding heart
To save my children from the o'erwhelming wrongs
That have for ten long years been heaped on me!
The fearful spectres of chicane and fraud   355
Have, Proteus-like, still changed their hideous forms
(As the law lent its plausible disguise),
Pursuing my faint steps, and I have seen
Friendship's sweet bonds (which were so early formed,
And once I fondly thought of amaranth   360
Inwove with silver seven times tried) give way
And fail, as these green fan-like leaves of fern
Will wither at the touch of autumn's frost.
Yet there are those whose patient pity still
Hears my long murmurs, who unwearied try   365
With lenient hands to bind up every wound
My wearied spirit feels, and bid me go
'Right onward'[22] – a calm votary of the nymph
Who from her adamantine rock points out
To conscious rectitude the rugged path   370
That leads at length to peace! Ah yes, my friends,
Peace will at last be mine, for in the grave
Is peace – and pass a few short years, perchance
A few short months, and all the various pain
I now endure shall be forgotten there,   375
And no memorial shall remain of me
Save in your bosoms; while even *your* regret
Shall lose its poignancy, as ye reflect
What complicated woes that grave conceals!
But if the little praise that may await   380
The mother's efforts should provoke the spleen
Of priest or Levite,[23] and they then arraign
The dust that cannot hear them, be it yours
To vindicate my humble fame, to say

---

[21] *flags* wild iris.
[22] 'Milton, Sonnet 22d' (Smith's note); see *To Mr Cyriack Skinner Upon his Blindness* 9.
[23] *Levite* contemptuous term for a clergyman.

That not in selfish sufferings absorbed 385
'I gave to misery all I had, my tears.'[24]
And if, where regulated sanctity
Pours her long orisons to heaven, my voice
Was seldom heard, that yet my prayer was made
To him who hears even silence – not in domes 390
Of human architecture filled with crowds,
But on these hills, where boundless yet distinct,
Even as a map, beneath are spread the fields
His bounty clothes, divided here by woods
And there by commons rude[25] or winding brooks, 395
While I might breathe the air perfumed with flowers
Or the fresh odours of the mountain turf,
And gaze on clouds above me, as they sailed
Majestic, or remark the reddening north
When bickering arrows of electric fire 400
Flash on the evening sky;[26] I made my prayer
In unison with murmuring waves that now
Swell with dark tempests, now are mild and blue
As the bright arch above, for all to me
Declare omniscient goodness, nor need I 405
Declamatory essays to incite
My wonder or my praise, when every leaf
That spring unfolds, and every simple bud
More forcibly impresses on my heart
His power and wisdom. Ah, while I adore 410
That goodness, which designed to all that lives
Some taste of happiness, my soul is pained
By the variety of woes that man
For man creates, his blessings often turned
To plagues and curses: saint-like Piety, 415
Misled by Superstition, has destroyed
More than Ambition, and the sacred flame
Of Liberty becomes a raging fire
When Licence and Confusion bid it blaze.
From thy high throne above yon radiant stars, 420
Oh power omnipotent, with mercy view
This suffering globe, and cause thy creatures cease,[27]
With savage fangs, to tear her bleeding breast;[28]
Restrain that rage for power that bids a man,
Himself a worm, desire unbounded rule 425

---

[24] 'Gray' (Smith's note), *Elegy* 123.
[25] *commons rude* coarse common land.
[26] *bickering arrows . . . sky* the aurora borealis or northern lights.
[27] *cause thy creatures cease* cause thy creatures [to] cease. Smith's somewhat affected diction allows this elision,

to which the reviewer in the *European Magazine* took exception.
[28] *This suffering globe . . . breast* As the reviewer in the *European Magazine* comments: 'to transmute the neutral noun "globe" into a female, and tear "her" breast, is a *licentia* not *sumpta pudenter*, and cannot be pardoned' (24 (1793) 44).

O'er beings like himself; teach the hard hearts
Of rulers that the poorest hind who dies
For their unrighteous quarrels in thy sight
Is equal to the imperious lord that leads
His disciplined destroyers to the field.   430
May lovely Freedom in her genuine charms,
Aided by stern but equal Justice, drive
From the ensanguined earth the hell-born fiends
Of Pride, Oppression, Avarice and Revenge
That ruin what thy mercy made so fair!   435
Then shall these ill-starred wanderers, whose sad fate
These desultory lines lament, regain
Their native country; private vengeance then
To public virtue yield, and the fierce feuds
That long have torn their desolated land   440
May (even as storms that agitate the air
Drive noxious vapours from the blighted earth)
Serve, all tremendous as they are, to fix
The reign of Reason, Liberty, and Peace!

From Beachy Head: with Other Poems (1807)[1]

BEACHY HEAD

On thy stupendous summit, rock sublime,
That o'er the channel reared, halfway at sea
The mariner at early morning hails,[2]
I would recline; while Fancy should go forth
And represent the strange and awful hour   5
Of vast concussion when the Omnipotent
Stretched forth his arm and rent the solid hills,[3]
Bidding the impetuous main flood rush between
The rifted shores, and from the continent
Eternally divided this green isle.   10
Imperial lord of the high southern coast,
From thy projecting headland I would mark

BEACHY HEAD
[1] The 'Advertisement' to this posthumous volume
states: 'The poem entitled *Beachy Head* is not com-
pleted according to the original design. That the
increasing debility of its author has been the cause of
its being left in an imperfect state will, it is hoped,
be a sufficient apology' (p. vii).
[2] 'In crossing the Channel from the coast of France,
Beachy Head is the first land made' (Smith's note).

[3] 'Alluding to the idea that this island was once
joined to the continent of Europe, and torn from
it by some convulsion of nature. I confess I never
could trace the resemblance between the two coun-
tries. Yet the cliffs about Dieppe resemble the chalk
cliffs on the southern coast. But Normandy has no
likeness whatever to the parts of England opposite to
it' (Smith's note).

Far in the east the shades of night disperse,
Melting and thinned, as from the dark blue wave
Emerging, brilliant rays of arrowy light   15
Dart from the horizon, when the glorious sun
Just lifts above it his resplendent orb.
Advances now, with feathery silver touched,
The rippling tide of flood; glisten the sands,
While, inmates of the chalky clefts that scar   20
Thy sides precipitous, with shrill harsh cry,
Their white wings glancing in the level beam,
The terns, and gulls, and tarrocks,[4] seek their food,
And thy rough hollows echo to the voice
Of the gray choughs[5] and ever-restless daws,   25
With clamour not unlike the chiding hounds,
While the lone shepherd and his baying dog
Drive to thy turfy crest his bleating flock.
  The high meridian[6] of the day is past,
And ocean now, reflecting the calm heaven,   30
Is of cerulean hue, and murmurs low
The tide of ebb upon the level sands.
The sloop, her angular canvas shifting still,
Catches the light and variable airs
That but a little crisp the summer sea,   35
Dimpling its tranquil surface.
                              Afar off,
And just emerging from the arch immense
Where seem to part the elements, a fleet
Of fishing vessels stretch their lesser sails,[7]
While more remote, and like a dubious spot   40
Just hanging in the horizon, laden deep,
The ship of commerce, richly freighted, makes
Her slower progress on her distant voyage,
Bound to the orient climates where the sun
Matures the spice within its odorous shell,   45
And, rivalling the grey worm's filmy toil,
Bursts from its pod the vegetable down,[8]
Which, in long turbaned wreaths, from torrid heat
Defends the brows of Asia's countless castes.[9]
There the earth hides within her glowing breast   50

---

[4] 'Terns: *sterna hirundo*, or sea swallow; gulls: *larus canus*; tarrocks: *larus tridactylus*' (Smith's note).
[5] 'Gray choughs: *corvus graculus*. Cornish choughs, or, as these birds are called by the Sussex people, saddle-backed crows, build in great numbers on this coast' (Smith's note).
[6] *high meridian* noon.

[7] *lesser sails* as they drag their nets, the fishing vessels proceed slowly through the sea, dependent only on their smaller sails.
[8] 'Cotton: *gossypium herbaceum*' (Smith's note).
[9] The Indiaman on the horizon is sailing to India to pick up cotton to take back to Europe. Lines 41–9 are inspired by *Paradise Lost* ii 636–42.

The beamy adamant[10] and the round pearl
Enchased[11] in rugged covering, which the slave,
With perilous and breathless toil, tears off
From the rough sea-rock deep beneath the waves.
These are the toys of nature, and her sport   55
Of little estimate in Reason's eye;
And they who reason, with abhorrence see
Man, for such gauds[12] and baubles, violate
The sacred freedom of his fellow man –
Erroneous estimate! As heaven's pure air,   60
Fresh as it blows on this aërial height,
Or sound of seas upon the stony strand,
Or inland, the gay harmony of birds,
And winds that wander in the leafy woods,
Are to the unadulterate taste more worth   65
Than the elaborate harmony brought out
From fretted stop, or modulated airs
Of vocal science.[13] So the brightest gems
Glancing resplendent on the regal crown,
Or trembling in the high-born beauty's ear,   70
Are poor and paltry to the lovely light
Of the fair star[14] that, as the day declines
Attendant on her queen, the crescent moon
Bathes her bright tresses in the eastern wave.

For now the sun is verging to the sea,   75
And as he westward sinks, the floating clouds
Suspended move upon the evening gale,
And gathering round his orb, as if to shade
The insufferable brightness, they resign
Their gauzy whiteness and, more warmed, assume   80
All hues of purple. There transparent gold
Mingles with ruby tints and sapphire gleams
And colours such as nature through her works
Shows only in the ethereal canopy.[15]
Thither aspiring fancy fondly soars,   85
Wandering sublime through visionary vales
Where bright pavilions rise, and trophies fanned
By airs celestial, and adorned with wreaths
Of flowers that bloom amid Elysian bowers.

---

[10] 'Diamonds, the hardest and most valuable of precious stones. For the extraordinary exertions of the Indians in diving for the pearl oysters, see the account of the pearl fisheries in Percival's *View of Ceylon*' (Smith's note). Robert Percival's *An Account of Ceylon* was first published in 1803.
[11] *Enchased* set.
[12] *gauds* showy ornaments, finery.

[13] Lines 57–68 are an attack on slavery. To reasonable people, the enslavement of men in exchange for jewels is an unequal transaction; just as, to the unadulterated sensibility, the delights of nature are worth more than the elaborate harmonies of music or the sound of the human voice.
[14] *fair star* Venus.
[15] *ethereal canopy* sky.

Now bright and brighter still the colours glow,   90
Till half the lustrous orb within the flood
Seems to retire, the flood reflecting still
Its splendour, and in mimic glory dressed;
Till the last ray, shot upward, fires the clouds
With blazing crimson, then in paler light   95
Long lines of tenderer radiance lingering yield
To partial darkness, and on the opposing side
The early moon distinctly rising throws
Her pearly brilliance on the trembling tide.
   The fishermen who at set seasons pass   100
Many a league off at sea their toiling night
Now hail their comrades from their daily task
Returning, and make ready for their own
With the night-tide commencing. The night tide
Bears a dark vessel on, whose hull and sails   105
Mark her a coaster from the north. Her keel
Now ploughs the sand, and sidelong now she leans,
While with loud clamours her athletic crew
Unload her, and resounds the busy hum
Along the wave-worn rocks. Yet more remote,   110
Where the rough cliff hangs beetling[16] o'er its base,
All breathes repose; the water's rippling sound
Scarce heard, but now and then the sea-snipe's cry[17]
Just tells that something living is abroad;
And sometimes crossing on the moon-bright line   115
Glimmers the skiff, faintly discerned awhile,
Then lost in shadow.
             Contemplation here,
High on her throne of rock, aloof may sit
And bid recording Memory[18] unfold
Her scroll voluminous, bid her retrace   120
The period when from Neustria's hostile shore[19]
The Norman launched his galleys, and the bay
O'er which that mass of ruin[20] frowns even now
In vain and sullen menace, then received
The new invaders – a proud martial race,   125
Of Scandinavia the undaunted sons
Whom Dogon, Fier-a-bras, and Humfroi led
To conquest, while Trinacria to their power
Yielded her wheaten garland, and when thou,

---

[16] *beetling* beetling (overhanging) cliffs recollect Thomson, *Spring* 454, who describes the hawk 'High, in the beetling Cliff'.

[17] 'In crossing the Channel this bird is heard at night, uttering a short cry, and flitting along near the surface of the waves. The sailors call it the sea-snipe,

but I can find no species of sea-bird of which this is the vulgar name. A bird so called inhabits the Lake of Geneva' (Smith's note).

[18] *recording Memory* history.

[19] *Neustria's hostile shore* Normandy.

[20] *ruin* Pevensey Castle.

Parthenope, within thy fertile bay   130
Received the victors.[21]
　　　　　　　　In the mailed ranks
Of Normans landing on the British coast
Rode Taillefer, and with astounding voice
Thundered the war-song daring Roland sang
First in the fierce contention; vainly brave,   135
One not inglorious struggle England made,
But failing, saw the Saxon heptarchy[22]
Finish for ever. Then the holy pile,
Yet seen upon the field of conquest, rose,[23]
Where to appease Heaven's wrath for so much blood,   140
The conqueror bade unceasing prayers ascend,
And requiems for the slayers and the slain.

---

[21] 'The Scandinavians (modern Norway, Sweden, Denmark, Lapland, etc.) and other inhabitants of the north, began towards the end of the eighth century to leave their inhospitable climate in search of the produce of more fortunate countries.

The north-men made inroads on the coasts of France and, carrying back immense booty, excited their compatriots to engage in the same piratical voyages; and they were afterwards joined by numbers of necessitous and daring adventurers from the coasts of Provence and Sicily.

In 844 these wandering innovators had a great number of vessels at sea and, again visiting the coasts of France, Spain, and England, the following year they penetrated even to Paris; and the unfortunate Charles the Bald, King of France, purchased at a high price the retreat of the banditti he had no other means of repelling.

These successful expeditions continued for some time till Rollo (otherwise Raoul) assembled a number of followers and, after a descent on England, crossed the Channel, and made himself master of Rouen, which he fortified. Charles the Simple, unable to contend with Rollo, offered to resign to him some of the northern provinces, and to give him his daughter in marriage. Neustria, since called Normandy, was granted to him, and afterwards Brittany. He added the more solid virtues of the legislator to the fierce valour of the conqueror; converted to Christianity, he established justice, and repressed the excesses of his Danish subjects, till then accustomed to live only by plunder. His name became the signal for pursuing those who violated the laws, as well as the cry of Haro, still so usual in Normandy. The Danes and Francs produced a race of men celebrated for their valour, and it was a small party of these that in 983, having been on a pilgrimage to Jerusalem, arrived on their return at Salerno, and found the town surrounded by Mahometans, whom the Salernians were bribing to leave their coast. The Normans represented to them the baseness and cowardice of such submission and, notwithstanding the inequality of their numbers, they boldly attacked the Saracen camp and drove the infidels to their ships. The Prince of Salerno, astonished at their successful audacity, would have loaded them with the marks of his gratitude but, refusing every reward, they returned to their own country from whence, however, other bodies of Normans passed into Sicily (anciently called Trinacria); and many of them entered into the service of the Emperor of the east, others of the Pope, and the Duke of Naples was happy to engage a small party of them in defence of his newly founded duchy. Soon afterwards three brothers of Coutance, the sons of Tancred de Hauteville – Guillaume Fier-a-bras, Drogon, and Humfroi – joining the Normans established at Aversa, became masters of the fertile island of Sicily and, Robert Guiscard joining them, the Normans became sovereigns both of Sicily and Naples (Parthenope). How William, the natural son of Robert, Duke of Normandy, possessed himself of England, is too well-known to be repeated here. William, sailing from St Valori, landed in the bay of Pevensey and at the place now called Battle met the English forces under Harold – an esquire (ecuyer) called Taillefer, mounted on an armed horse, led on the Normans, singing in a thundering tone the war song of Rollo. He threw himself among the English and was killed on the first onset. In a marsh not far from Hastings, the skeletons of an armed man and horse were found a few years since, which are believed to have belonged to the Normans, as a party of their horse, deceived in the nature of the ground, perished in the morass' (Smith's note).

[22] *Saxon heptarchy* the seven kingdoms established by the Angles and Saxons in Britain.

[23] 'Battle Abbey was raised by the Conqueror, and endowed with an ample revenue, that masses might be said night and day for the souls of those who perished in battle' (Smith's note).

But let not modern Gallia form from hence
Presumptuous hopes that ever thou again,
Queen of the isles, shalt crouch to foreign arms.   145
The enervate[24] sons of Italy may yield,
And the Iberian,[25] all his trophies torn
And wrapped in Superstition's monkish weed,
May shelter his abasement, and put on
Degrading fetters. Never, never thou,   150
Imperial mistress of the obedient sea!
But thou, in thy integrity secure,
Shalt now undaunted meet a world in arms.
   England, 'twas where this promontory rears
Its rugged brow above the channel wave,   155
Parting the hostile nations, that thy fame,
Thy naval fame, was tarnished, at what time
Thou, leagued with the Batavian, gavest to France
One day of triumph – triumph the more loud
Because even then so rare.[26] Oh well redeemed,   160
Since, by a series of illustrious men
Such as no other country ever reared,
To vindicate her cause. It is a list
Which, as Fame echoes it, blanches the cheek
Of bold Ambition, while the despot feels   165
The extorted sceptre tremble in his grasp.
   From even the proudest roll by glory filled,
How gladly the reflecting mind returns
To simple scenes of peace and industry
Where, bosomed in some valley of the hills,   170
Stands the lone farm, its gate with tawny ricks
Surrounded, and with granaries and sheds
Roofed with green mosses, and by elms and ash
Partially shaded; and not far removed
The hut of sea-flints built – the humble home   175
Of one who sometimes watches on the heights
When hid in the cold mist of passing clouds

---

[24] *enervate* weak, effeminate.

[25] As Curran observes, Napoleon had conquered Italy and the Iberian peninsula.

[26] 'In 1690, King William being then in Ireland, Tourville, the French admiral, arrived on the coast of England. His fleet consisted of 78 large ships, and 22 fire-ships. Lord Torrington, the English admiral, lay at St Helens with only 40 English and a few Dutch ships, and, conscious of the disadvantage under which he should give battle, he ran up between the enemy's fleet and the coast, to protect it. The Queen's Council, dictated to by Russell, persuaded her to order Torrington to venture a battle. The orders Torrington appears to have obeyed reluctantly: his fleet now consisted of 22 Dutch and 34 English ships. Evertson, the Dutch admiral, was eager to obtain glory; Torrington, more cautious, reflected on the importance of the stake. The consequence was that the Dutch rashly sailing on were surrounded, and Torrington, solicitous to recover this false step, placed himself with difficulty between the Dutch and the French. But three Dutch ships were burnt, two of their admirals killed, and almost all their ships disabled. The English and Dutch, declining a second engagement, retired towards the mouth of the Thames. The French, from ignorance of the coast and misunderstanding among each other, failed to take all the advantage they might have done of this victory' (Smith's note).

The flock, with dripping fleeces, are dispersed
O'er the wide down; then from some ridged point
That overlooks the sea, his eager eye   180
Watches the bark that for his signal waits
To land its merchandise. Quitting for this
Clandestine traffic his more honest toil,
The crook abandoning, he braves himself
The heaviest snowstorm of December's night,   185
When with conflicting winds the ocean raves,
And on the tossing boat unfearing mounts
To meet the partners of the perilous trade
And share their hazard.[27] Well it were for him
If no such commerce of destruction known,   190
He were content with what the earth affords
To human labour, even where she seems
Reluctant most. More happy is the hind[28]
Who with his own hands rears on some black moor
Or turbary[29] his independent hut   195
Covered with heather, whence the slow white smoke
Of smouldering peat arises. A few sheep,
His best possession, with his children share
The rugged shed when wintry tempests blow;
But when with spring's return the green blades rise   200
Amid the russet heath, the household live
Joint tenants of the waste throughout the day,
And often, from her nest among the swamps,
Where the gemmed sun-dew[30] grows, or fringed buck-bean,[31]
They scare the plover[32] that with plaintive cries   205
Flutters, as sorely wounded,[33] down the wind.
Rude, and but just removed from savage life,
Is the rough dweller among scenes like these
(Scenes all unlike the poet's fabling dreams
Describing Arcady).[34] But he is free;   210
The dread that follows on illegal acts
He never feels, and his industrious mate
Shares in his labour. Where the brook is traced
By crowding osiers,[35] and the black coot[36] hides

---

[27] 'The shepherds and labourers of this tract of country, a hardy and athletic race of men, are almost universally engaged in the contraband trade, carried on for the coarsest and most destructive spirits, with the opposite coast. When no other vessel will venture to sea, these men hazard their lives to elude the watchfulness of the Revenue officers, and to secure their cargoes' (Smith's note).

[28] *hind* peasant, farm labourer.

[29] *turbary* peat bog.

[30] 'sun-dew: *drosera rotundifolia*' (Smith's note).

[31] 'buck-bean: *menyanthes trifoliatum*' (Smith's note).

[32] 'plover: *tringa vanellus*' (Smith's note).

[33] *as sorely wounded* i.e. as if sorely wounded, so as to distract attention from her nest.

[34] *Arcady* the mountainous central Pelopennesus, named after Arcas, son of Zeus, who reigned here; the people were shepherd-musicians. Although the Greeks regarded it as barbaric, the Romans idealized it into a paradise of nymphs and shepherds. The 'poet' Smith has in mind is probably Virgil, who celebrates Arcadia at *Eclogues* x 31ff.

[35] *osiers* willow trees.

[36] 'coot: *fulica aterrima*' (Smith's note).

Among the plashy reeds her diving brood,   215
The matron wades, gathering the long green rush
That well prepared hereafter lends its light
To her poor cottage, dark and cheerless else
Through the drear hours of winter. Otherwhile
She leads her infant group where charlock[37] grows   220
'Unprofitably gay',[38] or to the fields
Where congregate the linnet and the finch
That on the thistles so profusely spread
Feast in the desert, the poor family
Early resort, extirpating[39] with care   225
These and the gaudier mischief of the ground;
Then flames the high-raised heap, seen afar off
Like hostile war-fires flashing to the sky.[40]
Another task is theirs. On fields that show
As[41] angry Heaven had rained sterility   230
Stony and cold, and hostile to the plough,
Where, clamouring loud, the evening curlew[42] runs
And drops her spotted eggs among the flints,
The mother and the children pile the stones
In rugged pyramids, and all this toil   235
They patiently encounter, well content
On their flock bed[43] to slumber undisturbed
Beneath the smoky roof they call their own.
Oh little knows the sturdy hind who stands
Gazing, with looks where envy and contempt   240
Are often strangely mingled, on the car
Where prosperous Fortune sits; what secret care
Or sick satiety is often hid
Beneath the splendid outside. *He* knows not
How frequently the child of luxury,   245
Enjoying nothing, flies from place to place
In chase of pleasure that eludes his grasp,
And that content is e'en less found by him
Than by the labourer whose pick-axe smooths
The road before his chariot, and who doffs   250
What *was* an hat; and, as the train pass on,
Thinks how one day's expenditure like this
Would cheer him for long months, when to his toil
The frozen earth closes her marble breast.

---

[37] *charlock* wild mustard.
[38] '"With blossomed furze, unprofitably gay", Goldsmith' (*Deserted Village* 194) (Smith's note).
[39] *extirpating* rooting out.
[40] 'The beacons formerly lighted up on the hills to give notice of the approach of an enemy. These signals would still be used in case of alarm, if the telegraph now substituted could not be distinguished on account of fog or darkness' (Smith's note). The semaphore, an upright post with moveable arms, was invented in 1792, and a chain erected along the south coast in 1795.
[41] *As* i.e. as if.
[42] 'Curlew: *charadrius oedicnemus*' (Smith's note).
[43] *flock bed* mattress stuffed with waste wool from shearing.

Ah, who *is* happy? Happiness! A word   255
That like false fire[44] from marsh effluvia born
Misleads the wanderer, destined to contend
In the world's wilderness with want or woe.
Yet *they* are happy who have never asked
What good or evil means: the boy   260
That on the river's margin gaily plays
Has heard that death is there; he knows not death,
And therefore fears it not, and venturing in
He gains a bullrush or a minnow – then,
At certain peril, for a worthless prize,   265
A crow's or raven's nest, he climbs the boll[45]
Of some tall pine, and of his prowess proud
Is for a moment happy. Are *your* cares,
Ye who despise him, never worse applied?
The village girl is happy who sets forth   270
To distant fair, gay in her Sunday suit,
With cherry-coloured knots and flourished shawl,
And bonnet newly-purchased. So is he,
Her little brother, who his mimic drum
Beats till he drowns her rural lovers' oaths   275
Of constant faith and still-increasing love.
Ah, yet a while, and half those oaths believed,
Her happiness is vanished, and the boy,
While yet a stripling, finds the sound he loved
Has led him on till he has given up   280
His freedom and his happiness together.[46]
I once was happy, when while yet a child,[47]
I learned to love these upland solitudes,
And, when elastic[48] as the mountain air,
To my light spirit care was yet unknown,   285
And evil unforeseen. Early it came,
And childhood scarcely passed, I was condemned,
A guiltless exile,[49] silently to sigh,
While Memory with faithful pencil drew
The contrast, and, regretting, I compared   290
With the polluted smoky atmosphere
And dark and stifling streets, the southern hills

---

[44] *false fire* the ignis fatuus, a phosphorescent light
seen hovering over marshy ground, believed to be
produced by the spontaneous combustion of inflam-
mable gas produced by decaying organic matter. The
phenomenon was frequently blamed by contemporary
poets for misleading lost travellers; see, e.g., Collins,
Ode on the Popular Superstitions of the Highlands 95–8;
Erasmus Darwin, *The Loves of the Plants* iv 53–4.
[45] *boll* trunk.

[46] *the boy . . . his happiness together* the boy becomes a
soldier with a real drum.
[47] Smith echoes her own *Sonnet V. To the South
Downs* 1: 'Ah hills beloved, where once, an happy
child . . .' See also line 368.
[48] *elastic* buoyant.
[49] Her father married Charlotte to Benjamin Smith,
a young merchant in the City of London, when she
was only sixteen, in 1765. Living over the business in
Cheapside, she felt herself to be in 'personal slavery'.

That to the setting sun their graceful heads
Rearing, o'erlook the frith[50] where Vecta[51] breaks
With her white rocks the strong impetuous tide,   295
When western winds the vast Atlantic urge
To thunder on the coast. Haunts of my youth!
Scenes of fond daydreams, I behold ye yet,
Where 'twas so pleasant by thy northern slopes
To climb the winding sheep-path, aided oft   300
By scattered thorns whose spiny branches bore
Small woolly tufts, spoils of the vagrant lamb
There seeking shelter from the noonday sun;
And pleasant, seated on the short soft turf,
To look beneath upon the hollow way   305
While heavily upward moved the labouring wain
And, stalking slowly by, the sturdy hind,
To ease his panting team, stopped with a stone
The grating wheel.
              Advancing higher still
The prospect widens, and the village church   310
But little, o'er the lowly roofs around
Rears its gray belfry and its simple vane;
Those lowly roofs of thatch are half concealed
By the rude arms of trees, lovely in spring[52]
When on each bough the rosy-tinctured bloom   315
Sits thick and promises autumnal plenty.[53]
For even those orchards round the Norman farms
Which, as their owners mark the promised fruit,
Console them for the vineyards of the south,
Surpass not these.
           Where woods of ash and beech   320
And partial copses fringe the green hill-foot,
The upland shepherd rears his modest home,
There wanders by a little nameless stream
That from the hill wells forth, bright now and clear,
Or after rain with chalky mixture gray,   325
But still refreshing in its shallow course
The cottage garden – most for use designed,
Yet not of beauty destitute. The vine
Mantles the little casement, yet the briar
Drops fragrant dew among the July flowers;   330

---

[50] *frith* firth; long narrow inlet from the sea.
[51] 'Vecta: the Isle of Wight, which breaks the force
of the waves when they are driven by south-west
winds against this long and open coast. It is some-
where described as "Vecta shouldering the western
waves"' (Smith's note).
[52] 'Every cottage in this country has its orchard, and
I imagine that not even those of Herefordshire or

Worcestershire exhibit a more beautiful prospect, when
the trees are in bloom, and the *Primavera candida e
vermiglia* is everywhere so enchanting' (Smith's note).
As Curran notes, Smith alludes to Petrarch, Sonnet
310, line 4 ('pure and rosy spring').
[53] *autumnal plenty* as Curran notes, apple harvests.

And pansies rayed and freaked,[54] and mottled pinks
Grow among balm, and rosemary and rue;
There honeysuckles flaunt, and roses blow
Almost uncultured – some with dark green leaves
Contrast their flowers of pure unsullied white;   335
Others, like velvet robes of regal state
Of richest crimson, while in thorny moss
Enshrined and cradled, the most lovely, wear
The hues of youthful beauty's glowing cheek.
With fond regret I recollect e'en now   340
In spring and summer what delight I felt
Among these cottage gardens, and how much
Such artless nosegays, knotted with a rush
By village housewife or her ruddy maid,
Were welcome to me, soon and simply pleased.   345
    An early worshipper at Nature's shrine,
I loved her rudest scenes – warrens and heaths,
And yellow commons, and birch-shaded hollows,
And hedgerows, bordering unfrequented lanes
Bowered with wild roses, and the clasping woodbine   350
Where purple tassels of the tangling vetch[55]
With bittersweet[56] and bryony[57] inweave,
And the dew fills the silver bindweed's[58] cups –
I loved to trace the brooks whose humid banks
Nourish the harebell and the freckled pagil,[59]   355
And stroll among o'ershadowing woods of beech,
Lending in summer, from the heats of noon,
A whispering shade; while haply there reclines
Some pensive lover of uncultured[60] flowers
Who from the tumps[61] with bright green mosses clad   360
Plucks the wood sorrel[62] with its light thin leaves,
Heart-shaped and triply folded, and its root
Creeping like beaded coral; or who there
Gathers the copse's pride, anémones[63]
With rays like golden studs on ivory laid   365
Most delicate, but touched with purple clouds –
Fit crown for April's fair but changeful brow.
    Ah, hills so early loved, in fancy still
I breathe your pure keen air, and still behold

---

[54] *pansies rayed and freaked* a recollection of *Lycidas*
144: 'the pansy freaked with jet' ('freaked' is Milton's
coinage).
[55] 'vetch: *vicia sylvatica*' (Smith's note).
[56] 'bittersweet: *solanum dulcamara*' (Smith's note).
[57] 'bryony: *bryonia alba*' (Smith's note).
[58] 'bindweed: *convolvulus sepium*' (Smith's note).
[59] 'harebell: *hyacinthus non scriptus*; pagil: *primula veris*'
(Smith's note).

[60] *uncultured* uncultivated; i.e. wildflowers.
[61] *tumps* humps.
[62] 'sorrel: *oxalis acetosella*' (Smith's note).
[63] 'anémones: *anemóne nemorosa*. It appears to be
settled on late and excellent authorities that this word
should not be accented on the second syllable, but on
the penultima. I have however ventured the more
known accentuation as more generally used, and suit-
ing better the nature of my verse' (Smith's note).

Those widely spreading views, mocking alike   370
The poet and the painter's utmost art.
And still, observing objects more minute,
Wondering remark the strange and foreign forms
Of sea-shells, with the pale calcareous[64] soil
Mingled, and seeming of resembling substance[65] –   375
Though surely the blue ocean (from the heights
Where the Downs westward trend,[66] but dimly seen)
Here never rolled its surge. Does Nature then
Mimic, in wanton mood, fantastic shapes
Of bivalves[67] and inwreathed volutes[68] that cling   380
To the dark sea-rock of the wat'ry world?
Or did this range of chalky mountains once
Form a vast basin where the ocean waves
Swelled fathomless?[69] What time these fossil shells,
Buoyed on their native element, were thrown   385
Among the embedding calx;[70] when the huge hill
Its giant bulk heaved, and in strange ferment
Grew up a guardian barrier 'twixt the sea
And the green level of the sylvan weald?[71]

     Ah, very vain is Science'[72] proudest boast,   390
And but a little light its flame yet lends
To its most ardent votaries; since from whence
These fossil forms are seen is but conjecture,
Food for vague theories or vain dispute,
While to his daily task the peasant goes   395
Unheeding such inquiry – with no care
But that the kindly change of sun and shower
Fit for his toil the earth he cultivates.
As little recks the herdsman of the hill,
Who, on some turfy knoll idly reclined,   400
Watches his wether[73] flock, that deep beneath
Rest the remains of men, of whom is left

---

[64] *calcareous* containing lime.

[65] 'Among the crumbling chalk I have often found shells, some quite in a fossil state and hardly distinguishable from chalk. Others appeared more recent – cockles, mussels, and periwinkles, I well remember, were among the number, and some whose names I do not know. A great number were like those of small land-snails. It is now many years since I made these observations. The appearance of sea-shells so far from the sea excited my surprise, though I then knew nothing of natural history. I have never read any of the late theories of the earth, nor was I ever satisfied with the attempts to explain many of the phenomena which call forth conjecture in those books I happened to have had access to on this subject' (Smith's note).

[66] *trend* incline, stretch.

[67] *bivalves* double-shelled molluscs; e.g. oyster, mussel.

[68] *volutes* spiral-shelled molluscs; e.g. periwinkles.

[69] 'The theory here slightly hinted at is taken from an idea started by Mr White' (Smith's note). Gilbert White's *Natural History of Selborne* (1789) concerns the countryside of south-east England.

[70] *calx* lime.

[71] *sylvan weald* wooded tract between the North and South Downs, including parts of Surrey, Sussex, and Kent.

[72] *Science'* the possessive case is indicated, but Smith elides the final 's' on account of the metre.

[73] *wether* castrated male sheep.

No traces in the records of mankind
Save what these half-obliterated mounds
And half-filled trenches doubtfully impart   405
To some lone antiquary, who on times remote,
Since which two thousand years have rolled away,
Loves to contemplate.[74] He perhaps may trace,
Or fancy he can trace, the oblong square
Where the mailed legions under Claudius[75] reared   410
The rampire[76] or excavated fossé[77] delved;
What time the huge unwieldy elephant
Auxiliary reluctant, hither led
From Afric's forest glooms and tawny sands,
First felt the northern blast, and his vast frame   415
Sunk useless – whence in after-ages found,
The wondering hinds on those enormous bones
Gazed;[78] and in giants dwelling on the hills
Believed and marvelled.[79]

                  Hither, ambition, come!
Come and behold the nothingness of all   420
For which you carry through the oppressed earth
War and its train of horrors – see where tread

---

[74] 'These Downs are not only marked with traces of encampments, which from their forms are called Roman or Danish, but there are numerous tumuli among them – some of which, having been opened a few years ago, were supposed by a learned antiquary to contain the remains of the original natives of the country' (Smith's note).

[75] 'That the legions of Claudius were in this part of Britain appears certain, since this Emperor received the submission of Cantii, Atrebates, Irenobates, and Regni, in which latter denomination were included the people of Sussex' (Smith's note).

[76] *rampire* rampart, barrier.

[77] *fossé* ditch, trench.

[78] 'In the year 1740 some workmen digging in the park at Burton in Sussex discovered, nine feet below the surface, the teeth and bones of an elephant. Two of the former were seven feet eight inches in length. There were, besides these, tusks, one of which broke in removing it, a grinder not at all decayed, and a part of the jaw-bone, with bones of the knee and thigh, and several others. Some of them remained very lately at Burton House, the seat of John Biddulph, Esq. Others were in possession of the Revd. Dr Langrish, minister of Petworth at that period, who was present when some of these bones were taken up, and gave it as his opinion that they had remained there since the universal deluge. The Romans under the Emperor Claudius probably brought elephants into Britain. Milton, in the second Book of his *History*, in speaking of the expedition, says that "He, like a great eastern king, with armed elephants, marched through Gallia." This is given on the authority of Dion Cassius, in his Life of the Emperor Claudius. It has therefore been conjectured that the bones found at Burton might have been those of one of these elephants, who perished there soon after its landing, or, dying on the high downs (one of which, called Duncton Hill, rises immediately above Burton Park), the bones might have been washed down by the torrents of rain and buried deep in the soil. They were not found together but scattered at some distance from each other. The two tusks were twenty feet apart. I had often heard of the elephant's bones at Burton, but never saw them, and I have no books to refer to. I think I saw, in what is now called the National Museum at Paris, the very large bones of an elephant, which were found in North America – though it is certain that this enormous animal is never seen in its natural state, but in the countries under the torrid zone of the old world. I have, since making this note, been told that the bones of the rhinoceros and hippopotamus have been found in America' (Smith's note).

[79] 'The peasants believe that the large bones sometimes found belonged to giants who formerly lived on the hills. The devil also has a great deal to do with the remarkable forms of hill and vale: the Devil's Punchbowl, the Devil's Leaps, and the Devil's Dyke, are names given to deep hollows, or high and abrupt ridges, in this and the neighbouring county.' (Smith's note) The 'neighbouring county' is Surrey.

The innumerous hoofs of flocks above the works
By which the warrior sought to register
His glory, and immortalize his name.   425
The pirate Dane, who from his circular camp
Bore in destructive robbery fire and sword
Down through the vale,[80] sleeps unremembered here;
And here, beneath the greensward, rests alike
The savage native who his acorn meal   430
Shared with the herds that ranged the pathless woods,[81]
And the centurion who, on these wide hills
Encamping, planted the Imperial Eagle.
All, with the lapse of time, have passed away,
Even as the clouds, with dark and dragon shapes,   435
Or, like vast promontories crowned with towers,
Cast their broad shadows on the Downs, then sail
Far to the northward, and their transient gloom
Is soon forgotten.
                           But from thoughts like these,
By human crimes suggested, let us turn   440
To where a more attractive study courts
The wanderer of the hills; while shepherd girls
Will from among the fescue[82] bring him flowers
Of wondrous mockery, some resembling bees
In velvet vest, intent on their sweet toil;[83]   445
While others mimic flies that lightly sport
In the green shade, or float along the pool,
But here seem perched upon the slender stalk
And gathering honey-dew;[84] while in the breeze
That wafts the thistle's plumed seed along,   450
Bluebells wave tremulous. The mountain thyme[85]
Purples the hassock of the heaving mole,[86]
And the short turf is gay with tormentil[87]

---

[80] 'The incursions of the Danes were for many ages the scourge of this island' (Smith's note).

[81] 'The aborigines of this country lived in woods, unsheltered but by trees and caves, and were probably as truly savage as any of those who are now termed so' (Smith's note).

[82] 'The grass called sheep's fescue (*festuca ovina*) clothes these downs with the softest turf' (Smith's note).

[83] '*Ophrys apifera*, bee ophrys, or orchis, found plentifully on the hills, as well as the next' (Smith's note).

[84] '*Ophrys muscifera*, fly orchis. Linnaeus, misled by the variations to which some of this tribe are really subject, has perhaps too rashly esteemed all those which resemble insects as forming only one species, which he terms ophrys insectifera. See *English Botany*' (Smith's note).

[85] 'Bluebells: *campanula rotundifolia*; mountain thyme: *thymus serpyllum*. "It is a common notion that the flesh

of sheep which feed upon aromatic plants, particularly wild thyme, is superior in flavour to other mutton. The truth is that sheep do not crop these aromatic plants unless, now and then, by accident, or when they are first turned on hungry to downs, heaths, or commons; but the soil and situations favourable to aromatic plants produce a short sweet pasturage, best adapted to feeding sheep, whom nature designed for mountains and not for turnip grounds and rich meadows. The attachment of bees to this, and other aromatic plants, is well known." Martyn's *Miller*' (Smith's note). Smith quotes Thomas Martyn, *The Gardener's and Botanist's Dictionary . . . by the late Philip Miller . . . To which are now added a complete enumeration and description of all plants* (1797–1807).

[86] *hassock of the heaving mole* molehill.

[87] 'Tormentil: *tormentilla reptans*' (Smith's note).

And birdsfoot trefoil, and the lesser tribes
Of hawkweed,[88] spangling it with fringed stars.   455
Near where a richer tract of cultured land
Slopes to the south, and burnished by the sun,
Bend in the gale of August floods of corn;
The guardian of the flock, with watchful care,[89]
Repels by voice and dog the encroaching sheep,   460
While his boy visits every wired trap[90]
That scars the turf, and from the pitfalls takes
The timid migrants[91] who, from distant wilds,
Warrens, and stone quarries, are destined thus
To lose their short existence. But unsought   465
By luxury yet, the shepherd still protects
The social bird[92] who, from his native haunts
Of willowy current or the rushy pool,
Follows the fleecy crowd, and flirts and skims
In fellowship among them.
                    Where the knoll   470
More elevated takes the changeful winds,
The windmill rears its vanes, and thitherward,
With his white load, the master travelling
Scares the rooks rising slow on whispering wings,
While o'er his head, before the summer sun   475
Lights up the blue expanse, heard more than seen,
The lark sings matins and, above the clouds
Floating, embathes his spotted breast in dew.
Beneath the shadow of a gnarled thorn
Bent by the sea-blast,[93] from a seat of turf   480
With fairy nosegays[94] strewn, how wide the view![95] –
Till in the distant north it melts away
And mingles indiscriminate with clouds;
But if the eye could reach so far, the mart
Of England's capital, its domes and spires   485
Might be perceived. Yet hence the distant range

---

[88] 'Birdsfoot trefoil: *trefolium ornithopoides*; hawkweed: *hieracium*, many sorts' (Smith's note).

[89] 'The Downs, especially to the south, where they are less abrupt, are in many places under the plough, and the attention of the shepherds is there particularly required to keep the flocks from trespassing' (Smith's note).

[90] 'Square holes cut in the turf, into which a wire noose is fixed, to catch wheatears. Mr White says that these birds (*motacilla oenanthe*) are never taken beyond the River Adur, and Beding Hill – but this is certainly a mistake' (Smith's note).

[91] 'These birds are extremely fearful and, on the slightest appearance of a cloud, run for shelter to the first rut, or heap of stones, that they see' (Smith's note).

[92] 'The yellow wagtail: *motacilla flava*. It frequents the banks of rivulets in winter, making its nest in meadows and cornfields. But after the breeding season is over, it haunts downs and sheepwalks, and is seen constantly among the flocks, probably for the sake of the insects it picks up. In France the shepherds call it *la bergeronette*, and say it often gives them, by its cry, notice of approaching danger' (Smith's note).

[93] 'The strong winds from the south-west occasion almost all the trees, which on these hills are exposed to it, to grow the other way' (Smith's note).

[94] *nosegays* perfumes, scents.

[95] 'So extensive are some of the views from these hills, that only the want of power in the human eye to travel so far, prevents London itself being discerned. Description falls so infinitely short of the reality, that only here and there distinct features can be given' (Smith's note).

Of Kentish hills[96] appear in purple haze,
And nearer undulate the wooded heights
And airy summits[97] that above the Mole[98]
Rise in green beauty, and the beaconed ridge   490
Of Blackdown[99] shagged with heath, and swelling rude
Like a dark island from the vale, its brow
Catching the last rays of the evening sun
That gleam between the nearer park's old oaks,
Then lighten up the river and make prominent   495
The portal and the ruined battlements
Of that dismantled fortress, raised what time
The Conqueror's successors fiercely fought,
Tearing with civil feuds the desolate land.[100]
But now a tiller of the soil dwells there,   500
And of the turret's looped and raftered halls
Has made an humbler homestead where he sees,
Instead of armed foemen, herds that graze
Along his yellow meadows, or his flocks
At evening from the upland driv'n to fold.   505
    In such a castellated mansion once
A stranger chose his home, and where hard by
In rude disorder fallen, and hid with brushwood,
Lay fragments gray of towers and buttresses,
Among the ruins often he would muse.   510
His rustic meal soon ended, he was wont
To wander forth, listening the evening sounds
Of rushing milldam[101] or the distant team,
Or nightjar chasing fern-flies;[102] the tired hind

---

[96] 'A scar of chalk in a hill beyond Sevenoaks in Kent is very distinctly seen of a clear day' (Smith's note).

[97] 'The hills about Dorking in Surrey, over almost the whole extent of which county the prospect extends' (Smith's note).

[98] The River Mole rises on the borders of Sussex and flows north to Dorking.

[99] 'This is an high ridge extending between Sussex and Surrey. It is covered with heath and has almost always a dark appearance. On it is a telegraph' (Smith's note).

[100] 'In this country there are several of the fortresses or castles built by Stephen of Blois in his contention for the kingdom, with the daughter of Henry I, the Empress Matilda. Some of these are now converted into farmhouses' (Smith's note).

[101] milldam dam constructed across a stream so as to raise its level, enabling it to power a mill-wheel.

[102] 'Dr Aikin remarks, I believe, in his essay "On the Application of Natural History to the Purposes of Poetry", how many of our best poets have noticed the same circumstance, the hum of the dor beetle (scaraboeus stercorarius) among the sounds heard by the evening wanderer. I remember only one instance in which the more remarkable, though by no means uncommon noise, of the fern owl, or goatsucker, is mentioned. It is called the nighthawk, the jar bird, the churn owl, and the fern owl, from its feeding on the scaraboeus solstitialis, or fern chafer, which it catches while on the wing with its claws, the middle toe of which is long and curiously serrated, on purpose to hold them. It was this bird that was intended to be described in the 42nd sonnet (Smith's Sonnets). I was mistaken in supposing it as visible in November; it is a migrant, and leaves this country in August. I had often seen and heard it, but I did not then know its name or history. It is called goatsucker (caprimulgus) from a strange prejudice taken against it by the Italians, who assert that it sucks their goats; and the peasants of England still believe that a disease in the backs of their cattle, occasioned by a fly which deposits its egg under the skin and raises a boil, sometimes fatal to calves, is the work of this bird, which they call a puckeridge. Nothing can convince them that their beasts are not injured by this bird, which they therefore hold in abhorrence' (Smith's note). Smith refers to An Essay on the Application of Natural History to Poetry (1777) by John Aikin, brother of Anna Laetitia Barbauld.

Passed him at nightfall, wondering he should sit   515
On the hilltop so late; they[103] from the coast
Who sought bye-paths with their clandestine load,
Saw with suspicious doubt the lonely man
Cross on their way; but village maidens thought
His senses injured, and with pity say   520
That he, poor youth, must have been crossed in love –
For often, stretched[104] upon the mountain turf
With folded arms, and eyes intently fixed
Where ancient elms and firs obscured a grange[105]
Some little space within the vale below,   525
They heard him as complaining of his fate,
And to the murmuring wind of cold neglect
And baffled hope he told. The peasant girls
These plaintive sounds remember, and even now
Among them may be heard the stranger's songs.   530

Were I a shepherd on the hill,
     And ever as the mists withdrew
Could see the willows of the rill
Shading the footway to the mill
     Where once I walked with you;   535

And as away night's shadows sail,
     And sounds of birds and brooks arise,
Believe that from the woody vale
I hear your voice upon the gale
     In soothing melodies;   540

And viewing from the Alpine height
     The prospect dressed in hues of air,
Could say, while transient colours bright
Touched the fair scene with dewy light,
     ''Tis that *her* eyes are there!'   545

I think I could endure my lot
     And linger on a few short years,
And then, by all but you forgot,
Sleep where the turf that clothes the spot
     May claim some pitying tears.   550

For 'tis not easy to forget
     One who through life has loved you still,
And you, however late, might yet
With sighs to memory giv'n, regret
     The shepherd of the hill.   555

---

[103]   *they* smugglers.
[104]   A verbal echo connects Smith's solitary with the melancholic poet of Gray's *Elegy*: 'His listless length at noontide would he stretch, / And pore upon the brook that babbles by' (ll. 103–4).
[105]   *grange* granary.

Yet otherwhile it seemed as if young Hope
Her flattering pencil gave to Fancy's hand,
And in his wanderings reared to soothe his soul
Ideal bowers of pleasure. Then, of solitude
And of his hermit life still more enamoured,   560
His home was in the forest, and wild fruits
And bread sustained him. There in early spring
The barkmen[106] found him ere the sun arose;
There at their daily toil, the wedgecutters[107]
Beheld him through the distant thicket move.   565
The shaggy dog following the truffle-hunter[108]
Barked at the loiterer, and perchance at night
Belated villagers from fair or wake,
While the fresh night-wind let the moonbeams in
Between the swaying boughs, just saw him pass –   570
And then in silence, gliding like a ghost
He vanished, lost among the deepening gloom!
But near one ancient tree, whose wreathed roots
Formed a rude couch, love-songs and scattered rhymes,
Unfinished sentences, or half-erased,   575
And rhapsodies like this, were sometimes found:

    Let us to woodland wilds repair
      While yet the glittering night-dews seem
    To wait the freshly-breathing air
      Precursive of the morning beam   580
    That, rising with advancing day,
    Scatters the silver drops away.

    An elm uprooted by the storm,
      The trunk with mosses gray and green
    Shall make for us a rustic form   585
      Where lighter grows the forest scene;
    And far among the bowery shades
    Are ferny lawns and grassy glades.

    Retiring May to lovely June
      Her latest garland now resigns;   590
    The banks with cuckoo-flowers[109] are strewn,
      The woodwalks blue with columbines,[110]

---

[106] 'As soon as the sap begins to rise, the trees intended for felling are cut and barked. At which time the men who are employed in that business pass whole days in the woods' (Smith's note).

[107] 'The wedges used in ship-building are made of beech wood, and great numbers are cut every year in the woods near the Downs' (Smith's note).

[108] 'Truffles are found under the beech woods by means of small dogs trained to hunt them by the scent' (Smith's note).

[109] 'Cuckoo-flowers: *lychnis dioica*. Columbines: *aquilegia vulgaris*. Shakespeare describes the cuckoo buds as being yellow. He probably meant the numerous ranunculi, or March marigolds (*caltha palustris*) which so gild the meadows in spring; but poets have never been botanists. The cuckoo-flower is the *lychnis floscuculi*.' (Smith's note).

[110] 'Columbines: *aquilegia vulgaris*' (Smith's note).

And with its reeds the wandering stream
Reflects the flag-flower's[111] golden gleam.

There, feathering down the turf to meet,   595
   Their shadowy arms the beeches spread,
While high above our sylvan seat
   Lifts the light ash its airy head;
And later leaved, the oaks between
Extend their boughs of vernal green.   600

The slender birch its paper rind
   Seems offering to divided love,
And shuddering even without a wind
   Aspens their paler foliage move,
As if some spirit of the air   605
Breathed a low sigh in passing there.

The squirrel in his frolic mood
   Will fearless bound among the boughs;
Yaffils[112] laugh loudly through the wood,
   And murmuring ring-doves tell their vows;   610
While we, as sweetest woodscents rise,
Listen to woodland melodies.

And I'll contrive a sylvan room
   Against the time of summer heat,
Where leaves, inwoven in nature's loom,   615
   Shall canopy our green retreat,
And gales that 'close the eye of day'[113]
Shall linger ere they die away.

And when a sear and sallow hue
   From early frost the bower receives,   620
I'll dress the sand rock cave for you,
   And strew the floor with heath and leaves,
That you, against the autumnal air
May find securer shelter there.

The nightingale will then have ceased   625
   To sing her moonlight serenade,
But the gay bird with blushing breast[114]
   And woodlarks still will haunt the shade,[115]

---

[111] 'Flag-flower: *iris pseudacorus*' (Smith's note).
[112] 'Yaffils: woodpeckers (*picus*); three or four species in Britain.' (Smith's note).
[113] '"And liquid notes that close the eye of day". Milton. The idea here meant to be conveyed is of the evening wind, so welcome after a hot day of summer, and which appears to soothe and lull all nature into tranquillity' (Smith's note). The quotation is form *Sonnet 1 5*.
[114] 'The robin (*motacilla rubecula*), which is always heard after other songsters have ceased to sing' (Smith's note).
[115] 'The woodlark (*alauda nemorosa*) sings very late' (Smith's note).

And by the borders of the spring
Reed-wrens will yet be carolling.[116]   630

The forest hermit's lonely cave
    None but such soothing sounds shall reach,
Or hardly heard, the distant wave
    Slow breaking on the stony beach,
Or winds that now sigh soft and low   635
Now make wild music as they blow.

And then before the chilling north
    The tawny foliage falling light
Seems as it flits along the earth
    The footfall of the busy sprite   640
Who, wrapped in pale autumnal gloom,
Calls up the mist-born mushroom.

Oh, could I hear your soft voice there,
    And see you in the forest green
All beauteous as you are, more fair   645
    You'd look amid the sylvan scene,
And in a wood-girl's simple guise
Be still more lovely in mine eyes.

Ye phantoms of unreal delight,
    Visions of fond delirium born,   650
Rise not on my deluded sight,
    Then leave me drooping and forlorn
To know such bliss can never be,
Unless Amanda[117] loved like me.

The visionary, nursing dreams like these,   655
Is not indeed unhappy. Summer woods
Wave over him, and whisper as they wave
Some future blessings he may yet enjoy.
And as above him sail the silver clouds,
He follows them in thought to distant climes   660
Where, far from the cold policy of this,
Dividing him from her he fondly loves,
He in some island of the southern sea
May haply build his cane-constructed bower
Beneath the breadfruit or aspiring palm   665
With long green foliage rippling in the gale.[118]

---

[116] 'Reed-wrens (*motacilla arundinacea*) sing all the summer and autumn, and are often heard during the night' (Smith's note).

[117] *Amanda* Smith leaves a blank at this point in the printed text; the present reading is conjectural.

[118] 'An allusion to the visionary delights of the new discovered islands where it was at first believed men lived in a state of simplicity and happiness, but where, as later enquiries have ascertained, that exemption from toil, which the fertility of the country gives them, produces the grossest vices, and a degree of corruption that late navigators think will end in the extirpation of the whole people in a few years' (Smith's note).

Oh, let him cherish his ideal bliss –
For what is life, when Hope has ceased to strew
Her fragile flowers along its thorny way?
And sad and gloomy are his days who lives   670
Of Hope abandoned!
               Just beneath the rock
Where Beachy overpeers the Channel wave,
Within a cavern mined by wintry tides
Dwelt one who, long disgusted with the world
And all its ways, appeared to suffer life   675
Rather than live;[119] the soul-reviving gale
Fanning the beanfield[120] or the thymy heath
Had not for many summers breathed on him;
And nothing marked to him the season's change
Save that more gently rose the placid sea,   680
And that the birds which winter on the coast
Gave place to other migrants; save that the fog,
Hovering no more above the beetling cliffs,
Betrayed not then the little careless sheep
On the brink grazing, while their headlong fall[121]   685
Near the lone hermit's flint-surrounded home
Claimed unavailing pity – for his heart
Was feelingly alive to all that breathed;
And outraged as he was, in sanguine youth,
By human crimes, he still acutely felt   690
For human misery.
               Wandering on the beach,
He learned to augur from the clouds of heaven,
And from the changing colours of the sea
And sullen murmurs of the hollow cliffs,
Or the dark porpoises[122] that near the shore   695
Gambolled and sported on the level brine
When tempests were approaching; then at night
He listened to the wind, and as it drove
The billows with o'erwhelming vehemence,
He, starting from his rugged couch, went forth   700
And hazarding a life too valueless
He waded through the waves with plank or pole

---

[119] 'In a cavern almost immediately under the cliff called Beachy Head, there lived, as the people of the country believed, a man of the name of Darby, who for many years had no other abode than this cave, and subsisted almost entirely on shellfish. He had often administered assistance to shipwrecked mariners, but venturing into the sea on this charitable mission during a violent equinoctial storm, he himself perished. As it is above thirty years since I heard this tradition of Parson Darby (for so I think he was called), it may now perhaps be forgotten' (Smith's note).

[120] *the soul-reviving gale . . . beanfield* Smith may have in mind Coleridge, *Eolian Harp* 9–10: 'How exquisite the scents / Snatched from yon beanfield!'

[121] 'Sometimes in thick weather the sheep, feeding on the summit of the cliff, miss their footing and are killed by the fall' (Smith's note).

[122] 'Dark porpoises: *delphinus phocoena*' (Smith's note).

Towards where the mariner in conflict dread
Was buffeting for life the roaring surge –
And now just seen, now lost in foaming gulfs,   705
The dismal gleaming of the clouded moon
Showed the dire peril. Often he had snatched
From the wild billows some unhappy man
Who lived to bless the hermit of the rocks.
But if his generous cares were all in vain,   710
And with slow swell the tide of morning bore
Some blue-swoln corse to land, the pale recluse
Dug in the chalk a sepulchre – above
Where the dank sea-wrack marked the utmost tide,
And with his prayers performed the obsequies[123]   715
For the poor helpless stranger.
                              One dark night
The equinoctial wind blew south by west
Fierce on the shore; the bellowing cliffs were shook
Even to their stony base, and fragments fell
Flashing and thundering on the angry flood.   720
At daybreak, anxious for the lonely man,
His cave the mountain shepherds visited,
Though sand and banks of weeds had choked their way:
He was not in it, but his drowned corse,
By the waves wafted, near his former home   725
Received the rites of burial. Those who read,
Chiselled within the rock these mournful lines,
Memorials of his sufferings, did not grieve
That, dying in the cause of charity,
His spirit, from its earthly bondage freed,   730
Had to some better region fled for ever.

Mary Scott (1751–1793)

Little is known of her life prior to the publication of *The Female Advocate* (1774). She was the daughter of a linen weaver and lived in Milborne Port, Somerset. She had a brother, Russell, who was the Unitarian minister at Portsmouth, 1788–1833. At the age of twenty-one she entered a poem into the commonplace book of her friend, Mary Steele; it reveals that her health was so bad that she could hardly write.

Mary met John Taylor when they were both twenty-two. He was then a student at Daventry Academy, a Unitarian institution in Coventry. For some reason Mary's mother disapproved of him, but he remained faithful to her until Mrs Scott's death in 1787. Mary's father died the following year. She married Taylor in May 1788, at around the same time as the publication of her second volume, *The Messiah*. Taylor became minister

---

[123] *obsequies* funeral rites.

of the chapel at Ilminster; she became a Unitarian, but he became a Quaker in 1790. She had two children; her son, John Edward Taylor (1791–1844), founded the *Guardian* newspaper in 1821. She died on 5 June 1793, at the age of forty-one, in Bristol, three weeks before delivery of a third child.

The Female Advocate is a supplement to John Duncombe's *The Feminiad* (1754), a celebration of women writers throughout the ages. Scott was inspired by a passionate sensitivity to the unjust exclusion of women from the intellectual circles in which men seemed to move so freely. She wanted to amplify Duncombe's work, celebrating women he had omitted or who had since come to prominence.[1] Throughout her forthright introduction, and the poem itself, the emphasis is firmly on the debarring of women from liberal studies. This is most clearly evident in the passage celebrating Anna Laetitia Aikin (later Barbauld), which envisages a future in which women are permitted to develop themselves as intellectuals, so that 'One turns the moral, one th' historic page, / Another glows with all a Shakespeare's rage!' (lines 449–50).

The Female Advocate has an obvious significance insofar as it both embodies the feminist subtext behind so much romantic poetry by women, and is an early attempt to alert readers to the existence of a distinctive female canon. Scott identifies the makers of such a canon as Phillis Wheatley, Anna Laetitia Aikin, and Hannah More. Not surprisingly, her poem spoke powerfully to the bluestockings, and may even have helped them formulate some of their aims; Mrs Montagu is known to have recommended it to Elizabeth Carter, for instance. Its critical reception was, given its uncompromising preface, surprisingly favourable. The *Monthly Review* commented with approval: 'This lady has done herself the honour to defend the literary privileges of her sex, and to assert the distinctions which those privileges bring along with them, against those vile usurpers *the Men*'.[2] The *Gentleman's Magazine* went further; the poem contained 'a spirit, an energy, which few of either sex have equalled. . . . Each of the above portraits seems drawn from the life, the skill and precision with which the features are distinguished (in so large a group, no easy task!) being equal to the glow and beauty of the colouring'.[3] And the *Critical Review* added its voice to the chorus of praise: 'Did no other instance exist of genius in a lady than that with which we are here presented, this production alone would afford incontestible proof that nature has not prohibited the fair from arriving at excellence in poetry. But Miss Scott has asserted the intellectual endowments of the sex by such a multitude of examples as fully establish their title to the favour of the muses, and an honourable rank in polite literature.'[4]

Further Reading

Moira Ferguson, *Eighteenth-Century Women Poets: Nation, Class, and Gender* (Albany, NY, 1995), chapter 3

——, '"The Cause of My Sex": Mary Scott and the Female Literary Tradition', *HLQ* 50 (1987) 359–77

Joyce Fullard, 'Notes on Mary Whateley and Mary Scott's *The Female Advocate*', *PBSA* 81 (1987) 74–6

---

[1] These included Margaret Cavendish, Duchess of Newcastle; Anne Killigrew; Katherine Philips; Elizabeth Tollet; Charlotte Lennox; and Catherine Macaulay.

[2] *Monthly Review* 51 (1774) 387–90, p. 387.
[3] *Gentleman's Magazine* 44 (1774) 375–7, pp. 375–6.
[4] *Critical Review* 38 (1774) 218–20, p. 218.

From The Female Advocate; A Poem. Occasioned by Reading Mr Duncombe's Feminiad (1774)

TO A LADY (EXTRACT)

Being too well acquainted with the illiberal sentiments of men in general in regard to our sex, and prompted by the most fervent zeal for their privileges, I took up the pen with an intention of becoming their advocate but, thinking myself unequal to the task, it was quickly laid aside, and probably never would have been resumed, had not your partiality to the author led you to have been pleased with the specimen which you saw.

It may perhaps be objected that it was unnecessary to write on this subject, as the sentiments of all men of sense relative to female education are now more enlarged than they formerly were. I allow that they are so; but yet those of the generality (of men of sense and learning I mean, for it would be absurd to regard the opinions of those who are not such) are still very contracted. How much has been said, even by writers of distinguished reputation, of the distinction of sexes in souls, of the studies, and even of the virtues proper for women? If they have allowed us to study the imitative arts, have they not prohibited us from cultivating an acquaintance with the sciences? Do they not regard the woman who suffers her faculties to rust in a state of listless indolence with a more favourable eye than her who engages in a dispassionate search after truth? And is not an implicit acquiescence in the dictates of their understandings esteemed by them as the sole criterion of good sense in a woman? I believe I am expressing myself with warmth, but I cannot help it; for when I speak or write on this subject, I feel an indignation which I cannot, and which indeed I do not, wish to suppress. It has folly and cruelty for its objects, and therefore must be laudable: folly, because if there really are those advantages resulting from a liberal education which it is insinuated they have derived from thence, the wider those advantages are diffused, the more will the happiness of society be promoted. And if the pleasures that flow from knowledge are of all others the most refined and permanent, it surely is extreme barbarity to endeavour to preclude us from enjoying them, when they allow our sensations to be far more exquisite than their own. But I flatter myself a time may come when men will be as much ashamed to avow their narrow prejudices in regard to the abilities of our sex, as they are now fond to glory in them. A few such changes I have already seen, for facts have a powerful tendency to convince the understanding – and, of late, female authors have appeared with honour in almost every walk of literature. Several have started up since the writing of this little piece; the public favour has attested the merit of Mrs Chapone's *Letters on the Improvement of the Mind*,[1] and of Miss More's elegant pastoral drama entitled *A Search After Happiness*.[2] *Poems by Phillis Wheatley, a Negro Servant to Mr Wheatley of Boston*,[3] and *Poems by a Lady*,[4] printed for G. Robinson in Paternoster Row, lately published, also possess considerable merit.

TO A LADY

[1] Hester Chapone (1727–1801), *Letters on the Improvement of the Mind* (1773), was dedicated to Mrs Montagu.
[2] *The Search After Happiness* (Bristol, 1773) was More's first publication. John Langhorne gave it a rapturous review, saying: 'The ingenious author of the poem before us in every respect merits our protection. Whether we consider the harmony of her verse, or the happiness

of her sentiments, her strength of thought, or her purity of expression, it equally excites our admiration: for this pastoral drama was written at the age of EIGHTEEN!' (*Monthly Review* 49 (1773) 202–4, p. 202).
[3] See pp. 136–42.
[4] Probably *Original Poems, Translations, and Imitations, from the French. By a Lady* (1773), published by G. Robinson (see Jackson 183).

If I should be thought to have spoken with severity of men in general, I flatter myself I have not suffered one line to escape me that can give pain to those of a more liberal turn of mind. For such, my heart feels all the esteem due to their exalted worth. They will approve of my design, and did they know how much years of ill-health have impaired every faculty of my mind, it might perhaps lead them to be favourable in their censures on the execution. My ear will, I hope, ever be attentive to the dictates of the candid critic, but I also hope I have spirit enough to despise the sneers of the narrow-minded pedant.

But zealous as I really am in the cause of my sex, yet I would not be understood to insinuate that every woman is formed for literature: the greatest part of both sexes are necessarily confined to the business of life. All I contend for is that it is a duty absolutely incumbent on every woman whom nature hath blessed with talents, of what kind soever they may be, to improve them; and that that is much oftener the case than it is usually supposed to be. As to those ladies whose situation in life will not admit of their engaging very deep in literary researches, it surely is commendable in them to employ part, at least, of their leisure hours in improving their minds in useful knowledge: the advantages of an understanding in any degree cultivated are too obvious to need pointing out.

[ON ELIZABETH MONTAGU]

Say, Montagu,[1] can this unartful verse
Thy genius, learning, or thy worth rehearse?
To paint thy talents justly should conspire
Thy taste, thy judgement, and thy Shakespeare's fire.   360
Well hath thy pen with nice discernment traced
What various pow'rs the matchless poet graced;
Well hath thy pen his various beauties shown,
And proved thy soul congenial to his own.
Charmed with those splendid honours of thy name,   365
Fain would the muse relate thy nobler fame;
Dear to Religion, as to Learning dear,
Candid, obliging, modest, mild, sincere;
Still prone to soften at another's woe,
Still fond to bless, still ready to bestow.   370
    Oh sweet philanthropy,[2] thou guest divine,
What permanent, what heartfelt joys, are thine!
Supremely blessed the maid whose generous soul
Bends all-obedient to thy soft control;

[ON ELIZABETH MONTAGU]

[1] 'Mrs Montagu, author of the "Essay on the Genius and Writings of Shakespeare, compared with the Greek and French dramatic poets"' (Scott's note). Elizabeth Montagu (1720–1800) published her *Essay on the Writings and Genius of Shakespeare* in 1769; its popularity was such that it was into its third edition by 1772, and had been praised by Reynolds, Lord Lyttelton and Lord Grenville.

[2] The account of Montagu leads naturally into an apostrophe to philanthropy, as Montagu was known for her generosity, particularly towards child chimney-sweeps, girls in need, and women writers such as Sarah Fielding. Having quoted these lines, the *Gentleman's Magazine* commented: 'By the above, our fair panegyrist, we see, is acquainted with the life, as well as the writings, of this excellent essayist; a life to which all literary fame, however great, must be subordinate' (*Gentleman's Magazine* 44 (1774) 375–7, p. 376).

Nature's vast theatre her eye surveys,   375
Studious to trace eternal wisdom's ways;
Marks what dependencies, what different ties
Throughout the spacious scale of beings rise;
Sees Providence's oft-mysterious plan,
Formed to promote the general good of man.   380
With noble warmth thence her expanded mind
Feels for the welfare of all humankind:
Thence flows each lenient art that soothes distress,
And thence the unremitting wish to bless!

[ON ANNA LAETITIA AIKIN]

Fired with the music, Aikin,[1] of thy lays,
To thee the muse a joyful tribute pays;   420
Transported dwells on that harmonious line
Where taste and spirit, wit and learning shine;
Where Fancy's hand her richest colourings lends,
And every shade in just proportion blends.
How fair, how beauteous to our gazing eyes   425
Thy vivid intellectual paintings rise!
We feel thy feelings, glow with all thy fires,
Adopt thy thoughts, and pant with thy desires.
Proceed, bright maid, and may thy polished page
Refine the manners of a trifling age: 430
Thy sex apprize of pleasure's treach'rous charms,
And woo them from the siren's fatal arms;
Teach them with thee on Fancy's wing to soar,
With thee, the paths of science to explore;
With thee, the open book of Nature scan,   435
Yet nobly scorn the little pride of man.
   Man, seated high on Learning's awful throne,
Thinks the fair realms of knowledge his alone;
But you, ye fair, his Salic law[2] disclaim:
Supreme in Science shall the tyrant reign   440
When every talent all-indulgent Heav'n
In lavish bounty to your share hath giv'n?
   With joy ineffable the muse surveys
The orient beams of more resplendent days:

[ON ANNA LAETITIA AIKIN]
[1] 'See Poems and Miscellaneous Pieces in Prose, by Miss Aikin (daughter of the Revd Mr Aikin, one of the tutors to the Academy at Warrington), lately married to the Revd Mr Rochemont Barbauld' (Scott's note). *Miscellaneous Pieces in Prose* (1773), which Anna co-authored with her brother John, won praise from the *Monthly Review*: 'Miss Aikin has an indisputable claim to originality, and may be classed as a genius of the higher order. . . . It is nothing to say she is a woman.

It is generally thought that minds are of no sex, but if they were distinguished as bodies are, it would not avail here, as we could never discover in Miss Aikin's compositions any peculiar touches of a feminine hand' (*Monthly Review* 49 (1773) 472–8, p. 472).
[2] *Salic law* fundamental law of the French monarchy by which females are excluded from succession to the crown; in this case, Scott uses it to mean a law by which women are excluded from 'the fair realms of knowledge'.

As on she raptured looks to future years,   445
What a bright throng to fancy's view appears!
To them see Genius her best gifts impart,
And Science raise a throne in every heart!
One turns the moral, one th' historic page,
Another glows with all a Shakespeare's rage!   450
With matchless Newton now one soars on high,
Lost in the boundless wonders of the sky;
Another now, of curious mind, reveals
What treasures in her bowels earth conceals;
Nature's minuter works attract her eyes –   455
Their laws, their pow'rs, her deep research descries.
From sense abstracted, some with arduous flight
Explore the realms of intellectual light;
With unremitting study seek to find
How mind on matter, matter acts on mind: 460
Alike in nature, arts, and manners read,
In every path of knowledge, see they tread! –
Whilst men, convinced of female talents, pay
To female worth the tributary lay.

Phillis Wheatley (Mrs John Peters) (*c.*1753–1784)

What is it that makes Phillis Wheatley a romantic? The question is begged because, despite her position in this volume, she died early, in the same year that Charlotte Smith published the first edition of *Elegiac Sonnets*. J. R. de J. Jackson is in no doubt: all her publications are listed in his *Romantic Poetry by Women* (1993).[1] Even if we do not regard her as quite the same kind of writer as Felicia Hemans or Letitia Landon, it would be appropriate to see her as one of the first of a series of poets who, in spite of a lack of formal education, to say nothing of social status, won respect for their work as writers; others in this group must include Ann Yearsley and Isabella Lickbarrow. More importantly, she is a precursor of the bluestockings, and helped prepare the ground for the acceptance of their writings. The story of romantic women writers is in large part that of the fight for the recognition of women's rights – the right to education, the right to associate with male intellectuals, and so forth. Phillis Wheatley's significance in that story is indicated by the fact that her *Poems* (1773) were savaged in the *Public Advertiser* for being part of 'a flood of female literature', and by the more appreciative comments of Mary Scott in *The Female Advocate* (see p. 133).

What clinches the argument, at least for me, is her preoccupation not just with the question of her rights but with literary ideas of concern to the romantics. Her poem *On Imagination* is admittedly of its time; it is not quite the same concept as that discussed in *Biographia Literaria* or Wordsworth's *Poems* (1815).[2] It is, in any case, essentially

---

[1] Jackson, pp. 366–9.   [2] See *Romanticism* 476–9, 574.

religious, as is so much of her verse. But it does show a writer of considerable power thinking about how the imagination operates and what it can achieve – and in terms which Wordsworth and Coleridge would have understood. Specifically, she conceives of the imagination as being, in Coleridgean terms, a unifying force: 'There in one view we grasp the mighty whole' (l. 21).

Her story is remarkable. She was born, probably in 1753, 'somewhere in Africa', as one of her bibliographers puts it,[3] possibly in Senegal. In 1761 she was taken from her family by slave traders, transported to New England, and sold on the streets of Boston. Despite all this, she was lucky in one respect: her new 'owners' were John and Susanna Wheatley, who treated her kindly. John was a well-to-do tailor in Boston, and he purchased Phillis as servant to his children, Nathaniel and Mary, twins who were about ten years older than her. Mary at once befriended Phillis, and when she saw her trying to form letters on a wall with a piece of chalk, began teaching her how to write. She turned out to have a formidable gift; she learned to read and write in sixteen months, and composed her first poem at the age of thirteen. In 1767 her first published poem appeared in the Newport *Mercury*. Three years later, she published *An Elegiac Poem on the Death of George Whitefield* (1770). It sold well, and besides several reprintings in America, enjoyed a modest sale in England after being published there in 1771. Soon after, Phillis was christened. She learnt Latin and read the classics. Proposals for publishing a volume by subscription in Boston in 1772 came to nothing. After a spell of particularly poor health she accompanied Nathaniel to London where he was doing business.

This visit to London in 1773 was one of the most important events of her short life. She moved in high society and was the toast of the town. Her own account, in a letter to David Wooster, conveys much of the excitement she felt:

I was received in England with such kindness, complaisance, and so many marks of esteem and real friendship as astonishes me on the reflection, for I was no more than six weeks there. Was introduced to Lord Dartmouth[4] and had near half an hour's conversation with his Lordship, with whom was Alderman Kirkman. Then to Lord Lincoln,[5] who visited me at my own lodgings with the famous Dr Solander,[6] who accompaned Mr Banks in his late expedition round the world. Then to Lady Cavendish[7] and Lady Carteret Webb, Mrs Palmer[8] – a poetess, an accomplished lady. To Dr Thomas Gibbons,[9] rhetoric professor. To Israel Mauduit, Esqr.,[10] Benjamin Franklin, Esqr. F.R.S.,[11] Greenville Sharp, Esqr.,[12] who attended

[3] Charles Frederick Heartman, *Phillis Wheatley (Phillis Peters): A Critical Attempt and a Bibliography of her Writings* (New York, 1915), p. 9.

[4] William Legge, 2nd Earl of Dartmouth (1731–1801), Secretary of State for the Colonies 1772–5.

[5] Henry Fiennes Clinton, 9th Earl of Lincoln (1720–94), Whig politician.

[6] Daniel Charles Solander (1736–82), botanist, engaged by Joseph Banks to accompany him on Cook's voyage in the *Endeavour*, 1768. In 1773 he was made Keeper of the Natural History Department of the British Museum.

[7] Catherine, Lady Cavendish, had married William Cavendish, 3rd Duke of Devonshire in 1718; she died 8 May 1777.

[8] Mary Palmer (1716–94), sister of Sir Joshua Reynolds, author of *Devonshire Dialogues* (1839).

[9] Thomas Gibbons (1720–85), author and dissenting minister; his *Rhetoric* was published in 1767.

[10] Israel Mauduit (1708–87), political pamphleteer and dissenter, supporter of American independence.

[11] Benjamin Franklin (1706–90), printer, author, philanthropist, inventor, statesman, diplomat, scientist.

[12] Granville Sharp (1735–1813), philanthropist, pamphleteer, and scholar, was one of the earliest agitators for liberation of slaves. He published a pamphlet on the subject in 1769, and was an advocate for James Somersett, whose case led to the judgement, in 1772, that once a slave set foot in British territory he became a free man.

me to the Tower and showed me the lions, panthers, tigers, etc., the horse armoury, small armoury, the crowns, sceptres, diadems, the fount for christening the royal family. Saw Westminster Abbey, British Museum, Coxe's Museum, Saddler's Wells, Greenwich Hospital, Park and Chapel, the Royal Observatory at Greenwich, etc., etc., too many things and places to trouble you with in a letter. The Earl of Dartmouth made me a compliment of five guineas, and desired me to get the whole of Mr Pope's works,[13] as the best he could recommend to my perusal. This I did; also got Hudibrass, Don Quixot, and Gay's Fables.[14]

She also met Selina Hastings, Countess of Huntingdon (1707–91), and the Lord Mayor of London, who gave her a copy of *Paradise Lost*, which she kept for the rest of her life. Shortly after, she published her first volume in London, *Poems on Various Subjects, Religious and Moral. By Phillis Wheatley, Negro Servant to Mr John Wheatley, of Boston, in New England* (1773). It was dedicated to Selina Hastings and carried a short testimony to her abilities by John Wheatley, as well as a letter signed by various notable personages of the time which vouched for the fact that all the poems were by her. It was a success, and has enjoyed numerous reprintings up to the present.

In 1774, with the deaths of John and Susanna Wheatley, she was given her freedom, and married John Peters, another freed slave. Not much is known about the marriage, but it seems to have been unhappy. Peters had been a lawyer, but lost property during the Revolution and by the time of the marriage was a poor man. She continued to compose poetry and in 1779 attempted to publish a subscription edition of her work, but without success. Her husband was eventually imprisoned for debt, and Phillis was forced to work in a black boarding-house, where she died alone and neglected in 1784.

Not all of those who reviewed *Poems on Various Subjects* (1773) were as kind or perceptive as those who encouraged its author. In fact, the engraving of Phillis at the front of the volume, and the various statements testifying as to the authenticity of its contents, made it virtually impossible for any of its reviewers to forget that its author was a black slave. It is useful to bear in mind that the campaign to abolish slavery had hardly begun, and it was very difficult for many people to conceive that someone in Phillis's situation could put pen to paper at all, let alone versify. Unfortunately some critics were blinded by these prejudices. John Langhorne, who had been so generous to Hannah More earlier that year (see p. 19), is a case in point; he reviewed the volume for the *Monthly Review*:

> If we believed, with the ancient mythologists, that genius is the offspring of the sun, we should rather wonder that the sable race have not been more distinguished by it, than express our surprise at a single instance. The experience of the world, however, has left to this part of mythology but little probability for its support; and, indeed, it appears to be wrong in its first principles. A proximity to the sun, far from heightening the powers of the mind, appears to enfeeble them in proportion as it enervates the faculties of the body. Thus we find the tropical regions remarkable for nothing but the sloth and languor of their inhabitants, their lascivious dispositions, and their deadness to invention.[15]

---

[13] Phillis often cited Pope as a chief influence.
[14] *The Collected Works of Phillis Wheatley* ed. John C. Shields (New York, 1988), pp. 169–70.

[15] *Monthly Review* 49 (1773) 457–9, pp. 457–8.

He goes on to comment: 'The poems written by this young negro bear no endemial[16] marks of solar fire or spirit. They are merely imitative; and, indeed, most of those people have a turn for imitation, though they have little or none for invention.'[17] Langhorne concludes his review with a swipe at the inhabitants of Phillis's home town, who were at that moment making life difficult for the English: 'We are much concerned to find that this ingenious young woman is yet a slave. The people of Boston boast themselves chiefly on their principles of liberty. One such act as the purchase of her freedom would, in our opinion, have done them more honour than hanging a thousand trees with ribbons and emblems.'[18]

After all this, it is a relief to come across the *Critical Review*, which responds directly to Langhorne's attack:

> The negroes of Africa are generally treated as a dull, ignorant, and ignoble race of men, fit only to be slaves, and incapable of any considerable attainments in the liberal arts and sciences. A poet or poetess amongst them, of any tolerable genius, would be a prodigy in literature. Phillis Wheatley, the author of these poems, is this literary phenomenon.... The pieces of which this little volume consists, are the productions of her leisure moments. And though they are not remarkably beautiful, they have too much merit to be thrown aside as trifling and worthless effusions.[19]

This critic concluded: 'The whole is indeed extraordinary, considered as the production of a young negro who was, but a few years since, an illiterate barbarian'.[20] Although not directly relevant to the critical reception of her work, it is worth noting the appearance of a letter by one 'Ancillariolus' in the *Public Advertiser* shortly after Phillis's volume was published. It began inauspiciously enough: 'Mercy upon us! What a flood of female literature pours in daily upon this learned nation! From that excellent gentlewoman in breeches, Mrs Macaulay, to that more than brown beauty, Phillis Wheatley, of Boston!'[21] From these comments it is evident that Ancillariolus means no good. He goes on to suggest that Phillis collaborate with Oliver Goldsmith, the playwright and poet, on a literary project, but uses terms that would have amused neither:

> Matrimony is the thing in poetry as well as in prose. What may not a male and female genius produce when they are properly joined together!... I could, therefore, wish that Phillis and Oliver would touch up something between them in the elegiac way before their hands are joined in wedlock. What might be contained in a few sheets before the ceremony would have more real fire in it than whole volumes of lazy operations after marriage. Though this is a kind of *black* business, I see already some light through it, if the Doctor will gird up his loins and set about it before Phillis leaves the literary circles here for the learned converse of Bostonian patriots.[22]

This unpleasant performance concludes with a comment that fully reveals its author's beliefs: 'though the importation of negroes has been considerable of late years, few of

---

[16] Endemic (belonging to a state or people).
[17] Ibid., p. 458.
[18] Ibid., pp. 458–9.
[19] *Critical Review* 36 (1773) 232–3, p. 232.
[20] Ibid., p. 233.
[21] *Public Advertiser* no. 12002, 6 October 1773.
[22] Ibid.

our ladies have yet arrived at any degree of African beauty beyond the mulatto tinge, whereas I am told our Sappho is of a deep jetty hue'.[23] The letter is, in fact, riddled with a fear of miscegenation, and expresses this anxiety through a tasteless skit at the expense of Goldsmith and Phillis. It is worth citing here as a reminder of the opinions of the world she inhabited; indeed, while turning the pages of the *Public Advertiser*, I was uncomfortably aware of the recurrent presence of the paper's 'Plantation News'. It is a kind of vindication that of all the writers in this volume Phillis is among those whose work is most frequently discussed today; the bibliography below lists only a very small fraction of the available criticism.

Further Reading

M. A. Richmond, *Bid the Vassal Soar* (Washington, D.C., 1974)
William H. Robinson, *Phillis Wheatley in the Black American Beginnings* (Detroit, 1975)
——, *Critical Essays on Phillis Wheatley* (Boston, 1982)
S. E. Ogude, *Genius in Bondage: A Study of the Origins of African Literature in English* (Ife-Ife, 1983)
William H. Robinson, *Phillis Wheatley and her Writings* (New York and London, 1984)
The Collected Works of Phillis Wheatley ed. John C. Shields (New York, 1988)
Black American Poets and Dramatists Before the Harlem Renaissance ed. Harold Bloom (New York, 1994), pp. 119–32
Julie Ellison, 'The Politics of Fancy in the Age of Sensibility', *RR* 228–55

From Poems on Various Subjects, Religious and Moral (1773)

PREFACE[1]

The following poems were written originally for the amusement of the author, as they were the products of her leisure moments. She had no intention ever to have published them, nor would they now have made their appearance, but at the importunity of many of her best, and most generous friends – to whom she considers herself as under the greatest obligations.

As her attempts in poetry are now sent into the world, it is hoped the critic will not severely censure their defects, and we presume they have too much merit to be cast aside with contempt, as worthless and trifling effusions.

As to the disadvantages she has laboured under, with regard to learning, nothing needs to be offered, as her master's letter in the following page will sufficiently show the difficulties in this respect she had to encounter.

With all the imperfections the poems are now humbly submitted to the perusal of the public.

THE FOLLOWING IS A COPY OF A LETTER SENT BY THE AUTHOR'S MASTER TO THE PUBLISHER

Phillis was brought from Africa to America in the year 1761, between seven and eight years of age. Without any assistance from school education, and by only what she was

---

[23] Ibid.

PREFACE
[1] The Preface is not, apparently, by Phillis.

taught in the family, she, in sixteen months time from her arrival, attained the English language (to which she was an utter stranger before), to such a degree as to read any, the most difficult parts of the sacred writings, to the great astonishment of all who heard her.

As to her writing, her own curiosity led her to it, and this she learnt in so short a time that in the year 1765 she wrote a letter to the Revd Mr Occom, the Indian minister, while in England.

She has a great inclination to learn the Latin tongue, and has made some progress in it. This relation is given by her master who bought her, and with whom she now lives.

John Wheatley
Boston, 14 November 1772

ON BEING BROUGHT FROM AFRICA TO AMERICA

'Twas Mercy brought me from my *pagan* land,
Taught my benighted soul to understand
That there's a God, that there's a Saviour too:
Once I redemption neither sought nor knew.
Some view our sable race with scornful eye –   5
'Their colour is a diabolic dye.'
Remember Christians, negroes black as Cain
May be refined, and join th' angelic train.

ON IMAGINATION

Thy various works, imperial queen,[1] we see;
How bright their forms! How decked with pomp by thee!
Thy wondrous acts in beauteous order stand,
And all attest how potent is thine hand.
  From Helicon's refulgent heights attend,   5
Ye sacred choir, and my attempts befriend;
To tell her glories with a faithful tongue,
Ye blooming graces, triumph in my song.
  Now here, now there, the roving fancy flies,
Till some loved object strikes her wand'ring eyes,   10
Whose silken fetters[2] all the senses bind,
And soft captivity involves the mind.
  Imagination, who can sing thy force,
Or who describe the swiftness of thy course?
Soaring through air to find the bright abode,   15
Th' empyreal palace of the thund'ring God,
We on thy pinions can surpass the wind,
And leave the rolling universe behind:
From star to star the mental optics rove,
Measure the skies, and range the realms above.   20

ON IMAGINATION
[1] *imperial queen* imagination.

[2] *silken fetters* possibly a recollection of Akenside, *Pleasures of Imagination* ii 562: 'The silken fetters of delicious ease'.

There in one view we gasp the mighty whole,[3]
Or with new worlds amaze th' unbounded soul.
   Though Winter frowns to fancy's raptured eyes,
The fields may flourish, and gay scenes arise,
The frozen deeps may break their iron bands,   25
And bid their waters murmur o'er the sands;
Fair Flora[4] may resume her fragrant reign,
And with her flow'ry riches deck the plain;
Sylvanus[5] may diffuse his honours round,
And all the forest may with leaves be crowned;   30
Show'rs may descend, and dews their gems disclose,
And nectar sparkle on the blooming rose.
   Such is the pow'r, nor are thine orders vain,
Oh thou the leader of the mental train;
In full perfection all thy works are wrought,   35
And thine the sceptre o'er the realms of thought.
Before thy throne the subject passions bow,
Of subject passions sov'reign ruler thou;
At thy command joy rushes on the heart,
And through the glowing veins the spirits dart.   40
   Fancy might now her silken pinions try
To rise from earth, and sweep th' expanse on high;
From Tithon's bed[6] now might Aurora rise,
Her cheeks all glowing with celestial dyes,
While a pure stream of light o'erflows the skies.   45
The monarch of the day I might behold,
And all the mountains tipped with radiant gold,
But I reluctant leave the pleasing views
Which fancy dresses to delight the muse;
Winter austere forbids me to aspire,   50
And northern tempests damp the rising fire;
They chill the tides of fancy's flowing sea,
Cease then, my song, cease the unequal lay.

Anne Grant (*née* Macvicar) (1755–1838)

Born in Glasgow, Anne left Scotland at the age of three, and travelled with her family
to America. Her father, Duncan Macvicar, was an officer in a highland regiment, the
77th Foot, and when they were assigned to America, he took his family to Albany, NY,
with the intention of settling there. Anne was taught to read by her mother, Catherine
Mackenzie; one of her father's colleagues, a sergeant in the same regiment, encouraged
her writing skills. By the age of six she was conversant with the Old Testament, and
eagerly devouring *Paradise Lost*. For several years Anne resided with the Schuyler family
in Albany, acquiring during that time a good knowledge of the Dutch language.

---

[3] *There in one view we grasp the mighty whole* cf. Edward
Young, *Night Thoughts* ix 1991, where rational people
'Can grasp creation with a single thought'.

[4] *Flora* Roman goddess of spring and gardens.
[5] *Sylvanus* god of the country, half-man, half-goat.
[6] *Tithon's bed* Tithon was the husband of Aurora.

A few years after the British conquest of Canada, Anne's father resigned from the army and became a settler in Vermont, where he received a grant of land to which he made additions by purchase. However, his increasing prosperity was interrupted by bad health and in 1768 he decided to return with his family to Scotland. Unfortunately for him he left without disposing of his property, which, on the outbreak of the American Revolution, was confiscated by the republic. Macvicar was thus dependent on the limited income he received as barrack-master of Fort Augustus. Stationed there was also the Revd. James Grant, a military chaplain and an accomplished scholar. Anne married him in 1779, when they moved to the parish of Laggan in Inverness, to which Grant was appointed. (For this reason Anne is often referred to as Anne Grant of Laggan, to distinguish her from the contemporary Mrs Grant of Carron.)

Anne was determined to help her husband in his work as much as she could, but as she was not a highlander immediately found herself up against a major obstacle: she had no knowledge of the native tongue. With much hard dedicated work she soon acquired sufficient Gaelic to converse with the people around her, and began a lifelong study of their culture. That developed into a fascination with the works that inspired, and provided much of the material for, James Macpherson's famous, and highly successful, 'translations' from Ossian. Grant's own translations of ancient Gaelic verse comprise some of her finest compositions. In time, the local people came to respect and accept her.

She had twelve children, of whom four died. In 1801 her husband also died, leaving her with eight children to bring up, while the manse in which they lived had to be yielded to his successor. On top of all this, she discovered that they had run up huge debts. Her solution was to publish the verses she had been writing since the age of nine. She managed to find no less than 3,000 subscribers for her first volume, and published it in 1803. It attracted favourable notices, and the sale was sufficient to discharge her debts at Laggan.

Having moved to Stirling, Anne set about publishing her *Letters from the Mountains* (1806), written from Laggan to a number of correspondents over the years. Their heady brew of highland scenery, characters, and legends, proved popular, and the volume went through several editions in succeeding years. In 1810 she moved to Edinburgh and became a frequenter of literary circles; friends included Francis Jeffrey, Walter Scott, and Henry Mackenzie. In 1811 she published her *Essays on the Superstitions of the Highlanders*, and in 1814 a long poem, *Eighteen Hundred and Thirteen* – a satirical exercise inspired by Barbauld's *Eighteen Hundred and Eleven* (see pp. 10–18).

Unlike the British, the Scots value their writers, and in 1825 Anne was granted a pension of £100 per annum, in recognition of her literary achievement. That, along with the profits from her writings and the legacies of deceased friends, left her free from financial worries for the remainder of her life. She died at the age of eighty-three.

From The Highlanders, and Other Poems (1810)

THE HIGHLANDERS (EXTRACT)

The Highland Poor; from Part II

Where yonder ridgy mountains bound the scene,   295
The narrow op'ning glens that intervene
Still shelter, in some lonely nook obscure,

One poorer than the rest, where all are poor –
Some widowed matron, hopeless of relief,
Who to her secret breast confines her grief,   300
Dejected sighs the wintry night away,
And lonely muses all the summer day.
Her gallant sons who, smit with honour's charms,
Pursued the phantom Fame through war's alarms,
Return no more – stretched on Hindostan's plain,   305
Or sunk beneath th' unfathomable main.
In vain her eyes the watry waste explore
For heroes fated to return no more!
Let others bless the morning's red'ning beam,
Foe to her peace – it breaks th' illusive dream   310
That, in their prime of manly bloom confessed,
Restored the long-lost warriors to her breast.
And as they strove with smiles of filial love
Their widowed parent's anguish to remove,
Through her small casement broke th' intrusive day,   315
And chased the pleasing images away!
No time can e'er her vanished joys restore,
For ah! a heart, once broken, heals no more.
The dewy beams that gleam from pity's eye,
The 'still small voice'[1] of sacred sympathy   320
In vain the mourner's sorrows would beguile,
Or steal from weary woe one languid smile.
Yet what they can, they do: the scanty store,
So often opened for the wandering poor,
To her each cottager complacent deals,   325
While the kind glance the melting heart reveals;
And still, when evening streaks the west with gold,
The milky tribute from the lowing fold
With cheerful haste officious children bring,
And every smiling flow'r that decks the spring.   330
Ah, little know the fond attentive train
That spring and flow'rets smile for her in vain;
Yet hence they learn to reverence modest woe,
And of their little all a part bestow.
Let those to wealth and proud distinction born,   335
With the cold glance of insolence and scorn
Regard the suppliant wretch, and harshly grieve
The bleeding heart their bounty would relieve.
Far different these; while from a bounteous heart
With the poor sufferer they divide a part;   340

THE HIGHLANDERS
[1]   *still small voice* an echo of I Kings 19:12: 'And after
the earthquake a fire; but the Lord was not in the
fire: and after the fire a still small voice.'

Humbly they own that all they have is given
A boon precarious from indulgent Heaven;
And the next blighted crop or frosty spring,
Themselves to equal indigence[2] may bring.

The Aged Bard's Wish (Translation of a Gaelic Poem Composed in the Isle of Skye)

As when a minstrel, taught by Heav'n to sing,
Awakes high raptures to the vocal string.

Pope's *Odyssey*[1]

Oh lay me by yon peaceful stream
    That glides away so softly slow,
Where boughs exclude the noonday beam,
    And early violets round me blow.[2]

And thou, oh sun, with friendly eye   5
    Regard my languid limbs of age;
While on the new sprung grass they lie,
    Their warmth restore, their pains assuage.

Then on the pure stream's sloping side,
    Wave soft thy wings, thou western gale;   10
Clear stream, how gently dost thou glide
    To wake the flow'rets of the vale.

The primrose pale, of lovely dye,
    Around my dewy bank be spread;
The daisy ope its modest eye,   15
    And golden blooms bedeck my bed.

From lofty banks that bound my glen
    Let blossomed branches softly bend,
While sweetly from each rocky den
    The little birds their love-notes blend.   20

Where from yon crag, with age so grey,
    The fresh stream bursts with rushing sound,
And echo bears the din away
    While ocean's distant waves resound.

---

[2] *indigence* penury.
THE AGED BARD'S WISH
[1] These lines do not come from Pope, although they are reminiscent of *Homer's Odyssey* iv 23–4.
[2] 'The first verse is so compressed in the original that it is not possible to confine the sense in an equal number of English lines. The second has also some peculiar epithets that cannot be transfused into English in the same bounds. Thus it becomes necessary to give the sense of these two in three English verses.

This explanation is meant for the direction of such readers as may have the curiosity to compare this close and often literal translation with the corresponding verses of the original poem. Betwixt the twelfth and fifteenth verses of the original are two highly figurative and poetical, but so much wrapped in the mist of local superstition that they are difficult to understand or translate, and could only excite interest in minds to which the wild solemnity they breathe is in some degree familiar' (Grant's note).

Each rock and hill returns the strain   25
  Of nature's joy that wakes around,
While sportive kids in frolic vein
  And roes in sprightly gambol bound.

The low of herds on yonder gale
  Comes pleasing to my aged ear,   30
And sweetly rural from the dale
  The bleating of their young I hear.

And near me let the hinds repose,
  And dappled fawns when tired of play,
Beside my brook's green margin close,   35
  Or where the dashing fountains play.

Oh wake the chase, where I may hear
  The hunter rouse th' impatient hounds;
Their voice is music to my ear –
  My cheek glows youthful at the sounds.   40

I feel youth's cheerful spirit rise
  To hear the bugle sound so shrill,
While triumph bursts in joyful cries,
  Where sinks the dun deer on the hill.

Then quick I see the goats rebound   45
  That morn and eve my steps pursue;
Yon mountain tops their cries resound
  Which I at hopeless distance view.[3]

I see Benard of lofty brow
  Amidst his green locks dream the roes,   50
A thousand hills appear below,
  And on his head the clouds repose.[4]

Above my glen I see the grove
  Where first is heard the cuckoo's song;
Where deer in peaceful freedom rove,   55
  And pines protect the harmless throng.

I see the lake where wild ducks play
  And lead about their tender young,
With water-lilies bordered gay,
  Its banks with evergreens o'erhung.   60

---

[3] 'The verses after this correspond with those of the same number in the original' (Grant's note).
[4] 'The fourteenth verse has great force in the original. Literally it runs thus: "I see Benard, chieftain of a thousand mountains; / Among his locks are the visions of the roes – / On his head is the sleep of the clouds"' (Grant's note).

The water-nymph, with bosom white,[5]
    Swims graceful on the swelling wave;
Her infant train, with new delight,
    Their downy breasts incessant lave.

And when she wings her lofty flight,   65
    Afar amidst the clouds to rise,
And when she quits my aching sight,
    Commixing with the northern skies,

She goes upon the southern gale,[6]
    Where vent'rous prow ne'er cut the waves,   70
Where never rose the flutt'ring sail,
    But ocean solitary raves.

Be thou, with snowy plumage soft,
    Oh swan, not far from my repose;
Even when I see thee soar aloft,   75
    Thy parting strain will soothe my woes.

Tell from what distant land the wind[7]
    Bears on its wings the sound of woe –
Sure 'tis his voice, who left behind
    His love to trace the realm of snow.   80

Stream thy bright eyes, oh virgin mild!
    For him on Lochlin's stormy coast
Who perished midst the tempest wild –
    To thee, to me, forever lost!

The graceful youth, in manly bloom,   85
    Who left my grey locks thus forlorn,
Far off to seek an early tomb –
    Dost thou with social sorrow mourn?

---

[5] 'Here the imagery grows so bold, and the expression so peculiar to the original language, that it becomes necessary to render the sense rather than the literal meaning, which again dilates two verses into three. The epithet translated "water" nymph is still bolder in the original, for there the swan is called "Lovely white-bosomed maid"' (Grant's note).

[6] 'For the reason above mentioned, I have marked the eighteenth verse so as to answer the corresponding verse of the original. I am thus attentive to minute particulars, because a faithful, though not constrained or literal, translation from nature's own genuine language, as it may justly be called, affords a double pleasure. The imagination is amused, and the heart affected, by the picturesque and pathetic powers of original poetry, and the understanding and judgement are exercised in tracing the operations of the untutored mind, and the powers of unassisted genius' (Grant's note).

[7] 'As there is very little frost or snow in the islands, great numbers of swans come there from Norway in the beginning of winter. Some stay to hatch, but they mostly go northward in summer. This furnishes the bard with the fine image, very strongly expressed in the original, of the north wind bearing towards him the moan of the departed, upon which he inquires of the swan from what cold country that well-known voice came. This affords him a pretence for digressing' (Grant's note).

Thy beauteous cheek, grown pale with grief,
   Still leans upon thy hand of snow,
Still heaves thy bosom for the chief   90
   Long in the narrow bed laid low.

Oh be his mem'ry ever blessed,
   Bright be the clouds of his repose;
Soon shall we share the hero's rest,   95
   Soon life, and love, and sorrow close.

Rise thou, whose soft melodious song
   Pours on my heart the balm of ease;
Ye plaintive echoes come along,
   And waft the notes, thou sighing breeze!   100

From ocean's breast, oh gale, arise!
   Bear on thy wings the dulcet strain,
Bear it where high on clouds he lies,
   Tell him he hears the fair complain.

Tell, ere thy strength be past, oh wind,   105
   Where weak in helpless age I lie,
Low on my rusty shield reclined,
   And view his fair flow'r with'ring nigh.

Lift me, oh you, whose arms are young!
   Lay me beneath yon broad oak's shade;   110
For now the noonday sun grows strong,
   Let not his rays my eyes invade.

Then wilt thou come, thou vision fair,
   Oft mingled with the stars of night;
Scenes of my youth shall rise in air,   115
   And times of manhood's active might.

Show to my soul the lovely maid,
   Beneath the oak, the forest's pride;
Her cheek let golden tresses shade,
   Her lover, smiling, grace her side.   120

May endless joy their spirits wait,
   And meteors waft th' enamoured pair!
Blessed be your souls, and blessed thy fate,
   Maid with the graceful locks so fair!

Leave not my soul, oh dream of joy!   125
   Oh turn again, once more return!
They hear me not, my darling boy;
   For thee, for her, not long I mourn!

Now lay me close by yonder fall
   That leaps in thunder o'er the rock;   130
My lyre and shell attend my call,
   The spear my sires in battle shook.

And come whence ocean's waters roll,
   Ye breezes mild that softly blow,
And bear away my parting soul   135
   Where sinks the sun at evening low.

Oh bear me to the happy isles[8]
   Where shades of mighty heroes rest,
Who, sunk in sleep, forget their toils,
   Or wake the music of the blessed.   140

Blind Ossian's[9] misty halls unfold;
   Your eyes no more the bard shall view.
Let me my harp and shell behold –
   And now, dear harp and shell, adieu!

From Essays on the Superstitions of the Highlanders of Scotland (1811)

METRICAL TRANSLATION OF THE SONG OF MACGREGOR NA RUARA

My sorrow, deep sorrow, incessant returning,
Time still as he flies adds increase to my mourning,
While I think on Macgregor, true heir of Glenlyon,
Where still to sad fancy his banners seem flying.

On Macgregor na Ruara, whose pipes far resounding,   5
With their true martial strain set each bosom a-bounding;
The badge of Strathspey from yon pine by the fountain
Distinguished the hero when climbing the mountain.

The plumes of the eagle gave wings to his arrow,
And destruction flew wide from the weapon so narrow;   10
His shafts, highly polished and bright, were a treasure
That the son of a king might have boasted with pleasure.

When the brave son of Murdoch so gracefully held them,
Well poised and directed, no weapon excelled them;
Now dead to the honour and pride I inherit,   15
Not the blow of a vassal could rouse my sad spirit.

---

[8] Grant has in mind the Elysian fields of classical Greek and Roman literature, the idyllic world where the souls of those honoured by the gods spent an afterlife of revelry, feasting, or exercise.

[9] *Ossian* James Macpherson (1736–96) travelled Scotland collecting the materials that contributed to *Fingal* (1762) and *Temora* (1763), purported to be the translations of an epic by Ossian, son of Finn, dating from some remote period of Scottish history.

Though insult or injury now should oppress me,
My protector is gone, and nought else can distress me;
Deaf to my loud sorrows, and blind to my weeping,
My aid and support in yon chapel lie sleeping.   20

In that cold narrow bed they shall slumber for ever,
Yet nought from my fancy their image shall sever,
He that shared the kind breast which my infancy nourished,
Now cold in the earth, leaves no trace where they flourished.

No obsequies[1] fitting, his pale corpse adorning,   25
No funeral honours to soothe our long mourning,
No virgins high-born, with their tears to bedew thee,
To deck thy pale corpse, and with flow'rets to strew thee.

My sorrow, deep sorrow, incessant returning,
Time still as it flies adds increase to my mourning.   30

Ann Yearsley (*née* Cromartie)   (1756–1806)

In December 1784 the *Gentleman's Magazine* published a letter 'from a gentleman, residing on Clifton Hill near Bristol, to a friend in London, dated 30 November 1784':

We have a phenomenon upon this hill: a poor woman, about the age of thirty, who has led hitherto the painful life of a milkmaid; has shown the most pious cares to a mother lately deceased; has proved a most excellent wife to a husband of no vice, but of very little capacity; and who has taken, and still takes, the care of her five children. In the midst of so laborious and so anxious a life, her passion for books, that began at the age of five years, has been supported, and has enabled her to show a taste in poetry, particularly in blank verse.... Her countenance bespeaks sense. She is gifted with a clear voice, and, I believe, of much compass. She warbles wild notes in a style that makes me believe (though, indeed, I am no judge) that, with instruction, she might have become a siren.[1]

Ann's passion for books may not have been supported by a formal education, but her brother had taught her to read, and her mother had borrowed books on her behalf. She had married John Yearsley in June 1774, by whom, within the space of six years, she had six children. During this time she managed to read and write poetry, some of which found its way to Hannah More, the leavings from whose table provided scraps for Ann's pig. It was as a result of Hannah's patronage that the letter appeared in the *Gentleman's Magazine* and that, in April 1785, one of her poems appeared in its pages with the note: 'A collection of the poems of this extraordinary woman has been advertised

---

METRICAL TRANSLATION OF THE SONG OF MACGREGOR
NA RUARA
[1] *obsequies* funeral rites.

ANN YEARSLEY (*NÉE* CROMARTIE)
[1] *Gentleman's Magazine* 54 (1784) 897. A 'siren' in this case is presumably a woman who sings beautifully.

for publication, by a 5 shilling subscription'.[2] In the Preface to Ann's first book, Hannah related her 'discovery', made after visiting Elizabeth Montagu[3] in Berkshire:

> On my return from Sandleford, a copy of verses was shown me, said to be written by a poor illiterate woman in this neighbourhood, who sells milk from door to door. The story did not engage my faith, but the verses excited my attention; for, though incorrect, they breathed the genuine spirit of poetry and were rendered still more interesting by a certain natural and strong expression of misery which seemed to fill the heart and mind of the author.[4]

With Montagu, Hannah organized a subscription list for Ann's *Poems, on Several Occasions*. It was an extraordinarily successful enterprise: over a thousand contributors were enrolled, including seven duchesses, sixteen countesses, Reynolds, Walpole, Burney, and most of the bluestockings. Hannah even sent her protégée on tour to meet her society friends; as she told a correspondent: 'Do you know that my poor milkwoman has been sent for to Stoke, to visit the Duchess of Beaufort and the Duchess of Rutland; and to Bath, to Lady Spencer, Mrs Montagu, etc.? I hope all these honours will not turn her head, and indispose her for her humble occupations'.[5] Among her admirers was Georgiana Cavendish, Duchess of Devonshire, who gave Ann a copy of John Bell's multi-volume *Poets of Great Britain complete from Chaucer to Churchill*. The condescension in Hannah's comments underlines the pleasure she took in the act of patronage; in retrospect she confessed: 'After having considered her character with admiration, a certain selfish principle (which can never be long suspended) suggested to me that I might obtain great pleasure if I could be the means of promoting her prosperity'.[6]

Ann's first volume of poems was published in June 1785 to considerable acclaim; charcteristically, the *Gentleman's Magazine* professed 'a very favourable opinion of these "wood-notes wild"',[7] and the *Monthly Review* said that it provided 'a very striking picture of a vigorous and aspiring genius'.[8] But by this time, strains were developing between poet and patroness. Hannah had placed the subscription money in a trust fund and appointed herself and Elizabeth Montagu as its trustees in order to prevent Ann's husband from gaining access to it. The scheme effectively made Ann and her children dependent on More for their income. Within a few months of the book's publication Ann's gratitude had turned to resentment. She agreed that she and her husband should not have access to the principal sum that had been collected, but thought they should get the interest, and wanted all the money divided among the children when they reached the age of twenty-one. She told her side of the story in an 'Autobiographical Narrative' added to the fourth edition of her *Poems* in 1786. The literary world was shocked, and reviewers made great play with the hostilities between the two poets; the *European Magazine* reprinted all of the 'Narrative', commenting:

> With good intentions, as we trust, on both sides, something appears to have been wanting. There seems to have been too much hauteur and too little delicacy on

---

[2] *Gentleman's Magazine* 55 (1785) 305. The poem was *To Stella, on a Visit to Mrs Montagu*, later published in the *Poems* (1785).

[3] Elizabeth Montagu (1720–1800), 'Queen of the blue-stockings'.

[4] Ann Yearsley, *Poems, on Several Occasions* (1785), p. iv.

[5] William Roberts, *Memoirs of the Life and Correspondence of Mrs Hannah More* (3rd edn, 4 vols, London, 1835), i 332.

[6] Ibid., i 368.

[7] *Gentleman's Magazine* 55 (1785) 812–13, p. 813.

[8] *Monthly Review* 73 (1785) 216–21, p. 221.

the part of the patroness, and perhaps too much jealousy and too little confidence on the part of the client. To use the words of Miss Betty More to Miss Yearsley, 'There is a manner in speaking', and, we may add, in acting, in which both the ladies seem to have erred.[9]

By reprinting all of the 'Narrative', the reviewer implicitly sided with Ann, and a number of others gave their support: 'if we are to believe what is here related, and we know not that it has ever been contradicted, Miss More's conduct to the poetical ward, since the first publication of her *Poems*, has cancelled every prior obligation, and what would otherwise have been deemed base ingratitude, and unwarrantable petulance, now appears a proper spirit, and just resentment.'[10] There was bitterness on both sides. Hannah commented that 'vanity, luxury, idleness, and pride, have entered the cottage the moment poverty vanished',[11] and told Mrs Montagu: 'Mrs Yearsley's conceit that you can envy her talents gives me comfort – for as it convinces me that she is mad, I build upon it a hope that she is not guilty in the all-seeing eye'.[12] She and Montagu hung on as trustees for a while (as she told Elizabeth Carter, 'My conscience tells me I ought not to give up my trust for these poor children, on account of their mother's wickedness'[13]) but they were eventually persuaded to resign, and the money passed to Ann through various intermediaries.

By 1786 she had a new patron, Frederick Augustus Hervey, Bishop of Derry and Earl of Bristol, who contributed £50 towards the costs of the fourth edition of the *Poems*, and to whom she dedicated her *Poem on the Inhumanity of the Slave-Trade* (1788). This was an important moment, as it marked the beginning of the numerous laws that led to abolition. On 21 May 1788, Sir William Dolben proposed a Bill to the House of Commons that limited the number of slaves which could be transported from Africa to British colonies in the West Indies. There was a good deal of opposition even to this comparatively mild proposal. On 26 May merchants and inhabitants of Liverpool presented a petition to the House, saying that Dolben's Bill would cause them financial ruin; all the same, the Bill was passed in both Houses. Ann's poem on the slave trade was composed and published in direct competition with Hannah More's *Slavery: A Poem* (see pp. 43–50), as a number of reviewers observed: 'Mrs Yearsley starts forward as a kind of competitor, to bend the Ulyssean bow with her quondam guardian friend and patroness'.[14] The poem is an important one, in that it shows how far she had come. There was a fierce, passionate, independent voice in Ann, that felt powerfully the pain of injustice, whether on a domestic or a political level. As time passed, that voice was becoming more articulate and intense. But the *Poem on the Inhumanity of the Slave-Trade* is also very much of its time, insofar as it contains many stylistic mannerisms which Ann had picked up from Milton and Young, whose poems she knew well; this is what the *Critical Review* meant when it observed that it is 'frequently rather turgid than sublime, but her sentiments are liberal, and often expressed with peculiar energy.'[15] The *European Magazine* took a similar line, concurring with the poem's aims, while expressing reservations about her literary style:

---

[9] *European Magazine* 11 (1787) 87–90, p. 87.

[10] *Critical Review* 64 (1787) 435–7, p. 435.

[11] William Roberts, *Memoirs of the Life and Correspondence of Mrs Hannah More*, i 368–9.

[12] Ibid., i 374.

[13] Ibid., i 391.

[14] *Critical Review* 65 (1788) 314.

[15] Ibid.

The piece certainly is not without beauties; but they are beauties which, we fear, will add little fresh lustre to her laurels. Before, we have seen her shine in rhyme, and now we see her obscure herself in blank verse. Mrs Inchbald proverbially tells us, 'such things are'; but from Mrs Ann Yearsley 'such things should not be' – nor, we hope, will be again. Everything considered, however, she claims our admiration as a woman of nice sensibility, fettered perhaps by poverty, if not by oppression herself, yet nobly contemning in others all the enjoyments that flow from usurped power, and from ill-gotten wealth.[16]

Perhaps the kindest review came from the *New Annual Register*, which said that the poem was 'entitled to our commendation, for the ardour with which she pleads on behalf of the oppressed Africans, the pathos by which she interests our sensibility, and the bold imagery by which her poetry is ornamented.'[17]

Another aspect of Ann's political personality emerges in the poems she wrote after the execution of Louis XVI. Wordsworth's response to this important moment in the French Revolution was to write a pamphlet in defence of regicide;[18] Ann's was to write a lament on behalf of 'Ill-fated Louis', who she regarded as unjustly murdered. Shortly after, she composed a similar poem lamenting the imprisonment of Marie Antoinette, who was to be executed in October. Her attitude compares with that of Charlotte Smith in *The Emigrants*, also published in 1793, and contrasts with that of more dedicated radicals like Helen Maria Williams. Both poems on the French royal family were sold at Ann's circulating library, which she opened in 1793. Her final volume of poems was *The Rural Lyre* (1796), a sizable collection which shows her deploying a variety of metres and stanza forms with considerable virtuosity; one of its subscribers was Charlotte Smith.

Ann had a gift – what a reviewer of her first volume called 'a strong and fervid imagination'.[19] That gift enabled her to feel intensely the injustices that had been done both to her and others, and it is what makes her poetry more than just the 'wild wood warblings' of a primitivist. She was a good deal more sophisticated than that, in technical terms alone. As the reviewer of her second volume in the *Critical Review* admitted: 'In regard to modulation of numbers, particularly in blank verse, we know few authors superior to the Bristol milk-woman. Her sentiments are often equally just and original, her diction strong and animated, and her pauses judiciously varied'.[20]

Further Reading

Moira Ferguson, 'The Unpublished Poems of Ann Yearsley', *Tulsa Studies in Women's Literature* 12 (1993) 13–46

——, *Eighteenth-Century Women Poets: Nation, Class, and Gender* (Albany, NY, 1995), chapters 4 and 5
Jerome J. McGann, *The Poetics of Sensibility: A Revolution in Literary Style* (Oxford, 1996), pp. 55–64
Patricia Demers, '"For mine's a stubborn and a savage will": "Lactilla" (Ann Yearsley) and "Stella" (Hannah More) Reconsidered', *HLQ* 56 (1993) 135–50
Alan Richardson, 'Darkness Visible: Race and Representation in Bristol Abolitionist Poetry, 1770–1810, *TWC* 27 (1996) 67–72

---

[16] *European Magazine* 13 (1788) 424.
[17] *New Annual Register* 9 (1788) 260.
[18] *A Letter to the Bishop of Llandaff*, not published in Wordsworth's lifetime.

[19] *Critical Review* 60 (1785) 148–9, p. 148.
[20] *Critical Review* 64 (1787) 435–7, p. 436.

From Poems, on Several Occasions (1785)

ON MRS MONTAGU

Why boast, oh arrogant, imperious man,
Perfection so exclusive?[1] Are thy powers
Nearer approaching deity? Canst thou solve
Questions which high Infinity[2] propounds,
Soar nobler flights, or dare immortal deeds   5
Unknown to woman, if she greatly dares
To use the powers assigned her? Active strength,
The boast of animals, is clearly thine;
By this upheld, thou think'st the lesson rare
That female virtues teach, and poor the height   10
Which female wit obtains. The theme unfolds
Its ample maze, for Montagu befriends
The puzzled thought and, blazing in the eye
Of boldest opposition, straight presents
The soul's best energies, her keenest powers,   15
Clear, vigorous, enlightened; with firm wing
Swift she o'ertakes *his* muse, which spread afar
Its brightest glories in the days of yore.
Lo! where she, mounting, spurns the steadfast earth
And, sailing on the cloud of science,[3] bears   20
The banner of perfection.
Ask Gallia's mimic sons[4] how strong her powers,
Whom, flushed with plunder from her Shakespeare's page,
She swift detects amid their dark retreats
(Horrid as Cacus[5] in their thievish dens);   25
Regains the trophies, bears in triumph back
The pilfered glories to a wond'ring world.[6]
So Stella[7] boasts; from her the tale I learned;
With pride she told it; I with rapture heard.
   Oh Montagu, forgive me if I sing   30
Thy wisdom tempered with the milder ray
Of soft humanity, and kindness bland!
So wide its influence, that the bright beams
Reach the low vale where mists of ignorance lodge,
Strike on the innate spark which lay immersed,   35
Thick-clogged, and almost quenched in total night.

ON MRS MONTAGU
[1] The abrupt opening of this poem, with its challenging question, makes one wonder whether Hannah More might have shown its author Mary Scott's *Female Advocate*, with its attack on anti-feminism; see pp. 133–6, above.
[2] *Infinity* God.
[3] *science* knowledge.

Gallia's mimic sons French imitators of Shakespeare.
[5] *Cacus* son of Vulcan and Medusa, a three-headed monster vomiting smoke and flames.
[6] In the *Essay on the Genius and Writings of Shakespeare* (1769), Montagu demonstrated how Corneille, in composing his *Cinna*, had borrowed from *Julius Caesar*.
[7] *Stella* Hannah More, who introduced Yearsley to Montagu.

On me it fell, and cheered my joyless heart.
   Unwelcome is the first bright dawn of light
To the dark soul; impatient, she rejects,
And fain would push the heavenly stranger back;   40
She loathes the cranny which admits the day;
Confused, afraid of the intruding guest,
Disturbed, unwilling to receive the beam
Which to herself her native darkness shows.
   The effort rude to quench the cheering flame   45
Was mine, and e'en on Stella could I gaze
With sullen envy and admiring pride,
Till, doubly roused by Montagu, the pair
Conspire to clear my dull, imprisoned sense,
And chase the mists which dimmed my visual beam.   50
   Oft as I trod my native wilds alone
Strong gusts of thought would rise, but rise to die;
The portals of the swelling soul ne'er oped
By liberal converse, rude ideas strove
Awhile for vent, but found it not, and died.   55
Thus rust the mind's best powers. Yon starry orbs,
Majestic ocean, flowery vales, gay groves,
Eye-wasting lawns, and heaven-attempting hills
Which bound th' horizon, and which curb the view –
All those, with beauteous imagery, awaked   60
My ravished soul to ecstasy untaught
To all the transport the rapt[8] sense can bear.
But all expired, for want of powers to speak;
All perished in the mind as soon as born,
Erased more quick than cyphers on the shore   65
O'er which the cruel waves, unheedful, roll.
   Such timid rapture as young Edwin seized
When his lone footsteps on the Sage obtrude,[9]
Whose noble precept charmed his wond'ring ear –
Such rapture filled Lactilla's[10] vacant soul   70
·When the bright moralist,[11] in softness dressed,
Opes all the glories of the mental world,
Deigns to direct the infant thought, to prune
The budding sentiment, uprear the stalk
Of feeble fancy, bid idea live,   75
Woo the abstracted spirit from its cares,
And gently guide her to the scenes of peace.
Mine was that balm, and mine the grateful heart,
Which breathes its thanks in rough but timid strains.

---

[8] *rapt* carried away in spirit.
[9] 'See *The Minstrel*' (Yearsley's note). James Beattie's
poem (1771–4), essentially autobiographical, described
the education and upbringing of a young Scottish poet.

[10] 'The author' (Yearsley's note).
[11] *the bright moralist* Montagu.

From Poems on Various Subjects (1787)

ADDRESSED TO SENSIBILITY

Oh Sensibility! Thou busy nurse
Of inj'ries once received, why wilt thou feed
Those serpents in the soul, their stings more fell
Than those which writhed round Priam's priestly son?[1]
I feel them here! They rend my panting breast,   5
But I will tear them thence – ah, effort vain!
Disturbed they grow rapacious, while their fangs
Strike at poor memory; wounded she deplores
Her ravished joys, and murmurs o'er the past.
  Why shrinks my soul within these prison walls[2]   10
Where wretches shake their chains? Ill-fated youth,
Why does thine eye run wildly o'er my form,
Pointed with fond enquiry? 'Tis not me
Thy restless thought would find; the silent tear
Steals gently down his cheek. Ah, could my arms   15
Afford thee refuge, I would bear thee hence
To a more peaceful dwelling! Vain the wish;
Thy pow'rs are all unhinged, and thou wouldst sit
Insensible to sympathy: farewell.
Lamented being, ever lost to hope,   20
I leave thee, yea, despair myself of cure.
  For oh, my bosom bleeds, while griefs like thine
Increase the recent pang. Pensive I rove,
More wounded than the hart whose side yet holds
The deadly arrow. Friendship, boast no more   25
Thy hoard of joys o'er which my soul oft hung
Like the too-anxious miser o'er his gold.
My treasures all are wrecked; I quit the scene
Where haughty Insult cut the sacred ties
Which long had held us. Cruel Julius, take   30
My last adieu! The wound thou gav'st is death,
Nor canst e'en thou recall my frighted sense
With friendship's pleasing sound; yet will I clasp
Thy valued image to my aching mind,
And, viewing that, forgive thee; will deplore   35
The blow that severed two congenial souls!
  Officious Sensibility, 'tis thine

ADDRESSED TO SENSIBILITY
[1] *Priam's priestly son* a reference to Laocoon, Trojan priest of Apollo, who attempted to dissuade the Trojans from admitting the wooden horse. For this, his sons were killed by sea-serpents, and he died in extreme agony while trying to save them.

[2] 'Bedlam' (Yearsley's note). The Hospital of St Mary of Bethlehem in London opened as a hospital for lunatics in 1402. As Yearsley indicates, treatment of the insane was, in the eighteenth century, little different from that of convicts.

To give the finest anguish, to dissolve
The dross of spirit till all essence, she
Refines on real woe; from thence extracts   40
Sad unexisting phantoms, never seen.
  Yet, dear ideal mourner, be thou near
When on Lysander's[3] tears I silent gaze;
Then, with thy viewless pencil, form his sigh,
His deepest groan, his sorrow-tinged thought,   45
Wish immature, impatience, cold despair,
With all the tort'ring images that play,
In sable hue, within his wasted mind.
  And when this dreary group shall meet my thought,
Oh throw my pow'rs upon a fertile space   50
Where mingles ev'ry varied soft relief.
Without thee, I could offer but the dregs
Of vulgar consolation; from her cup
He turns the eye, nor dare it soil his lip!
Raise thou my friendly hand; mix thou the draught   55
More pure than ether, as ambrosia[4] clear,
Fit only for the soul; thy chalice fill
With drops of sympathy, which swiftly fall
From my afflicted heart: yet – yet beware,
Nor stoop to seize from passion's warmer clime   60
A pois'nous sweet. Bright cherub, safely rove
Through all the deep recesses of the soul!
Float on her raptures, deeper tinge her woes,
Strengthen emotion, higher waft her sigh,
Sit in the tearful orb, and ardent gaze   65
On joy or sorrow. But thy empire ends
Within the line of spirit. My rough soul,
Oh Sensibility, defenceless hails
Thy feelings most acute. Yet ye who boast
Of bliss *I* ne'er must reach, ye who can fix   70
A rule for sentiment, if rules there are
(For much I doubt, my friends, if rule e'er held
Capacious sentiment), ye sure can point
My mind to joys that never touched the heart.
What is this joy? Where does its essence rest?   75
Ah, self-confounding sophists, will ye dare
Pronounce *that* joy which never touched the heart?
Does education give the transport keen,
Or swell your vaunted grief? No, nature feels
Most poignant, undefended; hails with me   80
The pow'rs of Sensibility untaught.

---

[3] Lysander was a Spartan general who routed the
Athenians in 405 BC. He was killed in the Corinthian
war, 395 BC.

[4] *ambrosia* in Greek myth, the food of gods and
immortals.

A Poem on the Inhumanity of the Slave-Trade (1788)

TO THE RIGHT HON. AND RIGHT REVD. FREDERICK, EARL OF BRISTOL, BISHOP OF DERRY,[1] ETC., ETC.

My Lord,

Being convinced that your ideas of justice and humanity are not confined to one race of men,[2] I have endeavoured to lead you to the Indian coast. My intention is not to cause that anguish in your bosom which powerless compassion ever gives; yet my vanity is flattered when I but *fancy* that your Lordship feels as I do.

    With the highest reverence, I am,

      My Lord,

        Your Lordship's much obliged,

          And obedient servant,

          ANN YEARSLEY

Bristol, thine heart hath throbbed to glory: slaves,
E'en Christian slaves, have shook their chains, and gazed
With wonder and amazement on thee.[3] Hence,
Ye grov'ling souls, who think the term I give
Of Christian slave, a paradox! To *you*   5
I do not turn, but leave you to conception
Narrow; with that be blessed, nor dare to stretch
Your shackled souls along the course of freedom.
    Yet, Bristol, list! nor deem Lactilla's soul
Lessened by distance; snatch her rustic thought,   10
Her crude ideas, from their panting state,
And let them fly in wide expansion; lend
Thine energy, so little understood
By the rude million, and I'll dare the strain
Of Heav'n-born Liberty till Nature moves   15
Obedient to her voice. Alas, my friend,
Strong rapture dies within the soul, while pow'r
Drags on his bleeding victims. Custom, law,
Ye blessings and ye curses of mankind,
What evils do ye cause? We feel enslaved,   20
Yet move in your direction. Custom, thou
Wilt preach up filial piety; thy sons
Will groan, and stare with impudence at heav'n,
As if they did abjure the act, where Sin
Sits full on Inhumanity; the church   25
They fill with mouthing, vap'rous sighs and tears,

TO THE RIGHT HON. AND RIGHT REVD. FREDERICK, EARL OF BRISTOL, BISHOP OF DERRY
[1] Frederick Augustus Hervey, 4th Earl of Bristol and 5th Baron Howard de Walden, Bishop of Derry (1730–1803), very active in Irish politics, was Yearsley's patron.

[2] i.e. the Irish.
[3] Bristol was deeply implicated in the slave trade. For years it had been one of the main ports which handled newly arrived slaves from abroad.

Which, like the guileful crocodile's, oft fall,
Nor fall but at the cost of human bliss.
   Custom, thou hast undone us, led us far
From godlike probity, from truth, and heaven.   30
   But come, ye souls who feel for human woe,
Though dressed in savage guise! Approach, thou son,
Whose heart would shudder at a father's chains,
And melt o'er thy loved brother as he lies
Gasping in torment undeserved. Oh sight   35
Horrid and insupportable, far worse
Than an immediate, an heroic death!
Yet to this sight I summon thee. Approach,
Thou slave of avarice, that canst see the maid
Weep o'er her inky sire! Spare me, thou God   40
Of all-indulgent mercy, if I scorn
This gloomy wretch, and turn my tearful eye
To more enlightened beings. Yes, my tear
Shall hang on the green furze, like pearly dew
Upon the blossom of the morn. My song   45
Shall teach sad Philomel a louder note,
When Nature swells her woe. O'er suff'ring *man*
My soul with sorrow bends! Then come, ye few
Who feel a more than cold, material essence;
Here ye may vent your sighs, till the bleak north   50
Find its adherents aided. Ah, no more!
The dingy youth comes on, sullen in chains;
He smiles on the rough sailor who aloud
Strikes at the spacious heav'n, the earth, the sea,
In breath too blasphemous – yet not to *him*   55
Blasphemous, for *he* dreads not either. Lost
In dear internal imag'ry, the soul
Of Indian Luco rises to his eyes,
Silent, not inexpressive; the strong beams
With eager wildness yet drink in the view   60
Of his too-humble home where he had left
His mourning father and his Incilanda.
   Curse on the toils spread by a Christian hand
To rob the Indian of his freedom! Curse
On him who from a bending parent steals   65
His dear support of age, his darling child –
Perhaps a son, or a more tender daughter –
Who might have closed his eyelids as the spark
Of life gently retired. Oh thou poor world,
Thou fleeting good to individuals! See   70
How much for thee they care, how wide they ope
Their helpless arms to clasp thee! Vapour thou,
More swift than passing wind! Thou leav'st them nought
Amid th' unreal scene, but a scant grave.

I know the crafty merchant will oppose   75
The plea of nature to my strain, and urge
His toils are for his children; the soft plea
Dissolves my soul – but when I sell a son,
Thou God of nature, let it be my own!
   Behold that Christian! See what horrid joy   80
Lights up his moody features, while he grasps
The wished-for gold, purchase of human blood!
Away, thou seller of mankind! Bring on
Thy daughter to this market, bring thy wife,
Thine aged mother (though of little worth),   85
With all thy ruddy boys! Sell them, thou wretch,
And swell the price of Luco! Why that start?
Why gaze as thou wouldst fright me from my challenge
With look of anguish? Is it *nature* strains
Thine heart-strings at the image? Yes, my charge   90
Is full against her, and she rends thy soul,
While I but strike upon thy pitiless ear,
Fearing her rights are violated. Speak,
Astound the voice of Justice! Bid thy tears
Melt the unpitying pow'r, while thus she claims   95
The pledges of thy love. Oh, throw thine arm
Around thy little ones, and loudly plead
Thou *canst not* sell thy children. Yet beware
Lest Luco's groan be heard; should *that* prevail,
Justice will scorn thee in her turn, and hold   100
Thine act against thy pray'r. 'Why clasp', she cries,
'That blooming youth? Is it because thou lov'st him?'
Why, Luco was beloved: then wilt thou feel,
Thou selfish Christian, for thy private woe,
Yet cause such pangs to him that is a father?   105
Whence comes thy right to barter for thy fellows?
Where are thy statutes? Whose the iron pen
That gave thee precedent? Give me the seal
Of virtue or religion for thy trade,
And I will ne'er upbraid thee; but if force   110
Superior, hard brutality alone
Become thy boast, hence to some savage haunt,
Nor claim protection from my social laws.
   Luco is gone; his little brothers weep,
While his fond mother climbs the hoary rock   115
Whose point o'erhangs the main. No Luco there,
No sound, save the hoarse billows. On she roves,
With love, fear, hope, holding alternate rage
In her too-anxious bosom. Dreary main!
Thy murmurs now are riot, while she stands   120
List'ning to ev'ry breeze, waiting the step
Of gentle Luco. Ah return, return,

Too hapless mother; thy indulgent arms
Shall never clasp thy fettered Luco more.
See Incilanda – artless maid, my soul   125
Keeps pace with thee and mourns. Now o'er the hill
She creeps, with timid foot, while Sol embrowns
The bosom of the isle, to where she left
Her faithful lover: here the well-known cave,
By nature formed amid the rock, endears   130
The image of her Luco; here his pipe,
Formed of the polished cane, neglected lies,
No more to vibrate; here the useless dart,
The twanging bow, and the fierce panther's skin,
Salute the virgin's eye. But where is Luco?   135
He comes not down the steep though he had vowed,
When the sun's beams at noon should sidelong gild
The cave's wide entrance, he would swift descend
To bless his Incilanda. Ten pale moons
Had glided by, since to his generous breast   140
He clasped the tender maid and whispered love.
     Oh mutual sentiment, thou dang'rous bliss,
So exquisite that Heav'n had been unjust
Had it bestowed less exquisite of ill;
When thou art held no more, thy pangs are deep,   145
Thy joys convulsive to the soul; yet all
Are meant to smooth th' uneven road of life.
     For Incilanda, Luco ranged the wild,
Holding her image to his panting heart;
For her he strained the bow, for her he stripped   150
The bird of beauteous plumage – happy hour,
When with these guiltless trophies he adorned
The brow of her he loved. Her gentle breast
With gratitude was filled, nor knew she aught
Of language strong enough to paint her soul,   155
Or ease the great emotion, whilst her eye
Pursued the gen'rous Luco to the field
And glowed with rapture at his wished return.
     Ah sweet suspense, betwixt the mingled cares
Of friendship, love, and gratitude – so mixed,   160
That ev'n the soul may cheat herself. Down, down,
Intruding memory! Bid thy struggles cease
At this soft scene of innate war. What sounds
Break on her ear? She, starting, whispers 'Luco?'
Be still, fond maid; list to the tardy step   165
Of leaden-footed woe. A father comes,
But not to seek his son who, from the deck,
Had breathed a last adieu; no, he shuts out
The soft, fallacious gleam of hope, and turns
Within upon the mind. Horrid and dark   170

Are his wild, unenlightened pow'rs; no ray
Of forced philosophy to calm his soul,
But all the anarchy of wounded nature.
Now he arraigns his country's gods, who sit,
In his bright fancy, far beyond the hills,   175
Unriveting the chains of slaves; his heart
Beats quick with stubborn fury, while he doubts
Their justice to his child. Weeping old man,
Hate not a Christian's God, whose record holds
Thine injured Luco's name. Frighted he starts,   180
Blasphemes the deity whose altars rise
Upon the Indian's helpless neck, and sinks,
Despising comfort, till by grief and age
His angry spirit is forced out. Oh guide,
Ye angel-forms, this joyless shade to worlds   185
Where the poor Indian, with the sage, is proved
The work of a Creator. Pause not here,
Distracted maid! Ah, leave the breathless form
On whose cold cheek thy tears so swiftly fall,
Too unavailing! 'On this stone', she cries,   190
'My Luco sat, and to the wand'ring stars
Pointed my eye, while from his gentle tongue
Fell old traditions of his country's woe.'
Where now shall Incilanda seek him? Hence,
Defenceless mourner, ere the dreary night   195
Wrap thee in added horror. Oh despair,
How eagerly thou rend'st the heart! She pines
In anguish deep and sullen: Luco's form
Pursues her, lives in restless thought, and chides
Soft consolation. Banished from his arms,   200
She seeks the cold embrace of death; her soul
Escapes in one sad sigh. Too hapless maid! –
Yet happier far than he thou lov'dst; his tear,
His sigh, his groan avail not, for they plead
Most weakly with a Christian. Sink, thou wretch,   205
Whose act shall on the cheek of Albion's sons
Throw shame's red blush; thou who hast frighted far
Those simple wretches from thy God, and taught
Their erring minds to mourn his partial love,[4]
Profusely poured on thee, while they are left   210
Neglected to *thy* mercy. Thus deceived,
How doubly dark must be their road to death!
    Luco is borne around the neighb'ring isles,
Losing the knowledge of his native shore

---

[4] 'Indians have been often heard to say, in their complaining moments, "God Almighty no love us well; he be good to buckera; he bid buckera burn us; he no burn buckera"' (Yearsley's note). 'Buckera', Yearsley explains in a further note, means 'white man'.

Amid the pathless wave, destined to plant   215
The sweet luxuriant cane.[5] He strives to please,
Nor once complains, but greatly smothers grief.
His hands are blistered, and his feet are worn,
Till ev'ry stroke dealt by his mattock[6] gives
Keen agony to life; while from his breast   220
The sigh arises, burdened with the name
Of Incilanda. Time inures the youth,
His limbs grow nervous, strained by willing toil,
And resignation, or a calm despair
(Most useful either) lulls him to repose.   225
   A Christian renegade that from his soul
Abjures the tenets of our schools, nor dreads
A future punishment, nor hopes for mercy,
Had fled from England to avoid those laws
Which must have made his life a retribution   230
To violated justice, and had gained,
By fawning guile, the confidence (ill-placed)
Of Luco's master. O'er the slave he stands
With knotted whip, lest fainting nature shun
The task too arduous, while his cruel soul   235
Unnat'ral, ever feeds, with gross delight,
Upon his suff'rings. Many slaves there were,
But none who could suppress the sigh and bend
So quietly as Luco. Long he bore
The stripes that from his manly bosom drew   240
The sanguine stream (too little prized); at length
Hope fled his soul, giving her struggles o'er,
And he resolved to die. The sun had reached
His zenith; pausing faintly, Luco stood,
Leaning upon his hoe, while mem'ry brought,   245
In piteous imag'ry, his aged father,
His poor fond mother, and his faithful maid.
The mental group in wildest motion set
Fruitless imagination. Fury, grief,
Alternate shame, the sense of insult, all   250
Conspire to aid the inward storm – yet words
Were no relief; he stood in silent woe.
   Gorgon, remorseless Christian, saw the slave
Stand musing mid the ranks and, stealing soft
Behind the studious Luco, struck his cheek   255
With a too-heavy whip that reached his eye,
Making it dark for ever. Luco turned
In strongest agony, and with his hoe
Struck the rude Christian on the forehead. Pride,
With hateful malice, seized on Gorgon's soul,   260

---

[5] *cane* sugar cane.   [6] *mattock* tool for loosening hard ground.

By nature fierce, while Luco sought the beach
And plunged beneath the wave. But near him lay
A planter's barge, whose seamen grasped his hair,
Dragging to life a wretch who wished to die.
   Rumour now spreads the tale, while Gorgon's breath   265
Envenomed aids her blast. Imputed crimes
Oppose the plea of Luco, till he scorns
Even a just defence, and stands prepared.
The planters, conscious that to fear alone
They owe their cruel pow'r, resolve to blend   270
New torment with the pangs of death, and hold
Their victims high in dreadful view, to fright
The wretched number left. Luco is chained
To a huge tree, his fellow-slaves are ranged
To share the horrid sight; fuel is placed   275
In an increasing train, some paces back,
To kindle slowly, and approach the youth,
With more than native terror. See, it burns!
He gazes on the growing flame, and calls
For 'Water, water!' The small boon's denied.   280
E'en Christians throng each other to behold
The different alterations of his face
As the hot death approaches. (Oh shame, shame
Upon the followers of Jesus! Shame
On him that dares avow a God!) He writhes,   285
While down his breast glide the unpitied tears,
And in their sockets strain their scorched balls.
'Burn, burn me quick! I cannot die!' he cries,
'Bring fire more close!' The planters heed him not,
But still prolonging Luco's torture, threat   290
Their trembling slaves around. His lips are dry,
His senses seem to quiver ere they quit
His frame for ever, rallying strong, then driv'n
From the tremendous conflict. Sight no more
Is Luco's, his parched tongue is ever mute;   295
Yet in his soul his Incilanda stays,
Till both escape together. Turn, my muse,
From this sad scene; lead Bristol's milder soul
To where the solitary spirit roves,
Wrapped in the robe of innocence, to shades   300
Where pity breathing in the gale dissolves
The mind, when fancy paints such real woe.
   Now speak, ye Christians (who for gain enslave
A soul like Luco's, tearing her from joy
In life's short vale – and if there be a hell,   305
As ye believe, to *that* ye thrust her down,
A blind, involuntary victim), where
Is your true essence of religion? Where
Your proofs of righteousness, when ye conceal

The knowledge of the Deity from those   310
Who would adore him fervently? Your God
Ye rob of worshippers, his altars keep
Unhailed, while driving from the sacred font
The eager slave, lest he should hope in Jesus.
    Is this your piety? Are these your laws,   315
Whereby the glory of the Godhead spreads
O'er barb'rous climes? Ye hypocrites, disown
The Christian name, nor shame its cause; yet where
Shall souls like yours find welcome? Would the Turk,
Pagan, or wildest Arab, ope their arms   320
To gain such proselytes? No. He that owns
The name of Mussulman[7] would start, and shun
Your worse than serpent touch; *he* frees his slave
Who turns to Mahomet.[8] The Spaniard stands
Your brighter contrast; he condemns the youth   325
For ever to the mine, but ere the wretch
Sinks to the deep domain, the hand of Faith
Bathes his faint temples in the sacred stream,
Bidding his spirit hope.[9] Briton, dost thou
Act up to this? If so, bring on thy slaves   330
To Calv'ry's mount, raise high their kindred souls
To him who died to save them:[10] this alone
Will teach them calmly to obey thy rage,
And deem a life of misery but a day,
To long eternity. Ah, think how soon   335
Thine head shall on earth's dreary pillow lie
With thy poor slaves, each silent, and unknown
To his once furious neighbour. Think how swift
The sands of time ebb out, for him and *thee.*
Why groans that Indian youth, in burning chains   340
Suspended o'er the beach? The lab'ring sun
Strikes from his full meridian on the slave
Whose arms are blistered by the heated iron
Which, still corroding, seeks the bone. What crime
Merits so dire a death? Another gasps   345
With strongest agony, while life declines
From recent amputation.[11] Gracious God!

---

[7] *Mussulman* Muslim.
[8] 'The Turk gives freedom to his slave on condition that he embraces Mahometism' (Yearsley's note).
[9] 'The Spaniard, immediately on purchasing an Indian, gives him baptism' (Yearsley's note).
[10] *him who died to save them* Christ, crucified on Calvary.
[11] 'A Coromantin slave in Jamaica (who had frequently escaped to the mountains) was, a few years since, doomed to have his leg cut off. A young practitioner from England (after the surgeon of the estate had refused to be an executioner) undertook the operation, but after the removal of the limb, on the slave's exclaiming, "You buckera! God Almighty made dat leg; you cut it off! You put it on again?" was so shocked, that the other surgeon was obliged to take up the vessels, apply the dressings, etc. The negro suffered without a groan, called for his pipe, and calmly smoked till the absence of his attendant gave him an opportunity of tearing off his bandages, when he bled to death in an instant. Many will call this act of the negro's stubbornness; under *such* circumstances, I dare give it a more glorious epithet, and that is *fortitude*' (Yearsley's note). Coromantin slaves came from the eastern coast of Madras.

Why thus in mercy let thy whirlwinds sleep
O'er a vile race of Christians, who profane
Thy glorious attributes? Sweep them from earth,   350
Or check their cruel pow'r; the savage tribes
Are angels when compared to brutes like these.
   Advance, ye Christians, and oppose my strain;
Who dares condemn it? Prove from laws divine,
From deep philosophy, or social love,   355
That ye derive your privilege. I scorn
The cry of Av'rice, or the trade that drains
A fellow-creature's blood; bid Commerce plead
Her public good, her nation's many wants,
Her sons thrown idly on the beach, forbade   360
To seize the image of their God and sell it.
I'll hear her voice, and Virtue's hundred tongues
Shall sound against her. Hath our public good
Fell rapine[12] for its basis? Must our wants
Find their supply in murder? Shall the sons   365
Of Commerce shiv'ring stand, if not employed
Worse than the midnight robber? Curses fall
On the destructive system that shall need
Such base supports! Doth England need them? No;
Her laws, with prudence, hang the meagre thief   370
That from his neighbour steals a slender sum,
Though famine drove him on. O'er *him* the priest,
Beneath the fatal tree,[13] laments the crime,
Approves the law, and bids him calmly die.
Say, doth this law that dooms the thief protect   375
The wretch who makes another's life his prey,
By hellish force to take it at his will?
Is this an English law, whose guidance fails
When crimes are swelled to magnitude so vast,
That Justice dare not scan them? Or does Law   380
Bid Justice an eternal distance keep
From England's great tribunal, when the slave
Calls loud on Justice only? Speak, ye few
Who fill Britannia's senate, and are deemed
The fathers of your country! Boast your laws,   385
Defend the honour of a land so fall'n
That Fame from ev'ry battlement is flown,
And heathens start e'en at a Christian's name.
   Hail, social love! True soul of order, hail!
Thy softest emanations – pity, grief,   390
Lively emotion, sudden joy, and pangs
Too deep for language – are thy own: then rise,
Thou gentle angel! Spread thy silken wings

---

[12] *rapine* plunder, robbery.   [13] *fatal tree* from which he is to be hung.

O'er drowsy man, breathe in his soul, and give
Her godlike pow'rs thy animating force   395
To banish inhumanity. Oh loose
The fetters of his mind, enlarge his views,
Break down for him the bound of avarice, lift
His feeble faculties beyond a world
To which he soon must prove a stranger! Spread   400
Before his ravished eye the varied tints
Of future glory; bid them live to Fame
Whose banners wave for ever. Thus inspired,
All that is great, and good, and sweetly mild,
Shall fill his noble bosom. He shall melt –   405
Yea, by thy sympathy unseen, shall feel
Another's pang; for the lamenting maid
His heart shall heave a sigh; with the old slave
(Whose head is bent with sorrow) he shall cast
His eye back on the joys of youth, and say,   410
'Thou once couldst feel, as I do, love's pure bliss;
Parental fondness, and the dear returns
Of filial tenderness were thine, till torn
From the dissolving scene.' Oh, social love,
Thou universal good, thou that canst fill   415
The vacuum of immensity, and live
In endless void! Thou that in motion first
Set'st the long lazy atoms, by thy force
Quickly assimilating, and restrained
By strong attraction – touch the soul of man;   420
Subdue him; make a fellow-creature's woe
His own by heartfelt sympathy, whilst wealth
Is made subservient to his soft disease.
      And when thou hast to high perfection wrought
This mighty work, say, 'Such is Bristol's soul.'   425

Reflections on the Death of Louis XVI (1793)[1]

> *Is it good*
> *For man to drain the sacred stream of life*
> *From his sad brother's heart? Oh 'tis a deed*
> *Unworthy such an immortal spirit! Where*
> *Shall meek neglected Mercy find a spot*
> *To weep in silence o'er her slaughtered sons?*

REFLECTIONS ON THE DEATH OF LOUIS XVI (1793)
[1] This poem was composed rapidly after the execu-
tion of Louis XVI in Paris on 29 January 1793; it was
on sale by the middle of the following month.

A pause of sorrow hangs upon the world,
    While heav'nly Pity sighs through all the air;
Too late she mourns! Fury her torch hath hurled,
    Man sickens with her heat, his wildest passions glare!

Yet, gentle Pity, stay! Though thy soft charms   5
    Are dimmed awhile, thy lustre shall return;
Murder shall tremble mid the din of arms,
    And o'er his victim the fierce soldier mourn.

Melted by thee, through many a lonely hour,
    E'en stoic Pride shall weep a murdered King;   10
Such tears are sacred to thy soft'ning pow'r,
    Then bathe in honest grief thy rosy wing

And shake the healing drops on ev'ry shore,
    Where mad Bellona² stings the troubled mind,
Where feeble mortals blindly would adore   15
    That airy vision Wisdom ne'er could find.

Where fancied Liberty with rude excess
    Courts man from sober joy, and lures him on
To frantic War, struck by her gaudy dress,
    His ardent soul is in the chase undone.   20

The ignis fatuus³ followed by the clown⁴
    Deceives not more than Liberty – her arms
Were never round the weary warrior thrown;
    He dies a victim to fallacious⁵ charms.

Ask ye where joyous Liberty resorts –   25
    In France, in Spain, or in Britannia's vale?
Oh no! She only with poor Fancy sports;
    Her richest dwelling is the passing gale.

Like echo, she exists in airy sound,
    Never possessed, ne'er to one rule confined;   30
Fix but one hair to mark her fairy ground,
    She vanishes, nor leaves a trace behind.

Yet for this vapour, gen'rous man must die,
    For this, he ventures on a world unknown;
For this, he braves the crime of sanguine dye;   35
    For this, he drags a monarch from his throne.

---

² *Bellona* Roman goddess of war.
³ *ignis fatuus* a phosphorescent light seen hovering
over marshy ground, believed to be produced by the
spontaneous combustion of inflammable gas produced
by decaying organic matter.
⁴ *clown* peasant.
⁵ *fallacious* delusive.

Ill-fated Louis! All thy pangs are o'er!
  Nature's keen agony hath left thy heart;
Thy childrens' groans by thee are heard no more,
  To hold thee back, when Murder cries 'Depart!'   40

Oh deep, deep struggle! Surely thou wert made
  To break the strongest ligament of woe;
To feel ere Death could thy full veins invade
  The finest torture humankind can know.

Yes, millions fall, but few so high are wrought   45
  By nature's working in the awful hour,
Few taste the cup with pain so deeply fraught –
  Ah Louis, thou hast proved the soul's sublimest pow'r!

Thy murd'rers live – what friendly arm shall ease
  The pillow which supports a guilty head,   50
When conscience nourishes the mind's disease,
  And mem'ry brings the shadow of the dead?

In that dread hour, much injured spirit, rise,
  And breathe forgiveness through thy murd'rer's soul;
Ah, bid him save thy children ere he dies,   55
  Then guide him to thy God, where worlds eternal roll!

From The Rural Lyre (1796)

EXTEMPORE ON HEARING A GENTLEMAN PLAY A HYMN ON HIS FLUTE, THURSDAY 31 JULY, ELEVEN AT NIGHT, 1795, NEAR THE AUTHOR'S WINDOW AT BRISTOL WELLS.

The moon now from old Avon's stream
Withdraws each pale and trembling beam
    That cheers the lonely night;
And as she leaves the weary flood,
Dark grow the vales, dark grows yon wood –   5
    E'en Fancy takes her flight.

Yet Philomel, that shuns the morn,
Sits list'ning on the dewy thorn
    And half forgets her woe;
Contemns her own melodious note   10
While o'er the wave the numbers float,
    That from thy breathing flow.

Oh, ——, there has been an hour,
When melody (enchanting pow'r)

Lured all my cares to rest;   15
My spirit drank her melting lay,
In sacred rapture died away
    And trembled to be blessed.

Those hours are flown, the transport's o'er!
Yet memory from her heav'nly store   20
    My lasting grief beguiles;
Amid the vigils of the night,
Thus tuned by thee to fine delight,
    O'er her pale vision smiles.

A little while when I may be   25
Estranged from all, forgot by thee,
    Prolong th' inspiring strain –
Hark, whisp'ring angels join my prayer,
They make thy tranquil mind their care
    And near thee will remain.   30

Ah, pardon me! With sorrow mute,
I take my pen – thy plaintive flute
    So charms my thinking soul.
On air my fancy seems to fly,
Spirits I long have mourned are nigh,   35
    And worlds beneath me roll.

Georgiana Cavendish, Duchess of Devonshire   (1757–1806)

'Of a lady on whom fortune has bestowed youth, wealth, and beauty, little of incident is to be expected',[1] opined the *European Magazine* in a profile of Georgiana Cavendish in April 1787. The author of that article was being highly ironic, for Georgiana's life was nothing if not full of extraordinary events. Born 9 June 1757, she was the eldest daughter of John, 1st Earl Spencer, and his wife Georgiana Poyntz, from whom, as the *European Magazine* said, she 'experienced a very careful and exemplary attention in her education'.[2] By the age of fifteen she was already known for her beauty. In 1773 she published her novel, *Emma, or the Unfortunate Attachment*, and a year later married William Cavendish, 5th Duke of Devonshire, who was said at the time to be the 'first match' in the kingdom. A good match he may have been but, according to Lady Caroline Lamb, it was not made from love: 'Lady Georgiana's marriage was one *de convenance*. Her delight was hunting butterflies. The housekeeper breaking a lath over her head reconciled her to the match [to become Duchess of Devonshire]. She was ignorant of everything.'[3]

After her marriage she became a prominent society hostess, 'distinguished as the leader of fashion, and the arbitress of taste, treading the gay round of amusements with

---

[1]   *European Magazine* 11 (1787) 219.

[2]   Ibid.

[3]   *Sydney Owenson, Lady Morgan's Memoirs: Autobiography, Diaries and Correspondence* (2 vols, London, 1862), ii 199.

easy dignity and cheerful innocence; partaking of entertainments adapted to her period of life; a pattern and example to the gay, the youthful, and the noble of her sex'.[4] She was an early style queen, setting the fashion when she exchanged hooped dresses for the simpler, flowing gowns for which she was known. Among her friends she counted Mary Delany, Elizabeth Montagu, Johnson, Sheridan, and Charles James Fox. Her friendship with Fox led her to pioneer the art of political canvassing among working-class voters in the Westminster election of 1784, going so far as to kiss a butcher in return for his vote. In 1779 she published her second novel, *The Sylph*, which was well received by reviewers.[5]

From 1782 the Duke and Duchess formed a *ménage à trois* with Lady Elizabeth Foster (1757–1824), who was separated from her husband and two sons. The women exchanged passionate letters, and both bore the Duke's children – Georgiana's first, in 1783, being described by some wags as the child of three people. She eventually had three children by the Duke, and Elizabeth two. Georgiana was an enthusiastic gambler, and by 1789 had run up debts of almost £60,000. But it was not this that was to get her into trouble. In 1791 an affair with Charles Grey (who, as Prime Minister in 1832, would be responsible for the Reform Bill) led to another pregnancy, at which point both Georgiana and Elizabeth were ordered to the continent by the Duke. From November 1791 to September 1793 she travelled from France, Switzerland and finally to Italy, before being allowed to return. During this period Elizabeth composed *A Journey through Switzerland*, and Georgiana her *Passage of the Mountain of St Gothard*. It was after her return that, for a brief period, she looked after her sister's child, the nine-year-old Caroline Ponsonby (and future Lady Caroline Lamb).

The poems written by both Elizabeth and Georgiana during their exile were pirated; editions of the *Passage* exist from as early as 1799, and some may have been printed even before that. It was widely reprinted in newspapers and periodicals, one of its earliest readers being Coleridge, who responded with *Ode to Georgiana, Duchess of Devonshire*, published in the *Morning Post*, 24 December 1799. Its earliest authorized publication came in 1802 when it appeared with a French translation by Jacques Delille; in 1803, a new edition appeared with an Italian translation by Gaetano Polidori. A French edition of 1816 featured illustrations by Elizabeth.

Georgiana died at Devonshire House, 30 March 1806, much burdened by gambling debts. Three years later the Duke married Elizabeth, before he died in 1811.

Georgiana was as fortunate with her reviewers as with those who wrote her profiles. As with the work of most of the women included in this volume, reviewers seem always to have connected the sex and social class of the writer with the poetry they produced. It is no surprise, therefore, to find the *Poetical Register* remarking that 'This elegant little poem does great honour to the taste, talent, and feeling of its noble authoress.'[6] The *Literary Journal* follows suit, announcing that 'This is the second instance[7] which our duty has occasioned us to notice, of a female high in rank and famed for her beauty, rising above the chilling influence of fashion, and becoming warmed and animated by the fervour of genius'.[8]

---

[4] *European Magazine* 11 (1787) 219.
[5] See notices in *Monthly Review* 60 (1779) 240; *Critical Review* 48 (1779) 319; *London Magazine* 48 (1779) 37–8; *Town and Country Magazine* 11 (1779) 568.
[6] *Poetical Register* 2 (1802) 437.

[7] In the issue for 6 January 1803, the same reviewer had commended *Poems on Several Occasions, By a Lady* (1803).
[8] *Literary Journal* 1 (10 March 1803) 313–14.

Further Reading

The Two Duchesses: Georgiana Duchess of Devonshire, Elizabeth Duchess of Devonshire ed. Vere Foster (1898) (contains poems and letters)

The Passage of the Mountain of St Gothard, A Poem (1802)

To my children

Ye plains where threefold harvests press the ground,[1]
Ye climes where genial gales incessant swell,
Where art and nature shed profusely round
    Their rival wonders – Italy, farewell.[2]

Still may thy year in fullest splendour shine,   5
Its icy darts in vain may winter throw!
To thee, a parent, sister, I consign,[3]
    And, winged with health, I woo thy gales to blow.

Yet pleased, Helvetia's rugged brows I see,[4]
And through their craggy steeps delighted roam,   10
Pleased with a people honest, brave and free,
    Whilst every step conducts me nearer home.

I wander where Tesino madly flows,[5]
From cliff to cliff in foaming eddies tossed;
On the rude mountain's barren breast he rose,   15
    In Po's broad wave now hurries to be lost.

THE PASSAGE OF THE MOUNTAIN OF ST GOTHARD,
A POEM (1802)
[1] 'We quitted Italy in August 1793, and passed into
Switzerland over the mountain of St Gothard. The
third crop of corn was already standing in Lombardy'
(Cavendish's note).
[2] 'The first stanza possesses very appropriate beauty
of idea, and exquisite harmony of metre, and the word
"Italy" is introduced with peculiar felicity of expres-
sion' (*Literary Journal* 1 (10 March 1803) 313–14).
[3] 'We left Lady Spencer and Lady Bessborough at
the Baths of Lucca, intending to pass the winter at
Naples' (Cavendish's note).
[4] 'The contrast between Switzerland and the Milanese
appeared very striking; the Milanese was infested with a
band of robbers that caused us some alarm, and obliged
us to use some precautions, but from the moment we
entered the mountains of Switzerland we travelled with-
out any fear, and felt perfectly secure. Death is the
punishment of robbery: this punishment however very
rarely occurs. At Lausanne there had been but one
execution in fifteen years' (Cavendish's note).

[5] 'On the 9th we embarked upon the Lago Maggiore
at the little town of Sesto, situated where the Tesino
runs out of the lake. In the course of two days' naviga-
tion we particularly admired the striking and colossal
statue of St Charles Boromeo (with its pedestal, 100
feet from the ground), the beautiful Boromean islands,
and the shores of the lake, interspersed with towns and
woods and crowned by the distant view of the Alps.
On the evening of the 10th we landed at Magadino,
one of the three Cisalpine Balliages belonging to Switzer-
land; and as the air was too noxious for us to venture
to sleep there, we sent for horses to conduct us to
Belinzona, a pretty town in the midst of high moun-
tains, under the jurisdiction of three of the Swiss
Cantons – Switz, Underwald, and Uri. From hence
(after having prepared horses, chairs and guides, and
having our carriages taken to pieces) we set out, on
the evening of the 12th, to enter the mountain, and
ascended gradually by a road which nearly followed
the course of the Tesino. The Tesino takes its rise
not far from the summit of St Gothard, and joins the
Po near Pavia' (Cavendish's note).

His shores, neat huts and verdant pastures fill,
　　And hills where woods of pine the storm defy;
While, scorning vegetation, higher still,
　　Rise the bare rocks coeval with the sky.　　　　　　　　20

Upon his banks a favoured spot I found,
　　Where shade and beauty tempted to repose;
Within a grove, by mountains circled round,
　　By rocks o'erhung, my rustic seat I chose.

Advancing thence, by gentle pace and slow,　　　　　　　25
　　Unconscious of the way my footsteps pressed,
Sudden, supported by the hills below,
　　St Gothard's summits rose above the rest.[6]

Midst towering cliffs and tracts of endless cold
　　Th' industrious path pervades the rugged stone,　　　30
And seems (Helvetia, let thy toils be told!)
　　A granite girdle o'er the mountain thrown.[7]

No haunt of man the weary traveller greets,
　　No vegetation smiles upon the moor,
Save where the flow'ret breathes uncultured sweets,[8]　　35
　　Save where the patient monk receives the poor.[9]

Yet let not these rude paths be coldly traced,
　　Let not these wilds with listless steps be trod,
Here fragrance scorns not to perfume the waste,
　　Here charity uplifts the mind to God.　　　　　　　　40

His humble board the holy man prepares,
　　And simple food, and wholesome lore bestows,

---

[6] 'St Gothard itself arises from the top of several other high mountains; some have given it 17,600 feet of perpendicular height from the level of the sea, but General Ptyffer, who completed the celebrated model of that part of Switzerland surrounding Lucerne, makes it only 9,075 feet above the Mediterranean. It is the centre of that collection of mountains which the ancients called by the name of Adula, and which separated the Rhaetian from the Poenian Alps. To us it appeared, owing to its gradual ascent, less high than the mountain of the great St Bernard' (Cavendish's note).

[7] 'Mr Coxe's editor (Mr Raymond) calls it a granite ribbon thrown over the mountain. This wonderful work is a road of nearly 15 feet in breadth, paved with granite, and executed even through the most difficult part of the mountain – sometimes suspended on the edge of a precipice; sometimes pierced through rocks, where no other passage offered; sometimes forming bold and light bridges, from rock to rock' (Cavendish's note).

[8] 'Soon after leaving Ayrollo and passing the last wood of firs, all vegetation ceases except the scanty grass and heath which creeps among the rocks; but there appears to be some wildflowers and, in particular, a very sweet one which I gathered, and which I think is called *Achillea mille folium*, but by the guides, *Mutterino*; and also a flossy flower, of which I could not learn the name' (Cavendish's note).

[9] 'There is a small convent at the top of the mountain where two monks reside, and who are obliged to receive and entertain the poor travellers that pass this way. Padre Lorenzo had lived there for twenty years, and seemed a sensible and benevolent man. They have a large dairy and make excellent cheese; five small lakes, which are at the top of the mountain, supply them with fish. The monks are Capuchins, and belong to a convent at Milan' (Cavendish's note).

Extols the treasures that his mountain bears,
And paints the perils of impending snows.

For whilst bleak winter numbs with chilling hand –   45
Where frequent crosses mark the traveller's fate[10] –
In slow procession moves the merchant band,[11]
And silent bends where tottering ruins wait.

Yet midst those ridges, midst that drifted snow
Can nature deign her wonders to display;   50
Here adularia shines with vivid glow,[12]
And gems of crystal sparkle to the day.

Here, too, the hoary mountain's brow to grace,
Five silver lakes in tranquil state are seen;
While from their waters many a stream[13] we trace   55
That, 'scaped from bondage, rolls the rocks between.

Hence flows the Reuss to seek her wedded love,[14]
And, with the Rhine, Germanic climes explore;
Her stream I marked, and saw her wildly move
Down the bleak mountain, through her craggy shore.   60

My weary footsteps hoped for rest in vain,
For steep on steep in rude confusion rose;
At length I paused above a fertile plain
That promised shelter and foretold repose.[15]

Fair runs the streamlet o'er the pasture green,   65
Its margin gay with flocks and cattle spread;

---

[10] 'When any lives have been lost from the falls of snow, a small cross is erected' (Cavendish's note).

[11] 'The whole trade from Switzerland to Italy passes over this mountain, and they often travel in bands of forty laden mules. The destruction occasioned by the avalanches, which also bring rocks along with them, is so much dreaded that they are obliged to keep the strictest silence, lest the vibration of the air should bring down the snow. The excellence of the road over the mountain of St Gothard is owing to its being kept up for this yearly commerce' (Cavendish's note).

[12] 'No mountain is more rich in its mineral productions, at least with regard to beauty. The treasures it possesses were brought into their present repute by Padre Pini, the chief of the cabinet at Milan. The adularia is a beautiful variety of the feldt spar, and is thus called after the ancient name of the mountain. The crystals of St Gothard are much celebrated; in it is also found the blue shoerl or sappar, as it has been named by young Mr de Saussure; and also a marble which has the singular quality of bending and being

phosporic. It is called dolomite, from the name of its discoverer, Dolomieu' (Cavendish's note).

[13] 'The Rhine, the Rhone, the Aar, the Tesino, and the Reuss, all rise in the mountain of St Gothard' (Cavendish's note).

[14] 'The Reuss unites with the Aar beyond the lake of Lucerne, and with him falls into the Rhine' (Cavendish's note).

[15] 'The valley of Ursera is celebrated for its fertility and verdure, and the placid manner in which the Reuss runs through it. It feeds a great number of cattle, and has two small towns. It was formerly woody, but the peasants believe that their forests were destroyed by a magician. They have only one wood above the town, which protects it from the avalanches; and, considering this wood as their palladium, it is said they forbid cutting down a tree on pain of death. The green pastures and placid appearance of the valley form a beautiful contrast with the rocks and precipices which surround it' (Cavendish's note).

Embowering trees the peaceful village screen,
And guard from snow each dwelling's jutting shed.

Sweet vale, whose bosom wastes and cliffs surround,
Let me awhile thy friendly shelter share –   70
Emblem of life, where some bright hours are found
Amidst the darkest, dreariest years of care.

Delved through the rock, the secret passage bends;[16]
And beauteous horror strikes the dazzled sight;
Beneath the pendent bridge the stream descends   75
Calm – till it tumbles o'er the frowning height.

We view the fearful pass, we wind along
The path that marks the terrors of our way;
Midst beetling rocks, and hanging woods among,
The torrent pours, and breathes its glitt'ring spray.   80

Weary at length, serener scenes we hail –
More cultured groves o'ershade the grassy meads,
The neat though wooden hamlets deck the vale,
And Altorf's spires recall heroic deeds.[17]

But though no more amidst those scenes I roam,   85
My fancy long each image shall retain;
The flock returning to its welcome home[18]
And the wild carol of the cowherd's strain.

Lucernia's lake[19] its glassy surface shows,
Whilst nature's varied beauties deck its side;   90

[16] 'The two outlets to this beautiful little valley are the rugged descent from St Gothard, and a passage of some yards in length, cut through the rock, on the Switzerland side. The traveller immediately, upon passing this aperture, finds himself on the celebrated Devil's Bridge, and beholds the Reuss dashing in a torrent under it. The Devil's Bridge is one of the five bridges that distinguish this road. It was so named from the people thinking it impossible to be the work of man; several other bridges in Switzerland have the same name given to them. The whole of this extraordinary road was supposed to have been performed by the Swiss soldiers after the revolution in 1313, which secured liberty to Switzerland; it is imagined the government thus employed them in order to keep them quiet' (Cavendish's note).

[17] 'The Revolution known by the name of the Swiss League began in its smallest canton, Switz, but the chief events happened at Altorf, capital of the canton of Uri. The original name of Switzerland was Helvetia; when united to the emperor, under Conrad the Salique, it was La haute Allemagne; and, after the revolution of 1313, it took the name of Switzerland, from the canton Suitz having been the cradle of its liberty' (Cavendish's note).

[18] 'The circumstance alluded to pleased me very much, though I saw it not in St Gothard but in the mountains of Bearn. At evening, a flock of goats returned to the market-place of the little town of Interlacken; immediately each goat went to its peculiar cottage, the children of which came out to welcome and caress their little comrade. The Rans des Vaches, sung by the Swiss cowherds, is a simple melody intermixed with the cry which they use to call the cows together' (Cavendish's note).

[19] 'The Lake of Lucerne is also called the Lake of the four Cantons, and is as diversified and beautiful as any of Switzerland. Embarking below Altorf, the first part of the navigation is narrow but romantic, bounded by the rocky shores of Uri and Underwald; after passing through the narrowest part, a large expanse presents itself, bounded to the right by Switz, to the left by Underwald, and having Lucerne and distant mountains in front' (Cavendish's note).

Here rocks and woods its narrow waves enclose,
And there, its spreading bosom opens wide.

And hail the chapel, hail the platform wild![20]
Where Tell directed the avenging dart
With well-strung arm, that first preserved his child,   95
Then winged the arrow to the tyrant's heart.

Across the lake, and deep embowered in wood,
Behold another hallowed chapel stand,[21]
Where three Swiss heroes lawless force withstood,
And stamped the freedom of their native land.   100

Their liberty required no rites uncouth,
No blood demanded and no slaves enchained;
Her rule was gentle and her voice was truth,
By social order formed, by laws restrained.

We quit the lake, and cultivation's toil   105
With nature's charms combined, adorns the way,

---

[20] 'The Emperor Albert, having the ambitious design of conquering Switzerland in order to make a patrimony of it for one of his younger sons, had by degrees succeeded in subduing the greater part; and, under false pretences, had sent arbitrary baillies or governors, who exercised much cruelty and oppression upon the people. The worst of these was Geissler, a rapacious and ferocious man, whose castle in Uri was a continued scene of barbarity and plunder. Discontents had already taken place, and the people not only murmured but had meetings on every fresh insult; when, in the year 1307, Geissler, to prove his power and indulge his vanity, erected his hat on a pole in the marketplace of Altorf, and insisted on the people bowing to it as they passed. William Tell refused. The tyrant, to revenge himself, ordered Tell's youngest son to be brought to the marketplace, and, tying him to a stake, placed an apple upon his head and desired the father to shoot at it with his crossbow. William Tell succeeded in hitting the apple, but when the tyrant asked him the reason of his having another arrow concealed in his dress, he replied, 'To have killed you, had I killed my son.' The offended governor had Tell seized and bound and placed in the same boat with himself, resolving to carry him across the lake to his own castle. A frightful storm (to which the Swiss lakes are liable) suddenly arose, and they were obliged to unchain the prisoner, who was celebrated for his skill as a mariner. He conducted them near a ridge of rocks and, vaulting from the boat with his crossbow in his hand, killed the tyrant. To this, Tell and Switzerland owed their deliverance. The chapel is built on the very spot, surrounded with picturesque woods; and the simple story of Tell, in the appropriate dresses, is painted within the chapel' (Cavendish's note).

[21] 'Opposite to Tell's chapel, in the woody and high shore of the opposite part of Uri, another little chapel just peeps from the surrounding grove. It was here, to avoid discovery, that the friends of liberty met, before the adventure of Tell and the death of Geissler facilitated their endeavours. The chiefs of them were three: Henry de Melchtal, whose father, an old peasant of Underwald, when ploughing his field, was insulted by the emissaries of Geissler, who told him that a wretch like him ought not to use oxen, but to be yoked himself. The son defended his father and the oxen, and was obliged to fly to secure his own life. They seized the helpless old man, and, as he refused to discover the retreat of his son, put out his eyes. Young Henry fled to Uri, to the house of a gentleman of the name of Walter Furst. Vernier de Staubach, a gentleman of the canton of Switz, joined in their meetings at the chapel; he also had been insulted by the tyrant. By the steady and uniform exertions of these men, and the three cantons, they at length took prisoners all the emperor's officers, but with this remarkable instance of humanity: that they banished them without any injury to their persons or possessions. The famous victory of Mongarten in 1315, where a small number of Swiss, from the advantage of their mountains, defeated the Imperial army under Leopold, son to Albert, established their liberty. The three cantons formed excellent laws, and promised friendship and assistance to each other, and by degrees, though at different periods, the thirteen cantons joined in *Ligue Suisse*' (Cavendish's note).

And well-earned wealth improves the ready soil,
And simple manners still maintain their sway.[22]

Farewell Helvetia, from whose lofty breast
Proud Alps arise, and copious rivers flow;   110
Where, source of streams, eternal glaciers rest,[23]
And peaceful science gilds the plains below.[24]

Oft on thy rocks the wondering eye shall gaze,
Thy vallies oft the raptured bosom seek –
There, nature's hand her boldest work displays;   115
Here, bliss domestic beams on every cheek.

Hope of my life, dear children of my heart!
That anxious heart, to each fond feeling true,
To you still pants each pleasure to impart,
And more – oh transport – reach its home and you.   120

Mary Robinson (*née* Darby) (1758–1800)

'She is a woman of undoubted genius', Coleridge told Southey in January 1800. 'She overloads everything, but I never knew a human being with so *full* a mind – bad, good, and indifferent, I grant you, but full and overflowing'.[1] It was not an unfair account, and was certainly more charitable than that of many of her contemporaries.

She was born and brought up in Bristol, the younger daughter of John Darby, a whaling captain from America, and Mary Seys. Mary's first school was that run in Bristol by Hannah More's sisters. When her father absconded to Labrador, ostensibly to set

---

[22] 'The domestic society and simple gaiety of most parts of Switzerland exist in spite of the inroads of strangers; indeed, it seems impossible not to seek rather to join in their happy amusements than to wish to introduce the dissipation of other countries amongst them' (Cavendish's note).

[23] 'The glaciers are formed probably by such an accumulation of ice, that the summer's sun only melts what is sufficient to supply the rivers without diminishing the original stores which are there congealed. This however varies their forms, which are sometimes very beautiful, in waves, arches, pinnacles, etc., and the light of the sun gives them prismatic colours. I saw the glacier of Grindelwald in August, and I might have touched the ice with one hand, and with the other gathered strawberries that grew at its foot' (Cavendish's note).

[24] 'The interesting literary characters in Switzerland are very numerous. At Geneva, M. de Saussure, the first who boldly reached and examined the summit of Mont Blanc; his daughter Madame de Germany, whose writings are said to be as lively and fanciful as Ariosto's, and who is celebrated as a botanist; Mr Hubert the blind observer of nature; Mr Senebier, etc. At Lausanne, Mr Constant the author of *Laure*; Madame de Montolieu, the author of *Caroline de Litchfield*; and, when I was there, the aimiable Dr Tissot, who delighted by the charms of his conversation as much as he was revered for his skill and humanity. At Zuric, Lavater, who adds to his genius and eccentricity, an enthusiastic pursuit of . every benevolent virtue. At Neuchatel, Madame Chariere, the interesting author of *Caliste ou Lettres de Lausanne* – not to omit Necker, du Tremblay, de Luc, Bonnet, and so many others who have been lately celebrated in Switzerland' (Cavendish's note).

MARY ROBINSON (*NÉE* DARBY)
[1] Griggs i 562.

up a whaling station, her mother moved her to school in Chelsea, where she was taught by the gifted but alcoholic Meribah Lorington. In later years Mary described Lorington as 'the most extensively accomplished female that I ever remember to have met with.' . . . All that I ever learned I acquired from this extraordinary woman'.[2] At a time when women were seldom educated, Lorington was remarkably erudite; besides knowing Latin, French and Italian, she was, according to Mary, 'a perfect arithmetician and astronomer'.[3] Later, when the Robinsons were strapped for cash, her mother set up a school at which, as a teenager, Mary worked as an assistant. She concluded her formal education at a finishing school in Marylebone. Her dancing master introduced her to luminaries in the theatrical world, including David Garrick, who encouraged her interest in acting. 'He would sometimes dance a minuet with me, sometimes request me to sing the favourite ballads of the day', she later recalled. She remembered him as tremendously charismatic: 'he appeared to me as one who possessed more power, both to awe and to attract, than any man I ever met with'.[4]

In April 1774 she married Thomas Robinson, an articled clerk at Lincoln's Inn, who was thought to be comfortably off. This was not, alas, the case, and within months he was driven out of the capital to evade his creditors. Mary gave birth to their daughter, Mary Elizabeth, in Wales, November 1774. In 1775 Robinson was imprisoned for debt and, like Charlotte Smith, Mary partook of her husband's punishment, nursing her daughter in the cells. During her incarceration she began to write; her first volume, *Poems* (1775), was partly funded by Georgiana Cavendish, Duchess of Devonshire, one of the few women to respond to her requests for assistance. She went on to publish *Captivity: A Poem* (1777).

Thanks to the good graces of Garrick and Sheridan, Mary found employment as an actress at Drury Lane Theatre on release from prison; she found fame almost immediately, when acting the part of Juliet in December 1776. In the next few years she enjoyed tremendous success as an actress; her starring roles included those of Ophelia, Viola, Rosalind, Lady Macbeth, and Perdita. It was, in fact, while playing Perdita, in late 1779, that she attracted the dubious attentions of the seventeen-year-old Prince of Wales. Their first assignation was, allegedly, in Kew Gardens: 'She had been concealed in the island opposite, and on a signal that the coast was clear, stepped into a boat, and was rowed across.'[5] She became his mistress in return for a promised £20,000, which was never paid.[6] He abandoned her the following year, leaving her to much ridicule in the press, which compelled her to retire from the stage. After lengthy negotiations she managed to coax £5,000 out of the royal family. Subsequent lovers included Charles James Fox, who secured an annuity for her of £500, and Colonel Bastre Tarleton, a war hero and veteran of the American War, who became the recipient of many letters and poems. Tarleton was the father of the child she was carrying when, at the age of twenty-four, she suffered the miscarriage that left her paralysed from the waist down.

After spending several years on the continent with Tarleton, she returned to England in 1788. By this time she relied increasingly on her writing for income, and in succeeding years her productivity was remarkable. Between 1775 and 1800 she produced six volumes of poetry, eight novels, and two plays, with remarkable success. Her gothic

[2] *Memoirs of the late Mrs Robinson* (2 vols, 1803), i 32–3.
[3] Ibid., i 33.
[4] Ibid., i 55.

[5] The Hon. Grantley F. Berkeley, *My Life and Recollections* (4 vols, London, 1865–6), iv 34.
[6] This is described in her own words, *Romanticism* 117.

chiller *Vancenza, or The Dangers of Credulity* (1792) sold out in a day. She often published her poetry in newspapers such as *The World* and *The Oracle*, usually under the names of 'Laura' and 'Laura Maria'. Her talent for engaging in poetical dialogues with the likes of Robert Merry (1755–98), aligned her for a while with the Della Cruscans – a band known for affected, sentimental, and highly ornamented verse. For a while they were very popular, and her biographer in the *Memoirs* records that 'During her poetical disguise, many complimentary poems were addressed to her: several ladies of the blue-stocking club, while Mrs Robinson remained unknown, even ventured to admire – nay, more, to recite her productions in their learned and critical coterie.'[7] But the popularity of the Della Cruscans did not endure, and by the mid-1790s the public was tiring of their mannered style. Although the association with them helped Mary to become known, it was to colour her critics' view of her poetry for years to come. Although she was already beginning to grow out of the Della Cruscan mode by the time she composed *Sappho and Phaon* (1796), included here, it nonetheless provides a good idea of the kind of diction and style by which it is typified.

Her *Poems* (1791) brought together her Della Cruscan poetry, and sold very well. Over 600 people, including the royal family, subscribed to it; even the critics approved. The *Gentleman's Magazine* found the poems 'elegant, harmonious, and correct; a spirit of pensiveness pervades them all'.[8] The *European Magazine* reported that they 'have experienced, as they deserved, a very favourable reception. They are elegant and pathetic'.[9] The *Monthly Review* gave a similarly positive report: 'This ingenious and celebrated lady has attracted the attention of the public both by her personal charms and her mental accomplishments – and who can withstand the united powers of beauty and of wit?'[10] On a personal level, however, things were not going so well. Tarleton attempted to abandon her in 1791 and succeeded in doing so in 1797. She found solace in her writing. Among numerous publications during the 1790s, *Sappho and Phaon* is one of the most accomplished. Sappho was significant to Robinson for a number of reasons. For one thing, she was a woman poet of universally acknowledged greatness, and that puts her in a very small but select company. It is Mary's contention that 'there has not been, during a long series of years, the smallest mark of public distinction bestowed on literary talents. Many individuals whose works are held in the highest estimation now that their ashes sleep in the sepulchre were, when living, suffered to languish and even to perish in obscure poverty, as if it were the peculiar fate of genius to be neglected while existing, and only honoured when the consciousness of inspiration is vanished for ever.' Most of these 'individuals', as Mary makes clear in her Preface to the poem, are women; Sappho's renown thus provides an example of how the world should receive the works of Robinson and her female contemporaries. More importantly, Sappho is the epitome of the impassioned poet. As Jean Jacques Barthélemy testifies, she loved her disciples 'to excess because it was impossible for her to love otherwise'; and in the tale of Sappho's fatal passion for Phaon Mary finds the perfect vehicle for some of her most effective and moving poetry about the pains of unrequited, and betrayed, love.

On the whole, the critical reception of *Sappho and Phaon* was favourable, if somewhat bemused. The critics had pigeonholed her as a Della Cruscan, and the sonnets are more sophisticated than this gave them to expect. As a result, even the more positive reviews sound reserved. The *Critcal Review* remarked: 'Of the talents of Mrs Robinson,

---

[7] *Memoirs of the late Mrs Robinson*, ii 125.

[8] *Gentleman's Magazine* 61 (1791) 560–1, p. 560.

[9] *European Magazine* 19 (1791) 439–41, p. 439.

[10] *Monthly Review* 6 (1791) 448–50, p. 448.

our readers have had frequent specimens. She certainly possesses a brilliancy of fancy and command of poetical language, but the ear is oftener addressed than the heart in her productions – a fault particularly striking in verses which are given under the name of the impassioned Sappho. It is however to her praise that the sonnets are perfectly chaste; they are, moreover, as she takes care to tell us, "legitimate sonnets".[11] Perhaps the most perceptive of the reviewers was that of the *Analytical*, who recognized that Mary was developing beyond her Della Cruscan roots: 'The subject of these sonnets is certainly well chosen to suit the powers of the writer. The varieties of Sappho's passion are expressed with tenderness and harmony not unworthy of the theme. If the poetess has not attained the simplicity of her model, she has at least the merit of avoiding, in a great measure, those playful conceits with which her earlier pieces too much abounded.'[12]

She was best known to the first-generation romantics as a contributor of verse to the *Morning Post*, where her poems appeared under the name 'Tabitha Bramble'. Coleridge, Southey, and Wordsworth were fellow contributors at the same time, and it was Coleridge who engaged in dialogue with her, in both verse and prose. Most famously, he sent her a manuscript copy of *Kubla Khan*, which in turn prompted *Mrs Robinson to the Poet Coleridge* (see *Romanticism* 117–19). In addition, her *The Snow-Drop* prompted Coleridge's poem of the same name, and her celebratory ode to the newborn Derwent Coleridge, *Ode Inscribed to the Infant Son of S. T. Coleridge*, sent to Coleridge in manuscript, inspired his address to her, *A Stranger Minstrel*.[13] Her *Lyrical Tales* (1800) were influenced by *Lyrical Ballads*, and almost persuaded Wordsworth to change the title of the second edition of his work.[14] By the time the reviews appeared, she was dead, and for that reason most of the critics felt obliged to compliment the volume, while hinting at deficiencies which they claimed to be too polite to mention. This, at least, was the tactic of the *Monthly Review*: 'She takes her harp from the willow on which it hung, to attune it to sounds of woe, to harrow up the soul, and to impress on the imagination the melancholy truth that human life is indeed a vale of tears. If she described it as she found it, we must not only forgive her, but lament her unfortunate destiny; yet we do not recommend it to our readers to cherish those gloomy representations of our present state, which the wounded mind feels a satisfaction in delineating.'[15] The *European Magazine* observed that 'The imagery and sentiment scattered among these little poems will be found generally poetical and just, and the versification spirited and harmonious, with sometimes' a cast of structure that pleasingly reminds us of our ancient poets.'[16] The *British Critic* commented: 'Mrs Robinson unquestionably possessed talents and accomplishments which might have adorned and improved society. We have had frequent occasion to commend, though incidentally just reason to censure, various publications of her pen, both in prose and verse. She had a lively imagination, and much practice taught her the art of writing with great facility and some elegance'.[17]

Mary's reputation did not die with her. It was kept alive by her daughter, Mary Elizabeth, who collected together some of her fugitive verses, along with those of other

---

[11] *Critical Review* 19 (1797) 114.
[12] *Analytical Review* 24 (1796) 602–5, p. 605.
[13] See EHC i 356–8, Griggs i 639–42, EHC i 350–2.
[14] It is worth noting that *Odes* ed. George Dyer (Ludlow, 1800), published just before her death, contains one of her poems, *To Meditation*.

[15] *Monthly Review* 36 (1801) 26–30, p. 26.
[16] *European Magazine* 38 (1800) 362.
[17] *British Critic* 18 (1801) 193.

poets, in *The Wild Wreath* (1804), and edited a complete edition of the *Poetical Works* (1806). In many respects the most impressive of these achievements is the 1806 edition, which was not, however, well received. One of the milder notices, in the *Poetical Register*, characterized her as a Della Cruscan: 'Mrs Robinson had a brilliant imagination, and a considerable command of language, but she was deficient in taste. A great number of her compositions are rendered disgusting by affectation and meretricious ornament. It is, however, but justice to say that her later poems are written in a much purer style than those which she published during the period of the Della Crusca madness.'[18] The harshest comments by far appeared in Arthur Aikin's *Annual Review*, and may have been written by Aikin himself. Their strategy was largely to ignore the literary merits of the work and instead to attack its author on ethical grounds:

Sensibility is a most bewitching power, and when sensibility, under the form of 'lovely woman', complains of the perfidy of false friends, the ingratitude of fickle lovers, the nothingness of pomp and pleasure, and the variety of nameless miseries that assail from every quarter the generous and feeling heart – who but must melt with compassion towards the charming sufferer, and glow with indignation against a base unfeeling world? But let us stop a moment to enquire from what description of people these pathetic lamentations most frequently proceed. Why from these very mistresses of colonels, captains, and ensigns – from that guilty, but much enduring class of woman who, rashly bartering away the good opinion of the world, the respect of friends, and the care of legal protectors, receive nothing in exchange but some vague and ineffectual claims on the gratitude, tenderness, or pity, of the most base, selfish, and profligate portion of mankind! Such a one was poor Mrs Robinson, and as an impressive lesson of the effects of such a course of conduct upon the mind, temper, and fortune, her prolix and querulous effusions, her 'miserable strain', may be recommended to the attention of thoughtless and inexperienced youth. But let not juvenile ignorance by deceived by sentimental misrepresentations and unprincipled concealments. Before a tender-hearted young lady has committed to memory the invocation to 'Apathy' or learned to recite with tragic emphasis the 'Ode to Ingratitude',[19] let her at least be aware from *what reflections* the author wished to take shelter in insensibility, and for *what favours* her lovers had proved ungrateful.[20]

The review concludes by reminding us that 'Mrs R. was one of the chief disciples of what was called the Della Cruscan School, a sect of harmonious drivellers, who bewitched the idle multitude for a time with a sweet sound which passed for fine poetry, and an extravagant and affected cant which was mistaken for the language of exquisite feeling.'[21]

These reviewers were unquestionably wrong. Mary Robinson is one of the most important poets of her time. It is not just the qualities that Coleridge noticed that single her out – the plenitude of energy, feeling, and so forth; it is also that she possessed a unique and original voice. She was certainly shaped by outside influences, such as the Della Cruscans, but, like all genuine talents, she developed beyond them to create

---

[18] *Poetical Register* 6 (1807) 540.
[19] The reviewer refers incorrectly, in both cases, to the poems entitled *To Apathy* and *Sonnet. To Ingratitude*.
[20] *Annual Review* 5 (1806) 516–19, pp. 516–17.
[21] Ibid., p. 517.

something new. Even the influence of Wordsworth and Coleridge is transmuted, in *Lyrical Tales*, into something which, though reminiscent of *Lyrical Ballads*, is distinct from it. This is precisely how Coleridge felt when he first read *The Haunted Beach* in the *Morning Post*, where it appeared on 28 February 1800. He wrote immediately to Southey, advising him to include it in his forthcoming *Annual Anthology*: 'if you should not have received that day's paper, write immediately that I may transcribe it – it falls off sadly to the last – wants tale and interest; but the images are new and very distinct – that "silvery carpet" is so *just* that it is unfortunate it should *seem* so bad, for it is *really* good – but the metre – aye, that woman has an ear!'[22] It is not hard to see why Coleridge enjoyed the poem so much. Like some of his own, it plays on our susceptibility to the uncanny, the sinister, the spooky; the gothicism is, perhaps, a little crude next to *Christabel* or *The Ancient Mariner*, but it nonetheless works. *The Haunted Beach* is, in its own quiet way, a haunting poem. The anonymous author of the biography appended to her *Memoirs* rcounted the circumstances of its composition:

> On one of these nights of melancholy inspiration, she discovered from her window a small boat struggling in the spray, which dashed against the wall of her garden. Presently two fishermen brought on shore in their arms a burden which, notwithstanding the distance, Mrs Robinson perceived to be a human body, which the fishermen, after covering it with a sail from their boat, left on the land and disappeared. But a short time elapsed before the men returned, bringing with them fuel, with which they vainly endeavoured to reanimate their unfortunate charge. Struck with a circumstance so affecting, which the stillness of the night rendered yet more impressive, Mrs Robinson remained for some time at her window, motionless with horror. At length, recovering her recollection, she alarmed the family, but before they could gain the beach, the men had again departed. The morning dawned, and day broke in upon the tragical scene. The bathers passed and repassed with little concern, while the corpse continued, extended on the shore, not twenty yards from the Steine. During the course of the day many persons came to look on the body, which still remained unclaimed and unknown. Another day wore away, and the corpse was unburied, the lord of the manor having refused to a fellow-being a grave in which his bones might decently repose, alleging as an excuse *that he did not belong to that parish*. Mrs Robinson, humanely indignant at the scene which passed, exerted herself, but without success, to procure by subscription a small sum for performing the last duties to a wretched outcast. Unwilling, by an ostentatious display of her name, to offend the higher and more fastidious powers, she presented to the fishermen her own contribution, and declined further to interfere. The affair dropped, and the body of the stranger, being dragged to the cliff, was covered by a heap of stones without the ceremony of a prayer.

> These circumstances made on the mind of Mrs Robinson a deep and lasting impression; even at a distant period she could not repeat them without horror and indignation. This incident gave rise to the poem entitled *The Haunted Beach*, written but a few months before her death.[23]

---

[22] Griggs i 576. See also Coleridge's letter to Mary Elizabeth Robinson, Griggs ii 903–6.

[23] *Memoirs of the late Mrs Robinson*, ii 121–4.

Further Reading

Robert Bass, *The Green Dragon: The Lives of Banastre Tarleton and Mary Robinson* (New York, 1957)

Stuart Curran, 'Mary Robinson's *Lyrical Tales* in Context', *RR* 17–35

Linda H. Peterson, 'Becoming an Author: Mary Robinson's *Memoirs* and the Origins of the Woman Artist's Autobiography', *RR* 36–50

Judith Pascoe, 'Mary Robinson and the Literary Marketplace', *RWW* 252–68

Jerome J. McGann, *The Poetics of Sensibility: A Revolution in Literary Style* (Oxford, 1996), pp. 94–116

Judith Pascoe, 'The Spectacular Flaneuse: Mary Robinson and the City of London, *TWC* 23 (1992) 165–71

Jacqueline Labbe, 'Selling One's Sorrows: Charlotte Smith, Mary Robinson, and the Marketing of Poetry, *TWC* 25 (1994) 68–71

Susan Luther, 'A Stranger Minstrel: Coleridge's Mrs Robinson', *SIR* 33 (1994) 391–409

Eleanor Ty, 'Engendering a Female Subject: Mary Robinson's (Re)Presentations of the Self', *English Studies in Canada* 21 (1995) 407–31

Lisa Vargo, 'The Claims of "real life and manners": Coleridge and Mary Robinson', *TWC* 26 (1995) 134–7

From The Wild Wreath ed. Mary Elizabeth Robinson (1804)

A LONDON SUMMER MORNING (COMPOSED 1794)

Who has not waked to 'list the busy sounds
Of summer morning in the sultry smoke
Of noisy London? On the pavement hot
The sooty chimney-boy, with dingy face
And tattered covering, shrilly bawls his trade,   5
Rousing the sleepy housemaid. At the door
The milk-pail rattles, and the tinkling bell
Proclaims the dustman's office, while the street
Is lost in clouds imperious.[1] Now begins
The din of hackney coaches,[2] wagons, carts;   10
While tinmen's shops, and noisy trunk-makers,
Knife-grinders, coopers, squeaking cork-cutters,
Fruit-barrows, and the hunger-giving cries
Of vegetable vendors, fill the air.
Now ev'ry shop displays its varied trade,   15
And the fresh-sprinkled pavement cools the feet
Of early walkers. At the private door
The ruddy housemaid twirls the busy mop,
Annoying the smart 'prentice,[3] or neat[4] girl
Tripping with bandbox[5] lightly. Now the sun   20
Darts burning splendour on the glitt'ring pane,
Save where the canvas awning throws a shade

A LONDON SUMMER MORNING

[1] *clouds imperious* commanding, or obscuring clouds of dust. Note the Miltonic inversion of noun and adjective.

[2] *hackney coaches* four-wheeled coaches, drawn by two horses, seated for six passengers.

[3] *'prentice* apprentice, probably a lawyer's clerk.

[4] *neat* smart, well-dressed.

[5] *bandbox* cardboard box for hats.

On the gay merchandise. Now spruce and trim
In shops where beauty smiles with industry,
Sits the smart damsel, while the passenger   25
Peeps through the window, watching ev'ry charm.
Now pastry dainties catch the eyes minute
Of hummy insects, while the slimy snare
Waits to enthral them. Now the lamp-lighter
Mounts the slight ladder, nimbly venturous,   30
To trim the half-filled lamp,[6] while at his feet
The pot-boy[7] yells discordant. All along
The sultry pavement, the old-clothes man cries
In tone monotonous, and sidelong views
The area for his traffic. Now the bag   35
Is slily opened, and the half-worn suit
(Sometimes the pilfered treasure of the base
Domestic spoiler) for one half its worth
Sinks in the green abyss. The porter now
Bears his huge load along the burning way,   40
And the poor poet wakes from busy dreams
To paint the summer morning.

Sappho and Phaon. In a Series of Legitimate Sonnets, with Thoughts on Poetical Subjects, and Anecdotes of the Grecian Poetess. (1796)

PREFACE

It must strike every admirer of poetical compositions that the modern sonnet, conclud-
ing with two lines winding up the sentiment of the whole, confines the poet's fancy,
and frequently occasions an abrupt termination of a beautiful and interesting picture,
and that the ancient (or what is generally denominated the 'legitimate'[1]) sonnet may be
carried on in a series of sketches, composing, in parts, one historical or imaginary subject,
and forming in the whole a complete and connected story.

With this idea, I have ventured to compose the following collection, not presuming
to offer them as imitations of Petrarch, but as specimens of that species of sonnet-
writing so seldom attempted in the English language, though adopted by that sublime
bard whose muse produced the grand epic of *Paradise Lost*, and the humbler effusion
which I produce as an example of the measure to which I allude, and which is termed
by the most classical writers the legitimate sonnet.

> Oh nightingale, that on yon bloomy spray
> Warblest at eve, when all the woods are still,
> Thou with fresh hope the lover's heart dost fill,
> While the jolly hours lead on propitious May.

---

[6] *trim the half-filled lamp* to prepare the streetlight for
burning after dark.

[7] *pot-boy* boy who serves beer to customers in a tavern.

PREFACE

[1] *legitimate* in the sense of 'correct, proper'.

Thy liquid notes that close the eye of day,
  First heard before the shallow cuckoo's bill,
  Portend success in love; oh if Jove's will
Have linked that amorous power to thy soft lay
  Now timely sing, ere the rude bird of hate
Foretell my hopeless doom in some grove nigh,
  As thou from year to year hast sung too late
For my relief, yet hadst no reason why;
  Whether the muse or love call thee his mate,
Both them I serve, and of their train am I.[2]

To enumerate the variety of authors who have written sonnets of all descriptions would be endless; indeed, few of them deserve notice and, where among the heterogeneous mass of insipid and laboured efforts, sometimes a bright gem sheds lustre on the page of poesy, it scarcely excites attention owing to the disrepute into which sonnets are fallen. So little is rule attended to by many who profess the art of poetry, that I have seen a composition of more than 30 lines ushered into the world under the name of sonnet, and that from the pen of a writer whose classical taste ought to have avoided such a misnomer.

Dr Johnson describes a sonnet as 'a short poem consisting of fourteen lines, of which the rhymes are adjusted by a particular rule'. He further adds, 'It has not been used by any man of eminence since Milton'.[3] Sensible of the extreme difficulty I shall have to encounter in offering to the world a little wreath gathered in that path which even the best poets have thought it dangerous to tread, and knowing that the English language is, of all others, the least congenial to such an undertaking (for I believe that the construction of this kind of sonnet was originally in the Italian, where the vowels are used almost every other letter), I only point out the track where more able pens may follow with success, and where the most classical beauties may be adopted and drawn forth with peculiar advantage.

---

[2] Milton, *Sonnet 1*, composed probably spring 1629; a Petrarchan sonnet, following the Italian metrical scheme of two quatrains and two tercets.

[3] The quotation is in fact Johnson's definition from his *Dictionary*, which states in full that the sonnet 'is not very suitable to the English language, and has not been used by any man of eminence since Milton'. 'Since the death of Dr Johnson a few ingenious and elegant writers have composed sonnets according to the rules described by him; of their merits the public will judge, and the literati decide. The following quotations are given as the opinions of living authors respecting the legitimate sonnet.

The little poems which are here called sonnets have, I believe, no very just claim to that title, but they consist of fourteen lines, and appear to me no improper vehicle for a single sentiment. I am told, and I read it as the opinion of very good judges, that the legitimate sonnet is ill-calculated for our language. The specimens Mr Hayley has given, though they form a strong exception, prove no more than that the difficulties of the attempt vanish before uncommon powers.

    (Mrs C. Smith's Preface to her
    Elegiac Sonnets [see p. 72])

Likewise, in the preface to a volume of very charming poems (among which are many legitimate sonnets) by Mr William Kendall of Exeter, the following opinion is given of the Italian rhythm, which constitutes the legitimate sonnet. He describes it as

a chaste and elegant model, which the most enlightened poet of our own country disdained not to contemplate. Amidst the degeneracy of modern taste, if the studies of a Milton have lost their attraction, legitimate sonnets, enriched by varying pauses, and an elaborate recurrence of rhyme, still assert their superiority over those tasteless and inartificial productions which assume the name, without evincing a single characteristic of distinguishing modulation.'

    (Robinson's note)

Sophisticated sonnets are so common (for every rhapsody of rhyme, from six lines to sixty, comes under that denomination) that the eye frequently turns from this species of poem with disgust. Every schoolboy,[4] every romantic scribbler, thinks a sonnet a task of little difficulty. From this ignorance in some, and vanity in others, we see the monthly and diurnal publications abounding with ballads, odes, elegies, epitaphs, and allegories, the nondescript ephemera from the heated brains of self-important poetasters, all ushered into notice under the appellation of 'sonnet'!

I confess myself such an enthusiastic votary of the muse that any innovation which seems to threaten even the least of her established rights makes me tremble, lest that chaos of dissipated pursuits which has too long been growing like an overwhelming shadow, and menacing the lustre of intellectual light, should, aided by the idleness of some, and the profligacy of others, at last obscure the finer mental powers, and reduce the dignity of talents to the lowest degradation.

As poetry has the power to raise, so has it also the magic to refine. The ancients considered the art of such importance that, before they led forth their heroes to the most glorious enterprizes, they animated them by the recital of grand and harmonious compositions. The wisest scrupled not to reverence the invocations of minds graced with the charm of numbers. So mystically fraught are powers said to be which look beyond the surface of events, that an admired and classical writer, describing the inspirations of the Muse, thus expresses his opinion:

> So when remote futurity is brought
> Before the keen inquiry of her thought,
> A terrible sagacity informs
> The poet's heart, he looks to distant storms,
> He hears the thunder ere the tempest low'rs,
> And armed with strength surpassing human pow'rs,
> Seizes events as yet unknown to man,
> And darts his soul into the dawning plan.
> Hence in a Roman mouth the graceful name
> Of prophet and of poet was the same,
> Hence British poets too the priesthood shared
> And ev'ry hallowed druid was a bard.[5]

That poetry ought to be cherished as a national ornament cannot be more strongly exemplified than in the simple fact that, in those centuries when the poets' laurels have been most generously fostered in Britain, the minds and manners of the natives have been most polished and enlightened. Even the language of a country refines into purity by the elegance of numbers: the strains of Waller[6] have done more to effect that than all the labours of monkish pedantry since the days of druidical mystery and superstition.

---

[4] To prove the point, Wordsworth's first published poem, which appeared in the *European Magazine* when he was a schoolboy of sixteen, was a sonnet.

[5] 'Cowper' (Robinson's note); the quotation is from *Table Talk* 492–503.

[6] Edmund Waller (1606–87), royalist politician, poet, and friend of Dryden. His poetry was renowned for its polished simplicity.

Though different minds are variously affected by the infinite diversity of harmonious effusions, there are, I believe, very few that are wholly insensible to the powers of poetic compositions. Cold must that bosom be which can resist the magical versification of *Eloisa to Abelard*,[7] and torpid to all the more exalted sensations of the soul is that being whose ear is not delighted by the grand and sublime effusions of the divine Milton! The romantic chivalry of Spenser vivifies the imagination, while the plaintive sweetness of Collins soothes and penetrates the heart. How much would Britain have been deficit[8] in a comparison with other countries on the scale of intellectual grace had these poets never existed! Yet it is a melancholy truth that here, where the attributes of genius have been diffused by the liberal hand of nature almost to prodigality, there has not been, during a long series of years, the smallest mark of public distinction bestowed on literary talents. Many individuals whose works are held in the highest estimation now that their ashes sleep in the sepulchre were, when living, suffered to languish and even to perish in obscure poverty, as if it were the peculiar fate of genius to be neglected while existing, and only honoured when the consciousness of inspiration is vanished for ever.

The ingenious mechanic has the gratification of seeing his labours patronised, and is rewarded for his invention while he has the powers of enjoying its produce. But the poet's life is one perpetual scene of warfare: he is assailed by envy, stung by malice, and wounded by the fastidious comments of concealed assassins. The more eminently beautiful his compositions are, the larger is the phalanx he has to encounter, for the enemies of genius are multitudinous.

It is the interest of the ignorant and powerful to suppress the effusions of enlightened minds. When only monks could write and nobles read, authority rose triumphant over right, and the slave, spellbound in ignorance, hugged his fetters without repining. It was then that the best powers of reason lay buried like the gem in the dark mine; by a slow and tedious progress they have been drawn forth, and must erelong diffuse an universal lustre – for that era is rapidly advancing when talents will tower like an unperishable column, while the globe will be strewed with the wrecks of superstition.

As it was the opinion of the ancients that poets possessed the powers of prophecy, the name was consequently held in the most unbounded veneration. In less remote periods the bard has been publicly distinguished; princes and priests have bowed before the majesty of genius. Petrarch was crowned with laurels, the noblest diadem in the Capitol of Rome; his admirers were liberal, his contemporaries were just, and his name will stand upon record with the united and honourable testimony of his own talents, and the generosity of his country.

It is at once a melancholy truth and a national disgrace that this island, so profusely favoured by nature, should be marked, of all enlightened countries, as the most neglectful of literary merit! And I will venture to believe that there are both poets and philosophers, now living in Britain, who, had they been born in any *other* clime, would have been honoured with the proudest distinctions, and immortalized to the latest posterity.

I cannot conclude these opinions without paying tribute to the talents of my illustrious countrywomen who, unpatronised by Courts, and unprotected by the powerful, persevere in the paths of literature, and ennoble themselves by the unperishable lustre of mental pre-eminence!

---

[7] A reference to Pope's poem, published 1717.   [8] *deficit* deficient.

To the Reader

The story of the Lesbian Muse,[9] though not new to the classical reader, presented to my imagination such a lively example of the human mind, enlightened by the most exquisite talents, yet yielding to the destructive control of ungovernable passions, that I felt an irresistible impulse to attempt the delineation of their progress, mingling with the glowing picture of her soul such moral reflections as may serve to excite that pity which, while it proves the susceptibility of the heart, arms it against the danger of indulging too luxuriant a fancy.

The unfortunate lovers, Heloise and Abelard, and the supposed platonic Petrarch and Laura, have found panegyrists in many distinguished authors. Ovid[10] and Pope have celebrated the passion of Sappho for Phaon, but their portraits, however beautifully finished, are replete with shades tending rather to depreciate than to adorn the Grecian poetess.

I have endeavoured to collect, in the succeeding pages, the most liberal accounts of that illustrious woman whose fame has transmitted to us some fragments of her works through many dark ages, and for the space of more than 2,000 years. The merit of her compositions must have been indisputable to have left all contemporary female writers in obscurity; for it is known that poetry was, at the period in which she lived, held in the most sacred veneration, and that those who were gifted with that divine inspiration were ranked as the first class of human beings.

Among the many Grecian writers, Sappho was the unrivalled poetess of her time: the envy she excited, the public honours she received, and the fatal passion which terminated her existence, will, I trust, create that sympathy in the mind of the susceptible reader which may render the following poetical trifles not wholly uninteresting.

Mary Robinson
St. James's Place, 1796

Account of Sappho

Sappho, whom the ancients distinguished by the title of the Tenth Muse, was born at Mytilene in the island of Lesbos, 600 years before the Christian era. As no particulars have been transmitted to posterity respecting the origin of her family, it is most likely she derived but little consequence from birth or connections. At an early period of her life she was wedded to Cercolus, a native of the isle of Andros; he was possessed of considerable wealth and, though the Lesbian Muse is said to have been sparingly gifted with beauty, he became enamoured of her – more perhaps on account of mental than personal charms. By this union she is said to have given birth to a daughter but, Cercolus leaving her while young in a state of widowhood, she never after could be prevailed on to marry.

The fame which her genius spread, even to the remotest parts of the earth, excited the envy of some writers who endeavoured to throw over her private character a shade which shrunk before the brilliancy of her poetical talents. Her soul was replete with harmony, that harmony which neither art nor study can acquire; she felt the intuitive superiority, and to the muses she paid unbounded adoration.

---

[9]   *Lesbian Muse* Sappho.

[10]   Ovid, 'Sappho Phaoni', was one of Mary's most important sources. It is the fifteenth of Ovid's *Epistles*, and takes the form of a letter from Sappho to Phaon.

The Mytilenians held her poetry in such high veneration, and were so sensible of the honour conferred on the country which gave her birth, that they coined money with the impression of her head, and at the time of her death paid tribute to her memory such as was offered to sovereigns only.

The story of Antiochus has been related as an unequivocal proof of Sappho's skill in discovering, and powers of describing, the passions of the human mind. That prince is said to have entertained a fatal affection for his mother-in-law, Stratonice – which, though he endeavoured to subdue its influence, preyed upon his frame and, after many ineffectual struggles, at length reduced him to extreme danger. His physicians marked the symptoms attending his malady, and found them so exactly correspondent with Sappho's delineation of the tender passion, that they did not hesitate to form a decisive opinion of the cause which had produced so perilous an effect.

That Sappho was not insensible to the feelings she so well described is evident in her writings but it was scarcely possible that a mind so exquisitely tender, so sublimely gifted, should escape those fascinations which even apathy itself has been awakened to acknowledge.

The scarce specimens now extant from the pen of the Grecian Muse have, by the most competent judges, been esteemed as the standard for the pathetic, the glowing, and the amatory. The ode, which has been so highly estimated, is written in a measure distinguished by the title of the Sapphic. Pope made it his model in his juvenile production beginning 'Happy the man whose wish and care . . .'[11]

Addison was of opinion that the writings of Sappho were replete with such fascinating beauties, and adorned with such a vivid glow of sensibility, that, probably, had they been preserved entire, it would have been dangerous to have perused them.[12] They possessed none of the artificial decorations of a feigned passion; they were the genuine effusions of a supremely enlightened soul labouring to subdue a fatal enchantment, and vainly opposing the conscious pride of illustrious fame against the warm susceptibility of a generous bosom.

Though few stanzas from the pen of the Lesbian poetess have darted through the shades of oblivion, yet those that remain are so exquisitely touching and beautiful that they prove beyond dispute the taste, feeling, and inspiration of the mind which produced them. In examining the curiosities of antiquity, we look to the perfections, and not the magnitude, of those relics which have been preserved amidst the wrecks of time. As the smallest gem that bears the fine touches of a master surpasses the loftiest fabric reared by the labours of false taste, so the precious fragments of the immortal Sappho will be admired, when the voluminous productions of inferior poets are mouldered into dust.

When it is considered that the few specimens[13] we have of the poems of the Grecian Muse have passed through three and twenty centuries, and consequently through the hands of innumerable translators, and when it is known that Envy frequently delights

---

[11] Pope's *Ode on Solitude* (1717), written, he said, when he was twelve.

[12] Addison's article on Sappho was one of Robinson's chief sources: 'I do not know, by the character that is given of her works, whether it is not for the benefit of mankind that they are lost. They were filled with such bewitching tenderness and rapture, that it might

have been dangerous to have given them a reading' (*Spectator* 223, 15 Nov. 1711; *The Spectator* ed. Donald F. Bond (5 vols, Oxford, 1965), ii 366).

[13] *few specimens* Addison's 1735 edition of the works consisted of two 'odes', six fragments, and two epigrams.

in the base occupation of depreciating merit which it cannot aspire to emulate, it may be conjectured that some passages are erroneously given to posterity, either by ignorance or design. Sappho, whose fame beamed round her with the superior effulgence which her works had created, knew that she was writing for future ages; it is not therefore natural that she should produce any composition which might tend to tarnish her reputation, or lessen that celebrity which it was the labour of her life to consecrate. The delicacy of her sentiments cannot find a more eloquent advocate than in her own effusions – she is said to have commended in the most animated panegyric the virtues of her brother Lanychus and, with the most pointed and severe censure, to have contemned the passion which her brother Charaxus entertained for the beautiful Rhodope. If her writings were, in some instances, too glowing for the fastidious refinement of modern times, let it be her excuse, and the honour of her country, that the liberal education of the Greeks was such as inspired them with an unprejudiced enthusiasm for the works of genius, and that, when they paid adoration to Sappho, they idolized the muse, and not the woman.

I shall conclude this account with an extract from the works of the learned and enlightened Abbé Barthelemi, at once the vindication and eulogy of the Grecian poetess:

Sappho undertook to inspire the Lesbian women with a taste for literature; many of them received instructions from her, and foreign women increased the number of her disciples. She loved them to excess because it was impossible for her to love otherwise, and she expressed her tenderness in all the violence of passion. Your surprise at this will cease when you are acquainted with the extreme sensibility of the Greeks, and discover that amongst them the most innocent connections often borrow the impassioned language of love.

A certain facility of manners she possessed, and the warmth of her expressions were but too well calculated to expose her to the hatred of some women of distinction, humbled by her superiority, and the jealousy of some of her disciples who happened not to be the objects of her preference. To this hatred she replied by truths and irony, which completely exasperated her enemies. She repaired to Sicily, where a statue was erected to her; it was sculptured by Silanion, one of the most celebrated staturists of his time. The sensibility of Sappho was extreme! She loved Phaon, who forsook her; after various efforts to bring him back, she took the leap of Leucata,[14] and perished in the waves!

Death has not obliterated the stain imprinted on her character; for Envy, which fastens on illustrious names, does not expire, but bequeaths her aspersions to that calumny which never dies.

Several Grecian women have cultivated poetry with success, but none have hitherto attained to the excellence of Sappho. And among other poets, there are few indeed who have surpassed her.[15]

---

[14] 'Leucata was a promontory of Epirus, on the top of which stood a temple dedicated to Apollo. From this promontory despairing lovers threw themselves into the sea, with an idea that, if they survived, they should be cured of their hopeless passions. The Abbé Barthelmi says that "many escaped, but others having perished, the custom fell into disrepute, and at length

was wholly abolished" – *vide Travels of Anacharsis the Younger*' (Robinson's note).

[15] The quotation consists of a series of extracted and revised sentences from Jean Jacques Barthélemy, *Travels of Anacharsis the younger in Greece* tr. W. Beaumont (2nd edn, 7 vols, 1794), ii 63–5.

Flendus amor meus est; elegeia flebile carmen;
Non facit ad lacrymas barbitos ulla meas.[1]

Ovid.

Love taught my tears in sadder notes to flow,
And tuned my heart to elegies of woe.

Pope.[2]

I. SONNET INTRODUCTORY

Favoured by Heav'n are those ordained to taste
  The bliss supreme that kindles fancy's fire,
  Whose magic fingers sweep the muses' lyre
In varying cadence, eloquently chaste!
Well may the mind, with tuneful numbers graced,   5
  To fame's immortal attributes aspire,
  Above the treach'rous spells of low desire
That wound the sense, by vulgar joys debased.
  For thou, blessed poesy, with godlike pow'rs
To calm the miseries of man wert giv'n;   10
  When passion rends, and hopeless love devours,
By mem'ry goaded, and by frenzy driv'n,
  'Tis thine to guide him midst Elysian bow'rs
And show his fainting soul a glimpse of heav'n.

II. THE TEMPLE OF CHASTITY

High on a rock, coeval[1] with the skies,
  A temple stands, reared by immortal pow'rs
  To chastity divine! Ambrosial flow'rs,
Twining round icicles, in columns rise,
Mingling with pendent gems of orient dyes!   5
  Piercing the air, a golden crescent tow'rs,
  Veiled by transparent clouds, while smiling hours[2]
Shake from their varying wings celestial joys!
  The steps of spotless marble, scattered o'er
With deathless roses armed with many a thorn,   10
  Lead to the altar; on the frozen floor,
Studded with teardrops petrified by scorn,
  Pale vestals kneel the goddess to adore,
While Love,[3] his arrows broke, retires forlorn.

III. THE BOWER OF PLEASURE[1]

Turn to yon vale beneath, whose tangled shade
  Excludes the blazing torch of noonday light

---

[1] *Heroides* xv 7–8: 'Unsuccessful love complains in sadder notes, and elegy is fittest to express my woe. No harp can serve to paint my flowing tears' (Ovid, *Epistles* 167).

[2] Pope, *Sapho to Phaon* (1712) 7–8.

II. THE TEMPLE OF CHASTITY

[1] *coeval* as old as, of the same age as.

[2] *hours* female divinities supposed to preside over the changing seasons.

[3] *Love* Cupid.

III. THE BOWER OF PLEASURE

[1] Cf. Spenser's Bower of Bliss, *Faerie Queene* II xii st.71–2.

Where sportive fawns and dimpled loves[2] invite,
The bow'r of pleasure opens to the glade;
Lulled by soft flutes, on leaves of violets laid,   5
    There witching beauty greets the ravished sight,
    More gentle than the arbitress of night
In all her silv'ry panoply arrayed!
The birds breathe bliss; light zephyrs kiss the ground,
Stealing the hyacinth's divine perfume;   10
    While from pellucid fountains glitt'ring round
Small tinkling rills bid rival flowrets bloom!
    Here laughing cupids bathe the bosom's wound,
There tyrant passion finds a glorious tomb!

IV. SAPPHO DISCOVERS HER PASSION

Why, when I gaze on Phaon's beauteous eyes,
    Why does each thought in wild disorder stray?
    Why does each fainting faculty decay,
And my chilled breast[1] in throbbing tumults rise?
Mute on the ground my lyre neglected lies,   5
    The muse forgot, and lost the melting lay;
    My downcast looks, my faltering lips betray
That, stung by hopeless passion, Sappho dies!
    Now on a bank of cypress[2] let me rest;
Come, tuneful maids, ye pupils of my care,   10
    Come, with your dulcet numbers soothe my breast;
And as the soft vibrations float on air,
    Let pity waft my spirit to the blest
To mock the barb'rous triumphs of despair!

V. CONTEMNS ITS POWER

Oh how can Love exulting Reason quell!
    How fades each nobler passion from his gaze!
    E'en fame, that cherishes the poet's lays,
That fame ill-fated Sappho loved so well.
Lost is the wretch who in his fatal spell   5
    Wastes the short summer of delicious days,
    And from the tranquil path of wisdom strays
In passion's thorny wild, forlorn to dwell.
    Oh ye who in that sacred temple smile
Where holy Innocence resides enshrined,   10
    Who fear not sorrow and who know not guile,

---

[2] *loves* cupids.
IV. SAPPHO DISCOVERS HER PASSION
[1] *my chilled breast* a recollection of Pope, *Sapho to Phaon* 126: 'Grief chilled my breast, and stopped my freezing blood'.

[2] *cypress* associated with death.

Each thought composed, and ev'ry wish resigned –
  Tempt not the path where Pleasure's flow'ry wile,
In sweet but pois'nous fetters, holds the mind.

VI. DESCRIBES THE CHARACTERISTICS OF LOVE

Is it to love, to fix the tender gaze,
  To hide the timid blush, and steal away?
  To shun the busy world, and waste the day
In some rude mountain's solitary maze?
Is it to chant *one* name in ceaseless lays,   5
  To hear no words that other tongues can say,
  To watch the pale moon's melancholy ray,
To chide in fondness, and in folly praise?
  Is it to pour th' involuntary sigh,
To dream of bliss, and wake new pangs to prove;   10
  To talk, in fancy, with the speaking eye,
Then start with jealousy, and wildly rove?
  Is it to loathe the light, and wish to die?
For these I feel, and feel that they are love.

VII. INVOKES REASON

Come, Reason, come, each nerve rebellious bind!
  Lull the fierce tempest of my fev'rish soul;
  Come with the magic of thy meek control
And check the wayward wand'rings of my mind!
Estranged from thee, no solace can I find;   5
  O'er my rapt brain, where pensive visions stole,
  Now passion reigns and stormy tumults roll –
So the smooth sea obeys the furious wind!
  In vain philosophy unfolds his store,
O'erwhelmed is ev'ry source of pure delight;   10
  Dim is the golden page of wisdom's lore;
All nature fades before my sick'ning sight:
  For what bright scene can fancy's eye explore
Midst dreary labyrinths of mental night?

VIII. HER PASSION INCREASES

Why, through each aching vein, with lazy pace
  Thus steals the languid fountain of my heart,
  While, from its source, each wild convulsive start
Tears the scorched roses from my burning face?
In vain, oh Lesbian vales, your charms I trace!   5
  Vain is the poet's theme, the sculptor's art;
  No more the lyre its magic can impart,
Though waked to sound, with more than mortal grace!
  Go, tuneful maids, go bid my Phaon prove
That passion mocks the empty boast of fame;   10

Tell him no joys are sweet but joys of love,
Melting the soul and thrilling all the frame!
Oh may th' ecstatic thought his bosom move,
And sighs of rapture fan the blush of shame!

IX. LAMENTS THE VOLATILITY OF PHAON

Ye who in alleys green and leafy bow'rs
   Sport, the rude children of fantastic birth,
   Where frolic nymphs and shaggy tribes of mirth
In clam'rous revels waste the midnight hours;
Who, linked in flaunting bands of mountain flow'rs,   5
   Weave your wild mazes o'er the dewy earth
   Ere the fierce lord of lustre[1] rushes forth
And o'er the world his beamy radiance pours –
   Oft has your clanking cymbal's madd'ning strain,
Loud ringing through the torch-illumined grove,   10
   Lured my loved Phaon from the youthful train
Through rugged dells, o'er craggy rocks to rove:
   Then how can she his vagrant heart detain,
Whose lyre throbs only to the touch of love?

X. DESCRIBES PHAON

Dang'rous to hear is that melodious tongue,
   And fatal to the sense those murd'rous eyes,
   Where in a sapphire sheath love's arrow lies,
Himself concealed the crystal haunts among!
Oft o'er that form enamoured have I hung,[1]   5
   On that smooth cheek to mark the deep'ning dyes,
   While from that lip the fragrant breath would rise –
That lip, like Cupid's bow with rubies strung!
   Still let me gaze upon that polished brow
O'er which the golden hair luxuriant plays;   10
   So on the modest lily's leaves of snow
The proud sun revels in resplendent rays!
   Warm as his beams this sensate[2] heart shall glow
Till life's last hour with Phaon's self decays!

XI. REJECTS THE INFLUENCE OF REASON

Oh Reason, vaunted sovereign of the mind,
   Thou pompous vision with a sounding name,
   Canst thou the soul's rebellious passions tame?
Canst thou in spells the vagrant fancy bind?

IX. LAMENTS THE VOLATILITY OF PHAON
[1] *lord of lustre* the sun.
X. DESCRIBES PHAON
[1] *hung* perhaps an echo of Adam's doting vision of
the sleeping Eve:

                    he on his side
Leaning half-raised, with looks of cordial love
Hung over her enamoured . . .
                    (*Paradise Lost* v 11–13)

[2] *sensate* feeling, full of sensibility.

Ah no, capricious as the wav'ring wind 5
   Are sighs of love that dim thy boasted flame,
   While folly's torch consumes the wreath of fame,
And Pleasure's hands the sheaves of truth unbind.
   Pressed by the storms of fate, Hope shrinks and dies,
Frenzy darts forth in mightiest ills arrayed, 10
   Around thy throne destructive tumults rise
And hell-fraught jealousies thy rights invade!
   Then what art thou? Oh idol of the wise –
A visionary theme, a gorgeous shade!

XII. Previous to her interview with Phaon

Now o'er the tessellated[1] pavement strew
   Fresh saffron steeped in essence of the rose,
   While down yon agate column gently flows
A glitt'ring streamlet of ambrosial dew!
My Phaon smiles; the rich carnation's hue 5
   On his flushed cheek in conscious lustre glows,
   While o'er his breast enamoured Venus throws
Her starry mantle of celestial blue!
   Breathe soft, ye dulcet flutes, among the trees
Where clust'ring boughs with golden citron[2] twine, 10
   While slow vibrations dying on the breeze
Shall soothe his soul with harmony divine!
   Then let my form his yielding fancy seize,
And all his fondest wishes blend with mine.

XIII. She endeavours to fascinate him

Bring, bring to deck my brow, ye sylvan girls,
   A roseate[1] wreath, nor for my waving hair
   The costly band of studded gems prepare
Of sparkling chrysolite[2] or orient pearls;[3]
Love o'er my head his canopy unfurls, 5
   His purple pinions fan the whisp'ring air;
   Mocking the golden sandal, rich and rare,
Beneath my feet the fragrant woodbine curls.
   Bring the thin robe to fold about my breast,
White as the downy swan; while round my waist 10
   Let leaves of glossy myrtle bind the vest –
Not idly gay, but elegantly chaste!
   Love scorns the nymph in wanton trappings dressed,
And charms the most concealed are doubly graced.

XII. Previous to her interview with Phaon
[1] *tessellated* formed out of mosaics.
[2] *citron* a kind of citrus fruit.
XIII. She endeavours to fascinate him
[1] Rose and myrtle together (see l. 11) indicate a coy defence of femininity, since Venus, Greek goddess of erotic love, often veiled herself in them when washing.
[2] *chrysolite* green gems.
[3] *orient pearls* pearls from the Indian Ocean, more beautiful and exotic that those from European mussels.

XIV. To the Aeolian harp[1]

Come, soft Aeolian harp, while zephyr plays
    Along the meek vibration of thy strings,
    As twilight's hand her modest mantle brings,
Blending with sober grey the western blaze!
Oh prompt my Phaon's dreams with tend'rest lays   5
    Ere night o'ershade thee with its humid wings,
    While the lorn Philomel his[2] sorrow sings
In leafy cradle, red with parting rays!
    Slow let thy dulcet tones on ether[3] glide,
So steals the murmur of the am'rous dove;   10
    The mazy legions swarm on ev'ry side,
To lulling sounds the sunny people[4] move!
    Let not the wise their little world deride –
The smallest sting can wound the breast of love.[5]

XV. Phaon awakes

Now round my favoured grot let roses rise
    To strew the bank where Phaon wakes from rest;
    Oh happy buds, to kiss his burning breast,
And die beneath the lustre of his eyes!
Now let the timbrels echo to the skies,   5
    Now damsels sprinkle cassia[1] on his vest,
    With od'rous wreaths of constant myrtle[2] dressed,
And flow'rs, deep-tinted with the rainbow's dyes!
    From cups of porphyry[3] let nectar flow,
Rich as the perfume of Phoenicia's vine!   10
    Now let his dimpling cheek with rapture glow
While, round his heart, love's mystic fetters twine;
    And let the Grecian lyre its aid bestow
In songs of triumph, to proclaim him mine!

XVI. Sappho rejects hope

Delusive hope, more transient than the ray
    That leads pale twilight to her dusky bed
    O'er woodland glen or breezy mountain's head,

XIV. To the Aeolian harp
[1] The eighteenth-century equivalent of wind-chimes, the Aeolian harp was left in front of an open window, or hung on a tree, where its strings would be 'played' by the wind (Aeolus is the Greek god of storms and winds); cf. Coleridge, *The Eolian Harp* (1795).
[2] *his* technically correct; despite the traditional identification of the nightingale with Philomela (see note 5, below), only male nightingales sing, as part of the courtship ritual.

[3] *ether* effectively air; upper regions of the sky.
[4] *sunny people* insects that fly around in the sun.
[5] Philomela was seduced, according to Ovid, by her brother-in-law, Tereus, King of Thrace. She was turned into a nightingale, and her sad song was said to be caused by a thorn in her breast.
XV. Phaon awakes
[1] *cassia* fragrant shrub.
[2] *myrtle* sacred to Venus, an emblem of love.
[3] *porphyry* beautiful and valuable purple stone.

Ling'ring to catch the parting sigh of day –
Hence with thy visionary charms, away!   5
  Nor o'er my path the flow'rs of fancy spread;
  Thy airy dreams on peaceful pillows shed,
And weave for thoughtless brows a garland gay.
  Farewell low vallies; dizzy cliffs, farewell!
Small vagrant rills that murmur as ye flow,   10
  Dark-bosomed labyrinth and thorny dell;
The task be mine all pleasures to forego,
  To hide where meditation loves to dwell
And feed my soul with luxury of woe![1]

XVII. THE TYRANNY OF LOVE

Love steals unheeded o'er the tranquil mind
  As summer breezes fan the sleeping main,
  Slow through each fibre[1] creeps the subtle pain,
Till closely round the yielding bosom twined;
Vain is the hope the magic to unbind,   5
  The potent mischief riots in the brain,
  Grasps ev'ry thought, and burns in ev'ry vein,
Till in the heart the tyrant lives enshrined.
  Oh victor strong, bending the vanquished frame,
Sweet is the thraldom that thou bidst us prove,   10
  And sacred is the tear thy victims claim,
For blessed are those whom sighs of sorrow move!
  Then nymphs, beware how ye profane my name,
Nor blame my weakness till like me ye love!

XVIII. TO PHAON

Why art thou changed, oh Phaon, tell me why?
  Love flies reproach when passion feels decay;
  Or I would paint the raptures of that day
When, in sweet converse, mingling sigh with sigh,
I marked the graceful languor of thine eye,   5
  As on a shady bank entranced we lay.
  Oh eyes, whose beamy radiance stole away
As stars fade trembling from the burning sky,
  Why art thou changed, dear source of all my woes?
Though dark my bosom's tint, through ev'ry vein   10
  A ruby tide of purest lustre flows,
Warmed by thy love or chilled by thy disdain;
  And yet no bliss this sensate being knows –
Ah, why is rapture so allied to pain?

XVI. SAPHO REJECTS HOPE
[1] *luxury of woe* this paradox exemplifies the emotional indulgence that characterized the Della Cruscan sensibility.

XVII. THE TYRANNY OF LOVE
[1] *fibre* i.e. of the body.

XIX. SUSPECTS HIS CONSTANCY

Farewell, ye coral caves, ye pearly sands,
  Ye waving woods that crown yon lofty steep;
Farewell, ye nereides[1] of the glitt'ring deep,
Ye mountain tribes, ye fawns, ye sylvan bands:
On the bleak rock your frantic minstrel stands,   5
  Each task forgot, save that to sigh and weep;
  In vain the strings her burning fingers sweep,
No more her touch the Grecian lyre commands!
  In Circe's[2] cave my faithless Phaon's laid,
Her daemons[3] dress his brow with opiate flow'rs;[4]   10
  Or, loit'ring in the brown pomgranate[5] shade,
Beguile with am'rous strains the fateful hours,
  While Sappho's lips to paly ashes fade
And sorrow's cank'ring[6] worm her heart devours!

XX. TO PHAON

Oh I could toil for thee o'er burning plains,
  Could smile at poverty's disastrous blow,
  With thee could wander midst a world of snow
Where one long night o'er frozen Scythia[1] reigns.
Severed from thee, my sick'ning soul disdains   5
  The thrilling thought, the blissful dream to know,
  And canst thou give my days to endless woe,
Requiting sweetest bliss with cureless pains?
  Away, false fear, nor think capricious fate
Would lodge a daemon in a form divine!   10
  Sooner the dove shall seek a tiger mate
Or the soft snowdrop round the thistle twine;
  Yet, yet, I dread to hope, nor dare to hate,
Too proud to sue,[2] too tender to resign![3]

XXI. LAMENTS HER EARLY MISFORTUNES

Why do I live to loathe the cheerful day,
  To shun the smiles of fame, and mark the hours
  On tardy pinions move, while ceaseless show'rs
Down my wan cheek in lucid currents stray?
My tresses all unbound, nor gems display,   5

XIX. SUSPECTS HIS CONSTANCY
[1] *nereides* sea-nymphs.
[2] Circe was an enchantress renowned for her seductiveness.
[3] *daemons* spirits.
[4] *opiate flow'rs* flowers that induce drowsiness and inaction.

[5] *pomgranate* this spelling is deliberate, but it was already archaic by Robinson's day.
[6] *cank'ring* consuming.
XX. TO PHAON
[1] *Scythia* ancient region extending over much of European and Asiatic Russia.
[2] *sue* pursue.
[3] *resign* give up.

Nor scents Arabian; on my path no flow'rs
Imbibe the morn's resuscitating pow'rs,
For one blank sorrow saddens all my way!
As slow the radiant sun of reason rose,
Through tears my dying parents saw it shine;[1]
    A brother's frailties swelled the tide of woes,[2]
And, keener far, maternal griefs were mine![3]
    Phaon, if soon these weary eyes shall close,
Oh must that task, that mournful task, be thine?

10

XXII. Phaon forsakes her

Wild is the foaming sea, the surges roar,
    And nimbly dart the livid[1] lightnings round!
    On the rent rock the angry waves rebound –
Ah me, the less'ning bark is seen no more!
Along the margin of the trembling shore,
    Loud as the blast my frantic cries shall sound,
    My storm-drenched limbs the flinty fragments wound,
And o'er my bleeding breast the billows pour!
    Phaon return! Ye winds, oh waft the strain
To his swift bark! Ye barb'rous waves forbear,
    Taunt not the anguish of a lover's brain,
Nor feebly emulate the soul's despair!
    For howling winds and foaming seas in vain
Assail the breast when passion rages there!

5

10

XXIII. Sappho's conjectures

To Etna's scorching sands my Phaon flies![1]
    False youth, can other charms attractive prove?
    Say, can Sicilian loves thy passions move,
Play round thy heart and fix thy fickle eyes,
While in despair the Lesbian Sappho dies?

5

XXI. Laments her early misfortunes
[1] "'Sex mihi natales ierant, cum lecta parentis / Ante diem lacrymas ossa bibere meas. / Arsit inops frater, victus meretricis amore; / Mistaque cum turpi damna pudore tulit." Ovid' (Robinson's note). The quotation is from *Heroides* xv 61–2, and translates: 'Scarce was I in my sixth year, when the ashes of a deceased parent drank my tears. My brother next, despising wealth and honour, burnt with an ignoble flame, and obstinately plunged himself into shameful distresses' (Ovid, *Epistles* 171).
[2] Sappho's brother, Charaxos, became involved with a courtesan called Rhodope, and squandered all his money on her.
[3] Sappho gave birth to a daughter, Cleis, named after her mother. Sappho's poems give no indication

of why she might have felt 'grief' for Cleis; possibly Robinson refers merely to the incidental pains of watching a daughter grow up, or perhaps she had read a fictionalized account of Sappho's life that included comments on a possible tragic end for Cleis.
XXII. Phaon forsakes her
[1] *livid* furiously angry.
XXIII. Sappho's conjectures
[1] *To Etna's scorching sands my Phaon flies* an echo of Pope, *Sapho to Phaon* 11: 'Phaon to Etna's scorching fields retires'. "'Arva Phaon celebat diversa Typhoidos Etnae" Ovid' (Robinson's note). The quotation is from *Heroides* xv 11: 'Phaon honours the distant fields of burning Etna' (Ovid, *Epistles* 167).

Has spring for thee a crown of poppies wove,
   Or dost thou languish in th' Idalian grove[2]
Whose altar kindles, fanned by lover's sighs?
   Ah think that, while on Etna's shores you stray,
A fire more fierce than Etna's fills my breast;[3]   10
   Nor deck Sicilian nymphs with garlands gay
While Sappho's brows with cypress wreaths are dressed;
   Let one kind word my weary woes repay,
Or in eternal slumbers bid them rest.

XXIV. HER ADDRESS TO THE MOON

Oh thou, meek orb that, stealing o'er the dale,
   Cheer'st with thy modest beams the noon of night,
   On the smooth lake diffusing silv'ry light,
Sublimely still and beautifully pale!
What can thy cool and placid eye avail   5
   Where fierce despair absorbs the mental sight,
   While inbred[1] glooms the vagrant thoughts invite
To tempt the gulf where howling fiends assail?
   Oh night, all nature owns thy tempered pow'r;
Thy solemn pause, thy dews, thy pensive beam;   10
   Thy sweet breath whisp'ring in the moonlight bow'r,
While fainting flowrets kiss the wand'ring stream!
   Yet vain is ev'ry charm, and vain the hour,
That brings to madd'ning love no soothing dream!

XXV. TO PHAON

Canst thou forget, oh idol of my soul,
   Thy Sappho's voice, her form, her dulcet lyre
   That, melting ev'ry thought to fond desire,
Bade sweet delirium o'er thy senses roll?
Canst thou so soon renounce the blest control   5
   That calmed with pity's tears love's raging fire,
   While Hope, slow breathing on the trembling wire,[1]
In every note with soft persuasion stole?
   Oh sov'reign of my heart, return, return!
For me no spring appears, no summers bloom,   10
   No sunbeams glitter and no altars burn!
The mind's dark winter of eternal gloom
   Shows midst the waste a solitary urn,
A blighted laurel[2] and a mould'ring tomb!

---

[2] *th' Idalian grove* grove near Mt Idalus in Cyprus, sacred to Venus.

[3] "'Me calor Etnaeo non minor igne coquit'" Ovid' (Robinson's note). From *Heroides* xv 12: 'while flames fierce as those of Etna prey upon my heart' (Ovid, *Epistles* 167).

XXIV. HER ADDRESS TO THE MOON
[1] *inbred* deeply ingrained.

XXV. TO PHAON
[1] *wire* string of the lyre.
[2] *laurel* usually a symbol of victory or distinction in poetry.

XXVI. Contemns philosophy

Where antique woods o'erhang the mountain's crest
  And midday glooms in solemn silence lour,
  Philosophy, go seek a lonely bow'r,
And waste life's fervid noon in fancied rest.
Go where the bird of sorrow weaves her nest,   5
  Cooing, in sadness sweet, through night's dim hour;
  Go cull the dewdrops from each potent flow'r
That med'cines to the cold and reas'ning breast!
  Go where the brook in liquid lapse steals by,
Scarce heard amidst the mingling echoes round,   10
  What time the moon fades slowly down the sky,
And slumb'ring zephyrs moan in caverns bound:
  Be these thy pleasures, dull Philosophy,
Nor vaunt[1] the balm to heal a lover's wound.

XXVII. Sappho's address to the stars

Oh ye bright stars that on the ebon[1] fields
  Of heav'n's vast empire trembling seem to stand,
  Till rosy morn unlocks her portal bland
Where the proud sun his fiery banner wields!
To flames less fierce than mine your lustre yields,   5
  And pow'rs more strong my countless tears command;
  Love strikes the feeling heart with ruthless hand,
And only spares the breast which dullness shields!
  Since, then, capricious nature but bestows
The fine affections of the soul to prove   10
  A keener sense of desolating woes,
Far, far from me the empty boast remove;
  If bliss from coldness, pain from passion flows –
Ah, who would wish to feel, or learn to love?

XXVIII. Describes the fascinations of love

Weak is the sophistry and vain the art
  That whispers patience to the mind's despair;
  That bids reflection bathe the wounds of care
While Hope, with pleasing phantoms, soothes their smart!
For mem'ry still, reluctant to depart   5
  From the dear spot once rich in prospects fair,
  Bids the fond soul enamoured linger there,
And its least charm is grateful to the heart![1]
  He never loved who could not muse and sigh,
Spangling the sacred turf with frequent tears,   10

XXVI. Contemns philosophy
[1] *vaunt* boast.
XXVII. Sappho's address to the stars
[1] *ebon* black.

XXVIII. Describes the fascinations of love
[1] *And its least charm is grateful to the heart* i.e. the heart
is grateful for the least charm which the prospects
possess.

Where the small rivulet that ripples by
Recalls the scenes of past and happier years,
When on its banks he watched the speaking eye,
And one sweet smile o'erpaid an age of fears!

XXIX. DETERMINES TO FOLLOW PHAON

Farewell, ye tow'ring cedars, in whose shade,
  Lulled by the nightingale, I sunk to rest,
  While spicy breezes hovered o'er my breast
To fan my cheek, in deep'ning tints arrayed;
While am'rous insects humming round me played,   5
  Each flow'r forsook, of prouder sweets in quest,
  Of glowing lips in humid fragrance dressed,
That mocked the sunny Hybla's[1] vaunted aid!
Farewell, ye limpid rivers, oh farewell!
  No more shall Sappho to your grots repair;   10
  No more your white waves to her bosom swell,
Or your dank weeds entwine her floating hair,
  As erst when Venus in her sparry cell[2]
Wept to behold a brighter goddess there!

XXX. BIDS FAREWELL TO LESBOS

O'er the tall cliff that bounds the billowy main
  Shad'wing the surge that sweeps the lonely strand,
  While the thin vapours break along the sand,
Day's harbinger[1] unfolds the liquid plain.[2]
The rude sea murmurs, mournful as the strain   5
  That love-lorn minstrels strike with trembling hand,
  While from their green beds rise the siren band[3]
With tongues aërial to repeat my pain!
The vessel rocks beside the pebbly shore,
  The foamy curls its gaudy trappings lave;   10
  Oh bark propitious, bear me gently o'er,
Breathe soft, ye winds; rise slow, oh swelling wave!
  Lesbos, these eyes shall meet thy sands no more;
I fly to seek my lover, or my grave!

XXXI. DESCRIBES HER BARK

Far o'er the waves my lofty bark shall glide,
  Love's frequent sighs the flutt'ring sails shall swell,[1]

XXIX. DETERMINES TO FOLLOW PHAON
[1] Hybla was a mountain near Syracuse, with a town
of the same name at its base.
[2] *sparry cell* cell made out of crystalline minerals.
XXX. BIDS FAREWELL TO LESBOS
[1] *Day's harbinger* the sun.
[2] *the liquid plain* the sea.

[3] *the siren band* two or three sea-nymphs whose sing-
ing was so seductive that all who heard forgot to eat
and died.
XXXI. DESCRIBES HER BARK
[1] Cf. Pope, *Sapho to Phaon* 253: 'Cupid for thee shall
spread the swelling sails'.

While to my native home[2] I bid farewell,
Hope's snowy hand the burnished helm shall guide!
Tritons[3] shall sport amidst the yielding tide,   5
   Myriads of cupids round the prow shall dwell,
   And Venus throned within her opal shell
Shall proudly o'er the glitt'ring billows ride![4]
Young dolphins, dashing in the golden spray,
Shall with their scaly forms illume the deep,   10
   Tinged with the purple flush of sinking day,
   Whose flaming wreath shall crown the distant steep;
   While on the breezy deck soft minstrels play,
And songs of love the lover soothe to sleep!

XXXII. Dreams of a rival

Blessed as the gods, Sicilian maid, is he,[1]
   The youth whose soul thy yielding graces charm;
   Who bound, oh thraldom sweet, by beauty's arm,
In idle dalliance fondly sports with thee!
Blessed as the gods that iv'ry throne to see,   5
   Throbbing with transports, tender, timid, warm,
   While round thy fragrant lips light zephyrs swarm
As op'ning buds attract the wand'ring bee!
   Yet short is youthful passion's fervid hour;
Soon shall another clasp the beauteous boy;   10
   Soon shall a rival prove, in that gay bow'r,
The pleasing torture of excessive joy!
   The bee flies sickened from the sweetest flow'r,
The lightning's shaft but dazzles to destroy!

XXXIII. Reaches Sicily

I wake! Delusive phantoms, hence, away!
   Tempt not the weakness of a lover's breast;
   The softest breeze can shake the halcyon's nest,[1]
And lightest clouds o'ercast the dawning ray!
'Twas but a vision! Now the star of day[2]   5
   Peers like a gem on Etna's burning crest!
   Welcome, ye hills, with golden vintage dressed,
Sicilian forests brown, and vallies gay!
   A mournful stranger from the Lesbian isle,

---

2 *my native home* Mytilene on Lesbos.
3 *Tritons* sea deities, half man, half dolphin.
4 Venus sprang from the foaming remains of Uranus,
scattered in the sea by Chronos, his son.
XXXII. Dreams of a rival
1 'Vide Sappho's Ode' (Robinson's note). This son-
net is an adaptation of Sappho, Φαίνεταί μοι κῆνος

ἴσος θέοισιν, translated by Addison as 'An Ode on a
Young Maid whom she loved'.
XXXIII. Reaches Sicily
1 *the halcyon's nest* the kingfisher was believed by
classical writers to breed in a nest out at sea, and that
it charmed the wind and the waves so that they
would be calm during that period.
2 *the star of day* the sun.

Not strange, in loftiest eulogy of song,   10
   She who could teach the Stoic's cheek to smile,[3]
Thaw the cold heart, and chain the wond'ring throng,
   Can find no balm, love's sorrows to beguile –
Ah, sorrows known too soon, and felt too long!

XXXIV. SAPPHO'S PRAYER TO VENUS

Venus, to thee the Lesbian muse shall sing
   The song which Mytilenian[1] youths admired,
   When Echo, am'rous of the strain inspired,
Bade the wild rocks with madd'ning plaudits ring![2]
Attend my prayer, oh queen of rapture, bring   5
   To these fond arms he whom my soul has fired –
   From these fond arms removed, yet still desired,
Though love exulting spreads his varying wing!
   Oh source of ev'ry joy, of ev'ry care,
Blessed Venus, goddess of the zone divine,[3]   10
   To Phaon's bosom Phaon's victim bear;
So shall her warmest, tend'rest vows be thine!
   For Venus, Sappho shall a wreath prepare,
And Love be crowned, immortal as the Nine![4]

XXXV. REPROACHES PHAON

What means the mist opaque that veils these eyes?
   Why does yon threat'ning tempest shroud the day?
   Why does thy altar, Venus, fade away,
And on my breast the dews of horror rise?
Phaon is false! Be dim, ye orient skies,   5
   And let black Erebus[1] succeed your ray;
   Let clashing thunders roll, and lightnings play –
Phaon is false, and hopeless Sappho dies!
   'Farewell, my Lesbian love', you might have said
(Such sweet remembrance had some pity proved),   10
   Or coldly thus: 'Farewell, oh Lesbian maid!'[2] –

---

[3] Robinson presumably took the line that Stoics were not easily moved to laughter.

XXXIV. SAPPHO'S PRAYER TO VENUS

[1] *Mytilenian* from Mytilene, Sappho's home city, on Lesbos.

[2] Echo's unrequited love for Narcissus persisted after death, when she survived as a voice.

[3] *the zone divine* Venus' power was enhanced by a magic belt (or zone), which inspired love even when worn by the most deformed.

[4] *Nine* the Muses.

XXXV. REPROACHES PHAON

[1] *Erebus* the god Erebus (darkness) married Night to produce Day and Upper Light (ether).

[2] 'Pope' (Robinson's note). Robinson acknowledges the fact that ll.9–11 are borrowed from Pope, *Sapho to Phaon* 113–14:

> 'Farewell my Lesbian love!' you might have said,
> Or coldly thus, 'Farewell oh Lesbian maid!'

She adds a further note: "'Si tam certus eras hinc ire, modestius isses, / Et modo dixesses Lesbi puella, vale" Ovid'. From *Heroides* xv 99–100: 'If you were determined to abandon me, it might yet have been done in a kinder way. Was it too much to say, "Farewell, my Lesbian maid"?' (Ovid, *Epistles* 173).

No task severe, for one so fondly loved!
The gentle thought had soothed my wand'ring shade,
From life's dark valley and its thorns removed!

XXXVI. HER CONFIRMED DESPAIR

Lead me, Sicilian maids, to haunted bow'rs,
   While yon pale moon displays her faintest beams
   O'er blasted woodlands and enchanted streams
Whose banks infect the breeze with pois'nous flow'rs;
Ah, lead me where the barren mountain tow'rs,   5
   Where no sounds echo but the night-owl's screams,
   Where some lone spirit of the desert gleams,
And lurid horrors wing the fateful hours!
   Now goaded frenzy grasps my shrinking brain,
Her touch absorbs the crystal fount of woe!   10
   My blood rolls burning through each gasping vein –
Away, lost lyre, unless thou canst bestow
   A charm to lull that agonizing pain
Which those who never loved can never know!

XXXVII. FORESEES HER DEATH

When, in the gloomy mansion of the dead,
   This with'ring heart, this faded form shall sleep;
   When these fond eyes at length shall cease to weep,
And earth's cold lap receive this fev'rish head;
Envy shall turn away, a tear to shed,   5
   And time's obliterating pinions sweep
   The spot where poets shall their vigils keep,
To mourn and wander near my freezing bed!
   Then my pale ghost upon th' Elysian shore[1]
Shall smile, released from ev'ry mortal care;   10
   While, doomed love's victim to repine[2] no more,
My breast shall bathe in endless rapture there!
   Ah no, my restless shade would still deplore,
Nor taste that bliss, which Phaon did not share!

XXXVIII. TO A SIGH

Oh sigh, thou steal'st, the herald of the breast,
   The lover's fears, the lover's pangs to tell;
   Thou bidd'st with timid grace the bosom swell,
Cheating the day of joy, the night of rest!
Oh lucid tears, with eloquence confessed,   5
   Why on my fading cheek unheeded dwell,

XXXVII. FORESEES HER DEATH
[1] Elysium is the idyllic world where the souls of those honoured by the gods spend their afterlives.

[2] *repine* complain.

Meek as the dewdrops on the flowret's bell
By ruthless tempests to the green sod pressed?
   Fond sigh be hushed; congeal, oh slighted tear!
Thy feeble pow'rs the busy Fates[1] control!   10
   Or if thy crystal streams again appear,
Let them, like Lethe's,[2] to oblivion roll;
   For Love the tyrant plays when hope is near,
And she who flies the lover, chains the soul!

XXXIX. TO THE MUSES

Prepare your wreaths, Aonian[1] maids divine,
   To strew the tranquil bed where I shall sleep;
   In tears, the myrtle and the laurel steep,
And let Erato's[2] hand the trophies twine.
No Parian marble[3] there, with laboured line   5
   Shall bid the wand'ring lover stay to weep;
   There holy silence shall her vigils keep
Save when the nightingale such woes as mine
   Shall sadly sing; as twilight's curtains spread,
There shall the branching lotus[4] widely wave,   10
   Sprinkling soft show'rs upon the lily's[5] head,
Sweet drooping emblem for a lover's grave!
   And there shall Phaon pearls of pity[6] shed
To gem the vanquished heart he scorned to save!

XL. VISIONS APPEAR TO HER IN A DREAM

On the low margin of a murm'ring stream,
   As rapt[1] in meditation's arms I lay,
   Each aching sense in slumbers stole away
While potent fancy formed a soothing dream;
O'er the Leucadian[2] deep a dazzling beam   5
   Shed the bland light of empyrean[3] day!
   But soon transparent shadows veiled each ray,
While mystic visions sprang athwart the gleam!

XXXVIII. TO A SIGH
[1] *Fates* The three sisters wove man's destiny and cut the thread of life at the moment of death.
[2] *Lethe* the river of forgetfulness in Hades, where souls drank and forgot their past existence.
XXXIX. TO THE MUSES
[1] Aonia was the seat of the Muses.
[2] Erato was the muse of lyric and love poetry, crowned with roses and myrtle.
[3] *Parian marble* Paros, one of the Cyclades islands between Greece and Turkey, was the home of some particularly fine marble.
[4] *lotus* In Homer's *Odyssey*, the lotus induces a state of dreamy forgetfulness and a loss of desire to return home.

[5] The lily is symbolic of purity.
[6] *pearls of pity* tears.
XL. VISIONS APPEAR TO HER IN A DREAM
[1] *rapt* entranced, enraptured.
[2] Leucadia is one of the Ionian islands off the west coast of Greece. It terminates in a promontory 2000 feet high, from which lovers who threw themselves into the sea were believed to be able to cure their infatuations.
[3] *empyrean* the highest heaven, residence of God and the angels; Mary presumably means that it is noon, which is 'bland' in the sense of 'soothing', 'restful'.

Now to the heaving gulf they seemed to bend,
And now across the sphery regions[4] glide; 10
  Now in mid air their dulcet voices blend,
'Awake, awake!' the restless phalanx cried,
  'See ocean yawns the lover's woes to end,
Plunge[5] the green wave, and bid thy griefs subside!'

XLI. RESOLVES TO TAKE THE LEAP OF LEUCATA

Yes, I will go where circling whirlwinds rise,
  Where threat'ning clouds in sable grandeur lour,
  Where the blast yells, the liquid columns pour,
And madd'ning billows combat with the skies!
There while the daemon of the tempest flies 5
  On growing pinions through the troublous[1] hour,
  The wild waves gasp impatient to devour,
And on the rock the wakened vulture cries!
  Oh dreadful solace to the stormy mind,
To me more pleasing than the valley's rest, 10
  The woodland songsters, or the sportive kind[2]
That nip the turf or prune the painted crest;
  For in despair alone the wretched find
That unction[3] sweet which lulls the bleeding breast!

XLII. HER LAST APPEAL TO PHAON

Oh canst thou bear to see this faded frame
Deformed and mangled by the rocky deep?
  Wilt thou remember, and forbear to weep
My fatal fondness, and my peerless fame?
Soon o'er this heart, now warm with passion's flame, 5
  The howling winds and foamy waves shall sweep;
  Those eyes be ever closed in death's cold sleep
And all of Sappho perish, but her name!
  Yet if the Fates suspend their barb'rous ire,
If days less mournful Heav'n designs for me, 10
  If rocks grow kind, and winds and waves conspire
To bear me softly on the swelling sea,
  To Phoebus only will I tune my lyre –
'What suits with Sappho, Phoebus, suits with thee!'[1]

---

[4] *the sphery regions* the sky.
[5] *Plunge* plunge into.
XLI. RESOLVES TO TAKE THE LEAP OF LEUCATA
[1] *troublous* disturbed.
[2] *the sportive kind* of bird.
[3] *unction* soothing influence.

XLII. HER LAST APPEAL TO PHAON
[1] 'Pope. "Grata lyram posui tibi Phoebe, poetria Sappho: / Convenit illa mihi, convenit illa tibi". Ovid' (Robinson's note). From *Heroides* xv 183–4: 'Grateful Sappho consecrates her harp to Phoebus, a gift that agrees both to the giver and the god' (Ovid, *Epistles* 179). As Mary acknowledges in her note, l. 14 is borrowed from Pope, *Sapho to Phaon* 216.

XLIII. Her reflections on the Leucadian rock before she perishes

While from the dizzy precipice I gaze,
    The world receding from my pensive eyes,
    High o'er my head the tyrant eagle flies,
Clothed in the sinking sun's transcendent blaze!
The meek-eyed moon midst clouds of amber plays   5
    As o'er the purpling plains of light[1] she hies,
    Till the last stream of living lustre dies
And the cool concave[2] owns her tempered[3] rays!
    So shall this glowing, palpitating soul
Welcome returning Reason's placid beam,   10
    While o'er my breast the waves Lethean[4] roll
To calm rebellious Fancy's fev'rish dream;
    Then shall my lyre disdain love's dread control,
And loftier passions prompt the loftier theme!

XLIV. Sonnet conclusive

Here droops the muse, while from her glowing mind
    Celestial Sympathy with humid[1] eye
    Bids the light sylph capricious Fancy fly,
Time's restless wings with transient flow'rs to bind!
For now with folded arms and head inclined,   5
    Reflection pours the deep and frequent sigh
    O'er the dark scoll of human destiny,
Where gaudy buds and wounding thorns are twined.
    Oh sky-born Virtue, sacred is thy name!
And though mysterious Fate with frown severe   10
    Oft decorates thy brows with wreaths of fame
Bespangled o'er with sorrow's chilling tear,
    Yet shalt thou more than mortal raptures claim –
The brightest planet of th' eternal sphere!

From Walsingham; or, the Pupil of Nature (1797)

Lines addressed by a young lady of fashion to a small green fly, which had pitched[1] on the left ear of Lady Amaranth's little white barbet,[2] Fidelio, on a summer evening, after a shower, near sunset

Little, barb'rous, cruel fly!
Tell me, tell me, tell me why

XLIII. Her reflections on the Leucadian rock
before she perishes
[1] *the purpling plains of light* as the sun sets.
[2] *concave* sky.
[3] *tempered* subdued, diminished.
[4] *Lethean* Lethe was the river of forgetfulness in
Hades, which souls drank from in order to forget
their past existence.

XLIV. Sonnet conclusive
[1] *humid* tearful.
Lines addressed by a young lady of fashion to
a small green fly . . .
[1] *pitched* settled.
[2] *barbet* poodle.

You to poor Fidelio bring,
To vex his ear, *so keen* a sting?
Little, barb'rous, cruel fly,   5
Haste away, or you must *die*!

'Soft!' I hear Fidelio say,
'Do not send the fly away;
Let him hover round and round,
Let him, let him, let him *wound*,   10
Lest the little rogue should sip
Honey from my lady's lip!'[3]

A THOUSAND TORMENTS WAIT ON LOVE

A thousand torments wait on love –
    The sigh, the tear, the anguished groan;
But he who never learnt to prove
    A jealous pang has nothing known!

For jealousy, supreme of woe,   5
    Nursed by distorted fancy's pow'r,
Can round the heart bid mis'ry grow,
    Which darkens with the ling'ring hour,

While shadows, blanks to reason's orb,[1]
    In dread succession haunt the brain,   10
And pangs, that ev'ry pang absorb,
    In wild, convulsive tumults reign.

At morn, at eve, the fever burns,
    While phantoms tear the aching breast;
Day brings no calm, and night returns   15
    To mark no soothing hour of rest.

Nor, when the bosom's wasted fires
    Are all extinct, is anguish o'er;
For *jealousy*, that ne'er expires,
    Still wounds, when *passion* lives no more.   20

From The Poetical Works of the Late Mrs Robinson (1806)

THE PROGRESS OF LIBERTY (COMPOSED 1798)

Conclusion to Book I

Superstition, more destructive still   725
Than plague or famine, tyranny or war!

---

[3] Robinson's text continues ironically: 'This extra-
ordinary effort of exalted genius was received by the
noble auditors with enthusiastic wonder and applause,
while every individual solicited to have a copy'.

A THOUSAND TORMENTS WAIT ON LOVE
[1] *orb* eye.

Thou palsying mischief, thou benumbing foe
To all the proudest energies of man!
Whence springs thy subtle desolating charm?
From pompous pageantry and bigot pride, 730
From mitred canopies and shrines of gold,
And bones of mould'ring monks? Can freezing nights
In cells where cold inanity[1] presides,
Clothed in religion's meek and sainted guise,
Or long-drawn pageantry of empty show, 735
Conceal the trembling soul from that dread pow'r
Which marks th' all-seeing? On Italia's shores,
On every plain, on ev'ry mountain-top,
The voice of nature speaks in mighty sounds
To bid thee tremble! Then, oh nature, say, 740
Shall rich Italia's bow'rs, her citron[2] shades,
Her vales prolific, mountains golden-clad,
And rivers fringed with nectar-teeming groves,
Re-echo with the mighty song of praise
To empyrean[3] space, while shackled still 745
The man of colour dies? Shall torrid suns
Shoot downward their hot beams on mis'ry's race,
And call forth luxuries to pamper pride,
Steeped in the Ethiop's tears, the Ethiop's blood?
Shall the caprice of nature, the deep tint 750
Of sultry climes, the feature varying,
Or the uncultured mind, endure the scourge
Of sordid tyranny, or heap the stores
Of his fair fellow man, whose ruddy cheek
Knows not the tear of pity; whose white breast 755
Conceals a heart than adamant more hard,
More cruel than the tiger's? Bend thy gaze,
Oh happy offspring of a tempered[4] clime,
On whom the partial[5] hand of nature set
The stamp of bloomy tints, proportions fine, 760
Unmixing with the goodly outside show
The mind appropriate; bend thy pitying gaze
To Zembla's[6] frozen sphere where, in his hut,
Roofed by the rocky steep, the savage smiles,
In conscious freedom smiles, and mocks the storm 765
That howls along the sky. Th' unshackled limb,
Clothed in the shaggy hide of uncouth bear,
Or the fleet mountain elk, bounds o'er the cliff,
The free-born tenant of the desert wild.

THE PROGRESS OF LIBERTY
[1] *inanity* hollowness.
[2] *citron* a kind of citrus fruit.
[3] *empyrean* the highest heaven.

[4] *tempered* moderate, temperate.
[5] *partial* kindly, well-disposed.
[6] *Zembla* Nova Zembla, islands in the Arctic Ocean, north of Archangel in Russia.

The glow of liberty through ev'ry vein 770
Bids sensate streams revolve; the dusky path
Of midnight solitudes no terror brings,
Because he fears no lord. The prowling wolf,
Whose eyeballs redden midst the world of gloom,
Yells fierce defiance, formed by nature's law 775
To share the desert's freedom. O'er the sky
The despot darkness reigns in sullen pride
Half the devoted year. His ebon[7] wing
O'ershadows the blank space; his chilling breath
Benumbs the breast of nature; on his brow, 780
Myriads of stars with lucid lustre gem
His boundless diadem! The savage cheek
Smiles at the potent spoiler, braves his frown;
And while the partial gloom is most opaque,
Still vaunts the mind unfettered! If for these 785
Indulgent nature breaks the bonds of woe,
Gilding the deepest solitudes of night
With the pure flame of liberty sublime;
If for the untaught sons of gelid[8] climes,
Health cheers the darkest hour with vig'rous age,[9] 790
Shall the poor African, the passive slave,
Born in the bland effulgence of broad day,
Cherished by torrid splendours, while around
The plains prolific teem with honeyed stores
Of Afric's burning soil – shall such a wretch 795
Sink prematurely to a grave obscure,
No tear to grace his ashes? Or suspire[10]
To wear submission's long and goading chain,
To drink the tear that down his swarthy cheek
Flows fast, to moisten his toil-fevered lip, 800
Parched by the noontide blaze? Shall he endure
The frequent lash, the agonizing scourge,
The day of labour, and the night of pain;
Expose his naked limbs to burning gales;
Faint in the sun, and wither in the storm; 805
Traverse hot sands, imbibe the morbid breeze
Winged with contagion, while his blistered feet,
Scorched by the vertical and raging beam,
Pour the swift life-stream[11]? Shall his frenzied eyes
(Oh worst of mortal miseries!) behold 810
The darling of his soul, his sable love,

---

[7] *ebon* black.
[8] *gelid* freezing.
[9] 'Buffon, speaking of the inhabitants of Nova Zembla, says, "they are seldom or never sick, and all arrive at extreme old age. Even the old men are so vigorous that it is difficult to distinguish them from the young"' (Robinson's note). Robinson has in mind Georges Louis Le Clerc, comte de Buffon, whose *Histoire Naturelle, générale et particuliere* ran to 38 volumes (1749–1804).
[10] *suspire* breathe – hence live, exist.
[11] *life-stream* blood.

Selected from the trembling, timid throng
By the wan tyrant, whose licentious touch
Seals the dark fiat[12] of the slave's despair?
Humanity, from thee the suppliant claims   815
The meed[13] of retribution! Thy pure flame
Would light the sense opaque, and warm the spring
Of boundless ecstasy, while nature's laws
So violated, plead, immortal-tongued,
For her dark-fated children; lead them forth   820
From bondage infamous! Bid reason own
The dignities of man whate'er his clime,
Estate, or colour. And, oh sacred truth!
Tell the proud lords of traffic that the breast,
Thrice ebon-tinted, bears a crimson tide   825
As pure, as clear, as Europe's sons can boast.
Then, liberty, extend thy thund'ring voice
To Afric's scorching climes, o'er seas that bound
To bear the blissful tidings, while all earth
Shall hail humanity – the child of Heav'n!   830

From Lyrical Tales (1800)

THE HAUNTED BEACH[1]

Upon a lonely desert beach
    Where the white foam was scattered,
A little shed upreared its head,
    Though lofty barks were shattered.
The seaweeds gath'ring near the door   5
    A sombre path displayed,
And all around, the deaf'ning roar
Re-echoed on the chalky shore,
    By the green billows made.

Above, a jutting cliff was seen   10
    Where seabirds hovered, craving,
And all around the crags were bound
    With weeds, forever waving;
And here and there, a cavern wide
    Its shad'wy jaws displayed,   15
And near the sands, at ebb of tide,
A shivered mast was seen to ride
    Where the green billows strayed.

---

[12] *fiat* decree.
[13] *meed* reward.

THE HAUNTED BEACH
[1] Robinson's biographer relates the story of how this poem came to be written, headnote, p. 182, above.

And often, while the moaning wind
   Stole o'er the summer ocean,   20
The moonlight scene was all serene,
   The waters scarce in motion;
Then while the smoothly slanting sand
   The tall cliff wrapped in shade,
The fisherman beheld a band   25
Of spectres gliding hand in hand,
   Where the green billows played.

And pale their faces were as snow,
   And sullenly they wandered;
And to the skies, with hollow eyes,   30
   They looked, as though they pondered.
And sometimes from their hammock shroud
   They dismal howlings made;
And while the blast blew strong and loud
The clear moon marked the ghastly crowd   35
   Where the green billows played.

And then above the haunted hut,
   The curlews, screaming, hovered;
And the low door, with furious roar,
   The frothy breakers covered.   40
For in the fisherman's lone shed
   A murdered man was laid,
With ten wide gashes on his head;
And deep was made his sandy bed
   Where the green billows played.   45

A shipwrecked mariner was he,
   Doomed from his home to sever,
Who swore to be, through wind and sea,
   Firm and undaunted ever;
And when the wave resistless rolled,   50
   About his arm he made
A packet rich of Spanish gold,
And, like a British sailor bold,
   Plunged where the billows played.

The spectre band, his messmates brave,   55
   Sunk in the yawning ocean,
While to the mast he lashed him fast
   And braved the storm's commotion.
The winter moon upon the sand
   A silv'ry carpet[2] made,   60

---

[2] *silv'ry carpet* For Coleridge's admiring comment on
this phrase, see headnote, p. 182, above.

And marked the sailor reach the land,
And marked his murd'rer wash his hand,
   Where the green billows played.

And since that hour the fisherman
   Has toiled and toiled in vain;   65
For all the night, the moony light
   Gleams on the spectred main.
And when the skies are veiled in gloom,
   The murd'rer's liquid way
Bounds o'er the deeply yawning tomb,   70
And flashing fires the sands illume
   Where the green billows play.

Full thirty years his task has been,
   Day after day more weary;
For Heaven designed his guilty mind   75
   Should feed on prospects dreary.
Bound by a strong and mystic chain,
   He has not pow'r to stray,
But destined mis'ry to sustain,
He wastes, in solitude and pain,   80
   A loathsome life away.

THE NEGRO GIRL

I
Dark was the dawn, and o'er the deep
   The boist'rous whirlwinds blew;
The seabird wheeled its circling sweep,
   And all was drear to view,
When on the beach that binds the western shore   5
The love-lorn Zelma stood, list'ning the tempest's roar.

II
Her eager eyes beheld the main,
   While on her Draco dear
She madly called, but called in vain –
   No sound could Draco hear   10
Save the shrill yelling of the fateful blast,
While ev'ry seaman's heart quick shuddered as it past.

III
White were the billows, wide displayed,
   The clouds were black and low;
The bittern shrieked, a gliding shade   15
   Seemed o'er the waves to go!
The livid flash illumed the clam'rous main
While Zelma poured, unmarked, her melancholy strain.

IV

'Be still!' she cried, 'Loud tempest cease!
   Oh spare the gallant souls!   20
The thunder rolls, the winds increase,
   The sea like mountains rolls,
While from the deck the storm-worn victims leap,
And o'er their struggling limbs the furious billows sweep.

V

'Oh barb'rous pow'r, relentless fate!   25
   Does Heaven's high will decree
That some should sleep on beds of state,
   Some in the roaring sea?
Some nursed in splendour deal Oppression's blow,
While Worth and Draco pine in slavery and woe.   30

VI

'Yon vessel oft has ploughed the main
   With human traffic fraught;
Its cargo, our dark sons of pain,
   For worldly treasure bought!
What had they done? Oh Nature tell me why   35
Is taunting scorn the lot of thy dark progeny?

VII

'Thou gav'st, in thy caprice, the soul
   Peculiarly enshrined;
Nor from the ebon[3] casket stole
   The jewel of the mind!   40
Then wherefore let the suff'ring negro's breast
Bow to his fellow man in brighter colours dressed.

VIII

'Is it the dim and glossy hue
   That marks him for despair,
While men with blood their hands embrue,[4]   45
   And mock the wretch's prayer?
Shall guiltless slaves the scourge of tyrants feel,
And, e'en before their God, unheard, unpitied kneel?

IX

'Could the proud rulers of the land
   Our sable race behold,   50
Some bowed by torture's giant hand
   And others basely sold,
Then would they pity slaves, and cry with shame,
"Whate'er their tints may be, their souls are still the same!"

---

[3] *ebon* black.   [4] *embrue* stain.

X

'Why seek to mock the Ethiop's face?   55
   Why goad our hapless kind?
Can features alienate the race?
   Is there no kindred mind?
Does not the cheek which vaunts the roseate hue
Oft blush for crimes that Ethiops never knew?   60

XI

'Behold, the angry waves conspire
   To check the barb'rous toil!
While wounded Nature's vengeful ire
   Roars round this trembling isle!
And hark, her voice re-echoes in the wind –   65
Man was not formed by Heav'n to trample on his kind!

XII

'Torn from my mother's aching breast,
   My tyrant sought my love,
But in the grave shall Zelma rest
   Ere she will faithless prove;   70
No, Draco, thy companion I will be
To that celestial realm where negroes shall be free!

XIII

'The tyrant white man taught my mind
   The lettered page to trace;
He taught me in the soul to find   75
   No tint, as in the face;
He bade my reason blossom like the tree,
But fond affection gave the ripened fruits to thee.

XIV

'With jealous rage he marked my love,
   He sent thee far away,   80
And prisoned in the plaintain grove
   Poor Zelma passed the day;
But ere the moon rose high above the main
Zelma and love contrived to break the tyrant's chain.

XV

'Swift o'er the plain of burning sand   85
   My course I bent to thee;
And soon I reached the billowy strand
   Which bounds the stormy sea.
Draco, my love! Oh yet thy Zelma's soul
Springs ardently to thee, impatient of control!   90

XVI

'Again the lightning flashes white
  The rattling cords among!
Now by the transient vivid light
  I mark the frantic throng!
Now up the tattered shrouds my Draco flies,   95
While o'er the plunging prow the curling billows rise.

XVII

'The topmast falls! Three shackled slaves
  Cling to the vessel's side!
Now lost amid the madd'ning waves,
  Now on the mast they ride –   100
See, on the forecastle my Draco stands!
And now he waves his chain, now clasps his bleeding hands.

XVIII

'Why, cruel white-man, when away
  My sable love was torn,
Why did you let poor Zelma stay   105
  On Afric's sands to mourn?
No! Zelma is not left, for she will prove
In the deep troubled main her fond, her faithful love!'

XIX

The lab'ring ship was now a wreck,
  The shrouds were flutt'ring wide;   110
The rudder gone, the lofty deck
  Was rocked from side to side;
Poor Zelma's eyes now dropped their last big tear,
While from her tawny cheek the blood recoiled with fear.

XX

Now frantic on the sands she roamed,   115
  Now shrieking stopped to view
Where high the liquid mountains foamed
  Around the exhausted crew,
Till from the deck, her Draco's well-known form
Sprung mid the yawning waves, and buffetted the storm.   120

XXI

Long on the swelling surge sustained,
  Brave Draco sought the shore,
Watched the dark maid, but ne'er complained –
  Then sunk, to gaze no more!
Poor Zelma saw him buried by the wave,   125
And, with her heart's true love, plunged in a wat'ry grave.

From The Wild Wreath ed. Mary Elizabeth Robinson (1804)

THE POET'S GARRET (COMPOSED 1800)

Come, sportive fancy, come with me and trace
The poet's attic home, the lofty seat
Of th' Heaven-tutored Nine,[1] the airy throne
Of bold imagination, rapture-fraught
Above the herd of mortals! All around,   5
A solemn stillness seems to guard the scene,
Nursing the brood of thought – a thriving brood
In the rich mazes of the cultured brain.
Upon thy altar, an old worm-eat board,
The panel of a broken door, or lid
Of a strong coffer, placed on three-legged stool,   10
Stand quires of paper, white and beautiful –
Paper by destiny ordained to be
Scrawled o'er and blotted, dashed and scratched and torn,
Or marked with lines severe, or scattered wide
In rage impetuous! Sonnet, song, and ode,   15
Satire and epigram, and smart charade;[2]
Neat paragraph or legendary tale
Of short and simple metre – each by turns
Will there delight the reader.
                              On the bed
Lies an old rusty[3] 'suit of solemn black',   20
Brushed threadbare and, with brown unglossy hue,
Grown rather ancient. On the floor is seen
A pair of silken hose,[4] whose footing bad
Shows they are travellers, but who still bear
Marks somewhat *holy*.[5] At the scanty fire   25
A chop. turns round, by packthread[6] strongly held;
And on the blackened bar a vessel shines
Of battered pewter, just half filled, and warm
With Whitbread's beverage pure.[7] The kitten purrs,
Anticipating dinner, while the wind   30
Whistles through broken panes, and drifted snow
Carpets the parapet with spotless garb
Of vestal[8] coldness. Now the sullen hour
(The fifth hour after noon) with dusky hand
Closes the lids of day. The farthing[9] light   35

THE POET'S GARRET
[1] *Nine* the muses.
[2] *charade* riddle in which each syllable of the answer
must be guessed.
[3] *rusty* shabby, worn.
[4] *hose* stockings.
[5] *holy* Robinson's italics are no doubt intended to
indicate the pun.

[6] *packthread* twine for securing boxes.
[7] *Whitbread's beverage pure* bitter. Samuel Whitbread
the elder (d. 1796) entered a London brewery as a
clerk and ended up as its proprietor.
[8] *vestal* chaste, pure.
[9] *farthing* small amount of.

Gleams through the cobwebbed chamber, and the bard
Concludes his pen's hard labour. Now he eats
With appetite voracious nothing sad
That the costly plate, nor the napkin fine,
Nor china rich, nor sav'ry viands greet   40
His eye or palate. On his lyric board
A sheet of paper serves for tablecloth;
A heap of salt is served (oh heav'nly treat!)
On Ode Pindaric, while his tuneful puss
Scratches his slipper for her fragment sweet   45
And sings her love-song soft, yet mournfully.
   Mocking the pillar Doric, or the roof
Of architecture Gothic, all around
The well-known ballads flit of Grub Street fame!
The casement broke gives breath celestial   50
To the long dying-speech, or gently fans
The love-inflaming sonnet. Round about
Small scraps of paper lie, torn vestiges
Of an unquiet fancy: here a page
Of flights poetic; here a dedication,   55
A list of *dramatis personae* bold,
Of heroes yet unborn and lofty dames
Of perishable compound, 'light as air',
But sentenced to oblivion!
                     On a shelf
Yclept a mantlepiece, a phial stands,   60
Half-filled with potent spirits, clear and strong,
Which sometimes haunt the poet's restless brain,
And fill his mind with fancies whimsical.
   Poor poet! Happy art thou, thus removed
From pride and folly! For in thy domain   65
Thou canst command thy subjects, fill thy lines
With the all-conqu'ring weapon Heav'n bestows
In the grey goose's wing which, tow'ring high,
Bears thy rich fancy to immortal fame!

From The Poetical Works of the Late Mrs Robinson (1806)

ODE INSCRIBED TO THE INFANT SON OF S. T. COLERIDGE, ESQ. BORN 14 SEPTEMBER 1800 AT KESWICK IN CUMBERLAND.[1]

Spirit of Light, whose eye unfolds
The vast expanse of Nature's plan;

ODE INSCRIBED TO THE INFANT SON OF S. T. COLERIDGE
[1] Derwent Coleridge (1800–83) was the second son of the poet, and would grow up to be a distinguished schoolteacher, the first Principal of St Mark's College, Chelsea, and, after the death of his sister Sara, one of the foremost editors of his father's works. He is the subject of Raymonde and Godfrey Hainton, *The Unknown Coleridge* (1997). His father had befriended Mary in London during the winter of 1799–1800, when he had read her *Kubla Khan*. This had inspired her poem, *Mrs Robinson to the Poet Coleridge* (*Romanticism* 117–19).

And from thy eastern throne[2] beholds
    The mazy paths of the lorn[3] traveller – man!
To thee I sing, Spirit of Light, to thee   5
Attune the varying strain of wood-wild minstrelsy!

Oh pow'r creative, but for thee
    Eternal chaos all things would enfold,
And black as Erebus[4] this system be,
    In its ethereal space, benighted, rolled.   10
But for thy influence, e'en *this day*
Would slowly, sadly, pass away;
Nor proudly mark the mother's tear of joy,
The smile seraphic of the baby boy,
The father's eyes, in fondest transport taught   15
To beam with tender hope, to speak the enraptured thought.

To thee I sing, Spirit of Light, to thee
Attune the strain of wood-wild minstrelsy.
Thou sail'st o'er Skiddaw's[5] heights sublime,
Swift borne upon the wings of joyous time!   20
The sunny train, with widening sweep,
Rolls blazing down the misty-mantled steep;
And far and wide its rosy ray
Flushes the dewy-silvered breast of day!
Hope-fost'ring day, which Nature bade impart   25
Heav'n's proudest rapture to the parent's heart.
Day! First ordained to see the baby pressed
Close to its beauteous mother's throbbing breast,
While instinct, in its laughing eyes, foretold
The mind susceptible, the spirit bold,   30
The lofty soul, the virtues prompt to trace
The wrongs that haunt mankind o'er life's tempestuous space.

Romantic mountains, from whose brows sublime
    Imagination might to frenzy turn,
Or to the starry worlds in fancy climb,   35
    Scorning this low earth's solitary bourn;[6]
Bold cataracts, on whose headlong tide
The midnight whirlwinds howling ride;
Calm-bosomed lakes that, trembling, hail
The cold breath of the morning gale,   40
And on your lucid mirrors wide display,

---

[2] *eastern throne* the sun rises in the east.
[3] *lorn* lonely, desolate.
[4] *Erebus* son of Chaos, associated with absolute darkness.
[5] *Skiddaw* oldest and fourth highest peak in the Lake District (3,053 ft). Robinson never saw the Lakes, and is dependent in this poem on Coleridge's descriptions.

She had written to him, at around the time she composed this poem: 'Oh Skiddaw! I think, if I could but once contemplate thy summit, I should never quit the prospect it would present till my eyes were closed for ever' (Griggs ii 669).
[6] *bourn* limit, boundary.

In colours rich, in dewy lustre gay;
Mountains and woodlands, as the dappled dawn
Flings its soft pearl-drops on the summer lawn;
Or paly moonlight, rising slow,   45
While o'er the hills the ev'ning zephyrs blow –
Ye all shall lend your wonders, all combine
To bless the baby boy with harmonies divine.

Oh baby, when thy unchained tongue
    Shall, lisping, speak thy fond surprise;   50
When the rich strain thy father sung
    Shall from thy imitative accents rise;
When through thy soul rapt[7] Fancy shall diffuse
The mightier magic of his loftier muse –
Thy wakened spirit, wond'ring, shall behold   55
Thy native mountains capped with streamy gold,
Thy native lakes, their cloud-topped hills among,
Oh hills made sacred by thy parent's song![8]
Then shall thy soul, legitimate,[9] expand,
And the proud lyre quick throb at thy command!   60
And Wisdom, ever watchful, o'er thee smile,
His white locks waving to the blast the while;
And pensive Reason, pointing to the sky,
Bright as the morning star her clear broad eye,
Unfold the page of Nature's book sublime –   65
The lore of ev'ry age, the boast of ev'ry clime!

Sweet baby boy, accept a stranger's song;
    An untaught minstrel joys to sing of thee!
And, all alone, her forest haunts among,
    Courts the wild tone of mazy harmony!   70
A stranger's song, babe of the mountain wild,
Greets thee as Inspiration's darling child!
Oh may the fine-wrought spirit of thy sire
Awake thy soul and breathe upon thy lyre!
And blessed, amid thy mountain haunts sublime,   75
    Be all thy days, thy rosy infant days,
And may the never-tiring steps of time
    Press lightly on with thee o'er life's disastrous maze.

Ye hills, coeval[10] with the birth of time!
    Bleak summits, linked in chains of rosy light!   80
    Oh may your wonders many a year invite
Your native son the breezy path to climb
Where, in majestic pride of solitude,

---

[7] *rapt* enraptured.
[8] *thy parent's song* probably a reference to *Frost at*
Midnight 59–63.

[9] *legitimate* genuine, intense.
[10] *coeval* the same age as; as old as.

Silent and grand, the hermit thought shall trace,
Far o'er the wild infinity of space,   85
The sombre horrors of the waving wood;
The misty glen; the river's winding way;
The last deep blush of summer's ling'ring day;
The winter storm that, roaming unconfined,
Sails on the broad wings of the impetuous wind.   90

Oh, whether on the breezy height
Where Skiddaw greets the dawn of light,
Ere the rude sons of labour homage pay
To summer's flaming eye or winter's banner grey;
Whether Lodore[11] its silver torrent flings   95
The mingling wonders of a thousand springs;
Whether smooth Bassenthwaite,[12] at eve's still hour,
    Reflects the young moon's crescent pale,
Or meditation seeks her silent bow'r
    Amid the rocks of lonely Borrowdale[13] –   100
Still may thy name survive, sweet boy, till Time
Shall bend to Keswick's vale thy Skiddaw's brow sublime!

THE SAVAGE OF AVEYRON (COMPOSED OCTOBER 1800)[1]

'Twas in the mazes of a wood,
The lonely wood of Aveyron,
I heard a melancholy tone:
    It seemed to freeze my blood!
A torrent near was flowing fast,   5
And hollow was the midnight blast
As o'er the leafless woods it passed
    While terror-fraught I stood!
Oh mazy woods of Aveyron,
    Oh wilds of dreary solitude!   10
    Amid thy thorny alleys rude
I thought myself alone!
    I thought no living thing could be
    So weary of the world as me,
While on my winding path the pale moon shone.   15

---

[11] *Lodore* large waterfall on the banks of Derwentwater, near Keswick.
[12] *Bassenthwaite* large lake, at one end of which is Keswick.
[13] *Borrowdale* the valley at the opposite end of Derwentwater from Keswick. The most famous description of it is probably that by Ann Radcliffe, *Romanticism* 156.
THE SAVAGE OF AVEYRON
[1] Judith Pascoe points out that this poem was probably inspired by reports in the *Morning Post* of the wild boy of Arveyron: 'He lived on potatoes, chestnuts, and acorns. . . . His features are regular, but without expression; every part of his body is covered with scars; these scars attest the cruelty of the persons by whom, it is presumed, he has been abandoned; or perhaps they are attributable only to the dangers of a solitary existence at a tender age, and in a rude tract of country' (*Morning Post* 3 October 1800; as quoted in Judith Pascoe, 'Mary Robinson and the Literary Marketplace', *RWW* 252–68, p. 266).

Sometimes the tone was loud and sad,
And sometimes dulcet, faint, and slow;
And then a tone of frantic woe:
   It almost made me mad.
The burden was 'Alone! Alone!'   20
And then the heart did feebly groan;
Then suddenly a cheerful tone
   Proclaimed a spirit glad!
Oh mazy woods of Aveyron,
   Oh wilds of dreary solitude!   25
   Amid your thorny alleys rude
I wished myself a traveller alone.

'Alone!' I heard the wild boy say,
And swift he climbed a blasted oak;
And there, while morning's herald woke,   30
   He watched the opening day.
Yet dark and sunken was his eye,
Like a lorn[2] maniac's, wild and shy,
And scowling like a winter sky,
   Without one beaming ray!   35
Then, mazy woods of Aveyron
   Then, wilds of dreary solitude,
   Amid thy thorny alleys rude
I sighed to be a traveller alone.

'Alone! Alone!' I heard him shriek –   40
'Twas like the shriek of dying man!
And then to mutter he began,
   But oh, he *could not speak*!
I saw him point to heav'n and sigh,
The big drop trembled in his eye;   45
And slowly from the yellow sky
   I saw the pale morn break.
I saw the woods of Aveyron
   Their wilds of dreary solitude;
   I marked their thorny alleys rude,   50
And wished to be a traveller alone!

His hair was long and black, and he
From infancy *alone* had been;
For since his fifth year he had seen,
   None marked his destiny!   55
No mortal ear had heard his groan,
For him no beam of hope had shone;
While sad he sighed, 'Alone! Alone!'

---

[2] *lorn* lonely, desolate, wretched.

Beneath the blasted tree.
And then, oh woods of Aveyron,   60
  Oh wilds of dreary solitude,
  Amid your thorny alleys rude
I thought myself a traveller alone.

And now upon the blasted tree
He carved three notches broad and long,   65
And all the while he sang a song
  Of nature's melody!
And though of words he nothing knew,
And though his dulcet tones were few,
Across the yielding bark he drew,   70
  Deep sighing, notches three.
Oh mazy woods of Aveyron,
  Oh wilds of dreary solitude,
  Amid your thorny alleys rude
Upon this blasted oak no sunbeam shone.   75

And now he pointed one, two, three;
Again he shrieked with wild dismay;
And now he paced the thorny way,
  Quitting the blasted tree.
It was a dark December morn,   80
The dew was frozen on the thorn,
But to a wretch so sad, so lorn,
  All days alike would be!
Yet mazy woods of Aveyron,
  Yet wilds of dreary solitude,   85
  Amid your frosty alleys rude
I wished to be a traveller alone.

He followed me along the wood
To a small grot his hands had made,
Deep in a black rock's sullen shade,   90
  Beside a tumbling flood.
Upon the earth I saw him spread
Of withered leaves a narrow bed,
Yellow as gold, and streaked with red –
  They looked like streaks of blood!   95
Pulled from the woods of Aveyron
  And scattered o'er the solitude
  By midnight whirlwinds strong and rude,
To pillow the scorched brain that throbbed alone.

Wild berries were his winter food,   100
With them his sallow lip was dyed;
On chestnuts wild he fed beside,

Steeped in the foamy flood.
Chequered with scars his breast was seen,
Wounds streaming fresh with anguish keen,   105
And marks where other wounds had been
    Torn by the brambles rude.
Such was the boy of Aveyron,
    The tenant of that solitude,
    Where still, by misery unsubdued,   110
He wandered nine long winters all alone.

Before the step of his rude throne,
The squirrel sported, tame and gay,
The dormouse slept its life away
    Nor heard his midnight groan.   115
About his form a garb he wore,
Ragged it was, and marked with gore,
And yet where'er 'twas folded o'er
    Full many a spangle shone!
Like little stars, oh Aveyron,   120
    They gleamed amid thy solitude;
    Or like, along thy alleys rude,
The summer dewdrops sparkling in the sun.

It once had been a lady's vest,
White as the whitest mountain's snow,   125
Till ruffian hands had taught to flow
    The fountain of her breast!
Remembrance bade the wild boy trace
Her beauteous form, her angel face,
Her eye that beamed with heavenly grace,   130
    Her fainting voice that blessed,
When in the woods of Aveyron
    Deep in their deepest solitude,
    Three barb'rous ruffians shed her blood,
And mocked, with cruel taunts, her dying groan.   135

Remembrance traced the summer bright,
When all the trees were fresh and green,
When lost the alleys long between,
    The lady passed the night;
She passed the night, bewildered wild,   140
She passed it with her fearless child
Who raised his little arms and smiled
    To see the morning light.
While in the woods of Aveyron
    Beneath the broad oak's canopy,   145
    She marked aghast the ruffians three
Waiting to seize the traveller alone!

Beneath the broad oak's canopy
The lovely lady's bones were laid;
But since that hour no breeze has played 150
    About the blasted tree!
The leaves all withered ere the sun
His next day's rapid course had run,
And ere the summer day was done
    It winter seemed to be. 155
And still, oh woods of Aveyron,
    Amid thy dreary solitude
    The oak a sapless trunk has stood,
To mark the spot where murder foul was done!

From her the wild boy learned 'Alone!' 160
She tried to say, 'My babe will die!'
But angels caught her parting sigh,
    The babe her dying tone.
And from that hour the boy has been
Lord of the solitary scene, 165
Wand'ring the dreary shades between,
    Making his dismal moan!
Till, mazy woods of Aveyron,
    Dark wilds of dreary solitude,
    Amid your thorny alleys rude 170
I thought myself alone.
    And could a wretch more wretched be,
    More wild or fancy-fraught than he,
Whose melancholy tale would pierce an heart of stone?

Helen Maria Williams (1761–1827)

Helen Maria Williams was born in London in 1761 to Charles Williams, an army officer, and Helen Hay. When her father died in 1769 she and her mother moved to Berwick-upon-Tweed, where her mother educated her at home. Her most formative years were spent in Scotland, where she fell in love with the people and the countryside. In exile in France in 1814, she remembered those early years with wistful affection in an apostrophe to 'Scotia':

Ah, lost to me thy fir-clad hills,
The music of thy mountain rills,
Yet ever shall the mem'ry last,
'Pleasant and mournful' of the past.[1]

---

[1] *The Travellers in Haste* 11–14, from *Poems on Various Subjects* (1823).

She returned to London in 1781 and, with the help of the dissenting minister Dr Andrew Kippis, published her first poem, *Edwin and Eltruda, A Legendary Tale* (1782). The entire episode, she later recalled, was fortuitous: 'My first production, the Legendary Tale of Edwin and Eltruda, was composed to amuse some solitary hours, and without any view to publication. Being shown to Dr Kippis, he declared that it deserved to be committed to the press, and offered to take upon himself the task of introducing it to the world.'[2] She had begun a successful career as a poet and rapidly became known in literary circles, counting among her friends Fanny Burney, William Hayley, Samuel Johnson, Elizabeth Montagu, Anna Seward, the Wartons, Samuel Rogers, and Charlotte Smith. In 1783 she published *An Ode on the Peace*, and in 1784 *Peru, A Poem. In Six Cantos*, which she dedicated to Elizabeth Montagu. Boswell recounts the story of her first meeting with Dr Johnson in May 1784, after publication of *An Ode on the Peace*: 'He had dined that day at Mr Hoole's, and Miss Helen Maria Williams being expected in the evening, Mr Hoole put into his hands her beautiful "Ode on the Peace". Johnson read it over, and when this elegant and accomplished young lady was presented to him, he took her by the hand in the most courteous manner, and repeated the finest stanza of her poem; this was the most delicate and pleasing compliment he could pay.'[3] More than 1,500 people subscribed to her collected *Poems* of 1786. It was read, among others, by the young William Wordsworth, then a schoolboy of sixteen at Hawkshead Grammar School. She was well known as a poet of sensibility, and it was at that moment fashionable to address sentimental sonnets to her in the periodicals of the day.[4] This is precisely what Wordsworth did: his first published poem, *Sonnet on Seeing Miss Helen Maria Williams Weep at a Tale of Distress*, appeared in the *European Magazine* for March 1787. It is also worth noting that the gothicism of his schoolboy poem, *The Vale of Esthwaite*, is strongly influenced by Williams's *Part of an Irregular Fragment, found in a Dark Passage of the Tower*. Interestingly, the *Irregular Fragment* was the poem which several of the reviewers of the *Poems* singled out as its finest work. The *European Magazine* observed that it was 'the poem which we esteem the best display of Miss Williams' poetical powers',[5] while the *Monthly Review* decided to reprint it, with the encomium:

> In the *Irregular Fragment* the writer rises on no feeble wing into the regions of fancy and passion. The piece has so much merit that we cannot deny ourselves the satisfaction of presenting it to our readers entire; after premising that it is founded on the idea of an apartment in the Tower, shut up for ages, in which are assembled the ghosts of all those whom history relates to have been murdered in that state prison, and of a murdered royal family, whose story is lost in the lapse of time.[6]

Even as late as 1823, one of the reviewers of her collected poems pronounced that 'an *Irregular Fragment* and her sonnets are all that the volume contains of real poetry.'[7]

---

[2] Preface, *Poems* (1786).
[3] *Boswell's Life of Johnson* ed. George Birkbeck Hill, rev. L. F. Powell (6 vols, Oxford, 1934–40), iv 282.
[4] See, for instance, *To Miss Helen Maria Williams: On her Poem of Peru, Gentleman's Magazine* 54 (1784) 532; Anna Seward's *Sonnet to Miss Williams on her Epic Poem, Peru, Gentleman's Magazine* 54 (1784) 613; and *Sonnet to Miss Helena-Maria Williams* by J. B———o in the *European*

Magazine 12 (1787) 144. James Averill has pointed to other contributions to the *European* including *Stanzas to Mrs Barbauld, Sonnet Addressed to Miss Seward*, and three sonnets to Charlotte Smith (*Wordsworth and the Poetry of Human Suffering* (Ithaca, NY, 1980), p. 33).
[5] *European Magazine* 10 (1786) 89–93, 177–80, p. 180.
[6] *Monthly Review* 75 (1786) 44–9, p. 44.
[7] *Literary Museum* 47 (15 March 1823) 166.

The *Fragment* is indeed a remarkable work; it may be the archetypal gothic poem of the eighteenth century. Its lurid imagery and skilfully contrived incoherent climax guaranteed it a renown for years afterwards. But what many of its readers seem not to have noticed is its political implications. In a volume dedicated to the Queen it must be regarded as surprising, to say the least, to find a poem which portrays the English monarchy as a succession of homicidal maniacs. The 1786 collection is, in fact, most notable for its articulation, via conventional literary forms, of a clearly defined radical intelligence. That radicalism came to the fore in her *Poem on the Bill lately passed for Regulating the Slave-Trade*, published towards the end of 1788, the same year in which Ann Yearsley and Hannah More published poems on the same subject (see pp. 158–67 and 43–50). This year saw a good deal of debate about the future of the slave trade partly because of a Bill proposed in the House of Commons on 21 May 1788 by Sir William Dolben, MP for the University of Oxford. It aimed to limit the number of slaves which could be transported from Africa to British colonies in the West Indies. Hardly a world-shaking proposal, one would have thought – but it was generally recognized that this was the beginning of an abolitionist movement. On 26 May merchants and inhabitants of Liverpool presented a petition to the House, saying that Dolben's Bill would cause them all financial ruin. And there was a good deal of argument from those MPs with slave owning interests. Fortunately, the Bill was passed in both Houses, and provided the occasion for Helen's *Poem on the Bill Lately Passed for Regulating the Slave-Trade*. It may not be her best work, being composed in an artificial manner that sounds stilted to modern ears, but it has a fervour and a passion of the moment, which deserves attention today for reasons other than its qualities as poetry. Its author evidently felt frustrated at the caution of the Bill, and uses its success as an argument for complete abolition. Reactions to the poem were generally favourable; the *Critical Review* was right to find the poem 'too figurative and highly ornamented',[8] but that opinion was not echoed by other commentators. The *English Review* was more moderate: 'There are passages in it that would do high credit to a meaner pen, and the style of the performance is constantly easy, flowing, and poetical. But we cannot discover in it that unity, that lucid arrangement, that compression, and that energy, which we should have expected.'[9] The *New Annual Register* was more positive: 'The style of this poem is easy and harmonious, and its language truly elegant and poetical';[10] *The Diary; or, Woodfall's Register* commented that it 'is not inferior to any of this lady's former productions and will rather add to, than diminish, her reputation'.[11] And the *Monthly Review* was most favourable of all: 'In easy, harmonious verse, she pours forth the sentiments of an amiable mind, nor do we recollect, among the poems which have lately attracted our attention, to have perused one with more pleasure than that which now lies before us.'[12]

Helen's *Julia, A Novel; Interspersed with Some Poetical Pieces* (1790) revised Rousseau's *Nouvelle Héloïse*, making the triangle one of a man, who dies, leaving two women to bring up a child together. In *The Bastille, A Vision* (one of those poetical pieces with which it is 'interspersed'), it revises the heady cocktail of gothicism and radicalism found in the *Irregular Fragment* so that this time the target is the French *ancien régime*, and its many injustices are symbolized by the Bastille, which had been stormed on 14 July 1789. As with the 1786 volume, Helen's reviewers seem to have missed the novel's politics; the *Monthly Review* commented that 'The pieces of poetry, occasionally introduced, are,

---

[8]   *Critical Review* 67 (1789) 314.
[9]   *English Review* 13 (1789) 133–5, p. 135.
[10]   *New Annual Register* 9 (1788) 260.
[11]   *The Diary; or, Woodfall's Register* (17 April 1789).
[12]   *Monthly Review* 80 (1789) 237–8, p. 237.

in general, elegant, and considerably enhance the value of the volumes'.[13] The *Analytical Review* found the poems 'ingenious and harmonious',[14] and the *Critical Review* merely noted that 'The poetry, interspersed, perhaps too frequently interspersed, deserves the character we have already had occasion to give of this lady's works; it is in general tender, pathetic, and pleasing.'[15]

By the time it was published Helen was renowned as one of the keenest supporters of the French Revolution, and it came as no suprise when she visited Paris and saw the ruins of the Bastille for herself – an experience described in her *Letters Written in France in the Summer of 1790* (1790).[16] Back in London she published a new edition of her *Poems* in 1791, before returning to France in July, explaining her reasons for doing so in *A Farewell, for Two Years, to England. A Poem* (1791). Her reasons were unashamedly political, and in this poem she reprises her opposition to the slave trade, and relates it to the quest by the revolutionary French for liberty. As with the *Poem on the Bill Lately Passed for Regulating the Slave-Trade*, this may not be her best poetical achievement, but it is once again the product of an intensely felt passion at a particular moment. Even the poem's title is a product of an optimism she would not feel again: she would not be able to return to England in 1793. And after her departure in 1791, she would be more or less exiled from her homeland for ever. It is not surprising, in view of all this, that she chose not to reprint this poem in her 1823 collected works. Reviews of her *Farewell to England* were positive; the *Analytical Review* remarked that 'The idea of visiting France, now become the first seat of freedom, fires her muse with more than usual ardour. The poem will be read with pleasure by those whose bosoms glow with kindred sentiments.'[17] The *Monthly Review* also presented her case sympathetically:

> Much of nature gives animation to this poem, much fond recollection of the inno-cent pleasures of early youth. She has, very properly, introduced her favourite sub-ject, the renovation of Gallic liberty, and has taken occasion, gently and tenderly, to expostulate with those of her countrymen who seem unwilling to allow their neighbours the blessing of that freedom which they so happily enjoy. She also adverts, very pathetically, to the late miscarriage of Mr Wilberforce's slave-bill, and, turning to France, exhorts her generously to espouse the cause of the poor Africans . . .[18]

Even when reviewers disagreed with her politics, as in the case of the *Critical Review*, she was indulged, probably because she was popular with readers, and things in Paris had not yet turned really ugly: 'Miss Williams' farewell numbers are extremely sweet and musical, and her enthusiasm in the cause of liberty shines with a lustre so bright and ardent as to excite our warm admiration. We cannot say that her principles always coin-cide with our own, or that her arguments are absolutely incontrovertible, but where they do not convince, we applaud the spirit with which they are delivered, and the numbers in which they are conveyed.'[19]

It is intriguing that when he visited Paris in 1791, Wordsworth obtained a letter of introduction to Helen from Charlotte Smith, though in the event he did not meet her until 1820. She was prominent in British circles in Paris, being acquainted with Thomas

[13] *Monthly Review* 2 (1790) 334–6, p. 335.
[14] *Analytical Review* 7 (1790) 97–100, p. 100.
[15] *Critical Review* 69 (1790) 592–3, p. 593.
[16] See *Romanticism* 139–40.

[17] *Analytical Review* 10 (1791) 188.
[18] *Monthly Review* 5 (1791) 341–2.
[19] *Critical Review* 2 (1791) 232.

Paine and Mary Wollstonecraft. The months following the execution of Louis XVI in January 1793 were difficult ones for English radicals. Wordsworth reacted by writing a pamphlet in defence of regicide which, fortunately for him, was not published; had it been, he and his publisher would probably have been tried for treason. Helen's support for the revolution did not waver, and that fidelity to her principles was to cost her dearly. One of the earliest warnings of what was to happen came with an open letter to her from Anna Seward who, until the execution, had publicly supported events in France. Seward's letter appeared in the *Gentleman's Magazine* for February 1793, and was prefaced by an explanation of how it was 'sent to Miss Helen Maria Williams a few days before the tidings of that demoniac transaction, the murder of the deposed and blameless Louis, reached this nation'.[20] She proceeded to articulate her revulsion at the execution of the king, and advised Helen: 'Oh return while yet you may, to the bosom of your native country, which has fostered your talents and enrolled your fame!'[21] She continued: 'Fly, dear Helen, that land of carnage! from the pernicious influence of that equalizing system which, instead of diffusing universal love, content and happiness, lifts every man's hand against his brother.'[22] The conclusion to the letter was more ominous: 'Adieu, my dear friend! Love and respect your country half as well as I love and respect you, and we shall soon cease to view you in a state of cold alienation, and of impending danger!'[23] From the point of view of personal survival this was excellent advice; the outbreak of war with Britain, Prussia, and Austria in February, and the Reign of Terror, which began in October 1793, made life precarious for English men and women in Paris. Helen, her mother and sister were arrested under the general order of 7 October, placing all British and Hanoverian subjects 'in a state of arrest in houses of security'.

While in confinement she translated St Pierre's *Paul and Virginia* (1796), and continued to record her impressions of revolutionary France in the *Letters Containing a Sketch of the Politics of France* (1795).[24] Although her account of the revolution has often been criticized for its inaccuracies, it is nonetheless valuable for its first-hand account of an energetic and emotional involvement in the affairs of the day. She emphasizes the part played by women in the revolution, their efforts to fight tyranny, and their fortitude, regarding these records of the revolution as among her most important works: 'My narratives make a part of that marvellous story which the eighteenth century has to record to future times, and the testimony of a witness will be heard. Perhaps, indeed, I have written too little of events which I have known so well; but the convulsions of states form accumulations of private calamity that distract the attention by overwhelming the heart, and it is difficult to describe the shipwreck when sinking in the storm.'[25] All of which did her little credit with her compatriots, who were coming to regard her as a traitor to the British cause; the *British Critic* commented, not untypically, of the 1795 *Letters*: 'As usual, the French are all wise, generous, good, great, etc. etc. etc. and every other nation, her own in particular, contemptible in the balance'.[26]

Helen and her family owed their eventual release from prison to Jean Debry, a humane deputy to the Convention, who risked much suspicion, and danger to himself, in pleading their cause. They were released in July 1794, when Helen left her family in Paris and joined John Hurford Stone in Switzerland. Stone, a Unitarian and fellow radical, was also a married man. Their affair scandalized London, and made it virtually

---

[20] *Gentleman's Magazine* 63 (1793) 108–10, p. 108.
[21] Ibid., p. 109.
[22] Ibid., p. 110.
[23] Ibid.
[24] *Romanticism* 142–3.
[25] *Poems on Various Subjects* (1823), p. x.
[26] *British Critic* 8 (1796) 321.

impossible for her ever to return. Reviewers now had two sticks with which to beat her: her politics and her morals. Her apparent loyalty to France was particularly incendiary in view of the fact that the war with England showed no sign of abating. In 1798, letters Helen and Stone had written to Joseph Priestley in America were intercepted by an English ship and published as evidence of her treachery; the *Anti-Jacobin Review* crowed: 'These self-transported *patriots* triumph, by anticipation, in the conquest of England, the downfall of her monarchy, and the consequent establishment of a republic, under which their pious friend, Dr Priestley, may live unmolested by *Kings*, by *tithes* or by *Bishops*'.[27] In the same year Helen's *Tour in Switzerland* was published; the reviews were equally harsh. The reviewer in the *British Critic* begins not with an account of the book, but a prejudiced account of her career, including the comment that she 'caught the infection of Gallic liberty' and was currently 'the *companion* of a man employed by the French government.... Miss or Mrs Williams felt no compunction at attending Mr S. on his excursion, who is, we are told, a married man, and has a wife living in this country'.[28]

She continued to express her radical views in her volumes on French history (1815, 1819), became a naturalized French citizen in 1817, and published her collected poems in 1823. The reviews for that last poetical appearance were surprisingly respectful. 'Anything from the pen of Miss Williams must be important', said the *Monthly Literary Register*. 'Without deeply entering into comparisons, we may remark that there appears through all her considerable works a sober and masculine propriety seldom encountered in the pages of her fair contemporaries'.[29] The *European Magazine* concurred: 'We think the volume a very acceptable offering to the public, and it will be valued by many as a reminiscence of a lady whose name was once so familiar to our studies, but whose pen has latterly kept no pace with the promise of her earlier productions.'[30] More grudgingly, the *Monthly Review* described her poetry as 'always above mediocrity though wanting in some of the higher characteristics of genius'.[31]

Vilified by the English, she died in Paris in 1827. Her obituarist in the *Monthly Review* offered the tart judgement: 'She wrote several works connected with France, which obtained for her a considerable degree of popularity in that country, as well as in this; but they have been already forgotten.'[32] She was buried next to John Hurford Stone, who she may secretly have married in 1794.

Further Reading

Mary A. Favret, *Romantic Correspondence: Women, Politics, and the Fiction of Letters* (Cambridge, 1993), chapter 3

Gary Kelly, *Women, Writing, and Revolution 1790–1827* (Oxford, 1993), chapters 2 and 6

Richard C. Sha, 'Expanding the Limits of Feminine Writing: The Prose Sketches of Sydney Owenson (Lady Morgan) and Helen Maria Williams', *RWW* 194–206

Chris Jones, 'Helen Maria Williams and Radical Sensibility', *Prose Studies* 12 (1989) 3–24

Deborah Kennedy, '"Storms of Sorrow": The Poetry of Helen Maria Williams', *Lumen* 10 (1991) 77–91

Nicola J. Watson, 'Novel Eloisas: Revolutionary and Counter-Revolutionary Narratives in Helen Maria Williams, Wordsworth and Byron', *TWC* 23 (1992) 18–23

Vivien Jones, 'Femininity, Nationalism, and Romanticism: The Politics of Gender in the Revolution Controversy', *History of European Ideas* 16 (1993) 299–305

---

[27] *Anti-Jacobin Review* 1 (1798) 146–51, p. 150.

[28] *British Critic* 12 (1798) 24–9, p. 24.

[29] *Monthly Literary Register* 3 (1823) 124–6, p. 124.

[30] *European Magazine* 83 (1823) 355–6, p. 356.

[31] *Monthly Review* 102 (1823) 20–31, p. 23.

[32] *Monthly Review* 7 (1828) 139.

From Poems (1786)

PART OF AN IRREGULAR FRAGMENT, FOUND IN A DARK PASSAGE OF THE TOWER

Advertisement

The following poem is formed on a very singular and sublime idea. A young gentleman, possessed of an uncommon genius for drawing, on visiting the Tower of London, passing one door of a singular construction, asked what apartment it led to, and expressed a desire to have it opened. The person who showed the place shook his head and answered, 'Heaven knows what is within that door; it has been shut for ages.' This answer made small impression on the other hearers, but a very deep one on the imagination of this youth. Gracious Heaven! An apartment shut up for ages – and in the Tower!

> Ye Towers of Julius! London's lasting shame,
> By many a foul and midnight murder fed.

Genius builds on a slight foundation, and rears beautiful structures on 'the baseless fabric of a vision.' The above transient hint dwelt on the young man's fancy, and conjured into his memory all the murders which history records to have been committed in the Tower: Henry VI, the Duke of Clarence, the two young Princes, sons of Edward IV, Sir Thomas Overbury, etc. He supposes all their ghosts assembled in this unexplored apartment, and to these his fertile imagination has added several others. One of the spectres raises an immense pall of black velvet, and discovers the remains of a murdered royal family whose story is lost in the lapse of time. The gloomy wildness of these images struck my imagination so forcibly that, endeavouring to catch the fire of the youth's pencil, this fragment was produced.

I

Rise, winds of night! Relentless tempests rise!
    Rush from the troubled clouds, and o'er me roll;
In this chill pause a deeper horror lies,
    A wilder fear appals my shudd'ring soul.
'Twas on this day,[1] this hour accursed,   5
    That Nature, starting from repose,
Heard the dire shrieks of murder burst –
    From infant innocence they rose
        And shook these solemn towers!
I shudd'ring pass that fatal room,   10
For ages wrapped in central gloom;
I shudd'ring pass that iron door
Which fate perchance unlocks no more;
Death, smeared with blood, o'er the dark portal lours.

PART OF AN IRREGULAR FRAGMENT
[1] 'The anniversary of the murder of Edward V, and his brother Richard, Duke of York' (Williams's note).

II

How fearfully my step resounds   15
  Along these lonely bounds;
Spare, savage blast, the taper's quiv'ring fires,
Deep in these gath'ring shades its flame expires.
  Ye host of heaven! The door recedes;
  It mocks my grasp – what unseen hands   20
    Have burst its iron bands?
  No mortal force this gate unbarred
  Where danger lives, which terrors guard –
  Dread powers! Its screaming hinges close
    On this dire scene of impious deeds.   25
  My feet are fixed! Dismay has bound
  My step on this polluted ground –
  But lo! the pitying moon a line of light
Athwart the horrid darkness dimly throws,
And from yon grated window chases night.   30

III

  Ye visions that before me roll,
That freeze my blood, that shake my soul,
    Are ye the phantoms of a dream?
Pale spectres, are ye what ye seem?
    They glide more near,   35
      Their forms unfold!
Fixed are their eyes, on me they bend –
  Their glaring look is cold!
  And hark, I hear
Sounds that the throbbing pulse of life suspend!   40

IV

  'No wild illusion cheats thy sight
With shapes that only live in night –
  Mark the native glories spread
    Around my bleeding brow!
The crown of Albion wreathed my head   45
  And Gallia's lillies[2] twined below;
When my father shook his spear,
  When his banner sought the skies,
Her baffled host recoiled with fear,
  Nor turned their shrinking eyes.   50
Soon as the daring eagle springs
  To bask in heav'n's empyreal light,

---

[2] 'Henry VI was crowned when an infant, at Paris'
(Williams's note).

The vultures ply their baleful wings,
  A cloud of deep'ning colour marks their flight,
    Staining the golden day;   55
But see, amid the rav'nous brood
  A bird of fiercer aspect soar.
The spirits of a rival race[3]
Hang on the noxious blast, and trace
  With gloomy joy his destined prey,   60
Inflame th' ambitious wish that thirsts for blood,
And plunge his talons deep in kindred gore.

V

'View the stern form that hovers nigh –
Fierce rolls his dauntless eye
  In scorn of hideous death;   65
Till starting at a brother's[4] name,
Horror shrinks his glowing frame,
  Locks the half-uttered groan,
    And chills the parting breath.
Astonished Nature heaved a moan   70
When her affrighted eye beheld the hands
She formed to cherish, rend her holy bands.[5]

VI

'Look where a royal infant[6] kneels,
  Shrieking and agonized with fear;
He sees the dagger pointed near   75
  A much-loved brother's[7] breast,
And tells an absent mother all he feels.
  His eager eye he casts around;
  Where shall her guardian form be found
    On which his eager eye would rest?   80
  On her he calls in accents wild
  And wonders why her step is slow
    To save her suff'ring child!
Robed in the regal garb, his brother stands
  In more majestic woe,   85
And meets the impious stroke with bosom bare,
Then fearless grasps the murd'rer's hands,
  And asks the minister of hell to spare
  The child whose feeble arms sustain
  His bleeding form from cruel death.   90

---

[3] 'Richard III, by murdering so many near relations, seemed to revenge the sufferings of Henry VI and his family, on the House of York' (Williams's note).
[4] 'Richard III, who murdered his brother, the Duke of Clarence' (Williams's note).

[5] i.e. by fratricide, an unnatural act.
[6] 'Richard Duke of York' (Williams's note).
[7] 'Edward V' (Williams's note).

In vain fraternal fondness pleads,
　　For cold is now his livid cheek,
And cold his last expiring breath.
　　And now with aspect meek,
The infant lifts its mournful eye,   95
And asks with trembling voice to die,
If death will cure his heaving heart of pain.
　　His heaving heart now bleeds!
Foul tyrant, o'er the gilded hour
That beams with all the blaze of power,   100
　　Remorse shall spread her thickest shroud;
The furies in thy tortured ear
　　Shall howl with curses deep and loud,
And wake distracting fear!
　　I see the ghastly spectre rise,   105
　　Whose blood is cold, whose hollow eyes
　　Seem from his head to start;
　　With upright hair and shiv'ring heart,
Dark o'er thy midnight couch he bends,
And clasps thy shrinking frame, thy impious spirit rends.'   110

VII
Now his thrilling accents die,
His shape eludes my searching eye;
But who is he,[8] convulsed with pain,
That writhes in every swelling vein?
　　Yet in so deep, so wild a groan,   115
A sharper anguish seems to live
　　Than life's expiring pang can give:
He dies deserted and alone.
　　If pity can allay thy woes,
　　Sad spirit, they shall find repose;   120
Thy friend, thy long-loved friend is near;
He comes to pour the parting tear,
　　He comes to catch the parting breath.
Ah heaven! no melting look he wears,
His altered eye with vengeance glares;   125
Each frantic passion at his soul;
'Tis he has dashed that venomed bowl
　　With agony and death.

VIII
But whence arose that solemn call?
　　Yon bloody phantom waves his hand   130
And beckons me to deeper gloom;
　　Rest, troubled form, I come –

---

[8] 'Sir Thomas Overbury, poisoned in the Tower by
Somerset' (Williams's note).

Some unknown power my step impels
To horror's secret cells.
   'For thee I raise this sable pall,   135
   It shrouds a ghastly band;
Stretched beneath, thy eye shall trace
    A mangled regal race.
A thousand suns have rolled since light
   Rushed on their solid night;   140
See, o'er that tender frame grim Famine hangs
   And mocks a mother's pangs!
The last, last drop which warmed her veins
    That meagre infant drains,
   Then gnaws her fond sustaining breast.   145
   Stretched on her feeble knees, behold
Another victim sinks to lasting rest;
Another yet her matron arms would fold,
Who strives to reach her matron arms in vain,
   Too weak her wasted form to raise.   150
   On him she bends her eager gaze;
    She sees the soft imploring eye
That asks her dear embrace, the cure of pain –
    She sees her child at distance die!
   But now her steadfast heart can bear   155
   Unmoved the pressure of despair.
When first the winds of winter urge their course
O'er the pure stream, whose current smoothly glides,
The heaving river swells its troubled tides;
But when the bitter blast with keener force   160
   O'er the high wave an icy fetter throws,
The hardened wave is fixed in dead repose.'

IX
'Say, who that hoary form? Alone he stands,
And meekly lifts his withered hands –
   His white beard streams with blood!   165
I see him with a smile deride
The wounds that pierce his shrivelled side
   Whence flows a purple flood;
   But sudden pangs his bosom tear –
    On one big drop, of deeper dye,   170
    I see him fix his haggard eye
   In dark and wild despair!
That sanguine drop which wakes his woe,
    Say, spirit, whence its source?'
'Ask no more its source to know –   175
    Ne'er shall mortal eye explore
   Whence flowed that drop of human gore,
   Till the starting dead shall rise
   Unchained from earth, and mount the skies,

And time shall end his fated course.   180
   Now th' unfathomed depth behold:
     Look but once! A second glance
    Wraps a heart of human mould
     In death's eternal trance.

X
'That shapeless phantom, sinking slow   185
Deep down the vast abyss below,
Darts through the mists that shroud his frame –
A horror nature hates to name!
Mortal, could thine eyes behold
All those sullen mists enfold,   190
Thy sinews at the sight accursed
Would wither, and thy heart-strings burst;
Death would grasp with icy hand
And drag thee to our grisly band!
Away! the sable pall I spread,   195
And give to rest th' unquiet dead;
Haste, ere its horrid shroud enclose
   Thy form, benumbed with wild affright,
   And plunge thee far through wastes of night,
    In yon black gulf's abhorred repose!'   200
    As, starting at each step, I fly,
    Why backward turns my frantic eye
     That closing portal past?
Two sullen shades, half-seen, advance!
   On me a blasting look they cast,   205
   And fix my view with dang'rous spells
   Where burning frenzy dwells!
Again! their vengeful look – and now a speechless –
     * * * * * * *

A Poem on the Bill Lately Passed for Regulating the Slave-Trade (1788)

The quality of mercy is not strained;
It droppeth, as the gentle rain from heav'n
Upon the place beneath. It is twice blessed;
It blesseth him that gives, and him that takes.

                 Shakespeare[1]

The hollow winds of night no more[2]
In wild unequal cadence pour

A POEM ON THE BILL LATELY PASSED FOR REGULATING
THE SLAVE-TRADE (1788)
[1] *The Merchant of Venice* IV i 180–3.
[2] The slaves' groans of severe agony will no longer
be heard by 'fancy' because Sir William Dolben's Bill
to limit the number of slaves that could be trans-
ported from Africa to British colonies in the West
Indies had been passed by the House of Commons
in May 1788.

On musing fancy's wakeful ear
The groan of agony severe
From yon dark vessel which contains   5
The wretch new-bound in hopeless chains,
Whose soul with keener anguish bleeds
As Afric's less'ning shore recedes;
No more where ocean's unseen bound
Leaves a drear world of waters round,   10
Between the howling gust shall rise
The stifled captive's latest sighs;
No more shall suffocating death
Seize the pent victim's sinking breath
(The pang of that convulsive hour   15
Reproaching man's insatiate power –
Man, who to Afric's shore has passed
Relentless as the annual blast
That sweeps the Western Isles and flings
Destruction from its furious wings).   20
And woman – she, too weak to bear
The galling chain, the tainted air,
Of mind too feeble to sustain
The vast accumulated pain,
No more in desperation wild   25
Shall madly strain her gasping child
With all the mother[3] at her soul;
With eyes where tears have ceased to roll,
Shall catch the livid[4] infant's breath,
Then sink in agonizing death.   30
    Britain, the noble blessed decree[5]
That soothes despair, is framed by thee!
Thy powerful arm has interposed,
And one[6] dire scene for ever closed;
Its horror shall no more belong   35
To that foul drama, deep with wrong.
Oh, first of Europe's polished lands
To ease the captive's iron bands;
Long as thy glorious annals shine,
This proud distinction shall be thine!   40
Not first alone when Valour leads
To rush on Danger's noblest deeds;[7]
When Mercy calls thee to explore
A gloomy path untrod before,

---

[3] *mother* i.e. maternal power.
[4] *livid* blue; the child is unable to breathe for lack of fresh air.
[5] *decree* law; a reference to the Bill to regulate transportation of slaves.

[6] *one* Williams's emphasis underlines the fact that the abolitionist cause had more battles to fight.
[7] *Not first alone . . . noblest deeds* Britain is first not just when valour is called for, in the face of danger, but also when Mercy is called for.

Thy ardent spirit springs to heal   45
And, greatly gen'rous, dares to feel!
Valour is like the meteor's light
Whose partial flash leaves deeper night,
While Mercy, like the lunar ray,
Gilds the thick shade with softer day.   50
    For this, in fame's immortal shrine,
A double wreath, oh Pitt,[8] is thine!
For this, while distant ages hear
With Admiration's sacred tear,
Of powers whose energy sublime   55
Disdained to borrow force from Time,
With no gradations marked their flight,
But rose at once to glory's height;
The deeds of mercy that embrace
A distant sphere, an alien race,   60
Shall Virtue's lips record, and claim
The fairest honours of thy name!
'Tis ever nature's gen'rous view,
Great minds should noble ends pursue,
As the clear sunbeam when most bright   65
Warms in proportion to its light.
And Richmond[9] – he who, high in birth,
Adds the unfading rays of worth,
Who stoops from scenes in radiance dressed
To ease the mourner's aching breast,   70
The tale of private woe to hear,
And wipe the friendless orphan's tear.
His bosom for the captive bleeds,
He, guardian of the injured, pleads
With all the force that genius gives   75
And warmth that but with Virtue lives,
For Virtue with divine control
Collects the various powers of soul
And lends, from her unsullied source,
The gems of thought their purest force.   80
    Oh blest decree, whose lustre seems
Like the sweet moon's reviving beams
That chase the hideous forms of night
And promise day more richly bright;
Great deed, that met consenting minds   85
In all but those whom av'rice binds,
Who creep in interest's crooked ways,
Nor ever pass her narrow maze,

---

[8]   William Pitt the younger (1759–1806), Prime Minister 1783–1801, 1804–6.

[9]   Charles Lennox, 3rd Duke of Richmond (1735–1806), Master-General of the Ordnance 1782–95, an energetic campaigner for reform.

Or those whom hard indiff'rence steels
To every pang another feels.   90
For *them*[10] has fortune round their bowers
Twined (partial[11] nymph!) her lavish flowers;
For *them*, from unsunned caves, she brings
Her summer ice; for *them* she springs
To climes where hotter suns produce   95
The richer fruit's delicious juice;
While *they*[12] whom wasted blessings tire
Nor leave *one* want to feed desire
With cool, insulting ease demand
Why, for yon hopeless captive band,   100
Is asked, to mitigate despair,
The mercy of the common air?
The boon of larger space to breathe,
While cooped that hollow deck beneath?
A lengthened plank, on which to throw   105
Their shackled limbs, while fiercely glow
The beams direct, that on each head
The fury of contagion shed?[13]
And dare presumptuous guilty man
Load with offence his fleeting span?[14]   110
Deform creation with the gloom
Of crimes that blot its cheerful bloom?
Darken a work so perfect made,
And cast the universe in shade?
    Alas, to Afric's fettered race   115
Creation wears no form of grace!
To them earth's pleasant vales are found
A blasted waste, a sterile bound,
Where the poor wand'rer must sustain
The load of unremitted pain;   120
A region in whose ample scope
His eye discerns no gleam of hope;
Where thought no kind asylum knows
On which its anguish may repose –
But death, that to the ravaged breast   125
Comes not in shapes of terror dressed,
Points to green hills where freedom roves,
And minds renew their former loves;
Or, louring in the troubled air,
Hangs the fierce spectre of Despair   130
Whose soul abhors the gift of life,
Who steadfast grasps the reeking[15] knife,

---

[10] *them* i.e. the consenting minds of line 85.
[11] *partial* kindly, friendly.
[12] *they* i.e. the avaricious of line 86.

[13] *The fury of contagion shed* the sun was believed to be an agent of disease.
[14] *span* i.e. of life.
[15] *reeking* smelling of blood.

Bids the charged heart in torrents bleed,
And smiles in frenzy at the deed –
So when rude winds the sailor urge   135
On polar seas near earth's last verge,
Long with the blast he struggles hard
To save his bark, in ice embarred,[16]
But finds at length, o'ercome with pain,
The conflict with his fate is vain;   140
Then heaves no more the useless groan,
But hardens like the wave to stone.[17]
    Ye noble minds who o'er a sky
Where clouds are rolled, and tempests fly,
Have bid the lambent lustre play   145
Of *one* pure, lovely, azure ray –
Oh far diffuse its op'ning bloom
And the wide hemisphere illume!
Ye who *one* bitter drop have drained
From slav'ry's cup with horror stained,   150
Oh let no fatal dregs be found,
But dash her chalice on the ground;[18]
Oh, while she links her impious chain
And calculates the price of pain,
Weighs Agony in sordid scales   155
And marks if death or life prevails,
In one short moment seals the doom
Of years, which anguish shall consume;
Decides how near the mangling scourge
May to the grave its victim urge –   160
Yet for awhile, with prudent care
The half-worn wretch, if useful, spare,
And speculates, with skill refined,
How deep a wound will stab the mind,
How far the spirit can endure   165
Calamity, that hopes no cure!
Ye who can selfish cares forego,
To pity those which others know,
As light that from its centre strays
To glad[19] all nature with its rays,   170
Oh ease the pangs ye stoop to share
And rescue millions from despair!

---

[16] *embarred* enclosed, imprisoned.
[17] The *English Review* quoted lines 135–42, with the comment: 'A single instance we perceive of bad taste, a tinsel brilliancy, as where suicide is illustrated by the following simile' (*English Review* 13 (1789) 133–5, p. 135). Interestingly, these lines were omitted when the poem was reprinted in Williams's 1823 collected poems.
[18] The *Critical Review* quoted lines 143–52, with the comment: 'This, we imagine, reduced to plain prose, would signify: "as you have gained one point, and the trade for slaves is better regulated, extend your kindness, and procure for them absolute freedom". The "ray", mentioned above, does not dazzle us with excess of light, but disgusts by its superfluity of epithets. "Azure" and "opening bloom", applied to it, are ungenial expressions, and to "drain a drop" an awkward one' (*Critical Review* 67 (1789) 314).
[19] *glad* gladden.

For you, while Morn in graces gay
Wakes the fresh bloom of op'ning day,
Gilds with her purple[20] light your dome,   175
Renewing all the joys of home –
Of home, dear scene, whose ties can bind
With sacred force the human mind;
That feels each little absence pain[21]
And lives but to return again;   180
To that loved spot, however far,
Points, like the needle to its star;
That native shed which first we knew,
Where first the sweet affections grew,
Alike the willing heart can draw   185
If framed of marble or of straw,
Whether the voice of pleasure calls
And gladness echoes through its walls,
Or to its hallowed roof we fly
With those we love to pour the sigh,   190
The load of mingled pain to bear,
And soften every pang we share!
Ah, think how desolate *his* state,
How *he* the cheerful light must hate,
Whom, severed from his native soil,   195
The morning wakes to fruitless toil,
To labours hope shall never cheer
Or fond domestic joy endear.
Poor wretch, on whose despairing eyes
His cherished home shall never rise,   200
Condemned (severe extreme) to live
When all is fled that life can give!
And ah, the blessings valued most
By human minds, are blessings lost!
Unlike the objects of the eye,   205
Enlarging as we bring them nigh,
Our joys at distance strike the breast
And seem diminished when possessed.
    Who from his far-divided shore
The half-expiring captive bore?   210
Those whom the traffic of their race
Has robbed of every human grace,
Whose hardened souls no more retain
Impressions nature stamped in vain,
All that distinguishes their *kind*,   215
For ever blotted from their mind;

---

[20] *purple* the colour of victory.

[21] *That feels each little absence pain* i.e. the mind feels
each little absence from home with pain.

As streams that once the landscape gave
Reflected on the trembling wave,
Their substance change when locked in frost
And rest in dead contraction lost;   220
Who view unmoved the look that tells
The pang that in the bosom dwells;
Heed not the nerves that terror shakes,
The heart convulsive anguish breaks;
The shriek that would their crimes upbraid,   225
But deem despair a part of trade.
Such only for detested gain
The barb'rous commerce would maintain.
   The gen'rous sailor, he who dares
All forms of danger, while he bears   230
The British flag o'er untracked seas
And spreads it on the polar breeze;
He who, in glory's high career,
Finds agony and death are dear,
To whose protecting arm we owe   235
Each blessing that the happy know –
Whatever charms the softened heart,
Each cultured grace, each finer art,
E'en thine, most lovely of the train,
Sweet poetry, thy heav'n-taught strain –   240
His breast,[22] where nobler passions burn
In honest poverty, would spurn
The wealth oppression can bestow,
And scorn to wound a fettered foe.
True courage in the unconquered soul   245
Yields to compassion's mild control,
As the resisting frame of steel
The magnet's secret force can feel.
   When borne at length to western lands,
Chained on the beach the captive stands,   250
Where man (dire merchandise!) is sold
And bartered life is paid for gold.
In mute affliction, see him try
To read his new possessor's eye;
If one blessed glance of mercy there,   255
One half-formed tear may check despair!
Ah, if that eye with sorrow sees
His languid look, his quiv'ring knees,
Those limbs which scarce their load sustain,
That form consumed in wasting pain,   260
Such sorrow melts his ruthless eye
Who sees the lamb he doomed to die,

---

[22]   *His breast* i.e. that of the sailor.

In pining sickness yield his life,
And thus elude the sharpened knife;
Or if where savage habit steels　　　　　　　　　　265
The vulgar mind, one bosom feels
The sacred claim of helpless woe,
If pity in that soil can grow –
Pity, whose tender impulse darts
With keenest force on nobler hearts,　　　　　　　270
As flames that purest essence boast,
Rise highest when they tremble most.
Yet *why* on one poor chance must rest
The interests of a kindred breast?
Humanity's devoted cause　　　　　　　　　　　275
Recline[23] on humour's[24] wayward laws?
To Passion's rules must Justice bend
And life upon Caprice depend?
　Ah ye, who one fixed purpose own,
Whose untired aim is *self* alone;　　　　　　　280
Who think in gold the essence lies
From which extracted bliss shall rise;
To whose dull sense no charm appears
In social smiles or social tears,
As mists that o'er the landscape sail,　　　　　　285
Its beauteous variations veil;
Or if, in some relenting hour,
When nature reassumes her power,
Your alms to Penury ye lend
Or serve, for once, a suff'ring friend;　　　　　290
Whom no weak impulse e'er betrayed
To give that friend incautious aid;
Who with exact precision pause
At that nice point which Int'rest draws;
Your watchful footsteps never found　　　　　295
To stray beyond that guarded bound –
Does fleeting life proportion bear
To all the wealth ye heap with care?
When soon your days in measured flight
Shall sink in death's terrific night,　　　　　　300
Then seize the moments in your power –
To mercy consecrate the hour!
Risk something in her cause at last,
And thus atone for all the past;
Break the hard fetters of the slave,　　　　　305
And learn the luxury to save![25]
Does Avarice, your god, delight
With agony to feast his sight?

---

[23] *Recline* depend.
[24] *humour* mood, temperament.

[25] *the luxury to save* i.e. the luxury of saving, or liberating, someone from slavery.

Does he require that victims slain,
And human blood his altars stain? 310
Ah, not alone of power possessed
To check each virtue of the breast,
As when the numbing frosts arise
The charm of vegetation dies;
His sway the hardened bosom leads 315
To cruelty's remorseless deeds
Like the blue lightning, when it springs
With fury on its livid wings,
Darts to its goal with baleful force,
Nor heeds that ruin marks its course. 320
   Oh eloquence, prevailing art,
Whose force can chain the list'ning heart,
The throb of sympathy inspire
And kindle every great desire,
With magic energy control 325
And reign the sov'reign of the soul,
That dreams, while all its passions swell,
It shares the power it feels so well,
As visual objects seem possessed
Of those clear hues by light impressed – 330
Oh skilled in every grace to charm,
To soften, to appal, to warm,
Fill with thy noblest rage the breast,
Bid on those lips thy spirit rest,
That shall, in Britain's senate, trace 335
The wrongs of Afric's captive race!
But fancy o'er the tale of woe
In vain one heightened tint would throw;
For ah, the truth is all we guess
Of anguish in its last excess! 340
Fancy may dress in deeper shade
The storm that hangs along the glade,
Spreads o'er the ruffled stream its wing
And chills awhile the flowers of spring,
But where the wintry tempests sweep 345
In madness o'er the darkened deep,
Where the wild surge, the raging wave,
Point to the hopeless wretch a grave,
And death surrounds the threat'ning shore –
Can fancy add one horror more? 350
   Loved Britain, whose protecting hand,
Stretched o'er the globe, on Afric's strand
The honoured base of freedom lays,
Soon, soon the finished fabric[26] raise!
And when surrounding realms would frame, 355

---

[26] *fabric* of laws to abolish slavery.

Touched with a spark of gen'rous flame,
Some pure, ennobling, great design,
Some lofty act, almost divine,
Which earth may hail with rapture high,
And Heav'n may view with fav'ring eye,   360
Teach them[27] to make all nature free,
And shine by emulating thee!

From Julia, A Novel (1790)

THE BASTILLE, A VISION[1]

I.1
'Drear cell, along whose lonely bounds
Unvisited by light
Chill silence dwells with night,
Save when the clanging fetter sounds!
Abyss where mercy never came,   5
Nor hope the wretch can find,
Where long inaction wastes the frame,
And half annihilates the mind!

I.2
'Stretched helpless in this living tomb,
Oh haste, congenial death!   10
Seize, seize this ling'ring breath,
And shroud me in unconscious gloom –
Britain, thy exiled son no more
Thy blissful vales shall see;
Why did I leave thy hallowed shore,   15
Distinguished land, where all are free?'

I.3
Bastille! within thy hideous pile
Which stains of blood defile,
Thus rose the captive's sighs,
Till slumber sealed his weeping eyes –   20
Terrific visions hover near!

---

[27] *them* i.e. the 'surrounding realms' of line 355.
THE BASTILLE, A VISION
[1] This poem is preceded in the novel by the following passage: 'Mr F. called at Mr Clifford's one evening, and finding Charlotte and Julia sitting at work, he desired their permission to read to them a poem written by a friend lately arrived from France, and who, for some supposed offence against the state, had been immured several years in the Bastille, but was at length liberated by the interference of a person in power. The horrors of his solitary dungeon were one night cheered by the following prophetic dream.' The prison of the Bastille had for years symbolized the injustice of the *ancien régime*, and its storming on 14 July 1789 (still celebrated today) was welcomed by many on both sides of the English Channel. Williams visited the ruins of the Bastille when she went to Paris in 1790; she describes it in her *Letters Written in France* (1790), extracted in *Romanticism* 139–40.

He sees an awful form appear
Who drags his step to deeper cells
Where stranger wilder horror dwells.

II.1

'Oh tear me from these haunted walls   25
Or those fierce shapes control,
Lest madness seize my soul;
That pond'rous mask of iron[2] falls,
I see.' 'Rash mortal, ha! Beware,
Nor breathe that hidden name!   30
Should those dire accents wound the air,
Know death shall lock thy stiff'ning frame.

II.2

'Hark, that loud bell which sullen tolls!
It wakes a shriek of woe
From yawning depths below;   35
Shrill through this hollow vault it rolls!
A deed was done in this black cell
Unfit for mortal ear;
A deed was done, when tolled that knell,
No human heart could live and hear!   40

II.3

'Rouse thee from thy numbing trance,
Near on thick gloom advance,
The solid cloud has shook;
Arm all thy soul with strength to look –
Enough! Thy starting locks have rose,   45
Thy limbs have failed, thy blood has froze;
On scenes so foul, with mad affright,
I fix no more thy fastened sight.'

III.1

'Those troubled phantoms melt away,
I lose the sense of care!   50
I feel the vital air –
I see, I *see* the light of day!
Visions of bliss, eternal powers!
What force has shook those hated walls?
What arm has rent those threat'ning towers?   55
It falls – the guilty fabric falls!'

---

[2] 'Alluding to the prisoner who has excited so many conjectures in Europe' (Williams's note). The man in the iron mask was a state prisoner during the reign of Louis XIV, and was confined in the Bastille. His identity was concealed and he wore a mask covered in black velvet; who he was remains a mystery.

III.2

'Now favoured mortal, now behold!
To soothe thy captive state
I ope the book of fate –
Mark what its registers unfold!   60
Where this dark pile in chaos lies,
With nature's execrations hurled,
Shall freedom's sacred temple rise
And charm an emulating world!

III.3

''Tis her awak'ning voice commands   65
Those firm, those patriot bands,
Armed to avenge her cause
And guard her violated laws!
Did ever earth a scene display
More glorious to the eye of day   70
Than millions with according mind
Who claim the rights of humankind?

IV.1

'Does the famed Roman page sublime
An hour more bright unroll
To animate the soul   75
Than this, loved theme of future time?
Posterity, with rev'rence meet,
The consecrated act shall hear;
Age shall the glowing tale repeat
And youth shall drop the burning tear!   80

IV.2

'The peasant, while he fondly sees
His infants round the hearth
Pursue their simple mirth
Or emulously climb his knees,
No more bewails their future lot   85
By tyranny's stern rod oppressed,
While freedom guards his straw-roofed cot
And all his useful toils are blessed.

IV.3

Philosophy,[3] oh share the meed
Of freedom's noblest deed!
'Tis thine each truth to scan,   90
Guardian of bliss and friend of man!

---

[3] The works of numerous philosophers, including Rousseau and Holbach, were credited with having generated an intellectual climate favourable to the Revolution.

'Tis thine all human wrongs to heal,
'Tis thine to love all nature's weal,
To give each gen'rous purpose birth   95
And renovate the gladdened earth.[4]

A Farewell, for Two Years, to England. A Poem. (1791)

Sweet spring, while others hail thy op'ning flowers,
The first young hope of summer's blushing hours,
Me they remind that when her ardent ray
Shall reach the summit of our lengthened day,
Then, Albion, far from thee, my cherished home,   5
To foreign climes my pensive steps must roam,
And twice shall spring, dispelling winter's gloom,
Shed o'er thy lovely vales her vernal bloom;
Twice shall thy village-maids, with chaplets gay
And simple carols, hail returning May;   10
And twice shall autumn, o'er thy cultured plain,
Pour the rich treasures of his yellow grain;
Twice shall thy happy peasants bear along
The lavish store, and wake the harvest-song,
Ere from the bounded deep my searching eye,   15
Ah, land beloved, shall thy white cliffs descry.
Where the slow Loire, on borders ever gay,
Delights to linger in his sunny way,
Oft, while I seem to count, with musing glance,
The murm'ring waves that near his brink advance,   20
My wand'ring thoughts shall seek the grassy side,
Parental Thames, where rolls thy ample tide;
Where on thy willowed bank, methinks, appears
Engraved the record of my passing years.
Ah, not like thine, their course is gently led,   25
By zephyrs fanned, through paths with verdure spread;
They flow, as urged by storms the mountain rill
Falls o'er the fragments of the rocky hill.
   My native scenes! Can aught in time or space
From this fond heart your loved remembrance chase?   30
Linked to that heart by ties for ever dear,
By joy's light smile, and sorrow's tender tear;
By all that ere my anxious hopes employed,
By all my soul has suffered or enjoyed!
Still blended with those well-known scenes, arise   35
The varying images the past supplies;

---

[4]   *And renovate the gladdened earth* Williams's language
in this line is full of millennial optimism; many be-
lieved that the French Revolution was the harbinger
of a universal spiritual revolution to come.

The childish sports that fond attention drew,
And charmed my vacant heart when life was new;
The harmless mirth, the sadness robbed of power
To cast its shade beyond the present hour –   40
And that dear hope which soothed my youthful breast,
And showed the op'ning world in beauty dressed;
That hope which seemed with bright unfolding rays
(Ah, vainly seemed!) to gild my future days;
That hope which, early wrapped in lasting gloom,   45
Sunk in the cold inexorable tomb!
And Friendship, ever powerful to control
The keen emotions of the wounded soul,
To lift the suff'ring spirit from despair,
And bid it feel that life deserves a care.   50
Still each impression that my heart retains
Is linked, dear land, to thee by lasting chains.
    She too, sweet soother of my lonely hours,
Who gilds my thorny path with fancy's flowers,
The muse who early taught my willing heart   55
To feel with transport her prevailing art,
Who deigned before my infant eyes to spread
Those dazzling visions she alone can shed –
She who will still be found where'er I stray
The loved companion of my distant way;   60
Midst foreign sounds, her voice that charms my ear,
Breathed in my native tongue, I still shall hear;
Midst foreign sounds, endeared will flow the song
Whose tones, my Albion, will to thee belong!
    And when with wonder thrilled, with mind elate,   65
I mark the change sublime in Gallia's state,
Where new-born Freedom treads the banks of Seine,
Hope in her eye, and Virtue in her train!
Pours day upon the dungeon's central gloom,
And leads the captive from his living tomb;   70
Tears the sharp iron from his loaded breast,
And bids the renovated[5] land be blessed –
My thoughts shall fondly turn to that loved isle
Where Freedom long has shed her genial smile.
Less safe in other lands the triple wall   75
And massy portal of the Gothic hall,
Than in that favoured isle the straw-built thatch
Where Freedom sits, and guards the simple latch.
    Yet, Albion, while my heart to thee shall spring,
To thee its first, its best affections bring;   80
Yet when I hear exulting millions pour

---

[5] *renovated* this picks up the millennial hope implied in the final line of the preceding poem. Universal spiritual renewal was one of the expected results of the French Revolution.

The shout of triumph on the Gallic shore,
Not without sympathy my pensive mind
The bounds of human bliss enlarged, shall find;
Not without sympathy my glowing breast   85
Shall hear, on any· shore, of millions blessed,
Scorning those narrow souls, whate'er their clime,
Who meanly think that sympathy a crime,
Who, if one wish for human good expand
Beyond the limits of their native land,   90
And from the worst of ills would others free,
Deem that warm wish, my country, guilt to thee.
Ah, why those blessings to one spot confine,
Which, when diffused, will not the less be thine?
Ah, why repine if far those blessings spread   95
For which so oft thy gen'rous sons have bled?
Shall Albion mark with scorn the lofty thought,
The love of liberty, herself has taught?
Shall *her* brave sons, in this enlightened age,
Assume the bigot-frown of papal rage,   100
Nor tolerate the vow to Freedom paid
If diff'ring from the ritual *they* have made?
Freedom, who oft on Albion's fost'ring breast
Has found *her* friends in stars and ermine dressed,
Allows that some among her chosen race   105
Should there the claim to partial honours trace,
And in the long-reflected lustre shine
That beams through ancestry's ennobled line;
While she, with guardian wing, can well secure
From each proud wrong the undistinguished poor.   110
On Gallia's coast, where oft the robe of state
Was trailed by those whom Freedom's soul must hate;
Where, like a comet, rank appeared to glow
With dangerous blaze that threatened all below –
There Freedom now, with gladdened eye, beholds   115
· The simple vest that flows in equal folds.
    And though on Seine's fair banks a transient storm[6]
Flung o'er the darkened wave its angry form,
That purifying tempest now has passed –
No more the trembling waters feel the blast;   120
The bord'ring images, confusedly traced
Along the ruffled stream, to order haste;[7]
The vernal dayspring bursts the partial gloom,
And all the landscape glows with fresher bloom.
    When, far around that bright'ning scene, I view   125

---

[6] *a transient storm* a reference to the storming of the Bastille, 14 July 1789, when the prison was not merely demolished, but many of its prisoners slaughtered.

Williams's views on this event are elucidated in her *Letters*; see *Romanticism* 139–40.
[7] *to order haste* hasten to order.

Objects of gen'ral bliss, to Gallia new,
Then, Albion, shall my soul reflect with pride
Thou wert her leading star, her honoured guide;
That, long in slav'ry sunk, when taught by thee,
She broke her fetters, and has dared be free;   130
In new-born majesty she seems to rise,
While sudden from the land oppression flies.
So, at the solemn hour of nature's birth,
When brooding darkness[8] veiled the beauteous earth,
Heaven's awful mandate pierced the solid night –   135
'Let there be light', it said, 'and there was light!'
 Ah, when shall reason's intellectual ray
Shed o'er the moral world more perfect day?
When shall that gloomy world appear no more
A waste, where desolating tempests roar?   140
Where savage Discord howls in threat'ning form,
And wild Ambition leads the madd'ning storm;
Where hideous Carnage marks his dang'rous way,
And where the screaming vulture scents his prey?
Ah, come, blest Concord, chase with smile serene   145
The hostile passions from the human scene.
May Glory's lofty path be found afar
From agonizing groans and crimson war,
And may the ardent mind that seeks renown
Claim not the martial, but the civic crown,   150
While pure Benevolence, with happier views
Of bright success, the gen'ral good pursues!
Ah, why, my country, with indignant pain,
Why in thy senate did she plead in vain?
Ah, why in vain enforce the captives' cause,   155
And urge humanity's eternal laws?
With fruitless zeal the tale of horror trace,
And ask redress for Afric's injured race?
Unhappy race! Ah, what to them availed
That touching eloquence whose efforts failed?   160
Though in the senate Mercy found combined
All who possess the noblest pow'rs of mind,
On other themes, pre-eminently bright,
They shine, like single stars, with sep'rate light –
Here, only *here*, with intermingled rays,   165
In one resplendent constellation blaze.
Yes, captive race, if all the force displayed
By glowing Genius, in Compassion's aid,
When with that energy she boasts alone,
She made your wrongs, your ling'ring tortures known,   170
Bade full in view the bloody visions roll,

---

[8] *brooding darkness* Miltonic; cf. *L'Allegro* 6: 'Where
brooding darkness spreads his jealous wings'.

Shook the firm nerves, and froze the shudd'ring soul,
As when the sun, in piercing radiance bright,
Dispelling the low mists of doubtful light,
Its lustre on some hideous object throws   175
And all its hateful horror clearly shows –
If Genius could in Mercy's cause prevail,
When Interest presses the opposing scale,
How swift had Britons torn your galling chain,
And from their country wiped its foulest stain!   180
But oh, since mis'ry, in its last excess,
In vain from British honour hopes redress,
May other lands the bright example show,
May other regions lessen human woe!
Yes, Gallia, haste! Though Britain's sons decline   185
The glorious power to save, that power is thine;
Haste, since, while Britain courts that dear-bought gold
For which her virtue and her fame are sold,
And calmly calculates her trade of death,
Her groaning victims yield in pangs their breath;   190
Then save some portion of that suff'ring race
From ills the mind can scarce endure to trace!
Oh, whilst with mien august thy leaders scan,
And guard with jealous zeal the rights of man,[9]
Forget not that to all kind Nature gives   195
Those common rights, the claim of all that lives.
But yet my filial heart its wish must breathe
That Britain first may snatch this deathless wreath;
First to the earth this act divine proclaim,
And wear the freshest palm of virtuous fame;   200
May I, in foreign realms, her glories hear,
Catch the loved sounds, and pour th' exulting tear!
   And when, the destined hour of exile past,
My willing feet shall reach their home at last;
When, with the trembling hope Affection proves,[10]   205
My eager heart shall search for those it loves,
May no sharp pang that cherished hope destroy,
And from my bosom tear the promised joy,
Shroud every object, every scene in gloom,
And lead my bleeding soul to Friendship's tomb!   210
But may that moment to my eyes restore
The friends whose love endears my native shore!
Ah, long may Friendship, like the western ray,
Cheer the sad evening of a stormy day,
And gild my shadowy path with ling'ring light,   215
The last dear beam that slowly sinks in night.

[9] *the rights of man* a reference to Thomas Paine's famous republican work (1791–2). Cf. the allusion in Susanna Blamire's rather different poem, *Joe and Ned* 20, p. 66.

[10] *proves* experiences.

From Paul and Virginia (1796)

SONNET TO THE STRAWBERRY

The strawberry blooms upon its lowly bed,
Plant of my native soil! The lime may fling
More potent fragrance on the zephyr's wing,
The milky cocoa richer juices shed,
The white guava lovelier blossoms spread –   5
But not like thee to fond remembrance bring
The vanished hours of life's enchanting spring,
Short calendar joys for ever fled!
Thou bidd'st the scenes of childhood rise to view,
The wild-wood path which fancy loves to trace   10
Where, veiled in leaves, thy fruit of rosy hue
Lurked on its pliant stem with modest grace.
But ah, when thought would later years renew,
Alas, successive sorrows crowd the space!

Joanna Baillie (1762–1851)

Joanna was the younger daughter of Dorothea Hunter and James Baillie, a presbyterian minister of Bothwell, Lanarkshire, later Professor of Divinity at the University of Glasgow (where a cache of her letters is now retained in the library). Her mother's family was distinguished: her aunt was Anne Hunter (1742–1821), the poet and bluestocking; her uncles were the famous surgeons, William and John Hunter. In 1783 William bequeathed his London house in Great Windmill Street to Matthew, Joanna's brother, a physician and anatomist. In 1784 his mother and sisters joined him there, and on his marriage in 1791 moved to Hampstead. After Mrs Baillie's death in 1806, Joanna lived with her sister for the remainder of her life.

Her first publication was the little-noticed *Poems; wherein it is attempted to describe certain views of nature and of rustic manners* (1790). The volume has much charm, and is in fact quite experimental, as the various poems not merely evoke different scenes, but different psychological states. All the same, they are apprentice pieces, and look forward to her *Series of Plays; in which it is attempted to delineate the stronger passions of the mind* (3 vols, 1798–1812), the work which attracts most critical attention today. The first volume contained two plays on hate, and two on love. It appeared anonymously, leading to widespread speculation about the identity of its author. Her authorship was acknowledged in 1800, the year that saw the first performance of *De Monfort* with Sarah Siddons in the starring role. (Georgiana Cavendish, Duchess of Devonshire, provided the epilogue.) She became widely known in literary circles, being acquainted with Wordsworth, Scott, Samuel Rogers, Anna Laetitia Barbauld (who included some of her poems from the 1790 volume in an anthology) and Maria Edgeworth. Her reputation went into decline after a particularly harsh review from Francis Jeffrey in 1803. In subsequent years she concentrated on poetry. In 1821 she published *Metrical Legends*, the result of a visit to Scotland; she edited an anthology of contemporary poetry in 1823; her *Fugitive Verses* appeared in 1840, containing several poems not hitherto published (it was reprinted in 1842); and *Ahalya Baee*, a long poem about a female Indian ruler, was published in 1849. A one-volume edition of her dramatic and poetical works appeared in 1851.[1] On its publication the reviewer in the *Eclectic* pointed out that her songs 'are only inferior to those of Burns, superior to those of Haynes Bayly, and Moore, and quite equal to those of Sir Walter Scott and Campbell. Need we speak of *The Gowan glitters on the Sward*, *Saw ye Johnny Coming?*, *Tam o' the Lin*, or *The Weary Pund o' tow*? Every Scotchman in the world worthy of the name knows these by heart – while, perhaps, thousands are ignorant that they are by Joanna Baillie'.[2] Her poetry is usually represented by work from the 1790 volume; this is not, I think, her best. The reviewer was right to observe that Joanna's finest poems are her songs. They are a good deal more energetic and compelling than the early verse, which has a rather studied feel to it. In the Preface to her 1840 *Fugitive Verses*, she explained the principles behind her poetry:

> Modern poetry, within these last thirty years, has become so imaginative, impassioned, and sentimental, that more homely subjects, in simple diction, are held in comparatively small estimation. This, however, is a natural progress of the art, and the obstacles it may cast in the way of a less gifted, or less aspiring genius, must be submitted to with good grace. Nay, they may even sometimes be read with more relish from their very want of the more elevated flights of fancy from our natural love of relaxation after having had our minds kept on the stretch, by following, or endeavouring to follow, more sublime and obscure conceptions. He who has been coursing through the air in a balloon, or ploughing the boundless ocean in the bark of some dauntless discoverer, or careering over the field on a warhorse, may be very well pleased after all to seat himself on a bench by his neighbour's door, and look at the meadows around him, or country people passing along the common from their daily work. Let me then be encouraged to suppose that something of this nature may, with the courteous reader, operate in my behalf.[3]

The belief in simplicity of subject-matter and diction is redolent of Wordsworth's Preface to *Lyrical Ballads*. No doubt this was something she discussed with Wordsworth when they became acquainted in literary circles in London in the 1810s, though critical investigation in recent years indicates that Wordsworth borrowed from her as early as 1799. A new complete edition of the plays and poetry is in preparation at the time of writing, edited by Keith Hanley and Amanda Gilroy.

Further Reading

Margaret S. Carhart, *The Life and Work of Joanna Baillie* (New Haven, 1923)
Daniel P. Watkins, *A Materialist Critique of English Romantic Drama* (Gainesville, Florida, 1993), chapter 3
Catherine B. Burroughs, 'English Romantic Women Writers and Theatre Theory: Joanna Baillie's Prefaces to the *Plays on the Passions*', RR 274–96
Marjean D. Purinton, *Romantic Ideology Unmasked: The Mentally-Constructed Tyrannies in Dramas of William Wordsworth, Lord Byron, Percy Shelley, and Joanna Baillie* (Newark and London, 1994)

---

[1] Jackson records an American edition of her complete poetical works in 1832 (Jackson 15).

[2] *Eclectic Review* 5th series 1 (1851) 407–23, p. 421.

[3] *Fugitive Verses* (1840), pp. vi–vii.

Catherine B. Burroughs, '"Out of the Pale of Social Kindred Cast": Conflicted Performance Styles in Joanna Baillie's *De Monfort*', *RWW* 223–35

Anne K. Mellor, 'Joanna Baillie and the Counter-Public Sphere', *SIR* 33 (1994) 559–67

William D. Brewer, 'Joanna Baillie and Lord Byron', *Keats-Shelley Journal* 44 (1995) 165–81

From Fugitive Verses (1840)

A SCOTCH SONG[1]

The gowan[2] glitters on the sward,[3]
  The lavrock's[4] in the sky,
And collie on my plaid[5] keeps ward,[6]
  And time is passing by.
    Oh no! sad and slow   5
And, lengthened on the ground,
  The shadows of our trysting bush,[7]
It wears so slowly round!

My sheep-bell tinkles frae the west,
  My lambs are bleating near,   10
But still the sound that I lo'e best,
  Alac! I canna' hear.
    Oh no! sad and slow,
The shadow lingers still,
  And like a lanely ghaist I stand   15
And croon upon the hill.

I hear below the water roar,
  The mill wi' clacking din,
And Lucky scolding frae her door,
  To ca' the bairnies[8] in.   20
    Oh no! sad and slow,
These are na' sounds for me,
  The shadow of our trysting bush,
It creeps sae drearily!

I coft[9] yestreen, frae chapman Tam,   25
  A snood[10] of bonny blue,

A SCOTCH SONG
[1] Other versions of this poem are entitled *The Shepherd's Song (The Lover's Watch)*.
[2] *gowan* daisy.
[3] *sward* turf.
[4] *lavrock* lark, as at Coleridge, *Ancient Mariner* (1798), 348.
[5] *plaid* long piece of twilled woollen cloth worn as an outer garment in the Highlands.

[6] *ward* watch, guard.
[7] *trysting bush* the bush where the shepherd is to meet his lover.
[8] *bairnies* children.
[9] *coft* bought.
[10] *snood* hair-band worn by young unmarried women in Scotland.

And promised when our trysting cam'
  To tie it round her brow.
    Oh no! sad and slow,
The mark it winna' pass;   30
  The shadow of that weary thorn
Is tethered on the grass.

Oh now I see her on the way,
  She's past the witch's knowe,[11]
She's climbing up the browny's[12] brae,   35
  My heart is in a lowe![13]
    Oh no! 'tis na' so,
'Tis glamrie[14] I have seen;
  The shadow of that hawthorn bush
Will move na' mair till e'en.   40

My book o' grace I'll try to read,
  Though conned wi' little skill;
When collie barks I'll raise my head,
  And find her on the hill;
    Oh no! sad and slow,   45
The time will ne'er be gane,
  The shadow of the trysting bush
Is fixed like ony stane.

SONG ('POVERTY PARTS GOOD COMPANY', FOR AN OLD SCOTCH AIR)

When my o'erlay was white as the foam o' the lin,[1]
And siller was chinkin my pouches within;
When my lambkins were bleatin on meadow and brae,
As I went to my love in new cleeding[2] sae gay,
  Kind was she, and my friends were free,   5
  But poverty parts good company.

How swift passed the minutes and hours of delight,
When piper played cheerly and crusie[3] burned bright,
And linked in my hand was the maiden sae dear,
As she footed the floor in her holy-day gear!   10
  Woe is me, and can it then be
  That poverty parts sic[4] company?

We met at the fair and we met at the kirk,
We met i' the sunshine, we met i' the mirk;

---

[11] *knowe* mound.
[12] *browny* fairy.
[13] *in a lowe* on fire.
[14] *glamrie* magic.

SONG
[1] *lin* waterfall.
[2] *cleeding* cladding, clothing.
[3] *crusie* the lamp.
[4] *sic* such.

And the sound o' her voice, and the blinks o' her een,[5]   15
The cheerin and life of my bosom hae been.
    Leaves frae the tree, at Mertimass flee,
    And poverty parts sweet company.

At bridal and infare[6] I braced me wi' pride,
The bruise[7] I hae won, and a kiss o' the bride;   20
And loud was the laughter good fellows among,
As I uttered my banter or chorused my song;
    Dowie and dree[8] are jestin and glee,
    When poverty spoils good company.

Wherever I gaed kindly lasses looked sweet,   25
And mithers and aunties were unco[9] discreet,
While kebbuck and beeker[10] were set on the board –
But now they pass by me, and never a word!
    Sae let it be, for the worldly and slee[11]
    Wi' poverty keep nae company.   30

But the hope of my love is a cure for its smart,
And the spae-wife[12] has tauld me to keep up my heart,
For wi' my last saxpence, her loof[13] I hae crossed,
And the bliss that is fated can never be lost.
    Though cruelly we may ilka[14] day see   35
    How poverty parts dear company.

SONG

What voice is this, thou evening gale,
That mingles with thy rising wail;
And as it passes, sadly seems
The faint return of youthful dreams?

Though now its strain is wild and drear,   5
Blithe was it once as skylark's cheer,
Sweet as the nightbird's sweetest song,
Dear as the lisp of infant's tongue.

It was the voice, at whose sweet flow
The heart did beat and cheek did glow,   10
And lip did smile and eye did weep,
And motioned love the measure keep.

---

[5] *een* eyes.
[6] *infare* housewarming.
[7] *bruise* race.
[8] *Dowie and dree* hard to beat.
[9] *unco* very.

[10] *kebbuck and beeker* cheese and beaker.
[11] *slee* sly.
[12] *spae-wife* fortune-teller.
[13] *loof* palm.
[14] *ilka* each, every.

Oft be thy sound, soft gale of even,
Thus to my wistful fancy given;
And as I list the swelling strain   15
The dead shall seem to live again.

From The Dramatic and Poetical Works of Joanna Baillie (1851)

TAM O' THE LIN

Tam o' the Lin was fu' o' pride,
And his weapon he girt to his valorous side,
A scabbard o' leather wi' deil-haet[1] within –
'Attack me wha daur!'[2] quo' Tam o' the Lin.

Tam o' the Lin he bought a mear,   5
She cost him five shilling, she was na' dear,
Her back stuck up and her sides fell in –
'A fiery yaud!'[3] quo' Tam o' the Lin.

Tam o' the Lin he courted a may,[4]
She stared at him sourly and said him nay,   10
But he stroked down his jerkin and cocked up his chin –
'She aims at a laird then', quo' Tam o' the Lin.

Tam o' the Lin he gaed to the fair,
Yet he looked wi' disdain on the chapman's ware,
Then chucked out a saxpence, the saxpence was tin –   15
'There's coin for the fiddlers', quo' Tam o' the Lin.

Tam o' the Lin wad show his lare,[5]
And he scanned o'er the book wi' a wiselike stare,
He muttered confusedly but didna begin –
'This is dominie's[6] business', quo' Tam o' the Lin. 20

Tam o' the Lin had a cow wi' ae horn,
That liket to feed on his neighbour's corn,
The stanes he threw at her fell short o' her skin –
'She's a lucky auld reiver',[7] quo' Tam o' the Lin.

Tam o' the Lin he married a wife,   25
And she was the torment, the plague o' his life;
'She lays sae about her, and makes sic a din –
She frightens the bailie',[8] quo' Tam o' the Lin.

TAM O' THE LIN
[1] *deil-haet* nothing.
[2] *wha daur* who dares.
[3] *yaud* old mare.
[4] *may* maiden.

[5] *lare* learning.
[6] *dominie* teacher.
[7] *reiver* raider.
[8] *bailie* bailiff, local sheriff.

Tam o' the Lin grew dowie and douce,[9]
And he sat on a stane at the end o' his house;   30
'What ails thee, auld chield?'[10] He looks haggard and thin –
'I'm no vera cheery', quo' Tam o' the Lin.

Tam o' the Lin lay down to die,
And his friends whispered softly and woefully,
'We'll buy you some masses to scour away sin';   35
'And drink at my latewake',[11] quo' Tam o' the Lin.

Ann Radcliffe (*née* Ward)   (1764–1823)

Ann Radcliffe was born in London on 9 July 1764, the only child of William Ward,
a haberdasher, and Ann Oates, who was thirty-six at the time of her daughter's birth.
Ward may have been a haberdasher by trade, but he was nonetheless well connected.
His uncle was William Cheselden, surgeon to George II, and Ann Oates was the cousin
of Sir Richard Jebb, a famous physician of the day. Her maternal uncle-in-law was
Thomas Bentley, of the pottery firm Wedgwood and Bentley. When Ann was seven,
the Wards moved to Bath, where William managed a branch of the Wedgwood and
Bentley china emporium. It is believed that, at around this time, Ann was introduced
to Elizabeth Montagu.

On 15 January 1787, at the age of twenty-two, Ann married William Radcliffe at
St Michael's Church in Bath. Radcliffe was an Oxford graduate who was training as
a lawyer at the Inner Temple. After their marriage, Ann joined him in London where
he gave up his training and became editor and proprietor of a newspaper, *The English
Chronicle*. The couple were to remain childless, but the marriage seems to have been
happy. In leisure hours Ann read, sang, and went to operas, oratorios and plays. She
also began to write. Six works appeared, with remarkable speed, between 1789 and 1797.
Her first three novels were published, anonymously, within three years.

The Castles of Athlin and Dunbayne, A Highland Story (1789) is comparatively short and
experimental, but it is full of the rugged landscapes that were to become the stock-
in-trade of the Radcliffe chiller. It received little critical attention, and no reviews that
she would have found encouraging. But Ann persisted. The following year she published
A Sicilian Romance, set in Catholic Europe, featuring a heroine who is the focus of
debased and perverted lust. All the same, it is still a step away from her best work
– the three novels that were to follow: *The Romance of the Forest* (1791), *The Mysteries of
Udolpho* (1794) and *The Italian* (1797). *The Romance of the Forest* was greeted with rave
reviews, which encouraged its anonymous author to reveal her identity on publication
of a second edition in 1792. This was the work that established her reputation beyond
doubt. *The Mysteries of Udolpho* was, if anything, even more successful. It received a luke-
warm reception from the reviewers, who criticized the poetry, anachronisms, improb-
abilities, and so forth (all the lumber of the gothic, in other words), but this had little
effect on sales. *Udolpho* was an enormous success with the reading public, selling in vast
numbers. Most of the reviewers had something to say about the poetry. The *Analytical
Review* commented that 'many of the little pieces have very great merit, but some abound

---

[9]   *dowie and douce* dull and quiet.   [11]   *latewake* watch kept at night over a dead body.
[10]   *auld chield* old man.

too much with monosyllables, which give feebleness to poetry'.[1] The *British Critic* found them superfluous to the narrative: 'However fond the reader may be of poetry, and however excellent the verses themselves, we will venture to assert that few will choose to peruse them whilst eagerly and anxiously pursuing the thread of the tale – a plain proof that, in such a situation, at least they are impertinent. Having said this, we are ready to confess that Mrs Radcliffe's poetical abilities are of the superior kind, and we shall be glad to see her compositions separately published.'[2] William Enfield in the *Monthly Review* agreed with this conclusion: 'Several of the pieces of poetry are elegant performances, but they would have appeared with more advantage as a separate publication.'[3]

After its publication, in the summer of 1794, the Radcliffes went on holiday to Holland, Germany and the Lake District. Travel books were all the rage, and as a result of the tour Ann wrote her own, *A Journey Made in the Summer of 1794* (1795). It contains some memorable landscape descriptions, particularly of the Lakes.[4] Ann never again went abroad, but the Radcliffes went on holiday, within England, at least once a year after this tour. In the years between *Udolpho* (1794) and The *Italian* (1797) Ann had eliminated the faults which critics had observed in the earlier novels, and she had read M. G. Lewis's *The Monk*. This combination of elements makes *The Italian* her most accomplished work, and it was greeted with acclaim by the reviewers.

Ann's father died on 24 July 1798, leaving her interests in the rents of property in Houghton-on-the-Hill, near Leicester; her mother died two years later, leaving most of her property to Ann. Combined with earnings from her novels, Ann found herself comfortably off for the first time in her life. She did not need to write for financial motives, and indeed published no more during her life. Of course, by the 1800s her novels were so well established in the literary world that they were attracting the attentions of satirists, imitators and those who, like Jane Austen in *Northanger Abbey*, disapproved of the 'debased' public appetite for the gothic. By 1810, when Coleridge made the following comment to Wordsworth, the Radcliffean gothic must have seemed very dated:

> I amused myself a day or two ago, on reading a romance in Mrs Radcliffe's style, with making out a scheme which was to serve for all romances *a priori*, only varying the proportions: a Baron or Baroness ignorant of their birth, and in some dependent situation – Castle on a rock – a sepulchre at some distance from the rock – deserted rooms – underground passages – pictures – a ghost, so believed, or a written record – blood on it! – a wonderful cut-throat – etc. etc. etc.[5]

Ann composed a final novel in 1802, *Gaston de Blondeville*, which was published after her death, in 1826. In subsequent years she continued to write poetry, but in seclusion, and with no expectation of publication. Her virtual disappearance from the public eye aroused speculation that the author of the gothic chillers of the 1790s had gone mad, or even that she had died. Sir Walter Scott for one was taken in by rumours that, 'in consequence of brooding over the terrors which she depicted, her reason had at length been overturned, and that the author of *The Mysteries of Udolpho* only existed as the melancholy inmate of a private madhouse'.[6] Her last twelve years were dogged by respiratory ailments, mainly asthma. She died in 1823.

[1] *Analytical Review* 19 (1794) 140–5, p. 144.
[2] *British Critic* 4 (1794) 110–21, p. 120.
[3] *Monthly Review* 15 (1794) 278–83, p. 281.
[4] See *Romanticism* 156–7.

[5] Griggs iii 294.
[6] Quoted Deborah D. Rogers, *Ann Radcliffe: A Bio-Bibliography* (1996), p. 13.

Today, she continues to attract much critical notice, primarily as a novelist. Given the magnitude of her achievement in the genre, that is entirely right and proper, but she is no mean poet. Who, for instance, can resist the charm of *The Butterfly to his Love*? And *A Sea-View* should be accounted a remarkable visionary feat, insofar as it evokes a landscape Radcliffe had never set eyes on. I have selected poems both from her early novels, and from *Gaston de Blondeville*.

Further Reading

Clare Frances McIntyre, *Ann Radcliffe in Relation to her Time* (New Haven, 1920)
Daniel Cottom, *The Civilised Imagination: A Study of Ann Radcliffe, Jane Austen, and Sir Walter Scott* (Cambridge, 1985)
The Critical Response to Ann Radcliffe ed. Deborah D. Rogers (Westport, CT, 1994)
Robert Miles, *Ann Radcliffe: The Great Enchantress* (Manchester and New York, 1995)
Deborah D. Rogers, *Ann Radcliffe: A Bio-Bibliography* (Westport, CT, 1996)

From The Romance of the Forest (1791)

Song of a Spirit

In the sightless[1] air I dwell,
  On the sloping sunbeams play;
Delve the cavern's inmost cell
  Where never yet did daylight stray;

Dive beneath the green sea waves   5
  And gambol in the briny deeps,
Skim ev'ry shore that Neptune[2] laves,
  From Lapland's plains to India's steeps.

Oft I mount with rapid force
  Above the wide earth's shadowy zone,   10
Follow the day-star's[3] flaming course
  Through realms of space to thought unknown;

And listen oft celestial sounds
  That swell the air unheard of men,
As I watch my nightly rounds   15
  O'er woody steep and silent glen.

Under the shade of waving trees,
  On the green bank of fountain[4] clear,
At pensive eve I sit at ease,
  While dying music murmurs near.   20

Song of a Spirit
[1] *sightless* unseen, dark.
[2] *Neptune* Roman god of the sea.
[3] *day-star* the sun.
[4] *fountain* spring, brook.

And oft, on point of airy clift
  That hangs upon the western main,
I watch the gay tints passing swift,
  And twilight veil the liquid plain.

Then, when the breeze has sunk away,   25
  And ocean scarce is heard to lave,
For me the sea-nymphs softly play
  Their dulcet shells beneath the wave.

Their dulcet shells, I hear them now,
  Slow swells the strain upon mine ear;   30
Now faintly falls, now warbles low,
  Till rapture melts into a tear.

The ray that silvers o'er the dew
  And trembles through the leafy shade,
And tints the scene with softer hue,   35
  Calls me to rove the lonely glade;

Or hie me to some ruined tower
  Faintly shown by moonlight gleam,
Where the lone wanderer owns my power
  In shadows dire that substance seem,

In thrilling sounds that murmur woe,   40
  And pausing silence make more dread;
In music breathing from below
  Sad solemn strains that wake the dead.

Unseen I move, unknown am feared!
  Fancy's wildest dreams I weave;   45
And oft by bards my voice is heard
  To die along the gales of eve.

From The Mysteries of Udolpho (1794)

THE BUTTERFLY TO HIS LOVE

What bowery dell with fragrant breath
Courts thee to stay thy airy flight,
Nor seek again the purple heath,
So oft the scene of gay delight?

Long I've watched i' the lily's bell,   5
Whose whiteness stole the morning's beam –
No fluttering sounds thy coming tell,
No waving wings at distance gleam.

But fountain fresh, nor breathing grove,
Nor sunny mead, nor blossomed tree,   10
So sweet as lily's cell shall prove –
The bower of constant love and me.

When April buds begin to blow,
The primrose and the harebell blue
That on the verdant moss-bank grow,   15
With violet cups that weep in dew;

When wanton[1] gales breathe through the shade
And shake the blooms and steal their sweets,
And swell the song of ev'ry glade,
I range the forest's green retreats.   20

There, through the tangled wood-walks play,
Where no rude urchin paces near,
Where sparely[2] peeps the sultry day,
And light dews freshen all the air.

High on a sunbeam oft I sport   25
O'er bower and fountain, vale and hill;
Oft ev'ry blushing flowret court
That hangs its head o'er winding rill.

But these I'll leave to be thy guide,
And show thee where the jasmine spreads   30
Her snowy leaf, where may-flow'rs hide
And rosebuds rear their peeping heads.

With me the mountain's summit scale,
And taste the wild thyme's honeyed bloom,
Whose fragrance, floating on the gale,   35
Oft leads me to the cedar's gloom.

Yet, yet, no sound comes in the breeze!
What shade thus dares to tempt thy stay?
Once, me alone thou wished to please,
And with me only thou wouldst stray.   40

But while thy long delay I mourn,
And chide the sweet shades for their guile,
Thou mayst be true, and they forlorn,
And fairy favours court thy smile.

THE BUTTERFLY TO HIS LOVE   [2]   *sparely* sparsely.
[1] *wanton* sportive, playful.

The tiny queen of fairyland   45
Who knows thy speed hath sent thee far
To bring, or ere the night-watch stand,
Rich essence for her shadowy ear;

Perchance her acorn-cups to fill
With nectar from the Indian rose,   50
Or gather, near some haunted rill,
May-dews that lull to sleep love's woes;

Or o'er the mountains bade thee fly
To tell her fairy love to speed,
When ev'ning steals upon the sky,   55
To dance along the twilight mead.

But now I see thee sailing low,
Gay as the brightest flow'rs of spring,
Thy coat of blue and jet I know,
And well thy gold and purple wing.   60

Borne on the gale, thou comst to me;
Oh welcome, welcome, to my home!
In lily's cell we'll live in glee,
Together o'er the mountains roam.

TO THE WINDS

Viewless,[1] through heaven's vast vault your course ye steer,
Unknown from whence ye come, or whither go!
Mysterious pow'rs, I hear ye murmur low
Till swells your loud gust on my startled ear
And, awful,[2] seems to say – some God is near!   5
I love to list[3] your midnight voices float
In the dread storm that o'er the ocean rolls,
And, while their charm the angry wave controls,
Mix with its sullen roar, and sink remote.
Then, rising in the pause, a sweeter note,   10
The dirge of spirits who your deeds bewail,
A sweeter note oft swells while sleeps the gale!
But soon, ye sightless pow'rs, your rest is o'er;
Solemn and slow, ye rise upon the air,
Speak in the shrouds,[4] and bid the sea-boy fear,   15
And the faint-warbled dirge is heard no more!
   Oh then I deprecate your awful reign,
The loud lament, yet bear not on your breath!

TO THE WINDS
[1] *Viewless* invisible.
[2] *awful* awe-inspiring.

[3] *list* hear.
[4] *shrouds* ropes, usually in pairs, leading from the head of a ship's mast.

Bear not the crash of bark far on the main,
Bear not the cry of men who cry in vain,   20
The crew's dread chorus sinking into death!
Oh give not these, ye pow'rs, I ask alone,
As rapt[5] I climb these dark romantic steeps,
The elemental roar, the billow's moan;
I ask the still, sweet tear that listening Fancy weeps!   25

From Gaston de Blondeville...with Some Poetical Pieces (1826)

A SEA-VIEW

A breeze is springing up. Mark yon grey cloud
That from th' horizon piles its Alpy steeps
Upon the sky; there the fierce tempest rides.
Our vessel owns the gale, and all her sails
Are full; the broad and slanted deck cuts with its edge   5
The foaming waves that roll almost within it,
And often bow their curling tops as if
In homage. Not so the onward billows;
For while, with steady force, the vexing prow
Flings wide the groaning waters, high rise they,   10
Darting their dragon-headed vengeance; now
Baffled they burst on either side with rage,
And dash their spray in the hard seaman's face.
The gale is rising, and the roughening waves
Show darker shades of green with, here and there,   15
Far out, white foamy tops, that rise and fall
Incessant. Storm-lights,[1] issuing from the clouds,
Mark distances upon the mighty deep;
There, in one gleam, a white sail scuds along –
Farther, those vessels seem to hang in shade,   20
And farther still, on the last edge of ocean,
Where falls a paler, mistier sunlight,
See where some port-town peeps above the tide
With its long, level ramparts, turret-crowned;
There a broad tower and there a slender spire   25
Stand high upon the light, while all between,
Of intermingled roofs, embattled gates,
Quays, ancient halls and smoking chimneys, sunk
Low, and all blended in one common mass,
Are undiscerned so far. There all is calm;   30
The waters slumber; the anchored keels repose;
And not a top-mast trembles;
While here the chafing billows mount the deck,

---

[5] *rapt* entranced.

A SEA-VIEW
[1] *Storm-lights* lurid light seen in a stormy sky.

Dash through the sturdy shrouds,[2] and with their foam
Buffet the braced sail. Toward that port   35
Our vessel steers, which from the seas and winds
May soon receive us.
But ah, while yet we gaze, the vision fades!
The high-piled ramparts, overtopped with turrets,
Vanish in shade before the searching eye,   40
Which nought but waves and sky can trace o'er all
The lone horizon! So on Calabria's shore,
Where the old Reggio spreads its walls
Beside the sea, the fairy's wand at eve
Is lifted – and behold, far on the waters   45
Another landscape rise![3] Wood-mantled steeps
And shadowy mountains soar, and turrets from
Some promontory's point hang o'er the vale
Where sleeps among its palms the hamlet low,
Hid from the bustling, ostentatious world,   50
Deep in the bosom of this silent scene.
    Ah, beauteous work of fairy,[4] that can paint
Unreal visions to th' admiring eye,
Charming it with distinct though faithless forms.
The magic sceptre dropped – behold, they vanish!   55
A desert world of water's only there!
*   *   *   *   *   *
And thus th' enchantress on the daily path
Of Youth attends, known only by her power
Unseen, and conjures up Hope, Joy and Bliss
To dance in the fresh bowers of fadeless spring.   60
At Reason's touch the airy dream dissolves;
We gaze, and wonder at such wild delusion,
Yet weep its loss, and court its forms again.
Hail, beauteous scenes of fairy, Fancy's world! –
Where Truth, so cold and colourless, comes not,   65
Or far away in lonely grandeur stands
Like the great snowy Alps, whose cloudy shapes
And aspect stern (deforming the horizon)
Make the still landscape, spread below, appear
More green, more gay, more cheering to our view.   70
Hail, beauteous scenes of fairy, Fancy's world!
And now, as if the spell had worked again,
The stormy shade far distant floats away.

---

2   *shrouds* ropes, usually in pairs, leading from the head of a ship's mast.
3   'This phenomenon is noticed in Swinburne's Travels in the Two Sicilies. The people of Reggio attribute it, all natural as it is, to the fairy Morgana, and run with shouts to the shore, to witness her wonders' (Radcliffe's note). Radcliffe refers to Henry Swinburne (1743–

1803), *Travels in the Two Sicilies* (2 vols, 1783–5), which almost certainly provided most of the information on which this poem is based. The fata Morgana is a mirage seen in the Straits of Messina, attributed to the agency of fairies.
4   *fairy* magic.

Again the spired city shines in light,
Peering beyond the waves, here shadowed yet   75
By the lingering storm. The pier outstretches
Its arm to meet us, and the lighthouse shows
Its column, and we see the lanthorn[5] high,
Suspended o'er the margin of the tide,
The star of the night-wandering mariner.   80
Hail, cheering port, first vision of the land –
Vision, but not illusion, hail again!

SCENE ON THE NORTHERN SHORE OF SICILY

Here from the castle's terraced site,
  I view, once more, the varied scene
  Of hamlets, woods, and pastures green,
And vales far stretching from the sight
Beneath the tints of coming night;   5
  And there is misty ocean seen
  With glancing oars and waves serene,
And stealing sail of shifting light.
Now let me hear the shepherd's lay,
  As on some bank he sits alone;   10
  That oaten reed of tender tone
He loves at setting sun to play.
It speaks in joy's delightful glee,
  Then pity's strains its breath obey,
  Or Love's soft voice it seems to be,   15
  And steals at last the soul away!
And now the village bells afar
  Their melancholy music sound
Mournfully o'er the waters round,
  Till twilight sends her trembling star.   20
Oft shall my pensive heart attend,
  As swell the notes along the breeze,
And weep anew the buried friend
  In tears that sadly, softly please;
And when pale moonlight tips the trees,   25
  On the dark castle's tower ascends,
Throws o'er its walls a silvery gleam,
  And in one soft confusion blends
Forest and mountain, plain and stream,
  I list[1] the drowsy sounds that creep   30
On night's still air to soothe the soul;
  The hollow moan of ocean's roll,
The bleat and bell of wandering sheep,
  The distant watchdog's feeble bark,

---

[5] *lanthorn* chamber at the top of the lighthouse in
which the light is located.

SCENE ON THE NORTHERN SHORE OF SICILY
[1] *list* hear.

The voice of herdsman pacing home 35
   Along the leafy labyrinth dark,
And sounds that from the castle come
   Of closing door that sullen falls,
And murmurs through the chambers high
   Of half-sung strains from ancient halls 40
That through the long, long galleries die.
And now the taper's flame I spy
   In antique casement, glimmering pale;
And now 'tis vanished from my eye,
   And all but gloom and silence fail. 45

Once more I stand in pensive mood,
   And gaze on forms that truth delude;
And still mid Fancy's flitting scene,
   I catch the streaming cottage-light
Twinkling the restless leaves between, 50
   And ocean's flood, in moonbeams bright.

The Snow-Fiend

Hark, to the snow-fiend's voice afar
That shrieks upon the troubled air!
Him by that shrilly call I know –
Though yet unseen, unfelt below –
And by the mist of livid grey 5
That steals upon his onward way.
He from the ice-peaks of the north
In sounding majesty comes forth,
Dark amidst the wondrous light
That streams o'er all the northern night. 10
A wan rime through the airy waste
Marks where unseen his car has passed,
And veils the spectre-shapes, his train,
That wait upon his vengeful reign.
Disease and Want and shuddering Fear, 15
Danger and Woe and Death are there.
Around his head for ever raves
A whirlwind cold of misty waves.
But oft, the parting surge between,
His visage keen and white is seen; 20
His savage eye and paly glare
Beneath a helm of ice appear;
A snowy plume waves o'er the crest,
And wings of snow his form invest.
Aloft he bears a frozen wand, 25
The ice-bolt trembles in his hand,
And ever, when on sea he rides,

An iceberg for his throne provides.
As fierce he drives his distant way,
Agents remote his call obey, 30
From half-known Greenland's snow-piled shore
To Newfoundland and Labrador,
O'er solid seas where nought is scanned
To mark a difference from land,
And sound itself does but explain 35
The desolation of his reign.
The moaning querulous and deep,
And the wild howl's infuriate sweep
Where'er he moves, some note of woe
Proclaims the presence of the foe, 40
While he, relentless, round him flings
The white shower from his flaky wings.
Hark, 'tis his voice – I shun his call
And shuddering seek the blazing hall.
Oh speak of mirth, oh raise the song, 45
Hear not the fiends that round him throng!
Of curtained rooms and firesides tell,
Bid Fancy work her genial spell
That wraps in marvel and delight
December's long tempestuous night; 50
Makes courtly groups in summer bowers
Dance through pale winter's midnight hours;
And July's eve its rich glow shed
On the hoar wreath that binds his head;
Or knights on strange adventure bent, 55
Or ladies into thraldom sent;
Whatever gaiety ideal
Can substitute for troubles real.
Then let the storms of winter sing,
And his sad veil the snow-fiend fling, 60
Though wailing lays are in the wind,
They reach not then the tranced[1] mind;
Nor murky form, nor dismal sound
May pass the high enchanted bound.

Ann Batten Cristall (born *c.*1769)

Ann was born at Penzance, Cornwall, to Joseph Alexander Cristall, ship's captain, and his wife Elizabeth Batten, daughter of John Batten, a local merchant. She was the eldest child in a family of four sons and two daughters. Her father, a Scotsman, was often

---

THE SNOW-FIEND
[1] *tranced* entranced, in a trance.

away from home, but eventually set up yards in Fowey and Penzance where he made sails, masts and blocks. It is said that he was of a jealous disposition, and that his time ashore was not pleasant for his family. The date of Ann's birth is not known, but she was baptized 7 December 1769 in Penzance. Thanks partly to their father's frequent absences, she and her younger sister Elizabeth were taught by their mother, who loved literature and classical mythology. When they were still quite small, the family moved to Rotherhithe, where their father opened another yard, and where Ann's brother Joshua found work as a dealer in china.

Ann became a schoolteacher in 1788, and by March of that year had encountered first Everina Wollstonecraft and, through her, her famous sister Mary. Both are listed among the subscribers to *Poetical Sketches*. By 1790 Joshua Cristall had moved on from dealing in china to become a painter of china in the potteries in Staffordshire and Shropshire operated by Thomas Turner, from which the Blue Willow and Brosely Blue Dragon patterns originate. He would later become a celebrated watercolourist, engraver, and, in 1804, founder member of the Society of Painters in Watercolours. He was in correspondence with Mary Wollstonecraft by 1790, when she reproached him for an occasion on which 'you selfishly forgot your sister's peace of mind', and exhorted him to look after her: 'I know that you earnestly wish to be the friend and protector of your amiable sister and hope no inconsiderate act or thoughtless mode of conduct will add to her cares – for her comfort very much depends on you.'[1] Later that year Wollstonecraft regretted that she herself may have hurt Ann's 'tender affectionate heart'.[2] It is likely, given her counsel, that Wollstonecraft was already in the habit of giving Joshua financial help (she regretted giving him 'all the money I had' in March 1797),[3] and equally likely that Ann was financially dependent on Joshua. Their father was paralysed by a stroke in the 1790s, and his business began to fail.

Ann's *Poetical Sketches* was published by Joseph Johnson in 1795, with a title page featuring an engraving made from a drawing by her brother, featuring her fictional character Holbain. The list of subscribers is a roll-call of distinguished dissenters and radicals of the day: it includes John Aikin; Amelia Alderson (later Opie); Anna Laetitia Barbauld; John Disney; George Dyer; William Frend (notorious Cambridge radical); Benjamin Flower (Cambridge radical publisher); Capel Lofft (radical pamphleteer and intellectual); James Losh (friend of Wordsworth); Benjamin Heath Malkin; Anna Maria Porter; Richard Porson (Cambridge intellectual); Samuel Rogers; John Tweddell (Cambridge intellectual and friend of Wordsworth); Mary and Everina Wollstonecraft; and Gilbert Wakefield. It is likely that Ann encountered Joseph Johnson through Wollstonecraft, and that Dyer secured a number of these distinguished subscribers.[4]

The poems themselves are, I think, startlingly original, though I cannot be the first to have noted that there are times when her verse sounds like that of Blake. As an acquaintance of Johnson and Wollstonecraft, Ann was of course moving in Blakean circles. Might she have seen Blake's own *Poetical Sketches*? Some of her characters have names that sound a shade Blakean – Eyezion, Thelmon, Carmel (though Macpherson is another likely influence here). And some of her poems occasionally catch the tone of Blake's *Songs* – as, for instance, in the case of *A Fragment: The Blind Man*. Her use

---

[1]   *Collected Letters of Mary Wollstonecraft* ed. Ralph M. Wardle (Ithaca, NY, 1979), p. 188.

[2]   Ibid., p. 196.

[3]   Ibid., p. 384.

[4]   Disney, Flower, Frend, Wakefield and Porson were Cambridge cronies of Dyer's; it is hard to know how else they would have heard about Ann's volume.

of language is original in a way that is sometimes highly redolent of Blake, as when one of her characters is said to have 'unzoned passions'.[5] But when her work is closely examined, the few suggestions as to influence appear rather tenuous, and the case for Ann's originality in her own right becomes stronger. For one thing, despite her dissenting friends, the religious world of her poems is more conventional than that of Blake's. She is in no doubt as to the existence of an omnipresent, benevolent deity. What is not so expected is the quasi-pantheistic manner in which her characters deliquesce into the natural world around them. Rosamonde's voice is, at one point, 'pinioned on the wind'[6] – a rather paradoxical way of describing how her song has detached itself from its physical source and assumed its own life. Later we are told that sorrow 'Racked her celestial system with its rage'[7] – an astonishing turn of phrase which breaks down the barrier between Rosamonde's physical being and the divinely-ordered cosmos in which she moves. Ann even harnesses Greek myth to her distinctive purpose, as when Iris, messenger of the gods, is invoked in her traditional guise as rainbow,

> Reflecting each celestial ray,
> As if the flowers that decked the May
> Were there exhaled, and through its watery pores did glow.[8]

That she should describe the rainbow as having pores is surprising enough – but 'watery pores'? There is a baroque element here, even something of the grotesque, but it works because it is, finally, part of an integrated vision of a universe in which man and nature comprise elements of the same living being – a 'concord', to use Ann's term. There is another, illuminating example of her use of Greek myth, when the Graces are said to 'stray' amid the locks of a woman's hair.[9] Again, the usage is peculiar, and verges on the excessive, but it has a logic about it, if the Graces are considered as part of a life-force that lends the hair its vibrancy. But the most telling phrases of all are those which describe that most pantheistic of elements – the air. In Ann's poems, the air is 'pregnant'[10] – a distinctive phrasing that manages not just to give it being, but to allude to its seed-bearing function. Elsewhere, we are told that the 'ambient air breathes nature's rich perfumes'[11] – a beautifully compact line that turns the air, decisively, into a physical entity, inhaling the odours of the flowers. It is in the matter of that heightened sensitivity to the numinous in nature that Ann is most romantic, at a moment when Wordsworth, moving in similar company, was still experimenting with an oddly politicized gothic mode, in *Adventures on Salisbury Plain*. The final stanza of one of the last poems in the volume, *An Ode*, tells us a great deal about the essential beliefs that inform her work:

> Stupendous nature – rugged, beauteous, wild!
>   Impressed with awe, thy wondrous book I read;
> Beyond this stormy tract, some realm more mild,
>   My spirit tells me, is for man decreed,
>   Where, unallayed, bliss reigns without excess –
> Thus hope eccentric points to happiness![12]

5   *Elegy on a Young Lady* 55.
6   *Morning. Rosamonde* 21.
7   Ibid., l. 113.
8   *Evening. Gertrude* 55–7.

9   *Holbain* 194.
10   *Verses Written in the Spring* 23.
11   *The Triumph of Superstition. Raphael and Ianthe* 82.
12   *An Ode* 25–30.

It is not so much that nature is central to her vision of human life, but that it is imperfect in its present state – 'Beasts, birds, fish, insects, war with cruel strife!'[13] What confirms her essential optimism is that within such a postlapsarian vision she comprehends a realm in which 'bliss reigns without excess'. We are very close to the millennial vision of Blake's work, and that of Wordsworth in *The Recluse* – and, indeed, Ann may well have believed, with many of her contemporaries, that the millennium was close at hand. But that does not have to be inferred here. What she is telling us is that the flawed, fallen world before her is a promise of future happiness. Paradoxically enough, that 'hope eccentric' provides the spiritual centre from which so much of her poetry emanates.

Poetical Sketches is original in a way that few other volumes are, and it seems right to include it here in its entirety so that modern readers can reach their own conclusions about it. Its biggest violation of contemporary expectation is announced in its running heads: 'Poetical Sketches, In Irregular Verse'. The irregularity of the verses is noted by all the reviewers as a fault, but all go on to say that the book as a whole contains the work of an original talent. The *Analytical Review* even goes so far as to argue that Ann's contravention of current poetical practices is an element of the book's charm:

> Poesy, the child of Nature, if sometimes improved, is also sometimes spoiled, by the moulding hand of art. In the present state of refinement, in which every effort of genius is subjected, with tyrannical rigour, to established rule, and in which poetry, in particular, is often rather the mechanical production of patient ingenuity, than the spontaneous offspring of a vigorous imagination, a poet, writing from the pure impulse of natural sensibility, and giving free range to an untutored fancy, is a phenomenon entitled to notice at least for its rarity. Productions thus fairly dug out of the mine of invention, thought presented to the public eye without the last polish of art, or even with some unsightly encrustations, ought not to be trampled upon with disdain.
>
> The small volume of poems here offered to the public are not written exactly according to the rules of art. The writer has not had it in her power to enrich either her fancy, or her vocabulary, from the treasures of antiquity. She has not been much indebted for imagery, or phraseology, to modern poets; she has not confined herself strictly to the established laws of English versification. We must add that she has not always been so careful as might have been wished, to choose perfect rhymes or to avoid prosaic diction. Nevertheless she has written many pieces which discover no inconsiderable portion of poetical feeling and energy. Her descriptions of nature are often such as could not have been produced without a lively fancy, and sometimes her verse gratifies the ear with a continued flow of melody. In those pieces in which the verse is irregular, and of which the principal business is to describe natural objects, or to express emotions or passions, Miss C. has succeeded best.[14]

The *British Critic*, too, admitted that there were infelicities in Cristall's technique, but argued that 'There is a great deal of genuine poetical spirit in these compositions, and they will be read with great satisfaction by all but the fastidious critic, who refuses to pardon, even in writers without experience, a seeming inattention to rhyme and the

---

[13] Ibid., l. 14.   [14] *Analytical Review* 21 (1796) 282–6, pp. 282–3.

structure of verse. In this respect there are some irregularities in Miss Cristall's perform-
ance but there is much genius and warmth of imagination. It is our fortune to meet
with so little good poetry that we are glad to take every opportunity of placing before
our readers the dawn of what may ripen into future excellence.'[15] The *Critical Review*
was equally ready to excuse Ann's unconventional versification: 'These sketches are evid-
ently the production of a young writer; the title is modest, but the work possesses con-
siderable merit. In the poetical sketches of a young poetess, we are not surprised to
meet with some redundancies, and a few inaccuracies. But where we clearly discover the
hand of genius, we can easily forgive a little extravagance; and where we survey many
beauties, we can overlook a few blemishes. We certainly think very favourably of Miss
Cristall's Sketches.'[16] The reviewer concludes, 'We recommend this ingenious young lady
to the patronage of the public, being convinced that she is the poetess of nature, and
that she will amply repay the attention of her readers.'[17] Although the *Gentleman's Magazine*
did not publish a review, it did reprint two poems from the volume.[18]

Ann met Robert Southey in March 1797, and in a letter to his Bristol publisher,
Joseph Cottle, he wrote enthusiastically, providing us with a glimpse of her in literary
London. Southey was introduced to her by their mutual friend, George Dyer:

> But Miss Christal, have you seen her Poems? A fine, artless, sensible girl. Now,
> Cottle, that word 'sensible' must not be construed here in its dictionary acceptation.[19]
> Ask a Frenchman what it means, and he will understand it, though, perhaps, he
> can by no circumlocution explain its French meaning. Her heart is alive. She loves
> poetry. She loves retirement. She loves the country. Her verses are very incorrect,
> and the literary circle say she has no genius, but she has genius, Joseph Cottle,
> or there is no truth in physiognomy.[20]

'Unknown, and nothing in the scale of things', Ann says of herself in one of her
poems[21] – and indeed, after her father's· death in 1802, she drifts into obscurity. One
of the kindest references to her occurs in Dyer's *Poems* (1801), where he comments:
'The names of Smith, More, Williams, Robinson, Carter, Seward, Opie, and Cristall, are
well known'.[22] If that was so in 1801, little was heard of her subsequently. She is named
in the *Biographical Dictionary of Living Authors* in 1816. Joshua too won praise from Dyer,
in *Poetics* (1812), where he was praised for his 'delicate classical hand',[23] so that it is
possible that Dyer was still acquainted with both Cristalls at that time. Joshua became
President of the Watercolour Society in 1812 and moved to Herefordshire in 1822,
where he remained until 1841. In that year he returned to London until his death in
1847. His household is said to have consisted of two young servants and 'two lady
wards, between whom and himself there existed a strong attachment'. These were, one
presumes, his sisters. Elizabeth is believed to have been alive in 1851; we do not know
when Ann died. She seems never to have married.

---

[15] *British Critic* 5 (1795) 423–4, p. 423.
[16] *Critical Review* 13 (1795) 286–92, p. 286.
[17] Ibid., p. 292.
[18] *Gentleman's Magazine* 65 (1795) reprinted *A Frag-
ment: The Blind Man* (p. 325), and *A Song* ('Through
spring-time walks') (p. 861).
[19] Southey means 'highly sensitive', as opposed to
'endowed with good sense'.

[20] Joseph Cottle, *Reminiscences of Samuel Taylor Coleridge
and Robert Southey* (London, 1847), p. 204.
[21] *An Ode* 19.
[22] *Poems* (1801), p. 301.
[23] *Poetics: or, A Series of Poems, and Disquisitions on
Poetry* (2 vols, 1812), ii 179.

Further Reading

Jerome J. McGann, *The Poetics of Sensibility: A Revolution in Literary Style* (Oxford, 1996), pp. 195–206

Poetical Sketches, in Irregular Verse (1795)

PREFACE

These light effusions of a youthful imagination, written at various times for the entertainment of my idle hours, I now present to such readers whose minds are not too seriously engaged; and should they afford any degree of amusement, my most sanguine expectations will be answered. To attempt more in an age like this, enlightened by authors whose lives have been devoted to the study of metaphysical and moral truth,[1] would be presumptuous, and my experience does not justify such efforts. Most of my days have been passed in solitude, and the little knowledge I have acquired cannot boast the authority of much experience; my opinions, therefore, would carry little weight – for though the dictates of nature may be sometimes more just than conclusions drawn from a partial knowledge of the world, yet even our most settled convictions are never, perhaps, unbiased by prejudice, or uninfluenced by affection.

From among my juvenile productions I have principally selected for this volume some poetical tales and unconnected sketches which a love for the beauties of nature inspired. The versification is wild, and still incorrect, though I have taken much pains to reduce it to some degree of order. They were written without the knowledge of any rules, of which their irregularity is the natural consequence. The subjects, also, are not always such as, on maturer reflection, I should have chosen, had they been originally intended for publication. The seeds scattered in my mind were casual; the productions spontaneous and involuntary. I can only say that what I have written is genuine, and that I am but little indebted either to ancient or modern poets. With the ancient poets, indeed, my acquaintance has been but small, and only obtained through the medium of translations. Whatever superiority those may enjoy who can boast an acquaintance with these great masters, and however ambitious they may be to copy these originals, yet I cannot help observing that we have many instances of modern poets who have succeeded without treading too closely in their steps. Of this, the truly poetic energy of Robert Burns, and the simple elegance of some of George Dyer's poems,[2] afford remarkable instances. The latter, though a professed admirer of those writers,[3] appears to have guarded against a servile imitation of them.[4]

Those who have ever felt the warm influence of the muse, must know that her inspirations are flattering and seductive; that she often raises the heart with vanity, and then overwhelms it with fears. Such will readily believe that with a fluctuating mind and a trembling heart, I address the public, without any pretence for being treated with

---

PREFACE

[1] Such authors would include a number of those who had subscribed to this volume, such as George Dyer, John Disney, William Frend, Capel Lofft, George Wakefield, and Mary Wollstonecraft.

[2] Ann could have known only Dyer's *Poems* (1792).

[3] *those writers* i.e. the ancient poets.

[4] Dyer specifically denies wishing to directly imitate the classical writers in his Preface to *Poems* (1792). Most of the poems have classical epigraphs, and make allusions to classical works, most of which Dyer annotates.

particular indulgence. A strong motive first influenced me to this attempt, before I had sufficiently considered its boldness, and, having once adventured, I found it too late to recede.

BEFORE TWILIGHT. EYEZION.

Dawn had not streaked the spacious veil of night,
When Eyezion, the light poet of the spring,
Hied from his restless bed to sing,
Impatient for the promised beams of light;
Sweetly his voice through woods and vallies rang,   5
While fleeting o'er the hills, these anxious notes he sang:

'Swift, swift, ye lingering hours,
   And wake the morning star;
Rouse from the dew-fraught flowers
   The shades, and drive them far.   10

'Quick on the wings of morning
   Dart the young glimmering light,
Th' horizon's verge adorning,
   With blushing radiance dight.[1]

'Rise, Phoebus,[2] from yon mountain,   15
   Your saffron robes display;
Warm every lake and fountain,
   And kindle up the day.

'My soul, fledged with desires,
   Flutters, and pants for morn,   20
To catch the orient fires –
   Light trembling o'er the lawn.

'When rays, o'er meadows blushing,
   Illumine Viza's eyes,
Her lily-bosom flushing   25
   Reflects the glowing skies.

'Oh soul, that dart'st through ages,
   And wing'st with subtle power,
Why weak, when ardour rages,
   To speed one slumbering hour?   30

'Its beams when morning glances,
   Viza unfolds her charms,
Spangled with dews advances,
   And glows within my arms.

BEFORE TWILIGHT. EYEZION.   [2] *Phoebus* the sun.
[1] *dight* arrayed.

'Midst rills she laves her tresses,   35
    And blooming beams delight;
Swift – love my soul oppresses –
    Why's thought more quick than light?

'All hung with stars, as scorning,
    Night lingers mid the skies;   40
Oh when will rise the morning?
    Oh when will Viza rise?'

These notes a sportive zephyr gently blew;
    The lovely Viza oped her star-like eyes;
Her dreams dissolving mid night's shadows flew,   45
    While sweet sensations in her bosom rise.
Her ears th' enchanting strains with pleasure greet;
She asks, 'Who sang so early, and so sweet?'

EYEZION
    From Viza's memory then is Eyezion flown?
And is the music she inspires unknown?   50
If still no trait on thy remembrance pours,
Listen, whilst I describe my mental powers.

A current of creative mind,
Wild as the wandering gusts of wind,
Mid fertile fancy's visions trained,   55
Unzoned[3] I shot, and o'er each limit strained;
Around in airy circles whirled
    By a genius infinite;
    While Love in wanton ringlets curled
        My tresses, passion to excite.   60

Music waited on my birth,
    And called itself the soul of verse;
And wildly, through the mazy earth,
    My lips its melodies rehearse.

Thus skimming o'er the tracts of life,   65
    Borne on light elements I bound;
Free from rage and coarser strife,
    I catch new beauties all around;
From Love's light wings I steal the tender down,
While each gay Muse my aspiring temples crown.   70

---

[3] *Unzoned* unconfined.

When Grief pursues with harpy wing,
    To whirl me to dark realms of care,
      Upon poetic spells I fly,
    Wafted afar from black despair,
      And as I sing,   75
      Am raised on high.
Young Joy with pleasure smooths the scene,
Of mortal eyes unseen;
    With these I fleet,
Amid the Loves and Smiles sweet flowrets wreathe;   80
And every sigh I waft, and every joy I breathe,
    Mixed with seraphic airs, fly on poetic feet.

VIZA
Thou sweet enthusiast! Say what brings thee here
Ere mounting larks have hailed the morning star?
Involving shades,[4] with cruel care,   85
    Now wrap thee in their womb,
Though here and there a glittering star
    Shoots through blank night, and breaks the gloom.

EYEZION
Drawn by what irresistless[5] power,
    Shall I with trembling notes recite,   90
Why, glowing like an opening flower,
    I fleet before the morning light?

Yet fancy paints a conscious blush
    O'er thy fair cheeks; nor need my tongue
With deeper dye thy beauties flush –   95
    Thou know'st I'm drawn by thee alone.

From distant tracts I bound along,
    Nor hills nor streams my course delay,
Whilst oft reverb'rating my song,
    Sweet echo with the Muses play.   100

VIZA
Methinks the fading night decays,
    And morning breezes fan the air.

EYEZION
Distinct I view the silvering rays
    O'er yonder mountain tops appear.

---

[4] *involving* enveloping.   [5] *irresistless* irresistible.

VISA

Soon as young light shall clear the heaven,   105
  Urged by the glowing rays of morn;
When circling mists are distant driven,
  Expect me on the dewy lawn.

MORNING. ROSAMONDE.

Wild midst the teeming buds of opening May,
Breaking large branches from the flow'ry thorn,
  O'er the ferned hills see Rosamonda stray,
Scattering the pearls which the gay leaves adorn;
  Her ringlets o'er her temples play,   5
Flushed with the orient splendour of the morn.
The sun broke forth, and wide its glories threw,
Blushing along the sky, and sparkling in the dew.
  The plains gay-glittered with ethereal light,
    And the field-melody,   10
    Nature's wild harmony,
Breathed love, and sang delight!

Fresh Rosamonde the glowing scene surveys,
  Her youthful bosom inly stung with pain;
Early amid the shadowy trees she strays,   15
  Her shining eyes the starting tears restrain;
While tyrant Love within her pulses plays,
  O'er the wet grass she flew with wild disdain.
She flew from thought, and far
She sang, and hailed the morning star.   20
  Her voice was pinioned[1] on the wind,
Which wafts her notes around;
Encircling zephyrs caught each sound,
And bore them echoing through the wood,
Where pleased offended Urban stood   25
  With archest smile, yet musical and kind.
Conquering the sigh, she gaily sung,
And scorn loud-trembled on her wiry tongue.

While Urban stood, and held her in his eyes,
He to his lips applies   30
  The soft-breathed flute
Whose notes, when touched with art,
Steal to the inmost heart,
And throw the tyrannizing spirit down
  While vanity and pride are charmed and mute.   35

MORNING. ROSAMONDE.

[1] *pinioned* bound to.

Those lays reached Rosamonda's ear –
She fluttering like a bird whom fear
Has drawn within the fascinating serpent's fangs,
Unable to conceal the pangs
Of pride conflicting with returning love,   40
To hide her blushes darts amid the grove.
   Sweet showers fast sprinkle from her lovely eyes
Which drown her short-lived scorn;
   But as she moves the young musician flies,
Leaves her all wild, sad, weeping, and forlorn!   45

NOON. LYSANDER.

The sun had thrown its noontide ray
Amid the flowers, and scorched the plains,
Which panted for refreshing rains;
While gaudy flies their golden wings display,
And bees culled sweets to cheer a wintry day.   5
   Each beam that darted down
Chased lingering shades,
Through the thick umbrage of the trees pervades,
   And universal splendour shed around;
The slippery grass, burnt brown with heat,   10
Unkindly scorched the traveller's feet.

And now, oppressed,
While every creature languid hied to rest,
Amid the blaze Lysander bounds along,
   Bold as a lion, scorched by many a clime;   15
Far off was heard the echoes of his song,
   Responsive to his clear and artless rhyme.
He seeks no shade, nor grotto's cool retreat,
   But on, amidst the furzy heath, he pressed;
The heart's warm passions through his pulses beat,   20
   And native fire inspires his manly breast.
He seeks the craggy shore which ocean laves,
And, seated on a rock, surveys the swelling waves;
The eminence th' horizon's scope commands,
The plains surrounding, and the burning strands.   25
O'er the wild scene he threw a happy look,
   Compares the present pleasure with the past;
Gladly he turns each page of Nature's book,
   And prays the freedom of his soul may last.
     He rolled his eyes   30
     Across the seas;
Now glancing o'er the glassy waves,
     Now mounting to the skies –
     Th' immortal prize
Of valiant souls who find deep watery graves.   35

Thus as he sat, by strong reflection bound,
Up the rough rock ascends a sound
   Which piercingly pervades his ears;
It seemed the frantic cry of woe
   Which struggling groaned without the aid of tears.   40
The sounds like lightning reached his heart, and flushed
With quick alarm he made no longer stay.
Ardently down the craggy steep he rushed;
Rough heights he leaped, impatient of delay,
And tow'rds the sufferer bent his eager way,   45
Till by the sea he reached some rocky caves
Lashed by the loud-resounding waves.

There a wild female rent her golden hair
   With raging passions blind,
Her sad young bosom bare,   50
   And frantic seemed her stormy mind.
Swift tow'rds the sea she flies
With direful cries,
Driven on by fierce despair,
Mid oozy waves to drown remaining sense of care.   55

Touched by each generous thought
   By strong humanity impressed,
The damsel in his arms he caught,
   And held her, struggling, to his breast.
'Why trembles thus thy soul, oh wretched maid?   60
   Oh agony, too piercing agony,
Is through thy miserable frame portrayed –
   Oh could my breast relieve thy misery!
Just heaven, if thou hast pity, ease her pain!
Her heart will burst, she faints within my arms –   65
Upon my bosom she reclines her charms;
My falling tears bedew her cheeks in vain!'
He stretched her on the shore,
   He fetched cool water from the seas
And sprinkled her all o'er,   70
   And fanning her with leaves collects the breeze,
Till on the heavens she oped her azure eyes
   And with returning thought and grief, looked up.
'Ah, wretched me!' she cried, with bursting sighs,
   'I've plenteous drank at sorrow's bitter cup!   75
To God I fly; no help on earth I find,
   And from my soul would tear the mortal part;
Such sad disorders fill the human mind,
   Such deep afflictions rive[1] my guilty heart.

NOON. LYSANDER.

[1] *rive* tear.

I far in vice have strayed　　　　　　　　　　80
　　And, too severe,
The parents who adored the maid
　　No sighs from my repentant heart would hear
Till, raging in despair,
　　I franticly resolved to die　　　　　　　　85
　　Rather than (sad alternative!) to lie
Amid the streets, and common insults share.'

Stung to the heart, she rose;
　　Tears streamed from her fair eyes;
Shame in her cheeks revived the damask rose,[2]　　90
　　And poignant sorrow burst in bitter sighs.
She wept all silently;
　　Lysander scarce could speak,
Though sometimes, 'Cruelty, oh cruelty!'
　　Forth from his lips would break.　　　　　95

With generous passions swelled his noble breast,
Passions too strong and deep to be expressed;
Pity and rage with equal strivings beat,
And sympathy, wrought high by nat'ral heat.
'By my true soul!' at length he cried,　　　　100
'As Nature's my director and my guide,
My heart, chained by thy woe,
Shall neither joy nor comfort know,
Till I've revenged thy wrongs, and giv'n thee ease,
And, by my love, have set thy troubled soul at peace.　　105
　　Oh let not misery o'erwhelm thy heart,
　　　　Nor the fair path of life and joy decline;
　　Vengeance shall find the authors of thy smart –
　　　　Oh fearless rest thy drooping soul on mine,
Which, like the oak, round which the ivy strays,　　110
With blessings yet may store thy future days.'

The damsel's sorrow, like a furious storm,
　　Racked her celestial[3] system with its rage;
　　Her desperate passions deadly warfare wage,
And the mild radiance of her charms deform.　　115
At length the vivid fires rushed to her heart,
　　Tingled in ev'ry vein, blazed from her eyes,
　　While sudden joys before her spirits rise,
And o'er her cheeks warm transient colours dart.
　　Fired by his zeal,　　　　　　　　　120
Ecstatic feelings tinge her frame,
　　Whose glow the passions of her breast reveal
Bright blossom of a future-ripening flame!

---

[2]　*damask rose* from Damascus, with pink or light red
flowers.

[3]　*celestial* an unusual usage, difficult to define; pos-
sibly it means 'angelic' or 'divine'.

EVENING. GERTRUDE.

In clouds drew on the evening's close,
Which 'cross the west in ranges stood,
As pensive Gertrude sought the wood,
And there the darkest thicket chose;
While from her eyes amid the wild-briar flows 5
A sad and briny flood.
  Dark o'er her head
Rolled heavy clouds, while showers,
Pefumed by summer's wild and spicy flowers,
  Their ample torrents shed. 10

Why does she mourn?
  Why droop, like flowret nipped in early spring?
Alas, her tenderness meets no return!
Love hovers round her with his airy wing
And warms her youthful heart with vain delight 15
While Urban's graceful form enchants her sight,
  And from his eyes shoots forth the poisonous sting;
Another's charms th' impassioned youth inspired –
The sportive Rosamonde his genius fired.

The drops which glide down Gertrude's cheeks 20
Mid bitter agonies did flow;
And though awhile her pallid lips might glow,
'Twas as a blossom blighted soon with woe.
  Her disregarded tresses, wet with tears,
Hung o'er her panting bosom straight and sleek; 25
  Her faithful heart was all despondency and fears.

The skies disgorged, their last large drops refrain,
  The cloudy hemisphere's no more perturbed;
The leafy boughs that had received the rain,
  With gusts of wind disturbed, 30
Shake wild their scattering drops o'er glade and plain;
They fall on Gertrude's breast, and her white garments stain.
Sighing, she threw her mantle o'er her head,
And through the brakes towards her mansion sped;
Unheedingly her vestments drew along, 35
Sweeping the tears that to the branches hung,
    And as she passed
O'er the soaked road, from off the shining grass,
In clods around her feet the moist earth clung.

The clouds dispersed, again to sight 40
The evening sun glowed lambent bright;
And forcing back the louring shades,
Spread its enlivening beams, and kindled mid the glades.

With high-wrought verdure every object glowed,
And purple hills their glittering mansions showed.   45
    The universal gleam invites to sport,
        For toil and care cease with the ebbing day;
    Th' industrious youths to plains or groves resort,
        Dance on the lawn, or o'er the hillocks stray.

    Gertrude, wandering up a lane   50
From among the winding trees,
Fanned by a refreshing breeze,
    Ascends upon the glistening plain.
Across gay Iris[1] flung her bow
    Reflecting each celestial ray,   55
    As if the flowers that decked the May[2]
Were there exhaled, and through its watery pores did glow.

From a fair covert, Urban's gay resort,
    A whistling pipe in warbling notes respired;
The well-known sound invites each youth to sport,   60
    And every heart its harmony inspired;
        While from each mead
        So thick with daisies spread,
The bounding nymphs with fairy lightness sprung,
And gaily wild their sportive sonnets sung;   65
The air was scented by the odorous flowers,
Bright-sprinkled with the dew of fresh-fall'n show'rs.

Of lively grace, and dimpled smiles,
    Slim Cynthia, the refined,
Came with neat Phillis, full of tricksome wiles,   70
    While Silvius strolled behind,
        Chased by the marble-hearted Rosalind,
The loud and witty large-mouthed Madge
With her obsequious servant Hodge.

Blithe from the mill which, briskly turning round,   75
Made the young zephyrs breathe a rural sound,
Leaped Charles, gay-glowing with industrious heat,
Active to lead in every rustic feat;
Back from his brows he shook his wavy locks,
    And turning quick his lively eyes   80
    His lovely, modest Peggy spies
Returning with her aged father's flocks.

EVENING. GERTRUDE.
[1] *Iris* in Greek myth, the goddess who was messenger of the gods, and appeared as the rainbow.

[2] *the May* despite the article, Ann means the month, rather than the hawthorn.

Straight with his hand he gave his heart sincere,
Devoid of order danced, and whistled loud and clear.
Hebe, a blooming, sprightly fair,   85
With shallow Ned (an ill-matched pair);
Simple Daphne, rosy John,
And ever-blundering Heleson;
From a large mansion, gloomed by shading trees,
Forth sprung the star-eyed Luisse;   90
Graceful her tresses flowed around,
    Like scattered clouds that catch the moon's pale beams;
Scarcely she seemed to touch the verdant ground,
    But, as inspired,³ along the plain she streams.
More join the flock – they spring in air,   95
Light as winged doves, and like to doves they pair;
The sun's last ray now lingered o'er their head,
And sweets delectable around were spread.

Poor Gertrude, hid amongst the trees, surveyed
Each ardent youth, each blooming maid,   100
    And as she gazed,
Pleasure by slow degrees within her senses steals;
    Her eyes, with tears impearled, she raised,
Her heart each sweet sensation feels;
    Lightly her feet the grassy meadows tread,   105
While music's power deludes her from her cares;
    Among the nymphs, by its soft influence led,
Her sympathetic breast their raptures shares.

Thus while she felt, and joined the lively throng,
    Lo! quick ascends the plain   110
    The glory of each swain,
Urban, with sportive song,
    Whose cheerful notes in frolic measures fled;
        While Rosamonde –
Fleet-footed, glowing Rosamonde – he led.   115
The rapture of the lark her voice sent forth –
Too well, ah, Gertrude knew its worth;
Dire tremblings soon her spirits seize.
Could she, vain untaught nymph, aspire to please?
Her body owns no grace;   120
No smiles, no dimples deck her eyes or face.
    She feels that she has nought to prize,
Yet totally devoid of art,
    Expression's charm was hers, with beaming eyes,
A voice far-reaching, and a feeling heart.   125

---

³ *as inspired* i.e. as if inspired.

She turned around –
The flying breezes loosened to the air
Her ill-beseeming vests,[4] her scattered hair.
   So sad she looked, so artless was her woe,
As from a thinking mind had drawn a tear;   130
But joy through every vein had stole,
   And mirth shut out the sympathetic glow.
The heart's gay dance admits of no control,
Sweet joys but seldom through our senses steal –
'Tis pity then we should forget to feel.   135

   Gay wicked wit amid the circle spread,
And wanton round the lively sallies[5] sped;
Each neat-trimmed maiden laughed with playful glee,
Whom whispering swains divert with mimicry.
   Fair Rosamonde, whose rival bosom burned,   140
With taunting mirth directs young Urban's eyes;
   He, with mischievous archness, smiles returned,
Amid whose circles wounding satires[6] rise;
   Their sportive feet still beat the flowery ground,
While wicked looks, and jests, and jeers went round.   145

Pierced by their insults, stung with bitter smart,
Sad fell poor Gertrude's tears, high-heaved her heart.
Distant she flew and, sitting on a stone
Concealed, gave sorrow vent, and wept alone,
   Till mid her grief, a virtuous just disdain   150
      Came to her aid, and made her bosom glow;
      With shame she burns, she blushes at her woe,
And wonders at her weakness and her pain.

'Unhappy maid!' she cried, 'thou art to blame,
Thus to expose thy virtuous breast to shame;   155
   Poor heart, thy love is laughed at for its truth;
Yet 'tis a holy treasure, though disdained,
And wantonly by thoughtlessness profaned.
   Ah, why then waste the blessings of thy youth?
No more fair reason's sacred light despise;   160
   Thy heart may blessings find
That dwell not in the eyes,
   But in the virtues of the feeling mind.'

NIGHT

Solemn is night, when Silence holds her reign,
And the hushed winds die on the heaving main;

---

[4]   *vests* loose outer garments.   [6]   *wounding satires* against Gertrude.
[5]   *sallies* witticisms, banter.

When no short gleam of scattered light appears,
Nor lunar beams make faint the nobler stars;
Then those whom inward cares deprive of rest   5
Pour forth the secret sorrows of the breast.
   Such was the night – smooth glides the bark along,
From whence young Henry breathed his thoughtful song;
Pacing the deck, he threw his eyes around
The thick-starred firmament and vast profound;   10
The patient winds scarce whistled o'er the waste
The burning waves the vessel's prow embraced;
The nitrous[1] air unclouded glowed on high,
With northern meteors trembling through the sky.
   'Eternal Power!' he cried, 'with justice fraught,   15
Oh teach a wretch to curb each stubborn thought,
Whose passions reason's powers no more restrain,
Grown wanton midst intolerable pain.
   Pierced by ingratitude, I rove forlorn,
My faithful heart by strong affection torn;   20
A willing exile on the dangerous main,
Unshook by storms, while calms breathe peace in vain.
Oft with unmanly tenderness I mourn
And, tortured by imagination, burn;
Sighs in a natural cadence close each song,   25
And tones of anguish vibrate on my tongue.
   All is now hushed, still as the silent grave,
The breeze scarce swells the smooth unruffled wave
Which, glittering with celestial lustre bright,
Reflects the spangled heaven's ethereal light.   30
Oh how sublime this tract, for man designed;
Vast the perceptions of his rapid mind!
Strongly to earth his young affections cling,
While Fancy waves her bright and various wing;
But soon each hope of earthly bliss is crossed,   35
Nipped in the bud, or in possession lost;
Blushing, our empty wishes we survey,
When we our passions with their motives weigh.
   Deeply I feel this still and solemn hour,
Impressed with God's immeasurable power,   40
While worlds unnumbered mid yon ether[2] burn,
And thoughts immense pour in where'er I turn.
How much man errs, whose soul, with thought sublime,
Looks on tow'rds endless bliss through boundless time,
When he to earthly passions gives dire sway,   45
Or mourns those joys which of themselves decay!'

NIGHT
[1] *nitrous* impregnated with nitre, an explosive sub-
stance; the air is full of it because of the meteors
'trembling through the sky'.

[2] *ether* outer space.

SONG

Wandering in the still of eve,
  While songsters homeward cleave the air,
With lively notes my voice I tuned
  To usher in the evening star;
But straying near a woody brake,   5
  Sweet sounds of melody ascend,
Oft intermixed with sighs and tears.
  Anxious a pitying ear I lend,
As from a vale below thus sad they rolled;
    'Ah, idiot Fortune, why   10
    Should genius smothered die,
When fled by base delusive gold?
When fled by base delusive gold?

Wavering in a doubtful state,
  Impelled by reason and desire,   15
Strongly I feel an innate pow'r
  Raising the sparks of youthful fire,
While warmer fancy, genuine art,
  Urged by the touch, break forth to flame
But, chilled by the cold worldling's frown,   20
  And starved by reason, sink again.
Bewildered now I see the book of fate unfold:
    Ah, idiot Fortune, why
    Should genius smothered die
When fled by base delusive gold?   25
When fled by base delusive gold?

Unerring Pow'r, dare I complain?
  Yet sure mysterious is thy way,
That the vile dust dug from the earth
  Should rule with such unbounded sway;   30
Should smother up the seeds of love,
  And check the emanating fire
That swells the rip'ning artist's breast,
  And wakes the soul-entrancing lyre!
Ah, sad disgrace to man's diviner mould!   35
    For, idiot Fortune, why
    Should genius smothered die,
When fled by base delusive gold?
When fled by base delusive gold?

Murmuring thus at partial fate,   40
  The wretch's comfort I pursue;
How sweet those plaintive moments pass,
  How tuneful but, alas, how few!

Courting the muses, here my lute
   Soft I attune, and hail the sky;   45
Reading the traits of heavenly love,
   Aloud I breathe this ardent sigh:
Ah, when to me will Nature's works unfold?
   Through, cruel Fortune, I
      In cankered rust may die,   50
If fled by thee, delusive gold!
If fled by thee, delusive gold!'

HOLBAIN

Down sunk the sun, nor shed one golden ray,
But rising mists shut in the louring day;
The tides o'erflown had drenched the swampy turf,
And drizzling rains bedewed the dreary earth;
The rising moon a bloody meteor seemed,   5
And, scarce observed, the muffled planets gleamed;
The winds were hushed in silence most profound,
And night's dim shades hung heavily around.
   Holbain, a youth benighted in his course,
Led o'er the marshy plains his fiery horse;   10
Involving[1] treacherous mists delude his sight,
While lost he wandered through the dreary night.
With speed his blood grew warm, his pulses beat,
The spirits to his panting heart retreat
Where tyrant fear with thrilling horror pressed,   15
Till now a stranger to his daring breast.
An unknown trackless waste before him lay,
And boggy marshes intercept his way;
His eager pace is checked by dangerous swamps,
Or stopping he is chilled by mizzling[2] damps.   20
Alone, his active mind conspired with fear,
And fancied forms impregnated the air;
Lightly he stepped, of every sound afraid,
And often startled by the steed he led,
Which as he curbed unruly reared and neighed.   25
Clearing the clouds, a sudden gust arose,
Sighed through the woods, and shook the wat'ry boughs;
Alarmed, his hand his courser's rein forsook,
Which free, impetuous o'er the meadows broke –
In bounding circles strove to heave along,   30
Clogged mid the slimy mud, and fiercely strong;
Snorting with direful rage, he madd'ning flies,
Then plunged and, smothered in a quagmire, dies.

HOLBAIN

[1] *Involving* enveloping.

[2] *mizzling* drizzling.

Grief pierced the youth, while idle terrors flew,
And gloomy fancies melted from his view.   35
He looked around – no spectres haunt his sight
(For rising winds had swept the misty night);
The moon amid the parting vapours rode,
And o'er the earth a varying light bestowed.
Mourning his generous friend,³ while sad he stood,   40
The sound of feet he heard and, turning, viewed
Near him a man, quick-passing o'er the plain,
His aspect peaceful, and his vestments plain;
So thin, he looked the image of decay,
And closely wrapped to keep night's chills away.   45
Holbain salutes him, and enquires what care
Tempts him through damps to trust the midnight air?
    'Say rather', he replied, 'what cause has led
Thy daring feet to cross this dangerous mead,
Where fenny⁴ quagmires, shrouded by the night,   50
Bury the traveller, and delude the sight?
But well I know the pass and I will set thee right.'
    O'erjoyed, the youth his proffered aid embraced,
Repeats his wanderings, and his fears retraced;
Tells how mid fogs, bewildered in his course,   55
He 'mongst the marshes lost his faithful horse,
Then names his destined journey, and the road
Which he, mistaking, had unwary trod.
    'Thou'rt far, alas, from home', the senior cried,
'The path so intricate I scarce can guide;   60
But if you'll be the partner of my way,
And deign beneath my humble roof to stay,
Soon as tomorrow shall return to light
My son shall tend thy steps, and set thee right.'
    Holbain his ardent gratitude confessed,   65
And oft-repeated thanks his joy expressed.
Onward together as their course they speed
The youth recounts the virtues of his steed;
The other patient listened, nor reproved,
For midst his warmth he traced a mind he loved.   70
    Quitting the plains, they pass where awful stood,
Grown thick with age, a wild majestic wood,
Where lofty trees their solemn branches spread,
And winds loud whistling sung around their head;
Th' autumnal blight the withered leaves had strewed,   75
And bright the moon her awful visage showed.
Rugged and long the way, and late the night,
But pleasing converse made the journey light.
    Beguiling time, the elder thus begun,

---

³   *his generous friend* i.e. his horse.   ⁴   *fenny* swampy.

While native sweetness on his accents hung: 80
'Say, youth, to what profession art thou bred –
By glory fired, or by the muses led?
Or does philosophy thy mind pervade,
Or seek you riches in the world of trade?'
    'Glory', replied the youth, 'has spread its charms;   85
I caught its rays, and chose to follow arms;
Impatient grew to signalize[5] my name,
And took the brightest road that led to fame.'
    'And what is fame?' the senior calm replies,
'Distinctly speak, that I may prove thee wise.'   90
    'Fame', Holbain cried, 'like a celestial light,
Irradiates truth, and makes e'en virtue bright;
The soul of mighty deeds, whose fires impart
Beams which through length of ages glorious dart.'
    'Ardent thou speak'st', with smiles rejoined the sire,   95
'Yet be not dazzled while thou dost aspire,
Though those whom Fame midst her bright glories place
Shine forth examples to the human race,
Whose every act the crowd with transports view
And indiscriminate their paths pursue,   100
Whether their tract a noble end displays
Or splendent[6] vices catch fame's dazzling rays.
But be it thine to check ambition's flame,
And closely link with justice love of fame –
Which, shining with intrinsic lustre bright,   105
With virtue's beams will dart th' immortal light.
Heroes too long, of human glory proud,
Insatiable have drenched the world with blood;
Too loud the bards their frantic deeds resound,
While blinded mortals ravished listen round.   110
Detested race! Yet oft I feel the fire
Which urged them on, and mental strength admire;
For, wanting strength, none e'er can reach the heights
Where Virtue sits, and Genius wings her flights;
But monstrous crimes in soils luxuriant grow,   115
Strong powers ill-governed sink us deep below.
Civilization, as it taught mankind,
To individuals different tasks assigned.
No more the appetites absorb our cares,
The mind breaks forth, and nobler functions shares;   120
The polished arts with active fancy rise,
And Nature's mazes draw our wondering eyes;
Genius finds wider scope and, mounting high,
Exploring truth dawns with divinity!
But shame, deep shame to the inventive mind,   125

---

[5] *signalize* distinguish.   [6] *splendent* great, grand.

Mid heavenly studies still to blood inclined,
And, hunting not our food, we hunt mankind!
Nature has countless wonders strewed around,
Through air, the pregnant[7] earth, and vast profound,[8]
Where latent truths, evading common view,   130
Open pure lessons to the thinking few –
Who, truly wise, while fiercer passions die,
Learn the frail state of their mortality.
The finer arts my admiration claim,
As inoffensive paths to boundless fame;   135
Hence Poesy supreme in glory soars,
Whose searching eye the heavens and earth explores!
Its rapid flight nor space nor time can bound
The world of spirits or the pow'rs of sound.
Nor does the painter vain exert his art,   140
Who, tracing Nature through each varying part,
Arrests the strongest passions in their course,
And gives us time to contemplate their force.
Friend to such arts as Nature's works portray,
No stormy passions cloud my evening ray.   145
Sorrow in vain has strove to break a heart
Whose wishes ne'er from simple truth depart;
The charm of life, its griefs, its date I know,
And from these lights my inward comforts flow;
For while my reason Nature's ways explores,   150
Religion strengthens, and my soul adores!'
    They now had reached the confines of the wood
Where, girt with trees, the stranger's mansion stood,
To which they bend; the shining moon was gone,
And scattered stars beamed through the heavens alone.   155
Soft at the door his stick the sire applies
Which, opening quick, light glanced against their eyes.
His children ran with eager arms t' embrace
Their welcome sire, and kiss his much-loved face,
Anxious to know what cause could him detain   160
In a drear night, chilled by autumnal rain.
Answering by turns, in pleasing tones he greets,
While he and Holbain midst them take their seats.
His daughters tend him with assiduous care,
And cheerful smiles domestic joys declare;   165
Artless their forms, with modest plainness dressed,
And education's power their mien confessed.
His eldest son the youthful stranger greets,
While he with smiles his happy chance repeats;
Two younger boys obey their sister's word,   170

---

[7] *pregnant* fertile.   [8] *vast profound* the sea; a Popean expression, as at
Pope, *Homer's Odyssey* iv 777.

And with refereshing viands spread the board.
Now Holbain's eyes attentively survey
Th' instructive partner of his rugged way.
Wasted by care, he viewed the placid sire,
His large light eyes still beamed with mental fire;   175
Submissively serene his pleasing brow,
His lips, though pale, with genial smiles could glow;
His manners simple, but his thoughts refined,
Nor elegance was wanting to his mind.
His guest he welcomes, and with pleasing voice   180
Prays him to share his board and homely joys.
The artless youth with cheerful smiles partook,
Then round the table threw a happy look.
As he observes the family by turns
His fine eyes sparkle and his bosom burns;   185
The elder youth, more silent than the rest,
Seemed with the recent marks of grief impressed.
One daughter near her father took her place,
Filial affection beaming in her face –
Her features plain, her cheeks no roses dye,   190
No radiance kindles in her modest eye,
But feeling, sense, and purity combine –
A powerful charm, and with expression shine.
Amid her sister's locks the Graces[9] stray –
Softened her eyes, and flushed her cheeks like May.   195
Holbain delighted shared the sweet repast
Which filial love, good sense, and beauty graced;
Unwilling he at last retired to rest,
With love for the whole family impressed.
    Soon as the beams which chase the glowing dawn   200
Played o'er the hills, and marked distinct the morn,
He sprung from rest, all eager to survey
The mansion where so many virtues lay.
Delighted he beheld the blessed retreat,
Where useful plainness, taste, and order meet.   205
Neat was the bounteous garden paled around,
Which autumn with her ripening tributes crowned.
As mid the thick-grown trees some fruits he sought,
The elder youth he met, absorbed in thought,
Perturbed within, irregular his pace,   210
And gushing tears streamed o'er his strong-marked face.
Striving to pass unseen, he met his eyes,
Nor could his heaving breast repress deep sighs.
Holbain confused strove quickly to depart

---

[9] *Graces* the Graces presided over gentleness, loveli-
ness and charm – qualities which presumably she is
being said to possess.

(Sacred he deemed the feelings of the heart).   215
    The other, following, said, 'With shame I glow,
To be surprised in this unmanly woe.
Serene my father each affliction bears,
But larger griefs impel my copious tears;
Fall'n low from state and envied happiness,   220
Deeply does grief this sanguine heart impress;
Bitter remorse mid sad reflections rise,
And joy in vain would shine to glad these eyes;
But listen, while my faltering lips impart
What may excuse this weakness of my heart –   225
Just woke from madness, thought astonished turns,
Feels the dire hand of fate, and inward burns.
    There stood a fabric,[10] deeply wrapped in woods,
Where hoarse resounded loud impetuous floods
Which from the hills in rapid torrents gushed   230
Mid the dark trees, and down the vallies rushed;
The ruined walls were round with ivy spread,
And gloomy shades wild Gothic grandeur shed.
The awful ocean's wondrous space was nigh,
Whose roarings waked a deep solemnity!   235
Often, with youth's romantic raptures fraught,
In meditation lost, these scenes I sought –
Here mused, here read; the muses courted here,
And strove to draw them from their tuneful sphere.
    Thus fired, my genius boundless scope employed,   240
Glanced o'er all Nature and her works enjoyed.
My mother (ever honoured be her name,
Warmed by whose force my spirit burst to flame –
Whose stronger passions, chastened by our sire,
Still fill her children's pulses with her fire)   245
Listened, whilst I its various beauties told,
And sought the Gothic structure to behold;
Her breast maternal in my joys took part,
My feelings were congenial to her heart.
At her request we went, nor marked on high   250
A threatening storm which gathered o'er the sky.
    I led my mother through the devious[11] wood
To where, involved with trees, the fabric stood;
With equal awe she viewed the solemn place,
While warmly I romantic dreams retrace;   255
The songs I here had tuned enrapt I read,
And hours upon their swiftest pinions fled.
Nature, in her still warm, diffused the fire
Which in her youth loud woke th' harmonic lyre.
I saw her charmed, and warmly urged her stay   260

---

[10] *fabric* building.   [11] *devious* remote, distant.

To blend her wisdom with my youthful lay,
Devoting to her son th' instructive day,
When from her lips a forced consent I drew;
I caught her words, and for refreshments flew
While she within the tottering castle stays, 265
And all the grandeur of the scene surveys.
Stupendous clouds were rolling o'er the heav'n,
Strong rushed large torrents by quick eddies driv'n.
    In curious[12] choice of dainty viands bent
(Oh never-pardoned folly!), far I went – 270
Too far, alas! A friend partook the way,
With whom in converse thoughtlessly I stray.
Pleased with myself, while partial[13] praise I sought,
The best of mothers vanished from my thought
Till roused by a tremendous storm, which broke 275
Through the vast heavens, and my remembrance woke.
    Strong gathered through the trees the whirling gale,
Blew bleak a while, then whistled in the vale;
Then on it came, and with redoubled force
Strove midst contending trees to wing its course; 280
Driv'n back again, loud-roaring it complains,
Or blustering thunders o'er the neighbouring plains.
Wildly I heard the stormy ocean roar,
Wave dashed on wave flew bellowing to the shore.
Grief for my mother fills my labouring breast – 285
Precipitate I flew, with fears oppressed.
The storm with tenfold fury still persists,
Scarce the strong oak its dreadful power resists;
Borne by its ravings, tossed aloft in air,
Uprooted, torn, the mangled wood lies bare. 290
Trembling and horrorstruck, I rapid flew,
Nor could my friend my hasty steps pursue;
As I advance th' o'erwhelming tide arose,
Deluged the plains, and round in surges flows;
So fierce the winds, my feet were scarcely stayed,[14] 295
While through encroaching waters on I wade;
My pulses with strong agitation beat,
While present death with thousand horrors threat.
And art thou, oh my mother, mid this storm?
What from the winds shall guide thy sacred form? 300
The ruined fabric totters at each breath –
Perhaps already has conspired thy death!
Four times I fell midst gushing waters thrown,
Borne on by tides, or dashed against huge stones;
Yet strong necessity had giv'n me force 305

---

[12] *curious* careful, fastidious.   [14] *stayed* hindered, impeded.
[13] *partial* kind, encouraging.

And, spite of obstacles, I speed my course.
When near advanced I stopped, and dared not go,
Arrested by foreboding sense of woe.
I called aloud on her who speaks no more,
Aloud the angry torrents thundering roar!   310
Still nearer on, I trembling called again;
Still roared the winds, and still my voice was vain!
Mad with despair, wild tow'rds the spot I rush,
Where all around the bellowing torrents gush;
No trace of Gothic arch or roof remains,   315
By winds and waters swept along the plains.
Deep the contending elements resound
While, lost to thought, my frantic brain turns round.
Still seeking what I knew I could not find,
My dreadful cries concorded[15] with the wind.   320
Myself I felt the cause – grief and dismay
Rushed on my brain, and snatch my sense away.
My friend preserved my life, a thankless load,
And bore me to my father from the wood;
I knew not how he found me, or where sought,   325
For long suspended were the powers of thought.
　　I viewed my father, though worn down by care,
Sublimely virtuous, keenest sufferings bear,
His best affections ravished from his breast,
And sanguine hopes by penury suppressed.   330
The day my mother died, on tempests tossed,
Loaded with wealth, his stranded ships were lost;
Winged with our fate one storm relentless blew,
Conspired our ruin, and each hope o'erthrew.
Yet strong within, to every ill resigned,   335
Nought shakes the steadfast basis of his mind;
For pious faith, and hope's seraphic eye
Unfold the joys of immortality!
Active in all his duties here below,
Strong perseverance blunts the edge of woe.   340
With industry he heaps our little stores,
And still great Nature's ample page explores;
T' instruct the children in his Maker's ways,
And show how all by slow degrees decays;
That though on earth God's hand is strong impressed,   345
Yet higher hopes should fill the human breast.
Oh blessed example of a pious mind!
Yet still my stubborn breast pants unresigned;
Not guiltlessly I draw this wretched breath,
Nor tranquilly behold the gulf of death.'   350
　　Thoughtful he paused, while Holbain silent prayed,

---

[15] *concorded* harmonized.

And with strong sympathy the youth surveyed.
'Mysterious do thy ways, oh God, appear,
But, born to suffer, man must learn to bear.
Divinely pour religion through the soul,   355
For that alone the passions can controul!'
Each stood absorbed till summoned to repair
Within the hall, the morn's repast to share;
Th' obtrusion gave them pain – awhile they stay,
Then, walking slow, wiped the hot tears away.   360
   Holbain again the virtuous father meets,
And with the morning's salutation greets;
As pensively around his eyes he throws,
Strong to his mind their loss and patience rose.
Then mid the family he took his place,   365
And charmed beheld the younger daughter's grace;
More sweet she looks by day, the lovely dye
Of her fair cheeks with brightest flowrets vie;
Her azure eyes shot forth a lucid ray,
O'er her white neck her amber ringlets stray.   370
An anxious wish warm-kindled in his breast,
Its noble fire his guileless eyes confessed;
A pleased remembrance of his wealth arose,
His breast benevolent with rapture glows.
   Lingering he strove to lengthen out his stay,   375
And tore himself at last by force away;
But first the sire's permission did obtain
To visit this delightful spot again
When, friendship strengthening, into union grew,
And happier scenes unfolded to their view.   380

SONG ON LEAVING THE COUNTRY EARLY IN THE SPRING

While joy reanimates the fields,
And spring her odorous treasures yields;
While love inspires the happy grove,
   And music breaks from every spray;
I leave the sweet retreat I love   5
   Ere bloss'ming hawthorn greets the May;
Sad destiny! Oh, let me plaintive pour
O'er the unopened bud an unrefreshing shower.

To yonder hills which bound the sight
Where blushing eve dissolves in night;   10
To the wild heath, o'er which the gale
   Bleak wafts each sweet perfume of spring,
And to the weed-grown briary vale
   Sorrowing the parting lay I sing:
'Sweet flowers of spring, enlivening day,   15
Nature's unfolding charms fleet fast away.'

At morn I've viewed the glimmering light
Break from the east and chase the night,
Then strayed amid the frosty dews,
   While soaring larks shrill chanting rise,   20
And marked the thousand varying hues
   That streak the glowing morning skies;
'Sweet air of spring, enlivening day,
Nature's unfolding charms fleet fast away.'

No daisied lawns shall greet my eye,   25
Reluctant from their sweets I fly;
No more, wild wandering o'er the plains,
   I share each innocent delight;
The tinkling flocks, the woodland strains,
   The rural dance no more invite.   30
Sad destiny! Oh, let me plaintive pour
O'er the unopened bud an unrefreshing shower.

VERSES WRITTEN IN THE SPRING

From yon fair hill, whose woody crest
The mantling[1] hand of spring has dressed,
Where gales imbibe the May perfume,
And strew the blushing almond's bloom,
I view the verdant plains below   5
And lucid streams which gently flow;
The opening foliage, drenched with showers,
Weeps o'er the odorous vernal flowers,
And while before my tempered eye
From glancing clouds swift shadows fly,   10
While nature seems serene and blessed,
And inward concord tunes my breast,
I sigh for those by fortune crossed
Whose souls to nature's charms are lost –
Whether by love of wealth betrayed,   15
Absorbed in all the arts of trade,
Or deep engrossed in mighty schemes,
Tossed in ambition's empty dreams,
Or proud amid the learned schools,
Stiffened by dull pedantic rules,   20
Or those who ne'er from forms depart,
The slaves of fashion[2] and of art.[3]
   Oh lost to bliss – the pregnant[4] air,
The rising sun, the ripening year,

VERSES WRITTEN IN THE SPRING

[1] *mantling* enveloping; cf. the 'mantling vine' at *Comus* 294.

[2] *fashion* outward action or display.

[3] *art* formulated rules, learning.

[4] *pregnant* fertile, fertilizing.

The embryos[5] that on every bush   25
Midst the wild notes of songsters blush;
The violet's scent, the varying hues
Which morn's light ray strikes mid the dews,
To them are lost – involved in care,
They cannot feel, they cannot share.   30
   I grieve when round I cast my eyes
And feel a thousand pleasures rise
That this fair earth, by Heaven bestowed
(Which human fury stains with blood),
Should teem with joys which reach the heart,   35
And man be thus absorbed in art.

WRITTEN IN DEVONSHIRE, NEAR THE DART

Hail, Devon! In thy bosom let me rest,
And pour forth music from my raptured breast;
   I'll stray thy meadowed hills
     And plains along,
     And loudly sing the widely-varied song,   5
   Tracing thy rivers and thy bubbling rills.

Oft rising from the sea, the tempest lours,
   And buoyed on winds the clouds majestic sail,
While scattering burst in wide and frequent showers,
   Swelling the streams which glide through every vale;   10
Yet are the marshy plains bedecked with flowers,
   And balmy sweets are borne on every gale.

Where Dart romantic winds its mazy course,
   And mossy rocks jet[1] 'neath the woody hills
   From whence each creeping rill its store distils,   15
And wandering waters join with rapid force,
   There Nature's hand has wildly strewn her flowers,
And varying prospects strike the roving eyes;
Rough-hanging woods o'er cultured hills arise,
Thick ivy spreads around huge antic[2] towers,   20
     And fruitful groves
Scatter their blossoms fast as falling showers,
Perfuming ev'ry stream which o'er the landscape pours.

Along the grassy banks how sweet to stray
   When the mild eve smiles in the glowing west,   25
And lengthened shades proclaim departing day,
   And fainting sunbeams in the waters play,

---

[5] *embryos* buds, as at Thomson, *Spring* 99–101: 'while
the promised fruit/Lies yet a little embryo, unperceived
/ Within its crimson folds'.

WRITTEN IN DEVONSHIRE, NEAR THE DART
[1] *jet* jut, protrude.
[2] *antic* ancient or fantastic.

When every bird seeks its accustomed rest!
How grand to see the burning orb descend,
And the grave sky wrapped in its nightly robes,   30
Whether resplendent with the starry globes
Or silvered by the mildly solemn moon,
When nightingales their lonely songs resume
    And folly's sons their babbling noise suspend!

Or when the darkening clouds fly o'er the sea   35
    And early morning beams a cheerful ray
Waking melodious songsters from each tree,
    How sweet beneath each dewy hill
    Amid the pleasing shades to stray,
Where nectared flowers their sweets distil,   40
    Whose watery pearls reflect the day;
To scent the jonquil's rich perfume;
    To pluck the hawthorn's tender briars,
As wild beneath each flowery hedge
Fair strawberries with violets bloom   45
    And every joy of spring conspires!

Nature's wild songsters from each bush and tree
    Invite the early walk, and breathe delight;
What bosom heaves not with warm sympathy
    When the gay lark salutes the newborn light?   50
Hark, where the shrill-toned thrush,
    Sweet whistling, carols the wild harmony!
The linnet warbles, and from yonder bush
    The robin pours soft strains of melody!

Hail Devon! While through thy loved woods I stray,   55
Oh let me loudly pour the grateful lay;
    Tell each luxuriant bank where violets grow,
Each mazy vale where fragrant woodbines wind,
    How much of their bewitching charms they owe
To the sweet peace which fills my happy mind.   60
Ah where again will it such pleasures find?
Oh loved society, the heartfelt lay
    Is all the humble muse can now bestow;
Thy praises still I sing, as on I stray,
    Writ in my heart amid each strain they flow.   65

SONG (TUNE: 'THE HEAVY HOURS')

The balmy comforts that are fled
    To me no more return,
Though nature's sweets around are shed
    Amid those sweets I mourn,

With organs framed to taste delight,   5
   My soul its functions tries;
I feel, I see, but from my sight
   The transient landscape flies.

The glimmering beams of opening day
   Shot through a watery sky,   10
Delusive glowing tints display,
   But soon o'erwhelmed they die.
'Twas thus my youth in brightness dawned,
   My passions caught the glow,
Some ray of bliss each cloud adorned   15
   Which teemed with future woe.

Torn from each joy that soothes the heart,
   All other pleasures fly;
My thoughts pursue the toils of art,
   My feelings music try.   20
Then oh, my soul, thy pow'rs divine
   Strengthened in virtue rear;
Pour from thy breast in songs sublime
   Thy grief – and learn to bear.

ELEGY ON A YOUNG LADY

Transcendent beauty moulders midst the earth!
   Exquisite tints fleet with the morning dews!
All nature teems with life, while blasting death
   Dissolves each form, but time again renews,
From the earth's fullness, fresh perpetual stores –   5
   But oh, the individual soul to us is lost,
   And unresigned we weep, by passions tossed,
While mid the tuneful spheres in bliss it soars!

If there is harmony below,
   If ever melancholy   10
     Touched by melody
   Her blackened veil withdrew,
I'll strike the chords whence solemn numbers flow,
And showers of softening tears shall ease my woe,
   Weeping the fairest flower that ever blew! –   15
   A flower whose bloom,
     By grief untimely nipped,
   Was hurried to the tomb.
     The spirit, of mortal lustre stripped,
Flew from its blighted frame below;   20
   Her virgin virtues were exhaled above,
While o'er the corpse sad streams of bitter woe
   Deluged the relic of our former love.

My breast awhile your potent sighs restrain,
  And as I sing   25
Ye scattered notes of harmony,
  Waft here on heavenly wing
The spiritual maid again.
Oh let me catch a glimpse by fancy's ray,
  And mentally behold the virgin fair,   30
Who was from our embraces snatched away,
  A martyr to despair.
      Seraphic, young, and free,
She smiled like morning op'ning on the heaven,
      Blessed   35
        And possessed
  Of earth's felicity;
      To her 'twas given
      To solace human cares;
      Her eyes, like shooting stars,   40
  Glanced swift as vivid lightning through the frame;
    Possessed of virtuous passion and beloved,
  Pure, unalloyed, strong, burnt the sacred flame.
        Oh bliss,
        To what excess   45
    Dost thou delude the heart!
      The ties most holy and most pure
      Cannot endure:
      We all must part!
When, bitter tears, will your sad source be dry?   50
  When through the mental world will concord shine?
Man is the wreck of man; the soul divine
        Passion uproots.
For frail mortality I heave the potent sigh!

Lo! unzoned[1] passions, brooking no control,   55
  Transgressing nature's laws, rush madly on,
Wounding the sacred mansion of the soul,
  And unresigned, in wild excess grow strong.
    With love's distracting smart,
    Which disappointments rash and desperate make,   60
    Lo! Jaspar wild assails the virgin's heart
  Whose constancy no energy can shake –
Though sweet his lays, as if the muses sung,
And love's warm passion harmonised his tongue.

Repulsed, his maddened spirit knew no bounds;   65
  Fierce in despair, to vengeance swift he flies,

ELEGY ON A YOUNG LADY
[1] *unzoned* unbounded.

And oft his rival's heart in fancy wounds
  While unreined passion flashes from his eyes;
  Wilder and wilder still resound his cries,
    By furies driven on   70
    To lengths before to him unknown,
  Till on his murd'rous sword his rival dies!
    Ill-fated son of earth,
    At thy dire birth
Heaven filled thee as a horn with sad calamity,   .75
  To scatter with thy breath
    Contagious sorrow round,
  Till the dire fiend internal, fraught with death,
    Threw thy young glories down!

  Sudden despair rushed on the virgin's heart;   80
    All that was mortal yielded to the stroke.
    Forth the pure spirit broke,
  Divided from its grosser earthly part,
And winged with love seraphic mounts on high.
  Oh flattering hope! – in immortality   85
    T' enjoy affections Nature tears away.
    All here on earth is subject to decay,
And every day our lessening comforts fly.
    Mysterious Power,
  To whose dread will I bend   90
    And tremblingly adore,
Forgive the tears which suffering mortals shed,
  Awed by our loss, and sacred virtue's pangs;
    Stronger on future blessings we depend,
And learn how weak the thread   95
  On which all human comfort hangs.
    Humbled by sorrow, low in earth I bend,
  And yield the spotless virgin to the skies;
Nor need revenge provoke the direful steel,
  For pierced by guilt the breathless culprit lies.   100

THE TRIUMPH OF SUPERSTITION. RAPHAEL AND IANTHE.

In Gothic[1] times, when feudal laws obtained,
And tyranny with superstition[2] reigned,
Mysterious rites with dazzling shows confined
To narrow bounds the darkened human mind;
Enslaving forms excluded truth's pure light,   5
And wrapped the world in shades of mental night.
Where genius dawned it shot forth sanguine gleams,

THE TRIUMPH OF SUPERSTITION. RAPHAEL AND IANTHE.   [2] *superstition* false religion, probably Catholicism.
[1] *Gothic* medieval.

Its fires infused ambition's frantic dreams;
Scared by the sword, fair Freedom distant flew,
And men machines to guilty conquerors grew   10
While gloomy ignorance the earth pervades,
And science³ flies to deep romantic shades.
Yet still the active mind retained some power,
The fruit was lost, but stronger bloomed the flower;
Poetic thoughts and deeds the brave combined,   15
And strong imagination seized the blind.
    But when amid those superstitious days
Some potent mind shed truth's obtrusive rays,
Suspicious priestcraft trembled at the sight,
And strove by horrid crimes t' eclipse the light.   20
    The fair Ianthe, bright as rising day,
Or the wild blossoms which unfold in May,
A victim fell to those tyrannic times,
Accused by priests of supernat'ral crimes,
Because some rays, with native genius fired,   25
Shot through her graceful eyes, and love inspired,
While still she dared be innocent and free,
With wisdom armed, and saintlike chastity.
    By virtuous precepts formed, this lovely maid
Was on the cold Helvetian⁴ mountains bred;   30
But thither chased, fled with her aged sire
From civil feuds, and persecutions dire.
They sought some spot where they might freely live,
And undisturbed fair nature's gifts receive.
Oh wanderers vain, to seek·for certain good,   35
Though kings and priests had stained the earth with blood –
Whose pride-swoln hearts, of tinselled virtues vain,
No feeling for men's miseries retain;
Hunting for fame, they idly sport with life,
While clashing interests urge perpetual strife.   40
    Ianthe's mind, pure, subtle, and profound,
With genuine force threw light on all around;
Through her clear eyes the fires of fancy glow,
While wisdom flourished beauteous on her brow.
Her nerves, with force and quick sensations strung,   45
Deepened her rosy lips, and fired her trembling tongue.
A glimpse of truth her native genius caught,
For all around woke analysing thought;
She saw, abhorrent, persecution's rod,
And in her heart she sought the unknown God –   50
The God who lights the heavens and rules the storm,
Mixed the pure elements and gave them form!
    Europe was in destructive wars engaged,

---

³ *science* knowledge.   ⁴ *Helvetian* Swiss.

Th' imperial eagle and the Pontiff raged;
The sword vast desolation spread around,   55
And swains unheeded felt the fatal wound.
Selmo (such was Ianthe's father's name)
Felt his blood freeze through his enfeebled frame;
Prone to repine, with age fastidious grown,
He made the sorrows of mankind his own.   60
Seeking for peace, through various realms they sped,
Still hopes of bliss like airy visions fled;
Ianthe saw with grief her father's mind,
While shunning ills, to nature's blessings blind.
Her youthful senses oft with pleasures glow,   65
She feels some good still mixed with human woe.
   On spring's sweet close, when fostering nature strews
The earth with flowers, and all creation glows,
They rested in Italia's pleasant vales
Till vernal showers were chased by warmer gales;   70
Then Selmo sought to rove, whom nought can charm,
Though placid peace here breathed a transient calm –
For still he saw, with acrimonious eye,
The powers of priestcraft and of tyranny;
With indignation heard th' uplifted rod   75
Of vile oppressors termed the hand of God.
   His fixed design when fair Ianthe found,
Involuntary sighs her bosom wound;
Suffused with tears, her eyes the fields survey,
She pressed his hand, and warmly urged his stay.   80
   'Look round', she cried, 'here smiling plenty blooms,
The ambient air breathes nature's rich perfumes.
Stay, oh my father, at my urgent prayer –
These vales obscure our Maker's bounties share.
The bliss we seek the world may not contain,   85
We rove romantic,[5] and our toils are vain;
In every spot we've various miseries found,
Though transient joys are scattered all around.'
   Ardent she spoke, while hope a ray diffused,
But, still resolved, the restless sire refused;   90
Long on life's troubled ocean he had tossed,
And now his relish of the calm was lost.
Ianthe's eyes streamed o'er the loved retreat,
Of all the world this spot alone seemed sweet;
Her heaving breast unusual anguish wrung,   95
And never so persuasive was her tongue.
   Whence in her bosom did those cares arise?
Say, was her genius fired by Raphael's eyes?
Or did the heavenly music of his song

---

[5] *romantic* quixotically, without determined aim.

Infuse its warmth to urge her glowing tongue?   100
Frequent their bland⁶ society he sought,
His genuine converse woke expanding thought,
Oft mingling lays with such transcendent art
As fired her fancy while they reached her heart.
Tears he saw glisten in Ianthe's eye,   105
Her bosom heaving with the parting sigh;
With quickest sympathy he caught her smart,
While mixed emotions vibrate in his heart.
Ianthe's fire, her form replete with grace,
The rosy blush which crimsoned o'er her face,   110
Pervade his soul; her graceful hand he pressed,
And, with consent, the feeble sire addressed,
Urging their stay – with fear he rapid speaks,
While anxious feelings tinged his ardent cheeks;
Though fretful anger from old Selmo broke,   115
With ardour irresistible he spoke.
Both plead at once, strong arguments they pour
With anxious tears, and each persuasive power;
His first resolves before their wishes melt,
For latent motives in their force he felt.   120
He yields; young Raphael points his piercing eyes,
Quick warm suffusions o'er Ianthe rise;
A sudden shower fell o'er her blushing cheeks
And her delight too eloquently speaks.
   Then Selmo chose a more obscure retreat   125
To build a humble mansion, plainly neat,
Distant from where the feudal lords reside,
Amid a wood, and on a hill's warm side;
Her wild profusions nature strewed around,
And friendly rills refreshed the shaggy ground.   130
Raphael assistance yields; his skilful hand
Hewed the rough trees, and ploughed th' unfurrowed land;
To nature true, by purest thought refined,
No idle scorn of toil debased his mind.
Ianthe with fine taste the flowers combines,   135
And round their mansion spreads the swelling vines.
   Oft Raphael works beside th' inspiring maid,
And tender passions all his powers invade;
Celestial was the music of her tongue –
He added force, and wrote th' ecstatic song.   140
His tuneful lays fair nature's works disclose,
And latent truth, drawn forth, reflected glows;
Mute on his burning lips love trembling hung,
While strong expression marked each feeling song;
Her kindling cheeks with deeper blushes glow,   145

---

⁶   *bland* genial.

And tremulous her warbling measures flow.
   The jealous Selmo views with watchful eyes
Their mutual passions as they strengthening rise;
A parent's care hung heavy at his breast,
Till freely they their artless loves confessed.   150
Then late he felt fresh happiness to dawn,
And midst life's winter viewed one glowing morn.
The eyes of Raphael, piercing as the light,
Spoke his whole soul, and sparkled with delight.
Ianthe strives her transports to conceal,   155
And midst her ringlets her deep blushes veil.
Old Selmo blessed them, while a grateful tear
Flowed from his eyes, and mingled with the prayer.
   One eve the kindling heavens resplendent shone,
While sinking Phoebus girds his crimson zone[7]   160
Whose glorious beams through tracts immense were shed,
And not one cloud o'er heaven's vast arch was spread.
Amongst the woods Ianthe strayed afar,
Marking the lustre of the evening star;
On her fair face the setting sunbeams glow,   165
To nature's God her songs enraptured flow.
As on she wandered, fearless of alarms,
Arno from far beheld her graceful charms.
   Arno, the child of fortune and of fame,
Whose nervous manhood early deeds proclaim;   170
A noble strength of thought his soul inspires,
But fostered passion fed vindictive fires;
In his large eyes strong sense and feeling glow,
But anger rose like thunder on his brow.
Vast his designs, with rising pride he strode,   175
And wild ambition taints his youthful blood;
Lawless he tramples o'er the peasant's corn,
O'erleaps the fence, and treads the flowery lawn.
At night he walks the woods, stole hours from sleep,
To give his thoughts a large unbounded sweep;   180
Mused on the bard[8] who godlike heroes sung,
And caught their fire from his inspired tongue;
Strong to endure, he nursed an ardent flame –
Mistaking virtue, called it thirst of fame;
Each generous thought his ample heart could move,   185
Though violent in hate, yet boundless in his love.
   While o'er the fields his rolling eyes he threw,
Ianthe like a seraph met his view;
Almost a vision of his brain she seemed
(Whose warmth indulged with thousand phantoms teemed);   190

---

[7] Phoebus (the sun) puts on a crimson belt that emits
red light as the sun sets.

[8] 'Homer' (Cristall's note).

Uncertain what she was, her path he crossed –
He stopped, he gazed, in admiration lost.
The fires of love seemed glancing from her eyes,
Her glowing cheeks were tinged with heavenly dyes;
O'er her light frame bewitching graces strayed,   195
And midst her smiles a thousand charms portrayed.
Entranced he gazed – at once her power confessed,[9]
And youthful transports fired his manly breast.
The blind restored scarce feel more strong delight
When heaven's vast orb first strikes th' astonished sight.   200
He caught her hand, and breathed impassioned sighs,
While fear and anger flushed her cheeks and eyes;
Quick from his grasp her hand she trembling drew,
And, winged with terror, swift as light she flew.
    Awed by the virtue sacred on her brow,   205
Unusual feelings through his bosom glow;
He saw her shoot before him as a star
Which, meteor-like, darts through the hemisphere;
Her magic limbs he viewed, while on the wind
Her long luxuriant tresses streamed behind.   210
Ardent he gazed, lost in romantic bliss,
And doomed with strong resolve Ianthe his.
    To boundless passion all his heart resigned,
He shook each shackle from his haughty mind,
And following quick, stung at his own delay,   215
Bounds o'er each barrier which obstructs his way.
The woods awhile conceal the flying fair –
Tortured he flew, more rapid from despair;
One glance he caught – to sight her mansion rose –
He saw her enter and the portal close.   220
Rash in resolve, and conscious of his power,
With mad tyrannic force he wrenched the door;
In fiercely rushed – but started as he viewed
Raphael, who by his loved Ianthe stood.
Spent with her flight, she on his arm reclined,   225
Smiled in his eyes, and calmed her fluttering mind.
The tyrant saw, but scarcely stopped to look:
His inmost soul with grief and anger shook.
Raphael he loved, had patronized his lays,
Raised him from want, and crowned with living bays;   230
Dare he, th' admitted partner of his board,
Triumphant thwart th' affections of his lord?
His horror-shedding brow in curls arose,
A threatening vengeance in his eyeballs glows;
Flashing with its ungovernable sway,   235
He like an angry tempest burst away.

---

[9] *confessed* admitted.

Selmo his eyes towards Ianthe raised –
Ianthe, conscious, trembled as he gazed;
Whate'er had passed with faltering lips declares,
Spent with fatigue, and shook with rising fears.   240
As Raphael heard, a secret pang possessed
His anxious mind, and agitates his breast;
But this repressing, her loved hand he took,
And from the ardour of his passion spoke;
Their nuptial day he urged, while inward smart   245
Toned each persuasive word, and fired her heart.
While yet he speaks loud tumults burst the door,
And soldiers entering, round young Raphael pour;
From Arno sent, his stern commands they brought,
Quick to convey him where his armies fought –   250
To distant regions, scenes to him unknown,
Where Arno's power upheld a tyrant's throne.
Thus forced along, resistance were as vain
As if a pebble strove to stem the main.
　　Raphael's pure breast, where virtue made abode,   255
By early thought with fortitude endowed,
Too deeply pierced, no longer could control
The desperate sorrow which o'erwhelmed his soul;
Those love-attractive orbs, his vivid[10] eyes,
Convulsive rolled, each thought confus'dly flies;   260
Scarcely the drowned words a passage broke,
While raving, thus with agony he spoke:
'Alas, each promised blessing torn away,
Ianthe falls the mighty victor's prey!
Oh dire effect of arbitrary power –   265
In vain their bitter tears the wretched pour!
Vainly thou beat'st thy breast, in vain thy cries;
Thy Raphael only guesses at thy sighs!'
　　Her quick-presaging mind foresaw the stroke,
And all her frame with inward tremblings shook;   270
Yet, struggling with her pangs, she powerful strove
To calm his fears, and prove her steadfast love;
Infused fair hope, to snatch him from despair,
And claimed protection of their Maker's care;
Vows of eternal constancy she paid,   275
And firmness midst her tenderest tears displayed.
　　He saw her virtue with such strength combined
That, trusting in the God who armed her mind,
He strove sublime to meet his fate resigned.
　　Selmo, by Arno's lawless power dismayed,   280
Far from his reach had borne th' unhappy maid;
But ruin threats him if he flies th' abode

---

[10] *vivid* lively, bright.

Where all his little wealth was now bestowed.
Ianthe's mind, with conscious worth elate,
Fearless decides her father's wavering state. 285
Secure within, though stung with deepest smart,
She feels resentment fire her daring heart;
She longs the tyrant's spirit to control,
To probe his vice, and humble his high soul;
And Selmo, proud of virtues he had reared, 290
Secure in them, no more the despot feared.
  Impassioned Arno, anxious to remove,
Unrivalled now, each barrier to his love,
Skilled in the world, and each seducing art,
Studies to wind around her widowed heart. 295
All means he tries – too well his ardent mind,
Fertile in thought, could varying pleasures find;
He forced a charm through ev'ry sense to steal,
And strove each baser motive to conceal;
Yet vain his powers, no passion they impart – 300
Her mind despises and pervades his art.
Till now his spirit ne'er had borne control;
She curbs his fires, but captivates his soul;
Still from her rosy lips sweet music flies,
And radiant glances still escape her eyes. 305
Seeking revenge, she triumphed in her power,
And taught the haughty tyrant to adore;
Wild satire[11] vibrates from her scornful tongue,
And pointed truths each conscious passion stung;
The flash of wit, inspiring and severe, 310
Displayed her hate, and filled him with despair.
Baffled and angered now, he sues no more,
But asks advice of saintly Theodore.
  'Alas!' replied the priest, 'why should my son
Consult with me, since power is all his own? 315
Nature t' adorn thy name with Fortune vies,
At thy command the unyielding rebel dies;
If such thy wishes, say what power restrains?
Oh force the bliss which ignorance disdains;
For must thy youth be blasted midst its bloom, 320
And all thy glories wither in the tomb?'
Thus spoke the priest – impetuous he complies,
And rushing joys burst from his large black eyes.
  Vile Theodore was early trained in sin,
But outward meekness hid the fiend within; 325
Religion's cloak close-veiled an atheist breast,
Which lust and grossest appetites possessed.
Soon a dire scheme his brain inventive laid,

---

[11] *satire* mockery.

And prompt to execute, he seeks the maid;
But soon as he beheld her glowing charms,   330
His own frail breast a guilty passion warms –
Her graceful eyes which glowed with innate fire,
Her mental powers, his wondering soul inspire.
To Arno soon he showed an altered mind,
And, pleading conscience, the base act resigned.   335
Th' impassioned Baron saw the vile intent,
Quick to perceive, and ardent to resent.
   'And whence', with burning rage aloud he cries,
'This new-born conscience? Whence so lately wise?
Oh fool, to trust my secrets to a breast   340
By falsehood, craft, and selfishness possessed!
Yet guard thy actions, lest my wrath be hurled,
And all thy crimes blaze forth before the world.'
   He spoke abrupt, and from his presence broke,
But stung with deep remorse in secret shook;   345
He felt the other's baseness, while deep shame
Paints his own crimes, and glows throughout his frame.
   With purer thoughts again he seeks the maid,
Passion and grief his noble breast pervade,
Not more by beauty than her virtues fired   350
And by her force and harmony inspired.
Sincerity and ardour fired his eyes,
His manly bosom heaved with potent sights;
Spite of herself, such force his flames impart
That all her constancy scarce saved her heart.   355
   Unknown of Arno, Theodore meanwhile
Oft visits Selmo, and with subtle guile
In vilest colours paints the Baron's mind,
And charges him with crimes himself designed.
Ianthe caught th' alarm, with deepest smart   360
Trembling perceives his power pervade her heart;
Stung to the quick, repentance wrung her breast –
Humbled, her mind its impotence confessed.
Blushing within, each though inflicts a wound,
And refuge oft near Theodore she found;   365
To him she flies, as an instructive friend
In whose sage converse all her powers extend.
   Arno repulsed, with wounded pride retires,
And sought with nobler thoughts to quench his fires;
Too long to idle grief a willing prey,   370
With strength of soul he curbed its powerful sway.
   To Theodore's intent Ianthe blind
Sought for instruction from his well-stored mind;
Her heart, for pure affections finely framed,
Seemed torpid when its tributes were unclaimed;   375
Unconscious of the flame which burnt his heart,

With him she strays, her opening thoughts t' impart –
And as he hears, beneath his shadowy brow
His eyes drank love, and swelling features glow.
    Once[12] in the bosom of a silent grove,   380
Th' unhallowed priest profanely urged his love.
Shocked and astonished while she calls for aid,
With lawless force he seized the struggling maid;
But her loud shrieks transpierced[13] the air around –
In vain he strove to suffocate the sound;   385
Advancing feet of men and horse he hears,
He starts confused, and flies, o'erwhelmed with fears.
Scarcely she breathes, her cheeks with anger flush,
O'er her whole frame deep spreads the crimson blush;
From those who proffered aid, with flashing eyes,   390
Confused, enraged, the trembling virgin flies.
    Her succourers advance, a noble train
Of royal hunters, bounding o'er the plain.
The Prince commands to stop her as she flies,
And asks from whence arose those piercing cries?   395
Panting and spent, the wretched nymph they caught,
And fainting to the Prince and nobles brought.
By men surrounded, pierced by curious eyes,
Her heart within her fluttering bosom dies;[14]
The wretch she names, his vile intention speaks,   400
Her quick'ning pulses throb, shame dyes her burning cheeks.
    Each youthful bosom, by her beauty fired,
Touched by her wrongs, was with revenge inspired;
But most the Prince, enraged, and threat'ning loud,
Destruction to the wretched miscreant vowed;   405
Charmed with her youth, he bade her not to fear,
Himself conducts her to her father's care.
Her eyes beamed thanks, her cheeks spoke modesty;
He gazed, and left her with an ardent sigh.
    By fair Ianthe into fury wrought,   410
The Prince with eager haste the culprit sought;
The soldiers seize him, at their lord's commands –
Humbly before th' assembled court he stands.
The priests surrounding cast a louring eye,
Aloud the youthful lords for justice cry;   415
The Prince, inflamed, a faithful witness bears,
And menacing, the vile attempt declares;
Dauntless he stood, as if to vice unknown
(For well he knew the weakness of the throne).
    'Thy will, oh God, be done!' he cried aloud,   420
Then to the court with low submission bowed;

---

12   *Once* i.e. as soon as they had arrived...   14 *Her heart...dies* i.e. she lost heart, felt afraid.
13   *transpierced* penetrated.

'But hear, just powers, a guiltless wretch resigned,
And guard from witchcraft the King's sacred mind;
Before her spells young Arno's bloom decays,
And fierce on me th' infernal poison preys.'   425
He said no more, but firmly raised his eyes,
And with mock prayers insults the awful skies.
    Then mid the priests rose up a reverend sire,
Whose rolling eyeballs flashed romantic fire –
The visionary Robert, friend of song,   430
Rapt in wild dreams – fanatic, rash, and strong;
Those powers which might have formed him wise and good,
Lost in the bigot, made him thirst for blood;
His brother he commands to speak more plain,
And fully his mysterious words explain.   435
    Then Theodore his crafty bosom bared:
'This heart', he cried, 'by innocence prepared,
Can firmly stand the test, or bravely bleed,
Should the base arts of hell o'er truth succeed;
Yet here I vow, by all my hopes in heav'n,   440
That by her spells to desperation driv'n,
I fled before her, scorched by mad desire,
Burnt by the flames of an internal fire;
Writhed to the soul, I smart with secret pains,
For still her magic arts infest my veins.'   445
    With trembling heart the bigot monarch hears,
Whose governed mind teemed with religious fears;
In him the slave and tyrant were combined –
Impotent, cruel, and with priestcraft blind;
Through his own veins he felt unusual heat,   450
And, as possessed, his nerves and pulses beat;
Fearful he sat, and dared not give command.
When Robert rose, to stretch a saving hand
O'er the vile priest, and bade him not to fear –
'Truth's sacred rays', he cried, 'shall falsehood clear' –   455
Then urged with zeal the sorc'ress should be tried,
And the just ordeal on her crimes decide.
    The Prince assents; th' ill-fated maid they sought,
And quickly, with her aged father, brought;
His wrinkled visage, washed in briny tears,   460
Dawned not a ray to chase his daughter's fears;
O'er her fair breast, by many sorrows wrung,
Her long light hair in waving tresses hung;
The purest innocence illumed her face,
And every action spoke superior grace.   465
An universal horror fills each breast,
All sue for her and criminate[15] the priest

---

[15]   *criminate* incriminate, charge with crime.

Who claims the sacred ordeal to decide,
And chides their zeal with priestly art and pride:
'That pity which you feel her spells inspire,   470
Her eyes will pierce you with their magic fire.'
   Her voice was silenced when she strove to speak;
The guiltless blood ran warmly through her cheek.
Devout, on high she raised her lucid eyes;
Resigned, on conscious innocence relies,   475
For well she knew the author of her breath
With lengthened life might curse, or bless with death.
   Vile Theodore each crafty engine plies,
To prove her guilty false expedients tries.
Virtue no justice on this earth commands;   480
Convicted by each trial now she stands
Past all dispute. Though grief assails each eye,
The prince condemns her as a witch to die.
   Selmo, whose restless mind and wavering breast
No strength from calm philosophy possessed,   485
Nor from religion resignation drew,
Desponding, wild, with fierce distraction flew.
The hoary sire beheld her dragged along,
While direful horror froze his speechless tongue;
With trembling hands he smote his hopeless breast,   490
His rolling eyes departing sense expressed;
Aghast he stood, his feeble brain turned round,
High swelled his heart, his thoughts no utterance found –
Then sudden flew, like one possessed and blind,
Or withered leaves of aspen driv'n by wind;   495
Felt not his age, with transient fury strong;
Loud cries broke forth, with which the mountains rung:
He climbs a cliff, on his Ianthe calls,
And, starting backward, from its summit falls.
   Confined, to solitude a lonely prey,   500
In dreary cells the saintlike sufferer lay,
By ardent prayer and deep reflection strove
From her warm heart to shake the ties of love
(Which to the earth her sweet affections bind),
And raise in hope tow'rds Heav'n her pious mind;   505
Yet her young breast oft pants with inward fears,
While love and nature force impassioned tears.
   Involved in science, Arno's injured mind
All pleasures and the pomp of courts resigned;
Strong disappointments noble lessons taught –   510
His heart he learned, and purified each thought.
To him when rumour those dire tidings bears,
His rage relapses while aghast he hears;
With passion fired, and wild resentment wrought,
His arméd force with eager haste he sought;   515

Through his swoln veins the blood in torrents flies,
While fury blazes from his threatening eyes;
Convulsive passion half suppressed his breath –
Burning he rushes on to snatch the maid from death.
    Summoned, his vassals all unite around,   520
And the earth trembles with the warlike sound;
His limbs he armed, and shook his well-tried spear,
Then flew impetuous, menacing from far.
    Raphael, compelled, in Arno's armies fought,
And 'mongst his troops promiscuously[16] was brought;   525
Ianthe's fate was still to him unknown –
Deep-stung, the past absorbs his thoughts alone;
Such strong dejection long had bound his mind,
He seemed struck off the chain of humankind;
Lost in a dreary retrospect of woes,   530
Of all unconscious, to the field he goes.
Arno impatient rushes o'er the plain,
And fires with fierce revenge the hostile train.
    This day was fair Ianthe doomed to bleed;
The long processions to the pile proceed.   535
Already on the baneful faggots reared,
With elevated soul the maid appeared;
Amid her fears one beam of ecstasy
Shot o'er her face, and lightened in her eye;
Fired by immortal hopes, each ardent thought   540
Aspired to heaven, and her Redeemer sought;
Her soul, resigned, trusts that each earthly tie
Will there unite in blessed eternity.
    The Prince with terror heard loud shouts from far,
And the dire sounds of unexpected war;   545
Soon selfish fears his coward heart dismayed.
With voice confused, unknowing what he said,
He bade the kindling flames to be allayed.
    Arno rushed on to snatch her from her fate,
And whelm in ruins the tyrannic state,   550
When Theodore, with quickness all his own,
Apart to Robert cries, 'To thee alone
The prince can safety owe; say, canst thou stand
And see a sacrilegious foe command?'
    'Short is his date', austere the priest replied;   555
'Soon shall the haughty rebel rue his pride.'
    A ponderous crucifix his right hand held,
The left a sacred pompous[17] relic filled;
Reverend his form, mysterious his attire,
His haggard[18] eyes teemed with religious fire;   560

---

[16] *promiscuously* unceremoniously.

[17] *pompous* ceremonial.

[18] *haggard* wild; Ann has in mind Gray, *The Bard* 18:
'With haggard eyes the poet stood'.

As one inspired he rushes on the plain,
And spreads his robes before the royal train;
Then rearing high the cross and holy band,
He hurled defiance with a fierce command.
   'Foes to your mother church – ah, whither driv'n?   565
Like fallen angels would ye war with Heav'n?
'Tis Satan leads ye on, thus proudly great;
Death is your portion, hell your lasting fate,
Unless ye timely bow to Heaven's commands
And seize yon ruffian with your hostile hands,   570
Which impiously against your God you've reared,
Nor his high laws, nor burning vengeance feared.
Heavens, while I speak convulsive pants my breath,
Lest God in wrath denounce some awful death!
Remember Korah's fate,[19] and trembling know   575
Judgements await each sacrilegious foe.'
   He spoke; amazed, they fling their arms away,
Some cross their breasts, whilst ardently they pray;
Some seize their chief but, brooking no control,
He felt despair's sharp sting inflict his soul.   580
   'Before unconquered, now shall priests subdue?
And shall Ianthe fall in Arno's view?
Can he midst flames behold the maid expire,
And want the power to quench the hellish fire?'
Wildly he raved; the priestly train advance   585
To lead him captive, and to seize his lance;
Sullen he turned, while rage and deadly smart
Swelled his proud breast, and almost burst his heart;
His powers, his spirit, can no aid afford –
Sudden he rushes on his desperate sword.   590
'Hold his rash hand!' commanding Robert cries,
But vain, for as he spoke the hero dies.
   A mingled murmur ran, some shout aloud,
The distant troops around their leader crowd;
Raphael indignant 'mongst the rest drew nigh,   595
And o'er the field threw an enquiring eye;
Far in the rear, unconscious he had been,
Till now too distant to survey the scene;
But as he looked around with dumb surprise,
Confused, a distant spectre seemed to rise –   600
Ianthe's form, in direful garbs arrayed,
Appeared on piles of kindling faggots laid:

---

[19] *Korah's fate* Korah was a leader of a rebellion against Moses; he was punished with other rebels in the appropriate manner: 'And the earth opened her mouth, and swallowed them up, and their houses, and all the men that appertained unto Korah, and all their goods. They, and all that appertained to them, went down alive into the pit, and the earth closed upon them, and they perished from among the congregation' (Numbers 16:32–3).

Wildly he flew towards the horrid shade.
By priests withheld, he rages like the wind
Within the hollow of a rock confined;   605
But strong as winds, with unremitting force
He breaks their hold, and wings his active course;
He ran, disarmed and wounded in the fray,
And to the pile forced his intrepid way;
No spectre mocks, no empty shade descends,   610
In horrid certainty the vision ends.
Bleeding and pale he gazed, with horror filled,
His soul was shook, and every nerve was thrilled;
Ere he can speak they tear him from the maid,
While round the pile the crackling flames invade.   615
She caught his eyes, her resignation shook;
She struck her breast, but the volum'nous smoke
Wild rising to the winds obscured her view,
And kindling flames to vivid fierceness blew.
Bloodthirsty bigotry exulting glows,   620
And Robert shouted as the flames arose.
Wild raged the fires, the crackling pile gives way,
Th' involving smoke obscures the face of day
And flames upon the crumbling ruins prey.
The priests triumphant hail the Heavenly King,   625
And e'en midst murder, songs of worship sing.
Raphael, whom virtue snatched from rash despair,
Now seemed the test of what the heart can bear;
As he beheld the barbarous flames ascend,
And o'er the pile the circling smoke extend,   630
Awhile, by each sublimer thought forsook,
All that was human in his bosom shook;
A frantic wish of death alone inspires
To mingle souls, and rush amid the fires.
Desp'rate he flew tow'rds where the faggots blazed,   635
But ere he plunged, from pious habit raised
His heart to God; that sacred name impressed
The sense of duty on his rebel breast;
He felt a power divine his rage control,
An inward voice restrain his daring soul;   640
Awful against self-murder conscience rose;
Trembling he stopped; his heart with horror froze:
'Can the rash suicide e'er hope to join
Ianthe's spirit in the realms divine?'
His heart he prostrates, though convulsed with woe,   645
And as a Christian bore the deadly blow,
Mingles amid a dreary world again,
Suff'ring a life of labour and of pain;
From sorrow more sublime, more firm from thought,
Those truths he studied which the Saviour taught;   650

And from reflection and the Gospel drew
Strength, which on faith and hope's firm basis grew,
And virtues pure, unmixed with bigotry,
Which breathed forbearance, justice, charity.
Illumed within, e'en in that bloody hour   655
When priestcraft reigned with arbitrary power,
He saw their sway dissolve all human ties,
And darkness veil the laws, and Truth's fair eyes,
Yet could impart no ray of sacred light,
So thick the mists which clouded human sight.   660
   Thus dark, in error wrapped, long groaned mankind,
Pleased with vain shows, and to oppression blind,
Till Freedom, dawning o'er the injured earth,
Cleared some rank weeds, and gave true knowledge birth.
Oh may we ever sanctify her fane   665
And ne'er her hallowed paths with slaughter stain!
Love of mankind, not novelty, be ours;
For general good may man exert his powers!

SONG

Repeat, oh muse, the virtuous song
    Of him whose bosom knew no art;
Whose native measures, wild and strong,
    Poured the free dictates of his heart.[1]

Tossed midst life's terrific storms,
    My soul on nature's centre clings,
Striving to taste each scattered bliss,
    And loudly grateful anthems sings.

When flying o'er the billowy deep,   5
    Upborne the sounding waves among,
While winds the boiling ocean sweep,
    And lightnings dart their fires along;

Absorbed, unmoved, resolved of mind,
    I dare the elements assault,   10
Midst roaring oceans ploughed by wind,
    While thunders burst through heaven's high vault.

On virtue's base, and buoyed by hope,
    I see peace beam through every cloud;
Benumbed upon the shattered rope   15
    Still grateful is my song, and loud;

SONG
[1]   These are the terms in which Burns was celebrated,
though Ann's source for this epigraph is unknown.

Grateful for being raised from nought
  To scenes where nature's blessings shine,
Endued with fancy, love, and thought,
  And dawnings of a soul divine.   20

A FRAGMENT: THE BLIND MAN

Say, reverend man, why midst this stormy night
Wander'st thou darkling and exposed, alone?
Alas, I would assist thee, though unknown.
  'Rash youth, that God which robbed my eyes of sight
Darts through my mind a ray of sacred light.   5
The winds I heed not, nor the lashing shower,
My sinewy frame is firm, my soaring mind has power.
This oaken staff feels out the dangerous way;
'Twas Heaven's fierce fire which swept my eyes away
And left an orbless trunk, that knows nor night nor day.   10
Yet strong ideas rooted in my brain
Form there an universe, which doth contain
Those images which Nature's hand displays –
The heavenly arch,[1] the morning's glowing rays;
Mountains and plains, the sea by tempests hurled,   15
And all the grandeur of this glorious world!'
  But ah, how wild drives on the rapid storm,
Dashing the rain against thy reverend form!
Yon swelling river, foaming tow'rds the main,
Smokes midst th' advancing waves and falling rain: 20
Oh father, my young soul is shook within,
Oh let me lead you from this horrid scene!
  'I yield, but let not fear thy mind deform –
Hark! 'tis God's voice which urges on the storm;
He to this world of elements gave form.   25
From them he moulded all, yet gave not peace,
  But broke the harmony, and bade them rage;
He meant not happiness should join with ease,
  But varied joys and pains should all the world engage.'

THELMON AND CARMEL: AN IRREGULAR POEM

Part the First

In Thelmon's breast contending passions rise,
While, with resentment stung, he proudly flies;
The harmonist divine, to madness fired,
Rashly to Carmel's youthful charms aspired;
But she, with virtue's awful power possessed,   5

A FRAGMENT: THE BLIND MAN
[1] *heavenly arch* sky.

Taught him to blush, and drove him from her breast.
First anger in his heated bosom rose,
With pride he burns, for speedy vengeance glows;
His instrument, of heaven-inspired sound,
Touched by dire discord wounds the air around;   10
Then vengeance dies, and fierce disdain succeeds –
He flies, while Carmel's heart with sorrow bleeds.
His agonies are changed to bitter scorn,
Nor can the lofty spirit stoop to mourn;
Disowning every tie that linked the heart,   15
He lost in vice the racking sense of smart;
He gave a scope to all his mad desires
(Perverted genius deepest crimes inspires).
The wanton chords he struck with loose delight,
And wit's strong flashes shed luxuriant[1] light,   20
Till, satiate with the empty joys of sense,
And oft disgusted with their impotence,
Wearied of follies reaped without control,
With self-reproach he smarted to the soul;
With shame and scorn from noisy pleasures flew,   25
And to the calms of solitude withdrew;
Nature exploring, and with music fired,
Lost in research he wandered as inspired.

Part the Second

Removed from man, and summer's tuneful groves,
    Alone harmonious Thelmon strays to muse;
O'er rugged hills, through long rough paths he roves,
To where, impelled by winds, the ocean roars,
Heaves its vast surges on the echoing shores,   5
    Foams mid the rocks, and dashes the thick ooze.

Now on the sounding beach, sublime in thought,
    He viewed the wonders of the horrid deep,
Which from the heavens the ponderous torrents caught,
While briny mountains brave the darkened sky,   10
Where lowering clouds replete with waters fly,
    And stormy winds the heavens and ocean sweep.

Nor jarring elements untuned his soul,
    Each natural cause still tracing to its source,
While driven on winds the waves tremendous roll;   15
Curious to meditate on nature's law,
The vast Creator in his works he saw,
    And contemplation guides his wandering course.

PART THE FIRST
[1] *luxuriant* excessive.

Humbled by youthful crimes and curbed desires,
   Abstracted through life's mazy paths he trod,   20
The love of science[1] damped his former fires;
And with a heart formed to converse with man,
A genius[2] raised on nature's noblest plan,
   He inward drew his powers, and sought his God.

Pond'ring on man's vain passions as he stood,   25
   He heard the transports of the empty wind,
The vain contentions of the mighty flood,
Till the tired storm scowled cross the heaving main;
The spray no more flies o'er the distant plain,
   And the faint sun through filmy vapours shined.   30

Calm midst advancing shades dissolved the day,
   The silenced winds scarce shook the showery leaves,
And through the heavens the watery vapours stray;
Then o'er the sea (tumultuous now no more)
Which beat the rocks, and gently dashed the shore,   35
   A solemn melody his spirit breathes.

Thelmon, whom passions now no more control,
To science and to music gave his soul;
Fair Carmel's charms alone his love had fired,
Unmarked the mind which every grace inspired,   40
With violence it flamed, but soon expired.
His heedless wanderings fate or chance decides,
But now again near Carmel's dwelling guides;
Of which unmindful, still he roved the plains,
And to the setting sun poured forth sublime his strains.   45

Part the Third

The grove is hushed, the saffron-tingéd clouds
   Shoot down their softening colours to the west;
Advancing night the sable mountains shrouds,
   And with her dewy feet are meads and flowrets pressed.

Slowly the solemn moon its full orb rears,   5
   And through the skies its lucid influence throws,
Each glittering star mid fleecy clouds appears,
And through th' immeasurable path of heaven
   The high galaxy glows.

The moonbeams glide serene across the lake   10
   Whose glassy bosom gloomy branches shade;

PART THE SECOND   [2] *genius* spirit.
[1] *science* knowledge.

The dying gales the murmuring sedges shake,
While sounds melodious, pouring through the grove,
   The solemn stillness of the night invade.

Cool as the eve, mild as the lucid spheres,   15
   Fair Carmel wanders mid the nightly dew,
But wondering stood, as through her well-tuned ears
   She listening soft harmonious numbers drew.

On the chaste moon she fixed her crystal eyes,
   Her ear attentive caught the trembling sounds;   20
Responsive her lone bosom uttered sighs,
While the musician pours his lofty strains;
They fill the woods, they echo o'er the plains,
   The distant air with heavenly notes resounds.

Song of Thelmon

'In the cool bosom of the solemn night   25
   With songs sublime I hail the Power Divine,
As from yon orb the quivering beams of light
Surround the shades, and through the ether bright
   Soften the scene, and o'er the trembling waters shine.

'Mid splendent[1] day oft jarring passions war,   30
   But calm at eve I tread the silent grove,
And feel delight from every brook and star;
Each solemn scene I view with sacred awe,
While from a mental glance of nature's law
   I learn the wonders of almighty love.   35

'Rude were the storms which deep through my sad breast
   Have striv'n the germs[2] of virtue to expel –
Rebellious passions robbed my soul of rest;
But in despondency's most baleful hour
I felt within a renovating power   40
   Strengthen my soul, and all at last is well.

'My mind no more in boisterous transports drowned,
   Reflective feels a bosom formed for love,
Senses which touch the strings of thought profound
And taste each bliss in nature's calm retreats;   45
While o'er this wilderness of thorny sweets
   Wandering, with harmony of soul I move.'

SONG OF THELMON
[1] *splendent* bright.
[2] *germs* seeds.

He ceased, and midst the thickets strayed along.
  The listening virgin's bosom swelled with woe,
Mid silent tears she heard the solemn song –   50
  Well did her soul his heavenly accents know.

Rekindled passions warm her heaving breast,
  While memory teems with proofs of former love;
Deep in her heart each accent is impressed,
  Scarce can she quit the lake, or shadowy-waving grove.   55

Her fancy hears amidst the murmuring gale
  Still the faint echoes of his music roll;
Homeward she bends at last, fatigued and pale,
  And vainly strives to calm her trembling soul.

Part the Fourth

The moon is sunk, and heaven's resplendent stars
  Glimmer mid nightly shades and morning grey;
O'er the low plains a whitish mist appears
While, silvering every eastern cloud, the dawn,
Infusing slow the promise of the morn,   5
  Faint-tinged the couch where Carmel thoughtful lay.

From her clear eyes large pearly drops descend,
  Unusual fires thrill through her trembling veins
As when the potent solar rays extend
O'er tracts where long congealing ice and snows   10
Like mountains rise, near polar circles froze,
  And melting by its heat wild deluge the vast plains.

Remembrance poured its influence through her soul;
  Her aching bosom heaved with bitter sighs,
Her agitated thoughts distracted roll;   15
And to her fev'rish fancy Thelmon rose –
Now lofty verse in strains harmonious flows,
  Now passion speaks in his all-potent eyes.

Like an imperfect dream the past appears:
  His errors fleet like a dissolving cloud,   20
His virtues shine like uneclipséd stars,
No more the sense of wrongs secures her heart –
Her bosom burns with unavailing smart,
  And all within the hopeless flame avowed.

Restless she lay, till o'er the mantling skies   25
  The dazzling radiance of the morning rose;
From the broad light she turned her weeping eyes

And, spent with passion and the weight of thought,
The transient comfort of soft sleep she sought,
    And listless sunk at length to half repose.   30

Thus a sad prey to misery, Carmel found
No kind resource to mitigate the wound;
Void of pursuits, her heart seeks no relief,
No active duty rouses her from grief.
Though calm she seemed, within the poison wrought,   35
And her affections quite absorbed each thought.
The light of day her sorrowing mind oppressed;
Night was alone congenial to her breast;
Each eve she strays to soothe her joyless soul,
And pleased beholds the lengthening shadows roll.   40

Part the Fifth

In the mild west dissolved the blaze of day;
    The rosy heavens rich varying tints o'erspread;
Bright shone the hills beneath the evening ray;
Amid the corn wild crimson poppies blow,
All nature wore a universal glow,   5
    And joy was echoed o'er th' illumined mead.

Untouched by every accent of delight,
    Amid the smiling harvest Carmel strayed,
Then climbed a craggy hill of towering height
Where hanging woods luxuriant foliage spread,   10
And wild-blown flowers their spicy odours shed;
    Thence she the grand extensive scene surveyed.

Night did not yet possess its dark domain,
    But gradual shades o'erspread the burning sky;
The solemn lake, the flower-enamelled plain   15
Catch the last rays of the descending orb
Whose fiery blaze the distant seas absorb,
    While through the western clouds the crimson glories fly.

Nature in glowing plenty smiled below,
    Above the clouds incessant varying roll;   20
As Carmel viewed the fertile landscape glow,
Touched by the view, the glorious work she praised,
And to the Universal Parent raised,
    Fervent in prayer, her energetic soul.

The fading landscape lessens on her sight;   25
    Amid the ether, stars celestial shine;
Some scattered clouds still catch the ebbing light

And by the glimmering rays distinct she viewed
Thelmon, who lost in contemplation stood,
   As if in converse with the heavenly Nine.[1]   30

She strove to speak, but all her powers were bound;
   O'er her fair breast fast flowed a silent flood,
While he with musing pace was wandering round
The rugged path, and passed regardless by;
He saw her not, but drew unconscious nigh,   35
   Then mingled in the umbrage of the wood.

In vain again to calm her breast she tries,
   Her livid[2] eyes surveyed the ruthess heaven;
The briny showers she shed, the deep-felt sighs
Which mixed with prayers, her wretched bosom heaved;   40
Alike amid a friendless void were breathed,
   Or by the winds to neighbouring mountains driven.

Now when the clouds rolled heavy o'er the stars,
   And chilling midnight spread a dreary gloom,
She dried the painful sluices of her tears;   45
Devoid of hope she wished not for its light
And, thoughtless of the dangers of the night,
   Restless returned in silence to her home.

Part the Sixth

The shades of night and glimmering dawn are fled,
   The rising sun the parting clouds has fired;
The purple hills illumined flame with red,
While Thelmon, fraught with praise, forsakes his bed,
   With love of nature and her truths inspired.   5

The waving corn, moist with the pearly dew,
   Glitters beneath the sun's refulgent rays;
Luxuriant o'er each hedge wild roses grew,
And ripening fruits prolific greet his view –
   All Nature smiled a thousand various ways.   10

Silent this morn was his melodious tongue,
   And listening to the songsters of the grove
He envied their sweet lays, as blithe they sung;
For with a transient pang his heart was wrung,
   Reflecting on their pure and artless loves.   15

PART THE FIFTH   [2] *livid* passionate.
[1] *the heavenly Nine* the Muses.

Bitter remembrance deep pervades his soul,
   The glistening lake, the high-grown trees he knew;
O'er the sweet plains his eyes rekindling roll,
'Here Carmel's virtues did his fires control' –
   Deeply he blushed, and quick his eyes withdrew.   20

Touched by her wrongs, his soul its guilt confessed;
   His breast, which heaved with deep remorse and smart,
Mourning past crimes, an anxious wish possessed,
A wish which no obtruding pride suppressed,
   To own the errors of his altered heart.   25

Part the Seventh

Carmel he seeks. The wandering maid he found,
And with each look inflicts a deeper wound;
She strove to veil her blushes from his sight,
And hide her terrors by a sudden flight,
Yet could not fly, nor scarce resolve to stay –   5
Her burning heart contending passions sway.
   Approaching her, with awe serene he spoke,
While from his eyes the light of virtue broke;
With humble dignity his crimes confessed –
No rage against himself his words expressed.   10
Too well he knew, when swelled by passion's tide,
How hard the task the throbbing heart to guide,
And penitence he felt, devoid of pride.
   He viewed her with surprise, for while he speaks,
Delight, not anger, flushed her modest cheeks;   15
Th' emotions of her soul her eyes portray,
Where transient fires in vivid flashes play.
Rekindling transports as he gazed arise,
Which tinged his lips, and fired his rapt'rous eyes;
New sympathies within his bosom sprung,   20
Which warm in hope impel his glowing tongue.
Pure and refined his passions now appear,
His virtues strengthened, and his heart sincere;
His voice sublime, his eyes alike inspire,
Pervade her soul, and fill her breast with fire.   25
Dubious no more, she seeks not to retreat,
Too strongly love did in her bosom beat;
Fast from her eyes the tears of transport flow,
Joy takes the language of her former woe;
Amid the shower a smile seraphic broke –   30
She gave her hand, and thus impassioned spoke:
   'I seek not to restrain my throbbing heart,
Nor veil its candour with the show of art;
Forgiveness beams upon thee from mine eyes,
While all thy virtues to my memory rise.   35

Within I feel such powerful sympathy,
Such strong attraction of my soul to thee,
That no false pride in this important hour
Swerves my pure heart with its tyrannic power.
With agony I saw excess control   40
A mind whose grandeur ever awed my soul;
Thy wondrous songs, replete with genuine fire,
The love of nature which those songs inspire,
Were in my heart impressed with power divine;
In vain I strove thine image to resign,   45
And mourned the fall of such a soul as thine.
But now thy penitence o'erjoyed I view,
And yield my heart, as to thy virtue due.'
    He heard while joy redoubled in his breast,
And strong emotions every look expressed;   50
Sublime his soul its ardent love portrayed,
But most his future life his gratitude displayed.

SONG

Come, let us dance and sing,
While our spirits lightly wing;
Youth's gay fantastic spring
    Wreathes the mystic bow'rs!
Bend here thy quivering feet,   5
Fancy thy smiles shall greet,
Dimples mid roses sweet,
    And fruits with glowing flowers!
        Glide along,
        Join my song,   10
        Meet me in the varied throng;
        Crowned with May,
        Laughing gay,
        Hailing like a lark the day!
Thus the sweet spring we taste   15
Ere our genial warmth shall waste;
With nature's blessing graced,
    We sport the hours away.

Life's an uncertain joy,
Let's the rosy hours employ;   20
Ere they our powers destroy
    They shall scatter charms.
Grey dawn shall see them rise,
Silvering the opening skies,
Sparkling with dewy eyes,   25
    And blushing spread their arms.
        Tripping gay,

They burst with day,
Blazing with a gaudy ray;
Midst the bowers,   30
Blooming flowers
Opening hail the noontide hours.
Then gliding down the hills,
Silent eve its dew distils,
With rapture each bosom thrills;   35
    Night's songstress music pours.

Deep then their blush appears
Mid their saffron-tingéd hairs,
Waved o'er the rising stars
    Dissolving into night.   40
Borne next on Cynthia's horns,[1]
Glittering mid the lakes and lawns,
Elves, sprites and sylvan fauns
    Dance in vapours dight.[2]
        Nightly beams,   45
        Northern gleams,
        Magic fire through ether streams;[3]
        Round the sky
        The hours fly,
        Launching to eternity!   50
Thus ever on the wing,
Come let us dance and sing,
Trampling on sorrow's sting,
    Laughing at each sigh.

SONG

The eve descends with radiant streaks,
    Sweetly serene and grandly gay,
While western tinges flush the cheeks,
    And insects mid the zephyrs play.

Young Cymon, with a rapt'rous heart,   5
    Whom woodland scenes and pleasure drew,
Roved while his sweet poetic art
    From nature stole its noblest hue.

On wild thyme banks the poet sung,
    Harmonious thither called his fair,   10
Where blooming roses clustering hung,
    And every sweet perfumed the air.

SONG
[1] *Cynthia's horns* the horns of the crescent moon.
[2] *dight* decked, arrayed.

[3] *Northern gleams . . . ether streams* Ann describes the
aurora borealis.

Attentive to the well-known song
   Whose warbled sounds pervade the grove,
Blushing she heard, and sped along,   15
   Her thrilling bosom fired with love.

As on the odorous bank he pours
   A lover's song, a lover's sighs,
He saw her glowing, decked with flowers,
   Affection beaming from her eyes.   20

As summer suns unfold the rose,
   Or heightening sweets embalm the grove,
So as he gazed she deeper glows,
   And every look was fraught with love.

While o'er her face the zephyrs play,   25
   A thousand charms delight each sense,
Joined to the blushing bloom of May –
   The sweeter hue of innocence.

Her lovely hands a garland bound,
   Then on his head she placed the wreath,   30
His locks with flowering myrtles crowned,
   Laurels and roses waved beneath.[1]

The vivid fires thrilled through his breast
   As energetic strains he sung;
Her artless eyes still more expressed   35
   Than the wild fervour of his tongue.

TO A LADY ON THE RISE OF MORN

Rise, blossom of the spring,
   The dews of morn
   Still linger on the barren thorn –
Arise and sing!

Oh join my rapt'rous song!   5
   And o'er the wild bleak hills
And unfledged fields along
   Pursue the trickling rills;
      Oh rise!
Clothed with that modest grace   10
That veils the glowing beauties of thy face,
   And downward points the radiance of thine eyes.
  I wait thee on the thawing mountains

SONG
[1] Myrtles and roses are symbols of love, being associated with Venus.

Where spring dissolves the lingering fountains;
Oh trace with me the opening flowers,   15
Brave the sharp breeze, damp dews, and vernal showers!
Wild various Nature strews her charms,
And storms surround her mildest calms;
  Oh to her frowns let us superior be,
Taste each delight, and hail the coming spring,   20
  Singing the heavenly song of liberty!

SONG

Through springtime walks with flowers perfumed,
  I chased a wild capricious fair
Where hyacinths and jonquils bloomed,
  Chanting gay sonnets through the air;
    Hid amid a briary dell   5
      Or 'neath a hawthorn tree,
    Her sweet enchantments led me on
      And still deluded me.

While summer's splendent[1] glory smiles
  My ardent love in vain essayed,   10
I strove to win her heart by wiles,
  But still a thousand pranks she played;
Still o'er each sunburnt furzy hill,
  Wild, playful, gay, and free,
She laughed and scorned, I chased her still,   15
  And still she bantered[2] me.

When autumn waves her golden ears[3]
  And wafts o'er fruits her pregnant[4] breath,
The sprightly lark its pinions rears;
  I chased her o'er the daisied heath,   20
Sweet harebells trembled in the vale,
  And all around was glee;
Still, wanton as the timid hart,
  She swiftly flew from me.

Now winter lights its cheerful fire,   25
  While jests with frolic mirth resound
And draws the wand'ring beauty nigher,
  'Tis now too cold to rove around;
The Christmas game, the playful dance,
  Incline her heart to glee –   30
Mutual we glow, and kindling love
  Draws every wish to me.

SONG
[1] *splendent* brightly shining.
[2] *bantered* made fun of.

[3] *ears* of corn.
[4] *pregnant* fruitful, capable of germinating.

SONG

Both gloomy and dark was the shadowy night,
   The leaden-surged ocean heaved slowly each wave,
Silence solemn as death succeeded the light,
   And each ravenous prowler stole forth from its cave.

Now to a sea-beach, where a black baleful yew   5
   O'er venomous weeds its dark shadows impressed,
Disordered by grief the wild Tamara flew –
   As the wind was her brain, as the ocean her breast.

Then frequent and loud were her cries o'er the main,
   With passion she heaved, with distraction was torn;   10
The dead shore long-murm'ring re-echoed in vain,
   Nor will peace e'er again to her bosom return.

She mourns for the dead, the cold senseless dead,
   Her love who beneath the salt billows doth lie,
And the deep grave she seeks where rests his fair head –   15
   Loose-flying her tresses, distracted her eye.

The night as it darkens increases her pain,
   Her mind teems with horrors which deepen the gloom;
She hears his loved voice, shrill it calls her again,
   And his cold breast she seeks in the billowy tomb.   20

Distracted and lost, her poor shattered heart
   With passions was urged, which no force could control;
Deep-plunging in death she subdues her fierce smart,
   And from its torn mansion thus freed her young soul.

ELEGY

Wander, my troubled soul, sigh mid the night thy pain,
While from my cloud-hung brow stream showers of briny rain;
My spirit flies the earth, the darkest gloom pervades,
Hovers around the dead, and mingles with the shades.

Oh friend of my breast, thou'rt entombed within my heart,   5
I still to thee alone my inmost thoughts impart;
Solaced no more by thee, vain is the power of song,
Sighs check each tuneful lay, and murmuring glide along.

Thou wert unto my soul what the sun is to my sight,
But thou art set in death, and I am lost in night;   10
All nature seems a void of element'ry strife,
Where the soul is all cloud, and fraught with pain all life.

When near thy faithful breast I heeded not the storm,
Nor thought of wasting time, nor death's consuming worm,
Thy genius woke my thought, as oft we strayed alone,   15
And raised me to that heaven to which thou now art flown.

Silent oft I mourn, sad wandering mid the gloom,
Or on the sea-beat shore I weep my bitter doom;
To thee, among the blessed, my feeble soul would soar,
And mid the starry spheres th' Almighty Pow'r adore.   20

WRITTEN WHEN THE MIND WAS OPPRESSED

Wandering amid the horrors of the night,
    Musing, my sighs mix with the whistling wind,
Dim watery shadows shroud my feeble sight,
    And deep reflection fills my labouring mind.

Alone amid the deadly midnight glooms,   5
    I hear the winds rush wildly through the waste,
My strengthened soul its various powers assumes,
    While painful feelings agitate my breast.

'Alas!' I thought, 'Where tends this toil of life,
Unhappy, vain, delusive, frail, and short,   10
    Enveloped mid disease, death, sin, and strife,
As if weak man was his Creator's sport?'

Beneath the thunder on the desert strand,
    I listen to the solemn ocean's roar,
Awed by the powerful elements I stand,   15
    And mid their fierce convulsions heaven adore.

But the more fatal storms which rage within
    With stronger fears my youthful mind dismay;
Follies and passions which engender sin
    Assail the soul, and on the reason prey.   20

To nature's sweet enchantments waked from nought,
    Chaos impenetrably dark behind,
Early possessed of consciousness and thought,
    Impelled by passions of a new-born mind,

Borne on by hope, our youthful transports fly;   25
    Absolute pain alone we deem an ill,
Unknowing that those dreary voids are nigh
    Which restless apathy alone may fill.

We dream not that, as blooms each flower or tree,
  We blossom, shoot, improve but to decay.   30
Some new-felt pleasure springs from all we see,
  Till rapid time doth nature's truths display.

Yet midst this beauteous world our sweetened state
  Would smile when soothed by friendship's kindly breath;
But a drear darkness terminates our fate,   35
  And every human bosom starts from death.

The Enthusiast. Arla.

The pious sire of Arla reared her youth
  Strongly to feel the great Creator's power;
In her pure bosom sowed the seeds of truth,
  And opened nature's inexhaustless[1] store.
    Early he led her mind   5
To pure religion's unadultered[2] stream;
The young musician caught th' ecstatic theme,
  And sung God's glories to the sounding wind.
    Called by his king to war,
      He left her young   10
    To those impressions which his tender care
    Had on her pliant heart imprinted strong.

Her lively senses music's influence found;
  Her fingers struck the sacred organ's keys;
  With pious hopes and heavenly ecstasies   15
Her soul flew upward, winged by lofty sound.
    So sweet she sung
That infidels would hear;
    The hallowed notes which fired her sacred tongue
Infused her faith, and taught them to revere;   20
Her soul was meek, her energy was strong,
And force divine fired each seraphic song.

Her simple frame no ornaments adorned,
  No earthly radiance blushed,
But every look her mental force informed;   25
The infant soul with beams immortal dawned,
  And breaking forth her eyes and bosom flushed.
Her temperament was so replete with fires
  She scarcely seemed to feel the earthly part;
Her genius with eccentric force aspires,   30
  Its boundless flights with strong conceptions dart.

The Enthusiast. Arla.   [2] *unadultered* unadulterated.
[1] *inexhaustless* inexhaustible.

But dazzled by its light, and led astray,
Her inexperienced reason fell a prey;
Th' entrancing muse seduced her early youth,
More fraught with energy than fed with truth.   35

Her soul, enriched by nature's noblest stores,
    Gave to wild fancy mad and sovereign sway;
Imagination drew her finer powers
    Until the balance of her soul gave way;
And, its pure tenor thus destroyed and broke,   40
The dormant passions of her nature woke –
For minds with innate force and quickness fired,
    To their own operations left in youth,
Too oft by fostered prejudice inspired,
    Are warped from the more simple paths of truth.   45
Strong inclination points the unknown way,
And licensed passions blindly lead astray.

Her strengthening muse still more enchanting glows;
    Deluded the frail mortal strains her powers,
While giant weeds in her rich soil arose,   50
    Vainly the self-supposéd saint adores.
    Till lost in feverish dreams
        Mid fancy's fires she heavenly visions saw,
    As rapt she sang her wild melodious themes,
        Nature she thought relaxed its rigid law;   55
Angels she saw descending from on high,
Unfolding all the wonders of the sky,
And caught a glimpse of the Divinity.

One noon amid the sea-girt rocks she strayed,
Th' expansive ocean and the heavens surveyed;   60
Her soul was awed while lost in zeal she stood,
And the majestic wilds of nature viewed.
The air condensed, to sullen mists transforms,
The sky frowned awful, big with threatening storms,
    And gathering clouds unite;   65
The blackening ocean foams upon the shore,
While distant thunders mid the mountains roar,
    And pelting drops fast o'er the rocks alight.

The angry clouds in troops convolving³ part,
    The dun horizon gleams with horrid dye;   70
From sulph'rous vapours bursting lightnings dart,
    And louder thunders echo through the sky.
Shelter amid the rocky caves she sought,

---

³ *convolving* rolling, coiling.

From the large shower and vivid flash retires,
While solemn peals woke every awful thought,   75
    And the fierce lightnings filled the cave with fires.
Still rolling on terrific o'er her head,
    The rain in hasty torrents burst the clouds,
Which spent like smoke 'cross the blue ether fled,
    Whose brightness following vapours dimly shroud;   80
Trembling her face amid the rocks she hides
Till the fierce horrors of the storm subsides.

Flushed by her fears, with awe she reared her head
    By all the grandeur of the scene inspired,
    As distantly the solemn clouds retired;   85
She quits the cave, and hailed them as they fled,
    With wild imagination strongly fired,
While lambent still the lightnings flashed around,
And the hoarse thunders rolled a sullen sound;
Her lifted eyes the clouded heavens transpierce –   90
Divinest strains she sang of heavenly verse.

Thus, with enthusiastic raptures blind,
A heavenly vision fired her feverish mind;
    God's voice she thought amid the tempest rolled,
And fancied streams of glory filled the skies!   95
    The fires of heaven the awful clouds unfold,
Ethereal essence flushed her mortal eyes!
More wild she dreams a cherub downward flew,
And dimmed the sun as tow'rds the earth he drew.
Her spirit saw him cut the ambient skies,   100
While ocean burns with radiance as he flies;
Such hues empyreal his bright frame adorn,
He seems a ray of the eternal morn!
So fraught with living fires, his ardent eyes
Shot forth long beams which sparkled through the skies;   105
From him bright emanations darted round,
And his waved pinions gave celestial sound!

Entranced, nor doubting what her fancy saw,
Her youthful bosom heaved with sacred awe;
    She viewed him on the strong rock's pointed height,   110
Thence breathing strains enchanting mortal ears
Such as he tuned amid th' eternal spheres,
    Genius immortal winged its ardent flight!
    The sea responsive mighty surges rolled,
Bearing each other on; a voice they found –   115
Heaving, inspired, they laboured with the sound,
    And awfully their wondrous nature told.
The winds which roll the clouds along the sky

In every blast sang forth the Maker's praise;
The spirit seemed descended from on high   120
To catch the song, and to th' Almighty raise.

Then, like a meteor, fierce he shot along
(Refulgence brake,[4] for mortal eyes too strong);
    Amidst the clouds emerged his radiant head,
Wafting the tributes which all nature pays;   125
    Day seemed as twilight while the spirit fled,
The amber clouds received his parting rays.
Then round the shore th' enthusiast throws her eyes
(Still foamed the main, and troubled were the skies);
    Dazzled, through clouds the watery sunbeams views,   130
While parting vapours wild and various stray;
    Faintly her lucid bow fair Iris shows;[5]
Arla conceived it a remaining ray,
And wildly stretched her arms t' implore its stay.

Not unobserved her ecstacies had flown,   135
Nor the vibrations of her heavenly tongue;
    For Edran mid the rocks surveyed her charms,
And the seraphic frenzy of her eyes —
    Her hair long-streaming o'er her trembling arms
As from her lips the note of rapture flies.   140
    He saw her with fanatic ardour blind
And smiled, while passion in his bosom wrought,
And mischief mingling in the villain's thought
    With triumphs o'er religion puffed his mind.

He in the world's base school had studied long,   145
    Vain of his parts, devotion to decry,
And learnt bewitching eloquence of tongue
    To palliate vice with shifting sophistry.
His ample front deep penetration shows;
Beneath his powerful brows   150
Strong flashed his eyes,
And with invention strength of action vies.

Potent in ill, he bent his subtle powers
    To draw young Arla in his wily snare;
Joined in her raptures, while sublime she pours   155
    Entrancing strains of music on his ear.
Her pious fancies he enriched with thought,
    She listened to the wisdom of his tongue
And from his eyes fresh inspiration caught,

---

[4] *Refulgence brake* broke; i.e. bright light ('effulgence')   [5] Iris was the Greek messenger to the gods, usually
emanated from him.   represented by a rainbow.

Whilst he enamoured on her accents hung. 160
Her passions were already set on fire,
 Without a guard her heart defenceless lay;
 Soon to his arts her virtues fell a prey;
Her sweet affections glide to his desire.

Ruined, he left her plunged in deep despair; 165
The loved delusions of her soul were broke;
 Mid anarchy and horror she awoke,
Tumultuous passions her sad bosom tear.
Love warmly lingering in her mem'ry sat,
Urging her wounded soul to desperate hate; 170
The rapt'rous dreams her heart had cherished long
Flew, like the empty echoes of a song.

Devoid of basis, all support decays,
 Her frantic mind can nowhere find relief;
The bubbles burst which shone with glittering rays, 175
 And nought remained save passion, guilt and grief.
Robed in religion, Edran won her heart;
 Her faith is broke while she resents the wrong,
Wild-panting with love's agonizing smart
She burns, convulsed with feelings deep and strong; 180
  And oft diseased
  With mingled passions, fiery ecstasies
Her trembling lips poured potently in song.

Songs of Arla

Song I

'Wild wing my notes, fierce passions urge the strain;
 Strong flame the fires that kindle in my soul; 185
I strike the wiry harp, nor will refrain;
Mad is despair, and scorns each feeble rein,
 Feelings like mine no virtue can control.
Stifled, th' inflated heart with pain respires,
 My crimson veins with struggling blood are pressed, 190
My cheeks are flushed with passion's transient fires;
My brain with agonies distracted flies
Till the fierce streams burst from my burning eyes,
 And drowning torrents cool my panting breast.'

Song II

'With awe my soul the wreck of nature views, 195
 The storm amid the echoing mountain hears;
 The sighs of autumn, mingling with my tears,
Mourn the sad ravages which time pursues.

Hear the wild roar of the tempestuous blast,
   Whirling the forest leaves to distant air! 200
See blooming flowers in scattered fragments cast,
   While torrents pouring thunder on the ear;
The sun's bright beam in dreary winter lost,
Not joyless is, as me, on passion's tempests tossed.

'My youthful charms fade 'neath my burning eyes, 205
The soul-entrancing morn of pleasure flies;
   A raging sorrow sweeps without control
Those germs of genius which alone inspire:
   The sensual passions which consumed my soul
Burn my distempered bosom with their fire. 210
   Long lightnings glance still from my streaming eyes,
Though vain around the fiery circles roll;
Virtue and pleasure vanish from my soul;
   The transient shadow of my glory flies.'

Song III

'Impassioned strains my trembling lips rehearse, 215
   Echoing my soul the numbers pierce the skies,
     I seem (delusions thus my mind impair)
   To catch the potent fires of Edran's eyes.
On loftiest pinions then, more noble verse
   Bursts into sound, and floats upon the air, 220
     Till memory bursts on my deluded heart,
   Mingling discordant strains of deep despair.
Distracting thoughts upon my spirit pour,
   No longer in delusive dreams I rest,
Such passions mingle with each bitter shower! 225
   A father's image meets my troubled breast –
   Ah, wandering heart, how bitterly distressed!
Consuming flames will soon thy strength o'erpower,
   And thou abandoned die, with guilt oppressed.'

Her father, soon returning, heard her fate 230
   Whilst he anticipates his child's embrace,
And empty hopes his joyful heart elate;
   O'erwhelmed at once, he's blasted with disgrace –
No deeper pang his bosom can endure.
   The laurels fade on his victorious brow; 235
From his uplifted arms, in fraud secure,
   The villain fled, and shunned th' impending blow.

The parent viewed his lost desponding child,
   But did not chase the sufferer from his breast,
For Christian charity, benign and mild, 240
   Was deeply on his noble heart impressed.
Patient enquiries taught him the base art

With which the vile seducer spread his snare,
The weakness of her lost deluded heart,
   And present struggles of her wild despair;   245
To snatch her from th' abyss with haste he ran,
And warmly thus the tender sire began:

FATHER

Oh tremble not to meet thy parent's eyes,
   But to mine open arms for refuge fly;
From dark despondency, oh Arla, rise –   250
   Child of my bosom, calm the struggling sigh.

ARLA

Fast fall, ye tears, till ye have drowned my sight;
   Quicken, ye pulses, your increasing fire;
Oh let me lose myself in endless night –
   I burn with shame, I sicken at the light.   255
      When will my passions in the grave expire?
Through wild excess my hopes are all o'erthrown,
My genius blighted, and each virtue flown.

FATHER

Alas, what fiend is harassing thy breast,
   Urging thy passions like impetuous wind?   260
Convulsively they rage, and unsuppressed
   Will wreck the nobler functions of thy mind:
Is pure religion then no longer known?
How is thine heart thus from thy Maker flown?

ARLA

Short-breathing, deep with recent wounds I smart,   265
And bursting in my bosom heaves mine heart;
In vain my soul th' o'erwhelming storm would calm,
Nor can the dreams of wild devotion charm.
      Delusive Faith, seducer of my youth!
Thy wilder transports my young fancy caught,   270
   Delirious visions led me far from truth,
Provoked my passions, and my misery wrought;
From ignorance I waked to bitter thought,
Saw clear the folly that had led astray –
Guilt's burning blushes met the dawning day.   275

FATHER

Talk not of day – oh, wrapped in darkest night!
   Still deepening the dire shades which truth should break;
Enthusiastic mists have dimmed thy sight,
   From which alone to guilt thou didst awake;
   Unknowing truth, religion you mistake: 280
'Tis not the raging of a zealot's fires,

Nor visions which from pampered fancies spring,
Nor strains which a distempered zeal inspires,
   Though harmony awaked its loftiest string.
Religion is the tribute of a heart   285
   Which strongly feels God's goodness and his power,
And humbly strives to strengthen its desert,
   And, firm in hope, his attributes t' adore.
'Twas thus I taught thee, when I fired thy soul
   With God's omnipotence and wondrous love,   290
But madly thou hast started from control,
   And o'erstrained raptures deadly poisons prove.
Prayers are but sounds that mount to heaven in vain,
   While uncurbed passions rage with boundless sway;
Strong principles must potent minds restrain,   295
   Or dire extremes will on the reason prey.

ARLA
With ineffectual sounds wound not mine ear,
   Light as the winds, they cannot reach the soul;
She, like a hollow blast, thy voice can hear,
   And folding on herself rebukes control.   300
   To death alone my spirit looks for aid,
For all around me teems with dire dismay;
Each earthly bliss, alas, is torn away,
   And fierce distractions my weak soul pervade.
Pierced by my fate, stung with delusion's power,   305
I pant for death, and urge the mortal hour.

FATHER
Thou hast forgot thy soul can never die,
   That to the virtuous only death is rest;
Covered with guilt, o'erwhelmed with infamy,
   While earthly passions canker at thy breast,   310
Wouldst thou thus rush into eternity?

The strong rebellious spirit heard him speak,
   As fixed on death her desperate passions wrought;
A sudden paleness smote her crimson cheek,
   And trembling horror chilled awak'ning thought.   315
She rolled her fiery eyes, but found no rest,
   Her panting heart congealed with sudden fears;
Then rushing on her father's suffering breast,
   Burst in an agonizing shower of tears.

Nor did he strive her anguish to control,   320
   But let it rage till all its force was spent,
Then touched the filial feelings of her soul,
   Till to his words a willing ear she lent;

And then the heavenly precepts he diffused
   Which breathe forgiveness to the guilty heart,   325
The simple tenets she had once abused
   Now snatch her from despondency and smart.
But ere the tumult of her soul had rest,
   The sun of truth her mental darkness cleared,
Burst the thick clouds which had her mind oppressed,   330
   While hope divine her woe-fraught bosom cheered.

To depths of solitude she would have flown
   To purify the passions of her breast,
To cherish truth sequestered and alone,
   With meditation's pensive pleasures blessed.   335
But her wise parent checked her erring mind,
Who piety with strong reflection joined.
He cried, 'What new delusions wouldst thou try?
To what romantic wilds would Arla fly?
A mind prone to extremes these wishes fires –   340
'Tis passion, and not virtue, which inspires.
Large powers, with deep experience, scarce are food
For the reflective cave of solitude.
O'er what would thy sad meditations roll?
Still idle dreams would rise and cloud thy soul   345
Which practical devotion must efface,
And the strong exercise of virtue chase.
Thy mind already on itself has preyed,
Blinded through inexperience, and betrayed;
From nature's grander traits conceptions caught   350
Have waked thy genius and enriched thy thought;
But weak at root, though lofty and o'ergrown,
Thy mind is by each casual blast o'erthrown;
Let strengthened virtue then each thought inspire,
And cherished reason check wild fancy's fire.'   355
   He spake, she felt the wisdom of his words;
Her heart, resigned, to simple truth accords.

A Song of Arla, Written during her Enthusiasm

Flushed, from my restless pillow I arose
To calm my thoughts, sad stranger to repose;
Wandering through woods, by night's dread shadows gloomed,
At every glade I pensive reared my eyes
And viewed the fleecy clouds fleet o'er the skies   5
Which gathering thick a thousand forms assumed.
Sudden, while yet I gazed, the heavens grew bright;
The graceful star of night
Shot midst the dark assembled host of clouds
A pure resplendent light.   10

The parting vapours floating on the air
Seemed spirits teeming with immortal fire –
Bright emanations of th' Eternal Sire
Unto my soul revealed by ardent prayer.

Clear by the moon, a numerous host I view;   15
Circling its orb, the unclad spirits wing,
On music's pinions mystic flights pursue,
Glide through the air, and heavenly numbers sing;
While from on high
Descend long beams of light;   20
A thousand visions crowd upon my sight;
I seem to mount and, borne along the sky,
Rapt'rous I sing, in frenzied ecstasy.

'Whither flies my soul amid the lunar night?
Glory rushes on my sight!   25
Seraphic music fills my ear,
Visionary forms appear
In solemn grandeur dight![1]
Drawn by silver rays
Round the all-attracting orb,   30
While Night her sable wings displays,
Which every vivid beam absorb.
Amid the sacred host I fly,
Fraught with solemn harmony.
Mingling with the lunar beams,   35
From every eye immortal genius gleams;
The soul of sound
Pervades the shadowy space around.
From each wild harp a nightly spirit springs,
And peals of heavenly music sings;   40
Grand clouds of darkness hurried by the wind
Bearing th' emanations of the mind.
The touch most fine,
The gleam most magic;
The voice most rapt'rously divine,   45
Strains most wild and energetic!
All, all combine,
They gather, stream;
The sounds increase, they join,
While still we fly the circle round,   50
We dart along, wake every sound,
And amidst the harmony, and light, and darkness, shine.'

A SONG OF ARLA, WRITTEN DURING HER ENTHUSIASM
[1] *dight* adorned.

Now oped the starry regions on my sight,
And 'thwart dark space shot radiant streams of light;
Th' aereal forms in mists dissolving rise,   55
Yet still I hear the grand concordant song
Echoed by all the offspring of the skies,
Who each in their eternal language sung,
While all around break forth ethereal rays.
From high I heard a new and awful sound,   60
Swelling with voice divine the song of praise.
My feeble sense no longer bears the light,
Opposed my eyelids close,
The heavenly forms I lose
Amid th' all-piercing light.   65

My ears resound no more, my pulses cease,
And for a while my soul was hushed to peace.

Till, waking in the fields, with chilled affright,
I feel a shivering being wandering in the night.

AN ODE

Almighty Power, who rul'st this world of storms,
    Eternal spirit of infinity
Whose wisdom nature's boundless space informs –
    Oh look with mercy on man's misery,
Who, tossed on all the elements by turns,   5
With languor droops, or with fierce passion burns.

Submissive to life's casualties I sing;
    Though short our mortal day, and stored with pains,
And strongly nature's truths conviction bring
    That no firm happiness this world contains,   10
Yet hope, sweet hope, supports the pious breast,
Whose boundless views no earthly griefs arrest.

What dire disorder ravages the world;
    Beasts, birds, fish, insects, war with cruel strife!
Created matter in contention whirled   15
    Spreads desolation as it bursts to life!
And men, who mental light from heaven enjoy,
Pierce the fraternal[1] breast, and impiously destroy.

AN ODE
[1] *fraternal* brotherly; it is possible that this line has an immediate political context, as *fraternité* was one of the ideals of the French Revolution which, by the time Ann was writing, had given way to the violence of the Terror.

Unknown, and nothing in the scale of things,
  Yet would I wisdom's ways aloud rehearse,   20
Touched by humanity, strike loud the strings,
  And pour a strain of more inspired verse;
But reason, truth, and harmony are vain,
No power man's boundless passions can restrain.

Stupendous Nature – rugged, beauteous, wild!   25
  Impressed with awe, thy wondrous book I read;
Beyond this stormy tract, some realm more mild,
  My spirit tells me, is for man decreed,
Where, unallayed, bliss reigns without excess –
Thus hope eccentric points to happiness!   30

ODE ON TRUTH: ADDRESSED TO GEORGE DYER[1]

Where fancy paints with nature's simplest hues,
  And music's soul-entrancing concords join,
There shall my numbers hail the modest muse,
  As fervently she pours the generous line,
While noblest thoughts mine ardent soul inspire   5
To catch a glimpse of truth, and glow with nature's fire.[2]

Oh truth, pure virtue's uncorrupted source!
  How long shall art refract thy glorious rays
Or prejudice repel thy genuine force
  Till mortal eyes can scarce endure the blaze?   10
How impious thus to quit the heavenly light
For folly's idle glare, and tapers of the night!

Ye in whose bosoms passion holds its sway,
  Whom wild ambition prompts to raise a name,
Who, wandering far from nature's sober way,   15
  Would rush impetuous to the mount of fame –
Know, while the steep with eager steps ye climb,
That truth must give you strength, truth only is sublime.

Whether ye mingle with th' ecstatic throng
  Who thrill with skilful touch the sounding wire,   20
Or dare the loftiest flights of heavenly song,
  Or to the painter's noble art aspire –
Whate'er the path, whatever means be tried,
Nature and truth your steps must always guide.

ODE ON TRUTH: ADDRESSED TO GEORGE DYER
[1] George Dyer (1755–1841) was a political pamph-
leteer and man of letters. By 1796, when he encour-
aged Ann in her poetry, he was well known as the
author of two important works: *The Complaints of the
Poor People of England* and *A Dissertation on the Theory*
and Practice of Benevolence. He was a Unitarian, and it
was no doubt these connections that drew Ann into
his circle.
[2] *nature's fire* almost certainly a recollection of Burns
(mentioned in her Preface), *Epistle to J. Lapraik, An Old
Scotch Bard* 73: 'Gie me ae spark o' Nature's fire ...'

Yet art thou hid, fair truth, from human eyes, 25
   Existing pure, yet ne'er unsullied found.
Oh clear those clouds which still infest our skies,
   Dissolve those specious shows which still confound,
Burst every limit which obstructs thy ray
And to the mental eye unfold a cloudless day. 30

Thou whom fraternal love and freedom fire,
   Whose wide benevolence unbounded flows,
Whose unaffected muse those truths inspire
   Which prove that nature in thy bosom glows –
Through thee has truth shot forth her potent beam, 35
And simple nature's praise resounded in thy theme.

That lyre which sweetly tuned its polished strain,
   And sung of pity, liberty and peace,
The muses shall invite to strike again,
   And may their virtuous votaries till increase! 40
Still truth, through thee, shall dart her purer rays,
And simple nature woo thy modest, plaintive lays.

Amelia Opie (*née* Alderson) (1769–1853)

Born at Norwich on 12 November 1769, Amelia Alderson was the only child of prosperous Unitarians, Amelia Briggs and the physician James Alderson. Although she had little formal education, she learnt French and was encouraged both as a musician and writer. Her mother was sickly, but gave Amelia, by her own account, a fairly disciplined upbringing. Amelia later recalled how she had been trained to conquer her fears: 'My mother, who was as firm from principle, as she was gentle in disposition, in order to cure me of my first fear, made me take a beetle in my hand, and so convince myself it would not hurt me. As her word was law, I obeyed her, though with a shrinking frame; but the point was carried, and when, as frequently happened, I was told to take up a beetle and put it out of the way of being trodden upon, I learnt to forget even my former fear.'[1] Another early anxiety was blacks. Her parents who, like many Dissenters, were politically radical, took care to train her out of this, as she recalled:

> The African of whom I was so terribly afraid was the footman of a rich merchant from Rotterdam, who lived opposite our house; and, as he was fond of children, Aboar (as he was called) used to come up to speak to little missey as I stood at the door in my nurse's arms, a civility which I received with screams, and tears, and kicks. But as soon as my parents heard of this ill behaviour, they resolved to put a stop to it, and missey was forced to shake hands with the black the

---

[1] Cecilia Lucy Brightwell, *Memorials of the Life of Amelia Opie* (Norwich, 1854), p. 12.

next time he approached her, and thenceforward we were very good friends. Nor did they fail to make me acquainted with negro history; as soon as I was able to understand, I was shown on the map where their native country was situated; I was told the sad tale of negro wrongs and negro slavery; and I believe that my early and ever-increasing zeal in the cause of emancipation was founded and fostered by the kindly emotions which I was encouraged to feel for my friend Aboar and all his race.[2]

This was an enduring lesson; even in middle and old age, when she had largely relinquished her early radicalism, Amelia continued to believe that slavery was an injustice.

Her mother died on 31 December 1784, at the age of thirty-nine. Thereafter Amelia took over the running of the household and her father adopted her as his constant companion, introducing her to the fashionable society of Norwich. She was writing poetry by 1790, and published in the Norwich-based Dissenting periodical, *The Cabinet* (1795). She had radical political views, and this was no doubt one of the factors that drew her to William Godwin, whom she first met in Norwich in 1793. She met him again when she visited London for the famous treason trials of 1794, at which a number of celebrated radicals, including John Thelwall and Thomas Holcroft, were threatened with capital punishment. The Aldersons shared many sympathies with the accused, and Amelia attended the trials in the anxiety that, if they were found guilty, many in her father's circle, perhaps even her father himself, would have to leave the country. In the wake of the declaration of war on France in February 1793, Pitt was administering an increasingly repressive regime; there were spies everywhere. Not surprisingly, Alderson thought it prudent to destroy all the letters his daughter sent him concerning the case.

She seems to have enjoyed at least a mild flirtation with Godwin, who wrote a love poem to her, probably in February 1796. Something of the excitement of this period is caught in a remark in one of her letters, in which she comments: 'Mrs Inchbald says the report of the world is that Mr Holcroft is in love with her, she with Mr Godwin, Mr Godwin with me, and I am in love with Mr Holcroft! A pretty story indeed!'[3] Ironically, Amelia would, in succeeding years, write two anti-Godwinian novels. Another acquaintance at this moment was Anna Laetitia Barbauld, who may have told her about an interesting new volume of poems that was being published by the Dissenting bookseller, Joseph Johnson – Ann Batten Cristall's *Poetical Sketches* (1795). She decided to subscribe; another subscriber was Mary Wollstonecraft, whom she met in spring 1796.

On 8 May 1798 she married the divorced painter John Opie and moved to London. After this point she began to distance herself from the radicals. Opie encouraged her writing, and she wrote a good deal of poetry during ensuing years. In London in May 1799 she met Robert Southey, who found her 'extremely civil',[4] and who solicited from her some poems for the first volume of his *Annual Anthology* (2 vols, 1799–1800). The first book-length work bearing her name on the title-page was *The Father and Daughter, a Tale in Prose* (1801). Other works followed, including her *Poems* (1802), which was in its sixth edition by 1811, and *The Warrior's Return, and Other Poems* (1808). In 1802, like many other English people, she took advantage of the temporary peace between Britain and France, and visited Paris. Here she met Charles James Fox, Helen Maria Williams, saw Napoleon, and visited the Louvre.

---

[2] Ibid., p. 13.
[3] Ibid., p. 57.

[4] *New Letters of Robert Southey* ed. Kenneth Curry (2 vols, 1965), i 184.

John Opie died on 9 April 1807, after which she returned to Norwich, visiting London for a few weeks each year. She edited his *Lectures on Painting* (1809), contributed to annuals, and wrote novels until 1825, when she became a Quaker and devoted herself to charitable works.

Most of those who reviewed Amelia's *Poems* (1802) must have been aware of its popularity, and this would have given them cause to treat it kindly. The comments of the *British Critic* are typical: 'The poetical talents of Mrs Opie (formerly Miss Alderson) are generally known, but whatever may have been thought of them, either from former proofs, or from the contents of the present volume, we are perfectly convinced that the perusal of the following poem will greatly heighten their estimation, with those who are capable of just discrimination.'[5] The *Monthly Review* was also supportive, identifying Amelia (not for the last time) as a sentimental writer: 'We have more than once announced and commended the poetic compositions of this lady. Pathos we deem one of her peculiar excellencies'.[6] A number of reviewers regarded the volume as proof of Amelia's pre-eminence among her peers; the *Poetical Register* commented: 'Among the female writers of the present day Mrs Opie is entitled to hold a distinguished rank. Her poems cannot fail of giving pleasure to every reader of taste. They are not deformed by any of those meretricious ornaments which are so profusely employed by some persons, but are characterized throughout by elegance, tenderness, and simplicity.'[7] The *Monthly Mirror* used the volume's success as an excuse for an interesting discussion of the proliferation of women poets in general: 'However fabulous the tale of Hesiod may be deemed, respecting the daughters of Mnemosyne, it cannot be denied in this our day that the Muses of Britain are become more numerous than ever the bard of Ascra[8] reported of ancient Greece. In the *Poetical Register* for 1801, we found a record of 15 living poetesses in Albion's favoured isle; and we think the number might be extended. Though "last, not least" distinguished, on that Parnassian roll is the fair authoress of the present publication, which composes an assemblage of heart-emaning[9] effusions on subjects of domestic interest, of classical elegance, or of general philanthropy.'[10] The *Critical Review* took a similar tack, taking the opportunity to rank Amelia alongside the major women poets of the day:

A century ago – notwithstanding we had never been altogether without female attempts, and those occasionally successful – it was still thought wonderful in England that a woman should versify; her poems were ushered into the world under the patronage of the great, and prefaced by the praise of the learned. She acquired fame equal to her wishes, and it perished with her. The females of our own age claim a more just and durable celebrity. Miss Seward, Mrs Barbauld, Charlotte Smith, will take their place among the English poets for centuries to come. Mrs Opie's talents are already known to the public. Her contributions to the *Annual Anthology* have been generally selected for commendation; and her *Father and Daughter* has been deservedly praised as a novel.

The productions of this lady are always in a melancholy strain, and therefore more effectually convey their moral import.[11]

---

5 *British Critic* 20 (1802) 553–5, p. 553.
6 *Monthly Review* 39 (1802) 434–5, p. 434.
7 *Poetical Register* 2 (1803) 430.
8 *the bard of Ascra* Hesiod, whose birthplace was Ascra.
9 *heart-emaning* issuing from the heart.
10 *Monthly Mirror* 14 (1802) 39–41, pp. 39–40.
11 *Critical Review* 36 (1802) 413–18, p. 413.

The *Critical Review* singled out *The Negro Boy's Tale* for praise, observing that it 'is told in the broken language of the slaves; peculiarities of this kind always excite the reader's attention, but when the language is thus dramatically preserved, the thoughts also should be in character. Zambo is too poetical.'[12] The reviewer quotes lines 69–80 to illustrate the point, and concludes: 'On the whole, we have derived considerable pleasure from this little volume.'[13] The *New Annual Register* thought sufficiently highly of the poem to reprint it entire in its selection from the year's poetry, and commented politely (if somewhat condescendingly) on the volume as a whole: 'We turn *con amore* to the ladies; and are pleased to receive from Mrs Opie a little volume of her poetic effusions. They consist for the most part of short pieces in a plaintive and melancholy strain, and are seldom devoid of merit.'[14] A more measured account appeared in the *Annual Review*: 'The characteristic merit is pathos and sentiment; the verse is easy, but negligent; the measure flowing, but not rich in harmony. Many of these pieces, if the author thought proper to bestow that attention and patient labour without which no degree of genius can rise to distinction, might be polished into higher poetic excellence...'[15] The main dissenting voice was that of the *Edinburgh Review*, which gave the volume limited praise: 'These are of very various species of composition, and are perhaps still more different in merit than in subject. In the tender song of sentiment and pathos there is uncommon elegance, but in pieces of greater length, which require dignity or even tenderness of expression, and an easy development of thoughts which rise complicated in the moment of fancy, there is a dissimilarity of character in every respect, which contrasts, without relieving, the sweetness of the simpler pictures.'[16] The reviewer went on to accuse Amelia of three main faults: 'her abuse of reflection, of inversion, and of personification'.[17] They went on to single out *The Negro Boy's Tale* for further comment: 'Of *The Negro Boy's Tale*, from the happiness with which the circumstances of the scene are imagined, much more ought to have been made. His argument on the natural equality of the negro, and his sarcasms against those who practise not what they preach, are more in the character of the poet than of the supposed speaker. Even had they been natural, as addressed to any other person, they certainly are not, as addressed to her who had always been his friend.'[18]

By 1808, when Amelia published *The Warrior's Return, and Other Poems*, the tide was beginning to turn against the kind of sentimental verse in which she specialized. Even the most laudatory of reviews, such as that in the *Gentleman's Magazine*, sounds lukewarm and distinctly condescending:

There is a description of poets and poetesses who become such through strong retentive powers of memory; those persons, extremely fond of the productions of our best writers, read them till they are enabled to repeat whole poems, and quote correctly the most beautiful passages from twenty different authors; they then proceed to write sonnets, elegies, and speak impromptus, which they publish, and the public immediately discover that every thought and every image may be appropriated, without the least difficulty, to the original owners from whom they were borrowed, almost unconsciously, by the unfortunate retailer, doomed to sink

12 Ibid., p. 416.
13 Ibid., p. 418.
14 *New Annual Register* 23 (1802) 317.
15 *Annual Review* 1 (1802) 669–70, p. 669.

16 *Edinburgh Review* 1 (1802) 113–21, p. 114.
17 Ibid., p. 117.
18 Ibid., p. 120.

with his or her books into oblivion. This fact, undoubted and incontrovertible, induces the real friend of the muse to exult when he meets with originality and polished metre, animated by the genuine fire of the poet; such is the case in the present instance. Mrs Opie, possessed of a mind disdaining imitation, and conscious of its own resources, has presented the community with the means of passing a leisure hour innocently and delightfully . . .'[19]

The reviewer then reprints, with approval, *To Mr Opie, on his having painted for me the picture of Mrs Twiss*. Many of the other reviewers were less satisfied with the idea of poetry that passed leisure hours 'innocently and delightfully'. The *Monthly Review* commented: 'Mrs Opie's mind is certainly imbued with the spirit of poetry, and her writings have acquired deserved reputation, but if her muse found more difficulty in satisfying herself, she would more effectually augment her fame.'[20] There was a general dissatisfaction with the title poem of the volume, which the reviewer in the *Monthly* found divorced 'from the walk of true nature, and from that style of poetry which is adapted to the habits and feelings of men and women of the present day.'[21] The *Universal Magazine* began its account of the volume by remarking that, 'though containing some pretty pieces, it seems to consist of the refuse of her writing desk, collected together simply for the purpose of making a volume.'[22] This was rather a negative way of treating the fact that the collection does reprint many of the poems that Amelia had published over the last twenty years; the reviewer goes on to criticize 'a great deal of turgidity and inversion in her style', and to accuse her of pompous obscurity.[23] Most of the poems, it is concluded, 'do not rise above mediocrity'.[24] The reviewer in the *Eclectic Review* was equally unenthusiastic: 'The principal merits of Mrs Opie's poetry are elegance and tenderness; its principal faults, feebleness and insipidity; merits and faults so congenial, that we rarely find the former, without an alloy of the latter.'[25] The *British Critic* evades detailed comment, merely remarking that 'Mrs Opie's poems are generally of the plaintive and melancholy cast, and are expressive of strong feeling, united with a natural taste for poetry',[26] before going on to recount the story of the title poem. Perhaps, at the end of the year, Amelia might have taken some comfort from the comments in her friend Arthur Aikin's *Annual Review*, which begins: 'Though Mrs Opie may not excel in the sublime, she is eminently successful in the pathetic. Her amatory poems are unrivalled; they display as much delicacy of sentiment and refined allusion as Petrarch can boast; with as much warmth of imagination as is consistent with perfect purity.'[27] It concludes: 'There are a number of songs and short love elegies contained in the present volume, many of which display great delicacy of feeling, and considerable command of language.'[28]

If the *Ode to Borrowdale in Cumberland* is very much of its time in terms of manner, it is revolutionary in its content. Inspired by Amelia's visit to the Lake District, it recalls the landscape through the lens of someone well read in the works of the picturesque theorist William Gilpin. It begins as a neoclassical fantasy, envisaging the 'genius of the storm' sitting on the mountains, recounts the poet's sensation of terror and delight, and concludes with the hope that the memory of the landscape will 'hush my tortured breast's alarms' – presumably a reference to the anxious response of radicals to the

---

[19] *Gentleman's Magazine* 78 (1808) 612–13, p. 612.
[20] *Monthly Review* 57 (1808) 436–8, p. 437.
[21] Ibid.
[22] *Universal Magazine* 9 (1808) 306–7, p. 306.
[23] Ibid.
[24] Ibid., p. 307.
[25] *Eclectic Review* 5 (1809) 274–7, p. 274.
[26] *British Critic* 34 (1809) 183–4, p. 183.
[27] *Annual Review* 7 (1808) 522–4, p. 522.
[28] Ibid., p. 524.

repression of Pitt's administration. In reposing its faith in the powers of memory to soothe one's anxieties, Amelia anticipates Wordsworth in *Tintern Abbey*, who describes precisely the same effect when remembering the Wye valley 'in lonely rooms, and mid the din / Of towns and cities'. *The Negro Boy's Tale* is Amelia's best-known anti-slavery poem. It describes the plight of slaves aware that if they escape to England they cannot be forced to return to slavery elsewhere. As an essentially sentimental work, it is typical of Amelia's poetry, and the sudden conversion of Anna's father to Zambo's cause is distinctly implausible. All the same, it is deeply felt; abolition was still five years in the future, and it was part of a fight that had intensified since Hannah More, Ann Yearsley and Helen Maria Williams composed their anti-slavery poems in 1788.

Further Reading

Cecilia Lucy Brightwell, *Memorials of the Life of Amelia Opie* (Norwich, 1854)

Ann H. Jones, *Ideas and Innovations: Best Sellers in Jane Austen's Age* (New York, 1986), chapter 2

Gary Kelly, 'Discharging Debts: The Moral Economy of Amelia Opie's Fiction', *TWC* 11 (1980) 198–203

——, 'Amelia Opie, Lady Caroline Lamb, and Maria Edgeworth: Official and Unofficial Ideology', *Ariel* 12 (1981) 3–24

Roxanne Eberle, 'Amelia Opie's *Adeline Mowbray*: Diverting the Libertine Gaze; or, The Vindication of a Fallen Woman', *Studies in the Novel* 26 (1994) 121–52

From The Warrior's Return, and Other Poems (1808)

ODE TO BORROWDALE IN CUMBERLAND (COMPOSED 1794)

Hail, Derwent's beauteous pride!
Whose charms rough rocks in threatening grandeur guard,
Whose entrance seems to mortals barred,
But to the genius of the storm thrown wide.

He on thy rock's dread height,   5
Reclined beneath his canopy of clouds,
His form in darkness shrouds,
And frowns as fixed to keep thy beauties from the sight.
But rocks and storms are vain;
Midst mountains rough and rude   10
Man's daring feet intrude,
Till lo, upon the ravished eye
Burst thy clear stream, thy smiling sky,
Thy wooded valley, and thy matchless plain!

Bright vale, the muse's choicest theme,   15
My morning thought, my midnight dream;
Still memory paints thee, smiling scene,
Still views the robe of purest green,
Refreshed by beauty-shedding rains,

Which wraps thy flower-enamelled plains;   20
Still marks thy mountains' fronts sublime,
Force graces from the hand of time;
Still I thy rugged rocks recall,
Which seem as nodding to their fall,
Whose wonders fixed my aching sight,   25
Till terror yielded to delight,[1]
And my surprises, pleasures, fears,
Were told by slow delicious tears.

But suddenly the smiling day
That cheered the valley, flies away;   30
The wooded rocks, the rapid stream,
No longer boast the noontide beam;
But storms athwart the mountains sail,
And darkly brood o'er Borrowdale.
The frightened swain his cottage seeks,   35
Ere the thick cloud in terror speaks –
And see, pale lightning flashes round!
While as the thunder's awful sound
On Echo's pinion widely flies,
Yon cataract's[2] roar unheeded dies;   40
And thee, sublimity, I hail,
Throned on the gloom of Borrowdale!

But soon the thunder dies away,
The flash withdraws its fearful ray;
Again upon the silver stream   45
Waves in bright wreaths the noontide beam.

Oh scene sequestered, varied, wild,
Scene formed to soothe Affliction's child,
How blessed were I to watch each charm
That decks thy vale in storm or calm!   50

To see Aurora's[3] hand unbind
The mists by night's chill power confined;
Upon the mountain's dusky brow
Then mark their colours as they flow,
Gliding the colder west to seek,   55
As from the east day's splendours break.[4]

ODE TO BORROWDALE IN CUMBERLAND
[1] *Till terror yielded to delight* Amelia uses the concepts and terminology of the Burkean sublime; see *British Literature 1640–1789* 1032.
[2] The cataract was that of Lodore, on the banks of Derwentwater.
[3] *Aurora* goddess of dawn.

[4] In lines 51–6, Amelia follows the picturesque writer William Gilpin in his approval of contrasting lights and shades in the mountains: 'It is an agreeable amusement to attend these vast shadows in their slow, and solemn march over the mountains – to observe how the morning sun sheds only a faint catching light upon the summits of the hills, through one general mass of hazy shade . . .' (*Observations on the Lakes* i 90).

Now the green plain enchants the sight,
Adorned with spots of yellow light;
While, by its magic influence, shade
With contrast seems each charm to aid,   60
And clothes the woods in deeper dyes
To suit the azure-vested skies.
While, lo, the lofty rocks above,
Where proudly towers the bird of Jove;[5]
See from the view yon radiant cloud   65
His broad and sable pinions shroud,
Till, as he onward wings his flight,
He vanishes in floods of light;
Where feathered clouds on ether[6] sail
And glittering hang o'er Borrowdale.   70
Or at still midnight's solemn hour,
When the dull bat revolves no more,
In search of nature's awful grace
I'd go, with slow and cautious pace,
Where the loud torrent's foaming tide   75
Lashes the rock's uneven side –
That rock which, o'er the stream below
Bending its moss-clad crumbling brow,
Makes pale with fear the wanderer's cheek,
Nor midnight's silence fails to break   80
By fragments from its aged head,
Which, rushing to the river's bed,
Cause, as they dash the waters round,
A dread variety of sound;
While I the gloomy grandeur hail   85
And awestruck rove through Borrowdale.

Yes, scene sequestered, varied, wild,
So formed to soothe Affliction's child,
Sweet Borrowdale, to thee I'll fly,
To hush my bosom's ceaseless sigh.   90
If yet in nature's store there be
One kind heart-healing balm for me,
Now the long hours are told by sighs,[7]
And sorrow steals health's crimson dyes –
If aught can smiles and bloom restore,   95
Ah, surely thine's the precious power!
    Then take me to thy world of charms,
And hush my tortured breast's alarms;[8]
Thy scenes with unobtrusive art

---

[5] *the bird of Jove* the eagle, now an endangered species in the Lake District.
[6] *ether* higher reaches of the atmosphere.
[7] *by sighs* as opposed to bells, which toll the hours.

[8] *alarms* presumably political; Pitt was waging a campaign of repression against radicals like Amelia and her father, of which the treason trials of 1794 were the most obvious manifestation.

Shall steal the mourner from her heart;　　　　　　　　　100
The hands in sorrow clasped unclose,
Bid her sick soul on Heaven repose,
And, soothed by time and nature, hail
Health, peace, and hope in Borrowdale.

From The Annual Anthology Vol. 1, ed. Robert Southey (Bristol, 1799)

TO MR OPIE, ON HIS HAVING PAINTED FOR ME THE PICTURE OF MRS TWISS[1]

Hail to thy pencil![2] Well its glowing art
Has traced those features painted on my heart;
Now, though in distant scenes she soon will rove,
Still shall I here behold the friend I love –
Still see that smile, 'endearing, artless, kind',　　　　　5
The eye's mild beam that speaks the candid mind
Which, sportive oft, yet fearful to offend,
By humour charms, but never wounds a friend.
　But in my breast contending feelings rise,
While this loved semblance fascinates my eyes;　　　10
Now pleased, I mark the painter's skilful line,
Now joy, because the skill I mark was thine:
And while I prize the gift by thee bestowed,
My heart proclaims I'm of the giver proud.
Thus pride and friendship war with equal strife,　　15
And now the friend exults, and now the wife.

From Poems (1802)

THE NEGRO BOY'S TALE[1]

'Haste, hoist the sails! Fair blows the wind;
Jamaica, sultry land, adieu!
Away, and loitering Anna find!
I long dear England's shores to view.'

The sailors gladly haste on board,　　　　　　　　5
Soon is Trevannion's voice obeyed,
And instant, at her father's word,
His menials seek the absent maid.

TO MR OPIE, ON HIS HAVING PAINTED FOR ME THE PICTURE OF MRS TWISS
[1] This poem was later reprinted, in slightly revised form, in *The Warrior's Return, and Other Poems* (1808).
[2] *pencil* paintbrush.

THE NEGRO BOY'S TALE
[1] The situation of this poem is that Zambo has been taken from his home in Africa, to be a slave in Jamaica. Jamaica was British territory from 1655, in whose hands slavery flourished under the plantation system, not to be abolished until the 1830s.

But where was 'loitering Anna' found?
Mute, listening to a negro's prayer,   10
Who knew that sorrow's plaintive sound
Could always gain her ready ear;

Who knew to soothe the slave's distress
Was gentle Anna's dearest joy,
And thence, an earnest suit to press,   15
To Anna flew the negro boy.

'Missa', poor Zambo cried, 'sweet land
Dey tell me dat you go to see,
Vere, soon as on de shore he stand,
De helpless negro slave be free.[2]   20

'Ah, dearest missa, you so kind!
Do take me to dat blessed shore,
Dat I mine own dear land may find,
And dose who love me see once more.

'Oh, ven no slave, a boat I buy,   25
For me a letel boat vould do,
And over wave again I fly,
Mine own loved negro land to view.

'Oh, I should know it quick like tink,[3]
No land so fine as dat I see,   30
And den perhaps upon de brink
My moder might be look for me!

'It is long time since lass ve meet,
Ven I was take by bad vite man,
And moder cry, and kiss his feet,   35
And shrieking after Zambo ran.

'Oh missa, long, how long me feel
Upon mine arms her lass embrace!
Vile in de dark, dark ship I dwell,
Long burn her tear upon my face.   40

'How glad me vas she did not see
De heavy chain my body bear,
Nor close, how close ve crowded be,
Nor feel how bad, how sick de air!

---

[2]   Zambo is aware of the law passed at the trial of the slave James Somersett in 1772 that, 'as soon as any slave sets his foot upon English territory, he becomes free'. This did not imply abolition; it merely meant that a former slave who arrived in England could not be forcibly removed and returned to slavery elsewhere.

[3]   *quick like tink* i.e. quick as thought.

'Poor slaves! But I had best forget.   45
Dey say (but tease me is deir joy)
Me grown so big dat ven ve meet
My moder vould not know her boy.

'Ah sure, 'tis false, but yet if no,
Ven I again my moder see,   50
Such joy I at her sight vould show
Dat she vould tink it must be me.

'Den, kindest missa, be my friend,
Yet dat indeed you long become;
But now one greatest favour lend –   55
Oh find me chance to see my home!

'And ven I'm in my moder's arms,
And tell de vonders I have know,
I'll say, most best of all de charms
Vas she who feel for negro's woe.   60

'And she shall learn for you dat prayer
Dey teach to me to make me good;
Though men who sons from moders tear,
She'll tink, teach goodness never could.

'Dey say me should to oders do   65
Vat I vould have dem do to me,
But if dey preach and practise too,
A negro slave me should not be.

'Missa, dey say dat our black skin
Be ugly, ugly to de sight;   70
But surely if dey look vidin,
Missa, de negro's heart be vite.

'Yon coconut no smooth as silk,
But rough and ugly is de rind;
Ope it, sweet meat and sweeter milk   75
Vidin that ugly coat ve find.

'Ah missa, smiling in your tear,
I see you know what I'd impart;
De cocoa husk de skin I vear,
De milk vidin be Zambo's heart.   80

'Dat heart love you, and dat good land
Vere every negro slave be free,
Oh if dat England understand
De negro wrongs, how wrath she be!

'No doubt dat ship she never send   85
Poor harmless negro slave to buy,
Nor vould she e'er de wretch befriend
Dat dare such cruel bargain buy.

'Oh missa's God dat country bless!'
Here Anna's colour went and came,   90
But saints[4] might share the pure distress,
For Anna blushed at others' shame.[5]

'But missa, say; shall I vid you
To dat sweet England now depart,
Once more mine own good country view,   95
And press my moder on my heart?'

Then on his knees poor Zambo fell,
While Anna tried to speak in vain;
The expecting boy she could not tell
He'd ne'er his mother see again.[6]   100

But while she stood in mournful thought,
Nearer and nearer voices came;
The servants 'loitering Anna' sought,
The echoes rang with Anna's name.

Ah then, o'ercome with boding fear,   105
Poor Zambo seized her trembling hand,
'Mine only friend', he cried, 'me fear
You go, and me not see my land.'

Anna returned the artless grasp;
'I cannot grant thy suit', she cries,   110
'But I my father's knees will clasp,
Nor will I, till he hears me, rise.

'For should thine anxious wish prove vain,
And thou no more thy country see,
Still pity's hand might break thy chain   115
And lighter bid thy labours be.

'Here wanton stripes, alas, are thine,
And tasks far far beyond thy powers;
But I'll my father's heart incline
To bear thee to more friendly shores.   120

---

[4] *saints* a pun; the campaigners for the abolition of slavery were called the 'saints'.
[5] Anna is aware that Britain was still, in 1802, one of the foremost slaving nations; abolition of the trade came only in 1807, after much agitation.

[6] '"I could not tell the imp he had no mother". Vide Series of Plays on the Passions, by Miss Baillie; *Count Basil*, page 111' (Opie's note).

'Come to the beach, for me they wait!'
Then, grasping Zambo's sable hand,
Swift as the wind, with hope elate,
The lovely suppliant reached the sand.

But woe betides an ill-timed suit;   125
His temper soured by her delay,
Trevannion bade his child be mute,
Nor dare such fruitless hopes betray.

'I know', she cried, 'I cannot free
The numerous slaves that round me pine;   130
But one poor negro's friend to be,
Might (blessed chance!), might now be mine.'

But vainly Anna wept and prayed,
And Zambo knelt upon the shore;
Without reply, the pitying maid   135
Trevannion to the vessel bore.

Meanwhile, poor Zambo's cries to still,
And his indignant grief to tame,
Eager to act his brutal will,
The negro's scourge-armed ruler came.   140

The whip is raised, the lash descends,
And Anna hears the sufferer's groan;
But while the air with shrieks she rends,
The signal's given – the ship sails on.

That instant, by despair made bold,   145
Zambo one last great effort tried,
He burst from his tormentor's hold,
He plunged within the foaming tide.

The desperate deed Trevannion views,
And all his weak resentment flies;   150
'See, see, the vessel he pursues,
Help him, for mercy's sake!' he cries.

'Out with the boat – quick, throw a rope!
Wretches, how tardy is your aid!'
While, pale with dread, or flushed with hope,   155
Anna the awful scene surveyed.

The boat is out, the rope is cast,
And Zambo struggles with the wave;
'Ha! He the boat approaches fast –
Oh father, we his life shall save!'   160

'But low, my child, and lower yet
His head appears, but sure he sees
The succour given, and seems to meet
The opposing waves with greater ease.'

'See, see, the boat, the rope he nears;   165
I see him now his arm extend!
My Anna, dry those precious tears,
My child shall be *one negro's friend*!'

Ah, fate was near, that hope to foil;
To reach the rope poor Zambo tries;   170
But ere he grasps it, faint with toil,
The struggling victim sinks and dies.

Anna, I mourn thy virtuous woe;
I mourn thy father's keen remorse;
But from my eyes no tears would flow   175
At sight of Zambo's silent corse.

The orphan from his mother torn,
And pining for his native shore –
Poor tortured slave, poor wretch forlorn,
Can I his early death deplore?   180

I pity those who live and groan;
Columbia[7] countless Zambos sees,
For swelled with many a wretch's moan
Is western India's sultry breeze.

Come Justice, come, in glory dressed,   185
Oh come, the woe-worn negro's friend,
The fiend-delighting trade arrest,
The negro's chains asunder rend!

'Charlotte Dacre' (Charlotte Byrne *née* King) (?1771/2–1825)

Rosa Matilda was 'one of the most licentious writers of romance of the time',[1] her books devoured eagerly in their thousands by the reading and borrowing public in the first two decades of the nineteenth century; as Charlotte Dacre she was the author of some of the most forthright, impressive love lyrics of the day – but she began life as

---

[7] *Columbia* not a reference to the South American country, which did not exist by that name in 1802, but to Colombo, a town on the west coast of Ceylon (now Sri Lanka), formerly Dutch territory, which had fallen into British hands by 1802.

'CHARLOTTE DACRE' (CHARLOTTE BYRNE *NÉE* KING)
[1] Cited Ann H. Jones, *Ideas and Innovations: Best Sellers of Jane Austen's Age* (New York, 1986), p. 224.

Charlotte King. She and her sister Sophia were daughters of the money-lender, black-mailer, and radical writer Jonathan King (aka Jacob Rey), and his wife Deborah Lara. An intimate of Godwin[2] and Holcroft in the 1790s, Jonathan King was a colourful character about whom witnesses are divided. One of his closest friends, John Taylor, remarked: 'I have heard many reflections on his character, but can truly say that I never observed anything in his conduct, or ever heard him utter a sentiment, that could be injurious to his reputation. He was hospitable and attentive.'[3] It is not easy to know how far the profile of him in *The Scourge* may be trusted, but its comments on his relations with his wife ought at least to be quoted; Deborah Lara, it claims,

> was the first dupe of his cunning, and afterwards the victim of his cruelty. As long as the friendship of her family was of any importance to the establishment of his plans he was a model of conjugal affection and fidelity, but no sooner did he discover that the restraints of domestic life might interrupt his pursuits, and that he had no further advantages to expect by prolonging the connection, than he began to treat her with the most brutal inhumanity, and had she not fled for refuge to the habitation of her father, both she, and the infant with whom she was pregnant, might have fallen an untimely sacrifice to manual violence.[4]

If *The Scourge* is to be believed, King was not only a wife-beater, but an adulterer as well, his amours including Mary Robinson: 'With Mrs Robinson, the poetess, so notorious a few years after under the name of Perdita, he was, if report says true, the first instrument of conjugal infidelity; and her pretended correspondence, which King vainly endeavoured to employ for the purposes of extortion from her then protector, Lord M., was afterwards published.'[5] Whatever the truth of this, there were evidently strains in his marriage, because an affair with Jane Brinsley, Lady Lanesborough,[6] led to divorce. *The Scourge* thought his motive was financial: 'She was in want of money and a lover; and our hero had no objection to the possession of her person, *and her jointure.*'[7] The divorce of their parents in 1785, by Jewish law, was no doubt a traumatic experience for Charlotte and Sophia; all the same, their father was the dedicatee of the first volume the two girls published together, *Trifles of Helicon* (1798), a collection of sentimental and gothic poems, to show 'the education you have afforded us has not been totally lost'.[8] Charlotte's poetic powers developed rapidly as she published her verses in the *Morning Herald*; evidently the sisters continued to work closely together. By 1804 Sophia had married and published under her married name of Fortnum; many of the subjects of her *Poems, Legendary, Pathetic, and Descriptive* (1804)[9] – mad people, distressed lovers, and so forth – appear also in Charlotte's work. Charlotte would no doubt have endorsed the *Remarks of the Author* which preface Sophia's *Poems*:

---

2 Godwin later explained his friendship with King as follows: 'My motive was simple – the study to which I had devoted myself was man, to analyse his nature as a moralist, and to delineate his passions as an historian, or a recorder of fictitious adventures; and I believed that I should learn from this man and his visitors some lessons which I was not likely to acquire in any other quarter' (C. Kegan Paul, *William Godwin: His Friends and Contemporaries* (2 vols, London, 1876), i 147).

3 *Records of my Life* (2 vols, 1832), ii 341.

4 *The Scourge* 1 (1811) 1–27, pp. 2–3.

5 Ibid., p. 13.

6 Wife of the 2nd Earl of Lanesborough, whom she had married 22 June 1754. She outlived King by several years and died in February 1828.

7 *The Scourge* p. 14.

8 Jonathan King died in Florence in 1823; his obituary appeared in the *Monthly Repository* 23 (1823) 672.

9 Subscribers included Ann Grant and Georgiana Cavendish, Duchess of Devonshire.

Tales of wonder, and of spectres, have been much in vogue since the poems of Mr Lewis; it is hoped therefore that now to offer such to the public will not be conceived a dereliction from good taste. The fairy worlds of ghosts and of magic offer, without doubt, sublime images in poetry. Amid the horrible and the extraordinary, the fantastic imagination roves unshackled, free from the more rigid discipline of reason, and perhaps the exuberances of the wildest fancy may often interest and chain the attention when the cold and puerile love-sonnets and invocations which have deluged the public may fail of exciting the least notice.

The gothic delights of Sophia's book include such gems as *The Dead White Mumps, or the Ghost of Skiddaw*. By the time it appeared, she was well-known as a novelist; Charlotte had contributed some verses to her 1801 novel, *The Fatal Secret*, and was working on a novel of her own, but before seeing it into print she published a further volume of poems, *Hours of Solitude* (1805). It was dedicated to John Penn, the politician and poet (1760–1834) ('the patron of literature, and the friend of mankind', as the Preface puts it), with the acknowledgement: 'To your valuable hints am I indebted for whatever of correctness or accuracy my labours may boast; to your condescension, in improving my taste; and to your goodness, in calling forth an exertion of the slight talents I may possess'. The volume also contains a poem addressed to him. Penn was the grandson of the founder of Pennsylvania, and had been known to the King sisters since at least 1804, as he was among the subscribers to Sophia's 1804 volume. Charlotte would have known his *Critical and Poetical Works* (1797) (which includes a poem in defence of women's rights) and his *Poems* (2 vols, 1801). By 1802 he was the MP for Helston, Cornwall, and in 1805 he became governor of Portland, Dorset.

Hours of Solitude begins with an engraved portrait of Charlotte, entitled 'Rosa Matilda'. This was the name by which she was best known, although the title page offers another pseudonym: *Hours of Solitude. A Collection of Original Poems, now First Published. By Charlotte Dacre, better known by the name of Rosa Matilda*. It was as Charlotte Dacre that she would publish most of her novels and become best known in the literary world; for many years it was believed to be her real name. The volume itself is varied. Some of the poems are early work, reprinted from *Trifles of Helicon*; others are exercises in skin-crawling gothicry, not unlike some of those in her sister's volume the year before – *The Skeleton Priest; or, the Marriage of Death* and *Julia's Murder; or, the Song of Woe*, for instance. But it would be a mistake to dismiss all of the gothic verses. *The Mistress to the Spirit of her Lover* appears once as a piece of Ossianic prose, and then as a curiously effective poem about a demon lover. The best poems in the volume are, in fact, love poems. Charlotte wrote persuasively, and forthrightly, about the psychology of love. It was evidently something she understood, and perhaps only Lady Caroline Lamb could rival her for conviction and persuasiveness.

In 1805 Charlotte embarked on a career as one of the most popular gothic novelists of the day, first with *The Confessions of the Nun of St Omer* (1805), dedicated to M. G. Lewis, and then the popular *Zofloya; or The Moor* (1806), an outrageous fifteenth-century tale about illicit love in the Apennines. The female protagonist ends up in the arms of the vicious moor Zofloya, who reveals himself as Satan and throws her over a precipice: 'he grasped more firmly the neck of the wretched Victoria – with one push he whirled her headlong down the dreadful abyss! As she fell, his loud demoniac laugh, his yells of triumph, echoed in her ears, and a mangled corse, she was received into the foaming waters below!'[10] It was in this context that Charlotte was best known to her contemporaries: Shelley read the novel at Eton, and it was a strong influence on his *Zastrozzi* (1811), and Byron alludes to her in *English Bards and Scotch Reviewers* (1808):

> Far be't from me unkindly to upbraid
> The lovely Rosa's prose in masquerade,
> Whose strains, the faithful echoes of her mind,
> Leave wondering comprehension far behind.[11]

He added a note to these lines, which reveals that he had seen *Hours of Solitude*: 'This lovely little Jessica, the daughter of the noted Jew K[ing],[12] seems to be a follower of the Della Cruscan School, and has published two volumes of very respectable absurdities in rhyme, as times go; besides many novels in the style of the first edition of *The Monk*'.[13]

There were more novels to come. *The Libertine* went through three editions in the year of its publication, 1807, and she published another novel, *The Passions*, in 1811. There was a final volume of poetry, *George the Fourth, a Poem . . . To which are added Lyrics designed for various melodies*, in 1822.

Charlotte's private life was, apparently, eventful. She had three children, William, Charles and Mary, in 1806, 1807, and 1809, who were baptized in June 1811 at St Paul's Covent Garden. Her partner at this time was Nicholas Byrne, editor of the *Morning Post* from 1803–33, who was still married. After the death of his wife Louisa they married at St James, Westminster, on 1 July 1815. Charlotte died on 7 November 1825, 'after a long and painful illness', according to *The Times* (9 November 1825).

Charlotte's novels are brilliantly written, full of event, and exemplify what Wordsworth, in his funless way, described as the 'degrading thirst after outrageous stimulation'.[14] Her mature poetry is written with a freshness and a force that few can match, but it went largely unappreciated by the reviewers. Perhaps because of the presence of a poem to Mary Robinson in *Hours of Solitude*, they tended to identify her as a very out-of-date Della Cruscan and castigated her accordingly; hence, the *British Critic* begins:

> It is now long since we heard of Della Crusca, Anna Maria, or any of that swarm of insect poets, which the *Baviad*[15] put to flight. Rosa Matilda must surely be a pupil of the same school. Whether Miss Rosa has other views than that of having her poetry admired, we cannot say; but she advertises, by means of Mr Buck's engraver,[16] that she has an attractive person, as well as a poetical pen; and she takes care to tell the public, in a short advertisement, that she is still only three and twenty.[17]

---

[10] *Zofloya; or, The Moor* (3 vols, 1806), iii 234–5.

[11] Lines 755–8.

[12] The 'Jew King' was one of Jonathan King's soubriquets.

[13] *The Complete Poetical Works* ed. Jerome J. McGann and Barry Weller (7 vols, Oxford, 1980–93), i 413.

[14] In the Preface to *Lyrical Ballads*; see *Romanticism* 254.

[15] Satirical work by William Gifford (1791), ridiculing Della Cruscan excess.

[16] A reference to the engraving of Charlotte at the beginning of the volume.

[17] *British Critic* 27 (1806) 428–9. There is a short notice 'To the Public' at the beginning of the volume: 'Those poems in the subsequent collection, where the age at which they were written is not mentioned at the head, are of a recent date. At the age of three-and-twenty, therefore, having no longer extreme youth to plead in extenuation of their errors, I must merely recommend them to mercy.' It is clear, from her burial records, that Charlotte was reducing her age somewhat; she was fifty-three at the time of her death and must therefore have been born in 1771 or 2.

The reviewer concludes grumpily: 'The poems chiefly relate to love, of which poor Rosa seems to have felt all the vicissitudes. That she has also poetical feelings in her hours of solitude, we are far from attempting to deny, but she has not been instructed how much a few productions of high finish are preferable to a number of unequal effusions.'[18] The *Monthly Mirror* was equally unreceptive, also accusing her of Della Cruscan tendencies:

> Miss Dacre, alias Rosa, is 'better known by' being of the Della Cruscan school, than by having composed any copy of verses much above mediocrity. These 'now first published' are a piece of the same stuff, and the public mind is so made up with respect to its quality, that those who approved of her manufactory before, will continue to approve of it, while those ('a mighty host') who disapproved of it, will not, by anything we say, be induced to change their opinion. If we had been consulted – but alas! authors never come to us till they have done wrong, and require whipping. If this fair Rosa had enquired our sentiments on the business, we should have recommended to her, after Mr Gifford's trimming, to have kept all the future disclosures of her muse in the 'hours of solitude' and secrecy *sub rosa*.[19]

The *Poetical Register* was just as schoolmarmish in tone: 'Rosa Matilda has some imagination, some command of language, and some talent for rhyming and versifying, but she is, at present, lamentably deficient in taste and judgement. She would, we think, have acted more wisely had she excluded from her collection nearly one half of her poems, and bestowed on the remainder a careful revision. It is quality, not quantity, that gains the poetical crown.'[20] It was left to the *Annual Review* to sweeten the pill, with some fairly unpersuasive comment about the juvenilia being among the best poems in the book: 'A considerable proportion of these poems were written at the ages of sixteen, seventeen, and eighteen; some in maturer years, and not a few in the season of childhood, at the early age of thirteen, fourteen, and fifteen! Some of these latter, we think, are among the best, and give indications of a poetic genius, from the cultivation of which we should have anticipated future superiority.'[21]

The poems selected here present something of the range of verse in *Hours of Solitude*. *The Poor Negro Sadi* is very much a product of the moment. At the time of publication, abolition was still two years away, and the slave-trade, in spite of some serious blows – notably the Slave Trade Regulating Act of 1788, and the Slave Carrying Bill of 1799 (both of which severely limited the number of slaves that could be transported) – was still going strong. In the predominantly conservative climate that had followed the outbreak of war with the French in 1793, and the French invasion of Switzerland in 1798, it was not surprising that several motions to abolish the trade were defeated between 1791 and 1802. In 1805, there was still everything to fight for; it would take first Pitt's death in 1806 and then the determination of the Talents Ministry to bring about abolition in 1807. But Charlotte's attention, like that of Amelia Opie in *The Negro Boy's Tale* (which she may have known) is focused on a peculiarity in British law. The trial of the slave James Somersett in 1772 had determined that once a slave had set foot in British territory he could not be forcibly returned to slavery elsewhere. Like Zambo in Opie's poem, Sadi in Charlotte's is aware of this ruling, and seeks to take advantage of it. Unlike Zambo, Sadi succeeds and gets to England where, although liberated, he is nonetheless destitute, and finally perishes through need.

[18] Ibid., p. 429.
[19] *Monthly Mirror* 21 (1806) 392–3.
[20] *Poetical Register* 6 (1806) 508.
[21] *Annual Review* 4 (1805) 620–1, p. 620.

The Female Philosopher is one of several poems which Charlotte composed in the persona of a man; it is, in effect, a kind of dramatic monologue. It was a technique she found useful for exploring moral dilemmas – in this case, the man is presented with the prospect of 'friendship' with a woman 'formed for love'. Can he resist her? Can a woman so seductive satisfy herself merely with 'philosophic friendship'? The poem provides no conclusive answer, but offers a protagonist who takes the decision to abide by her request. *We Can Love But Once* is another such poem, but this one is written in the persona of a woman whose affections are solicited by a man who has betrayed someone else. The moral of the poem is that a betrayer knows nothing about fidelity, and everything about inconstancy.

Adriana Craciun reminds us that Charlotte's pen-name, Rosa Matilda, was borrowed from the demon lover in Lewis's *The Monk*.[22] Such associations remind us of two works she composed on the theme of the mistress addressing the spirit of her lover. The first is an Ossianic prose fragment entitled, in full, *The Mistress to the Spirit of her Lover, Which, in a Frenzy Occasioned by his Loss, She Imagined to Pursue Continually her Footsteps*. The second, a poem entitled *The Mistress to the Spirit of her Lover*, follows the prose fragment in *Hours of Solitude*, and is included here. The poem is remarkable for the portrayal of the mistress who aspires to mingle – literally, to transform – herself into the spirit of her lover 'in an embrace that is suggestive of both necrophilia and sexual ecstasy'.[23] The poem reworks the gothic in a manner that is just as sophisticated as *Christabel*.

Between 1805 and 1810 Charlotte was a regular contributor of poetry to the *Morning Post*, no doubt at the encouragement of Nicholas Byrne. *Wine, I say! I'll Drink to Madness!* was one of her earliest contributions, and is written in the persona of a betrayed male lover. Once again, Charlotte is writing what is essentially a dramatic monologue. This is not how it seems at first; beginning with one of the oldest clichés in the book, 'Let's drink today, and die tomorrow', only gradually does the poem set up an opposition between the girl serving drink to the speaker, and the woman who has deceived him. And then, as in *The Mistress to the Spirit of her Lover*, it becomes evident that the speaker is in the grip of a kind of possession:

> Before my 'witched eyes laughs a gay covered plain,
> While fancy forms visions that fire my brain!

The visions of the intoxicated lover reprise, in a particularly hellish manner, the 'Vision of beauty, vision of love' by which the mistress had been haunted. In both cases Charlotte is interested in exploring emotional extremes that torment, rather than inspire. These poems bring into sharp focus the psychological element discussed at greater length in Charlotte's novels.

Further Reading

Ann H. Jones, *Ideas and Innovations: Best Sellers of Jane Austen's Age* (New York, 1986), chapter 8
Adriana Craciun, '"I hasten to be disembodied": Charlotte Dacre, the Demon Lover, and Representations of the Body', *ERR* 6 (1995) 75–97
Charlotte Dacre, *Zofloya* ed. Adriana Craciun (Peterborough, Ontario, 1997)

---

[22] '"I hasten to be disembodied": Charlotte Dacre, the Demon Lover, and Representations of the Body', *ERR* 6 (1995) 75–97, p. 75.

[23] Ibid., p. 86.

From Hours of Solitude (1805)

THE UNFAITHFUL LOVER (IMPROMPTU)[1]

How dare you say that *still* you love?
   In truth you'll move my rage,
Or, likelier far, my scorn you'll prove
   If deeper you engage.

Be warned, in time *I* love no more   5
   Nor can I ever change;
One pang I felt, but now 'tis o'er,
   And *you* may freely range.

Cold, cold I feel to all your sighs,
   Cold, cold to all your tears,   10
Indiff'rence arms my altered eyes
   And apathy my ears.

Hard as the flinty rock I seem,
   The form no longer charms,
That, wand'ring in a fev'rish dream,   15
   Dwelt in the wanton's arms.

Go, satiate there – *my* love so pure
   Shall never more be yours;
Let meretricious charms allure,
   And wing your worthless hours.   20

Seduction from those eyes no more
   My conscious nerves will feel;
And while your sorrows I deplore,
   I have no wish to heal.

I know another *still* might say   25
   Your heart remained her own;
I think the senses cannot stray
   Indiff'rent and alone.

For 'tis the senses that delude,
   That vitiate the heart;   30
Refinement dies as they intrude
   And love conceals his dart.

THE UNFAITHFUL LOVER

[1] *impromptu* composed on the spur of the moment,
extempore.

Your *friend* perhaps I still may be –
Your mistress, never, never;
The flame that dazzled you from me   35
Leaves you more lost than ever.

THE POOR NEGRO SADI

Ah, poor negro Sadi, what sorrows, what anguish
    Oppress the lone victim fate dooms for a slave!
What eye or what heart o'er those sorrows shall languish?
    What finger point out the lone African's grave?

First torn like a wretch from his innocent dwelling,   5
    And torn from Abouka, the wife of his soul,
Then forced, while his heart was indignantly swelling,
    To bow his proud neck to the despot's control.

Think not, European, though dark his complexion,
    Dark, dark as the hue of the African's fate,   10
That his *mind* is devoid of the light of reflection
    And knows not distinctions of love or of hate.

And believe, when you see him in agony bending
    Beneath the hard lash, if he fainting should pause,
That pure are to heaven his sorrows ascending,   15
    And dear must you pay for the torture you cause.

Mark, mark the red blood that, so eloquent streaming,
    Appeals to the godhead thou sayest is thine!
Mark, mark the sunk eye that on heaven is beaming,
    It calls deep revenge on oppression and crime.   20

The poor negro Sadi – what horror befell him,
    To slavery dragged in the bloom of his years!
To the food he disdains, the vile lash must compel him –
    Ah, food doubly bitter when moistened by tears!

At length in a moment of anguish despairing,   25
    Poor Sadi resolves to escape, or he dies;
He plunged in the ocean, not knowing nor caring
    If e'er from its waves he was doomed to arise.[1]

He skims light as down, when at distance espying
    A vessel, its refuge he struggles to gain;   30
And nearly exhausted, just sinking, just dying,
    Escapes from a grave in the pitiless main.

THE POOR NEGRO SADI
[1] Sadi is probably aware of the ruling dating from 1772 that if a slave arrives in English territory he becomes free, and cannot be forcibly enslaved again; his motive is the same as that of Zambo in Opie's *The Negro Boy's Tale* (pp. 353–8).

But vainly preserved, sable victim of sorrow,
 An end far more dreadful thine anguish must have;
Though a moment from hope it faint lustre may borrow,   35
 Soon, soon must it sink in the gloom of the grave.

Soft, soft blew the gale, and the green billows swelling,
 Gay sailed the light vessel for Albion's shore;
Poor Sadi sighed deep for his wife and his dwelling –
 That wife and that dwelling he ne'er must see more.   40

Oh Britons, so famed in the annals of glory,
 The poor negro Sadi is cast on your plains;
Oh Britons, if just be your fame or your glory,
 The poor negro Sadi shall bless your domains.

As yet see he wanders forlorn and in sadness,   45
 By many scarce seen, and unpitied by all;
No glance yet his sunk heart has fluttered with gladness,
 Nor voice sympathetic on him seemed to call.

In vain, wretched negro, thou lookest around thee;
 In vain, wretched negro, so lowly dost bend;   50
Though a thousand cold faces for ever surround thee,
 Among them not one is, poor Sadi, thy friend.

Three nights and three days had he wandered despairing,
 No food nor no shelter the victim had found;
The pangs of keen hunger his bosom were tearing,   55
 When, o'erpowered with torture, he sunk on the ground.

He clasped his thin hands, now no longer imploring
 The succour which all had so basely denied,
In hopeless submission had finished deploring
 The suff'rings he felt must so shortly subside.   60

On the step of a door his faint body reclining
 Had sought unmolested to yield up its breath,
But hell-born tormentors forbade his resigning
 Within their vile precincts, his sorrows to death.

They dragged the lone victim, in misery lying,   65
 From off the cold stone where he languished to rest,
Defenceless they dragged him, unpitied though dying,
 His last wretched moments with horror oppressed!

Now keen blew the tempest, and keener still blowing,
 His shrunk heart scarce fluttered, scarce heaved his faint breath;   70
His blood was congealed, and his tears no more flowing
 Had froze on his eyelids, now closing in death.

Oh Heaven, that seest this sad wretch expiring
   By famine's keen tortures, unaided, alone,
Pure, pure to *thy* throne his last sighs are aspiring,   75
   Though sable his skin, though unchristian his tone.

Oh poor negro Sadi, what sorrows, what anguish
   Oppress the lone victim fate dooms for a slave!
What eye or what heart for those sorrows shall languish?
   What finger point out the lone African's grave?   80

THE FEMALE PHILOSOPHER

You tell me, fair one, that you ne'er can love,
   And seem with scorn to mock the dangerous fire;
But why then, trait'ress, do you seek to move
   In others what *your* breast can ne'er inspire?

You tell me you my *friend* alone will be,   5
   Yet speak of friendship in a voice so sweet
That, while I struggle to be coldly free,
   I feel my heart with wildest throbbings beat.

Vainly indiff'rence would you bid us feel,
   While so much languor in those eyes appear;   10
Vainly the stoic's happiness reveal,
   While soft emotion all your features wear.

Oh formed for love! Oh wherefore should you fly
   From the seducing charm it spreads around?
Oh why enshrine your soul with apathy,   15
   Or wish in frozen fetters to be bound?

Life is a darksome and a dreary day,
   The solitary wretch no pleasure knows,
Love is the star that lights him on his way,
   And guides him on to pleasure and repose.   20

But oft, forgetful of thy plan severe,
   I've seen thee fondly gaze, I've heard thee sigh;
I've marked thy strain of converse, sadly dear,
   While softest rapture lightened from thine eye.

Then have I thought some wayward youth employed   25
   Thy secret soul, but left thee to despair,
And oft with pleasing sorrow have enjoyed
   The task of chasing thy corrosive care.

Yet pride must save me from a dastard love,
   A grov'ling love that cannot hope return;
A soul like mine was never formed to prove   30
   Those viler passions with which some can burn.

Then fear not me, for since it is thy will,
   Adhere with stubborn coolness to thy vow;
Grant me thy philosophic friendship still –   35
   I'll grant thee *mine* with all the powers I know.

WE CAN LOVE BUT ONCE

Truant! You love me not – the reason this,
   You told me that you loved a maid before;
And though perchance you many more may kiss,
   True love, felt *once*, can never be felt *more*.
   Then ask not me to credit what you swore,   5
Nor e'er believe that I can give you bliss;
   Go, go to her who taught you how to love –
   Repeat to *her* your vows, and not to me;
For sooth I think, who can inconstant prove
   To his *first* love, will ever faithless be.   10
   In gaining wayward hearts no pride I see,
Nor have I pride in kindling in the breast
   That meteor flame called passion – no, not I;
The *heart* I aim at, and of that possessed,
   Make it my castle, and all arts defy,   15
   For that once filled, no longer roves the eye.

THE MISTRESS TO THE SPIRIT OF HER LOVER

Wilt thou follow me into the wild?
   Wilt thou follow me over the plain?
Art thou from earth or from heaven exiled?
   Or how comes thy spirit at large to remain?

Vision of beauty, vision of love,   5
   Follow me, follow me over the earth;
Ne'er leave me, bright shadow, wherever I rove,
   For dead is my soul to the accents of mirth.

Thou formest my pleasure, thou formest my pain;
   I see thee, but woe is my eyesight to me;   10
Thy heavenly phantom doth near me remain,
   But ah! thy *reality* where shall I see?

In the darkness of night as I sit on the rock,
   I see a thin form on the precipice brink;
Oh lover illusive, my senses to mock,   15
   'Tis madness presents if I venture to think.

Unreal that form which now hovers around,
    Unreal those garments which float on the wind,
Unreal those footsteps that touch not the ground,
    Unreal those features, wan vision, I find.   20

Oh vain combination, oh embodied mist!
    I dare not to lean on thy transparent form;
I dare not to clasp thee, though sadly I list –
    Thou wouldst vanish, wild spirit, and leave me forlorn.

Ah wilt thou not fall from that edge of the steep?   25
    The pale moon obliquely shines over the lake;
The shades are deceptive, below is the deep,
    And I see thy fair form in its clear waters shake.

Yet ah! I forget, *thou* art light as a breath;
    That aerial form which no atoms combine   30
Might dizzily sport down the abyss of death
    Or tremble secure on the hazardous line.

That hand unsubstantial, oh might it but press
    These temples which beat with the madness of love;
Oh let, if thou seest my frantic distress,   35
    Some sign of emotion thy consciousness prove.

Lo! see thy dim arms are extending for me;
    Thy soul then exists, comprehends, and is mine;
The life now is ebbing which mine shall set free –
    Ah, I feel it beginning to mingle with thine.   40

From The Morning Post No. 11,563 (10 September 1805, published under the name 'Rosa Matilda')

WINE, I SAY! I'LL DRINK TO MADNESS!

Wine's a sov'reign cure for sorrow,
    Let's drink today, and die tomorrow;
No wonder the bottle should mortals enslave,
    Since it snatches the soul from the brink of the grave!

Gentle creature, hither bring   5
    Wine to soothe my love's despair;
Then in merry accents sing,
    Woman *false* as she is fair!

Wine, I say! I'll drink to madness!
Wine, my girl, to cure my sadness! 10
And tell me no more there is folly in drinking –
Can anything equal the folly of thinking?

Magic soother, sparkling wine!
What is nectar, drink divine?
What is nectar to champagne? 15
Fill the goblet, fill again!

No more, no more of am'rous folly,
From me fly black melancholy;
And, tyrant, take heed how you come in my view,
Lest in my distraction your boldness you rue! 20

Smiling ruin, lovely woman,
Fit companions in our wine;
For in reason, surely no man
Comes within your fatal line.

Bring fresh bottles, bring fresh glasses, 25
From my soul how sorrow passes!
Before my 'witched eyes laughs a gay covered plain,
While fancy forms visions that fire my brain!

Then wine, I say! I'll drink to madness!
Wine, my girl, to cure my sadness! 30
And tell me no more there's folly in drinking –
Can anything equal the folly of thinking?

Mary Tighe (*née* Blachford) (1772–1810)

Mary Tighe was born in Dublin on 9 October 1772, the daughter of the Methodist leader Theodosia Tighe and the Revd William Blachford, a clergyman and landowner who was librarian of Marsh's Library and St Patrick's Library in Dublin. Her mother was a granddaughter of John Bligh, 1st Earl of Darnley, and a lineal descendant of Edward Hyde, 1st Earl of Clarendon. Theodosia was self-educated, as governesses were out of fashion during her childhood. Her husband died early, in May 1773, and, as a keen believer in a liberal education for women, she devoted herself to educating both her daughter and Mary's brother, John. Unusually for the day, Mrs Blachford was against rote learning, believing that it was better to teach spelling by writing. She made Mary learn the language by copying poems and prose by distinguished writers; Mary also translated passages by French authors and memorized poetry. Outside tutors were brought in to teach her music and drawing. Theodosia herself took responsibility for Mary's strict religious education (she herself was a Wesleyan, and founded the House of Refuge for Unprotected Female Servants in Dublin).

In 1793 Mary married her first cousin Henry Tighe, of Woodstock, County Wicklow, who represented the borough of Inistioge, Kilkenny, in the Irish Parliament. She did not love him, and never would. The marriage was unhappy, and they had no children. In fact, she was in love with someone else, but felt unable to decline Henry's proposal. Theodosia viewed Mary's suffering sympathetically, as she recorded in her journal: 'I saw my poor child struggling with a foolish and violent passion half insensible to the tenderness of a heart that was unwilling, indeed seemingly unable to wound by a positive refusal, though she saw her favourite lover at her feet'.[1]

Henry had a yearly allowance of £1,000. As this was thought inadequate, the newly married couple went to London, where he was to read for the bar. But he lacked the application and settled into an unproductive life, mingling with other uncommitted trainee lawyers, most of whom flocked to the Tighes' house so as to dally with his beautiful wife. Mary clearly felt an unease about this attention; an entry in her diary for 1796 reads: 'Very unhappy in my mind – yet I find it impossible to resist the temptations of being admired and showing the world that I am so. My conscience has this day been disturbed.'[2] Theodosia spent a good deal of time in London with them during the 1790s, and her presence may partly have been responsible for Mary's feelings of guilt. As Theodosia's own journal reveals, she was well aware of what was going on: 'I often thought him much to be pitied as he saw that his wife did not love him though he loved her. She always spent her mornings in study and it was from her hours of study with him that she acquired her knowledge of Latin. To her industry in this respect may be attributed the fact that she was afterwards able to undertake the difficult task of composing *Psyche*.'[3]

In 1801 the Tighes returned to Ireland, and it was here that Mary composed *Psyche*. Contrary to her *DNB* entry, there was no 1795 edition of the poem; Theodosia's journal clearly states that it was 'finished aṅd copied out fair some time before the end of 1803'.[4] At the same time that she composed *Psyche*, Mary also wrote a novel, *Selena*, which was never published, the manuscript of which is now at the National Library of Ireland. Partly autobiographical, it concerns a heroine, Selena, tricked by parental manoeuvring into marrying her first cousin with whom she is not in love.

From 1802 onwards *Psyche* – or parts of it – were circulating in manuscript. One of its earliest readers was Thomas Moore, who was inspired by it to compose his 1802 lyric, *To Mrs Henry Tighe on Reading her 'Psyche'*. It was privately published in a limited edition of fifty copies in 1805, by which time Mary had contracted the consumption that was to kill her. Her health took a serious turn for the worse in 1804; in Dublin for much of her illness, she was visited by Thomas Moore, Lady Morgan (then Sydney Owenson), Sir Arthur Wellesley (later Duke of Wellington), William Parnell, Lady Charlemont, William Henry Brooke, and Lady Argyll. Her final years were spent at Dublin and Rosanna, County Wicklow. Her final poem, *On Receiving a branch of Mezereon*

---

[1] Patrick Henchy, *The Works of Mary Tighe, Published and Unpublished* (Dublin, 1957), pp. 5–6.

[2] Ibid., p. 5.

[3] Ibid., p. 6.

[4] Ibid., p. 7.

which flowered at Woodstock, December 1809, was written months before her death at Woodstock, 24 March 1810. Countess de Charleville told Sydney Owenson that Mary had been 'the first genius of her day'.[5] In future years her grave would be visited by many admirers of her poetry, including Felicia Hemans, who had composed a poem based on her visit, *The Grave of a Poetess*.[6]

Psyche was given wider circulation after her death, when it was published with other poems in 1811, edited by her cousin and brother-in-law, William Tighe. Profits went to Theodosia's House of Refuge. In the same year William published *Mary, a Series of Reflections During Twenty Years*, a privately printed series of facsimiles of poems by Mary copied out in his hand.

The 1811 edition of *Psyche* was an immediate success, and had entered a fourth edition within the year. One of its readers was Keats, who enjoyed its subdued eroticism,[7] and it seems to have influenced Shelley as well. But *Psyche* is an extraordinary poem in its own right, irrespective of its influence on other writers. Its primary source is the story of Psyche as told by Apuleius. According to him, Psyche's beauty was so great that she distracted from the worship of Venus. Venus arranged for Cupid to make Psyche fall in love with 'some base wretch to foul disgrace allied'.[8] Her lover (Cupid himself) promised that she would give birth to 'an immortal boy'[9] so long as she did not look at him or seek to discover his identity. Out of jealousy, her sisters persuaded her that she was in fact sleeping with a monster, and urged her to kill him.[10] With a lamp and a knife close by, she discovered her lover to be Cupid ('Love's all-potent charms divinely stood confessed').[11] He is scared away when she drops the lamp and deserts her ('A desert solitude alone appears').[12] At this point in Apuleius Psyche is scolded by Venus and given a series of hard and worthless labours, such as sorting grain, that ultimately cause her death. But Mary sends her heroine off on an allegorical journey in which she is tested by encounters with such personages as Vanity, Flattery (Canto III), Credulity, Jealousy (Canto IV), and Indifference (Canto VI), before being reunited with Love. It is a kind of latter-day odyssey (making, incidentally, a number of references to that of Ulysses), which aims to value love as a romantic ideal. Despite the allegorical framework, there is nothing abstract about this; it is a genuinely moving work. Furthermore, Mary's handling of the Spenserian stanza is expert: the poetry is carried effortlessly by strong, fluent rhythms, and a language and a style that is plainer, and in some ways more engaging, than Spenser's. *Psyche* is one of the great love poems in the language, and does not deserve, as Jonathan Wordsworth has pointed out, to 'be consigned to dark oblivion'.[13]

The entire text is presented here, edited from the 1805 edition; as the 1811 text has usually provided the source for facsimile reprints of the work, a word is in order about the textual situation. There are a number of differences, the most important being:

---

5   Sydney Owenson, *Lady Morgan's Memoirs: Autobiography, Diaries and Correspondence* (2 vols, London, 1862), i 384.
6   See *Romanticism* 989–91.
7   Numerous echoes of Tighe are noted by Earle Vonard Weller in *Keats and Mary Tighe: The Poems of Mary Tighe with Parallel Passages from the work of John Keats* (New York, 1928). The more persuasive of these are included in my footnotes, below.
8   *Psyche* i 124.
9   Ibid., i 560.
10 Ibid., ii 118–26.
11 Ibid., ii 198.
12 Ibid., ii 254.
13 *Psyche 1811* introduced by Jonathan Wordsworth (Spelsbury, 1992).

(1) a number of substantive differences, including revisions, in the 1811 text. Not all of these can securely be attributed to Mary, and some may have been effected by the editor, William Tighe; for instance, 'blames' (1805) and 'blamed' (1811), at Canto IV, line 459, and 'Locendra' (1805) and 'Locendro' (1811), at Canto VI, line 182.

(2) a number of clearly erroneous readings in the 1811 text; for instance, 'why' in 1805 becomes 'while' in 1811 (Canto I, line 227).

(3) A number of Mary's notes are omitted from the 1811 edition.

Taken together, these distinctions make 1805 the preferable copy-text for any version of *Psyche* that attempts to present the work as Mary wished it to be read. Except where otherwise stated, all substantive readings are from 1805.

So far as I can find, the 1805 edition was not reviewed. It was not until 1811 that the critics had their say. They were almost all favourable. The most influential notice was probably that in the *Quarterly Review* which, in a rather donnish way, offered qualified praise:

> The most obvious characteristics of the poem before us are a pleasing repose of style and manner, a fine purity and innocence of feeling, and a delightful ease of versification. Passages certainly occur, distinguished by force of expression, or by considerable descriptive energy, but these are not predominant, and their effect is quenched by the not uncommon intervention of languor. With several individual exceptions, therefore, the poem is, on the whole, pleasing rather than great, amiable rather than captivating. In the judicious and affectionate address prefixed to it by the editor, we are told that, even in the lifetime of the author, it was borrowed with avidity and read with delight; and that the partiality of friends has already been outstripped by the applause of admirers. Whether the future progress of its fame will correspond with the past, we will not undertake to determine, but of this we are confident, that no reader who has sufficient taste and feeling to bestow on it the applause of an admirer, will be able to help regarding the memory of the author with the partiality of a friend.[14]

On a technical level too, the reviewer was appreciative: 'the author before us has done full justice to the structure of her verse. Her strains are sounding and numerous, without constraint or excessive complication, nor would it be difficult to extract from the poem many passages as flowing and musical as the finest in the *Fairy Queen* or the *Castle of Indolence*.'[15]

The 1811 edition presented Mary's work in the context of her untimely decease; it was prefaced by a brief introduction by William Tighe reminding the reader of 'the unhappy lot of a suffering frame and a premature death', and a vignette of Mary herself, her face bearing an expression of forlorn resignation. It is not surprising that most of the reviewers mention her death before going on, almost, one suspects, out of a sense of propriety, to compliment the poem. The writer in the *New Annual Register*

---

[14] *Quarterly Review* 5 (1811) 471–85, p. 478. [15] Ibid.

commented: 'The fair writer of this elegant allegory, after six years of protracted illness, expired 24 March 1810. We have hence perused it with a pleasing melancholy, and perhaps some prejudice of favour. Yet in sober truth we can fairly assert that it stands in need of no adventitious event to fix the reader's approbation'.[16] Most of the reviewers were aware of the 1805 edition, and the limited popularity that the poem had gained in the intervening years, as the *British Critic* noted: 'The elegant poem of *Psyche* was so long circulated in one or two private editions, that to descant upon it as a new performance would be to repeat only what the majority of our readers already know, and to accumulate superfluous praise where abundance has been already bestowed. The fair author is, alas, no more, and the talents and amiable sensibility which produced this allegory, corresponding with the interesting form which is prefixed to this volume, must have left a regret upon the minds of her relatives and friends which no public approbation could alleviate.'[17] Other reviewers pointed out the enormous popularity enjoyed by the poem at the time of writing, as for instance that in the *Poetical Register*: 'Alas! The harp which gave these delightful tones is now silent for ever! Mrs Tighe did not live to enjoy that general applause which the merit of her work has gained for her. At the time we are writing this, *Psyche* has, we believe, reached a fourth edition. This rapid sale of Mrs Tighe's poem is honourable to the public taste. The story is exquisitely told; the language is poetical; and the stanza, which is that of Spenser, is managed with great felicity.'[18] Several of the reviewers had appreciative and detailed comments to make about Mary's technical skill. The *Monthly Review* begins in the usual way (by reminding the reader of her untimely death) before going on to observe:

> Having proposed to herself the noble model of Spenser's versification, but having judiciously avoided all his antiquated phraseology, our poetess has composed a work which is calculated to endure the judgement of posterity, long after the possessors of an ephemeral popularity shall have faded away into a well-merited oblivion. While the hearts of our countrymen shall beat at the sweetest sounds of their native language, conveying, as nature dictates, the feelings of the purest passions, so long shall this tale of Psyche dwell on their ears, and they shall think the angel still is speaking![19]

The reviewer goes on: 'So far from thinking that the stanza as managed by this writer is tiresome, we are delighted with the variety and beauty of its construction.'[20] By contrast, the *British Review*, a new periodical, was one of the few that expressed negative views on Mary's handling of allegory: '. . . we lament the allegorical cast of the chief poem in this collection, and whilst we acknowledge, we cannot help also regretting the skill that has been bestowed on threading a mystical maze, and in counteracting the disadvantages of a stanza ill adapted to our language. Adorn it as you will, allegory, extended beyond certain limits, must pall upon the sense. It is becoming as an ornament, but cumbrous as a garb.'[21] It was not completely critical, however; the reviewer proceeds to approve of the poem's presentation of love: 'The vein of sentiment which runs through the poem under our consideration is far superior to that which pervades the generality of

[16] *New Annual Register* 32 (1811) 364.
[17] *British Critic* 38 (1811) 631–2, p. 631.
[18] *Poetical Register* 8 (1811) 604.
[19] *Monthly Review* 66 (1811) 138–52, p. 139.
[20] Ibid., 147–8.
[21] *British Review* 1 (1811) 277–93, pp. 277–8.

those compositions which may be termed romantic. It is not only elevated and refined, but pure and correct; chastened by good sense, and directed by a constant reference to the realities of life. Many an useful lesson may here be learnt in an art too little studied, the art of conjugal love.'[22] The mode of allegory was also a problem for the reviewer in the *Critical Review*, who began: 'The choice of subject forms the chief drawback on the merits of *Psyche*. Allegory, and especially that kind which is founded on classical mythology, has lost its novelty, and with its novelty its principal charms. In its nature it is cold and artificial, and formal even in its utmost luxuriance.'[23] This reviewer was not particularly taken by the poem, but seems to have felt uneasy about condemning it in view of its author's recent decease:

> Mrs Tighe wanted neither taste nor feeling. But she whose spirit was broken with actual grief, might fear to touch a string which would vibrate too long and too painfully. Withdrawing from real and even fictitious sorrow, when it bore the appearance of reality, she might fancy a relief in sharing the imaginary distresses of the phantoms of an ideal world. Thus she dissolved the substance of sorrow into a sound, while she pursued with enthusiasm the aerial and melodious harpings created by her own imagination.
>
> The style of *Psyche* is far superior to the fable; it is delicate, simple, and unaffected (if affectation consist in unsuccessful imitation). The diction for the most part is pure and classical, plain yet rarely prosaic, never mean; and the verse flows with a liquid and unbroken melody. In a word, the author of *Psyche* takes a middle flight, between earth and heaven, and preserves an even elevation with unfatigued wing. She seldom thrills, surprises, or deeply engages her reader, but often casts him into a voluptuous and soothing trance, and the effect of the whole may be not unaptly compared to a dream of sweet music.[24]

The *Eclectic Review* provided a respectful and appreciative account of the poem,[25] and the *Gentleman's Magazine* remarked that 'the memory of this regretted lady will long be celebrated by the admirers of genuine poetry, and unaffected modesty and worth'.[26]

Further Reading

Keats and Mary Tighe: The Poems of Mary Tighe, with Parallel Passages from the Work of John Keats ed. Earle Vonard Weller (New York, 1928)

Marlon B. Ross, *The Contours of Masculine Desire: Romanticism and the Rise of Women's Poetry* (New York, 1989), pp. 153–67

Mary Tighe, *Psyche 1811* introduced by Jonathan Wordsworth (Spelsbury, 1992)

Greg Kucich, 'Gender Crossings: Keats and Tighe', *Keats-Shelley Journal* 44 (1995) 29–39

Harriet Kramer Linkin, 'Romanticism and Mary Tighe's *Psyche*: Peering at the Hem of Her Blue Stockings', *SIR* 35 (1996) 55–72

---

[22] Ibid., 287–8.

[23] *Critical Review* 4th series 1 (1812) 606–9, p. 606.

[24] Ibid., p. 607.

[25] *Eclectic Review* 9 (1813) 217–29.

[26] *Gentleman's Magazine* 82 (1812) 464–7, p. 465.

Psyche; or, the Legend of Love (1805)

Castos docet et pios amores.[1]

Martial

PREFACE

The author who dismisses to the public the darling object of his solitary cares, must be prepared to consider, with some degree of indifference, the various reception it may then meet. But from those who write only for the more interested eye of friendship, no such indifference can be expected. I may therefore be forgiven the egotism which makes me anxious to recommend to my readers the tale with which I present them, while I endeavour to excuse in it all other defects but that which I fear cannot be excused – the deficiency of genius.

In making choice of the beautiful ancient allegory of Love and the Soul, I had some fears lest my subject might be condemned by the frown of severer moralists. However, I hope that if such have the condescension to read through a poem which they may perhaps think too long, they will yet do me the justice to allow that I have only pictured innocent love, such love as the purest bosom might confess. 'Les jeunes femmes, qui ne veulent point paroitre coquettes, ne doivent jamais parler de l'amour comme d'une chose ou elles puissent avoir part', says La Rochefoucauld.[2] But I believe it is only the false refinement of the most profligate court which could give birth to such a sentiment, and that love will always be found to have had the strongest influence where the morals have been purest.

I much regret that I can have no hope of affording any pleasure to some, whose opinion I highly respect, whom I have heard profess themselves ever disgusted by the veiled form of allegory, and yet

> Are not the choicest fables of the poets,
> Who were the fountains and first springs of wisdom,
> Wrapped in perplexed allegories?

But if I have not been able to resist the seductions of the mysterious fair, who perhaps never appears captivating except in the eyes of her own poet, I have however remembered that my verse cannot be worth much consideration, and have therefore endeavoured to let my meaning be perfectly obvious. The same reason has deterred me from using the obsolete words which are to be found in Spenser and his imitators.

Although I cannot give up the excellence of my subject, I am yet ready to own that the stanza which I have chosen has many disadvantages, and that it may perhaps be as tiresome to the reader as it was difficult to the author. The frequent recurrence of the same rhymes is by no means well adapted to the English language, and I know not whether I have a right to offer as an apology the restraint which I had imposed

---

PREFACE

[1] '...teaches chaste and reverent loves'.

[2] 'Young women who do not wish to appear flirtatious should never speak of love as something in which

they might be involved' (*Maximes* 418). François, duc de La Rochefoucauld (1613–80), is the best known of the French *moralistes*.

upon myself of strictly adhering to the stanza which my partiality for Spenser first inclined me to adopt.

The loves of Cupid and Psyche have long been a favourite subject for poetical allusion, and are well known as related by Apuleius:[3] to him I am indebted for the outline of my tale in the two first cantos; but, even there, the model is not closely copied, and I have taken nothing from Moliere,[4] La Fontaine,[5] Du Moustier, or Marino.[6] I have seen no imitations of Apuleius except by those authors, nor do I know that the story of Psyche has any other original.[7]

I should willingly acknowledge with gratitude those authors who have perhaps supplied me with many expressions and ideas, but if I have subjected myself to the charge of plagiarism, it has been by adopting the words or images which floated upon my mind, without accurately examining, or being indeed able to distinguish, whether I owed them to my memory or my imagination,

> Si id est peccatum, peccatum imprudentia est
> Poetae, non qui furtum facere studuerit.[8]

(Terentius)

And when I confess that all I have is but the fruit of a much-indulged taste for that particular style of reading, let me be excused if I do not investigate and acknowledge more strictly each separate obligation.

Rossana, January 1802

SONNET ADDRESSED TO MY MOTHER

Oh thou, whose tender smile most partially
  Hath ever blessed thy child – to thee belong
  The graces which adorn my first wild song,
If aught of grace it knows, nor thou deny
Thine ever-prompt attention to supply.   5
  But let me lead thy willing ear along
  Where virtuous love still bids the strain prolong
His innocent applause since, from thine eye,
  The beams of love first charmed my infant breast,
And from thy lip Affection's soothing voice   10
  That eloquence of tenderness expressed,
Which still my grateful heart confessed divine –
Oh ever may its accents sweet rejoice
The soul which loves to own whate'er it has is thine!

---

[3] Apuleius was writing *The Golden Ass* c.AD 155, one of the most famous episodes of which dealt with Cupid and Psyche.

[4] Molière (1622–73), the great French comic playwright, combined tragedy with ballet in his *Psyché* (1671).

[5] Jean de la Fontaine (1621–95) retold Apuleius in *Les Amours de Psyché et de Cupidon* (1669).

[6] Giambattista Marino (1569–1625), whose most ambitious work, *Adone* (1623), is a long mythological work about the love of Venus and Adonis.

[7] *original* source.

[8] 'If that is a sin, the sin is the inadvertence of the poet; he did not intend to steal something'.

Chi pensa quanto un bel desio d' amore
Un spirto pellegrin tenga sublime;
Non vorria non averne acceso il core;
Chi gusta quanto dolce il creder sia
Solo esser caro a chi sola n'e cara,
Regna in un stato a cui null' altro e pria.[1]

Ariosto, *Elegia* XII

CANTO I

Argument

Proem – Psyche introduced – her royal origin – envy of Venus – her instructions to
Cupid – the island of Pleasure – the fountains of Joy and of Sorrow – the appearance of
Love – Psyche asleep – mutually wounded – Psyche reveals her dream to her mother –
the oracle consulted – Psyche abandoned on the rock by its decree – carried by zephyrs
to the island of Pleasure – the Palace of Love – banquet of Love – marriage of Cupid
and Psyche – Psyche's daily solitude – her request to her lover – his reluctant consent

PROEM

Let not the rugged brow the rhymes accuse,
Which speak of gentle knights and ladies fair,
Nor scorn the lighter labours of the muse –
Who yet for cruel battles would not dare
The low-strung chords of her weak lyre prepare,   5
But loves to court repose in slumbery lay,
To tell of goodly bowers and gardens rare,
Of gentle blandishments and amorous play,
And all the lore of love in courtly verse essay.[1]

And ye whose gentle hearts in thraldom held   10
The power of mighty love already own,
When you the pains and dangers have beheld
Which erst your lord hath for his Psyche known,
For all your sorrows this may well atone –
That he you serve the same hath suffered;   15
And sure, your fond applause the tale will crown
In which your own distress is pictured,
And all that weary way which you yourselves must tread.

Most sweet would to my soul the hope appear,
That sorrow in my verse a charm might find,
To smooth the brow long bent with bitter cheer,   20

---

[1] The sentiment is intricate and involved, but it
may be rendered: 'He who thinks that a beautiful
lover can lift a sad spirit, will want to set her heart
on fire; he who knows how sweet it is to know that
he is loved only by her, is the sole ruler in this
state'.

CANTO I
[1] *essay* attempt.

Some short distraction to the joyless mind
Which grief, with heavy chain, hath fast confined
To sad remembrance of its happier state;
For to myself I ask no boon more kind   25
Than power another's woes to mitigate,
And that soft soothing art which anguish can abate.

And thou, sweet sprite, whose sway doth far extend,
Smile on the mean historian of thy fame!
My heart in each distress and fear befriend,   30
Nor ever let it feel a fiercer flame
Than innocence may cherish free from blame,
And hope may nurse, and sympathy may own;
For as thy rights I never would disclaim,
But true allegiance offered to thy throne,   35
So may I love but one, by one beloved alone.

That anxious torture may I never feel
Which, doubtful, watches o'er a wandering heart –
Oh who that bitter torment can reveal
Or tell the pining anguish of that smart?   40
In those affections may I ne'er have part,
Which easily transferred can learn to rove;
No, dearest Cupid, when I feel thy dart,
For thy sweet Psyche's sake may no false love
The tenderness I prize lightly from me remove!   45

Canto I

Much wearied with her long and dreary way,
And now with toil and sorrow well-nigh spent,
Of sad regret and wasting grief the prey,
Fair Psyche through untrodden forests went
To lone shades uttering oft a vain lament.   5
And oft in hopeless silence sighing deep,
As she her fatal error did repent,
While dear remembrance bade her ever weep,
And her pale cheek in ceaseless showers of sorrow steep.

Mid the thick covert of that woodland shade,   10
A flowery bank there lay undressed by art,
But of the mossy turf spontaneous made;
Here the young branches shot their arms athwart,
And wove the bower so thick in every part
That the fierce beams of Phoebus² glancing strong   15
Could never through the leaves their fury dart;

---

² *Phoebus* the sun.

But the sweet creeping shrubs that round it throng,
Their loving fragrance mix, and trail their flowers along.

And close beside a little fountain played
Which through the trembling leaves all joyous shone,   20
And with the cheerful birds sweet music made,
Kissing the surface of each polished stone
As it flowed past – sure as her favourite throne
Tranquillity might well esteem the bower,
The fresh and cool retreat have called her own,   25
A pleasant shelter in the sultry hour,
A refuge from the blast and angry tempest's power.

Wooed by the soothing silence of the scene
Here Psyche stood, and looking round, lest aught
Which threatened danger near her might have been,   30
Awhile to rest her in that quiet spot
She laid her down, and piteously bethought
Herself on the sad changes of her fate,
Which in so short a space so much had wrought,
And now had raised her to such high estate,   35
And now had plunged her low in sorrow desolate.

Oh how refreshing seemed the breathing wind
To her faint limbs, and while her snowy hands
From her fair brow her golden hair unbind,
And of her zone[3] unloose the silken bands,   40
More passing bright unveiled her beauty stands;
For faultless was her form as beauty's queen,
And every winning grace that Love demands,
With mild attempered dignity was seen
Play o'er each lovely limb, and deck her angel mien.   45

Though solitary now, dismayed, forlorn,
Without attendant through the forest rude,
The peerless maid of royal lineage born
By many a royal youth had oft been wooed;
Low at her feet full many a prince had sued,   50
And homage paid unto her beauty rare;
But all their blandishments her heart withstood,
And well might mortal suitor sure despair,
Since mortal charms were none which might with hers compare.

Yet nought of insolence or haughty pride   55
Found ever in her gentle breast a place;
Though men her wondrous beauty deified,

---

3   *zone* silk hair-band.

And rashly deeming such celestial grace
Could never spring from any earthly race,
Lo, all forsaking Cytherea's[4] shrine,   60
Her sacred altars now no more embrace,
But to fair Psyche pay those rites divine
Which, goddess, are thy due, and should be only thine.

But envy of her beauty's growing fame
Poisoned her sisters' hearts with secret gall,   65
And oft with seeming piety they blame
The worship which they justly impious call;
And oft, lest evil should their sire befall,
Besought him to forbid the erring crowd
Which hourly thronged around the regal hall   70
With incense, gifts, and invocations loud
To her whose guiltless breast ne'er felt elation proud.

For she was timid as the wintry flower
That, whiter than the snow it blooms among,
Droops its fair head submissive to the power   75
Of every angry blast which sweeps along,
Sparing the lovely trembler, while the strong
Majestic tenants of the leafless wood
It levels low. But ah, the pitying song
Must tell how, than the tempest's self more rude,   80
Fierce wrath and cruel hate their suppliant prey pursued.

Indignant quitting her deserted fanes,
Now Cytherea sought her favourite isle,
And there from every eye her secret pains
Mid her thick myrtle bowers concealed awhile;   85
Practised no more the glance or witching smile,
But nursed the pang she never felt before
Of mortified disdain; then to beguile
The hours which mortal flattery soothed no more,
She various plans revolved her influence to restore.   90

She called her son with unaccustomed voice,
Not with those thrilling accents of delight
Which bade so oft enchanted Love rejoice,
Soft as the breezes of a summer's night;
Now choked with rage its change could Love affright;   95
As all to sudden discontent a prey,
Shunning the cheerful day's enlivening light,
She felt the angry power's malignant sway
And bade her favourite boy her vengeful will obey.

---

4   *Cytherea* Venus.

Bathed in those tears which vanquish human hearts,   100
'Oh son beloved!' the suppliant goddess cried,
'If e'er thy too indulgent mother's arts
Subdued for thee the potent deities
Who rule my native deep, or haunt the skies;
Or if to me the grateful praise be due   105
That to thy sceptre bow the great and wise,
Now let thy fierce revenge my foe pursue,
And let my rival scorned her vain presumption rue.

'For what to me avails my former boast
That, fairer than the wife of Jove confessed,   110
I gained the prize thus basely to be lost?
With me the world's devotion to contest
Behold a mortal dares; though on my breast
Still vainly brilliant shines the magic zone.[5]
Yet, yet I reign; by you my wrongs redressed,   115
The world with humbled Psyche soon shall own
That Venus, beauty's queen, shall be adored alone.

'Deep let her drink of that dark, bitter spring
Which flows so near thy bright and crystal tide;
Deep let her heart thy sharpest arrow sting,   120
Its tempered barb in that black poison dyed.
Let her for whom contending princes sighed
Feel all the fury of thy fiercest flame
For some base wretch to foul disgrace allied,
Forgetful of her birth and her fair fame,   125
Her honours all defiled, and sacrificed to shame.'

Then with sweet pressure of her rosy lip,
A kiss she gave bathed in ambrosial dew;
The thrilling joy he would for ever sip,
And his moist eyes in ecstasy imbrue.[6]   130
But she whose soul still angry cares pursue
Snatched from the soft caress her glowing charms;
Her vengeful will she then enforced anew,
As she in haste dismissed him from her arms,
The cruel draught to seek of anguish and alarms.   135

Mid the blue waves by circling seas embraced
A chosen spot of fairest land was seen;
For there with favouring hand had Nature placed
All that could lovely make the varied scene;
Eternal spring there spread her mantle green,   140

---

[5]   *the magic zone* Venus' power was assisted by a   [6]   *imbrue* saturate.
magic belt which inspired love even when worn by
the most deformed person.

There high surrounding hills deep-wooded rose
O'er placid lakes, while marble rocks between
The fragrant shrubs their pointed heads disclose
And balmy breathes each gale which o'er the island blows.

Pleasure had called the fertile lawns her own   145
And thickly strewed them with her choicest flowers,
Amid the quiet glade her golden throne
Bright shone with lustre through o'erarching bowers.
There her fair train, the ever-downy Hours,[7]
Sport on light wing with the young Joys entwined;   150
While Hope, delighted, from her full lap showers
Blossoms whose fragrance can the ravished mind
Inebriate with dreams of rapture unconfined.

And in the grassy centre of the isle,
Where the thick verdure spreads a damper shade,   155
Amid their native rocks concealed awhile,
Then o'er the plains in devious streams displayed,
Two gushing fountains rise – and thence conveyed,
Their waters through the woods and vallies play,
Visit each green recess and secret glade,   160
With still unmingled, still meandering way,
Nor widely wandering far, can each from other stray.

But of strange contrast are their virtues found,
And oft the lady of that isle has tried
In rocky dens and caverns underground   165
The black deforméd stream in vain to hide;
Bursting all bounds her labours it defied,
Yet many a flowery sod its course conceals
Through plains where deep its silent waters glide,
Till secret ruin all-corroding steals,   170
And every treacherous arch the hideous gulf reveals.

Forbidding every kindly prosperous growth
Where'er it ran, a channel bleak it wore;
The gaping banks receded, as though loath
To touch the poison which disgraced their shore;   175
There deadly anguish pours unmixed his store
Of all the ills which sting the human breast,
The hopeless tears which past delights deplore,
Heart-gnawing jealousy which knows no rest,
And self-upbraiding shame, by stern remorse oppressed.   180

---

[7] *Hours* the three daughters of Jupiter representing
spring, summer and winter, often shown accompany-
ing Venus and the Graces.

Oh how unlike the pure transparent stream
Which near it bubbles o'er its golden sands!
Th' impeding stones with pleasant music seem
Its progress to detain from other lands;
And all its banks, enwreathed with flowery bands,   185
Ambrosial fragrance shed in grateful dew.
There young Desire enchanted ever stands,
Breathing delight and fragrance ever new,
And bathed in constant joys of fond affection true.[8]

But not to mortals is it e'er allowed   190
To drink unmingled of that current bright;
Scarce can they taste the pleasurable flood,
Defiled by angry Fortune's envious spite;
Who from the cup of amorous delight
Dashes the sparkling draught of brilliant joy,   195
Till, with dull sorrow's stream despoiléd quite,
No more it cheers the soul nor charms the eye,
But mid the poisoned bowl distrust and anguish lie.

Here Cupid tempers his unerring darts
And in the fount of bliss delights to play;   200
Here mingle balmy sighs and pleasing smarts,
And here the honeyed draught will oft allay[9]
With that black poison's all-polluting sway,
For wretched man. Hither, as Venus willed,
For Psyche's punishment he bent his way;   205
From either stream his amber vase he filled,
For her were meant the drops which grief alone distilled.

His quiver, sparkling bright with gems and gold,
From his fair-plumed shoulder graceful hung,
And from its top in brilliant cords enrolled   210
Each little vase resplendently was slung.
Still as he flew, around him sportive clung
His frolic train of wingéd zephyrs light,
Wafting the fragrance which his tresses flung,
While odours dropped from every ringlet bright,   215
And from his blue eyes beamed ineffable delight.

Wrapped in a cloud unseen by mortal eye[10]
He sought the chamber of the royal maid;
There, lulled by careless soft security,
Of the impending mischief nought afraid,   220

---

[8] Jonathan Wordsworth points out that this stanza provides a source for Keats, *Ode on a Grecian Urn* 21–30 (*Psyche 1811* introduced by Jonathan Wordsworth (Spelsbury, 1992)).

[9] *allay* mix.

[10] *unseen by mortal eye* cf. the sylphs in Pope's *Rape of the Lock* ii 61, 'too fine for mortal sight'.

Upon her purple couch was Psyche laid,
Her radiant eyes a downy slumber sealed;
In light transparent veil alone arrayed,
Her bosom's opening charms were half-revealed,
And scarce the lucid folds her polished limbs concealed.   225

A placid smile plays o'er each roseate lip:
Sweet severed lips, why thus your pearls disclose
That, slumbering thus, unconscious she may sip
The cruel presage of her future woes?
Lightly, as fall the dews upon the rose,   230
Upon the coral gates of that sweet cell[11]
The fatal drops he pours – nor yet he knows,
Nor, though a god, can he presaging tell
How he himself shall mourn the ills of that sad spell!

Nor yet content, he from his quiver drew,   235
Sharpened with skill divine, a shining dart;
No need had he for bow, since thus too true
His hand might wound her all-exposéd heart;
Yet her fair side he touched with gentlest art,
And half relenting on her beauties gazed: 240
Just then awaking with a sudden start
Her opening eye in humid lustre blazed –
Unseen he still remained, enchanted and amazed.

The dart which in his hand now trembling stood
As o'er the couch he bent with ravished eye,   245
Drew with its daring point celestial blood
From his smooth neck's unblemished ivory.
Heedless of this, but with a pitying sigh
The evil done now anxious to repair,
He shed in haste the balmy drops of joy   250
O'er all the silky ringlets of her hair,
Then stretched his plumes divine, and breathed celestial air.

Unhappy Psyche! Soon the latent wound
The fading roses of her cheek confess;
Her eyes' bright beams, in swimming sorrows drowned,   255
Sparkle no more with life and happiness,
Her parents' fond exulting hearts to bless;
She shuns adoring crowds, and seeks to hide
The pining sorrows which her soul oppress,
Till to her mother's tears no more denied,   260
The secret grief she owns, for which she lingering sighed.

---

[11]   *the coral gates . . . cell* i.e. her lips, the 'cell' being her
mouth.

A dream of mingled terror and delight
Still heavy hangs upon her troubled soul;
An angry form still swims before her sight,
And still the vengeful thunders seem to roll;   265
Still crushed to earth she feels the stern control
Of Venus unrelenting, unappeased.
The dream returns, she feels the fancied dole;[12]
Once more the furies on her heart have seized,
But still she views the youth who all her sufferings eased.   270

Of wondrous beauty did the vision seem,
And in the freshest prime of youthful years;
Such at the close of her distressful dream
A graceful champion to her eyes appears;
Her loved deliverer from her foes and fears   275
She seems in grateful transport still to press;
Still his soft voice sounds in her ravished ears;
Dissolved in fondest tears of tenderness
His form she oft invokes her waking eyes to bless.

Nor was it quite a dream,[13] for as she woke   280
Ere heavenly mists concealed him from her eye,
One sudden transitory view she took
Of Love's most radiant bright divinity;
From the fair image never can she fly,
As still consumed with vain desire she pines,   285
While her fond parents heave the anxious sigh,
And to avert her fate seek holy shrines,
The threatened ills to learn by auguries and signs.

And now, the royal sacrifice prepared,
The milk-white bull they to the altar lead,[14]   290
Whose youth the galling yoke as yet had spared,
Now destined by the sacred knife to bleed –
When lo, with sudden spring his horns he freed,
And headlong rushed amid the frighted throng,
While from the smoke-veiled shrine such sounds proceed   295
As well might strike with awe the soul most strong,
And thus divinely spoke the Heaven-inspiréd tongue:

'On nuptial couch, in nuptial vest arrayed,
On a tall rock's high summit Psyche place,
Let all depart, and leave the fated maid   300

---

[12] *dole* grief, distress.
[13] *Nor was it quite a dream* this episode would have had an obvious interest for Keats, who reworks the 'dreaming' of a lover into reality in *The Eve of St Agnes*, and who describes the imagination as being like Adam's dream: 'He awoke and found it truth' (*Romanticism* 1014).
[14] Weller suggests that lines 289–90 inspired Keats, *Ode on a Grecian Urn* 31–3.

Who never must a mortal hymen[15] grace.
A wingéd monster of no earthly race
Thence soon shall bear his trembling bride away;
His power extends o'er all the bounds of space,
And Jove himself has owned his dreaded sway,   305
Whose flaming breath sheds fire, whom earth and heaven obey.'

With terror, anguish, and astonishment
The oracle her wretched father hears;
Now from his brow the regal honours rent,
And now in frantic sorrow wild appears;   310
Nor threatened plagues, nor punishment he fears,
Refusing long the sentence to obey,
Till Psyche, trembling with submissive tears,
Bids them the sacrifice no more delay,
Prepare the funeral couch, and leave the destined prey.   315

Pleased by th' ambiguous doom the Fates promulge,[16]
The angry goddess and enamoured boy[17]
Alike content their various hopes indulge;
He still exploring with an anxious eye
The future prospect of uncertain joy,   320
Plans how the tender object of his care
He may protect from threatened misery –
Ah, sanguine Love, so oft deceived, forbear
With flattering tints to paint illusive[18] hope so fair!

But now what lamentations rend the skies!   325
In amaracine wreaths[19] the virgin choir
With 'Io Hymen'[20] mingle funeral cries;
Lost in the sorrows of the Lydian[21] lyre
The breathing flutes' melodious notes expire;
In sad procession pass the mournful throng   330
Extinguishing with tears the torches' fire,
While the mute victim weeping crowds among,
By unknown fears oppressed, moves silently along.

But on such scenes of terror and dismay
The mournful muse delights not long to dwell;   335
She quits well pleased the melancholy lay,
Nor vainly seeks the parents' woes to tell;
But what to wondering Psyche then befell

---

15 *hymen* marriage.
16 *promulge* formally announce.
17 *The angry goddess and enamoured boy* Venus and Cupid.
18 *illusive* deceptive, illusory.
19 *amaracine wreaths* wreaths composed, apparently, of amaranths, the imaginary flower reputed never to fade.

20 *Io Hymen* used to invoke the god of marriage at wedding ceremonies.
21 *Lydian* Lydia was a country of eastern Turkey famed for its music.

When thus abandoned, let her rather say,
Who shuddering looks to see some monster fell   340
Approach the desert rock to seize his prey,
With cruel fangs devour, or tear her thence away.

When lo, a gentle breeze began to rise,
Breathed by obedient zephyrs round the maid;
Fanning her bosom with its softest sighs   345
Awhile among her fluttering robes it strayed,
And boldly sportive latent charms displayed;
And then, as Cupid willed, with tenderest care
From the tall rock where weeping she was laid,
With gliding motion through the yielding air   350
To Pleasure's blooming isle their lovely charge they bear.

On the green bosom of the turf reclined,
They lightly now th' astonished virgin lay –
To placid rest they soothe her troubled mind;
Around her still with watchful care they stay,   355
Around her still in quiet whispers play,
Till lulling slumbers bid her eyelids close,
Veiling with silky fringe each brilliant ray,
While soft tranquillity divinely flows
O'er all her soul serene, in visions of repose.   360

Refreshed she rose, and all enchanted gazed
On the rare beauties of the pleasant scene.
Conspicuous far a lofty palace blazed
Upon a sloping bank of softest green –
A fairer edifice was never seen;   365
The high-ranged columns own no mortal hand,
But seem a temple meet for beauty's queen;
Like polished snow the marble pillars stand
In grace-attempered majesty, sublimely grand.

Gently ascending from a silvery flood,   370
Above the palace rose the shaded hill,
The lofty eminence was crowned with wood,
And the rich lawns, adorned by nature's skill,
The passing breezes with their odours fill;
Here ever-blooming groves of orange glow,   375
And here all flowers which from their leaves distil
Ambrosial dew in sweet succession blow,
And trees of matchless size a fragrant shade bestow.

The sun looks glorious mid a sky serene
And bids bright lustre sparkle o'er the tide;   380
The clear blue ocean at a distance seen

Bounds the gay landscape on the western side,
While closing round it with majestic pride,
The lofty rocks mid citron groves arise.
'Sure some divinity must here reside',   385
As, tranced in some bright vision, Psyche cries,
And scarce believes the bliss, or trusts her charméd eyes.

When lo, a voice divinely sweet she hears,
From unseen lips proceeds the heavenly sound:
'Psyche approach, dismiss thy timid fears,   390
At length his bride thy longing spouse has found,
And bids for thee immortal joys abound;
For thee the palace rose at his command,
For thee his love a bridal banquet crowned;
He bids attendant nymphs around thee stand,   395
Prompt every wish to serve, a fond obedient band.'

Increasing wonder filled her ravished soul,
For now the pompous portals opened wide;
There, pausing oft, with timid foot she stole
Through halls high-domed, enriched with sculptured pride,   400
While gay saloons appeared on either side
In splendid vista opening to her sight;
And all with precious gems so beautified,
And furnished with such exquisite delight
That scarce the beams of heaven emit such lustre bright.   405

The amethyst was there of violet hue,
And there the topaz shed its golden ray,
The chrysoberyl, and the sapphire, blue
As the clear azure of a sunny day,
Or the mild eyes where amorous glances play;   410
The snow-white jasper, and the opal's flame,
The blushing ruby, and the agate grey,
And there the gem which bears his luckless name[22]
Whose death, by Phoebus mourned, ensured him deathless fame.

There the green emerald, there cornelians glow,   415
And rich carbuncles pour eternal light
With all that India and Peru can show,
Or Labrador can give so flaming bright
To the charmed mariner's half-dazzled sight.
The coral-paved baths with diamonds blaze,   420
And all that can the female heart delight
Of fair attire, the last recess displays,
And all that Luxury can ask, her eye surveys.

---

[22] *his luckless name* Hyacinth, the Spartan youth loved
by Apollo (Phoebus), who brought him up. As they
were playing with a discus, the wind Zephyrus blew
it so that it killed Hyacinth.

Now through the hall melodious music stole,
And self-prepared the splendid banquet stands;   425
Self-poured the nectar sparkles in the bowl,
The lute and viol touched by unseen hands
Aid the soft voices of the choral bands;
O'er the full board a brighter lustre beams
Than Persia's monarch at his feast commands;   430
For sweet refreshment all-inviting seems
To taste celestial food, and pure ambrosial streams.[23]

But when meek Eve hung out her dewy star,
And gently veiled with gradual hand the sky,
Lo, the bright folding doors retiring far   435
Display to Psyche's captivated eye
All that voluptuous ease could e'er supply
To soothe the spirits in serene repose.
Beneath the velvet's purple canopy,
Divinely-formed, a downy couch arose,   440
While alabaster lamps a milky light disclose.

Once more she hears the hymeneal[24] strain,
Far other voices now attune the lay;
The swelling sounds approach, awhile remain,
And then, retiring faint, dissolved away.   445
The expiring lamps emit a feebler ray,
And soon in fragrant death extinguished lie;
Then virgin terrors Psyche's soul dismay,
When through the obscuring gloom she nought can spy,
But softly-rustling sounds declare some being nigh.   450

Oh you for whom I write, whose hearts can melt
At the soft thrilling voice whose power you prove,[25]
You know what charm, unutterably felt,
Attends the unexpected voice of Love.
Above the lyre, the lute's soft notes above,   455
With sweet enchantment to the soul it steals
And bears it to Elysium's[26] happy grove;
You best can tell the rapture Psyche feels
When Love's ambrosial lip the vows of Hymen seals.

---

[23] The reviewer in the *Gentleman's Magazine* was particularly impressed by this passage: 'The description of the ideal palace reared for Psyche, after the oracle had decreed she should be exposed on a tall rock's high summit, is fanciful and rich as a brilliant imagination can well depict; and the magic operations of her attendants are described with an exuberance of taste peculiar to herself, and equal to the manner in which she relates the impression made upon the heart of Cupid by the charms of Psyche when he executed the harsh commands of his mother' (*Gentleman's Magazine* 82 (1812) 464–7, p. 466). This stanza in particular may have given Keats the idea for the description of the banquet-room magically supplied with music and food, *Lamia* ii 117–31.

[24] *hymeneal* nuptial.

[25] *prove* i.e. by being susceptible to its power.

[26] *Elysium* idyllic world where the souls of the glorious dead spent an afterlife of revelry.

'''Tis he, 'tis my deliverer! Deep impressed   460
Upon my heart those sounds I well recall',
The blushing maid exclaimed; and on his breast
A tear of trembling ecstasy let fall.
But ere the breezes of the morning call
Aurora[27] from her purple humid bed,   465
Psyche in vain explores the vacant hall;
Her tender lover from her arms is fled,
While sleep his downy wings had o'er her eyelids spread.

Again the band invisible attend,
And female voices soothe the mournful bride;   470
Light hands to braid her hair assistance lend,
By some she sees the glowing bracelet tied;
Others officious hover at her side,
And each bright gem for her acceptance bring,
While some, the balmy air diffusing wide,   475
Fan softer perfumes from each odorous wing
Than the fresh bosom sheds of earliest, sweetest spring.

With songs divine her anxious soul they cheer,
And woo her footsteps to delicious bowers;
They bid the fruit more exquisite appear   480
Which at her feet its bright profusion showers.
For her they cull unknown celestial flowers;
The gilded car[28] they bid her fearless guide,
Which at her wish self-moved with wondrous powers,
The rapid bird's velocity defied,   485
While round the blooming isle it rolled with circuit wide.

Again they spread the feast, they strike the lyre,
But to her frequent questions nought reply,
Her lips in vain her lover's name require,
Or wherefore thus concealed he shuns her eye.   490
But when reluctant twilight veils the sky
And each pale lamp successively expires,
Again she trembling hears the voice of joy,
Her spouse a tender confidence inspires,
But with a fond embrace ere dawn again retires.   495

To charm the languid hours of solitude
He oft invites her to the muse's lore,[29]
For none have vainly e'er the muse pursued,
And those whom she delights, regret no more

---

[27] *Aurora* goddess of dawn and morning, often described rising from the bed of Tithonus, her husband.
[28] *car* chariot.

[29] *He oft invites her to the muse's lore* i.e. encouraged her to write poetry.

The social joyous hours, while rapt they soar   500
To worlds unknown, and live in fancy's dream.
Oh muse divine, thee only I implore,
Shed on my soul thy sweet inspiring beams,
And pleasure's gayest scene insipid folly seems!

Silence and solitude the Muses love   505
And whom they charm they can alone suffice,
Nor ever tedious hour their votaries prove.
This solace now the lonely Psyche tries,
Or, while her hand the curious needle plies,
She learns from lips unseen celestial strains;   510
Responsive now with their soft voice she vies,
Or bids her plaintive harp express the pains
Which absence sore inflicts where Love all potent reigns.

But melancholy poisons all her joys,
And secret sorrows all her hopes depress,   515
Consuming languor every bliss destroys,
And sad she droops repining, comfortless.
Her tender lover well the cause can guess,
And sees too plain inevitable fate
Pursue her to the bowers of happiness.   520
'Oh Psyche, most beloved, ere yet too late,
Dread the impending ills and prize thy tranquil state.'

In vain his weeping love he thus advised;
She longs to meet a parent's sweet embrace.
'Oh, were their sorrowing hearts at least apprised   525
How Psyche's wondrous lot all fears may chase,
For whom thy love prepared so fair a place!
Let but my bliss their fond complaints repress,
Let me but once behold a mother's face,
Oh spouse adored, and in full happiness   530
This love-contented heart its solitude shall bless.

'Oh, by those beauties I must ne'er behold!
The spicy-scented ringlets of thine hair;
By that soft neck my loving arms enfold,
Crown with a kind consent thy Psyche's prayer!   535
Their dear embrace, their blessing let me share;
So shall I stain our couch with tears no more,
But, blessed in thee, resign each other care,
Nor seek again thy secret to explore
Which yet, denied thy sight, I ever must deplore.'   540

Unable to resist her fond request,
Reluctant Cupid thus at last complied,

And sighing clasped her closer to his breast.
'Go then, my Psyche; go, my lovely bride!
But let me in thy faith at least confide   545
That by no subtle, impious arts betrayed,
Which, ah, too well I know will all be tried,
Thy simply trusting heart shall e'er be swayed
The secret veil to rend which fate thy screen hath made.

'For danger hovers o'er thy smiling days,   550
One only way to shield thee yet I know;
Unseen, I may securely guard thy ways
And save thee from the threatened storm of woe;
But forced, if known, my Psyche to forego,
Thou never, never must again be mine!   555
What mutual sorrows hence must ceaseless flow,
Compelled thy dear embraces to resign,
While thou to anguish doomed for lost delights shalt pine.

'Solace thy mind with hopes of future joy:
In a dear infant thou shalt see my face,   560
Blessed mother soon of an immortal boy.
In him his father's features thou shalt trace;
Yet go, for thou art free, the bounds of space
Are none for thee. Attendant zephyrs stay,
Speak but thy will, and to the wished-for place   565
Their lovely mistress swift they shall convey –
Yet hither, ah, return, ere fades the festive day.'

'Light of my soul, far dearer than the day!'
Exulting Psyche cries in grateful joy,
'Me all the bliss of earth could ill repay   570
For thy most sweet divine society;
To thee again with rapture will I fly,
Nor with less pleasure hail the star of eve
Than when in tedious solitude I sigh;
My vows of silent confidence believe,   575
Nor think thy Psyche's faith will e'er thy love deceive.'

Her suit obtained, in full contentment blessed,
Her eyes at length in placid slumbers close.
Sleep, hapless fair! Sleep on thy lover's breast –
Ah, not again to taste such pure repose!   580
Till thy sad heart by long experience knows
How much they err who, to their interest blind,
Slight the calm peace which from retirement flows;
And while they think their fleeting joys to bind,
Banish the tranquil bliss which heaven for man designed!   585

CANTO II

Argument

Introduction – dangers of the world – Psyche conveyed by zephyrs awakes once more in the paternal mansion – envy of her sisters – they plot her ruin – inspire her with suspicion and terror – Psyche's return to the Palace of Love – her disobedience – Love asleep – Psyche's amazement – the flight of Love – sudden banishment of Psyche from the island of Pleasure – her lamentations – comforted by Love – temple of Venus – task imposed on Psyche conditional to her reconciliation with Venus – Psyche soothed and attended by Innocence – Psyche wandering as described in the opening of the first Canto

Oh happy you[1] who, blessed with present bliss,
See not with fatal prescience future tears,
Nor the dear moment of enjoyment miss
Through gloomy discontent, or sullen fears
Foreboding many a storm for coming years;   5
Change is the lot of all. Ourselves with scorn
Perhaps shall view what now so fair appears;
And wonder whence the fancied charm was born
Which now with vain despair from our fond grasp is torn!

Vain schemer, think not to prolong thy joy!   10
But cherish while it lasts the heavenly boon;
Expand thy sails! Thy little bark shall fly
With the full tide of pleasure; though it soon
May feel the influence of the changeful moon,
It yet is thine! Then let not doubts obscure   15
With cloudy vapours veil thy brilliant noon,
Nor let suspicion's tainted breath impure
Poison the favouring gale which speeds thy course secure!

Oh Psyche, happy in thine ignorance,
Couldst thou but shun this heart-tormenting bane!   20
Be but content, nor daringly advance
To meet the bitter hour of threatened pain.
Pure spotless dove, seek thy safe nest again;
Let true affection shun the public eye
And quit the busy circle of the vain,   25
For there the treacherous snares concealéd lie;
Oh timely-warned escape – to safe retirement fly!

Bright shone the morn, and now its golden ray
Dispelled the slumbers from her radiant eyes,

CANTO II
[1]   *Oh happy you* Weller notes similar phrasing in Keats,
Ode to Psyche 22, *Ode on a Grecian Urn* 21.

Yet still in dreams her fancy seems to play,   30
For lo, she sees with rapture and surprise
Full in her view the well-known mansion rise,
And each loved scene or first endearment hails;
The air that first received her infant sighs
With wondering ecstasy she now inhales,   35
While every trembling nerve soft tenderness assails.

See from the dear pavilion where she lay,
Breathless she flies with scarce-assuréd feet,
Swift through the garden wings her eager way,
Her mourning parents' ravished eyes to greet   40
With loveliest apparition strange and sweet.
Their days of anguish all o'erpaid they deem
By one blessed hour of ecstasy so great;
Yet doubtingly they gaze, and anxious seem
To ask their raptured souls, 'Oh is this all a dream?'   45

The wondrous tale attentively they hear,
Repeated oft in broken words of joy;
She in their arms embraced, while every ear
Hangs on their Psyche's lips, and earnestly
On her is fixed each wonder-speaking eye;   50
Till the sad hour arrives which bids them part,
And twilight darkens o'er the ruddy sky;
Divinely urged they let their child depart,
Pressed with a fond embrace to each adoring heart.

Trusting that wedded to a spouse divine   55
Secure is now their daughter's happiness,
They half-contentedly their child resign,
Check the complaint, the rising sigh suppress,
And wipe the silent drops of bitterness.
Nor must she her departure more delay,   60
But bids them now their weeping Psyche bless;
Then back to the pavilion bends her way
Ere in the fading west quite sinks expiring day.

But while her parents listen with delight,
Her sisters' hearts the Furies[2] agitate;   65
They look with envy on a lot so bright,
And all the honours of her splendid fate,
Scorning the meanness of their humbler state;
And how they best her ruin may devise
With hidden rancour much they meditate,   70
Yet still they bear themselves in artful guise,
While mid the feigned caress, concealed the venom lies.

---

[2] *Furies* spirits of the earth bearing an implacable curse.

By malice urged, by ruthless envy stung,
With secret haste to seize their prey they flew,
Around her neck as in despair they clung;　　　　　　75
Her soft complying nature well they knew,
And trusted by delaying to undo;
But when they found her resolute to go,
Their well-laid stratagem they then pursue,
And, while they bid their treacherous sorrows flow,　　80
Thus fright her simple heart with images of woe.

'Oh hapless Psyche, thoughtless of thy doom!
Yet hear thy sisters who have wept for thee
Since first a victim to thy living tomb;
Obedient to the oracle's decree,　　　　　　　　85
Constrained we left thee to thy destiny.
Since then no comfort could our woes abate;
While thou wert lulled in false security
We learned the secret honours of thy fate,
And heard prophetic lips thy future ills relate.　　90

'Yet fearing never to behold thee more,
Our filial care would fain the truth conceal;
But from the sage's cell this ring we bore,
With power each latent magic to reveal.
Some hope from hence our anxious bosoms feel　　95
That we from ruin may our Psyche save,
Since Heaven propitious to our pious zeal,
Thee to our frequent prayers in pity gave,
That warned, thou yet mayst shun thy sad untimely grave.

'Oh how shall we declare the fatal truth?　　　　100
How wound thy tender bosom with alarms?
Tell how the graces of thy blooming youth,
Thy more than mortal, all-adoréd charms
Have lain enamoured in a sorcerer's arms?
Oh Psyche, seize on this decisive hour,　　　　105
Escape the mischief of impending harms!
Return no more to that enchanted bower,
Fly the magician's arts, and dread his cruel power.

'If yet reluctant to forego thy love,
Thy furtive joys and solitary state,　　　　　　110
Our fond officious care thy doubts reprove,
At least let some precaution guard thy fate,
Nor may our warning love be prized too late.
This night thyself thou mayst convince thine eyes:
Hide but a lamp, and cautiously await　　　　　115
Till in deep slumber thy magician lies,
This ring shall then disclose his foul deformities.

'That monster by the oracle foretold,
Whose curséd spells both gods and men must fear,
In his own image thou shalt then behold,   120
And shuddering hate what now is prized so dear;
Yet fly not then, though loathsome he appear,
But let this dagger to his breast strike deep;
Thy coward terrors then thou must not hear,
For if with life he rouses from that sleep   125
Nought then for thee remains, and we must hopeless weep.'

Oh have you seen, when in the northern sky
The transient flame of lambent lightning plays,
In quick succession lucid streamers fly,
Now flashing roseate, and now milky rays,[3]   130
While struck with awe the astonished rustics gaze?
Thus o'er her cheek the meeting signals move,
Now pale with fear, now glowing with the blaze
Of much indignant, still confiding love,
Now horror's lurid hue with shame's deep blushes strove.   135

On her cold passive hand the ring they place,
And hide the dagger in her folding vest,
Pleased the effects of their dire arts to trace
In the mute agony that swells her breast,
Already in her future ruin blessed –   140
Conscious that now their poor deluded prey
Should never taste again delight or rest,
But, sickening in suspicion's gloom decay,
Or urged by terrors rash, their treacherous will obey.

While yet irresolute with sad surprise,   145
Mid doubt and love she stands in strange suspense;
Lo, gliding from her sisters' wondering eyes
Returning zephyrs gently bear her thence;
Lost all her hopes, her joys, her confidence,
Back to the earth her mournful eyes she threw   150
As if imploring pity and defence;
While bathed in tears her golden tresses flew,
As in the breeze dispersed they caught the precious dew.

Illumined bright now shines the splendid dome,
Melodious accents her arrival hail;   155
But not the torches' blaze can chase the gloom,
And all the soothing powers of music fail;
Trembling she seeks her couch with horror pale,
But first a lamp conceals in secret shade,

---

[3] Tighe describes the aurora borealis, or northern
lights.

While unknown terrors all her soul assail.   160
Thus half their treacherous counsel is obeyed,
For still her gentle soul abhors the murderous blade.

And now, with softest whispers of delight,
Love welcomes Psyche still more fondly dear;
Not unobserved, though hid in deepest night,   165
The silent anguish of her secret fear.
He thinks that tenderness excites the tear
By the late image of her parents' grief,
And half-offended seeks in vain to cheer;
Yet while he speaks, her sorrows feel relief,   170
Too soon more keen to sting from this suspension brief!

Allowed to settle on celestial eyes,
Soft Sleep exulting now exerts his sway,
From Psyche's anxious pillow gladly flies
To veil those orbs, whose pure and lambent ray   175
The powers of heaven submissively obey.
Trembling and breathless then she softly rose
And seized the lamp where it obscurely lay,
With hand too rashly daring to disclose
The sacred veil which hung mysterious o'er her woes.   180

Twice, as with agitated step she went,
The lamp expiring shone with doubtful gleam,
As though it warned her from her rash intent;
And twice she paused, and on its trembling beam
Gazed with suspended breath, while voices seem   185
With murmuring sound along the roof to sigh;
As one just waking from a troublous dream,
With palpitating heart and straining eye,
Still fixed with fear remains, still thinks the danger nigh.

Oh, daring muse, wilt thou indeed essay   190
To paint the wonders which that lamp could show?
And canst thou hope in living words to say
The dazzling glories of that heavenly view?
Ah well I ween, that if with pencil true
That splendid vision could be well expressed,   195
The fearful awe imprudent Psyche knew
Would seize vith rapture every wondering breast,
When Love's all-potent charms divinely stood confessed.[4]

All imperceptible to human touch,
His wings display celestial essence light,   200

---
[4]   *confessed* revealed.

The clear effulgence of the blaze is such,
The brilliant plumage shines so heavenly bright
That mortal eyes turn dazzled from the sight;
A youth he seems in manhood's freshest years;
Round his fair neck, as clinging with delight, 205
Each golden curl resplendently appears,
Or shades his darker brow, which grace majestic wears.

Or o'er his guileless front the ringlets bright
Their rays of sunny lustre seem to throw –
That front than polished ivory more white! 210
His blooming cheeks with deeper blushes glow
Than roses scattered o'er a bed of snow,
While on his lips, distilled in balmy dews
(Those lips divine that even in silence know
The heart to touch), persuasion to infuse 215
Still hangs a rosy charm that never vainly sues.[5]

The friendly curtain of indulgent sleep
Disclosed not yet his eyes' resistless sway,
But from their silky veil there seemed to peep
Some brilliant glances with a softened ray, 220
Which o'er his features exquisitely play,
And all his polished limbs suffuse with light.
Thus through some narrow space the azure day
Sudden its cheerful rays diffusing bright,
Wide darts its lucid beams, to gild the brow of night. 225

His fatal arrows and celestial bow
Beside the couch were negligently thrown,
Nor needs the god his dazzling arms to show
His glorious birth, such beauty round him shone
As sure could spring from Beauty's self alone; 230
The gloom which glowed o'er all of soft desire,
Could well proclaim him Beauty's cherished son;
And Beauty's self will oft these charms admire,
And steal his witching smile, his glance's living fire.

Speechless with awe, in transport strangely lost, 235
Long Psyche stood with fixed adoring eye;
Her limbs immoveable, her senses tossed
Between amazement, fear, and ecstasy,

---

[5] The reviewer in the *Gentleman's Magazine* thought that female readers would be particularly impressed with this description: 'The consequences of the advice of the sisters afforded Mrs Tighe an opportunity for the display of a fancy, seldom excelled, in detailing the caution, terror, and trepidation of Psyche, who at length, by means of the magic lamp with which she had been furnished, sees Cupid in all the effulgence of his celestial nature; and we trust the description of his manly form and features will excite many warm emotions in the breasts of the female readers of this poem' (*Gentleman's Magazine* 82 (1812) 464–7, p. 466).

She hangs enamoured o'er the deity,
Till from her trembling hand extinguished falls   240
The fatal lamp – he starts – and suddenly
Tremendous thunders echo through the halls,
While ruin's hideous crash bursts o'er the affrighted walls.

Dread horror seizes on her sinking heart,
A mortal chillness shudders at her breast,   245
Her soul shrinks fainting from death's icy dart,
The groan scarce uttered dies but half expressed,
And down she sinks in deadly swoon oppressed.
But when at length awaking from her trance,
The terrors of her fate stand all confessed,   250
In vain she casts around her timid glance,
The rudely frowning scenes her former joys enhance.

No traces of those joys, alas, remain;
A desert solitude alone appears.
No verdant shade relieves the sandy plain,   255
The widespread waste no gentle fountain cheers,
One barren face the dreary prospect wears;
Nought through the vast horizon meets her eye
To calm the dismal tumult of her fears,
No trace of human habitation nigh: 260
A sandy wild beneath; above, a threatening sky.

The mists of morn yet chill the gloomy air
And heavily obscure the clouded skies;
In the mute anguish of a fixed despair
Still on the ground immoveable she lies;   265
At length, with lifted hands and streaming eye,
Her mournful prayers invoke offended Love:
'Oh let me hear thy voice once more', she cries,
'In death at least thy pity let me move,
And death, if but forgiven, a kind relief will prove.   270

'For what can life to thy lost Psyche give,
What can it offer but a gloomy void?
Why thus abandoned should I wish to live?
To mourn the pleasure which I once enjoyed,
The bliss my own rash folly hath destroyed?   275
Of all my soul most prized, or held most dear,
Nought but the sad remembrance doth abide,
And late repentance of my impious fear –
Remorse and vain regret what living soul can bear?

'Oh art thou then indeed for ever gone?   280
And art thou heedless of thy Psyche's woe?

From these fond arms for ever art thou flown,
And unregarded must my sorrows flow!
Ah, why too happy did I ever know
The rapturous charms thy tenderness inspires?   285
Ah why did thy affections stoop so low?
Why kindle in a mortal breast such fires,
Or with celestial love inflame such rash desires?

'Abandoned thus for ever by thy love,
No greater punishment I now can bear,   290
From fate no farther malice can I prove;
Not all the horrors of this desert drear,
Nor death itself can now excite a fear;
The peopled earth a solitude as vast
To this despairing heart would now appear;   295
Here then, my transient joys for ever past,
Let thine expiring bride thy pardon gain at last!'

Now prostrate on the bare unfriendly ground,
She waits her doom in silent agony;
When lo, the well-known soft celestial sound   300
She hears once more with breathless ecstasy.
'Oh yet too dearly loved, lost Psyche! Why
With cruel fate wouldst thou unite thy power,
And force me thus thine arms adored to fly?
Yet cheer thy drooping soul, some happier hour   305
Thy banished steps may lead back to thy lover's bower.

'Though angry Venus we no more can shun,
Appease that anger and I yet am thine!
Lo, where her temple glitters to the sun;
With humble penitence approach her shrine,   310
Perhaps to pity she may yet incline;
But should her cruel wrath these hopes deceive,
And thou, alas, must never more be mine,
Yet shall thy lover ne'er his Psyche leave,
But, if the Fates allow, unseen thy woes relieve.   315

'Stronger than I, they now forbid my stay;
Psyche beloved, adieu!' Scarce can she hear
The last faint words, which gently melt away;
And now more faint the dying sounds appear,
Borne to a distance from her longing ear;   320
Yet still attentively she stands unmoved
To catch those accents which her soul could cheer,
That soothing voice which had so sweetly proved
That still his tender heart offending Psyche loved!

And now the joyous sun had cleared the sky,   325
The mist dispelled revealed the splendid fane;
A palmy grove majestically high
Screens the fair building from the desert plain;
Of alabaster white and free from stain
Mid the tall trees the tapering columns rose;   330
Thither, with fainting steps and weary pain,
Obedient to the voice at length she goes,
And at the threshold seeks protection and repose.

Round the soft scene immortal roses bloomed,
While lucid myrtles in the breezes play;   335
No savage beast had ever yet presumed
With foot impure within the grove to stray,
And far from hence flies every bird of prey;
Thus, mid the sandy Garamantian wild,[6]
When Macedonia's lord[7] pursued his way,   340
The sacred temple of great Ammon smiled,
And green encircling shades the long fatigue beguiled.

With awe that fearfully her doom awaits
Still at the portal Psyche timid lies,
When lo, advancing from the hallowed gates   345
Trembling she views with reverential eyes
An aged priest. A myrtle bough supplies
A wand, and roses bind his snowy brows.[8]
'Bear hence thy feet profane!' he sternly cries,
'Thy longer stay the goddess disallows;   350
Fly, nor her fiercer wrath too daringly arouse!'

His pure white robe imploringly she held,
And, bathed in tears, embraced his sacred knees;
Her mournful charms relenting he beheld,
And melting pity in his eye she sees.   355
'Hope not', he cries, 'the goddess to appease;
Retire at awful distance from her shrine,
But seek the refuge of those sheltering trees,
And now thy soul with humble awe incline
To hear her sacred will, and mark the words divine.   360

'Presumptuous Psyche, whose aspiring soul
The god of Love has dared to arrogate;[9]
Rival of Venus, whose supreme control

---

[6] *the sandy Garamantian wild* the deserts of modern-
day northern Libya.
[7] *Macedonia's lord* Alexander the Great, whose birth
was attributed to the miraculous intervention of the

Egyptian god Ammon, to whose temple Alexander
made a famous pilgrimage.
[8] *A myrtle bough . . . snowy brows* Venus often shrouded
herself in rose and myrtle when washing.
[9] *arrogate* adopt, claim.

Is now asserted by all-ruling fate,
No suppliant tears her vengeance shall abate   365
Till thou hast raised an altar to her power
Where perfect happiness, in lonely state,
Has fixed her temple in secluded bower,
By foot impure of man untrodden to this hour!

And on the altar must thou place an urn   370
Filled from immortal beauty's sacred spring,
Which foul deformity to grace can turn,
And back to fond affection's eyes can bring
The charms which fleeting fled on transient wing;
Snatched from the rugged steep where first they rise,   375
Dark rocks their crystal source o'ershadowing,
Let their clear water sparkle to the skies
Where cloudless lustre beams which happiness supplies!

To Venus thus for ever reconciled
(This one atonement all her wrath disarms),   380
From thy loved Cupid then no more exiled
There shalt thou, free from sorrow and alarms,
Enjoy for ever his celestial charms.
But never shalt thou taste a pure repose
Nor ever meet thy lover's circling arms   385
Till all subdued that shall thy steps oppose –
Thy perils there shall end, escaped from all thy foes.'

With meek submissive woe she heard her doom,
Nor to the holy minister replied;
But in the myrtle grove's mysterious gloom   390
She silently retired her grief to hide.
Hopeless to tread the waste without a guide,
All unrefreshed and faint from toil she lies;
When lo, her present wants are all supplied –
Sent by the hand of Love a turtle[10] flies   395
And sets delicious food before her wondering eyes.

Cheered by the favouring omen, softer tears
Relieve her bosom from its cruel weight.
She blames the sad despondence of her fears;
When still protected by a power so great,   400
His tenderness her toils will mitigate.
Then with renewéd strength at length she goes,
Hoping to find some skilled in secret fate,
Some learnéd sage who haply might disclose
Where lay that blissful bower, the end of all her woes.   405

---

[10] *turtle* turtle-dove.

And as she went – behold, with hovering flight
The dove preceded still her doubtful way;
Its spotless plumage of the purest white,
Which shone resplendent in the blaze of day,
Could even in darkest gloom a light display –   410
Of heavenly birth, when first to mortals given,
Named Innocence. But ah, too short its stay;
By ravenous birds it fearfully was driven
Back to reside with Love, a denizen of heaven.

Now through the trackless wild, o'er many a mile   415
The messenger of Cupid led the fair
And cheered with hope her solitary toil,
Till now a brighter face the prospects wear;
Past are the sandy wastes and deserts bare,
And many a verdant hill and grassy dale,   420
And trace that mortal culture might declare,
And many a wild wood dark and joyous vale
Appeared her soul to soothe, could soothing scenes avail.

But other fears her timid soul distress
Mid strangers unprotected and alone,   425
The desert wilderness alarmed her less
Than cities, thus unfriended and unknown;
But where the path was all by moss o'ergrown,
There still she chose her solitary way,
Where'er her faithful dove before had flown   430
Fearful of nought she might securely stray,
For still his care supplied the wants of every day.

And still she entered every sacred grove
And homage paid to each divinity,
But chief the altar of almighty Love   435
Weeping embraced with fond imploring eye;
To every oracle her hopes apply,
Instructions for her dangerous path to gain –
Exclaiming oft, with a desponding sigh,
'Ah, how through all such dangers, toil and pain,   440
Shall Psyche's helpless steps their object e'er attain?'

And now remote from every peopled town
One sultry day a cooling bower she found;
There, as I whilom[11] sung, she laid her down,
Where rich profusion of gay flowers around   445
Had decked with artless show the sloping ground;
There the wild rose and modest violet grow,

---

[11]   *whilom* formerly.

There all thy charms, Narcissus,[12] still abound!
There wrapped in verdure fragrant lilies blow,
Lilies that love the vale, and hide their bells of snow.　　　　　450

Thy flowers, Adonis,[13] bright vermilion show;
Still for his love the yellow crocus pines;
There, while indignant blushes seem to glow,
Beloved by Phoebus his Acanthus[14] shines;
Reseda[15] still her drooping head reclines　　　　　455
With faithful homage to his golden rays,
And, though mid clouds their lustre he resigns,[16]
An image of the constant heart displays,
While silent still she turns her fond pursuing gaze.

And every sweet that Spring with fairy hands　　　　　460
Scatters in thy green path, enchanting May,
And every flowering shrub there clustering stands
As though they wooed her to a short delay,
Yielding a charm to soothe her weary way;
Soft was the tufted moss, and sweet the breeze,　　　　　465
With lulling sound the murmuring waters play,
With lulling sound from all the rustling trees
The fragrant gale invites to cool refreshing ease.

There as she sought repose, her sorrowing heart
Recalled her absent love with bitter sighs;　　　　　470
Regret had deeply fixed the poisoned dart
Which ever rankling in her bosom lies;
In vain she seeks to close her weary eyes –
Those eyes still swim incessantly in tears,
Hope in her cheerless bosom fading dies,　　　　　475
Distracted by a thousand cruel fears,
While banished from his love for ever she appears.

Oh thou best comforter of that sad heart
Whom fortune's spite assails – come, gentle sleep,
The weary mourner soothe! For well the art　　　　　480
Thou knowest in soft forgetfulness to steep
The eyes which sorrow taught to watch and weep;
Let blissful visions now her spirits cheer,
Or lull her cares to peace in slumbers deep,
Till from fatigue refreshed and anxious fear　　　　　485
Hope like the morning star once more shall reappear.

---

[12] *Narcissus* beautiful youth who fell in love with his own image and committed suicide, with the result that he was turned into a flower.
[13] *Adonis* killed by a boar while hunting, he was changed into an anemone.

[14] *Acanthus* Acantha was a nymph loved by Apollo (Phoebus) and given immortality in the flower Acanthus.
[15] *Reseda* 'reseda luteola' (Tighe's note). Reseda is an English garden plant also known as Mignonette.
[16] *mid clouds their lustre he resigns* in the midst of clouds, the sun surrenders the lustre of his 'golden rays'.

CANTO III

Argument

Praise of Love – Psyche's champion, with his attendant Constance, described – the knight assumes the command of Passion, who appears as a lion – Psyche proceeds under the protection of the knight – persuaded to repose in the bower of loose Delight – her escape from thence – led by Innocence to retirement – Psyche meets Vanity and Flattery – betrayed by them into the power of Ambition – rescued by her knight

Oh who art thou who darest of Love complain?
He is a gentle spirit and injures none!
His foes are ours; from them the bitter pain,
The keen, deep anguish, the heart-rending groan,
Which in his milder reign are never known.   5
His tears are softer than the April showers,
White-handed Innocence supports his throne;
His sighs are sweet as breath of earliest flowers,
Affection guides his steps, and Peace protects his bowers.

But scarce admittance he on earth can find,   10
Opposed by Vanity, by Fraud ensnared,
Suspicion frights him from the gloomy mind,
And Jealousy in vain his smiles has shared,
Whose sullen frown the gentle godhead scared;
From Passion's rapid blaze in haste he flies,   15
His wings alone the fiercer flame has spared;
From him Ambition turns his scornful eyes,
And Avarice, slave to gold, a generous lord denies.

But chief Inconstancy his power destroys;
To mock his lovely form, an idle train   20
With magic skill she dressed in transient toys,
By these the selfish votaries she can gain
Whom Love's more simple bands could ne'er detain.
Ah, how shall Psyche through such mortal foes
The fated end of all her toils attain?   25
Sadly she ponders o'er her hopeless woes,
Till on the pillowy turf she sinks to short repose.

But as the careless lamb whom playful chance
Thoughtless of danger has enticed to rove,
Amidst her gambols casts a sudden glance   30
Where lurks her wily foe within the grove,
Anxious to fly, but still afraid to move,
All hopeless of escape – so looks the maid,
Such dread her half-awakened senses prove,
When roused from sleep before her eyes dismayed   35
A knight all armed appears close mid the embowering shade.

Trembling she gazed, until the stranger knight
Tempering with mildest courtesy the awe
Which majesty inspired, low in her sight
Obeisance made; nor would he nearer draw, 40
Till, half-subdued surprise and fear, he saw
Pale terror yielding to the rosy grace,
The pure congealed blood begin to thaw,
And flowing through her crystal veins apace
Suffuse with mantling blush her mild celestial face. 45

Gently approaching then with fairest speech
He proffered service to the lonely dame,
And prayed her that she might not so impeach
The honour of his youth's yet spotless fame
As aught to fear which might his knighthood shame; 50
But if her unprotected steps to guard,
The glory of her champion he might claim,
He asked no other guerdon or reward
Than what bright honour's self might to his deeds award.

Doubting and musing much within her mind, 55
With half-suspicious, half-confiding eye,
Awhile she stood; her thoughts bewildered find
No utterance, unwilling to deny
Such proffered aid, yet bashful to reply
With quick assent, since though concealed his face 60
Beneath his helm, yet might she well espy
And in each fair proportion plainly trace
The symmetry of form, and perfect youthful grace.

Hard were it to describe the nameless charm
That o'er each limb, in every action played; 65
The softness of that voice, which could disarm
The hand of fury of its deadly blade.
In shining armour was the youth arrayed,
And on his shield a bleeding heart he bore,
His lofty crest light plumes of azure shade, 70
There shone a wounded dragon bathed in gore,
And bright with silver beamed the silken scarf he wore.

His milk-white steed with glittering trappings blazed,
Whose reins a beauteous boy attendant held,
On the fair squire with wonder Psyche gazed, 75
For scarce he seemed of age to bear the shield,
Far less a ponderous lance or sword to wield;
Yet well this little page his lord had served,
His youthful arm had many a foe repelled,
His watchful eye from many a snare preserved, 80
Nor ever from his steps in any danger swerved.

Graced with the gift of a perpetual youth,
No lapse of years had power his form to change;
Constance was named the boy, whose matchless truth,
Though oft enticed with other lords to range,   85
Nor fraud nor force could from that knight estrange;[1]
His mantle of celestial blue was made,
And its bright texture wrought with art so strange
That the fresh brilliant gloss could never fade,
And lustre yet unknown to Psyche's eyes displayed.   90

Thus while she gazed, behold with horrid roar
A lion from the neighbouring forest rushed;
A golden chain around his neck he bore
Which richly glowing with carbuncles blushed,
While his fierce eyeballs fiery rage had flushed.   95
Forth steps the youth before the affrighted fair,
Who in his mighty paw already crushed
Seems in the terrors of her wild despair,
And her mute quivering lips a deathlike paleness wear.

But scarce the kingly beast the knight beheld,   100
When crouching low, submissive at his feet,
His wrath extinguished, and his valour quelled,
He seemed with reverence and obeisance sweet
Him as his long-acknowledged lord to greet;
While, in acceptance of the new command,   105
Well-pleased the youth received the homage meet,
Then seized the splendid chain with steady hand
Full confident to rule, and every foe withstand.

And when at length recovered from her fear
The timid Psyche mounts his docile steed   110
Much prayed,[2] she tells to his attentive ear
(As on her purposed journey they proceed)
The doubtful course the oracle decreed,
And how, observant of her friendly guide,
She still pursued its flight with all the speed   115
Her fainting strength had hitherto supplied –
What pathless wilds she crossed! What forests darkling wide!

Which having heard, the courteous knight began
With counsel sweet to soothe her wounded heart;
Divinely eloquent, persuasion ran   120
The herald of his words ere they depart

CANTO III
[1] *could from that knight estrange* i.e. could estrange him
from that knight.

[2] *Much prayed* Psyche has been praying for the safety
of the knight.

His lips, which well might confidence impart,
As he revealed how he himself was bound
By solemn vow, that neither force nor art
His helmet should unloose, till he had found 125
The bower of happiness, that long-sought fairy ground.

'I too', he said, 'divided from my love,
The offended power of Venus deprecate;[3]
Like thee, through paths untrodden, sadly rove
In search of that fair spot prescribed by fate, 130
The blessed term of my afflicted state,
Where I the mistress of my soul shall find,
For whose dear sake no toil to me seems great,
Nor any dangers to my search assigned
Can from its purpose fright my ardent longing mind. 135

'Psyche, thy soft and sympathising heart
Shall share the rapture of thy loyal knight;
He too, in thy content shall bear a part,
Blessed witness of thy new-restored delight;
My vows of true allegiance here I plight, 140
Ne'er to forsake thee till thy perils end,
Thy steps to guard, in thy protection fight,
By counsel aid, and by my arm defend,
And prove myself in all thy champion and thy friend.'

So on they went, her cheerless heart revived 145
By promised succour in her doubtful way;
And much of hope she to herself derived,
From the warm eagerness his lips display
In their pursuit to suffer no delay.
'And sure', she softly sighed, 'my dearest Lord,[4] 150
Thy watchful love still guides me as I stray;
Not chance alone could such an aid afford –
Lo, beasts of prey confess the heaven-assisted sword!'

Now from his crystal urn, with chilling hand,
Vesper[5] had sprinkled all the earth with dew, 155
A misty veil obscured the neighbouring land
And shut the fading landscape from their view;
A beaten path they eagerly pursue
(For now refreshment and repose they need
As Psyche weary of long travel grew) 160
Where by a river's bank it seemed to lead,
Along its sinuous course they heedlessly proceed.

---

[3] *deprecate* plead against.
[4] *Lord* Cupid.
[5] *Vesper* Venus, the evening star, visible in the west after sunset.

At length the lordly beast that bore the knight
Explored the river's depth with sudden bound;
Psyche, who heard the plunge with strange affright,   165
Her champion reassured with welcome sound
That he the other bank had safely found;
And while he spoke, emerging from the shade,
A joyous goodly train appear around
Of many a gallant youth and white-robed maid,   170
Who grateful welcome gave, and courteous greeting paid.

Quick through the trees a thousand torches blazed,
The gloom to banish, and the scene disclose
To Psyche all irresolute, amazed:
A bridge with stately arch at distance rose.   175
Thither at once the gay assembly goes
Not unattended by the charméd knight,
Inviting Psyche to partake repose,
Pointing where shone their bower illumined bright –
Their bower so passing fair, the bower of loose Delight.   180

At length with timid foot the bridge she passed
And to her guardian knight clung fearfully,
While many a doubting glance around she cast
If still her watchful dove she might espy;
Feebly it seemed on labouring wing to fly   185
Till, dazzled by the sudden glare around,
In painful trance is closed its dizzy eye –
And had it not fair Psyche's bosom found,
Its drooping pinion soon had touched the unhallowed ground.

Hence there arose within her heart sore dread   190
Which no alluring pleasure could dispel;
The splendid hall with luscious banquet spread,
The soft-breathed flutes which in sweet concert swell
With melody of song unspeakable;
Nor the light-dancing troop in roses dressed   195
Could chase the terrors which she dared not tell,
While, fondly cherished in her anxious breast,
She strove in vain to soothe the fluttering bird to rest.

On a soft downy couch the guests are placed
And close behind them stands their watchful page,   200
But much his strict[6] attendance there disgraced,[7]
And much was scorned his green and tender age,
His calm fixed eye, and steady aspect sage.
But him nor rude disdain nor mockery,
Nor soothing blandishments could e'er engage,   205

---

[6] *strict* disciplined.   [7] *disgraced* i.e. put everyone else to shame.

The wanton mazes of their sports[8] to try,
Or from his lord to turn his firm adhering eye.

White-bosomed nymphs around with loosened zones
All on the guests obsequiously tend;
Some sing of love with soft expiring tones,   210
While Psyche's melting eyes the strain commend;
Some o'er their heads the canopy suspend,
Some hold the sparkling bowl, while some with skill
Ambrosial showers and balmy juices blend,
Or the gay lamps with liquid odours fill,   215
Whose many-coloured fires divinest sweets distil.

And now a softer light they seemed to shed,
And sweetest music ushered in their Queen;
Her languid steps by winged boys[9] are led,
Who in their semblance might have Cupids been –   220
Close-wrapped in veils her following train was seen.
Herself looked lovely in her loose attire,
Her smiling eyes gave lustre to the scene,
And still, where'er they turned their wanton fire,
Each thrilling nerve confessed the rapture they inspire.   225

The stranger guests she viewed with welcome glad,
And crowned the banquet with reception sweet,
To fill the glowing bowl her nymphs she bade,
And graceful rising from her splendid seat
She would herself present the sparkling treat –   230
When lo, the dove alarmed with sudden start,
Spurned the bright cup and dashed it at her feet!
For well he knew 'twas mixed with treacherous art
To sting his Psyche's breast with agonizing smart.

Regardless of her supplicating tears,   235
Each eye with vengeful rage the insult sees –
Her knight's protection now in vain appears.
The offended sovereign anxious to appease,
A thousand hands prepare the dove to seize;
Nor was this all, for as the tumult rose,   240
Sudden more thick than swarm of summer bees,
The secret dens their venomed hoards disclose,
And horror at the sight her vital spirits froze.

Hissing aloud with undulations dire,
Their forkéd tongues unnumbered serpents show;   245
Their tainted breath emitting poisonous fire,

---

[8] *sports* pastimes.

[9] *winged boys* As Weller points out, Keats uses the same phrase at *Ode to Psyche* 21.

All turn on Psyche as their mortal foe;
But he whose arm was never weak or slow
Now rushed before her with resistless spring,
On either side the oft-repeated blow   250
Repulsed the malice of their deadly sting,
While sparks of wrathful fire from their fierce jaws they fling.

'Fly, Psyche! These are slander's hellish brood!
Contest I know is vain', her champion cried.
Her passage now the opposing train withstood;   255
Struck with disgust their hideous forms she spied,
For lo, each silken veil is thrown aside,
And foul deformity and filth obscene
With monstrous shapes appear on every side;
But vanished is their fair and treacherous Queen,   260
And with her every charm that decked the enchanted scene.

Meanwhile the dove had soared above their reach,
But hovered still in anxious Psyche's sight;
Precursor of escape, it seemed to teach
Whither she safest might direct her flight,   265
And find a passport[10] in her foes' despite;
One rugged path there lay with briars o'ergrown,
Then dark and dismal with the shades of night –
Thither the dove on rapid wing had flown,
Conspicuous mid the gloom its silver plumage shone.   270

Yet she delayed, o'ercome by terror's power,
And scarce her fainting form the knight could shield,
When lo, still active in the trying hour,
Constance rushed fearless through the dreadful field!
With breastplate firm invulnerably steeled,   275
He heeded not the storms which round him press;
To any perils he disdained to yield,
Endued with prudence as with hardiness,
And ever skilled to bring due succour in distress.

Lo, swift returning on his master's steed,   280
In his right hand he held the lion's chain,
The mighty beast his gentleness could lead,
Though little used to bear the curb or rein
And mid those groves accustomed to remain;
Yet now prepared, with sweet submissive grace,   285
He ready stands the knight to bear again,
While trembling Psyche on the steed they place,
Which swift as lightning flies far from the dreadful chase.

---

[10]   *passport* safe passage.

Rough was the rude wild way, and many a thorn
Tore her loose garments in their rapid flight;   290
O'er many a league the panting fair is borne
Till now, emerging from the shades of night,
The grey-eyed morn stole forth her pallid light.
Then first she paused, unable to proceed,
Exhausted with fatigue, and pain, and fright.   295
'Turn, Psyche', cried the youth, 'relax thy speed,
And see thyself at length from thy pursuers freed.'

Mid the thick forest was a lonely dell
Where foot of man was seldom known to tread,
The sloping hills all round in graceful swell   300
The little green with woods environéd[11] –
Hither the dove their passive course had led.
Here the thin smoke blue rising mid the trees,
Where broad and brown the deepest umbrage spread,
Spoke the abode of safe retired ease,   305
And Psyche gladly there her dove descending sees.

In lowly cottage, walled with mossy sod,
Close by a little spring's perpetual rill,
A hermit dwelt, who many a year had trod
With sacred solitude that pine-clad hill,   310
And loved with holy images to fill
His soul enrapt, yet courteous them besought
Awhile secluded here to rest; and still
Replete with kind and hospitable thought,
To a sequestered bower the wearied Pysche brought.   315

Skilled in the virtue of each healing flower,
And the wild fruit's restoring juice to blend,
He spreads the frugal fare of wholesome power,
And heedfully his cares their wants attend;
A docile ear to his advice they lend,   320
And sage instruction from his precepts take,
Which much their future journey may befriend;
Wisdom with soothing eloquence he spake,
Pleased to resolve their doubts, and all their cares partake.

In those sweet placid scenes awhile they rest   325
Till Psyche finds her fainting strength revive,
And here her dove, as in a quiet nest,
Delighted seems to sportive joy alive –
And hence they surest confidence derive.

---

[11] *environéd* pronounced with four syllables, so as to
rhyme with 'tread'.

He plumes his wings, and through his swelling throat   330
(No more a ruffled, fearful fugitive)
In gentle murmurs pours his dulcet note,
While Psyche listening sits in some still vale remote.

Oh have you never known the silent charm
That undisturbed retirement yields the soul,   335
Where no intruder might your peace alarm,
And tenderness hath wept without control,
While melting fondness o'er the bosom stole?
Did fancy never, in some lonely grove,
Abridge the hours which must in absence roll?   340
Those pensive[12] pleasures did you never prove,
Oh you have never loved! You know not what is love!

They do not love who can to these prefer
The tumult of the gay, or folly's roar;
The muse they know not, nor delight in her   345
Who can the troubled soul to rest restore –
Calm contemplation. Yes, I must deplore[13]
Their joyless state, even more than his who mourns
His love for ever lost; delight no more
Unto his widowed heart indeed returns –   350
Yet, while he weeps, his soul their cold indifference spurns.

But if soft hope illumines fancy's dream,
Assuring him of love and constancy,
How exquisite do then the moments seem,
When he may hide himself from every eye   355
And cherish the dear thought in secrecy!
While sweet remembrance soothes his thrilling heart,
And brings once more past hours of kindness nigh,
Recalls the look of love when forced to part,
And turns to drops of joy the tears that sadly start.   360

Forgetful of the dangers of her way,
Imagination oft would Psyche bear
To her long travel's end, and that blest day
When Love unveiled should to her eyes appear;
When she might view his charms exempt from fear,   365
Taste his pure kisses, feel his balmy sighs,
Rest in the fond embrace of arms so dear,
Gaze with soft rapture on his melting eyes,
And hear his voice divine, the music of the skies!

---

[12] *pensive* meditative.   [13] *deplore* lament.

Their destined course impatient to achieve, 370
The knight is urgent onward to proceed;
Cheered with recruited strength they take their leave
Of their kind host, and pay their grateful meed
Of warmest thanks sincere; onward they speed
Their sunless journey long through forests green, 375
And tangled thickets rank with many a weed;
And when at closing day a hut is seen,
They seek the humble roof, nor scorn its welcome mean.[14]

It happened once that, early roused from sleep
(Ere her damp veil the virgin morn had cast 380
From her pale face, not yet with blushes deep
Lovely suffused, as when approaching fast
His herald star proclaims her spouse at last),
Psyche forsaking soon her homely bed
Alone had fearless the low threshold passed 385
And, to beguile the hours which lingering fled,
Light o'er the dewy plain walked forth with nimble tread.

Yet though the knight close-wrapped in slumber lay,
Her steps at distance still the page pursued,
Fearful that danger might befall her way, 390
Or lest, entangled in the mazy wood,
Returning she should miss the pathway rude.
The lark now hails the sun with rapturous song,
The cheerful earth resounds with gratitude,
O'er the gay scene, as Psyche tripped along, 395
She felt her spirits rise, her lightened heart grow strong.

And hark, soft music steals upon the ear –
'Tis woman's voice, most exquisitely sweet!
Behold, two female forms approaching near
Arrest with wonder Psyche's timid feet; 400
On a gay car, by speckled panthers fleet
Is drawn in gallant state a seeming queen,
And at her foot on low but graceful seat
A gentle nymph of lovely form is seen
In robe of fairest white, with scarf of pleasant green. 405

In strains of most bewitching harmony,
And still adapted to her sovereign's praise,
She filled the groves with such sweet melody
That, quite o'ercome with rapture and amaze,
Psyche stood listening to the warbled lays; 410

---

[14] *mean* lowly, humble.

Yet with a sullen, scarce-approving ear,
Her mistress sits, but with attentive gaze
Her eyes she fixes on a mirror clear
Where still, by fancy's spell, unrivalled charms appear.

And as she looked with aspect ever new,   415
She seemed on change and novel grace intent,
Her robe was formed of ever-varying hue,
And whimsically placed each ornament;
On her attire, with rich luxuriance spent,
The treasures of the earth, the sea, the air,   420
Are vainly heaped her wishes to content;
Yet were her arms and snowy bosom bare,
And both in painted pride shone exquisitely fair.

Her braided tresses in profusion dressed,
Circled with diadem and nodding plumes,   425
Sported their artful ringlets o'er her breast,
And to the breezes gave their rich perfumes;
Her cheek with tint of borrowed roses blooms.
Used to receive from all rich offerings,
She quaffs with conscious right the fragrant fumes   430
Which her attendant from a censer flings,
Who graceful feeds the flame with incense while she sings.

Soon as her glance fair Psyche's form had caught,
Her soft attendant smiling she addressed:
'Behold, Lusinga! Couldst thou e'er have thought   435
That these wild woods were so in beauty blest?
Let but that nymph in my attire be dressed
And scarce her loveliness will yield to mine!
At least invite her in our bower to rest,
Before her eyes let all my splendour shine;   440
Perhaps to dwell with us her heart we may incline.'

With softest smile applauding all she heard,
Lusinga bowing left her golden seat,
And Psyche, who at first in doubt had feared
While listening to the lay so silver-sweet,   445
Now passive followed with unconscious feet –
Till Constance, all alarmed, impatient flew,
And soft his whispers of the maid entreat
To fly the siren's song, for well he knew
What lurking dangers hence would to his Lord ensue.   450

'Oh, do not trust her treacherous lips', he cried,
'She is the subtle slave of Vanity,
Her queen, the child of folly and of pride,

To lure thee to her power each art will try,
Nor ever will release thee peaceably.'   455
He spoke, but spoke in vain, for lo, from far,
Of giant port they fast approaching spy
A knight, high-mounted on a glittering car,
From whose conspicuous crest flames wide a dazzling star.

'Psyche, escape! Ambition is at hand!'   460
The page exclaims, while swift as thought he flies;
She would have followed, but with parley bland
Lusinga soon her terrors pacifies.
'Fair nymph, ascend my car', the sovereign cries,
'I will convey thee where thy wishes lead;   465
Haply the safest course I may advise
How thou thy journey mayst perform with speed,
For ne'er in woods to dwell such beauty was decreed.'

So gently urgent her consent they wooed
With much persuasion of the stranger knight,   470
That yielding Psyche now no more withstood,
But pointing out to her observant sight
The humble cot where she had passed the night,
She prayed her kind conductress there to turn,
And promised to herself what vast delight   475
Her wondering knight would feel at her return,
And with what blushing shame the timid page would burn.

But scarcely had she climbed the fatal car
When swifter than the wind the panthers flew;
The traversed plains and woods, receding far,   480
Soon shut from trembling Psyche's anxious view
The spot where she had left her guardian true;
With desperate efforts, all in vain she tries
To escape the ills which now too sure she knew
Must from her ill-placed confidence arise: 485
Betrayed – ah, self-betrayed! A wretched sacrifice.

She strove to quit the car with sudden bound –
Ah, vain attempt! She now perceived too late
A thousand silken trammels,[15] subtly wound
O'er her fair form, detained her as she sate.   490
Lost in despair she yields to her sad fate,
And silent hears but with augmented fright
The Queen describe her brother's splendid state,
Who now outstripped them by his rapid flight,
And pressed his foaming steeds to gain the arduous[16] height.   495

---

[15]   *trammels* bonds.   [16]   *arduous* lofty.

High o'er the spacious plain a mountain rose,
A stately castle on its summit stood;
Huge craggy cliffs behind their strength oppose
To the rough surges of the dashing flood;
The rocky shores a boldly rising wood   500
On either side conceals; bright shine the towers
And seem to smile upon the billows rude.
In front the eye, with comprehensive powers,
Sees wide-extended plains enriched with splendid bowers.

Hither they bore the sad reluctant fair   505
Who mounts with dizzy eye the awful steep;
The blazing structure seems high-poised in air,
And its light pillars tremble o'er the deep.
As yet the heavens are calm, the tempests sleep,
She knows not half the horrors of her fate,   510
Nor feels the approaching ruin's whirlwind sweep –
Yet with ill-boding fears she passed the gate,
And turned with sickening dread from scenes of gorgeous state.

In vain the haughty master of the hall
Invites her to partake his regal throne;   515
With cold indifference she looks on all
The gilded trophies, and the well-wrought stone
Which in triumphal arches proudly shone.
And as she casts around her timid eye,
Back to her knight her trembling heart is flown,   520
And many an anxious wish, and many a sigh
Invoke his gallant arm protection to supply.

Sudden the lurid heavens obscurely frown,
And sweeping gusts the coming storm proclaim;
Flattery's soft voice the howling tempests drown,   525
While the roofs catch the greedy lightning's flame.
Loud in their fears, the attendant train exclaim
The light-built fabric ne'er can stand the blast,
And all its insecure foundations blame.
Tumultuously they rush: the chief aghast   530
Beholds his throne o'erturned, his train dispersing fast.

Psyche dismayed, yet thoughtful of escape,
In anxious silence to the portal pressed,
And freedom would have hailed in any shape,
Though seen in death's tremendous colours dressed.   535
But ah, she feels the knight's strong grasp arrest
Her trembling steps. 'Think not', he cries, 'to fly
With yon false crowd who by my favours blessed
Can now desert me when with changeful eye
Inclement fortune frowns from yon dark angry sky.'   540

While yet he spoke loud bursts the groaning hall,
With frightful peal the thundering domes resound,
Disjointed columns in wild ruin fall
While the huge arches tremble to the ground.
Yet unappalled amid the crush is found   545
The daring chief: his hold he firm maintains
Though hideous devastation roars around.
Plunged headlong down his prey he still sustains,
Who in his powerful grasp in deathlike swoon remains.

Down sinks the palace with its mighty lord,   550
Hurled from the awful steep with vehemence
Even to the floods below, which angry roared
And gaping wide received the weight immense.
Indignant still, with fearless confidence
He rose, high-mounting o'er the heaving waves;   555
Against their rage one arm is his defence,
The other still his lovely burden saves –
Though strong the billows beat, and fierce the tempest raves.

The blazing star yet shone upon his brow,
And flamed triumphant o'er the dashing main;   560
He rides secure the watery waste, and now
The sheltering shore he might in safety gain;
The sheltering shore he shuns with proud disdain,
And breasts the adverse tide. Ah, rash resource!
Yon vessel, Prince, thou never shalt attain –   565
For plunging mid the deep, with generous force,
See where the lion's lord pursues thy hardy course!

Psyche a well-known voice to life restores,
Once more her eyes unclosing view the light,
But not the waters, nor receding shores,   570
One only object can arrest her sight;
High o'er the flood she sees her valiant knight,
And sudden joy, and hopes (scarce trusted) cheer
Even in that awful moment's dread affright;
Her feeble cry indeed he cannot hear,   575
But sees her outstretched arms, and seems already near.

In vain the giant knight exerts his strength;
Urged by the impetuous youth the lion pressed,
And gaining fast upon his flight, at length
Prepared his daring progress to arrest,   580
And seized with furious jaw his struggling breast;
Gasping he loosed his hold – and Psyche lost
The o'erwhelming wave with ruin had oppressed,
But Constance, ever near when needed most,
The sinking beauty caught and bore her to the coast.   585

Stung with the shame of the relinquished prey,
Mad with revenge, and hate, and conscious pride,
The knight recovers from his short dismay,
And dashed resistless through the foaming tide;
The billows yielding to his arm divide,   590
As rushing on the youth he seeks the shore;
But now a combat strange on either side
Amid the waves begins; each hopes no more
The engulfing deep his foe shall e'er to light restore.

Beside the cold inhospitable lands   595
Where suns long absent dawn with lustre pale,
Thus on his bark the bold Biscayen stands,[17]
And bids his javelin rouse the parent whale;
Fear, pain, and rage at once her breast assail,
The agitated ocean foams around   600
Lashed by the sounding fury of her tail,
Or as she mounts the surge with frightful bound,
Wide echoing to her cries the bellowing shores resound.

Fierce was the contest, but at length subdued,
The youth exulting sees his giant foe.   605
With wonder still the enormous limbs he viewed
Which lifeless now the waves supporting show;
His starréd helm, that now was first laid low,
He seized as trophy of the wondrous fight,
And bade the sparkling gem on Constance glow,   610
While Psyche's eyes, soft-beaming with delight,
Through tears of grateful praise applaud her gallant knight.

CANTO IV

Argument

Introduction – sympathy – suspicion – Psyche benighted – Credulity represented,
according to a picture by Apelles, as an old woman the devoted prey of Slander, or the
Blatant Beast – contest between the knight and Slander – the knight wounded – Slander
flies – Credulity leads Psyche to the castle of Suspicion – Psyche deluded, laments the
desertion of her knight to the train of Inconstancy – Psyche betrayed by Suspicion into
the power of Jealousy – persuaded by him that her knight, by whom she was then
abandoned, was indeed Love – Psyche delivered by her knight – reconciliation

Full gladsome was my heart erewhile to tell
How proud Ambition owned[1] superior Love;
For ah, too oft his sterner power could quell

---

[17] 'The whale fishery, on the coast of Greenland,
was first carried on by the sailors of the Bay of
Biscay. See Goldsmith's Animated Nature, Vol. 6'
(Tighe's note). Tighe refers to Oliver Goldsmith,

An History of the Earth, and Animated Nature (8 vols,
1774).
CANTO IV
[1] *owned* i.e. admitted that Love was superior.

The mild affections which more gently move,
And rather silent fled than with him strove.   5
For Love content and tranquil saw with dread
The busy scenes Ambition's schemes approve,
And, by the hand of Peace obscurely[2] led,
From pride of public life disgusted ever fled.

There are who know not the delicious charm   10
Of sympathising hearts; let such employ
Their active minds; the trumpet's loud alarm
Shall yield them hope of honourable joy,
And courts may lure them with each splendid toy.
But ne'er may vanity or thirst of fame   15
The dearer bliss of loving life destroy!
Oh, blind to man's chief good who Love disclaim,
And barter pure delight for glory's empty name!

Blest Psyche, thou hast 'scaped the tyrant's power!
Thy gentle heart shall never know the pain   20
Which tortures Pride in his most prosperous hour.
Yet dangers still unsung for thee remain,
Nor must thou unmolested hope to gain
Immortal beauty's never-failing spring –
Oh no, nor yet tranquillity attain.   25
But though thy heart the pangs of doubt may sting,
Thy faithful knight shall yet thy steps in safety bring.

Warned by late peril now she scarcely dares
Quit for one moment his protecting eye;
Sure in his sight, her soul of nought despairs,   30
And nought looks dreadful when that arm is nigh
On which her hopes with confidence rely.
By his advice their constant course they bend,
He points where hidden danger they should fly;
On him securely, as her heaven-sent friend,   35
She bids her grateful heart contentedly depend.

Oh who the exquisite delight can tell
The joy which mutual confidence imparts?
Or who can paint the charm unspeakable
Which links in tender bands two faithful hearts?   40
In vain assailed by fortune's envious darts,
Their mitigated woes are sweetly shared,
And doubled joy reluctantly departs.
Let but the sympathising heart be spared,
What sorrow seems not light, what peril is not dared?[3]   45

---

[2] *obscurely* inconspicuously.

[3] *Let but . . . dared?* i.e. if you have a sympathetic companion, any sorrow, however heavy, can be faced, and any peril can be hazarded.

Oh never may suspicion's gloomy sky
Chill the sweet glow of fondly trusting love!
Nor ever may he feel the scowling eye
Of dark distrust his confidence reprove!
In pleasing error may I rather rove,   50
With blind reliance on the hand so dear,
Than let cold prudence from my eyes remove
Those sweet delusions, where nor doubt nor fear
Nor foul disloyalty nor cruel change appear.

The noble mind is ever prone to trust,   55
Yet love with fond anxiety is joined,
And timid tenderness is oft unjust;
The coldness which it dreads too prompt to find,
And torture the too-susceptible mind.
Hence rose the gloom which oft o'er Psyche stole   60
Lest he she loved, unmindful or unkind,
Should careless slight affection's soft control,
Or she, long absent, lose her influence o'er his soul.

'Twas evening, and the shades which sudden fell
Seemed to forebode a dark unlovely night;   65
The sighing wood-nymphs from their caves foretell
The storm which soon their quiet shall affright;
Nor cheering star nor moon appears in sight,
Nor taper twinkles through the rustling leaves
And sheds afar its hóspitable light.   70
But hark, a dismal sound the ear receives,
And through the obscuring gloom the eye strange forms perceives!

It was a helpless female who exclaimed,
Whose blind and aged form an ass sustained;
Misshaped and timorous, of light ashamed,   75
In darksome woods her hard-earned food she gained
And her voracious appetite maintained,
Though all devouring, yet unsatisfied;
Nor aught of hard digestion she disdained –
Whate'er was offered greedily she tried,   80
And meanly served, as slave, whoever food supplied.

A cruel monster now her steps pursued,
Well known of yore and named the Blatant Beast;
And soon he seized his prey with grasp so rude,
So fiercely on her feeble body pressed,   85
That had the courteous knight not soon released
Her unresisting limbs from violence,
She must have sunk by his rough jaws oppressed.
The spiteful beast, enraged at the defence,
Now turned upon the knight with foaming vehemence.   90

But when his fury felt the couchéd spear,
On Psyche's unarmed form he bellowing flew –
'Twas there alone the knight his rage could fear.
Swifter than thought his flaming sword he drew,
And from his hand the doubtful javelin threw   95
Lest erring it might wound the trembling fair:
Eager the cruel monster to subdue
He scorned to use his shield's protecting care,
And rashly left his side in part exposed and bare.

Sharp were the wounds of his avenging steel,   100
Which forced the roaring beast to quit the field;
Yet ere he fled, the knight unused to feel
The power of any foe, or e'er to yield
To any arm which sword or spear could wield,
Perceived the venom of his tooth impure;   105
But, with indignant silence, unrevealed[4]
The pain he bore, while through the gloom obscure
The beast, in vain pursued, urged on his flight secure.

And now the hag, delivered from her fear,
Her grateful thanks upon the knight bestowed,   110
And, as they onward went, in Psyche's ear
Her tongue with many a horrid tale o'erflowed,
Which warned her to forsake that venturous[5] road,
And seek protection in the neighbouring grove
Where dwelt a prudent dame who oft bestowed   115
Her sage advice when pilgrims, doomed to rove,
Benighted there, had else[6] with lurking dangers strove.

The knight now softly bade his charge beware,
Nor trust Credulity, whom well he knew;
Yet he himself, harassed with pain and care,   120
And heedful of the storm which fiercer grew,
Yielded, a path more sheltered to pursue.
Now soon entangled in a gloomy maze
Psyche no longer has her knight in view,
Nor sees his page's star-crowned helmet blaze;   125
Close at her side alone the hag loquacious stays.

Fearful she stops, and calls aloud in vain,
The storm-roused woods roar only in reply;
Anxious her loved protector to regain
She trembling listens to Credulity,   130
Who points where they a glimmering light may spy,

---

[4]   *unrevealed* concealing.   [6]   *else* otherwise.
[5]   *venturous* hazardous, risky.

Which, through the shade of intervening trees
And all the misty blackness of the sky,
Casting a weak and dubious ray she sees,
And fain by this would seek her terrors to appease.   135

Yet hoping that, allured by that same light
Which singly seemed through all the gloom to shine,
She there at last might meet her wandering knight,
Thither her footsteps doubtingly incline,
As best the uncertain path they could divine,   140
All tangled as it wound through brake and briar;
While to affright her soul at once combine
A thousand shapeless forms of terror dire –
Here shrieks the ill-omened bird, there glares the meteor's fire.[7]

In the deep centre of the mazy wood,   145
With matted ivy and wild vine o'ergrown,
A gothic castle solitary stood,
With massive walls built firm of murky stone;
Long had Credulity its mistress known,
Meagre her form and tawny was her hue,   150
Unsociably she lived, unloved, alone,
No cheerful prospects gladdened e'er her view,
And her pale hollow eyes oblique their glances threw.

Now had they reached the sad and dreary bower
Where dark Disfida held her gloomy state.   155
The grated casements strong with iron power,
The huge portcullis creaking o'er the gate,
The surly guards that round the drawbridge wait,
Chill Psyche's heart with sad foreboding fears;
Nor ever had she felt so desolate   160
As when at length her guide the porter hears
And at the well-known call reluctantly appears.

In hall half-lighted with uncertain rays,
Such as expiring tapers transient shed,
The gloomy princess sat, no social blaze   165
The unkindled hearth supplied, no table spread
Cheered the lone guest who weetless[8] wandered,[9]
But melancholy silence reigned around,
While on her arm she leaned her pensive head
And anxious watched, as sullenly she frowned,   170
Of distant whispers low to catch the doubtful sound.

---

[7] Meteors were believed to portend disaster.
[8] *weetless* unknowing, unaware.

[9] *wandered* all three syllables are pronounced, so as to rhyme with 'spread'.

Startled to hear an unaccustomed noise,
Sudden she rose, and on the intruders bent
Her prying eye askance; but soon the voice
Of her old slave appeased her discontent,   175
And a half-welcome to her guests she lent.
Her frequent questions satisfied at last,
Through all the neighbouring woods her scouts she sent
To seek the knight, while Psyche's tears flowed fast,
And all the livelong night in anxious woe she passed.   180

The sullen bell had told the midnight hour,
And sleep had laid the busy world to rest –
All but the watchful lady of that bower
And wretched Psyche; her distracted breast
The agony of sad suspense oppressed.   185
Now to the casement eagerly she flies,
And now the wished-for voice her fancy blessed;
Alas, the screaming nightbird only cries;
Only the drear obscure there meets her straining eyes!

Has thy heart sickened with deferréd hope   190
Or felt the impatient anguish of suspense?
Or hast thou tasted of the bitter cup
Which disappointment's withered hands dispense?
Thou knowest the poison which o'erflowed from hence
O'er Psyche's tedious, miserable hours.   195
The unheeded notes of plaintive Innocence
No longer soothe her soul with wonted powers,
While false Disfida's tales her listening ear devours.

Of rapid torrents and deep marshy fens,
Of ambushed foes and unseen pits they tell,   200
Of ruffians rushing from their secret dens,
Of foul magicians and of wizard spell,
The poisoned lance and net invisible;
While Psyche shuddering sees her knight betrayed
Into the snares of some enchanter fell,   205
Beholds him bleeding in the treacherous shade,
Or hears his dying voice implore in vain for aid.

At length the cruel messengers return,
Their trampling steeds sound welcome in her ear;
Her rapid feet the ground impatient spurn,   210
As eagerly she flies their news to hear.
Alas, they bring no tidings which may cheer
Her sorrowing soul oppressed, disconsolate!
'Dismiss', they cry, 'each idly timid fear!
No dangers now thy faithless knight await,   215
Lured by a wanton fair to bowers of peaceful state.

'We saw him blithely follow where she led,
And urged him to return to thee in vain.
Some other knight, insultingly he said,
Thy charms might soon for thy protection gain,   220
If still resolved to tread with weary pain
The tedious road to that uncertain land.
But he should there contentedly remain;
No other bliss could now his heart demand
Than that new lady's love and kindly proffered hand.'   225

Awhile she stood in silent wonder lost,
And scarce believes the strange abandonment;
No fears like this her heart had ever crossed,
Nor could she think his mind so lightly bent
Could swerve so quickly from its first intent;   230
Till sudden bursting forth in angry mood
Disfida gave her indignation vent,
'Ah, well I know', she cried, 'that wicked brood
Whose cursed ensnaring arts in vain my cares withstood:

'Vile Varia's fickle and inconstant train,   235
Perpetual torments of my harassed days.
Their nightly thefts my fruits, my flowers sustain,
Their wanton goats o'er all my vineyards graze,
My corn lies scattered, and my fences blaze,
My friends, my followers they basely lure;   240
I know their mischievous detested ways.
My castle vainly have I built so sure
While from their treacherous wiles my life is insecure.

'But I will lead thee to the glittering sands
Where shines their hollow many-coloured fane;   245
There, as the circling group fantastic[10] stands,
Thy truant knight perhaps thou mayst regain
From the light arts of that seductive train.'
She paused – but Psyche spoke not in reply;
Her noble heart, which swelled with deep disdain,   250
Forbade the utterance of a single sigh,
And shamed the indignant tear which started to her eye.

At length with firm but gentle dignity,
And cold averted eye, she thus replies:
'No, let him go. Nor power nor wish have I   255
His conduct to control. Let this suffice;
Before my path a surer guardian flies
By whose direction onward I proceed

---

[10] *fantastic* grotesque.

Soon as the morn's first light shall clear the skies.'
She ceased, then, languishing her griefs to feed,   260
Her cold dark chamber sought from observation freed.

'Twas there regret indulged the bitter tear;
She feels herself forsaken and alone.
'Behold', she cries, 'fulfilled is every fear,
Oh wretched Psyche, now indeed undone!   265
Thy love's protecting care no more is shown,
He bids his servant leave thee to thy fate,
Nor longer will the hopeless wanderer own.
Some fairer, nobler spouse, some worthier mate,
At length by Venus given shall share his heavenly state.   270

'Oh most adored, oh most regretted love!
Oh joys that never must again be mine,
And thou lost hope, farewell! Vainly I rove,
For never shall I reach that land divine,
Nor ever shall thy beams celestial shine   275
Again upon my sad unheeded way!
Oh let me here with life my woes resign,
Or in this gloomy den for ever stay,
And shun the scornful world, nor see detested day.

'But no, those scenes are hateful to mine eyes,   280
And all who spoke or witnessed my disgrace;
My soul with horror from this dwelling flies
And seeks some tranquil, solitary place
Where grief may finish life's unhappy race!'
So passed she the long night, and soon as morn   285
Had first begun to show his cheerful face,
Her couch, which care had strewn with every thorn,
With heavy heart she left, disquieted, forlorn.

Not thus Disfida suffered her to part,
But urged her there in safety to remain,   290
Repeating oft to her foreboding heart
That fairy land she never could attain.
But when she saw dissuasion was in vain,
And Psyche bent her journey to pursue,
With angry brow she called a trusty train   295
And bade them keep the imprudent fair in view,
And guard her dangerous path with strict observance true.

In vain their proffered service she declines,
And dreads the convoy of the scowling band;
Their hateful presence with her loss combines,   300
She feels betrayed to the destroyer's hand,

And trembling wanders o'er the dreary land.
While as she seeks to escape Disfida's power,
Her efforts still the officious guards withstand,
Led in vain circles many a tedious hour,[11]   305
Undistanced still she sees the gloomy turrets lour.

Till, wearied with her fruitless way, at length
Upon the ground her fainting limbs she threw;
No wish remained to aid exhausted strength,
The mazy path she cared not to pursue,   310
Since unavailing was the task she knew.
Her murmuring guards to seek for food prepare,
Yet mindful of their charge, still keep in view
The drooping victim of their cruel care,
Who sees the day decline in terror and despair.   315

Hark! – a low hollow groan she seems to hear
Repeated oft; wondering she looks around.
It seemed to issue from some cavern near,
Or low hut hidden by the rising ground;
For, though it seemed the melancholy sound   320
Of human voice, no human form was nigh;
Her eye no human habitation found,
But as she listening gazed attentively,
Her shuddering ears received the deep and long-drawn sigh.

The guard who nearest stood now whispering said,   325
'If aught of doubt remain within thy mind,
Or wish to know why thus thou wert betrayed,
Or what strange cause thy faithless knight inclined
To leave the charge he with such scorn resigned,
Each curious thought thou now mayst satisfy,   330
Since here the entrance of a cave we find
Where dwells, deep hid from day's too-garish eye,[12]
A sage whose magic skill can solve each mystery.'

He stayed[13] not her reply, but urged her on
Reluctant to the dark and dreary cave;   335
No beam of cheerful heaven had ever shone
In the recesses of that gloomy grave
Where screaming owls their daily dwelling crave.
One sickly[14] lamp the wretched master showed –
Devouring fiend! Who now the prey shall save   340
From his fell gripe,[15] whose hands in blood imbrued,[16]
In his own bosom seek his lacerated food?

---

[11]   *tedious hour* Weller notes the same phrase in Keats,
The Eve of St Agnes 79.
[12]   *day's too-garish eye* the sun.
[13]   *stayed* awaited.

[14]   *sickly* weak, failing.
[15]   *fell gripe* cruel grasp.
[16]   *imbrued* stained.

On the damp ground he sits in sullen woe,
But wildly rolls around his frenzied eye
And gnaws his withered lips, which still o'erflow   345
With bitter gall; in foul disorder lie
His black and matted locks; anxiety
Sits on his wrinkled brow and sallow cheek;
The wasted form, the deep-drawn, frequent sigh
Some slow-consuming malady bespeak,   350
But medicinal skill the cause in vain shall seek.

'Behold', the treacherous guard exclaimed, 'behold,
At length Disfida sends thy promised bride!
Let her, deserted by her knight, be told
What peerless lady lured him from her side;   355
Thy cares her future safety must provide.'
Smiling maliciously as thus he spoke,
He seemed her helpless anguish to deride;
Then swiftly rushing from the den he broke,
Ere from the sudden shock astonished she awoke.   360

She too had fled, but when the wretch escaped
He closed the cavern's mouth with cruel care,
And now the monster placed his form misshaped
To bar the passage of the affrighted fair.
Her spirits die, she breathes polluted air,   365
And vaporous visions swim before her sight;
His magic skill the sorcerer bids her share,
And lo, as in a glass, she sees her knight
In bower remembered well – the bower of loose Delight!

But oh, what words her feelings can impart,   370
Feelings to hateful envy near allied!
While on her knight her anxious glances dart,
His plumed helmet, lo! he lays aside;
His face with torturing agony she spied,
Yet cannot from the sight her eyes remove;   375
No mortal knight she sees had aid supplied,
No mortal knight in her defence had strove –
'Twas Love, 'twas Love himself, her own adoréd Love!

Poured in soft dalliance at a lady's feet,
In fondest rapture he appeared to lie,   380
While her fair neck with inclination sweet
Bent o'er his graceful form her melting eye,
Which his looked up to meet in ecstasy.
Their words she heard not; words had ne'er expressed
What well her sickening fancy could supply,   385
All that their silent eloquence confessed,
As breathed the sigh of fire from each impassioned breast.

While thus she gazed, her quivering lips turn pale;
Contending passions rage within her breast,
Nor ever had she known such bitter bale,   390
Or felt by such fierce agony oppressed.
Oft had her gentle heart been sore distressed,
But meekness ever has a lenient power
From anguish half his keenest darts to wrest;
Meekness for her had softened sorrow's hour,   395
Those furious fiends subdued which boisterous souls devour.

For there are hearts that, like some sheltered lake,
Ne'er swell with rage, nor foam with violence;
Though its sweet placid calm the tempests shake,
Yet will it ne'er with furious impotence   400
Dash its rude waves against the rocky fence
Which Nature placed the limits of its reign.
Thrice blessed who feel the peace which flows from hence,
Whom meek-eyed gentleness can thus restrain;
Whate'er the storms of fate, with her let none complain!   405

That mild associate Psyche now deserts,
Unlovely passions agitate her soul,
The vile magician all his art exerts,
And triumphs to behold his proud control.
Changed to a serpent's hideous form, he stole   410
O'er her fair breast to suck her vital blood;
His poisonous involutions[17] round her roll.
Already is his forked tongue imbrued[18]
Warm in the stream of life, her heart's pure purple flood.

Thus wretchedly she falls Geloso's prey,   415
But her, once more, unhoped-for aid shall save!
Admitted shines the clear blue light of day
Upon the horrors of that gloomy grave.
Her knight's soft voice resounds through all the cave –
The affrighted serpent quits his deadly hold   420
Nor dares the vengeance of his arm to brave,
Shrunk to a spider's form, while many a fold
Of self-spun web obscene the sorcerer vile enrolled.

Scarce had the star of his attendant youth
Blazed through the cavern and proclaimed the knight,   425
When all those spells and visions of untruth,
Bred in dark Erebus[19] and nursed in night,
Dissolving vanished into vapour light;
While Psyche, quite exhausted by her pains,

---

[17] *involutions* tangles, coils.   [19] *Erebus* darkness.
[18] *imbrued* plunged, embedded.

And hardly trusting her astonished sight,   430
  Now faint and speechless in his arms remains,
Nor memory of the past, nor present sense retains.

Borne from the cavern and to life restored,
  Her opening eyes behold her knight once more,
  She sees whom lost with anguish she deplored;   435
  Yet a half-feigned resentment still she bore,
  Nor sign of joy her face averted wore,
  Though joy unuttered panted at her heart;
  In sullen silence much she pondered o'er
What from her side induced him to depart,   440
And all she since had seen by aid of magic art.

Was it then all a false deluding dream
  That wore the semblance of celestial Love?
  On this her wavering thoughts bewildered seem
  At length to rest; yet onward as they move,   445
  Though much his tender cares her doubts reprove,
  And though she longs to hear and pardon all,
  Silence she still preserves; awhile he strove
  Her free and cheerful spirits to recall,
But found the task was vain – his words unnoticed fall. 450

Now in his turn offended and surprised,
  The knight in silence from her side withdrew;
  With pain she marked it, but her pain disguised,
  And heedless seemed her journey to pursue,
  Nor backward deigned to turn one anxious view   455
  As oft she wished; till, mindful of his lord,
  Constance alarmed affectionately flew,
  Eager to see their mutual peace restored,
And blames her cold reserve in many a soft-breathed word.

'Oh Psyche, wound not thus thy faithful knight   460
  Who fondly sought thee many an anxious hour,
  Though bleeding yet from that inglorious fight,
  Where thou wert rescued from the savage power
  Of that fell beast who would thy charms devour;
  Still faint with wounds, he ceased not to pursue   465
  Thy heedless course. Let not displeasure lour
  Thus on thy brow; think not his heart untrue!
Think not that e'er from thee he willingly withdrew!'

With self-reproach and sweet returning trust,
  While yet he spoke, her generous heart replies,   470
  Soft-melting pity bids her now be just
  And own the error which deceived her eyes;

Her little pride she longs to sacrifice
And ask forgiveness of her suffering knight –
Her suffering knight, alas, no more she spies,   475
  He has withdrawn offended from her sight,
Nor can that gentle voice now hope to stay his flight.

Struggling no more her sorrows to restrain,
Her streaming eyes look round with anxious fear –
Nor are those tender showers now shed in vain.   480
Her soft lamenting voice has reached his ear
Where latent he had marked each precious tear;
Sudden as thought behold him at her feet.
Oh reconciling moment, charm most dear!
What feeling heart thy pleasures would repeat,   485
Or wish thy dearly purchased bliss, however sweet?

The smiles of joy which swell her glowing cheek,
And o'er her parting lips divinely play,
Returning pleasure eloquently speak,
Forgetful of the tears which lingering stay   490
(Like sparkling dewdrops in a sunny day),
Unheeded tenants of rejoicing eyes.
His wounds her tender care can well repay;
There grateful kindness breathes her balmy sighs –
Beneath her lenient hand how swiftly suffering flies!   495

Freed from the mazes of Disfida's groves,
The opening landscape brightens to their view;
Psyche, with strength revived, now onward moves
In cheerful hope, with courage to renew
Repeated toils, and perils to pursue.   500
Thus when some tender plant neglected pines,
Shed o'er its pendent head the kindly dew –
How soon refreshed its vivid lustre shines!
Once more the leaf expands, the drooping tendril twines.

Thus cheered, the knight entreats her to impart   505
The dangers which her way had since befell;
Her timid lips refuse to speak the art
Which clothed him in a form she loved so well:
That she had thought him Love, she blushed to tell!
Confused she stopped, a gentle pause ensued;   510
What chance had brought him to the demon's cell
She then enquires; what course he had pursued,
And who his steps had led throughout the mazy wood.

Sooth he had much to say, though modest shame
His gallant deeds forbade him to declare;   515

For while through those bewildering woods he came,
Assisted by his page's active care,
He had detected Varia's wily snare,
And forced her wanton retinue to flee.
With like disgrace, malignant in despair,   520
Disfida's slaves their plots defeated see,
Their feeble malice scorned, their destined victims free.

But he had marked the traces of their feet,
And found the path which to the cavern led;
Whence now, rejoicing in reunion sweet,   525
Their way together cheerfully they tread,
Exempt awhile from danger and from dread;
While Psyche's heart, with confidence more bold,
Full oft the hour of rapture pictured
When those celestial charms she should behold,   530
And feel the arms of Love once more his bride enfold.

Canto V

Argument

Introduction – charm of poetry – Psyche beholds the Palace of Chastity – pleads for the admission of her knight – obtains it through the intervention of Hymen – hymn celebrating the triumphs of Chastity – Psyche, enraptured, desires to devote herself solely to the service of Chastity – entrusted by her to the protection of the knight – Psyche's voyage – tempest – coast of Spleen – Psyche received and sheltered by Patience

Delightful visions of my lonely hours!
Charm of my life and solace of my care!
Oh would the muse but lend proportioned powers,
And give me language equal to declare
The wonders which she bids my fancy share,   5
When rapt in her to other worlds I fly,
See angel forms unutterably fair,
And hear the inexpressive harmony
That seems to float on air, and warble through the sky.

Might I the swiftly glancing scenes recall,   10
Bright as the roseate clouds of summer's eve,
The dreams which hold my soul in willing thrall
And half my visionary days deceive,
Communicable shape might then receive,
And other hearts be ravished with the strain!   15
But scarce I seek the airy threads to weave,
When quick confusion mocks the fruitless pain,
And all the fairy forms are vanished from my brain.

Fond dreamer, meditate thine idle song!
But let thine idle song remain unknown;   20
The verse which cheers thy solitude, prolong;
What though it charm no moments but thine own?
Though thy loved Psyche smile for thee alone,
Still shall it yield thee pleasure, if not fame,
And when, escaped from tumult, thou hast flown   25
To thy dear silent hearth's enlivening flame,
There shall the tranquil muse her happy votary claim!

My Psyche's wanderings then she loves to trace;
Unrolls the glowing canvas to my sight;
Her chaste calm eye, her soft attractive grace,   30
The lightning of her heavenly smile so bright,
All yield me strange and unconceived delight.
Even now entranced her journey I pursue,
And gaze enraptured on her matchless knight –
Visions of love, pure, innocent and true;   35
Oh may your graceful forms for ever bless my view!

See as they tread the green, soft-levelled plain,
Where never weed, nor noxious plant was found!
Psyche, enchanted, bids her knight explain
Who rules that lovely and well-cultured ground   40
Where fairest flowers and purest springs abound.
'Oh object of my anxious cares', he cried,
As with a half-breathed sigh he gazed around,
'A stranger here, full oft I vainly tried
Admittance to obtain, and soothe the sovereign's pride. 45

'Here Castabella reigns, whose brow severe
Oft chilled my sanguine spirit by its frown;
Yet have I served her with adoring fear,
Though her ungrateful scorn will oft disown
The faithful homage by her servant shown;   50
Me she hath banished from her fair domain
For crimes my loyal heart had never known;
While thus excluded vainly I complain,
And feel another's guilt my injured honour stain.

'With false assumption of my arms and name,   55
Knight of the Bleeding Heart miscalled too long,
A vile impostor has disgraced my fame,
And much usurped by violence and wrong,
Which to the virgin Queen by right belong.
On me her irritated vengeance falls –   60
On me, repulsed by force of arms so strong
That, never suffered to approach her walls,
Unheard, indignant truth in vain for justice calls.

'Yet she alone our progress can assist,
And thou, oh Psyche, must her favour gain;   65
Nor from thy soft entreaties e'er desist
Till thou free entrance for thy knight obtain.
Here let his faithful services remain
Fixed on thy grateful heart, nor thou consent,
Nor let their force thy gentleness constrain   70
To leave him, thus disgraced, yet innocent,
Thine undeserved neglect forsaken to lament.'

While yet he speaks, before her ravished eyes
The brilliant towers of Castabella shine.
The sun that views them from unclouded skies   75
Sheds not through heaven a radiance more divine;
The adamantine walls with strength combine
Inimitable lustre ever clear.
Celestial temple, 'tis not lips like mine
Thy glories can reveal to mortal ear,   80
Or paint the unsullied beams which blaze for ever here.

Approaching now the well-defended gates
Which, placed at distance, guard the sacred fane,
Their lowly suit a stern repulse awaits;
The timid voice of Psyche pleads in vain,   85
Nor entrance there together can they gain.
While yet they stay, unwilling to retreat,
The dove, swift-sailing through the ethereal plain,[1]
Has reached already Castabella's seat,
And in her spotless breast has found a welcome sweet.   90

Caressing oft her well-remembered guest,
Serener smiles illumed her softened brow;
The heaven-sent messenger her soul confessed,
And mildly listened to his murmurs low,
Which seemed in pleading eloquence to flow;   95
His snowy pinions then he wide displayed,
And gently lured her from her throne to go
Even to the gates, where Psyche blushing stayed
Beside her awestruck knight half-doubtingly afraid.

That form majestic might the bravest awe,   100
Yet Psyche gazed with love unmixed with fear,
And felt those charms her soul attracted draw
As to maternal tenderness most dear.
Congenial souls! They at one glance appear

CANTO V
[1] *the ethereal plain* the sky.

Linked to each other by a mutual tie;   105
Her courteous voice invites her to draw near.
And lo, obedient to their sovereign's eye,
To Psyche's willing steps the barriers open fly!

But to the lion and his gallant lord
Sudden the affrighted guards the portals close.   110
Psyche looks back and, mindful of her word,
Mindful of him who saved her from her foes,
Guide of her course and soother of her woes,
The tear that started to her downcast eye,
The deepening blush which eloquently rose,   115
Silent assistant of the pleading sigh,
To speed the unuttered suit their powers persuasive try.

And now the knight, encouraged to approach,
Asserts his injured fame, and justice claims,
Confutes each charge, repels each foul reproach,   120
And each accusing falsehood boldly shames,
While conscious innocence his tongue inflames.
A firm attachment to her reign he vows,
The base impostor's guilty madness blames,
And, while the imputed crimes his spirit rouse,   125
No intercourse with him his nobler soul allows.

Meantime his faithful page had not been mute,
And he had found a ready warm ally –
For while his master urged the eager suit,
As through the goodly train[2] he cast his eye,   130
He chanced exulting mid the group to spy
A joyous youth, his fondly-cherished friend,
Hymen, the festive, love-attending boy,
Delighted his assistance hastes to lend,
Laughing unbars the gates, and bids the parley end.   135

Around their Queen the timid virgins crowd,
Who half-consentingly receives the knight,
And checks her sportive boy, whose welcome loud
Speaks his gay triumph and his proud delight.
Yet graceful smiles her happy guests invite   140
To share the feast with sacred honours blessed;
The palace opens to their dazzled sight;
Still as they gazed, the adoring eye confessed
That wondering awe which filled each consecrated breast.

---

[2]   *train* of attendants.

All was divine, yet still the fairest Queen   145
Like Dian[3] mid her circling nymphs appeared,
Or as Minerva[4] on Parnassus[5] seen,
When condescendingly with smiles she cheered
.The silent Muses who her presence feared.
A starry crown its heavenly radiance threw   150
O'er her pale cheek; for there the rose revered
The purer lilies of her saint-like hue,
Yet oft the mantling blush its transient visits knew.

The hand of Fate, which wove of spotless white
Her wondrous robe, bade it unchangeable   155
Preserve unsullied its first lustre bright,
Nor e'er might be renewed that sacred spell
If once destroyed – wherefore, to guard it well,
Two handmaids she entrusts with special care,
Prudence and Purity, who both excel,   160
The first in matron dignity of air,
The last in blooming youth unalterably fair.

Favourite of heaven, she at her birth received
With it the brilliant zone that bound her waist,
Which, were the earth of sun and stars bereaved,   165
By its own light beneficently cast
Could cheer the innocent, and guide the chaste.
Nor armour ever had the virgin bore,
Though oft in warlike scenes her youth she passed,
For while her breast this dazzling cestus[6] wore,   170
The foe who dared to gaze beheld the light no more.

But when her placid hours in peace are spent,
Concealed she bids its latent terrors lie,
Sheathed in a silken scarf, with kind intent
Wove by the gentle hand of Modesty;   175
And see, the blushing maid with downcast eye
Behind her mistress bides her charms retired!
While foremost of the group, of stature high,
Firm Courage lifts her brow by Truth inspired,
Who holds a crystal lamp in flames celestial fired.   180

See, fresh as Hebe,[7] blooming Temperance stand,
Present the nectared fruits, and crown the bowl!

---

[3] *Dian* virgin goddess of the moon, permitted by
Zeus to have a train of sixty Oceanides and twenty
other nymphs, all virgins.
[4] *Minerva* daughter of Zeus.

[5] *Parnassus* mountain sacred to the Muses.
[6] *cestus* belt.
[7] *Hebe* Juventas, goddess of youth.

While bright-eyed Honour leads the choral band,
Whose songs divine can animate the soul,
Led willing captive to their high control.   185
They sing the triumphs of their spotless Queen,
And proudly bid immortal fame enrol
Upon her fairest page such as had been
The champions of her cause, the favourites of her reign.

From Pallas[8] first begins the lofty song,   190
And Cynthia,[9] brightest goddess of the skies;
To her the virgin deities belong,
And each beholds her with a sister's eyes;
The mystic honours next of Fauna[10] rise,
Her solemn rites which purest hands require;   195
And Vesta,[11] who her virgins taught to prize,
And guard the sacred symbols of the fire
Which earth could ne'er revive if suffered to expire.

Emblem divine of female purity,
Whose trust betrayed to like sad fate shall doom;   200
Pursued by scorn, consigned to infamy,
The hapless victims perish in their bloom
Mid the dark horrors of a living tomb;
Effulgent Queen, thou wilt the pure defend
From the dark night of this opprobrious gloom;   205
Nor even with life thy favouring smiles shall end;
They bid illustrious fame beyond the grave extend.

First of the noble youths whose virtue shone,
Conspicuous chief in Castabella's train,
They sing the firm unmoved Bellerophon,[12]   210
And Peleus flying the Magnesian plain[13]
Pursued by all a wanton's fierce disdain.
You too, Hippolytus,[14] their songs employ –
Beloved by Phaedra, but beloved in vain –

---

[8] *Pallas* Minerva, mentioned at l. 147 above.
[9] *Cynthia* Diana, the moon.
[10] 'Fauna, called also the Bona Dea, during her life was celebrated for the exemplary purity of her manners, and after death was worshipped only by women' (Tighe's note).
[11] *Vesta* goddess of hearth and home, in whose round temple there burned continuously a flame tended by virgins. The extinguishing of the fire was believed to presage national disaster.
[12] *the firm unmoved Bellerophon* Stenobaea, in love with Bellerophon, denounced him to her husband Proetus when he did not respond to her advances.

[13] At this point Tighe inserted a note quoting what is effectively her source, Horace, *Ode* III vii 13–18:

Ut Praetum mulier perfida credulum
Falsis impulerit criminibus, nimis
    Casto Bellerophonti
    Maturare necem, refert,
Narrat pene datum Pelea Tartaro,
Magnessam Hyppolyten dum fugit abstinens.

Peleus aroused the ire of Acastus, king of Iolchos, when the king's wife, Astydamia, having failed to seduce him, accused him of raping her.
[14] *Hippolytus* was loved by Phaedra, the wife of his father, Theseus, but he did not return her love.

With the chaste honours of the Hebrew boy,[15]　　　　　　　215
Which time shall ne'er obscure, nor idle scorn destroy.

Nor was unsung whom on Hymettus' brow[16]
The bright Aurora wooed with amorous care;
He, mindful of his sacred nuptial vow,
Refused the goddess though celestial fair,　　　　　　　220
Breathing pure perfumes and ambrosial air.
Of wanton Circe's baffled arts they tell,
And him, too wise her treacherous cup to share,
Who scorned the enchantress and her mystic spell,[17]
And all the sirens' arts could gloriously repel.[18]　　　　225

The long-tried virtue of his faithful spouse[19]
Now sweetly animates the tuneful string –
Unsullied guardian of her virgin vows,
Who twice ten years had wept her wandering king.
Acastus' mourning daughter[20] next they sing,　　　　230
The chaste embrace which clasped her husband's shade;
And thee, Dictynna,[21] who, with daring spring,
Called from the Cretan rock on Dian's aid –
And still the goddess loves her favourite luckless maid.

Pleased to assume herself a name so dear　　　　　　235
She bids her altars to Dictynna rise;
Thus called, she ever turns, with willing ear,
To aid each nymph who for her succour cries.
See how the trembling Arethusa[22] flies
Through pathless woods, o'er rocks and open plains;　　240
In vain to escape the ravisher she tries –
Fast on her rapid flight Alpheus gains,
And scarce her fainting strength the unequal course sustains.

---

[15] 'Joseph' (Tighe's note).

[16] 'Cephalus' (Tighe's note). Though married to Procris, a princess of Athens, Cephalus was pursued by Aurora. Hymettus is a mountain two miles southeast of Athens, known for its honey.

[17] Circe was an enchantress, daughter of the sun, who turned half of Ulysses' men to stone; Ulysses himself defied her arts by the use of the herb moly.

[18] The sirens were sea-nymphs whose singing was so seductive that all who heard them forgot to eat and died. Ulysses was tied to the mast while his companions stopped their ears with wax.

[19] *faithful spouse* Penelope who, while Ulysses was fighting in the Trojan wars, was beseiged by suitors who she kept at bay by pretending to be weaving a shroud for her father-in-law Laertes. Ulysses slaughtered them all on his return.

[20] 'Laodamia' (Tighe's note). She was the daughter of Acastus, King of Iolchus, and wife of Protesilaus, a Thessalian king, the first of the Greeks to land at Troy, immediately killed by Hector. She so missed him that Hermes restored him to her for three hours, after which she stabbed herself.

[21] 'A virgin of Crete, who threw herself from a rock into the sea when pursued by Minos. The Cretans, not contented with giving her name to the rock which she had thus consecrated, were accustomed to worship Diana by the name of her unfortunate votary' (Tighe's note).

[22] *Arethusa* a nymph pursued by the god of the River Alpheus, who fell in love with her; she was turned into a fountain by Diana.

And now more near his dreaded step she hears,
His lengthened shadow flies before her feet;   245
Now o'er her neck his panting breath appears
To part her locks which, in disorder sweet,
Ambitious seemed to fan the fervid heat
That flushed her glowing cheek and heightened charms.
Hear how her gasping sighs for aid entreat!   250
'Dictynna, pitying see my just alarms,
And snatch thy fainting maid from those polluting arms.'

The goddess hears, and in a favouring cloud
Conceals her suppliant from Alpheus' sight;
In vain he looks around and calls aloud,   255
And wondering seeks the traces of her flight.
Enveloped, still she views him with affright –
An icy coldness creeps o'er all her frame,
And soon, dissolving in a current bright,
The silver stream retains her honoured name,   260
And still unmingled flows, and guards its virgin fame.

'Twas thus Castalia's sacred fountain[23] sprung,
Once a fair nymph by bright Apollo loved;
To Daphne[24] too his amorous strain he sung,
But sung in vain – her heart remained unmoved,   265
No vain delight her modest virtue proved
To be the theme of all his wanton lays.
To shun the god the sylvan scene she roved,
Nor prized the flattery of his tuneful praise,
Nor one relenting smile his splendid gifts could raise.   270

Yet were his lips with eloquence endued,
And melting passion warbled o'er his lyre,
And had she yielding listened as he wooed,
The virgin sure had caught the kindling fire
And fallen a victim to impure desire;   275
For safety cautious flight alone remained,
While tears of trembling innocence require
Her parents' aid – and lo, that aid obtained,
How suddenly her charms immortal laurels gained!

Dear to the Muses still her honours live,   280
And they too glory in their virgin name;
To pure delights their tranquil hours they give,
And fear to mingle with a grosser flame

---

[23] *Castalia's sacred fountain* fons Castalius, a spring rising in Mt Parnassus, near Castalia. The fountain was sacred to the Muses and Apollo.

[24] *Daphne* nymph with whom Apollo fell in love. He pursued her down the banks of the River Peneus; she was saved by being turned into a laurel.

The chaster fires which heaven hath bid them claim.
They smiled when Pan,[25] on Ladon's banks deceived,   285
The fair Syringa clasped who, snatched from shame,
Already had her tuneful form received,
And to the breathing winds in airy music grieved.

Still in that tuneful form[26] to Dian dear
She bids it injured innocence befriend,   290
Commands her train the sentence to revere,
And in her grove the vocal reeds suspend
Which Virtue may from calumny defend.
Self-breathed, when virgin purity appears,
What notes melodious they spontaneous send!   295
While the rash guilty nymph with horror hears
Deep groans declare her shame to awestruck wondering ears.

The spotless virgins shall unhurt approach
The stream's rude ordeal,[27] and the sacred fire.
See the pure maid, indignant of reproach,   300
The dreadful test of innocence require
Amid the holy priests and virgin choir!
See her leap fearless on the blazing shrine!
The lambent flames, bright-circling, all aspire
Innoxious[28] wreaths around her form to twine,   305
And crown with lustrous beams the virgin's brow divine.

Nor was the daring Clusia[29] then unsung
Who plunged illustrious from the lofty tower;
The favouring winds around the virgin clung,
And bore her harmless from the tyrant's power;   310
Nor those whom Vesta in the trying hour[30]
Protects from slander, and restores to fame;

---

[25] Pan pursued Syrinx, an Arcadian nymph, but at the River Ladon she was changed by the gods into a reed. The Ladon was a tributary of the River Alpheus in Arcadia.

[26] 'In a grove, sacred to Diana, was suspended a syrinx (the pipe into which the nymph Syringa had been metamorphosed) which was said to possess the miraculous power of thus justifying the calumniated' (Tighe's note).

[27] 'The trial of the Stygian fountain, by which the innocent were acquitted, and the guilty disgraced; the waters rising in a wonderful manner, so as to cover the laurel wreath of the unchaste female, who dared the examination' (Tighe's note).

[28] *Innoxious* harmless.

[29] 'Who, to avoid the violence of Torquatus, cast herself from a tower, and was preserved by the winds which, swelling her garments, supported her as she gently descended to the earth' (Tighe's note).

[30] 'Claudia, a vestal who, having been accused of violating her vow, attested her innocence by drawing up the Tiber a ship bearing a statue of the goddess, which many thousand men had not been able to remove. Æmilia, who was suspected of unchastity from having inadvertently suffered the sacred flame to expire, by entrusting it to the care of a novice, but, imploring Vesta to justify her innocence, she tore her linen garment, and threw it upon the extinguished ashes of the cold altar; when, in the sight of priests and virgins, a sudden and pure fire was thus enkindled. Tucia who, being falsely accused, carried water from the Tiber to the forum in a sieve, her accuser miraculously disappearing at the same time' (Tighe's note).

Nor Clelia,[31] shielded from the arrowy shower;
Nor thou whose purest hands[32] the sibyls claim,
And bid the modest fane revere Sulpicia's name.   315

O'er her soft cheek how arch the dimples play,
While pleased the goddess bears Sinope's wiles![33]
How oft she mocked the changeful lord of day,
And many a sylvan god who sought her smiles –
But chief when Jove her innocence beguiles.   320
'Grant me a boon', the blushing maid replies,
Urged by his suit. Hope o'er his amorous toils
Exulting dawns. 'Thine oath is past', she cries;
'Unalterably pure, thy spotless virgin dies!'

Rome shall for ages boast Lucretia's name![34]   325
And while its temples moulder into dust
Still triumph in Virginia's rescued fame,[35]
And Scipio's[36] victory over baffled lust.
Even now the strain, prophetically just,
In unborn servants bids their Queen rejoice,   330
And in her British beauties firmly trust.
Thrice happy fair, who still adore her voice,
The blushing virgin's law, the modest matron's choice!

Psyche with ravished ear the strain attends,
Enraptured hangs upon the heaven-strung lyre;   335
Her kindling soul from sensual earth ascends;
To joys divine her purer thoughts aspire;
She longs to join the white-robed spotless choir
And there for ever dwell a hallowed guest.
Even Love himself no longer can inspire   340
The wishes of the soft enthusiast's breast
Who, filled with sacred zeal, would there for ever rest.

---

[31] A Roman hostage held by the Etruscans, Cloelia swam the Tiber with other hostages to escape Porsenna, 508 BC.
[32] 'Sulpicia, a Roman lady of remarkable chastity; chosen by the sibyls to dedicate a temple to Venus Verticordia, in order to obtain greater purity for her contemporary countrywomen' (Tighe's note).
[33] 'The nymph Sinope, being persecuted by the addresses of Jupiter, at length stipulated for his promise to grant her whatever she might ask, and having obtained this promise, claimed the gift of perpetual chastity. "Sinope / Nympha prius, blandosque Jovis quæ luserat ignes / Coelicolis inmota procis" (Val. Flac. lib. v. ver. 110)' (Tighe's note). 'Sinope, once a nymph and one who mocked Jove's ardent wooing,

unmoved by heavenly suitors', Valerius Flaccus, *Argonautica* v 109–11.
[34] Lucretia was a celebrated Roman beauty, of the fifth century BC, who won a contest as to the best representative of womanly virtues. Her rape led to a popular uprising.
[35] A similar story: Virginia's father tried to force her into the arms of Appius Claudius, even though she was engaged to another man whom she loved. In the end her father stabbed her, precipitating a popular uprising.
[36] *Scipio* Publius Cornelius Scipio (236–184 BC), Roman general who distinguished himself in the Punic Wars and was accused of debauchery and corruption in later life. Mary would have known of him from her reading of the Roman historian, Livy.

Despising every meaner low pursuit,
And quite forgetful of her amorous care,
All heedless of her knight who, sad and mute,   345
With wonder hears the strange ungrateful fair,
A prostrate suppliant, pour the fervent prayer
To be received in Castabella's train,
And that in tranquil bliss secluded there,
Her happy votary still she might remain,   350
Free from each worldly care, and each polluting stain.

With gracious smile the Queen her favourite heard,
And fondly raised, and clasped her to her breast;
A beam of triumph in her eye appeared,
While ardent Psyche offered her request,   355
Which to the indignant knight her pride confessed.
'Farewell, mistaken Psyche!' he exclaims,
Rising at length with grief and shame oppressed,
'Since thy false heart a spouse divine disclaims,
I leave thee to the pomp which here thy pride inflames.'   360

'Yet stay, impetuous youth', the Queen replies,
Abashed, irresolute as Psyche stands,
'My favourite's happiness too dear I prize,
Far other services my soul demands .
Than those which here in these sequestered lands   365
Her zeal would pay; no, let her bear my fame
Even to the bowers where Love himself commands.
There shall my votary reign secure from blame,
And teach his myrtle groves to echo to my name.

'My lovely servant still defend from harms,   370
And stem with her yon strong opposing tide –
Haste, bear her safely to her lover's arms!
Be it thy care with steady course to guide
The light-winged bark I will myself provide.
Depart in peace, thou chosen of my heart;   375
Leave not thy faithful knight's protecting side.
Dear to me both, oh may no treacherous art
Your kindred souls divide, your fair alliance part!

'Here rest tonight; tomorrow shall prepare
The vessel which your destined course shall speed.   380
Lo, I consign my Psyche to thy care,
Oh gallant youth, for so hath fate decreed,
And Love himself shall pay the generous meed',
She said, and joined their unreluctant hands.
The grateful knight, from fear and sorrow freed,   385
Receives with hope revived the dear commands,
And Psyche's modest eye no other law demands.

Now Peace with downy step and silent hand
Prepares for each the couch of soft repose –
Fairest attendant; she with whispers bland   390
Bids the obedient eye in slumbers close.
She too the first at early morning goes
With light-foot Cheerfulness the guests to greet
Who, soothed by quiet dreams, refreshed arose,
Ready the labours of the day to meet,   395
But first due homage pay at Castabella's feet.

Bright was the prospect which before them shone;
Gay danced the sunbeams o'er the trembling waves.
Who that the faithless ocean had not known,
Which now the strand in placid whispers laves,   400
Could e'er believe the rage with which it raves
When angry Boreas bids the storm arise,
And calls his wild winds from their wintry caves?
Now soft Favonius breathes his gentlest sighs,[37]
Auspicious omens wait, serenely smile the skies.   405

The eager mariners now seize the oar,
The streamers flutter in the favouring gale.
Nor unattended did they leave the shore;
Hymen, whose smiles shall o'er mischance prevail,
Sits at the helm, or spreads the swelling sail.   410
Swift through the parting waves the vessel flies,
And now at distance scarce can Psyche hail
The shore, so fast receding from her eyes,
Or bless the snowy cliffs which o'er the coast arise.

Pleased with her voyage and the novel scene,   415
Hope's vivid ray her cheerful heart expands.
Delighted now she eyes the blue serene,
The purple hills, and distant rising lands,
Or, when the sky the silver queen commands,
In pleasing silence listens to the oar   420
Dashed by the frequent stroke of equal hands,
Or asks her knight if yet the promised shore
May bless her longing eyes when morn shall light restore?

The impatient question oft repeated thus
He smiling hears, and still with many a tale,   425
Or song of heavenly lore unknown to us
Beguiles the livelong night, or flagging sail
When the fresh breeze begins their bark to fail.
Strong ran the tide against the vessel's course,

---

[37] Boreas is the north wind, Favonius the west wind.

And much they need the kind propitious gale 430
Steady to bear against its rapid force
And aid the labouring oars, their tedious last resource.

But lo, the blackening surface of the deep
With sullen murmurs now begins to swell,
On ruffled wing the screaming sea-fowl sweep 435
The unlovely surge, and piteous seem to tell
How from the low-hung clouds with fury fell
The demons of the tempest threatening rage;
There, brooding future terrors, yet they dwell,
Till with collected force dread war they wage, 440
And in convulsive gusts the adverse winds engage.

The trembling Psyche, supplicating Heaven,
Lifts to the storm her fate-deploring eye,
Sees o'er her head the livid lightnings driven;
Then, turned in horror from the blazing sky, 445
Clings to her knight in speechless agony.
He all his force exerts the bark to steer,
And bids the mariners each effort try
To escape the rocky coast which threatens near,
For Hymen taught the youth that dangerous shore to fear. 450

Who has not listened to his tuneful lay,
That sings so well the hateful cave of Spleen?
Those lands, submitted to her gloomy sway,
Now open to their view a dreary scene,
As the sad subjects of the sullen Queen 455
Hang o'er the cliffs, and blacken all the strand;
And where the entrance of the cave is seen
A peevish, fretful, melancholy band,
Her ever-wrangling slaves in jarring concert stand.

Driven by the hurricane they touch the shore, 460
The frowning guards prepare to seize their prey,
The knight (attentive to the helm no more)
Resumes his arms, and bids his shield display
Its brilliant orb. 'Psyche, let no dismay
Possess thy gentle breast', he cheerly cries, 465
'Behind thy knight in fearless safety stay,
Smile at the dart which o'er thee vainly flies,
Secure from each attack their powerless rage despise.

'Soon shall the fury of the winds be past,
Serener skies shall brighten to our view; 470
Let us not yield to the imperious blast
Which now forbids our vessel to pursue

Its purposed course. Soon shall the heavens renew
Their calm clear smile, and soon our coward foes,
Despairing thus our courage to subdue,   475
Shall cease their idle weapons to oppose,
And unmolested peace restore our lost repose.'

Still as he spoke, where'er he turned his shield
The darts drop quivering from each slackened bow;
Unnerved each arm, no force remains to wield   480
The weighty falchion, or the javelin throw;
Each voice half-choked expires in murmurs low,
A dizzy mist obscures their wondering sight,
Their eyes no more their wonted fury know,
With stupid awe they gaze upon the knight,   485
Or, as his voice they hear, trembling disperse in flight.

Yet raged the storm with unabated power;
A little creek the labouring vessel gains;
There they resolve to endure the blustering hour,
The dashing billows, and the beating rains.   490
Soon as the bark the sheltering bay attains,
And in the shallows moored securely rides,
Attentive still to soften all her pains,
The watchful knight for Psyche's ease provides;
Some fisher's hut perchance the shelving harbour hides. 495

Deep in the sterile bank a grotto stood,
Whose winding caves repel the inclement air,
Worn in the hollowed rock by many a flood
And sounding surge that dashed its white foam there,
The refuge now of a defenceless fair   500
Who, issuing thence, with courteous kind intent
Approached the knight, and kindly bade him share
Whatever good indulgent Heaven had lent
To cheer her hapless years in lonely suffering spent.

More sweet than health's fresh bloom the wan hue seemed 505
Which sat upon her pallid cheek; her eye,
Her placid eye, with dove-like softness beamed;
Her head unshielded from the pitiless sky,
Loose to the rude wild blast her tresses fly;
Bare were her feet which pressed the shelly shore   510
With firm unshrinking step; while smilingly
She eyes the dashing billows as they roar,
And braves the boisterous storms so oft endured before.

Long had she there in silent sorrow dwelt,
And many a year resigned to grief had known;   515
Spleen's cruel insolence she oft had felt,

But never would the haughty tyrant own,
Nor heed the darts which, from a distance thrown,
Screened by her cavern she could safely shun;
The thorny brakes she trod for food alone,   520
Drank the cold stream which near the grotto run,
And bore the winter's frosts and scorching summer's sun.

In early youth, exchanging mutual vows,
Courage had wooed and won his lovely bride;
Tossed on those stormy seas, her daring spouse   525
From her fond arms the cruel waves divide,
And dashed her fainting on that rock's rough side.
Still hope she keeps, and still her constant heart
Expects to hail with each returning tide
His dear remembered bark; hence can no art   530
From those unlovely scenes induce her to depart.

When the vexed seas their stormy mountains roll,
She loves the shipwrecked mariner to cheer;
The trembling wretch escaped from Spleen's control,
Deep in her silent cell conceals his fear,   535
And panting finds repose and refuge here;
Benevolently skilled each wound to heal,
To her the sufferer flies, with willing ear
She woos them all their anguish to reveal,
And while she speaks, they half forget the woes they feel.   540

Now to her cave has Patience gently brought
Psyche, yet shuddering at the fearful blast;
Largely she heaped with hóspitable thought
The blazing pile, and spread the pure repast;
O'er her chilled form her own soft mantle cast,   545
And soothed her wearied spirits to repose
Till all the fury of the storm is past,
Till swift receding clouds the heavens disclose,
And o'er subsiding waves pacific[38] sunshine glows.

CANTO VI

Argument

Introduction – the power of Love to soften adversity – exhortation to guard Love from
the attacks of ill-temper, which conduct to indifference and disgust – Psyche becalmed
– Psyche surprised and carried to the island of Indifference – pursued and rescued by
her knight – the voyage concluded – Psyche brought home beholds again the temple
of Love – is reunited to her lover, and invited by Venus to receive in heaven her
apotheosis – conclusion

---

[38] *pacific* peaceful.

When pleasure sparkles in the cup of youth,
And the gay hours on downy wing advance,
Oh then 'tis sweet to hear the lip of truth
Breathe the soft vows of love, sweet to entrance
The raptured soul by intermingling glance   5
Of mutual bliss; sweet amid roseate bowers,
Led by the hand of Love, to weave the dance,
Or unmolested crop[1] life's fairy flowers,
Or bask in joy's bright sun through calm unclouded hours.

Yet they who light of heart in Mayday pride   10
Meet Love with smiles and gaily amorous song
(Though he their softest pleasures may provide,
Even then when pleasures in full concert throng) –
They cannot know with what enchantment strong
He steals upon the tender suffering soul,   15
What gently soothing charms to him belong,
How melting sorrow owns his soft control,
Subsiding passions hushed in milder waves to roll.

When vexed by cares and harassed by distress,
The storms of fortune chill thy soul with dread,   20
Let Love, consoling Love, still sweetly bless,
And his assuasive balm benignly shed.
His downy plumage o'er thy pillow spread
Shall lull thy weeping sorrows to repose;
To Love the tender heart hath ever fled,   25
As on its mother's breast the infant throws
Its sobbing face, and there in sleep forgets its woes.

Oh fondly cherish then the lovely plant
Which lenient Heaven hath given thy pains to ease;
Its lustre shall thy summer hours enchant,   30
And load with fragrance every prosperous breeze,
And when rude winter shall thy roses seize,
When nought through all thy bowers but thorns remain,
This still with undeciduous[2] charms shall please,
Screen from the blast and shelter from the rain,   35
And, still with verdure, cheer the desolated plain.

Through the hard season Love with plaintive note,
Like the kind redbreast, tenderly shall sing,
Which swells mid dreary snows its tuneful throat,
Brushing the cold dews from its shivering wing,   40
With cheerful promise of returning spring

CANTO VI   [2]   *undeciduous* enduring, permanent.
[1]   *crop* pick, pluck.

To the mute tenants of the leafless grove.
Guard thy best treasure from the venomed sting
Of baneful peevishness – oh, never prove
How soon ill-temper's power can banish gentle Love!   45

Repentance may the storms of passion chase,
And Love, who shrunk affrighted from the blast,
May hush his just complaints in soft embrace,
And smiling wipe his tearful eye at last.
Yet when the wind's rude violence is past,   50
Look what a wreck the scattered fields display!
See on the ground the withering blossoms cast,
And hear sad Philomel with piteous lay
Deplore the tempest's rage that swept her young away.

The tears capricious Beauty loves to shed,   55
The pouting lip, the sullen silent tongue,
May wake the impassioned lover's tender dread,
And touch the spring that clasps his soul so strong;
But ah, beware, the gentle power too long
Will not endure the frown of angry strife;   60
He shuns contention, and the gloomy throng
Who blast the joys of calm domestic life,
And flies when Discord shakes her brand with quarrels rife.

Oh he will tell you that these quarrels bring
The ruin, not renewal of his flame;   65
If oft repeated, lo, on rapid wing
He flies to hide his fair but tender frame –
From violence, reproach, or peevish blame
Irrevocably flies. Lament in vain!
Indifference comes the abandoned heart to claim,   70
Asserts for ever her repulsive reign,
Close followed by Disgust and all her chilling train.

Indifference, dreaded power, what art shall save
The good so cherished from thy grasping hand?
How shall young Love escape the untimely grave   75
Thy treacherous arts prepare? Or how withstand
The insidious foe who, with her leaden band,
Enchains the thoughtless, slumbering deity?
Ah, never more to wake or e'er expand
His golden pinions to the breezy sky,   80
Or open to the sun his dim and languid eye.

Who can describe the hopeless, silent pang
With which the gentle heart first marks her sway?
Eyes the sure progress of her icy fang

Resistless, slowly fastening on her prey;   85
Sees rapture's brilliant colours fade away,
And all the glow of beaming sympathy;
Anxious to watch the cold averted ray
That speaks no more to the fond meeting eye
Enchanting tales of love, and tenderness, and joy.   90

Too faithful heart, thou never canst retrieve
Thy withered hopes; conceal the cruel pain!
O'er thy lost treasure still in silence grieve,
But never to the unfeeling ear complain:
From fruitless struggles dearly-bought refrain,[3]   95
Submit at once – the bitter task resign,
Nor watch and fan the expiring flame in vain;
Patience, consoling maid, may yet be thine,
Go seek her quiet cell, and hear her voice divine!

But lo, the joyous sun, the soft-breathed gales   100
By zephyrs sent to kiss the placid seas,
Curl the green wave, and fill the swelling sails;
The seamen's shouts which jocund hail the breeze
Call the glad knight the favouring hour to seize.
Her gentle hostess Psyche oft embraced,   105
Who still solicitous her guest to please
On her fair breast a talisman had placed,
And with the valued gem her parting blessing graced.

How gaily now the bark pursues its way
Urged by the steady gale, while round the keel   110
The bubbling currents in sweet whispers play,
Their force repulsive now no more they feel;
No clouds the unsullied face of heaven conceal,
But the clear azure one pure dome displays,
Whether it bids the star of day reveal   115
His potent beams, or Cynthia's milder rays
On deep cerulean skies invite the eye to gaze.

Almost unconscious they their course pursue,
So smooth the vessel cuts the watery plain;
The wide horizon to their boundless view   120
Gives but the sky and Neptune's ample reign.
Still the unruffled bosom of the main
Smiles undiversified by varying wind;
No toil the idle mariners sustain

---

[3]   *From fruitless struggles dearly-bought refrain* i.e. refrain
from dearly-bought struggles that will turn out to be
fruitless.

While, listless, slumbering o'er his charge reclined,   125
The pilot cares no more the unerring helm to mind.

With light exulting heart glad Psyche sees
Their rapid progress as they quit the shore,
Yet weary languor steals by slow degrees[4]
Upon her tranquil mind; she joys no more   130
The never-changing scene to wander o'er
With still admiring eye; the enchanting song
Yields not that lively charm it knew before,
When first enraptured by his tuneful tongue
She bade her vocal knight the heavenly strain prolong.   135

A damp chill mist now deadens all the air,
A drowsy dullness seems o'er all to creep;
No more the heavens their smile of brightness wear.
The winds are hushed, while the dim glassy deep
Oppressed by sluggish vapours seems to sleep;   140
See his light scarf the knight o'er Psyche throws,
Solicitous his lovely charge to keep
From still increasing cold, while deep repose
Benumbs each torpid sense and bids her eyelids close.

Now as with languid stroke they ply the oars   145
While the dense fog obscures their gloomy way,
Hymen, well-used to coast these dangerous shores,
Roused from the dreaming trance in which he lay,
Cries to the knight in voice of dread dismay,
'Steer hence thy bark, oh yet in time beware;   150
Here lies Petrea, which with baneful sway
Glacella rules – I feel the dank cold air,
I hear her chilling voice, methinks it speaks despair!'

Even while he speaks, behold the vessel stands
Immoveable! In vain the pilot tries   155
The helm to turn; fixed in the shallow strands,
No more obedient to his hand it lies;
The disappointed oar no aid supplies
While sweeping o'er the sand it mocks their force.
The anxious knight to Constance now applies,   160
To his oft-tried assistance has recourse,
And bids his active mind design some swift resource.

Debating doubtfully awhile they stood,
At length on their united strength rely

---

[4]   *by slow degrees* Weller notes that Keats borrows this
phrase, *The Eve of St Agnes* 13.

To force the bark on the supporting flood: 165
They rouse the seamen who half-slumbering lie,
Subdued and loaded by the oppressive sky;
Then, wading mid the fog, with care explore
What side the deepest waters may supply,
And where the shallows least protect the shore,   170
While through their darksome search the star sheds light before.

Meantime deep slumbers of the vaporous mist
Hang on the heavy eyelids of the fair;
And Hymen too, unable to resist
The drowsy force of the o'erwhelming air,   175
Laid at her feet at length forgets his care –
When lo, Glacella's treacherous slaves advance,
Deep wrapped in thickest gloom! The sleeping fair[5]
They seize, and bear away in heedless trance,
Long ere her guardian knight suspects the bitter chance.   180

Thus the lorn traveller imprudent sleeps
Where his high glaciers proud Locendra[6] shows;
Thus o'er his limbs resistless torpor creeps,
As yielding to the fatal deep repose
He sinks benumbed upon the Alpine snows   185
And sleeps no more to wake, no more to view
The blooming scenes his native vales disclose,
Or ever more the craggy path pursue,
Or o'er the lichened steep[7] the chamois chase renew.

Lo, to their Queen they bear their sleeping prey,   190
Deep in her ice-built castle's gloomy state;
There on a pompous couch they gently lay
Psyche, as yet unconscious of her fate,
And when her heavy eyes half-opening late
Dimly observe the strange and unknown scenes,   195
As in a dream she views her changed estate,[8]
Gazing around with doubtful, troubled mien –
Now on the stupid crowd, now on their dull proud Queen.

With vacant smile, and words but half-expressed,
In one ungracious, never-varying tone,   200

---

[5] *fair* 'fair' (1811); 'pair' (1805). Although my copy-text is 1805, I have here preferred the reading of 1811. There is nothing to suggest that Hymen is also abducted by Glacella's slaves. When he next appears, at lines 358–60, he appears to have remained on board throughout.
[6] 'The immense glaciers, which crown the summit of the mountain of Locendra, supply a lake, and, issuing from this source, the river Reuss flows through the valley of St Gothard' (Tighe's note).
[7] 'The lichen, which is the exclusive winter food of the reindeer in Lapland, contributes also very considerably to the subsistence of the Alpine chamois' (Tighe's note).
[8] *estate* state, condition.

Glacella welcomes her bewildered guest,
And bids the chief supporter of her throne
Approach and make their mighty mistress known –
Proud Selfishness, her dark ill-favoured lord!
Her gorgeous seat, which still he shared alone,   205
He slowly leaves obedient to her word,
And ever as he moved the cringing train adored.

Nought of his shapeless form to sight appears;
Impenetrable furs conceal each part;
Harsh and unpleasing sounds in Psyche's ears   210
That voice which had subdued full many a heart;
While he, exerting every specious art,
Persuades her to adore their Queen's control;
Yet would he not Glacella's name impart,
But with false title (which she artful stole   215
From fair Philosophy) deludes the erring soul.

'Rest, happy fair', he cries, 'who here hast found
From all the storms of life a safe retreat,
Sorrow thy breast henceforth no more shall wound,
Nor care invade thee in this quiet seat.   220
The voice of the distressed no more shall meet
The sympathising ear; another's woes
Shall never interrupt the stillness sweet
Which here shall hush thee to serene repose,
Nor damp the constant joys these scenes for thee disclose.   225

'Fatigue no more thy soft and lovely frame
With vain benevolence and fruitless care;
No deep-heaved sigh shall here thy pity claim,
Nor hateful want demand thy wealth to share;
For thee shall Independence still prepare   230
Pleasures unmingled, and for ever sure;
His lips our sovereign's peaceful laws declare,
Centre existence in thyself secure,
Nor let an alien shade thy sunshine e'er obscure.'

He spoke, and lo, unnumbered doors unfold,   235
And various scenes of revelry display;
Here Grandeur sunk beneath the massive gold;
Here discontented Beauty pined away
And, vainly conscious, asked her promised sway;
Here Luxury prepared his sumptuous feast   240
While lurking Apathy behind him lay
To poison all the insipid food he dressed,
And shake his poppy crown o'er every sated guest.

The hireling minstrels strike their weary lyre
And slumber o'er the oft-repeated strain;   245
No listless youth to active grace they fire,
Here Eloquence herself might plead in vain,
Nor one of all the heartless crowd could gain.
And thou, oh sweeter than the Muses' song,
Affection's voice divine, with cold disdain   250
Even thou art heard, while mid the insulting throng
Thy daunted, shivering form moves timidly along!

Thus o'er the oiléd surface softly slides
The unadmitted stream, rapid it flows,
And from the impervious plain pellucid glides;   255
Repulsed with gentle murmurs thus it goes,
Till in the porous earth it finds repose,
Concealed and sheltered in its parent's breast –
Oh man's best treasure in this vale of woes!
Still cheer the sad, and comfort the distressed,   260
Nor ever be thy voice by Selfishness oppressed!

Psyche with languid step he leads around,
And bids her all the castle's splendour see.
Here Dissipation's constant sports abound,
While her loose hand, in seeming bounty free,   265
Her scentless roses, painted mimicry,
Profusely sheds; here Pride unheeded tells
To nodding crowds his ancient pedigree,
And Folly with reiterated spells
To count her spotted cards the yawning group compels.   270

'See how, attentive to her subjects' ease',
To their reluctant prey exclaims her guide,
'Each meeting joy⁹ of life she bids them seize,
Anxious for each gay pastime to provide;
See her fast-spreading power increasing wide,   275
Adored and worshipped in each splendid dome!
Lo, Beauty glows for ever at her side!
She bids her cheek the unvarying rose assume
And Bacchus sees for her his votive ivy bloom.¹⁰

'Is aught then wanting in this fairy bower?   280
Or is there aught which yet thy heart can move?'
That heart, unyielding to their sovereign's power,
In gentle whispers sighing, answers, 'Love!'
While scornful smiles the fond reply reprove,

---

⁹ *meeting joy* joyful reveller approaching each subject.   ¹⁰ Bacchus, god of wine and vegetation, is usually represented with a crown of ivy leaves.

'Lo!' he exclaims, 'thy vanquished Cupid view: 285
He oft with powerful arms had vainly strove
Our sovereign's rocky fortress to subdue;
Now, subject to her reign, he yields obedience due.'

Wondering she gazed around and, where he points,
An idiot child in golden chains she spies,   290
Rich cumbrous gems load all his feeble joints,
A gaudy bandage seels[11] his stupid eyes,
And foul Desire his short-lived torch supplies.
By the capricious hand of Fashion led,
Her sudden starts with tottering step he tries   295
Submissive to attend; him had she bred,
And Selfishness himself the nursling ever fed.

With lustre false his tinsel arms to deck
Ungraceful ornaments around him shone
(Gifts of his sportive guide);[12] she round his neck   300
A glittering cord insultingly had thrown,
Loading its pendent purse with many a stone
And worthless dross, and, ever as he went,
His leaden darts, with wanton aim unknown,
Now here, now there, in careless chance she sent,   305
That oft their blunted force in empty air was spent.

Shocked, from the gross imposture Psyche turned
With horror and disgust her fearful eye;
Her fate forlorn in silent anguish mourned,
And called her knight with many a hopeless sigh.   310
But see, the crowds in sudden tumult fly!
The doors, fast closing to exclude some foe,
Proclaim to Psyche's hopes her hero nigh –
Escaping from her guard she flies, when lo!
His form the bursting gates in awful beauty show.   315

'Fly from these dangerous walls', his page exclaims,
'Swift let us haste our floating bark to gain!
See thy knight's wondrous dart in terror flames;
Soon shall these ice-built walls no shape retain,
Nor can their Queen his dreaded sight sustain.'   320
Scarcely she heard while rapidly she fled,
Even as a bird, escaped the wily train[13]
The fowler with destructive art had spread,
Nor panting stays its flight, nor yet foregoes its dread.

---

[11] *seels* blindfolds; spelled in this way, it recalls the   [12] *his sportive guide* Fashion.
practice of sewing up the eyes of hawks when train-   [13] *train* snare, trap.
ing them.

See how astonished now the crowd supine,   325
Roused by his potent voice, confused arise;
In tottering masses o'er their heads decline
Dissolving walls; they gaze with wild surprise,
And each affrighted from the ruin flies.
Pitying he views the vain unfeeling band   330
Beneath his care, a vile and worthless prize;
Their Queen alone his vengeful arms demand,
But unknown force was hers his terrors to withstand.

A shield she had of more than gorgon[14] power,
And whom she would she could transform to stone,   335
Nor ever had it failed her till that hour.
She proves his form invincible alone,
And calls its force petrific[15] on her own.
Amazed he sees the indurated[16] train,
The callous tenants of the silent throne,   340
And all the marble subjects of their reign,
Inviolably hard, their breathless shape retain.

The magic shield he thence in triumph bore,
Resolved, in pity to the human race,
Her noxious hands its might should guide no more,   345
And bade the seas conceal its Hydra[17] face.
Oh kindly meant, though much-defeated grace!
For though the o'erwhelming weight of sounding waves
Conceal its rugged orb a little space,
Snatched by Glacella from the dark deep caves,   350
Once more the arm of Love with potent spell it braves.

But Psyche, rescued from their cruel scorn,
Urges her knight to hasten from the shore;
The buoyant vessel on the billows borne
Rides proudly o'er the mounting surge once more;   355
Again they spread the sails, the feathered oar
Skims with impatient stroke the sparkling tide;
The blushing Hymen now their smiles restore
Again to frolic gaily at their side,
Though still their playful taunts reproach their slumbering guide.   360

Psyche looks back with horror on the coast –
Black, drear, and desolate is all the scene.

---

[14] *gorgon* the gorgons were three sisters who had   [16] *indurated* hardened.
serpents in their hair, and could turn into stone anyone   [17] *Hydra* a monster with many heads, each of which
on whom they looked.   were replaced by two or more if cut off.
[15] *petrific* capable of turning something to stone.

The rocky cliffs still human shape may boast;
There the sad victims of the cruel Queen,
Memorials of her baneful power, are seen.   365
No vine-crowned hills, no glowing vales appear,
Nor the white cottage laughs upon the green;
The black and leafless thorn alone is there,
And the chill mountains lift their summits wild and bare.

Her spirits lighten as they leave behind   370
The dreary prospect of Glacella's isle;
She blessed with gladdened heart the light-winged wind
That bears her swiftly from a scene so vile;
With glistening eye, and hope's prophetic smile,
She hears her knight foretell their dangers o'er,   375
That sure success shall crown their fated toil,
And soon arriving at that happy shore
Love shall again be found, and leave his bride no more.

Now, from light slumbers and delicious dreams,
The jocund cry of joy aroused the fair;   380
The morn that kissed her eyes with golden beams
Bade her the universal transport share;
Divinely breathed the aromatic air,
And Psyche's heart, half-fainting with delight,
In the peculiar odour wafted there   385
Recalled the breezes which, o'er scenes most bright,
Their wings of perfume shook, and lingering stayed their flight.

The lovely shore the mariners descry
And many a gladsome cheer the prospect hails;
Its graceful hills rise full before the eye,   390
While eagerly expanding all their sails
They woo the freshness of the morning gales.
The approaching scenes new opening charms display,
And Psyche's palpitating courage fails –
She sees arrived at length the important day,   395
Uncertain yet of power the mandate to obey.

But one dear object every wish confines,
Her spouse is promised in that bower of rest;
And shall the sun, that now so cheerful shines,
Indeed behold her to his bosom pressed,   400
And in his heavenly smiles of fondness blessed?
Oh 'tis too much! Exhausted life she fears
Will struggling leave her agitated breast,
Ere to her longing eyes his form appears,
Or the soft hand of Love shall wipe away her tears.   405

Oh how impatience gains upon the soul
When the long-promised hour of joy draws near!
How slow the tardy moments seem to roll!
What spectres rise of inconsistent fear!
To the fond doubting heart its hopes appear   410
Too brightly fair, too sweet to realize;
All seem but daydreams of delight too dear!
Strange hopes and fears in painful contest rise,
While the scarce-trusted bliss seems but to cheat the eyes.

But safely anchored in the happy port,   415
Led by her knight the golden sands she pressed.
His heart beat high, his panting breath heaved short,
And sighs proclaim his agitated breast
By some important secret thought oppressed.
'At length', he cries, 'behold the fated spring!   420
Yon rugged cliff conceals the fountain blest
(Dark rocks its crystal source o'ershadowing)
And Constance swift for thee the destined urn shall bring.'

He speaks but scarce she hears, her soul intent
Surveys as in a dream each well-known scene.   425
Now from the pointed hills her eye she bent
Inquisitive o'er all the sloping green:
The graceful temple meet for Beauty's queen,
The orange groves that ever-blooming glow,
The silvery flood, the ambrosial air serene,   430
The matchless trees that fragrant shade bestow,
All speak to Psyche's soul, all seem their Queen to know.

Let the vain rover who his youth hath passed
Misled in idle search of happiness,
Declare, by late experience taught at last,   435
In all his toils he gained but weariness,
Wooed the coy goddess but to find that less
She ever grants where dearest she is bought;
She loves the sheltering bowers of home to bless,
Marks with her peaceful hand the favourite spot,   440
And smiles to see that Love has home his Psyche brought.

On the dear earth she kneels the turf to press,
With grateful lips and fondly streaming eyes.
'Are these the unknown bowers of Happiness?
Oh justly called, and gained at last!' she cries,   445
As eagerly to seize the urn she flies.
But lo, while yet she gazed with wondering eye
Constance ascends the steep to gain the prize,

The eagle's eyrie is not built so high
As soon she sees his star bright blazing to the sky.   450

    With light and nimble foot the boy descends,
    And lifts the urn triumphant in his hand;
    Low at the turf-raised altar Psyche bends,
    While her fond eyes her promised Love demand;
    Close at her side her faithful guardians stand,   455
    As thus with timid voice she pays her vows:
    'Venus, fulfilled is thine adored command,
    Thy voice divine the suppliant's claim allows,
The smile of favour grant, restore her heavenly spouse.'

    Scarce on the altar had she placed the urn,   460
    When lo, in whispers to her ravished ear[18]
    Speaks the soft voice of Love! 'Turn, Psyche, turn,
    And see at last, released from every fear,
    Thy spouse, thy faithful knight, thy lover here!'
    From his celestial brow the helmet fell;   465
    In joy's full glow, unveiled his charms appear,
    Beaming delight and love unspeakable,
While in one rapturous glance their mingling souls they tell.

    Two tapers thus, with pure converging rays,
    In momentary flash their beams unite,   470
    Shedding but one inseparable blaze
    Of blended radiance and effulgence bright,
    Self-lost in mutual intermingling light;
    Thus, in her lover's circling arms embraced,
    The fainting Psyche's soul, by sudden flight,   475
    With his its subtlest essence interlaced;
Oh bliss too vast for thought! By words how poorly traced!

    Fond youth, whom Fate hath summoned to depart,
    And quit the object of thy tenderest love,
    How oft in absence shall thy pensive heart   480
    Count the sad hours which must in exile move,
    And still their irksome weariness reprove?
    Distance with cruel weight but loads thy chain
    With every step which bids thee further rove,
    While thy reverted eye, with fruitless pain,   485
Shall seek the trodden path its treasure to regain.

    For thee what rapturous moments are prepared!
    For thee shall dawn the long-expected day!
    And he who ne'er thy tender woes hath shared,

---

[18]   *ravished ear* a phrase borrowed by Keats, as Weller
observes, *Lamia* i 268.

Hath never known the transport they shall pay   490
To wash the memory of those woes away.
The bitter tears of absence thou must shed
To know the bliss which tears of joy convey,
When the long hours of sad regret are fled,
And in one dear embrace thy pains compensated!   495

Even from afar beheld, how eagerly
With rapture thou shalt hail the loved abode!
Perhaps already, with impatient eye,
From the dear casement she hath marked thy road,
And many a sigh for thy return bestowed.   500
Even there she meets thy fond enamoured glance;
Thy soul with grateful tenderness o'erflowed,
Which firmly bore the hand of hard mischance,
Faints in the stronger power of joy's o'erwhelming trance.

With Psyche thou alone canst sympathise,   505
Thy heart benevolently shares her joy!
See her unclose her rapture-beaming eyes,
And catch that softly pleasurable sigh
That tells unutterable ecstasy!
While hark, melodious numbers[19] through the air   510
On clouds of fragrance wafted from the sky,
Their ravished souls to pious awe prepare!
And lo, the herald doves the Queen of Love declare!

With fond embrace she clasped her long-lost son,
And gracefully received his lovely bride,[20]   515
'Psyche, thou hardly[21] hast my favour won!'
With roseate smile her heavenly parent cried,
'Yet hence thy charms immortal, deified,
With the young Joys, thy future offspring fair,
Shall bloom for ever at thy lover's side;   520
All ruling Jove's high mandate I declare,
Blessed denizen of Heaven, arise its joys to share!'

She ceased, and lo, a thousand voices, joined
In sweetest chorus, Love's high triumph sing!
There, with the Graces and the Hours entwined,   525
His fairy train their rosy garlands bring,
Or round their mistress sport on halcyon wing;
While she enraptured lives in his dear eye
And drinks immortal love from that pure spring
Of never-failing full felicity,   530
Bathed in ambrosial showers of bliss eternally!

---

[19] *numbers* music.   [21] *hardly* boldly, daringly.
[20] *lovely bride* Weller notes a recollection in Keats,
The Eve of St Agnes 334.

Dreams of Delight, farewell! Your charms no more
Shall gild the hours of solitary gloom!
The page remains – but can the page restore
The vanished bowers which Fancy taught to bloom?   535
Ah no! Her smiles no longer can illume
The path my Psyche treads no more for me;
Consigned to dark oblivion's silent tomb
The visionary scenes no more I see –
Fast from the fading lines the vivid colours flee!   540

From Psyche, with Other Poems (third edition, 1811)

ON RECEIVING A BRANCH OF MEZEREON[1] WHICH FLOWERED AT WOODSTOCK, DECEMBER 1809[2]

Odours of spring, my sense ye charm
  With fragrance premature;
And mid these days of dark alarm,
  Almost to hope allure.
Methinks with purpose soft ye come   5
  To tell of brighter hours,
Of May's blue skies, abundant bloom,
  Her sunny gales and showers.

Alas, for me shall May in vain
  The powers of life restore;   10
These eyes that weep and watch in pain
  Shall see her charms no more.
No, no, this anguish cannot last,
  Beloved friends, adieu!
The bitterness of death were past,   15
  Could I resign but you.

But oh, in every mortal pang
  That rends my soul from life,
That soul, which seems on you to hang
  Through each convulsive strife,   20
Even now, with agonizing grasp
  Of terror and regret,
To all in life its love would clasp
  Clings close and closer yet.

ON RECEIVING A BRANCH OF MEZEREON
[1] *Mezereon* a species of the Daphne shrub unusual in that it produces sweet scented flowers very early in the year on dead-looking, leafless stems.
[2] William Tighe, the editor of the 1811 volume, appended the following note to this poem: 'The concluding poem of this collection was the last ever composed by the author, who expired at the place where it was written, after six years of protracted malady, on 24 March 1810, in the thirty-seventh year of her age. Her fears of death were perfectly removed before she quitted this scene of trial and suffering, and her spirit departed to a better state of existence, confiding with heavenly joy in the acceptance and love of her Redeemer'.

Yet why, immortal, vital spark, 25
    Thus mortally oppressed?
Look up, my soul, through prospects dark,
    And bid thy terrors rest;
Forget, forego thy earthly part,
    Thine heavenly being trust – 30
Ah vain attempt! my coward heart
    Still shuddering clings to dust.

Oh ye who soothe the pangs of death
    With love's own patient care,
Still, still retain this fleeting breath, 35
    Still pour the fervent prayer;
And ye whose smile must greet my eye
    No more, nor voice my ear,
Who breathe for me the tender sigh
    And shed the pitying tear, 40

Whose kindness (though far far removed)
    My grateful thoughts perceive,
Pride of my life, esteemed, beloved,
    My last sad claim receive!
Oh do not quite your friend forget, 45
    Forget alone her faults;
And speak of her with fond regret
    Who asks your lingering thoughts.

Sydney Owenson, Lady Morgan (1777–1859)

Sydney Owenson was one of the most prolific and successful writers of her time, producing over seventy volumes of fiction, poetry, non-fictional prose, and even an opera. Her total profits from her writing are estimated to have been £25,000 – an enormous amount for the time. And she was the first woman to be awarded a pension for her services to literature – £300 per annum, granted by Lord Melbourne (widowed husband of Lady Caroline Lamb) in 1837.

She was apparently born on Christmas Day[1] aboard the Dublin packet in the Irish Sea, the eldest child of the actor and singer Robert MacOwen by his wife Jane Hill, the daughter of a prosperous Shrewsbury tradesman and staunch Methodist (MacOwen later anglicized his name at the behest of a patron). A proud nationalist, she always regarded the location of her birth as having been Ireland; as she put it in her auto-biography: 'My father was a Celtic Irishman, my mother was a Saxon; and "I had the

---

[1] The year of her birth is disputed. Lionel Stevenson argues for 1776, while S. C. Hall who as a personal friend had reason to know, says it was 1777. This is the date favoured by John Andrew Hamilton in the *DNB*, and in the absence of more reliable evidence it is the date I have accepted. It should be noted, however, that Ann Jones favours 1780–?82, while Gayla S. McGlamery chooses ?1778.

good fortune", as Paddy O'Carrol says, "to come over to Ireland to be borned"'.[2] In early childhood, she was, like so many women of her time, educated by her mother who, she recalled, 'had received as much education as women of her class ever received in England – and no more. She had no accomplishments, no artistic tendencies, but she was a good English scholar, and was thoroughly well acquainted with the popular English literature of her time. She was familiar with the works of Pope, Addison (she had his *Spectator* by heart), all Shenstone's innocent pastorals, which she discordantly hummed, and taught us to the music of Jackson of Exeter.'[3] After Sydney's mother died in 1789, she was sent first to the school of Madame Terson at Clontarf (one of the best schools in Ireland), and later to a finishing school in Dublin. She grew up feeling pride for her country's traditions and heritage. Although a Protestant, she became passionately committed at a young age to the cause of Catholic emancipation; that, and her support of republican governments, was to win her the hatred of Tory reviewers such as Gifford and Croker in later years.

Brought up among theatrical people, it was no doubt from them that she acquired her enduring love of Shakespeare. She is said to have appeared on stage herself, but this cannot be confirmed. Certainly she accompanied her father in Irish society, mainly in Sligo and Dublin, and from 1798 to 1800 was a governess in the family of Featherstone of Bracklin Castle, Westmeath, and elsewhere. Throughout this time she was cultivating her talent for accompanying herself on the harp, dancing and writing.

Her *Poems* first appeared in 1801, published in both Dublin and London. She also collected a number of Irish tunes, composed lyrics, and published them. They enjoyed much popularity and her example was copied by Thomas Moore.[4] In 1803 she embarked on a wildly successful career as a novelist with *St Clair, or the Heiress of Desmond*, which her entry in the *DNB* describes as 'a trashy imitation of the *Sorrows of Werther*'. Her payment for this work was four complimentary copies of the novel – a state of affairs that would not prevail for long. The following year she published *The Novice of St Dominick*, which met with tremendous success, and is said to have given Pitt solace on his deathbed (he died in 1806). Such was the success of these novels that Richard Phillips, her publisher, was happy to offer her £300 for her third, *The Wild Irish Girl* (1806). Though not her best, it did even better than its predecessors, and Charles Maturin attempted to cash in on its success by calling his next fiction *The Wild Irish Boy* (1808).

Her opera, *The First Attempt*, was staged at the Theatre Royal, Dublin, 4 March 1807, where it ran several nights and made £400. Later that year she published *The Lay of an Irish Harp; or Metrical Fragments*, her most important volume of poems. She made no claims as a poet, and the two epigraphs to the volume indicate her own valuation: 'trifles light as air' (Shakespeare) and 'vrai papillon de Parnasse' (La Fontaine). Just in case the reader was in any doubt, she refers to her poems, in an exculpatory 'Prefatory Sketch', as being no more than 'trifles':

> Neither the Moorish loftiness of the Spanish, nor the elevated gravity of the Italian literature, has exempted them from that species of sportive composition which, though generally the effect of minor talent (tasteful in its mediocrity) is

---

[2] *Sydney Owenson, Lady Morgan's Memoirs: Autobiography, Diaries and Correspondence* (2 vols, London, 1862), i 40.
[3] Ibid., i 71. William Jackson (1730–1803), a composer, essayist, organist and painter, lived at Exeter for most of his working life.

[4] Most notably in his *Irish Melodies*; see *Romanticism* 664–5.

sometimes the effusion of superior genius, in the absence of its higher inspiration. But I believe the French language above any other abounds with those metrical trifles which, as the offspring of minds elegantly gay and intimately associated, have obtained the name of 'vers de societe', and which frequently possess an exquisite finesse of thought that does not exclude nature, and is most happily adapted to the delicate idiom of the language in which it flows.

On the surface, this is a highly self-effacing statement, but it is intriguing to find her using the same concepts that Wordsworth used to justify *Lyrical Ballads*. The 'exquisite finesse of thought that does not exclude nature', despite its excessively reserved manner, must refer to the same quality that Wordsworth more exuberantly describes as 'the spontaneous overflow of powerful feelings',[5] and when she calls for such 'finesse of thought' to be 'happily adapted to the delicate idiom of the language in which it flows', she seems to echo his desire for a language 'arising out of repeated experience and regular feelings'.[6] It is not clear whether she had read Wordsworth by 1807, much less whether she was influenced by him (though, in later years, he certainly read her[7]), but the important point is that her deferential 'Prefatory Sketch' is in its own way as innovatory as Wordsworth's more famous Preface. The poems themselves are as deeply felt as anything in Moore, ranging from the patriotic melancholy of *The Irish Harp*[8] to the whimsical lightness of *The Irish Jig*. As for her love poems, there can be few writers so adept at infusing a languid eroticism into, for instance, the conventional eighteenth-century personification of Twilight:

> But steal the softer hour between,
> When Twilight drops her mystic veil,
> And brings the anxious mind's repose,
> And leaves the sentient heart to feel.[9]

The reviewers were appropriately respectful of the volume. Given her popularity with the reading public, there can have been little doubt that it would do well, whatever they said. In fact, most begin by mentioning her success as a novelist; the *Oxford Review* is in this respect typical: 'The name of Miss Owenson is familiar to all readers of taste; to all who admire brilliancy of imagination and fertility of genius. The short poems in this volume are chiefly on trifling subjects, but display no less simplicity of thought than felicity of execution. We observe here and there some thoughts borrowed from the French and Italian poets, with whom our authoress appears to be very conversant; but they are borrowed in such a manner as to become her own, and to be frequently improved by the adoption.'[10] Sydney's success as a novelist was also on the mind of the reviewer in the *British Critic*: 'Miss Owenson has distinguished herself as a writer of novels somewhat above the middle class, and evidently possesses a warm and creative imagination. She now appears before the public as a writer of poetry, and it must be observed that her compositions have much animation, and will please many readers. They are principally of the amatory cast, too much so indeed for our gravity.'[11] Some reviewers noted faults in her style and language; the *Poetical Register* commented: 'In most

---

[5]   In the Preface to *Lyrical Ballads*; see *Romanticism* 253.

[6]   Ibid., p. 252.

[7]   See my *Wordsworth's Reading 1800–1815* (Cambridge, 1995), p. 268.

[8]   See *Romanticism* 636–9.

[9]   *The Boudoir* 13–16.

[10]   *Oxford Review* 2 (1807) 550–2, p. 550.

[11]   *British Critic* 33 (1809) 75–7, p. 75.

of these little poems there is great elegance, fancy, command of language, and melody of versification. Their chief fault is an occasional glitter and gaudiness, which, in her future compositions, Miss Owenson will do well to avoid. Let her beware of ridicule, by enlisting in the band of Della Cruscan rhymes. She has talents to entitle her to hold a respectable rank among female authors.'[12] The Della Cruscan qualities in her writing were noted also by the reviewer in *La Belle Assemblee*: '. . . though she is evidently in pursuit of a false taste, and invading the peculiar soil and demesnes of Della Crusca and Laura Maria, there is, nevertheless, a great deal of true poetic spirit, and much elegance and delicacy of sentiment. . . . It is too wild in some parts, and too careless and tame in others; but, upon the whole, it has that sort of merit which we expected from her pen, and we incur no hazard of having our judgement disputed, by earnestly recommending it to our readers.'[13] Some of these criticisms have a political dimension, of course, as her nationalism was controversial – which may account for the comment that the *Lays* were 'wild in some parts'. This may also be the cause of the reviewer's unease in the *Monthly Review*: 'We scarcely ever catch her in an indifferent mood; she is always completely awake, generally warm, and often fervid; and writing from feeling, she frequently commands the feelings of her readers. It is here, indeed, that, if we were to hint at a general fault, we ought to mention it: since this fault is, in our opinion, the language of feeling carried to excess.'[14] Political hostility provides the only way to account for the virulence of the notice in the *Annual Review*, which begins: 'A disgraceful farrago of passionate, unfeminine, and scarcely decorous rant, disgusting affectation, and the very quintessence of sentimental nonsense. . . . It is scarcely worthwhile to remark that this precious book is thickly bestrewn with French and Italian quotations, scarcely a line of which is rightly printed.'[15]

Sydney went on to write many more successful novels and non-fiction works, including *The Missionary* (1811), an Indian novel, with which Percy Bysshe Shelley was delighted. 'Will you read it?' he asked Thomas Jefferson Hogg in June 1811, 'It is really a divine thing. . . . Since I have read this book I have read no other – but I have thought strangely'.[16] She married Sir Charles Morgan in 1812, reluctantly, but the two seem to have enjoyed a happy marriage, despite having no children. Curiously, they drew up beforehand what today would be called a prenuptial agreement by which Sydney was allowed to keep for herself the £500 she had saved from the proceeds of her writing, while her husband's fortune was settled upon the daughter of his first marriage. Together they visited France, as research for a non-fiction work – *France* (1818), a collection of historical materials, cultural observation, and anecdotes. Notwithstanding the republicanism which it so fearlessly promoted, it was a success with English readers (though not with her arch-enemy John Wilson Croker, who wrote a vitriolic review in the *Quarterly Review*), and her publisher, Henry Colburn, offered her £2,000 to write *Italy* (1821). The resulting work won praise even from such curmudgeonly readers as Byron: 'Her work is fearless and excellent on the subject of Italy', he told Thomas Moore, 'and I know the country.'[17] She was a friend of Mary Tighe, Lady Caroline Lamb and Madame de Staël, and her *Memoirs* and *Autobiography* are a mine of information about people and events of her time. Among the delights of the latter is a note to herself, dating from 1818: 'I never looked half so well, and am grown quite fat, fair, and – a beauty!!!'[18]

---

[12] *Poetical Register* 6 (1807) 539.

[13] *La Belle Assemblee* supplement to 2 (1807) 43.

[14] *Monthly Review* 57 (1808) 374–8.

[15] *Annual Review* 6 (1807) 547.

[16] *The Letters of Percy Bysshe Shelley* ed. Frederick L. Jones (2 vols, Oxford, 1964), i 107.

[17] Marchand viii 189.

[18] *Passages from my Autobiography* (1859), p. 46.

She died 14 April 1859, her age a mystery even to her closest friends, leaving a fortune of between £15,000 and £16,000 to be divided between her nieces. She was buried in the Old Brompton cemetery.

Further Reading

Ann H. Jones, *Ideas and Innovations: Best Sellers of Jane Austen's Age* (New York, 1986), chapter 7

James Newcomer, *Lady Morgan the Novelist* (Lewisburg, PA, 1990)

Jeanne Moskal, 'Gender, Nationality, and Textual Authority in Lady Morgan's Travel Books', *RWW* 171–93

Richard C. Sha, 'Expanding the Limits of Feminine Writing: The Prose Sketches of Sydney Owenson (Lady Morgan) and Helen Maria Williams', *RWW* 194–206

Joseph W. Lew, 'Sydney Owenson and the Fate of Empire', *Keats-Shelley Journal* 39 (1990) 39–65

From The Lay of an Irish Harp; or Metrical Fragments (1807)

FRAGMENT X. THE BOUDOIR

To * * * * * * * *
La, vers le fin du jour la simple verite
Honteux de paroitre nud
Pour cacher sa rougeur, cherche l'obscurité.
La, sa confidence legitime rapproche deux amis.[1]

De Mouslier

I

What needst *thou* ask, or *I* reply?
Mere words are for the stupid many;
I've ever thought a speaking look
The sweetest eloquence of any!

II

Yes, thou may'st come, and at the hour 5
We consecrate to pensive pleasures,
When feeling, fancy, music, taste,
Profusely shed their dearest treasures.

III

Yet come not ere the sun's last beam
Sleeps on the west wave's purpled breast, 10
Nor wait thee till the full-orbed moon
Resplendent lifts her silver crest.

FRAGMENT X. THE BOUDOIR
[1] 'There, at the end of the day, simple truth, ashamed of appearing naked, seeks darkness to hide her blushes. There, her licit confidence brings two friends together.'

IV

But steal the softer hour between,
When Twilight drops her mystic veil,
And brings the anxious mind's repose,   15
And leaves the sentient heart to feel.

V

Yet turn not towards the flaunting bow'r
That echoes to the joyless laugh
Of gossip dames, nor seek the hall
Where Riot's sons her goblet quaff.   20

VI

But with a stilly noiseless step
Glide to the well-known fairy room,
Where fond affection visits oft,
And never finds the heart from home.

VII

Fear not to meet intruders there,   25
Thou'lt only find my harp and me,
Breathing perhaps some pensive song,
And waiting anxiously for thee.

VIII

And I will wear the vestal robe[2]
Thou lov'st, I know, to see me wear;   30
And with that sweet wreath formed by thee
(Though faded now) I'll bind my hair.

IX

And round my harp fresh buds I'll twine,
O'er which departing day has wept;
As wildly soft its chords I'll touch   35
As though a sigh its chords had swept.

X

And I will hum the song thou lov'st,
Or thou each bosom-chord shalt thrill
With thine own soul-dissolving strain –
Or silent,[3] we'll be happier still.   40

---

[2] *the vestal robe* a pure, virginal robe, like that worn
by a priestess of Vesta.
[3] 'Le secret d'ennuyer est celui de tout dire'
(Owenson's note). 'The secret of being dull is to tell

all'; the quotation is from Voltaire, *Discours en vers sur
l'homme.*

XI

Well now, thou know'st the time, the place,
And – but I merely meant to tell thee
That thou might'st come! Yet still I write
As though some witchcraft charm befell me.

FRAGMENT XIX. L'AMANT MUTIN

Sans depit sans legerte je quitte un amant volage,
Et je reprend ma liberte – sans regreter mon esclavage.[1]

Bernard le Jeune

I

Nay, if you threaten, all is over –
Ne'er dart that rebel look at me!
I languish too, to turn a rover,
So take your shackles – both are free.

II

No galling steel that chain composes,   5
Which once I fondly wove for thee;
See, it is formed of breathing roses,
And dewed with tears love stole from me.

III

But now if o'er its bloomy flushing[2]
Indiff'rence sheds her chilling air,   10
And o'er each bud (still faintly blushing)
Congeals each tear that lingers there.

IV

Why break at once the useless fetter,
Since round thy heart no more 'tis bound;
But while its roses thus you scatter,   15
Think not its thorns my breast shall wound.

V

And yet hadst thou still been that lover
That all I hoped to find in thee,
I ne'er had turned a careless rover,
I ne'er had been thus idly free.   20

VI

But o'er my lip, in fondness dying,
No sigh of love e'er breathed its soul,
Until some heart more fondly sighing,
My sigh into existence stole.

FRAGMENT XIX. L'AMANT MUTIN   [2] *bloomy flushing* the springing forth of new blooms.
[1] 'Without spite or insincerity I leave a flighty lover,
and I regain my freedom without regretting my slavery.'

VII

And if some tender pangs I cherished,   25
From thee I caught the pleasing anguish;
But when with thee those sweet pangs perished,
I felt them in my bosom languish.

FRAGMENT XXXV. THE IRISH JIG

And send the soul upon a jig to heaven.

Pope[1]

I

Old Scotia's jocund Highland reel
Might make an hermit play the deel,[2]
　　　So full of gig![3]
Famed for its cotillions gay France is,
But e'en give me the dance of dances –   5
　　　An Irish jig.

II

The slow *pas grave*, the brisk *coupée*,
The rigadoon, the light *chassée*,[4]
　　　Devoid of gig
I little prize; or saraband[5]   10
Of Spain, or German allemande[6] –
　　　Give me a jig![7]

III

When once the frolic jig's begun,[8]
Then hey, for spirit, life, and fun!
　　　And with some gig,   15
Trust me, I too can play my part,

FRAGMENT XXXV. THE IRISH JIG
[1] *Epistle to Burlington* 144.
[2] *deel* devil.
[3] *gig* fun, merriment.
[4] *The slow pas grave . . . chassée* names of various dances.
A rigadoon is a lively and complicated dance for two,
named after Rigaud, dancing-master at Marseilles.
[5] *saraband* slow and stately Spanish dance in triple
time.
[6] *allemande* name given to various German dances.
[7] 'This trifle is given as it was written, impromptu,
in the first flush of triumph, after having "simply
gained renown", by tiring out two famous jig dancers,
at the seat of a particular friend in Tipperary. There
are few countries whose inhabitants are strictly natives,
that have not a national dance, as well as a national
song: "This must have peculiarly been the case in
Ireland", says Noverre, in his *Essay on Dancing*, "for
such a natural and native taste for music as I have
spoken of, is usually accompanied by, or includes in it,

a similar one for dancing"' (Owenson's note). Owenson
refers to Jean Georges Noverre, *Lettres sur la danse, et
sur le ballet* (1760).
[8] 'The influence which an Irish jig holds over an
Irish heart is strongly illustrated in the following
singular anecdote borrowed from the appendix of Mr
Walker's interesting *Memoir of the Irish Bards*: "The
farce of the *Half-Pay Officer* having been brought out
at Drury Lane Theatre, the part of an old grand-
mother was assigned to Mrs Fryer, an Irish woman,
who had quitted the stage in the reign of Charles II,
and had not appeared on it for fifty years; during the
representation she exerted her utmost abilities; when
however she was called on to dance a jig at the age
of 85, she loitered, and seemed overcome; but as
soon as the music struck up the Irish trot, she footed
it as nimbly as any girl of five and twenty"' (Owenson's
note). Owenson refers to Joseph Cooper Walker,
Historical Memoirs of the Irish Bards (1786), who in turn
refers to Charles Molloy, *The Half-Pay Officers* (1720).

And dance with all my little heart
    The Irish jig.

IV

Now through the mazy figure flying,
With some (less active) partner vying,   20
    And full of gig;
Now warm with exercise and pleasure,
Each pulse beats wildly to the measure
    Of the gay jig!

V

New honours to the saint be given[9]   25
Who taught us first to dance to heaven!
    I'm sure of gig,
And laugh and fun his soul was made,
And that he often danced and played
    An Irish jig.   30

VI

I think 'tis somewhere clearly proved
That some great royal prophet loved
    A little gig;[10]
And though with warrior fire he glowed,
The prowess of his heel he showed   35
    In many a jig!

VII

Nay, somewhere too I know they tell
How a fair maiden danced so well,
    With so much gig,
That (I can scarce believe the thing)   40
She won a saint's head from a king
    For one short jig![11]

VIII

But I (so little my ambition)
Will fairly own, in meek submission
    (And with some gig),   45
That for no holy head I burn;
One poor lay heart[12] would serve my turn
    For well-danced jig.

---

[9] 'At Limages not long ago the people used to dance round the choir of the church, which is under the invocation of their patron saint, and at the end of each psalm, instead of the gloria patria, they sung as follows: "Saint Marcel, pray for us, and we will dance in honour of you" (Gallini)' (Owenson's note). Owenson refers to Giovanni Andrea Gallini, *A Treatise on the Art of Dancing* (1762).

[10] King David exhorted his listeners to 'Praise [God] with the timbrel and dance' (Psalms 150:4).
[11] Salome asked for the head of John the Baptist from King Herod in return for her dance; see Mark 6:21–8.
[12] lay heart i.e. the heart of someone not in holy orders.

IX
Since then we know from 'truths divine'
That saints and patriarchs did incline   50
    To fun and gig,
Why let us laugh and dance for ever
And still support with best endeavour
    The Irish jig!

Isabella Lickbarrow (1784–1847)

Isabella Lickbarrow was born on 5 November 1784, the eldest daughter of James Lickbarrow and Mary Bristo, Quakers, of Kendal; she had three sisters, Rachel (b. 1786), Hannah (b. 1787), and Margaret (b. 1789). Her father was a schoolmaster, probably in Kendal; he had died by 1814, when Isabella published her *Poetical Effusions*, which declares her to be an orphan. Her mother died on 12 May 1790, when Isabella was five and a half. Besides this, lamentably little is known of her.[1] But it is sufficient to establish beyond doubt that she was not a 'working-class' poetess, as she is sometimes said to have been. She reveals something of herself in her last book-length work, *A Lament Upon the Death of Her Royal Highness the Princess Charlotte* (1818):

> The following pieces were written by a young female in humble life, a native of Kendal, to beguile her leisure moments. She is an orphan, unlettered, and of exemplary character. Her friends have recommended the present publication, and they would hope that it will not be found unworthy of the notice and kindness of a liberal public. Self-instructed, she is indebted to herself only, for what little knowledge she may possess; and this circumstance, it is hoped, will disarm, as candour must deprecate, the severity of criticism.

These particulars are corroborated by what we learn about her from the Preface to her earlier volume, *Poetical Effusions* (1814), in which she tells us: 'The benevolence of kind friends suggested the present publication to the authoress who, after the domestic employments of the day, had secretly indulged herself in 'wooing the Muse' at intervals stolen from repose. And the intention of those kind friends was to assist the humble labours of herself and her orphan sisters, by raising from the generosity of the public a little fund, which would increase their family comforts and better their condition in life.' Poverty seems, therefore, to provide the background to Isabella's career. Her chief supporter seems to have been Isaac Steele, founder and editor of her local newspaper, the *Westmorland Advertiser, or Kendal Chronicle*, which began publishing in 1811. Steele was a Unitarian, and had been baptized in Kendal in July 1774. His newspaper was a weekly broadsheet of four pages carrying advertisements on the front page and local

---

[1] I am indebted to Constance Parrish for much of the information about Isabella Lickbarrow contained in this headnote.

and national news inside; on its back page there was always a box for poetry. Alongside extracts from such blockbusters as Byron's *Giaour* and *Childe Harold's Pilgrimage*, Steele published local poets, including Lickbarrow.

The first poem that can be securely identified as hers appeared anonymously in the nineteenth issue of the paper, 2 November 1811; it was entitled *Lines on the Comet*. Steele evidently encouraged her to write more, and she became a regular contributor, appearing in the paper twice or more times a month. She had published no less than sixty poems in the *Advertiser* by June 1815. It was a remarkable and, so far as I can find, unique example of literary patronage. Without the encouragement first of Steele, and later of his successors, M. and R. Branthwaite, Isabella's talent would probably not have developed so rapidly.

It seems likely that the plan for *Poetical Effusions* came, in the first instance, from the Branthwaites, who took over the *Advertiser* in January 1813. They solicited subscriptions in the paper in February 1814, and published the volume themselves, using the same paper and font used for the *Advertiser*, in July. Subscribers included Wordsworth, De Quincey, and Southey. Two local admirers of the volume wrote complimentary poems to Isabella, which were published in the paper, and Anna Laetitia Barbauld reviewed it briefly in the *Monthly Review*: 'The introduction to these verses is written with a simplicity and humility which are sufficient to mollify the severest critic; and the compositions, though brilliant, display much chastened feeling, and a poetical perception of the beauties of nature.'[2] There were, so far as I have been able to find, no other notices.

Isabella continued to publish poetry in the *Advertiser* until June 1815.[3] She must by then have been well known locally, and it is hard to see why the association with the paper should suddenly have ceased. Perhaps there was some falling-out not unlike that which had occurred between Ann Yearsley and Hannah More (see pp. 151–2), or perhaps the Branthwaites became less interested in poetry; by 1816, they were publishing more extracts from Byron, Scott, and Moore than previously, and by 1817 even those had given way to verse riddles and acrostics. Isabella published her last volume, the 1818 *Lament*, with 'G. F. Harris' Widow and Brothers, Water Street, Liverpool' (according to the title page).

This was not her last appearance in print, as was once thought. She published at least four more poems: also in 1818, her *Lines Occasioned by the Death of Dr Thomson, of Leeds*, appeared in the *Monthly Repository*,[4] and in 1820 three poems turned up in the *Lonsdale Magazine – Song of the Spirit of the Rock, Reply of the Wood Nymph* and *Cyndyllan's Hall*.[5] In the same periodical, another admirer of her work, one James Grocott, published a tribute to her, *To Miss Lickbarrow, On her Ode to Sensibility* (presumably a reference to the poem published below, pp. 474–5).[6] There are probably more poems in contemporary periodicals and newspapers waiting to be discovered.

Of the remainder of her life very little of consequence is known, but there are some intriguing clues. She lived for the remainder of her life in Kendal with her sisters Rachel and Margaret. In June 1843, the distinguished scientist John Dalton drafted a codicil to his will, leaving, 'in trust for my relations, Isabella, Margaret, and Rachel Lickbarrow, £900 in equal third shares'; he died the following year. Isabella's precise relation to

[2] *Monthly Review* 76 (1815) 211.
[3] Some of these poems, otherwise unavailable, are reprinted in my 'Isabella Lickbarrow and the *Westmorland Advertiser*', *TWC* 27 (1996) 118–26.

[4] *Monthly Repository* 13 (1818) 523.
[5] *Lonsdale Magazine* 1 (1820) 124–5, 174–5, and 227, respectively.
[6] Ibid., p. 272.

Dalton has yet to be determined. She died in Kendal on 15 February 1847, and her remains were interred at the Castle Street burial ground. Rachel and Margaret Lickbarrow remained at the family house in Highgate, Kendal, until their respective deaths (Rachel d. 1870; Margaret d. 1871).

She is little-known even now, at a time when women poets of the period are a source of considerable critical interest; that obscurity belies her talent. *On Sensibility: A Fragment* (which was first published in the *Westmorland Advertiser*, 19 June 1813) reworks the familiar eighteenth-century theme in a distinctively feminist context. Where Hannah More had been more concerned with censuring forms of sensibility which she regarded as debased, Isabella is concerned to show how it makes life so much harder when 'enshrined within a female frame'. The absence of a 'guardian and protector' was evidently something she felt deeply. *On Esthwaite Water* (first published *Westmorland Advertiser*, 11 September 1813) takes its cue from the picturesque writer William Gilpin, and his approving comments on the lakes he observed on his tour of Cumberland and Westmorland: 'But when the sky is splendid, and at the same time calm, the water (being then a perfect mirror) will glow all over with correspondent tints, unless other reflections, from the objects around, intervene and form more vivid pictures.'[7] But Isabella's repeated use of the words 'calm', 'repose', and 'tranquil', suggest that the poem is not purely loco-descriptive: the small lake of Esthwaite, which is doomed finally to lose 'The lovely visions of repose', has by the final line become an image of the psyche glimpsed in *On Sensibility*, too burdened by the intrusive cares of the world to remain at peace. There was as much need for agitation to combat slavery in 1814 as there had been in 1788 when Hannah More, Ann Yearsley, and Helen Maria Williams had written poems against it. By 1814 several laws had been passed drastically limiting slavery, including the Foreign Slave Bill of 1806, which destroyed 75 per cent of the trade at a stroke, and the Abolition Bill, which had abolished the trade once and for all, passed 1 May 1807. But conditions actually worsened for many existing slaves; with new supplies cut off, old women and children were often compelled to perform arduous tasks formerly given to men. And slavery continued in foreign countries. Britain and America had united in the Treaty of Ghent in 1812 in wishing to suppress the trade internationally, but their efforts tended to be half-hearted and ineffectual. It is against slavery overseas that Isabella writes in 1814, addressing most of her remarks to Thomas Clarkson, thanks partly to whose efforts abolition had taken place in 1807. *Patterdale* was Isabella's final poem to appear in the *Advertiser*, and it is one of her best. It reprises the theme of *On Esthwaite Water*, as the landscape is registered as an image of the perceiving mind. But then Isabella takes the conceit one step further – a step that confirms her as essentially romantic and even Wordsworthian. In *Patterdale* the landscape is imprinted, all its 'shadowy forms' intact, on the mind, to be invoked ever after by the involuntary action of 'The powers of fancy'.

Further Reading

Isabella Lickbarrow, *Poetical Effusions, 1814* (Spelsbury, 1994)
Stuart Curran, 'Isabella Lickbarrow and Mary Bryan: Wordsworthian Poets', *TWC* 27 (1996) 113–18
Duncan Wu, 'Isabella Lickbarrow and the *Westmorland Advertiser*', *TWC* 27 (1996) 118–26

---

[7] *Observations on the Lakes* i 99.

From Poetical Effusions (1814)

ON SENSIBILITY: A FRAGMENT

Oh sensibility, thou dangerous gift,
Which, like Pandora's fabled box,[1] contains
Compounded good and ill, the fountain-head
And source whence flow the sweet and bitter springs,
The pleasures and the pains of human life –   5
Exquisite joys, but woe more exquisite!
Whoe'er possessed thee yet, that did not wish,
In some unhappy moments of their lives,
They could exchange thy quick and throbbing pulse
For the dull sluggish tide which scarcely flows   10
Along the veins of torpid apathy,
Thy keen susceptibility of soul
For the cold marble of indifference?
   Oh ye who have from nature's hand received
That glowing spark of Promethean fire,[2]   15
That ardent inextinguishable flame
Which not the pressure of adversity
Nor poverty's benumbing touch can quench;
If doomed through desolate and rugged paths
Of life's obscurest wilderness to toil,   20
How much have you[3] to dread and to endure?
Much from the common casualties of life,
Untoward accidents, beneath whose weight
The man of fervent feelings soonest bends;
Much from the strength of your own warm affections,   25
Believing all sincere, and doubting none;
And oft, perhaps, mistaking warm professions
For firm and lasting friendship, only find
Repulsive coldness where you looked for welcome;
And much from disappointed hope, whose smile   30
With fairy sunshine for a moment gilds
Your dreary views, then vanishes for ever.
   Ye sons of sorrow, thus condemned to pine,
Unknown, unpitied, by a busy world,
Heaven be your friend, when other friends you've none.   35
And if enshrined within a female frame
That spirit dwells – oh, how much more unfit
To struggle through the thorny paths of life,
If she can find no kind and generous friend

ON SENSIBILITY: A FRAGMENT
[1] *Pandora's fabled box:* Pandora, the first woman, bore
a box of gifts which, when opened, released all the
evils of the world, leaving Hope inside.

[2] *That glowing spark of Promethean fire* i.e. sensibility.
When Jupiter took fire away from the earth, Prometheus
stole replacement fire from the chariot of the sun.
[3] *you* those with sensibility ('ye' in line 14).

In whom her confidence she may repose,   40
Her guardian and protector through a world
Where oft her weakness will require support.
Poor Mary, hapless orphan, where art thou?
Thy heart was formed for tenderness and love;
Thy mind, a beam of light breaking through clouds,   45
Shone like a meteor, with unsteady ray,
Irregular and bright, but shone in vain.
And now perhaps its energy is lost
And all its powers are buried in despair;
Perhaps thy struggles with misfortune past,   50
From life's rough storm thou hast a shelter found,
A lasting peaceful home within the grave.
  If such thy fate, ill-fated maid, farewell!
There is a world where sensibility,
So oft on earth the fruitful source of grief,   55
Will be the source of purest happiness.

ON ESTHWAITE WATER

O'er Esthwaite's lake, serene and still,
    At sunset's silent peaceful hour,
Scarce moved the zephyr's softest breath,
    Or sighed along its reedy shore.

The lovely landscape on its sides,   5
    With ev'ning's soft'ning hues impressed,
Shared in the gen'ral calm, and gave
    Sweet visions of repose and rest.

Inverted on the waveless flood,
    A spotless mirror smooth and clear,   10
Each fair surrounding object shone
    In softer beauty imaged there.

Brown hills and woods of various shades,
    Orchards and sloping meadows green,
Sweet rural seats and sheltered farms   15
    Were in the bright reflector seen.[1]

Ev'n lofty Tilberthwaite[2] from far
    His giant shadow boldly threw,
His rugged, dark, high-tow'ring head
    On Esthwaite's tranquil breast to view.   20

ON ESTHWAITE WATER
[1] See Gilpin's approving comments on the reflecting
powers of lakes, headnote, p. 473, above.
[2] *Tilberthwaite* modern-day Tilberthwaite is a valley
between Coniston and Ambleside ('thwaite' means

valley). Isabella probably means the mountain today
called Wetherlam, which is an extension of the
Tilberthwaite high fells, and which is clearly visible
from Esthwaite.

Struck with the beauty of the scene,
　　I cried, 'Oh may my yielding breast
Retain but images of peace
　　Like those, sweet lake, on thine impressed!'

Ne'er may it feel a ruder gale　　　　　　　　　　　　　25
　　Than that which o'er thy surface spreads,
When sportive zephyrs briskly play,
　　And whisper through thy bord'ring reeds;

When dancing in the solar beam,
　　Thy silv'ry waves the margin seek　　　　　　　　　30
With gently undulating flow,
　　And there in softest murmurs break.

Vain wish! O'er Esthwaite's tranquil lake
　　A stronger gale full frequent blows,
The soothing prospect disappears,　　　　　　　　　　35
　　The lovely visions of repose.

From The Westmorland Advertiser; or Kendal Chronicle (23 July 1814) Vol. 4, No. 161

On the Slave-Trade

Spirit of pure benevolence, descend
To earth to counsel senators and kings,
To teach mankind in kindness to delight,
And sweet compassion in their breasts implant,
That war, and its attendant train of ills,　　　　　　　5
May never more with misery fill the earth;
Teach those by heaven endowed with power or wealth
That not for them and for their good alone
Were they so far above their fellows placed;
Oh teach them what a privilege is theirs,　　　　　　　10
The glorious privilege to make others blessed;
Oh tell them what exalted bliss attends
The man of active warm benevolence
Whose bosom glows with love of humankind!
But chief, blessed spirit, now thy influence try　　　　15
To move the powers of Europe[1] in that cause
For which thy champion[2] toiled through many a year –

On the Slave-Trade
[1] *the Powers of Europe* Britain abolished slave trading in 1807; it was still permitted in other countries throughout Europe.

[2] 'Clarkson' (Lickbarrow's note). Thomas Clarkson lived near Ullswater, was a friend of Coleridge and Wordsworth, and may have been acquainted with Lickbarrow.

The cause of Africa's much-injured sons!
Ne'er may thy sacred spark inactive lie,
Ne'er may thy Heav'n-inspiréd flame decay,   20
Till sealed their charter for the rights of man,[3]
Till law protects them from the spoiler's hand,[4]
And years of slavery – a lingering death!
   And thou, my native land, whose honoured name,
Whose welfare to my heart will still be dear,   25
Unwearied be thy patience and thy zeal,
And firm thy voice against that barb'rous trade,
The curse of Afric, Europe's foul disgrace,
That the great Power who doth delight in mercy[5]
May approve – and, if again to sweep the earth,   30
War's dreadful whirlwind in its fury rise,
He may preserve thee[6] in the evil day.

From The Westmorland Advertiser; or Kendal Chronicle (3 June 1815) Vol. 5, No. 206

PATTERDALE[1] (COMPOSED 21 MAY 1815)

Mid western mountains far away,
Where soft the star of evening gleams
On glassy lakes and silver streams,
   A mild and melancholy ray,

A lovely vale, deep-bosomed, lies,   5
Of mountain dales the matchless queen,
A gem of softest, brightest green
   Beneath those cloudy northern skies.

Nursling of mountains – far around
Their heads those rugged guardians rear   10
To shield this quiet valley dear,
   Which they in wild confusion bound.

Proudly they rise to meet the storm
Whose fury threatens her repose,
And their stern, rock-crowned brows oppose,   15
   In many a rude and varied form.

---

[3] *their charter for the rights of man* Isabella alludes, of course, to Paine's *Rights of Man* (1791–2), although the phrase had become a commonplace by 1814.
[4] *the spoiler's hand* i.e. the hand of those who would enslave them.

[5] *the great Power who doth delight in mercy* God.
[6] *thee* i.e. 'my native land', line 24.
PATTERDALE
[1] This was the last of Lickbarrow's poems to appear in the *Westmorland Advertiser*.

But when the storm is hushed to rest,
And o'er the wild and lovely scene
The gladsome sun looks forth serene,
    And earth in gayer robes is dressed,   20

Then every steep and rugged pile
Throws by its frown and threat'ning air,
And on this lovely valley fair,
    Looks with a fond parental smile.

Their darling and their pride is she,   25
The vale that's cradled in their arms –
Exulting in her matchless charms,
    They wave their woods with joyous glee.

The sun in all his mighty round,
Where'er his radiant beams are shed,   30
On lowly plain or mountain's head,
    A lovelier scene has never found.

The spring in all her long career
May visit many a verdant isle
To bless it with her genial smile,   35
    Yet spot more beauteous or more dear

Than this sweet dale she has not seen;
Nor from the bounty of her store
Has given one sweeter, fairer flower,
    Or tint of lovelier, livelier green,   40

Or aught that might more charming be
To other vales – but all around
This little spot of fairy ground
    Has strewed her choicest favours free.

To me, like magic visions fair,   45
Of which an image would be faint,
Sublime above my power to paint,
    Sweet lonely dale, thy features were.

Like the wild wonders of a dream
Which strike with sudden, strong surprise,   50
Then vanish from our ravished eyes,
    Did thy romantic features seem.

Scarce from astonishment awoke,
And silent raptures of delight,
Ere like enchantment from my sight,   55
    Thy scenes were gone – the spell was broke.

And who from views like thine could part?
From views that fill th' astonished mind
With high-toned feelings undefined,
    And feel no sorrow at the heart.   60

I gave thee my adieus in sighs,
As fast retreating from the shore,
Each motion of the dashing oar
    Removed thee further from my eyes.

Yet long will shadowy forms remain   65
Of views, majestic all, and wild,
Around thee, Nature's favourite child,
    Lone Eden, of her mountain reign.

And oft o'er memory's magic glass,
When sleep, her opiate, tries in vain,   70
The powers of fancy to restrain,
    In wild confusion will they pass.

Lady Caroline Lamb (*née* Ponsonby) (1785–1828)

Caroline was the fourth child and only daughter of Frederick Ponsonby, 3rd Earl of Bessborough, and of his wife Lady Henrietta Frances Spencer (sister of Georgiana Cavendish, Duchess of Devonshire). At the age of three she was sent to Italy for six years and brought up by a servant. On her return she was sent to Devonshire House where she was brought up with her cousins by her aunt, who treated her kindly, and whom she always remembered affectionately; she later told Lady Morgan: 'I was a trouble, not a pleasure, all my childhood, for which reason, after my return from Italy, where I was from the age of four until nine, I was ordered by the late Dr Warre neither to learn anything nor see anyone, for fear the violent passions and strange whims they found in me should lead to madness; of which, however, he assured everyone there were no symptoms. I differ, but the end was, that until fifteen I learned nothing.'[1] Her account of her childhood as told to Lady Morgan is worth quoting:

> She gave curious anecdotes of high life – children neglected by their mothers – children served on silver in the morning, carrying down their plate to the kitchen – no one to attend to them – servants all at variance – ignorance of children on all subjects – thought all people were dukes or beggars – or had never to part with their money – did not know bread, or butter, was made – wondered if horses fed on beef – so neglected in her education, she could not write at ten

---

[1] *Sydney Owenson, Lady Morgan's Memoirs: Autobiography, Diaries and Correspondence* (2 vols, London, 1862), ii 211.

years old. Lady Georgiana Cavendish took her away, and she was sent to live with her godmother, Spencer, where the housekeeper, in hoop and ruffles, had the rule over seventy servants, and always attended her ladies in the drawing-room.[2]

Caroline married the Hon. William Lamb (later Lord Melbourne) in 1805, by whom she had three children, of which two died. The only one to survive was their son, George Augustus Frederick, born 11 August 1807. He was mentally ill throughout his life, and in a letter she blamed herself for this: 'my only child is afflicted; it is the will of God. I have wandered from right, and been punished.'[3] The marriage itself was not easy, though in later years Lamb took care of her, and she would describe him as 'the only noble fellow I ever met'.[4] At first, though, things were difficult, as Lady Morgan remembered: 'Her passion for William Lamb – would not marry him – knew herself to be a fury – wanted to follow him as a clerk, etc. Ill tempers on both sides broke out together after marriage – both loved, hated, quarrelled, and made up. "He cared nothing for my morals", she said. "I might flirt and go about with what men I pleased. He was privy to my affair with Lord Byron, and laughed at it. His indolence rendered him insensible to everything. When I ride, play, and amuse him, he loves me. In sickness and suffering, he deserts me. His violence is as bad as my own."'[5]

Her affair with Byron was in many respects one of the most important episodes in her life. Once again, her account of it, as related by Lady Morgan, is worth quoting:

Rogers[6] said 'you should know the new poet', and he offered me the MS of *Childe Harold* to read. I read it, and that was enough. Rogers said, 'He has a club-foot, and bites his nails'. I said, 'If he was ugly as Aesop I must know him'. I was one night at Lady Westmoreland's; the women were all throwing their heads at him. Lady Westmoreland led me up to him. I looked earnestly at him, and turned on my heel. My opinion, in my journal was, 'mad – bad – and dangerous to know'. A day or two passed; I was sitting with Lord and Lady Holland, when he was announced. Lady Holland said, 'I must present Lord Byron to you'. Lord Byron said, 'That offer was made to you before; may I ask why you rejected it?' He begged permission to come and see me. He did so the next day. Rogers and Moore[7] were standing by me: I was on the sofa. I had just come in from riding. I was filthy and heated. When Lord Byron was announced, I flew out of the room to wash myself. When I returned, Rogers said, 'Lord Byron, you are a happy man. Lady Caroline has been sitting here in all her dirt with us, but when you were announced, she flew to beautify herself.' Lord Byron wished to come and see me at eight o'clock, when I was alone; that was my dinner-hour. I said he might. From that moment, for more than nine months, he almost lived at Melbourne House. It was then the centre of all gaiety, at least in appearance.[8]

One hesitates to make too much of the affair with Byron, but the fact of the matter is that Caroline would spend the rest of her life remembering the time she had spent

[2] Ibid., ii 199.
[3] Ibid., ii 212.
[4] Ibid., ii 213.
[5] Ibid., ii 199–200.
[6] Samuel Rogers (1763–1855), poet, banker, and mutual friend of Caroline and Byron.

[7] Thomas Moore (1779–1852), poet; see *Romanticism* 664.
[8] Sydney Owenson, *Lady Morgan's Memoirs: Autobiography, Diaries and Correspondence*, ii 200–1.

with him, unable to believe that it was over. The affair began in March 1812 and ended in November, but it would cast a shadow over the rest of her life. Byron concluded it in a particularly brutal manner, by sending her a letter bearing the seal of his new conquest, Lady Oxford. She told Lady Morgan that 'It destroyed me: I lost my brain. I was bled, leeched; kept for a week in the filthy Dolphin Inn, at Rock. On my return, I was in great prostration of mind and spirit.'[9] For a long time she was effectively what we would today describe as a 'stalker', following him wherever he went, even waiting in the street when she knew he was attending a party inside. 'You talked to me about keeping her out', Byron told Lady Melbourne in June 1814, 'it is impossible – she comes at all times – at any time – and the moment the door is open in she walks – I can't throw her out of the window'.[10] He struck back in rhyme, making her the subject of one of the most memorable hate-poems in the language, *Remember me*.

Her revenge was also literary. She claimed that her first novel, *Glenarvon* (1816), was written in secret, at night, in the space of a month. It portrayed Byron as the evil and depraved Earl of Glenarvon, and even reprinted, word for word, the letter he had sent her when he ended their affair.[11] Though published anonymously, it was known to have come from her, and that its characters were thinly-veiled portrayals of real people. That, and Byron's popularity, which was then at its height, guaranteed a brisk sale. As the *Monthly Review* observed: 'This is altogether a strange publication. It is generally understood to proceed from the pen of a lady of rank and eccentricity, the daughter of an Irish Earl, and wife to the heir to an English Viscount; and to contain a delineation of her own life, as well as of the lives of the principal personages introduced. We have even on our table an index to the real and fictitious names, as they are commonly identified in the circles of fashion and of literary gossiping.'[12]

Perhaps Caroline's greatest literary achievement was *A New Canto* (1819), a remarkable act of literary appropriation in which, borrowing the same stanza that Byron had used in *Don Juan* Cantos I and II (the *ottava rima*), she ridiculed the society from which she felt increasingly excluded.[13] Some of the poems here are selected from the novels that followed: *Graham Hamilton* (1822) and *Ada Reis* (1823), both published anonymously. In general, the reviewers were fairly respectful of *Graham Hamilton*. Some described it as an improvement on *Glenarvon*, and the *Gentleman's Magazine* even went so far as to say that 'We have seldom derived greater pleasure from the perusal of a work of the same nature, than from that which is now before us.'[14] The only dissenting voice was that of the *Monthly Literary Register*, which commented: 'it is almost impossible to conceive a narrative so meagre in incident, and altogether so uninteresting.'[15]

The reviews of *Ada Reis* were more colourful. The novel itself was a preposterous oriental concoction claiming to be the translation of a manuscript found on the banks of the River Oronoko. 'Q' in the *Examiner* was enchanted by it: 'If these volumes be

---

[9] Ibid., ii 201.

[10] Marchand iv 132.

[11] It is worth quoting what the Baron de Bonstettin told Lady Morgan, when giving an example of Madame de Staël's 'want of tact and her great *naïveté*, which were extraordinary': "'I was present that day", said he, "when, across a crowded dinner table at Copet, she asked Lord Byron whether he was not the original of Lady C. Lamb's portrait of Glenarvon. He answered coolly, "C'est possible, Madame, mais je n'ai jamais posé"' (Sydney Owenson, Lady Morgan, *Passages from my Autobiography* (1859), pp. 311–12).

[12] *Monthly Review* 80 (1816) 217–18, p. 217. George Barker publishes one of these 'skeleton keys' to *Glenarvon* in *N&Q* (7th series) 10 (1890) 125.

[13] For a full text of the poem see *Romanticism* 695–703; it is discussed in my 'Appropriating Byron: Lady Caroline Lamb's *A New Canto*', *TWC* 26 (1995) 140–6.

[14] *Gentleman's Magazine* 92 (1822) 441–2, p. 441.

[15] *Monthly Literary Register* 1 (1822) 28–30, p. 30.

not the production of that gifted child of the Lakes, the Opium-eater,[16] they certainly ought to be, for we can conceive nothing more answerable to a series of his dreams, and the style of narrative adds exceedingly to the similarity. *Ada Reis* appears to us to be concocted by opium and a wayward imagination out of the whole series of Eastern Tales, and the wide range of kindred works of imagination, as Vathek, Faust, the Stories of Wieland, Anastasius, Don Juan, and even Quevedo, and Le Diable Boiteux.'[17] 'C', the reviewer in the *New Monthly Magazine*, sounded similarly bemused: 'The events succeed each other with the rapidity, and with something of the wildness of a dream. They have, consequently, but little sustained interest, but amidst the most unreined extravagance of the story, there are perceptible glimpses of the human heart, which are not the less interesting because they are somewhat out of place and proportion.'[18] Others were less susceptible; the critic in the *British Magazine* identified it as 'an imitation of Mr Beckford's *Vathek*; and we need not scruple to add that it is in every respect inferior to that surprising and interesting romance'.[19] The poetry, this reviewer thought, was 'pitiably dull and bad'.[20] The *Literary Gazette* took a similar line: 'To us the tale appears to be a wild, inconsistent medley, but the initiated may be able to trace characters and circumstances in what, to our limited sense, seems little more rational than the indigested and morbid visions of the nightmare.'[21] Caroline took all this quite hard, and shortly after seeing the reviews she told Lady Morgan: 'your kindness about *Ada Reis* I feel the more, as everybody wishes to run down and suppress the vital spark of genius I have, and, in truth, it is but small'.[22]

Critics and scholars have often attacked her; one has observed that 'She set herself up as a sort of professional injured female, and she never tired of lamenting her self-styled destruction',[23] while George Barker, the author of her entry in the *DNB*, comments that she was 'inordinately vain, and excitable to the verge of insanity'. But she was also extremely charismatic and, I suspect, rather brilliant; at least, that is the implication of the testimonies of those who knew her. Bulwer Lytton, with whom she enjoyed a prolonged flirtation, recalled:

> There was, indeed, a wild originality in her talk, combining great and sudden contrasts, from deep pathos to infantine drollery: now sentimental, now shrewd, it sparkled with anecdotes of the great world, and of the eminent persons with whom she had been brought up, or been familiarly intimate; and, ten minutes after, it became gravely eloquent with religious enthusiasm, or shot off into metaphysical speculations – sometimes absurd, sometimes profound – generally suggestive and interesting.[24]

Lady Morgan remembered her as 'tall and slight in her figure, her countenance was grave, her eyes dark, large, bright; her complexion fair; her voice soft, low, caressing,

[16]   the Opium-eater Thomas De Quincey, whose *Confessions of an English Opium-Eater* had been published in 1822.

[17]   *Examiner* 796 (27 April 1823) 284.

[18]   *New Monthly Magazine* 8 (1823) 317–21, p. 319.

[19]   *British Magazine* 1 (1823) 87–92, p. 87.

[20]   Ibid., p. 92.

[21]   *Literary Gazette* 323 (29 March 1823) 198–200, p. 198.

[22]   Sydney Owenson, *Lady Morgan's Memoirs: Autobiography, Diaries and Correspondence*, ii 210–11.

[23]   James O Hoge, Jr, 'Lady Caroline Lamb on Byron and her own wasted life: two new letters', *N&Q* 21 (1974) 331–3, p. 333.

[24]   *The Life, Letters, and Literary Remains of Edward Bulwer, Lord Lytton* (2 vols, London, 1883), i 328.

that was at once a beauty and a charm, and worked much of that fascination that was peculiarly hers; it softened down her enemies the moment they listened to her. She was eloquent, most eloquent, full of ideas, and of graceful gracious expression; but her subject was always herself.'[25] The impression one has of her character is further rounded by her letters, which are frequently charming, and always readable.[26] Besides her wit, they also reveal her to have been, from time to time, a manic-depressive. Typical is a remark to Lady Morgan that 'The only thoughts that ever can make me lose my senses are these: a want of knowledge as to what is really true; a certainty that I am useless; a fear that I am worthless; a belief that all is vanity and vexation of spirit, and that there is nothing new under the sun.'[27] Nonetheless, she evidently possessed an energy and a brilliance that could, on occasion, produce powerful and inventive poetry.

Further Reading

Elizabeth Jenkins, *Lady Caroline Lamb* (London, 1932)
Henry Blyth, *Caro: The Fatal Passion* (London, 1972)
Nicola J. Watson, 'Trans-figuring Byronic Identity', *Limits* 185–206
Malcolm Kelsall, 'The Byronic Hero and Revolution in Ireland: The Politics of *Glenarvon*', *The Byron Journal* 9 (1981) 4–19
Peter W. Graham, 'Fictive Biography in 1816: The Case of *Glenarvon*', *The Byron Journal* 19 (1991) 53–68
James Soderholm, 'Lady Caroline Lamb: Byron's Miniature Writ Large', *Keats-Shelley Journal* 40 (1991) 24–46
Annette Peach, ' "San Fedele Alla Mia Biondetta": A Portrait of Lord Byron Formerly Belonging to Lady Caroline Lamb', *Bodleian Library Record* 14 (1993) 285–95
Duncan Wu, 'Appropriating Byron: Lady Caroline Lamb's *A New Canto*', *TWC* 26 (1995) 140–6

BY THOSE EYES WHERE SWEET EXPRESSION (EDITED FROM MS; COMPOSED *c.*1816)[1]

By those eyes where sweet expression
Many a deep design conceal;
By those lips which preach discretion
Whilst they others' thoughts reveal;

---

[25] *Sydney Owenson, Lady Morgan's Memoirs: Autobiography, Diaries and Correspondence*, ii 254.
[26] Her letters may be found in the following: C. Kegan Paul, *William Godwin: His Friends and Contemporaries* (2 vols, London, 1876), ii 266–8, 285–6, 302–4 (letters to Godwin); *Fugitive Pieces and Reminiscences of Lord Byron* ed. Isaac Nathan (London, 1829), pp. 150, 153, 155–6 (letters to Nathan); *Sydney Owenson, Lady Morgan's Memoirs: Autobiography, Diaries and Correspondence*, i 442–3; ii 174–9, 203–4, 206–13, 240 (letters to Morgan); Sydney Owenson, Lady Morgan, *Passages from my Autobiography* (London, 1859), pp. 49–50, 66–71; W. M. Torrens, *Memoirs of the Right Honourable*

William Second Viscount Melbourne (2 vols, London, 1878), i 297, 171–2, 173–4, ii 130–1; James O Hoge, Jr, 'Lady Caroline Lamb on Byron and her own wasted life: two new letters', *N&Q* 21 (1974) 331–3 (letters to Bulwer Lytton); and my 'Appropriating Byron: Lady Caroline Lamb's *A New Canto*', *TWC* 26 (1995) 140–6.
[27] *Sydney Owenson, Lady Morgan's Memoirs: Autobiography, Diaries and Correspondence*, ii 303.
BY THOSE EYES WHERE SWEET EXPRESSION
[1] The MS, in Caroline's hand, is now at SUNY at Buffalo. Its contents lead me to believe that it was composed early, perhaps *c.*1816.

By Biondetta's[2] wrongs and woes,   5
Ah, ne crede[3] Byron's[4] vows.

Yes, by those oaths which made me blessed
And left me now the wretch you see;
Yes, by that smile which oft expressed
A love he never felt for me;   10
By every pang I hourly prove –
Ah, never trust in Byron's love.

By every gift which sought to cover
Falsehoods treacherous, dangerous art;
By every look the fondest lover   15
Could offer to the purest heart;
By all Biondetta's wrongs and woes,
Ah, ne crede Byron's vows.

From Graham Hamilton (1822)

'IF THOU COULDST KNOW WHAT 'TIS TO WEEP'

If thou couldst know what 'tis to weep,
    To weep unpitied and alone
The livelong night, whilst others sleep,
Silent and mournful watch to keep,   5
    Thou wouldst not do what I have done.

If thou couldst know what 'tis to smile,
    To smile whilst scorned by everyone,
To hide by many an artful wile,
A heart that knows more grief than guile,   10
    Thou wouldst not do what I have done.

And oh, if thou couldst think how drear,
    When friends are changed and health is gone,
The world would to thine eyes appear,
If thou like me to none wert dear,   15
    Thou wouldst not do what I have done.

---

[2] *Biondetta's* Caroline's name for herself, taken from the heroine of Jaques Cazotte's *Le Diable Amoreux* (1772), translated by John Miller as *The Enamoured Spirit* (1810). Biondetta in Cazotte's novel was a spirit of the devil disguised as a page, whose livery does not conceal her sex. Caroline used the same disguise to assignate with Byron, and even had her portrait painted in page's attire.

[3] *ne crede* do not believe. The phrase subverts the Byron family motto, 'crede Byron'. Byron gave Caroline a locket containing his portrait, with the motto engraved on the back. After his abandonment of her she had the word 'ne' engraved in front of the rest of the motto. See Annette Peach, '"San Fedele Alla Mia Biondetta": A Portrait of Lord Byron Formerly Belonging to Lady Caroline Lamb', *Bodleian Library Record* 14 (1993) 285–95.

[4] *Byron's* Caroline does not actually write this name into the poem, instead leaving a blank in the MS.

From Ada Reis (1823)

'SING NOT FOR OTHERS, BUT FOR ME'

I

Sing not for others, but for me,
In every thought, in every strain,
Though I perchance am far from thee,
And we must never meet again;
Though I may only weep for thee,   5
Sing not for others, but for me.

II

My spirit still is hovering nigh!
Then breathe for me that sacred sigh,
The sacred sigh, the thrilling tone
Which tells of time for ever gone –   10
Oh, when the heart's tear dims thine eye,
Think that my spirit hovers nigh.

III

In starry night or soft moonbeam,
By mossy bank or rippling stream,
In balmy breeze, in fragrant flower,   15
Though dearer hands may deck thy bower,
In all that's sweet or fair to thee,
Think not of others, but of me.

IV

If e'er thou sing'st thy native lay,
As thou wert wont in happier day,   20
That lay which breathed of love and truth
And all the joys of early youth;
Though all those joys are past for thee,
Sing not for others, but for me.

V

I've marked the struggles of thy mind,   25
Like bird in gilded cage confined;
Vain was the costly jewelled chain –
The heart breathed forth a mournful strain;
The spirit panted to be free,
And I could only weep for thee.   30

VI

Farewell! Alas, I may no more
Than weep and blame – and yet adore.
Thy hour is come – I cannot save –

But we shall meet beyond the grave;
The sinner's prayer may reach to heaven – 35
Pray then, and mayst thou be forgiven.

'WEEP FOR WHAT THOU HAST LOST, LOVE'

Weep for what thou hast lost, love,
Weep for what thou has won;
Weep for what thou didst not do,
And more for what thou hast done.

Time that's gone returneth never, 5
Keen repentance lasteth ever;
Heart that's pierced refuseth gladness,
Melancholy causeth madness.

Yet if tears avail not,
Tears of fond regret, 10
Arm thy mind and proudly, girl,
Endeavour to forget.

Shouldst thou spend thy days in grieving,
What is past there's no retrieving;
Once the hour of passion over, 15
Tear nor frown recalls a lover.

Weep for what thou hast lost, love,
Weep for what thou hast won;
Weep for what thou didst not do,
And more for what thou hast done. 20

DUET

The kiss that's on thy lip impressed
Is cold as parting kiss should be,
And he who clasps thee to his breast
Again can never feel for thee;
The chain I gave – a true love-token – 5
Thou see'st in every link is broken;
Then since 'tis so, 'twere best to part;
    I here renounce the oaths I swore –
Correct thy faults, amend thy heart,
    And let us meet no more. 10
The Answer
I go, but ere I go from thee,
    Give back what thou hast ta'en from me –
A heart that knew nor care nor guile,
A parent's fond approving smile,

The hopes which dared aspire to heav'n –   15
  Give these, and thou shalt be forgiv'n.
Take back the ring, take back the chain;
  Thy gifts, thy oaths I will resign;
Take back thy heart, since pledged in vain,
  But oh, restore what once was mine!   20

Hope not for this, thy course is run –
  All that is left thee is to die;
The dew drops with the setting sun,
  And see the winds pass scornful by.
So when thou'rt left by me, thou'lt find   25
  The world as scornful as the wind;
A stamp is set upon thy name,
  A blight clouds o'er thy early fame;
There's nothing now thy fate can save –
  Live scorned, or hide thee in the grave!   30

From Fugitive Pieces and Reminiscences of Lord Byron with Some Original Poetry, Letters and Recollections of Lady Caroline Lamb ed. Isaac Nathan (1829)

'LET THE HARP BE MUTE FOR EVER'

Let the harp be mute for ever,
  Rosa wakes no more the strain,
All its strings asunder sever,
  Rosa will not sing again;
Let those blooming chaplets perish   5
  That crowned it in its hour of joy,
Nor aught remain the thought to cherish,
  Of her that could my peace destroy.

Oh may no wand'ring breeze awaken
  The echo of its slumb'ring strings;   10
When by the zephyr's pinion shaken,
  It seems as if a spirit sings!
Why should I feel a thrill of pleasure,
  Condemned from every hope to part?
Why dote on melody's soft measure   15
  With desolation in my heart?

WILLIAM LAMB'S RETURN FROM PARIS, ASKING ME MY WISH

You ask my wish – the boon I crave,
Oh grant it, leave me what I have:
Leave me to rest upon my bed
With broken heart, and weary head.

No stormy passions now arise,   5
Nor tears relieve these suffering eyes;
No age, no love disturbs me now –
To God's avenging power I bow.

You've yielded to a wicked crew
Who ruin me, and laugh at you;   10
Sweep out the gore, and while you can,
Think for yourself, and be a man.

Felicia Dorothea Hemans (*née* Browne) (1793–1835)

Felicia Dorothea Browne was born at 118 Duke Street, Liverpool, on 25 September 1793,[1] the daughter of George Browne, merchant, and Felicity Wagner, daughter of Benedict Park Wagner of North Hall, Wigan (of mingled German, Italian, and Lancashire descent). She had three brothers: Sir Thomas Henry Browne, KCH (1787–1855), distinguished in the Peninsular Wars; Lieut.-Col. George Baxter Browne, CB, also distinguished in the Peninsular, and later Chief Commissioner of Police in Ireland; and Claude Scott Browne, Deputy Assistant Commissary-General in Upper Canada. Her father suffered business problems in 1800, and moved his family to Gwyrch (pronounced 'Gooirch'), near Abergele, North Wales, where Felicia was largely brought up, her education being supervised by her mother (they moved again, to Bronwhylfa, near St Asaph, in 1809). She learned Latin, modern languages, and drawing, and is said to have had a phenomenal memory. Her sister recalled that 'She could repeat pages of poetry from her favourite authors, after having read them but once over.... One of her earliest tastes was a passion for Shakespeare, which she read, as her choicest recreation, at six years old'.[2]

She began writing poetry at an early age, and published her first volume of poems, by subscription, when she was still only fourteen, in 1808.[3] Subscribers included John Wilson Croker, Reginald Heber, Thomas Medwin, and William Roscoe. The reviews are said to have been harsh, and, according to her biographer, 'so affected her, as to confine her to her bed for several days'.[4] In fact, the critics were fair; they were certainly firm, but all of them found encouraging words for the author. Anna Laetitia Barbauld in the *Monthly Review* commented, not unfairly, that some of the poems were 'jejune', and that they 'contain some erroneous and some pitiable lines', but added that 'we must praise the *Reflections on a Ruined Castle*, and the poetic strain in which they are delivered'. In concluding, she remarked that, 'if the youthful author were to content herself for some years with reading instead of writing, we should open any future work from her pen with an expectation of pleasure, founded on our recollection of this

---

[1] The year of her birth is variously given as 1793, 1794 and 1795. I have followed the dating given by her sister, Harriet Hughes, in her memoir in *The Works of Mrs Hemans* (7 vols, Edinburgh and London, 1839).
[2] *The Works of Mrs Hemans*, i 6.

[3] It is worth noting that the co-publisher was G. F. Harris, whose widow published Isabella Lickbarrow's final volume of poems a decade later.
[4] Henry F. Chorley, *Memorials of Mrs Hemans* (2 vols, 1836), i 37.

publication'.[5] The *Annual Review* took the same tack: 'An excellent ear this youthful candidate for the bays has acquired already; time only can discover whether she is capable of adding soul to sound, for the present her partial friends would certainly do more wisely in exhorting her to read, than tempting her to write'.[6] And the *Poetical Register* found in the poems 'promise of something better in future. . . . They are pretty, and not devoid of poetical ideas'.[7] In the same year Felicia published *England and Spain; or, Valour and Patriotism*, inspired by her brothers' involvement in the Peninsular campaign. One of the subscribers to the 1808 *Poems* was the young Thomas Medwin, who had met its author in North Wales. He showed them to his friend, Percy Bysshe Shelley, who in turn wrote to Thomas Jefferson Hogg, 28 July 1811: 'Now there is Miss F. D. Browne (certainly a tyger); yet she surpasses my sister in poetical talents, this your dispassionate criticism *must* allow'.[8] Shelley myth has it that the young man bombarded Miss F. D. Browne with letters but that, recognizing trouble when she saw it, Felicia's mother forbade her from replying.[9] Evidence for this story, however, is lacking.

If Felicia's sister is to be believed, the family was not much happier with Captain Alfred Hemans, whom she had met when she was fifteen. He was a soldier, and fought in the Peninsular campaign with her brothers. In 1811 he returnd to her, carrying scars sustained in the British withdrawal from Corunna in 1809, and a fever contracted during the Walcheren expedition. While still Felicia Dorothea Browne, she published *The Domestic Affections* in 1812, shortly before marrying him. For a while they lived at Daventry, a place she detested, before returning to her maternal home in Wales. They were evidently ill-suited; Captain Hemans is reported to have said that 'it was the curse of having a literary wife that he could never get a pair of stockings mended'.[10] After having no less than five children they separated in 1818, when Hemans went to live in Rome, in search of improved health, never to see her again.

Although her mother and sister helped her raise her children, the need to provide for them meant that she had to keep publishing. She was caught in a trap from which she was never to escape. 'Her poetry was often written with a readiness approaching improvisation', W. M. Rossetti wrote many years later, 'this she felt as in some degree a blemish, and towards the close of her life she regretted having often had to write in a haphazard way, so as to supply means for the education of her sons.'[11] The rush in which her poems were composed is clearly seen in her manuscripts; few carry corrections, revisions, or even deletions. Her working life was one of furious productivity, undertaken in spare moments from household chores; works included *Tales, and Historic Scenes in Verse* (1819); *Stanzas to the Memory of the Late King* (1820); *Welsh Melodies* (1822); *The Siege of Valencia, and Other Poems* (1823); *The Forest Sanctuary* (1825); *Lays of Many Lands* (1826); *Records of Woman* (1828), and *Songs of the Affections* (1830) – an astonishing publication record. She also contributed poems and essays to a wide range of periodicals and magazines; in 1823 she became a regular contributor to the *New Monthly Magazine*. Her usual practice was to publish poems first in periodicals, and then collect them in volume form. By this means she maximized her income, and became well known to readers of annuals, such that the *Monthly Review* commented, in 1828, 'Mrs Hemans maintains

[5] *Monthly Review* 60 (1809) 323.
[6] *Annual Review* 7 (1808) 525–6, p. 526.
[7] *Poetical Register* 7 (1808) 550.
[8] *The Letters of Percy Bysshe Shelley* ed. Frederick L. Jones (2 vols, Oxford, 1964), i 129.

[9] See Newman Ivey White, *Shelley* (2 vols, London, 1947), i 61.
[10] *A Short Sketch of the Life of Mrs Hemans* (1835), p. 32.
[11] *The Poetical Works of Mrs Felicia Hemans* ed. W. M. Rossetti (London, 1873), p. xxv.

her reputation among the annuals; for almost every one of them she has written verses which no one can pass over without reading.'[12] Reviews were, generally, favourable. She was a tremendously popular poet, and reviewers tended to acknowledge this when commenting on her work. As early as 1819, the *Edinburgh Monthly Review* commented: 'The more we become acquainted with Mrs Hemans as a poet, the more we are delighted with her productions, and astonished by her powers.'[13] The reviewer becomes quite rapturous: 'With an exquisite airiness and spirit, with an imagery which quite sparkles, are touched her lighter delineations; with a rich and glowing pencil her descriptions of visible nature: a sublime eloquence is the charm of her sentiments of magnanimity; while she melts into tenderness with a grace in which she has few equals.'[14] And, reviewing *The Siege of Valencia* in 1823, the *British Critic* remarked: 'When a woman can write like this, she *ought* to write. Her mind is national property. In the grand scheme of a popular literature, there are many departments which can alone be filled by the emanations of female genius.'[15] In 1826 the *Literary Chronicle* called her 'the first poetess of the day'.[16]

The most important of the many reviews she received was that by Francis Jeffrey for the second editions of *Records of Woman* and *The Forest Sanctuary*. He had a gendered view of female literature, regarding women as capable of writing well only about certain 'feminine' subjects;[17] Felicia, he believed, exemplified the female poet – though his enthusiasm for her work must also have something to do with the compatibility of their politics:

> It may not be the best imaginable poetry, and may not indicate the very highest or most commanding genius; but it embraces a great deal of that which gives the very best poetry its chief power of pleasing; and would strike us, perhaps, as more impassioned and exalted, if it were not regulated and harmonized by the most beautiful taste. It is infinitely sweet, elegant, and tender – touching, perhaps, and contemplative, rather than vehement and overpowering; and not only finished throughout with an exquisite delicacy, and even serenity of execution, but informed with a purity and loftiness of feeling, and a certain sober and humble tone of indulgence and piety, which must satisfy all judgements, and allay the apprehensions of those who are most afraid of the passionate exaggerations of poetry.[18]

In the meantime her work sold in vast quantities both in England and America, where a collected edition appeared in 1825. At about this time Ann Grant wrote to Felicia, telling her that she was 'Praised by all that read you, loved by all that praise you, and known, in some degree, wherever our language is spoken.'[19] At the height of her fame, Bishop Reginald Heber, friend and literary advisor, encouraged her to write a five-act tragedy, *The Vespers of Palermo*, which was staged at Covent Garden Theatre on 12 December 1823; it was, alas, a failure, although it was staged the following year in Edinburgh, with an epilogue by Sir Walter Scott, with some success.

---

[12] *Monthly Review* 9 (1828) 380.

[13] *Edinburgh Monthly Review* 2 (1819) 194–209, p. 194.

[14] Ibid., p. 207.

[15] *British Critic* 20 (1823) 50–61, p. 53.

[16] *Literary Chronicle* 379 (19 August 1826) 518–19, p. 518.

[17] For more on this, see Introduction, especially p. xxii, above.

[18] *Edinburgh Review* 50 (1829) 32–47, p. 34.

[19] *The Works of Mrs Hemans*, i 120.

Her mother's death in 1827 was a terrible blow, by which time her own health, ravaged by years of unrelenting hard work, was beginning to fail. She moved to Liverpool, where she found her celebrity wearisome, but still managed to compose. In need of a break, she toured Scotland and the Lakes in 1830, meeting Sir Walter Scott and Wordsworth along the way. Scott's epilogue for *The Vespers at Palermo* had led to a correspondence that led, in turn, to their encounter. As for Wordsworth, Hemans was always an admirer of his verse. His lines, she once wrote, 'quite haunt me, and I have a strange feeling as if I must have known them in my childhood, they come over me so like old melodies'.[20] Cumbria impressed her deeply, as she reported to a friend: 'I seem to be writing to you almost from the spirit-land; all is here so brightly still, so remote from everyday cares and tumults, that I sometimes can scarcely persuade myself I am not dreaming. It scarcely seems to be "the light of common day" that is clothing the woody mountain before me; there is something almost *visionary* in its soft gleams and ever-changing shadows. I am charmed with Mr Wordsworth, whose kindness to me has been quite a soothing influence over my spirits.'[21] The two writers evidently got on, and it was on the basis of this meeting that Wordsworth lamented her death in the 1837 text of his *Extempore Effusion on the Death of James Hogg*:

> Mourn rather for that holy spirit,
> Sweet as the spring, as ocean deep;
> For her who, ere her summer faded,
> Has sunk into a breathless sleep.

Friends included Maria Jane Jewsbury and Joanna Baillie, to whom she dedicated *Records of Woman*. She moved to Dublin to be closer to her brother, George, in 1831. In spite of her declining health, she continued to write, and to educate her sons. She died 16 May 1835, of tuberculosis, and was buried in St Anne's Church, Dublin.

It is useful to bear in mind that Britain was at continuous war with France from the year of Felicia's birth to 1815: she spent the first two decades of her life in a country waging war with Napoleon. There were two ways of reacting to this. If, like Anna Laetitia Barbauld, you clung to the ideals of the French Revolution, you were likely to denounce the wars, as she did in *Eighteen Hundred and Eleven*; if, on the other hand, your brothers and husband had seen service in them, as was true of Felicia, you were more likely to strike an appropriately patriotic attitude. This was partly the cause of Felicia's popularity, and explains why her work was acceptable to Tory critics like Croker and Jeffrey, who attacked Barbauld, Keats, Owenson, and Wordsworth for ideological reasons. But it would be a mistake to dismiss Felicia as merely jingoistic; even her early poetry is concerned with much more than love of her country. For one thing, there is the question of her Welshness. Wales was her adopted home, but she felt a profound attachment to it that runs throughout her work. In *The Rock of Cader Idris* that famous mountain, like the Druid bards who once thronged its summits, is freighted not just with a Welshness that she felt to the core of her being, but stands as a symbol of heroic independence against the incursions of 'The crested Roman in his hour of pride'.[22] Such defiant protectiveness towards one's national and personal identity is a crucial element in her thinking about the concept of heroism: she does

---

[20]   Henry F. Chorley, *Memorials of Mrs Hemans*, i 175.   [22]   *The Meeting of the Bards* 10.
[21]   *A Short Sketch of the Life of Mrs Hemans* (1835), p. 26.

not doubt that her brother's efforts in the Peninsular wars are on behalf of 'Cambria's vales and mountains far away'.[23] Heroism is not merely a patriotic pose well struck; it entails the 'ennobled thought'[24] that can dignify even the debased pastimes of the Roman empire in its decline, and it is what redeems Mark Antony's doomed soldiers who, on the eve of their slaughter, hide their anxiety with smiles:

> In every face
> Some shadow from the tempest of the mind,
> Rising by fits, the searching eye might trace,
> Though vainly masked in smiles which are not mirth,
> But the proud spirit's veil thrown o'er the woes of earth.[25]

Pride, defiance, courage in the face of inevitable defeat, even love: these are the virtues that pervade Felicia's poems. All of them provide the justification for that most reviled of monarchs, George III. There was a good deal to criticize in his career; he had, after all, lost America, and his madness had, for long periods, made him an ineffectual ruler. But Felicia views him with compassion; she is straightforward about his illness, but sees him as responsible for having saved Britain from invasion – in other words, as both a guardian of the nation, and a bulwark of patriotic strength: 'Still by thine arm upheld, our ancient landmarks stood'.[26]

Her *Records of Woman* (all of which are included here) famously concentrate on the hardships faced specifically by women. She had a good deal to say on the subject, having been under pressure to support her large family from the moment her husband abandoned her. 'My life after eighteen became so painfully, laboriously domestic, that it was an absolute duty to crush intellectual tastes', she once confided, 'I could neither read nor write legitimately till the day was over'.[27] Many of the *Records of Woman* are concerned with the plight of those lumbered with feckless, unreliable, weak, or ineffectual men: Seymour saves himself, but fails to save Arabella Stuart; Werner Stauffacher is saved only by 'the entreaties of his wife, a woman who seems to have been of an heroic spirit'; Properzia Rossi lavishes her love and art on a man not worthy of her; the Indian Woman is deserted by her husband for another woman, and so forth. But it would be a mistake to describe Felicia as having feminist designs; the other side to these poems is the high value their author places on the relationship between the sexes. *Gertrude, or Fidelity till Death* is about precisely that: Gertrude nurses her husband in his final tormented hours with what Felicia calls 'the most heroic devotedness'. In so doing, she becomes an exemplar for a mode of behaviour that, in spite of her own sad experience, Felicia valorized. Even Juana, despite the neglect with which her husband had treated her, is praised for wifely devotion after his death: 'Surely that humble, patient love *must* win back at last!'[28] It is easy now to laugh at the sentimentality of the boy on the burning deck – *Casabianca* has lost much of its power through the philistine over-familiarity with which the English, in their embarrassment, have treated it. But if read without readiness to scoff, it emerges as a moving story of someone who remains true to their word, even if it means the ultimate sacrifice. None of this, it seems to me, is at all 'feminine', which is how she was categorized by such reviewers as that in the

---

[23] *To my Eldest Brother, with the British Army in Portugal* 30.
[24] *The Statue of the Dying Gladiator* 34.
[25] *The Last Banquet of Antony and Cleopatra* 16–20.
[26] *Stanzas to the Memory of the Late King* 200.
[27] Henry F. Chorley, *Memorials of Mrs Hemans*, i 166, 175.
[28] *Juana* 32.

British Critic who remarked: 'She is especially excellent in painting the strength and the weaknesses of her own lovely sex, and there is a womanly nature throughout all her thoughts and her aspirations, which is new and inexpressibly touching.'[29] Not that any of this is wrong, but the characterization of her as someone who specialized in portraying 'womanly' strengths and weaknesses seriously misrepresents her. The moral questions at the heart of her work are not gender-specific; they extend beyond those barriers into areas of life that concern everyone.

Hemans was deeply Wordsworthian, in that she shared Wordsworth's sense of the numinous. The portent that heralds Antony's downfall in her 1819 poem is as real to her as the second sight which is celebrated in her poem of 1830. No doubt her love of nature as a child had much to do with this (her hatred of Daventry stemmed partly from the lack of green spaces). In this light, her last great poem, *Despondency and Aspiration*, is of particular interest. Composed during her final illness, it is a valedictory that attempts to trace her poetic talent to its roots:

> And then a glorious mountain-chain uprose,
>   Height above spiry height!
> A soaring solitude of woods and snows,
>   All steeped in golden light!
> While as it passed, those regal peaks unveiling,
>   I heard, methought, a waving of dread wings
> And mighty sounds, as if the vision hailing,
>   From lyres that quivered through ten thousand strings . . .[30]

The 'glorious mountain-chain' is Welsh, and the lyres those of the Druid bards she so revered. It is a vision that is morally and ideologically loaded. The mountain range exemplifies the virtues of steadfastness and fidelity she celebrates in her poetry, and which comprise

> The deep religion, which hath dwelt from yore,
> Silently brooding by lone cliff and lake,
>   And wildest river shore![31]

Further Reading

Peter W. Trinder, *Mrs Hemans* (Wales, 1984)

Norma Clarke, *Ambitious Heights: Writing, Friendship, Love – The Jewsbury Sisters, Felicia Hemans, and Jane Welsh Carlyle* (London, 1990)

Nanora Sweet, 'History, Imperialism, and the Aesthetics of the Beautiful: Hemans and the Post-Napoleonic Moment', *Limits* 170–84

Susan J. Wolfson, '"Domestic Affections" and "the spear of Minerva": Felicia Hemans and the Dilemma of Gender', *RR* 128–66

Anthony John Harding, 'Felicia Hemans and the Effacement of Woman', *RWW* 138–49

Jerome J. McGann, *The Poetics of Sensibility: A Revolution in Literary Style* (Oxford, 1996), pp. 174–94

---

[29] *British Critic* 20 (1823) 50–61, p. 52.

[30] *Despondency and Aspiration* 75–82.

[31] Ibid., ll. 141–3.

From Poems (1808)

WRITTEN ON THE SEA-SHORE

How awful, how sublime this view,
Each day presenting something new;
Hark! now the seas majestic roar,
And now the birds their warblings pour;
Now yonder lark's sweet notes resound,   5
And now an awful stillness reigns around.

F.D.B. aged ten

From The Domestic Affections, and Other Poems (1812)

THE STATUE OF THE DYING GLADIATOR

Commanding pow'r, whose hand with plastic art
Bids the rude stone to grace and being start,
Swell to the waving line the polished form,
And only want Promethean fire to warm;
Sculpture, exult, thy triumph proudly see,   5
The Roman slave immortalized by thee!
No suppliant sighs, no terrors round him wait,
But vanquished valour soars above his fate!
In that fixed eye still proud defiance lours,
In that stern look indignant grandeur towers!   10
He sees e'en death, with javelin barbed in pain,
A foe but worthy of sublime disdain!
Too firm, too lofty for one parting tear,
A quiv'ring pulse, a struggle, or a fear!

Oh fire of soul, by servitude disgraced,   15
Perverted courage, energy debased!
Lost Rome, thy slave, expiring in the dust,
Tow'rs far above patrician[1] rank, august!
While that proud rank, insatiate, could survey
Pageants that stained with blood each festal day!   20

Oh had that arm, which graced thy deathful show
With many a daring feat and nervous blow,

THE STATUE OF THE DYING GLADIATOR
[1] *patrician* those who derive from the original families of Rome, from whom senators and other members of the governing class were drawn.

Waved the keen sword and reared the patriot-shield,
Firm in thy cause, on glory's laureate[2] field,
Then, like the marble form, from age to age,　　　　　25
His *name* had lived in history's brightest page,
While death had but secured the victor's crown
And sealed the suffrage of deserved renown,
That gen'rous pride, that spirit unsubdued,
That soul with honour's high-wrought sense imbued　　30
Had shone, recorded in the song of fame,
A beam, as now a blemish, on thy name![3]
　　Yet here, so well has art majestic wrought
Sublimed expression and ennobled thought,
A dying hero we behold alone,　　　　　　35
And mind's bright grandeur animates the stone!
'Tis not th' arena's venal champion bleeds,
No – 'tis some warrior famed for matchless deeds!
Admiring rapture kindles into flame,
Nature and art the palm divided claim!　　　　40
Nature (exulting in her spirit's pow'r
To rise victorious in the dreaded hour)
Triumphs, that death and all his shadowy train
Assail a mortal's constancy in vain!
And art, rejoicing in the work sublime,　　　　45
Unhurt by all the sacrilege of time,
Smiles o'er the marble, her divine control
Moulded to symmetry, and fired with soul!

To my Eldest Brother, with the British Army in Portugal[1]

How many a day in various hues arrayed,
Bright with gay sunshine, or eclipsed with shade –
How many an hour on silent wing is passed,
Oh my loved brother, since we saw thee last?
Since *then* has childhood ripened into youth,　　　5
And fancy's dreams have fled from sober truth,
Her splendid fabrics[2] melting into air,[3]

---

[2] *laureate* deserving of honour.
[3] *Oh had that arm . . . on thy name* i.e. had the man fought on the battlefield (rather than in the gladiatorial arena) he would be celebrated by name, and would illuminate Rome's fame, rather than blemish it, as he does now.

To my Eldest Brother, with the British Army in Portugal
[1] Napoleon conquered Portugal in late 1807; the British landed there 1 August 1808, conquered Lisbon, and forced the evacuation of the French with the Convention of Cintra at the end of the month. However, the French returned the following year, and waged numerous battles and campaigns for the next two years. Wellington successfully defended his base in Portugal, and in 1812 began reclaiming Spain from the French. The Battle of Vitoria, 21 June 1813, decided the issue with the defeat of the French.

[2] *fabrics* buildings.
[3] *Her splendid fabrics melting into air* a borrowing from Prospero, who remarks that 'the baseless fabric of this vision', like spirits, 'Are melted into air, into thin air' (*Tempest* IV i 150–1).

As sage Experience waved the wand of care!
Yet *still* thine absence wakes the tender sigh
And the tear trembles in Affection's eye!   10
When shall we meet again? With glowing ray
Heart-soothing Hope illumes some future day,
Checks the sad thought, beguiles the starting tear,
And sings benignly still – *that* day is near!
She, with bright eye and soul-bewitching voice,   15
Wins us to smile, inspires us to rejoice,
Tells that the hour approaches to restore
Our cherished wanderer to his home once more,
Where sacred ties his manly worth endear
To faith still true, affection still sincere!   20
Then the past woes, the future's dubious lot,
In that blessed meeting shall be *all* forgot,
And joy's full radiance gild that sun-bright hour,
Though all around th' impending storm should lour!
    Now distant far, amidst th' intrepid host,   25
Albion's firm sons on Lusitania's[4] coast
(That gallant band, in countless danger tried,
Where glory's pole-star beams their constant guide),
Say, do *thy* thoughts, my brother, fondly stray
To Cambria's[5] vales and mountains far away?   30
Does fancy oft in busy daydreams roam,
And paint the greeting that awaits at home?
Does memory's pencil oft, in mellowing hue,
Dear social scenes, departed joys renew,
In softer tints delighting to retrace   35
Each tender image and each well-known face?
Yes, wanderer, yes, thy spirit flies to those
Whose love unaltered, warm and faithful glows!
    Oh, could that love, through life's eventful hours,
Illume thy scenes and strew thy path with flow'rs!   40
Perennial joy should harmonize thy breast,
No struggle rend thee, and no cares molest!
But though our tenderness can but bestow
The wish, the hope, the prayer averting woe,
Still shall it live, with pure unclouded flame,   45
In storms, in sunshine, far and near – the same;
Still dwell enthroned within th' unvarying heart,
And firm and *vital*, but with life depart!

Bronwhylfa,[6] 8 February 1811

---

4   *Lusitania* Portugal.
5   *Cambria* Wales.

6   *Bronwhylfa* near St Asaph, Flintshire, North Wales,
Browne family home since 1809.

From Tales, and Historic Scenes, In Verse (1819)

THE LAST BANQUET OF ANTONY AND CLEOPATRA[1]

Antony, concluding that he could not die more honourably than in battle, determined to attack Caesar at the same time both by sea and land. The night preceding the execution of this design, he ordered his servants at supper to render him their best services that evening, and fill the wine round plentifully, for the day following they might belong to another master, whilst he lay extended on the ground, no longer of consequence either to them or to himself. His friends were affected, and wept to hear him talk thus; which, when he perceived, he encouraged them by assurances that his expectations of a glorious victory were at least equal to those of an honourable death. At the dead of night, when universal silence reigned through the city, a silence that was deepened by the awful thought of the ensuing day, on a sudden was heard the sound of musical instruments, and a noise which resembled the exclamations of Bacchanals.[2] This tumultuous procession seemed to pass through the whole city, and to go out at the gate which led to the enemy's camp. Those who reflected on this prodigy[3] concluded that Bacchus, the god whom Antony affected to imitate, had then forsaken him.

Langhorne's *Plutarch*[4]

Thy foes had girt[5] thee with their dread array,
  Oh stately Alexandria,[6] yet the sound
Of mirth and music, at the close of day,
  Swelled from thy splendid fabrics,[7] far around
O'er camp and wave. Within the royal hall,   5
  In gay magnificence the feast was spread,
And, brightly streaming from the pictured wall,
  A thousand lamps their trembling lustre shed
O'er many a column, rich with precious dyes
That tinge the marble's vein, 'neath Afric's burning skies.   10

And soft and clear that wavering radiance played
  O'er sculptured forms that round the pillared scene
Calm and majestic rose, by art arrayed
  In godlike beauty, awfully serene.
Oh how unlike the troubled guests, reclined   15

THE LAST BANQUET OF ANTONY AND CLEOPATRA
[1] Mark Antony (82/81 BC–August 30 BC, Alexandria) was a Roman general under Julius Caesar and triumvir (43–30 BC). He was defeated by Octavian (future Emperor Augustus) in the last of the civil wars that destroyed the Roman republic. Cleopatra VII (69–30 BC) was the lover of Julius Caesar and the wife of Mark Antony (40 BC onwards). Felicia would have known their story both from Plutarch and from Shakespeare's *Antony and Cleopatra*.

[2] *Bacchanals* devotees of Bacchus, god of wine.
[3] *prodigy* omen.
[4] *Plutarch's Lives* tr. John and William Langhorne (6 vols, 1770); this popular translation had reached a ninth edition in 1805. Plutarch's Life of Antony is one of his longest and most vivid.
[5] *girt* surrounded.
[6] *Alexandria* in Egypt; Antony had allied his forces with those of Cleopatra.
[7] *fabrics* buildings.

Round that luxurious board! In every face
Some shadow from the tempest of the mind,
    Rising by fits, the searching eye might trace,
Though vainly masked in smiles which are not mirth,
But the proud spirit's veil thrown o'er the woes of earth.   20

Their brows are bound with wreaths[8] whose transient bloom
    May still survive the wearers, and the rose
Perchance may scarce be withered, when the tomb
    Receives the mighty to its dark repose!
The day must dawn on battle, and may set   25
    In death – but fill the mantling[9] wine-cup high!
Despair is fearless, and the Fates e'en yet
    Lend her one hour for parting revelry.
They who the empire of the world possessed
Would taste its joys again, ere all exchanged for rest.   30

Its joys – oh mark yon proud triumvir's[10] mien,
    And read their annals on that brow of care!
Midst pleasure's lotus-bowers his steps have been;
    Earth's brightest pathway led him to despair.
Trust not the glance that fain would yet inspire   35
    The buoyant energies of days gone by;
There is delusion in its meteor-fire,
    And all within is shame, is agony!
Away the tear in bitterness may flow,
But there are smiles which bear a stamp of deeper woe.   40

Thy cheek is sunk and faded as thy fame,
    Oh lost, devoted Roman! Yet thy brow
To that ascendant and undying name
    Pleads with stern loftiness thy right e'en now.
Thy glory is departed, but hath left   45
    A lingering light around thee – in decay
Not less than kingly, though of all bereft,
    Thou seem'st as empire had not passed away.
Supreme in ruin, teaching hearts elate,
A deep prophetic dread of still mysterious fate!   50

But thou, enchantress-queen,[11] whose love hath made
    His desolation – thou art by his side,
In all thy sovereignty of charms arrayed,
    To meet the storm with still unconquered pride.

---

[8] *wreaths* laurel wreaths symbolized victory.
[9] *mantling* sparkling.

[10] The triumvirate of Octavian, Antony and Lepidus
ruled the Roman empire.
[11] *enchantress-queen* Cleopatra.

Imperial being, e'en though many a stain   55
   Of error be upon thee, there is power
In thy commanding nature, which shall reign
   O'er the stern genius of misfortune's hour;
And the dark beauty of thy troubled eye
E'en now is all illumed with wild sublimity.   60

Thine aspect, all impassioned, wears a light
   Inspiring and inspired – thy cheek a dye
Which rises not from joy, but yet is bright
   With the deep glow of feverish energy.
Proud siren of the Nile! Thy glance is fraught   65
   With an immortal fire – in every beam
It darts, there kindles some heroic thought,
   But wild and awful as a sibyl's[12] dream;
For thou with death hast communed, to attain
Dread knowledge of the pangs that ransom from the chain.[13]   70

And the stern courage by such musings lent,
   Daughter of Afric, o'er thy beauty throws
The grandeur of a regal spirit, blent
   With all the majesty of mighty woes;
While he, so fondly, fatally adored,   75
   Thy fallen Roman, gazes on thee yet,
Till scarce the soul, that once exulting soared,
   Can deem the daystar of its glory set;
Scarce his charmed heart believes that power can be
In sovereign fate, o'er him, thus fondly loved by thee.   80

But there is sadness in the eyes around,
   Which mark[14] that ruined leader, and survey
His changeful mien, whence oft the gloom profound
   Strange triumph chases haughtily away.
'Fill the bright goblet, warrior guests!' he cries,   85
   'Quaff, ere we part, the generous[15] nectar deep!
Ere sunset gild once more the western skies,
   Your chief, in cold forgetfulness, may sleep,
While sounds of revel float o'er shore and sea,
And the red bowl again is crowned – but not for me.   90

---

[12] *sibyl* prophetess, fortune teller.
[13] 'Cleopatra made a collection of poisonous drugs, and being desirous to know which was least painful in the operation, she tried them on the capital convicts. Such poisons as were quick in their operation, she found to be attended with violent pain and convulsions; such as were milder were slow in their effect. She therefore applied herself to the examination of venomous creatures, and at length she found that the bite of the asp was the most eligible kind of death, for it brought on a gradual kind of lethargy. See Plutarch' (Hemans's note).
[14] *mark* regard.
[15] *generous* abundant.

'Yet weep not thus; the struggle is not o'er,
  Oh victors of Philippi,[16] many a field
Hath yielded palms to us! One effort more,
  By one stern conflict must our doom be sealed!
Forget not, Romans, o'er a subject world   95
  How royally your eagle's wing hath spread,
Though from his eyrie of dominion hurled,
  Now bursts the tempest on his crested head!
Yet sovereign still, if banished from the sky,
The sun's indignant bird, he must not droop, but die.'   100

The feast is o'er. 'Tis night, the dead of night;
  Unbroken stillness broods o'er earth and deep;
From Egypt's heaven of soft and starry light
  The moon looks cloudless o'er a world of sleep.
For those who wait the morn's awakening beams,   105
  The battle signal to decide their doom,
Have sunk to feverish rest and troubled dreams –
  Rest, that shall soon be calmer in the tomb,
Dreams, dark and ominous, but *there* to cease,
When sleep the lords of war in solitude and peace.   110

Wake, slumberers, wake! Hark! Heard ye not a sound
  Of gathering tumult? Near and nearer still
Its murmur swells. Above, below, around,
  Bursts a strange chorus forth, confused and shrill.
Wake, Alexandria! Through thy streets the tread   115
  Of steps unseen is hurrying, and the note
Of pipe and lyre and trumpet, wild and dread,
  Is heard upon the midnight air to float;
And voices, clamorous as in frenzied mirth,
Mingle their thousand tones, which are not of the earth.   120

These are no mortal sounds; their thrilling strain
  Hath more mysterious power, and birth more high;
And the deep horror chilling every vein
  Owns them of stern, terrific augury.
Beings of worlds unknown, ye pass away,   125
  Oh ye invisible and awful throng!
Your echoing footsteps and resounding lay
  To Caesar's camp exulting move along.
Thy gods forsake thee, Antony! The sky
By that dread sign reveals thy doom: 'Despair and die!'[17] 130

---

[16] *Philippi* At the Battle of Philippi, 42 BC, the combined forces of the triumvirate defeated their enemies, Marcus Brutus and Cassius, who later killed themselves.

[17] '"Tomorrow in the battle think on me, / And fall thy edgeless sword; despair and die!" Richard III' (Hemans's note). See *Richard III*, V iii 163–4.

Stanzas to the Memory of the Late King (1820)

Among many nations was there no King like him.

Nehemiah[1]

Know ye not that there is a prince and a great man fallen this day in Israel!

Samuel[2]

Another warning sound! The funeral bell,
   Startling the cities of the isle once more
With measured tones of melancholy swell,
   Strikes on th' awakened heart from shore to shore.
He at whose coming monarchs sink to dust[3]   5
   The chambers of our palaces hath trod,
And the long-suffering spirit of the just,
   Pure from its ruins, hath returned to God![4]
Yet may not England o'er her father weep –
Thoughts to her bosom crowd, too many and too deep.   10

Vain voice of reason, hush! They yet must flow,
   The unrestrained, involuntary tears;
A thousand feelings sanctify the woe,
   Roused by the glorious shades of vanished years.
Tell us no more 'tis not the time for grief   15
   Now that the exile of the soul is past,
And Death, blest messenger of Heaven's relief,
   Hath borne the wanderer to his rest at last;
For him, eternity hath tenfold day,
We feel, we know 'tis thus – yet nature will have way.   20

What though amidst us, like a blasted oak,
   Sadd'ning the scene where once it nobly reigned,
A dread memorial of the lightning stroke,
   Stamped with its fiery record, he remained;[5]
Around that shattered tree still fondly clung   25
   Th' undying tendrils of our love,[6] which drew
Fresh nurture from its deep decay, and sprung
   Luxuriant thence, to glory's ruin true,

STANZAS TO THE MEMORY OF THE LATE KING (1820)
[1] Nehemiah 13:26, on Solomon, for reforming the abuses of the Sabbath.
[2] II Samuel 3:38; words spoken by King David, lamenting the death of Abner.
[3] *He at whose coming monarchs sink to dust* i.e. death.
[4] George III, born 4 June 1738, died 29 January 1820 at Windsor Castle.

[5] Hemans refers to George III's inherited disease, porphyria, that caused agonizing pain, overactivity, paralysis and delirium. He suffered it in acute form at least four times during his reign; it is the subject of Alan Bennett's play, *The Madness of George III*.
[6] *Th' undying tendrils of our love* the peoples' love is like ivy, clinging to the trunk of the shattered tree (the King), drawing from it the strength with which to fight.

While England hung her trophies on the stem
That desolately stood, unconscious e'en of *them*.[7]   30

Of *them* unconscious! Oh mysterious doom![8]
Who shall unfold the counsels of the skies?[9]
His was the voice which roused, as from the tomb,
The realm's high soul to loftiest energies![10]
His was the spirit o'er the isles[11] which threw   35
The mantle[12] of its fortitude, and wrought
In every bosom, powerful to renew
Each dying spark of pure and generous thought;
The star of tempests beaming on the mast,[13]
The seaman's torch of hope, midst perils deepening fast.   40

Then from th' unslumbering influence of his worth,
Strength, as of inspiration, filled the land;
A young but quenchless flame went brightly forth,
Kindled by him – who saw it not expand!
Such was the will of Heaven: the gifted seer,[14]   45
Who with his God had communed, face to face,[15]
And from the house of bondage[16] and of fear,
In faith victorious, led the chosen race –
He through the desert and the waste their guide,
Saw dimly from afar the promised land, and died.[17]   50

Oh full of days and virtues! On thy head
Centred the woes of many a bitter lot:
Fathers have sorrowed o'er their beauteous dead;
Eyes, quenched in night,[18] the sunbeam have forgot;
Minds have striv'n buoyantly with evil years,   55
And sunk beneath their gathering weight at length;
But Pain for thee had filled a cup of tears
Where every anguish mingled all its strength;
By thy lost child[19] we saw thee weeping stand,
And shadows deep around fell from th' Eternal's hand.   60

---

[7] *them* i.e. the trophies of war with France.
[8] *doom* fate.
[9] *counsels of the skies* i.e. will of the gods.
[10] *loftiest energies* a reference, presumably, to the wars with America and France, prosecuted under George III's reign. This was not the light in which Anna Laetitia Barbauld viewed these events, in *Eighteen Hundred and Eleven* (see pp. 10–18).
[11] *isles* the British isles.
[12] *mantle* cloak.
[13] 'The glittering meteor, like a star, which often appears about a ship during tempests, if seen upon the main-mast, is considered by the sailors as an omen of good weather. See Dampier's *Voyages*' (Hemans's note).

William Dampier (1652–1715) published his *A New Voyage round the World* in 1697.
[14] *the gifted seer* the prophet Moses.
[15] Moses conversed with God on Mount Sinai, Exodus 19:21–4.
[16] *house of bondage* a biblical expression; see Exodus 13:14. The Israelites were led out of Egypt, the house of bondage, by Moses.
[17] Moses died in the land of Moab, within sight of Israel, at the age of 120, Deuteronomy 34:5.
[18] *Eyes, quenched in night* an effect of the King's ailment was that he went blind in his last years.
[19] *thy lost child* Princess Amelia died in 1810.

Then came the noon of glory,[20] which thy dreams
    Perchance of yore had faintly prophesied;
But what to *thee* the splendour of its beams?
    The ice-rock glows not midst the summer's pride!
Nations leaped up to joy, as streams that burst,   65
    At the warm touch of spring, their frozen chain,
And o'er the plains, whose verdure once they nursed,
    Roll in exulting melody again;
And bright o'er earth the long majestic line
Of England's triumphs swept, to rouse all hearts – but thine.   70

Oh what a dazzling vision, by the veil
    That o'er thy spirit hung, was shut from thee,
When sceptred chieftains thronged with palms to hail
    The crowning isle, th' anointed of the sea![21]
Within thy palaces the lords of earth   75
    Met to rejoice – rich pageants glittered by,
And stately revels imaged, in their mirth,
    The old magnificence of chivalry.
They reached not thee – amidst them, yet alone,
Stillness and gloom begirt one dim and shadowy throne.   80

Yet there was mercy still; if joy no more
    Within that blasted circle might intrude,
Earth had no grief whose footstep might pass o'er
    The silent limits of its solitude!
If all unheard the bridal song awoke   85
    Our hearts' full echoes, as it swelled on high,
Alike unheard the sudden dirge, that broke
    On the glad strain, with dread solemnity!
If the land's rose unheeded wore its bloom,
Alike unfelt the storm that swept it to the tomb!   90

And she[22] who, tried through all the stormy past,
    Severely, deeply proved, in many an hour,
Watched o'er thee, firm and faithful to the last,
    Sustained, inspired, by strong affection's power;
If to thy soul her voice no music bore,   95
    If thy closed eye and wandering spirit caught
No light from looks that fondly would explore
    Thy mien for traces of responsive thought –
Oh thou wert spared the pang that would have thrilled
Thine inmost heart, when death that anxious bosom stilled.   100

---

[20] *the noon of glory* The French were defeated in 1815, after the accession of the Prince Regent in 1811.
[21] *The crowning isle, th' anointed of the sea* i.e. England.

[22] *she* Queen Charlotte, whose marriage with George III lasted over fifty years, mainly through her strength of character.

Thy loved ones fell around thee – manhood's prime;
  Youth, with its glory; in its fullness, age –
All at the gates of their eternal clime
  Lay down and closed their mortal pilgrimage;
The land wore ashes[23] for its perished flowers,   105
  The grave's imperial harvest. Thou, meanwhile,
Didst walk unconscious through thy royal towers,
  The one that wept not in the tearful isle,
As a tired warrior on his battle-plain
Breathes deep in dreams amidst the mourners and the slain.   110

And who can tell what visions might be thine?
  The stream of thought, though broken, still was pure!
Still o'er that wave the stars of heaven might shine,
  Where earthly image would no more endure!
Though many a step, of once-familiar sound,   115
  Came as a stranger's o'er thy closing ear,
And voices breathed forgotten tones around,
  Which that paternal heart once thrilled to hear,
The mind hath senses of its own, and powers
To people boundless worlds in its most wandering hours.   120

Nor might the phantoms to thy spirit known
  Be dark or wild, creations of remorse;
Unstained by thee, the blameless past had thrown
  No fearful shadows o'er the future's course:
For thee no cloud, from memory's dread abyss,   125
  Might shape such forms as haunt the tyrant's eye,
And, closing up each avenue of bliss,
  Murmur their summons, to 'despair and die!'[24]
No! E'en though joy depart, though reason cease,
Still virtue's ruined home is redolent of peace.   130

They might be with thee still – the loved, the tried,
  The fair, the lost – they might be with thee still!
More softly seen, in radiance purified
  From each dim vapour of terrestrial ill;
Long after earth received them, and the note   135
  Of the last requiem o'er their dust was poured,
As passing sunbeams o'er thy soul might float
  Those forms, from us withdrawn – to thee restored!
Spirits of holiness, in light revealed,
To commune with a mind whose source of tears was sealed!   140

---

[23] *ashes* token of mourning.

[24] 'Tomorrow in the battle think on me, / And fall thy edgeless sword; despair and die!' (*Richard III*, V iii 163–4).

Came they with tidings from the worlds above,
  Those viewless regions where the weary rest?
Severed from earth, estranged from mortal love,
  Was thy mysterious converse with the blessed?
Or shone their visionary presence bright   145
  With human beauty? Did their smiles renew
Those days of sacred and serene delight,
  When fairest beings in thy pathway grew?
Oh, Heaven hath balm for every wound it makes,
Healing the broken heart; it smites, but ne'er forsakes.   150

These may be fantasies – and this alone,
  Of all we picture in our dreams, is sure:
That rest, made perfect, is at length thine own –
  Rest, in thy God immortally secure!
Enough for tranquil faith; released from all   155
  The woes that graved[25] Heaven's lessons on thy brow,
No cloud to dim, no fetter to enthral,
  Haply thine eye is on thy people now,
Whose love around thee still its offerings shed,
Though vainly sweet as flowers, grief's tribute to the dead.[26]   160

But if th' ascending, disembodied mind,
  Borne on the wings of morning to the skies,
May cast one glance of tenderness behind
  On scenes once hallowed by its mortal ties,
How much hast thou to gaze on! – all that lay   165
  By the dark mantle[27] of thy soul concealed,
The might, the majesty, the proud array
  Of England's march o'er many a noble field,
All spread beneath thee, in a blaze of light,
Shine like some glorious land viewed from an Alpine height.   170

Away, presumptuous thought! Departed saint,
  To thy freed vision what can earth display
Of pomp, of royalty, that is not faint,
  Seen from the birthplace of celestial day?
Oh pale and weak the sun's reflected rays,   175
  E'en in their fervour of meridian[28] heat,
To him who in the sanctuary[29] may gaze
  On the bright cloud that fills the mercy-seat![30]
And thou may'st view, from thy divine abode,
The dust of empires flit before a breath of God.   180

---

[25] *graved* engraved.
[26] *grief's tribute to the dead* i.e. tears.
[27] *mantle* the same cloak as at line 36.
[28] *meridian* noonday.

[29] *the sanctuary* heaven, as at *Paradise Lost* vi 672: 'the sanctuary of heaven secure'.
[30] *the mercy-seat* the golden covering placed upon the Ark of the Covenant, regarded as the resting place of God.

And yet we mourn thee! Yes, thy place is void
   Within our hearts – there veiled thine image dwelt,
But cherished still; and o'er that tie destroyed,
   Though faith rejoice, fond nature still must melt.
Beneath the long-loved sceptre of thy sway,   185
   Thousands were born who now in dust repose,
And many a head, with years and sorrows grey,
   Wore youth's bright tresses when thy star arose;
And many a glorious mind, since that fair dawn,
Hath filled our sphere with light, now to its source withdrawn.   190

Earthquakes have rocked the nations;[31] things revered,
   Th' ancestral fabrics[32] of the world, went down
In ruins, from whose stones Ambition reared
   His lonely pyramid of dread renown.
But when the fires that long had slumbered,[33] pent   195
   Deep in men's bosoms, with volcanic force,
Bursting their prison-house, each bulwark rent
   And swept each holy barrier from their course,
Firm and unmoved amidst that lava-flood,
Still by thine arm upheld, our ancient landmarks stood.   200

Be they eternal! Be thy children found
   Still, to their country's altars, true like thee!
And, while 'the name of Briton' is a sound
   Of rallying music to the brave and free,
With the high feelings, at the word which swell,   205
   To make the breast a shrine for Freedom's flame,
Be mingled thoughts of him who loved so well,
   Who left so pure, its heritage of fame!
Let earth with trophies guard the conqueror's dust,
Heaven in our souls embalms the memory of the just.   210

All else shall pass away – the thrones of kings,
   The very traces of their *tombs* depart;
But number not with perishable things
   The holy records virtue leaves the heart,
Heirlooms from race to race! And oh, in days   215
   When, by the yet unborn, thy deeds are blessed,
When our sons learn, 'as household words', thy praise,
   Still on thine offspring may thy spirit rest!
And many a name of that imperial line,
Father and patriot, blend in England's songs, with thine!   220

---

[31] *Earthquakes have rocked the nations* Recent earthquakes famous for their devastation included those in Lisbon (1755), Iran (1780) and Mexico (1811).
[32] *fabrics* houses.

[33] *the fires that long had slumbered* a reference to the American and French Revolutions, both of which occurred under George III's reign.

From Welsh Melodies (1822)

THE ROCK OF CADER IDRIS[1]

It is an old tradition of the Welsh bards that, on the summit of the mountain Cader Idris, is an excavation resembling a couch, and that whoever should pass a night in that hollow would be found in the morning either dead, in a state of frenzy, or endowed with the highest poetical inspiration.

I lay on that rock where the storms have their dwelling,
   The birthplace of phantoms, the home of the cloud;
Around it for ever deep music is swelling,
   The voice of the mountain-wind, solemn and loud.
'Twas a midnight of shadows all fitfully streaming,   5
   Of wild waves and breezes that mingled their moan,
Of dim shrouded stars, as from gulfs faintly gleaming,
   And I met the dread gloom of its grandeur alone.

I lay there in silence – a spirit came o'er me;
   Man's tongue hath no language to speak what I saw: 10
Things glorious, unearthly, passed floating before me,
   And my heart almost fainted with rapture and awe.
I viewed the dread beings around us that hover,
   Though veiled by the mists of mortality's breath;
And I called upon darkness the vision to cover,   15
   For a strife was within me of madness and death.

I saw them – the powers of the wind and the ocean,
   The rush of whose pinion bears onward the storms;
Like the sweep of the white-rolling wave was their motion,
   I *felt* their dim presence, but knew not their forms!   20
I saw them – the mighty of ages departed –
   The dead were around me that night on the hill:
From their eyes, as they passed, a cold radiance they darted –
   There was light on my soul, but my heart's blood was chill.

I saw what man looks on, and dies – but my spirit   25
   Was strong, and triumphantly lived through that hour;
And as from the grave, I awoke to inherit
   A flame all immortal, a voice, and a power!
Day burst on that rock with the purple cloud crested,
   And high Cader Idris rejoiced in the sun –   30
But oh, what new glory all nature invested,
   When the sense which gives soul to her beauty was won!

THE ROCK OF CADER IDRIS
[1] *Cader Idris* (Chair of Idris), a long mountain ridge,
reaching a height of 2,927ft, at Pen-y-Gader.

From The Siege of Valencia; a Dramatic Poem. The Last
Constantine: With Other Poems (1823)

THE MEETING OF THE BARDS. WRITTEN FOR AN EISTEDDFOD, OR MEETING
OF WELSH BARDS, HELD IN LONDON, 22 MAY 1822[1]

The Gorseddau, or meetings of the British bards, were anciently ordained to be held
in the open air, on some conspicuous situation, whilst the sun was above the horizon;
or, according to the expression employed on these occasions, 'in the face of the sun,
and in the eye of light'.[2] The places set apart for this purpose were marked out by
a circle of stones, called the circle of federation. The presiding bard stood on a large
stone (Maen Gorsedd, or the stone of assembly) in the centre. The sheathing of a sword
upon this stone was the ceremony which announced the opening of a Gorsedd, or
meeting. The bards always stood in their unicoloured robes, with their heads and feet
uncovered, within the circle of federation. See Owen's *Translation of the Heroic Elegies of
Llywarç Hen.*[3]

> Where met our bards of old, the glorious throng,
> They of the mountain and the battle song?
> They met – oh, not in kingly hall or bower,
> But where wild nature girt herself with power:
> They met where streams flashed bright from rocky caves, 5
> They met where woods made moan o'er warriors' graves,
> And where the torrent's rainbow spray was cast,
> And where dark lakes were heaving to the blast,
> And midst th' eternal cliffs, whose strength defied
> The crested Roman in his hour of pride;[4] 10
> And where the carnedd,[5] on its lonely hill,
> Bore silent record of the mighty still;
> And where the Druid's[6] ancient cromlech[7] frowned,
> And the oaks breathed mysterious murmurs round.

THE MEETING OF THE BARDS
[1] This poem was first published in the *Cambro-Briton*
3 (1822) 502–3, as *Lines on the Eisteddfod of the
Cymmrodorion.* It was read out at the Eisteddfod, as the
Cambro-Briton reported. It is worth noting that when
published in *The Siege of Valencia* (1823), the *British Critic*
commented: 'There are many pieces in this volume
which we shall not mention that had been better left
in the *Monthly,* or *Edinburgh Magazines,* or deposited in
the archives of that foolish body of people, who meet
in London, under the name of Eisteddvod (as we
copy it), and celebrate Welsh bardism, and Far Faliessin
and Hoel, and so forth, "in the sun's face, beneath
the eye of light", forsooth; when it is an even wager
that these precious Bards must pay for candles to
read their speeches by. This and Mr Irving's preach-
ing are the two greatest humbugs in London' (*British
Critic* 20 (1823) 50–61, p. 59).

[2] When the poem appeared in the *Cambro-Briton,* the
editor appended a note to this line: 'This is a literal
translation of the Bardic expression, "Yn wyneb haul
a llygad goleuni"'.
[3] William Owen (later William Owen Pughe) (1759–
1835) published *The Heroic Elegies and Other Pieces of
Llywarç Hen* in 1792.
[4] Caesar invaded Britain 55 or 54 BC. Wales was
inhabited by the Ordovices and Silures who, with the
renegade British leader Caractacus, were notori-
ously resistant to Roman invaders. Wales was finally
conquered by 78 AD.
[5] *carnedd* 'a stone barrow, or cairn' (Hemans's note).
[6] The Druids were the learned class among the
ancient Celts, who frequented oak forests and acted
as priests and teachers.
[7] *cromlech* 'a Druidical monument, or altar. The word
means a stone of covenant' (Hemans's note).

There thronged th' inspired of yore! On plain or height,   15
In the sun's face, beneath the eye of light,
And, baring unto heaven each noble head,
Stood in the circle, where none else might tread.
    Well might their lays be lofty! Soaring thought
From nature's presence tenfold grandeur caught;   20
Well might bold freedom's soul pervade the strains
Which startled eagles from their lone domains,
And, like a breeze in chainless triumph, went
Up through the blue resounding firmament.
    Whence came the echoes to those numbers high?   25
'Twas from the battlefields of days gone by,
And from the tombs of heroes laid to rest
With their good swords upon the mountain's breast;
And from the watchtowers on the heights of snow,
Severed by cloud and storm from all below;   30
And the turf-mounds,[8] once girt by ruddy spears,
And the rock-altars of departed years.
    Thence, deeply mingling with the torrent's roar,
The winds a thousand wild responses bore;
And the green land, whose every vale and glen   35
Doth shrine[9] the memory of heroic men,
On all her hills awakening to rejoice,
Sent forth proud answers to her children's voice.
For us, not ours the festival to hold
Midst the stone-circles, hallowed thus of old;   40
Not where great nature's majesty and might
First broke, all-glorious, on our infant sight;
Not near the tombs, where sleep our free and brave,
Not by the mountain-llyn,[10] the ocean wave,
In these late days we meet – dark Mona's[11] shore,   45
Eryri's[12] cliffs resound with harps no more!
But as the stream (though time or art may turn
The current, bursting from its caverned urn,
To bathe soft vales of pasture and of flowers,
From Alpine glens, or ancient forest bowers)   50
Alike, in rushing strength, or sunny sleep,
Holds on its course, to mingle with the deep –
Thus, though our paths be changed, still warm and free,
Land of the bard, our spirit flies to thee!
To thee our thoughts, our hopes, our hearts belong,   55
Our dreams are haunted by thy voice of song!

---

[8] 'The ancient British chiefs frequently harangued their followers from small artificial mounds of turf. See Pennant' (Hemans's note). Thomas Pennant (1726–98) published his *Tour in Wales*, 1778–81.
[9] *shrine* enshrine.
[10] *llyn* 'a lake or pool' (Hemans's note).

[11] *Mona* Isle of Anglesey at the north-west tip of Wales. It was a famous Druid centre and stronghold of resistance to the Romans.
[12] *Eryri* 'Snowdon' (Hemans's note). At 3,560 ft, Snowdon is the highest peak in England and Wales.

Nor yield our souls one patriot feeling less
To the green memory of thy loveliness
Than theirs whose harp-notes pealed from every height,
In the sun's face, beneath the eye of light!   60

THE VOICE OF SPRING[1]

I come, I come – ye have called me long;
I come o'er the mountains with light and song!
Ye may trace my step o'er the wakening earth,
By the winds which tell of the violet's birth,
By the primrose-stars in the shadowy grass,   5
By the green leaves, opening as I pass.

I have breathed on the south, and the chestnut flowers
By thousands have burst from the forest-bowers,
And the ancient graves and the fallen fanes
Are veiled with wreaths[2] on Italian plains –   10
But it is not for me, in my hour of bloom,
To speak of the ruin or the tomb!

I have looked o'er the hills of the stormy north
And the larch has hung all his tassels forth,
The fisher is out on the sunny sea,   15
And the reindeer bounds o'er the pastures free,
And the pine has a fringe of softer green,
And the moss looks bright, where my foot hath been.

I have sent through the wood-paths a glowing sigh,
And called out each voice of the deep blue sky;   20
From the night-bird's lay through the starry time
In the groves of the soft Hesperian[3] clime,
To the swan's wild note by the Iceland lakes,
When the dark fir-branch into verdure breaks.

From the streams and founts I have loosed the chain,   25
They are sweeping onto the silvery main,
They are flashing down from the mountain brows,
They are flinging spray o'er the forest-boughs,
They are bursting fresh from their sparry caves,
And the earth resounds with the joy of waves!   30

THE VOICE OF SPRING

[1] 'Originally published in the *New Monthly Magazine*' (Hemans's note). In her memoir, Felicia's sister quotes a letter in which Felicia remarks that '*The Voice of Spring* expresses some peculiar feelings of my own, although my life has yet been unvisited by any affliction so deeply impressive, in all its circumstances, as the one you have been called upon to sustain. Yet I cannot but feel every year, with the return of the violet, how much the shadows of my mind have deepened since its last appearance; and to me the spring, with all its joy and beauty, is generally a time of thoughtfulness rather than mirth' (*The Works of Mrs Hemans* (7 vols, Edinburgh and London, 1839), i 66).
[2] *wreaths* of past glories.
[3] *Hesperian* Italian, as at *Paradise Lost* i 520: 'the Hesperian fields'.

Come forth, oh ye children of gladness, come!
Where the violets lie may be now your home;
Ye of the rose lip and dew-bright eye,
And the bounding footstep, to meet me fly!
With the lyre, and the wreath, and the joyous lay,   35
Come forth to the sunshine, I may not stay.

Away from the dwellings of careworn men,
The waters are sparkling in grove and glen!
Away from the chamber and sullen hearth,
The young leaves are dancing in breezy mirth!   40
Their light stems thrill to the wildwood strains,
And youth is abroad in my green domains.

But ye! Ye are changed since ye met me last!
There is something bright from your features passed!
There is that come over your brow and eye   45
Which speaks of a world where the flowers must die!
Ye smile, but your smile hath a dimness yet –
Oh what have you looked on since last we met?

Ye are changed, ye are changed! And I see not here
All whom I saw in the vanished year!   50
There were graceful heads, with their ringlets bright,
Which tossed in the breeze with a play of light;
There were eyes, in whose glistening laughter lay
No faint remembrance of dull decay!

There were steps that flew o'er the cowslip's head,   55
As if for a banquet all earth were spread;
There were voices that rung through the sapphire sky,[4]
And had not a sound of mortality!
Are they gone? Is their mirth from the mountains passed?
Ye have looked on death since ye met me last!   60

I know whence the shadow comes o'er you now,
Ye have strewn the dust on the sunny brow!
Ye have given the lovely to earth's embrace,
She hath taken the fairest of beauty's race,
With their laughing eyes and their festal crown,   65
They are gone from amongst you in silence down!

They are gone from amongst you, the young and fair,
Ye have lost the gleam of their shining hair!
But I know of a land where there falls no blight,

---

[4] *the sapphire sky* cf. *Paradise Lost* iv 605, where the
sky glows 'With living sapphires'.

I shall find them there, with their eyes of light!   70
Where Death midst the blooms of the morn may dwell,
I tarry no longer – farewell, farewell!

The summer is coming, on soft winds borne,
Ye may press the grape, ye may bind the corn!
For me, I depart to a brighter shore,   75
Ye are marked by care, ye are mine no more;
I go where the loved who have left you dwell,
And the flowers are not death's – fare ye well, farewell!

From The Forest Sanctuary; and Other Poems (1825)

THE STRANGER IN LOUISIANA

An early traveller mentions a people on the banks of the Mississippi who burst into
tears at the sight of a stranger. The reason of this is that they fancy their deceased
friends and relations to be only gone on a journey and, being in constant expectation
of their return, look for them vainly amongst these foreign travellers.

Picart's *Ceremonies and Religious Customs*[1]

'J'ai passé moi-meme', says Chateaubriand in his *Souvenirs d'Amerique*,[2] 'chez une peuplade
indienne qui se prenait à pleurer à la vue d'un voyageur, parce qu'il lui rappelait des
amis partis pour la *Contrée des Ames*, et depuis long-tems *en voyage*.'[3]

We saw thee, oh stranger, and wept!
We looked for the youth of the sunny glance
Whose step was the fleetest in chase or dance!
The light of his eye was a joy to see,
The path of his arrows a storm to flee!   5
But there came a voice from a distant shore:
He was called – he is found midst his tribe no more!
He is not in his place when the night-fires burn,
But we look for him still – he will yet return!
His brother sat with a drooping brow   10
In the gloom of the shadowing cypress bough:
We roused him, we bade him no longer pine,
For we heard a step – but the step was thine.

We saw thee, oh stranger, and wept!
We looked for the maid of the mournful song –   15
Mournful, though sweet, she hath left us long!

THE STRANGER IN LOUISIANA
[1] Bernard Picart, *The Ceremonies and Religious Customs
of the World* was first published in English in 1733.
[2] François-René, Vicomte de Chateaubriand (1768–
1848) visited America 1791–2, and produced his *Sou-
venirs d'Italie, d'Angleterre, et d'Amerique* in 1815.

[3] 'I myself came across an Indian tribe whose
members began to weep at the sight of a traveller
because it reminded them of friends who had left for
the land of souls, and had been a long time on the
way there.'

We told her the youth of her love was gone,
And she went forth to seek him – she passed alone;
We hear not her voice when the woods are still,
From the bower where it sang like a silvery rill.   20
The joy of her sire with her smile is fled,
The winter is white on his lonely head,
He hath none by his side when the wilds we track,
He hath none when we rest, yet she comes not back!
We looked for her eye on the feast to shine,   25
For her breezy step – but the step was thine!

     We saw thee, oh stranger, and wept!
We looked for the chief who hath left the spear
And the bow of his battles forgotten here!
We looked for the hunter whose bride's lament   30
On the wind of the forest at eve is sent:
We looked for the first-born, whose mother's cry
Sounds wild and shrill through the midnight sky!
Where are they? Thou'rt seeking some distant coast –
Oh ask of them, stranger, send back the lost!   35
Tell them we mourn by the dark blue streams,
Tell them our lives but of them are dreams!
Tell how we sat in the gloom to pine,
And to watch for a step – but the step was thine!

ANCIENT GREEK SONG OF EXILE

Where is the summer with her golden sun?
   That festal glory hath not passed from earth;[1]
For me alone the laughing day is done!
   Where is the summer with her voice of mirth?
     Far in my own bright land!   5

Where are the fauns,[2] whose flute-notes breathe and die
   On the green hills? The founts, from sparry caves[3]
Through the wild places bearing melody?
   The reeds, low whispering o'er the river waves?
     Far in my own bright land!   10

Where are the temples, through the dim wood shining,
   The virgin-dances, and the choral strains?
Where the sweet sisters of my youth, entwining
   The spring's first roses for their sylvan fanes?
     Far in my own bright land!   15

ANCIENT GREEK SONG OF EXILE
[1] *passed from earth* an echo of Wordsworth, *Ode*, where
'I know, where'er I go / That there hath passed away
a glory from the earth' (ll. 17–18).

[2] *fauns* countryside deities with the legs and ears of
goats.
[3] *sparry caves* caves lined with spar (crystalline minerals).

Where are the vineyards, with their joyous throngs,
The red grapes pressing when the foliage fades?
The lyres, the wreaths, the lovely Dorian songs,
And the pine forests, and the olive shades?
Far in my own bright land!   20

Where the deep haunted grots, the laurel bowers,
The dryad's[4] footsteps and the minstrel's dreams?
Oh that my life were as a southern flower's!
I might not languish then by these chill streams,
Far from my own bright land!   25

From Records of Woman: With Other Poems (1828)

ARABELLA STUART

'The Lady Arabella' (as she has been frequently entitled) was descended from Margaret, eldest daughter of Henry VII, and consequently allied by birth to Elizabeth, as well as James I. This affinity to the throne proved the misfortune of her life, as the jealousies which it constantly excited in her royal relatives, who were anxious to prevent her marrying, shut her out from the enjoyment of that domestic happiness which her heart appears to have so fervently desired. By a secret, but early discovered union with William Seymour, son of Lord Beauchamp, she alarmed the cabinet of James, and the wedded lovers were immediately placed in separate confinement. From this they found means to concert a romantic plan of escape and, having won over a female attendant, by whose assistance she was disguised in male attire, Arabella, though faint from recent sickness and suffering, stole out in the night, and at last reached an appointed spot where a boat and servants were in waiting. She embarked and, at break of day, a French vessel, engaged to receive her, was discovered and gained. As Seymour, however, had not yet arrived, she was desirous that the vessel should lie at anchor for him; but this wish was overruled by her companions who, contrary to her entreaties, hoisted sail, 'which', says Disraeli,

> occasioned so fatal a termination to this romantic adventure. Seymour, indeed, had escaped from the Tower; he reached the wharf, and found his confidential man[1] waiting with a boat, and arrived at Lee.[2] The time passed; the waves were rising; Arabella was not there; but in the distance he descried a vessel. Hiring a fisherman to take him on board, he discovered, to his grief, on hailing it, that it was not the French ship charged with his Arabella; in depair and confusion he found another ship from Newcastle which, for a large sum, altered its course and landed him in Flanders.

---

[4] *dryad* wood-nymph.   [2] *Lee* town in Kent, six miles south-east of London.
ARABELLA STUART
[1] *confidential man* servant entrusted with a confidential task.

Arabella, meantime, whilst imploring her attendants to linger, and earnestly looking out for the expected boat of her husband, was overtaken in Calais Roads[3] by a vessel in the King's service, and brought back to a captivity, under the suffering of which her mind and constitution gradually sank.

What passed in that dreadful imprisonment cannot perhaps be recovered for authentic history, but enough is known; that her mind grew impaired, that she finally lost her reason, and, if the duration of her imprisonment was short, that it was only terminated by her death. Some effusions, often begun and never ended, written and erased, incoherent and rational, yet remain among her papers.

Disraeli's *Curiosities of Literature*[4]

The following poem, meant as some record of her fate, and the imagined fluctuations of her thoughts and feelings, is supposed to commence during the time of her first imprisonment, whilst her mind was yet buoyed up by the consciousness of Seymour's affection, and the cherished hope of eventual deliverance.

> *And is not love in vain*
> *Torture enough without a living tomb?*[5]

Byron

> *Fermossi al fin il cor che balzò tanto.*

Pindemonte[6]

I

'Twas but a dream! I saw the stag leap free
  Under the boughs where early birds were singing;
I stood o'ershadowed by the greenwood tree,[7]
  And heard, it seemed, a sudden bugle ringing
Far through a royal forest: then the fawn[8]   5
Shot, like a gleam of light, from grassy lawn
To secret covert; and the smooth turf shook,
And lilies quivered by the glade's lone brook,
And young leaves trembled as, in fleet career,
A princely band with horn and hound and spear,   10
Like a rich masque swept forth. I saw the dance
Of their white plumes[9] that bore a silvery glance
Into the deep wood's heart, and all passed by
Save one – I met the smile of *one* clear eye,
Flashing out joy to mine. Yes, *thou* wert there,   15
Seymour! A soft wind blew the clustering hair
Back from thy gallant brow, as thou didst rein
Thy courser, turning from that gorgeous train,

---

[3] *Roads* sheltered piece of water near the shore where vessels lie at anchor.

[4] Isaac Disraeli (1766–1848) published his *Curiosities of Literature* in 1791.

[5] *The Prophecy of Dante* iii 147–8.

[6] 'The heart that had beaten so much finally stopped'. Ippolito Pindemonte (1753–1828).

[7] *the greenwood tree* Hemans probably has in mind the sylvan setting of *As You Like It* II v 1.

[8] *fawn* young fallow deer.

[9] *white plumes* in their hats.

And fling, methought, thy hunting-spear away
And, lightly graceful in thy green array,   20
Bound to my side; and we, that met and parted,
  Ever in dread of some dark watchful power,
Won back to childhood's trust and, fearless-hearted,
  Blent the glad fullness of our thoughts that hour,
Even like the mingling of sweet streams beneath   25
Dim woven leaves, and midst the floating breath
Of hidden forest flowers.

II

                    'Tis past! I wake,
  A captive, and alone, and far from thee,
My love and friend! Yet fostering, for thy sake,
  A quenchless hope of happiness to be,   30
And feeling still my woman's spirit strong,
In the deep faith which lifts from earthly wrong
A heavenward glance. I know, I know our love
Shall yet call gentle angels from above
By its undying fervour; and prevail,   35
Sending a breath as of the spring's first gale
Through hearts now cold; and, raising its bright face,
With a free gush of sunny tears, erase
The characters of anguish. In this trust
I bear, I strive, I bow not to the dust,   40
That I may bring thee back no faded form,
No bosom chilled and blighted by the storm,
But all my youth's first treasures, when we meet,
Making past sorrow, by communion, sweet.

III

And thou too art in bonds! Yet droop thou not,   45
Oh, my beloved! There is *one* hopeless lot,
But one, and that not ours. Beside the dead
There sits the grief that mantles up its head,
Loathing the laughter and proud pomp of light,
When darkness, from the vainly-doting sight,   50
Covers its beautiful![10] If thou wert gone
  To the grave's bosom with thy radiant brow;
If thy deep-thrilling voice, with that low tone
  Of earnest tenderness, which now, ev'n now,
Seems floating through my soul, were music taken   55
For ever from this world – oh thus forsaken
Could I bear on? Thou liv'st, thou liv'st, thou'rt mine!

---

[10] "'Wheresoever you are, or in what state soever you be, it sufficeth me you are mine. *Rachel wept, and would not be comforted, because her children were no more.* And that, indeed, is the remediless sorrow, and none else!" From a letter of Arabella Stuart's to her husband. See *Curiosities of Literature*' (Hemans's note).

With this glad thought I make my heart a shrine
And, by the lamp which quenchless there shall burn,
Sit, a lone watcher for the day's return.   60

IV
And lo, the joy that cometh with the morning,
    Brightly victorious o'er the hours of care!
I have not watched in vain, serenely scorning
    The wild and busy whispers of despair!
Thou hast sent tidings, as of heaven. I wait   65
    The hour, the sign, for blessed flight to thee.
Oh for the skylark's wing that seeks its mate
    As a star shoots! But on the breezy sea
We shall meet soon. To think of such an hour!
    Will not my heart, o'erburdened by its bliss,   70
Faint and give way within me, as a flower
    Borne down and perishing by noontide's kiss?
Yet shall I *fear* that lot, the perfect rest,
The full deep joy of dying on thy breast
After long-suffering won? So rich a close   75
Too seldom crowns with peace affection's woes.

V
Sunset! I tell each moment – from the skies
    The last red splendour floats along my wall
Like a king's banner! Now it melts, it dies!
    I see one star – I hear – 'twas not the call,   80
Th' expected voice; my quick heart throbbed too soon.
I must keep vigil till yon rising moon
Shower down less golden light. Beneath her beam,
Through my lone lattice[11] poured, I sit and dream
Of summer lands afar, where holy love,   85
Under the vine or in the citron-grove,
May breathe from terror.
                            Now the night grows deep
And silent as its clouds, and full of sleep.
I hear my veins beat. Hark, a bell's slow chime!
My heart strikes with it. Yet again – 'tis time!   90
A step! A voice! Or but a rising breeze?
Hark, haste – I come to meet thee on the seas!
*   *   *   *   *   *   *   *   *   *   *

VI
Now never more, oh never, in the worth
Of its pure cause, let sorrowing love on earth
Trust fondly – never more! The hope is crushed   95

---

[11] *lattice* window.

That lit my life, the voice within me hushed
That spoke sweet oracles, and I return
To lay my youth, as in a burial-urn,
Where sunshine may not find it. All is lost!
No tempest met our barks, no billow tossed;   100
Yet were they severed, ev'n as we must be
That so have loved, so striven our hearts to free
From their close-coiling fate! In vain, in vain –
The dark links meet and clasp themselves again,
And press out life. Upon the deck I stood,   105
And a white sail came gliding o'er the flood
Like some proud bird of ocean; then mine eye
Strained out, one moment earlier to descry
The form it ached for, and the bark's career
Seemed slow to that fond yearning. It drew near,   110
Fraught with our foes! What boots it to recall
The strife, the tears? Once more a prison-wall
Shuts the green hills and woodlands from my sight,
And joyous glance of waters to the light,
And thee, my Seymour, thee!
                     I will not sink!   115
   Thou, *thou* hast rent the heavy chain that bound thee,
And this shall be my strength – the joy to think
   That thou mayst wander with heaven's breath around thee,
And all the laughing sky! This thought shall yet
Shine o'er my heart, a radiant amulet   120
Guarding it from despair. Thy bonds are broken,
And unto me, I know, thy true love's token
Shall one day be deliverance, though the years
Lie dim between, o'erhung with mists of tears.

VII
My friend, my friend, where art thou? Day by day,   125
Gliding, like some dark mournful stream, away
My silent youth flows from me. Spring the while
   Comes and rains beauty on the kindling boughs
Round hall and hamlet; summer, with her smile,
   Fills the green forest; young hearts breathe their vows;   130
Brothers long parted meet; fair children rise
Round the glad board; Hope laughs from loving eyes –
All this is in the world! These joys lie sown,
The dew of every path; on *one* alone
Their freshness may not fall – the stricken deer,[12]   135
Dying of thirst with all the waters near.

---

[12]   *the stricken deer* borrowed from Cowper's description of himself as 'a stricken deer that left the herd / Long since' (*Task* iii 108–9).

VIII

Ye are from dingle and fresh glade, ye flowers,
   By some kind hand to cheer my dungeon sent!
O'er you the oak shed down the summer showers,
   And the lark's nest was where your bright cups bent,   140
Quivering to breeze and raindrop like the sheen
Of twilight stars. On you heaven's eye[13] hath been,
Through the leaves pouring its dark sultry blue
Into your glowing hearts; the bee to you
Hath murmured, and the rill. My soul grows faint   145
With passionate yearning, as its quick dreams paint
Your haunts by dell and stream – the green, the free,
The full of all sweet sound, the shut from me!

IX

There went a swift bird singing past my cell –
   Oh love and freedom, ye are lovely things!   150
With you the peasant on the hills may dwell,
   And by the streams, but I – the blood of kings,
A proud unmingling river, through my veins
Flows in lone brightness, and its gifts are chains!
Kings! I had silent visions of deep bliss,   155
Leaving their thrones far distant, and for this
I am cast under their triumphal car,[14]
An insect to be crushed. Oh, heaven is far –
Earth pitiless!

Dost thou forget me, Seymour? I am proved[15]   160
So long, so sternly! Seymour, my beloved!
There are such tales of holy marvels done
By strong affection, of deliverance won
Through its prevailing power! Are these things told
Till the young weep with rapture, and the old   165
Wonder, yet dare not doubt – and thou, oh thou,
   Dost thou forget me in my hope's decay?
Thou canst not! Through the silent night, ev'n now,
   I that need prayer so much, awake and pray
Still first for thee. Oh gentle, gentle friend!   170
How shall I bear this anguish to the end?

Aid! Comes there yet no aid? The voice of blood
Passes heaven's gate, ev'n ere the crimson flood
Sinks through the greensward! Is there not a cry
From the wrung heart, of power, through agony,   175
To pierce the clouds? Hear, Mercy, hear me! None

---

13   *heaven's eye* the sky.   15   *proved* tested.
14   *car* chariot.

That bleed and weep beneath the smiling sun
Have heavier cause – yet hear! My soul grows dark –
Who hears the last shriek from the sinking bark
On the mid seas, and with the storm alone,   180
And bearing to th' abyss, unseen, unknown,
Its freight of human hearts? Th' o'ermastering wave!
Who shall tell how it rushed – and none to save?

Thou hast forsaken me![16] I feel, I know,
There would be rescue if this were not so.   185
Thou'rt at the chase, thou'rt at the festive board,
Thou'rt where the red wine free and high is poured,
Thou'rt where the dancers meet! A magic glass
Is set within my soul, and proud shapes pass,
Flushing it o'er with pomp from bower and hall;   190
I see one shadow, stateliest there of all –
Thine! What dost thou amidst the bright and fair,
Whispering light words, and mocking my despair?
It is not well of thee! My love was more
Than fiery song may breathe, deep thought explore;   195
And there thou smilest while my heart is dying,
With all its blighted hopes around it lying;
Ev'n thou, on whom they hung their last green leaf –
Yet smile, smile on – too bright art thou for grief!

Death! What, is death a locked and treasured thing   200
Guarded by swords of fire?[17] A hidden spring,
A fabled fruit, that I should thus endure
As if the world within me held no cure?
Wherefore not spread free wings – Heaven, Heaven control
These thoughts – they rush – I look into my soul   205
As down a gulf, and tremble at th' array
Of fierce forms crowding it! Give strength to pray,
So shall their dark host pass.

                              The storm is stilled.
    Father in heaven, thou, only thou canst sound   210
The heart's great deep, with floods of anguish filled,
    For human line[18] too fearfully profound.
Therefore forgive, my Father, if thy child,
Rocked on its heaving darkness, hath grown wild
And sinned in her despair! It well may be   215

---

[16]   *Thou hast forsaken me* an echo of Christ's words on
the cross: 'My God, my God, why hast thou forsaken
me?' (Matthew 27:46).
[17]   '"And if you remember of old, *I dare die.* Con-
sider what the world would conceive, if I should be
violently enforced to do it." *Fragments of her Letters*'
(Hemans's note).
[18]   *line* mariners 'plumb' the depths with a plumb-
line, a cord with a weight on the end; in Felicia's
metaphor, only God is capable of plumbing the depths
of the human heart.

That thou wouldst lead my spirit back to thee,
By the crushed hope too long on this world poured,
The stricken love which hath perchance adored
A mortal in thy place! Now let me strive
With thy strong arm no more! Forgive, forgive –   220
Take me to peace!

     And peace at last is nigh.
 A sign is on my brow, a token sent
Th' o'erwearied dust from home: no breeze flits by,
 But calls me with a strange sweet whisper blent
Of many mysteries.

     Hark! The warning tone   225
Deepens – its word is *Death*. Alone, alone,
And sad in youth, but chastened, I depart,
Bowing to Heaven. Yet, yet my woman's heart
Shall wake a spirit and a power to bless,
Ev'n in this hour's o'ershadowing fearfulness –   230
Thee, its first love! Oh tender still, and true!
Be it forgotten if mine anguish threw
Drops from its bitter fountain on thy name,
Though but a moment.

     Now, with fainting frame,
With soul just lingering on the flight begun,   235
To bind for thee its last dim thoughts in one,
I bless thee! Peace be on thy noble head,
Years of bright fame, when I am with the dead!
I bid this prayer survive me, and retain
Its might, again to bless thee, and again!   240
Thou hast been gathered into my dark fate
Too much; too long, for my sake, desolate
Hath been thine exiled youth; but now take back,
From dying hands, thy freedom, and retrack
(After a few kind tears for her whose days   245
Went out in dreams of thee) the sunny ways
Of hope, and find thou happiness! Yet send,
Ev'n then in silent hours, a thought, dear friend,
Down to my voiceless chamber; for thy love
Hath been to me all gifts of earth above,   250
Though bought with burning tears! It is the sting
Of death to leave that vainly-precious thing
In this cold world! What were it then, if thou,
With thy fond eyes, were gazing on me now?
Too keen a pang! Farewell, and yet once more,   255
Farewell! The passion of long years I pour
Into that word: thou hear'st not, but the woe

And fervour of its tones may one day flow
To thy heart's holy place; there let them dwell –
We shall o'ersweep the grave to meet – farewell!   260

THE BRIDE OF THE GREEK ISLE[1]

Fear! I'm a Greek, and how should I fear death?
A slave, and wherefore should I dread my freedom? . . .
I will not live degraded.

Sardanapalus[2]

I

Come from the woods with the citron-flowers,
Come with your lyres for the festal hours,
Maids of bright Scio! They came, and the breeze
Bore their sweet songs o'er the Grecian seas;
They came, and Eudora stood robed and crowned,   5
The bride of the morn, with her train around.
Jewels flashed out from her braided hair
Like starry dews midst the roses there;
Pearls on her bosom quivering shone,
Heaved by her heart through its golden zone;[3]   10
But a brow, as those gems of the ocean pale,
Gleamed from beneath her transparent veil;
Changeful and faint was her fair cheek's hue,
Though clear as a flower which the light looks through;
And the glance of her dark resplendent eye,   15
For the aspect of woman at times too high,
Lay floating in mists, which the troubled stream
Of the soul sent up o'er its fervid beam.
     She looked on the vine at her father's door
Like one that is leaving his native shore;   20
She hung o'er the myrtle once called her own,
As it greenly waved by the threshold stone;
She turned – and her mother's gaze brought back
Each hue of her childhood's faded track.
Oh hush the song, and let her tears   25
Flow to the dream of her early years!
Holy and pure are the drops that fall
When the young bride goes from her father's hall;
She goes unto love yet untried and new,
She parts from love which hath still been true;   30
Mute be the song and the choral strain

THE BRIDE OF THE GREEK ISLE
[1] 'Founded on a circumstance related in the Second
Series of the *Curiosities of Literature*, and forming part
of a picture in the *Painted Biography*, there described'
(Hemans's note).

[2] Byron, *Sardanapalus* I ii 479–80, 629.
[3] *its golden zone* the golden band round her bosom is
set with pearls.

Till her heart's deep wellspring is clear again!
She wept on her mother's faithful breast
Like a babe that sobs itself to rest;
She wept – yet laid her hand awhile   35
In *his* that waited her dawning smile,
Her soul's affianced, nor cherished less
For the gush of nature's tenderness!
She lifted her graceful head at last –
The choking swell of her heart was past;   40
And her lovely thoughts from their cells found way
In the sudden flow of a plaintive lay.[4]

The Bride's Farewell

Why do I weep? To leave the vine
    Whose clusters o'er me bend,
The myrtle (yet, oh call it mine!),   45
    The flowers I loved to tend;
A thousand thoughts of all things dear
    Like shadows o'er me sweep,
I leave my sunny childhood here –
    Oh therefore let me weep!   50

I leave thee, sister, we have played
    Through many a joyous hour,
Where the silvery green of the olive shade
    Hung dim o'er fount and bower.
Yes, thou and I, by stream, by shore,   55
    In song, in prayer, in sleep,
Have been as we may be no more –
    Kind sister, let me weep!

I leave thee, father! Eve's bright moon
    Must now light other feet,   60
With the gathered grapes and the lyre in tune,
    Thy homeward step to greet.
Thou in whose voice, to bless thy child,
    Lay tones of love so deep,
Whose eye o'er all my youth hath smiled –   65
    I leave thee! Let me weep!

Mother, I leave thee! On thy breast,
    Pouring out joy and woe,
I have found that holy place of rest
    Still changeless – yet I go!   70

---

[4] 'A Greek bride, on leaving her father's house, take leave of her friends and relatives frequently in extemporaneous verse. See Fauriel's *Chants Populaires de la Grèce Moderne*' (Hemans's note). Claude Fauriel (1772–1844) published his *Chants* 1824–5.

Lips that have lulled me with your strain,
  Eyes that have watched my sleep!
Will earth give love like *yours* again?
  Sweet mother, let me weep!

And like a slight young tree that throws 75
The weight of rain from its drooping boughs,
Once more she wept. But a changeful thing
Is the human heart, as a mountain spring
That works its way through the torrent's foam,
To the bright pool near it, the lily's home! 80
It is well! The cloud on her soul that lay
Hath melted in glittering drops away.
Wake again, mingle, sweet flute and lyre!
She turns to her lover, she leaves her sire.
Mother, on earth it must still be so, 85
Thou rearest the lovely to see them go!
  They are moving onward, the bridal throng,
Ye may track their way by the swells of song;
Ye may catch through the foliage their white robes' gleam
Like a swan midst the reeds of a shadowy stream. 90
Their arms bear up garlands, their gliding tread
Is over the deep-veined violet's bed;
They have light leaves around them, blue skies above,
An arch for the triumph of youth and love!

II
Still and sweet was the home that stood 95
In the flowering depths of a Grecian wood,
With the soft green light o'er its low roof spread,
As if from the flow of an emerald shed,
Pouring through lime-leaves that mingled on high,
Asleep in the silence of noon's clear sky. 100
Citrons amidst their dark foliage glowed,
Making a gleam round the lone abode;
Laurels o'erhung it, whose faintest shiver
Scattered out rays like a glancing river;
Stars of the jasmine its pillars crowned, 105
Vine-stalks its lattice and walls had bound,
And brightly before it a fountain's play
Flung showers through a thicket of glossy bay
To a cypress[5] which rose in that flashing rain,
Like one tall shaft of some fallen fane. 110
  And thither Ianthis had brought his bride,
And the guests were met by that fountain-side;

---

[5] *cypress* rather a portentous sight, as it is associated
with death.

They lifted the veil from Eudora's face,
It smiled out softly in pensive grace
With lips of love and a brow serene,   115
Meet for the soul of the deep wood-scene.
Bring wine, bring odours, the board is spread!
Bring roses, a chaplet for every head!
The wine-cups foamed, and the rose was showered
On the young and fair from the world embowered;   120
The sun looked not on them in that sweet shade,
The winds amid scented boughs were laid;
But there came by fits, through some wavy tree,
A sound and a gleam of the moaning sea.

   Hush, be still! Was that no more   125
   Than the murmur from the shore?
   Silence! Did thick raindrops beat
   On the grass like trampling feet?
   Fling down the goblet and draw the sword –
   The groves are filled with a pirate-horde!   130
   Through the dim olives their sabres shine;
   Now must the red blood stream for wine!

The youths from the banquet to battle sprang,
The woods with the shriek of the maidens rang;
Under the golden-fruited boughs   135
There were flashing poniards and dark'ning brows,
Footsteps o'er garland and lyre that fled,
And the dying soon on a greensward bed.
   Eudora, Eudora! *Thou* dost not fly!
She saw but Ianthis before her lie,   140
With the blood from his breast in a gushing flow,
Like a child's large tears in its hour of woe,
And a gathering film in his lifted eye,
That sought his young bride out mournfully.
She knelt down beside him, her arms she wound   145
Like tendrils his drooping neck around,
As if the passion of that fond grasp
Might chain in life with its ivy-clasp.
But they tore her thence in her wild despair,
The sea's fierce rovers, they left him there;   150
They left to the fountain a dark-red vein,
And on the wet violets a pile of slain,
And a hush of fear through the summer-grove –
So closed the triumph of youth and love!

III
   Gloomy lay the shore that night   155
   When the moon, with sleeping light,

Bathed each purple Sciote hill –
Gloomy lay the shore, and still.
O'er the wave no gay guitar
Sent its floating music far;   160
No glad sound of dancing feet
Woke, the starry hours to greet.
But a voice of mortal woe
In its changes wild or low
Through the midnight's blue repose,   165
From the sea-beat rocks arose,
As Eudora's mother stood
Gazing o'er th' Aegean flood
With a fixed and straining eye –
Oh, was the spoilers' vessel nigh?   170
Yes, there becalmed in silent sleep,
Dark and alone on a breathless deep,
On a sea of molten silver, dark,
Brooding – it frowned, that evil bark!
There its broad pennon a shadow cast,   175
Moveless and black from the tall still mast,
And the heavy sound of its flapping sail
Idly and vainly wooed the gale.
Hushed was all else; had ocean's breast
Rocked e'en Eudora that hour to rest?   180

To rest? The waves tremble! What piercing cry
Bursts from the heart of the ship on high?
What light through the heavens, in a sudden spire,
Shoots from the deck up? Fire, 'tis fire!
There are wild forms hurrying to and fro,   185
Seen darkly clear on that lurid glow;
There are shout, and signal-gun, and call,
And the dashing of water, but fruitless all!
Man may not fetter, nor ocean tame
The might and wrath of the rushing flame!   190
It hath twined the mast like a glittering snake
That coils up a tree from a dusky brake;
It hath touched the sails, and their canvas rolls
Away from its breath into shrivelled scrolls;
It hath taken the flag's high place in air,   195
And reddened the stars with its wavy glare,
And sent out bright arrows, and soared in glee
To a burning mount midst the moonlight sea.
The swimmers are plunging from stern and prow –
Eudora, Eudora – where, where art thou?   200
The slave and his master alike are gone;
Mother, who stands on the deck alone?
The child of thy bosom! And lo, a brand
Blazing up high in her lifted hand!

And her veil flung back, and her free dark hair   205
Swayed by the flames as they rock and flare;
And her fragile form to its loftiest height
Dilated, as if by the spirit's might,
And her eye with an eagle-gladness fraught –
Oh, could this work be of woman wrought?   210
Yes, 'twas her deed! By that haughty smile
It was hers – she hath kindled her funeral pile!
Never might shame on that bright head be –
Her blood was the Greek's, and hath made her free.

   Proudly she stands, like an Indian bride   215
On the pyre with the holy dead beside;
But a shriek from her mother hath caught her ear,
As the flames to her marriage-robe draw near,
And starting, she spreads her pale arms in vain
To the form they must never enfold again.   220
   One moment more, and her hands are clasped,
Fallen is the torch they had wildly grasped,
Her sinking knee unto Heaven is bowed,
And her last look raised through the smoke's dim shroud,
And her lips as in prayer for her pardon move –   225
Now the night gathers o'er youth and love![6]

THE SWITZER'S WIFE

Werner Stauffacher, one of the three confederates of the field of Grutli, had been alarmed by the envy with which the Austrian bailiff,[1] Landenberg, had noticed the appearance of wealth and comfort which distinguished his dwelling. It was not, however, until roused by the entreaties of his wife, a woman who seems to have been of an heroic spirit, that he was induced to deliberate with his friends upon the measures by which Switzerland was finally delivered.

> *Nor look nor tone revealeth aught*
> *Save woman's quietness of thought;*
> *And yet around her is a light*
> *Of inward majesty and might.*

M.J.J.[2]

> *Wer solch ein Herz an seinen Busen drückt,*
> *Der kann fur Herd und Hof mit Freuden fechten.*[3]

Willholm Tell[4]

---

[6] 'Originally published, as well as several other of these *Records*, in the *New Monthly Magazine*' (Hemans's note).

THE SWITZER'S WIFE

[1] *bailiff* law officer.

[2] Maria Jane Jewsbury, *Arria* 5–8, which Hemans knew from Jewsbury's *Phantasmagoria* (1825). Jewsbury (1800–33) was a friend and correspondent of Hemans, and they saw a good deal of each other when Jewsbury

visited Wales in the summer of 1828. Many of the poems which she wrote that summer appeared in her *Lays of the Leisure Hours* (1829), which was dedicated to Hemans 'in remembrance of the summer passed in her society'.

[3] 'Whoever presses such a heart to his bosom can with joy fight for hearth and home.'

[4] Schiller's *Wilhelm Tell* was first published in 1804, and first translated into English in 1825.

It was the time when children bound to meet
  Their father's homeward step from field or hill,
And when the herd's returning bells are sweet
  In the Swiss valleys, and the lakes grow still,
And the last note of that wild horn swells by   5
Which haunts the exile's heart with melody.

And lovely smiled full many an Alpine home,
  Touched with the crimson of the dying hour,
Which lit its low roof by the torrent's foam,
  And pierced its lattice through the vine-hung bower;   10
But one, the loveliest o'er the land that rose,
Then first looked mournful in its green repose.

For Werner sat beneath the linden tree
  That sent its lulling whispers through his door,
Ev'n as man sits, whose heart alone would be   15
  With some deep care, and thus can find no more
Th' accustomed joy in all which evening brings,
Gathering a household with her quiet wings.

His wife stood hushed before him – sad, yet mild
  In her beseeching mien; he marked it not.   20
The silvery laughter of his bright-haired child
  Rang from the greensward round the sheltered spot,
But seemed unheard; until at last the boy
Raised from his heaped-up flowers a glance of joy,

And met his father's face: but then a change   25
  Passed swiftly o'er the brow of infant glee,
And a quick sense of something dimly strange
  Brought him from play to stand beside the knee
So often climbed, and lift his loving eyes
That shone through clouds of sorrowful surprise.   30

Then the proud bosom of the strong man shook;
  But tenderly his babe's fair mother laid
Her hand on his, and with a pleading look,
  Through tears half-quivering, o'er him bent, and said,
'What grief, dear friend, hath made thy heart its prey,   35
That thou shouldst turn thee from our love away?

'It is too sad to see thee thus, my friend!
  Mark'st thou the wonder on thy boy's fair brow,
Missing the smile from thine? Oh cheer thee! Bend
  To his soft arms, unseal thy thoughts e'en now!   40
Thou dost not kindly to withhold the share
Of tried affection in thy secret care.'

He looked up into that sweet earnest face,
　　But sternly, mournfully; not yet the band
Was loosened from his soul, its inmost place　　　　　45
　　Not yet unveiled by love's o'ermastering hand.
'Speak low!' he cried, and pointed where on high
The white Alps glittered through the solemn sky.

'We must speak low amidst our ancient hills
　　And their free torrents, for the days are come　　50
When tyranny lies couched by forest rills
　　And meets the shepherd in his mountain-home.
Go pour the wine of our own grapes in fear,
Keep silence by the hearth – its foes are near.

'The envy of th' oppressor's eye hath been　　　　　55
　　Upon my heritage.[5] I sit tonight
Under my household tree, if not serene,
　　Yet with the faces best beloved in sight;
Tomorrow eve may find me chained, and thee –
How can I bear the boy's young smiles to see?'　　　60

The bright blood left that youthful mother's cheek;
　　Back on the linden-stem she leaned her form,
And her lip trembled, as it strove to speak,
　　Like a frail harp-string, shaken by the storm.
'Twas but a moment, and the faintness passed,　　　65
And the free Alpine spirit woke at last.

And she, that ever through her home had moved
　　With the meek thoughtfulness and quiet smile
Of woman, calmly loving and beloved,
　　And timid in her happiness the while,　　　　　　70
Stood brightly forth, and steadfastly, that hour,
Her clear glance kindling into sudden power.

Aye, pale she stood, but with an eye of light,
　　And took her fair child to her holy breast,
And lifted her soft voice, that gathered might　　　75
　　As it found language. 'Are we thus oppressed?
Then must we rise upon our mountain-sod,
And man must arm, and woman call on God!

'I know what thou wouldst do – and be it done!
　　Thy soul is darkened ·with its fears for me.　　　80
Trust me to Heaven, my husband! This, thy son,
　　The babe whom I have born thee, must be free!'

---

[5]　*heritage* inherited property.

And the sweet memory of our pleasant hearth
May well give strength – if aught be strong on earth.

'Thou hast been brooding o'er the silent dread   85
    Of my desponding tears; now lift once more,
My hunter of the hills, thy stately head,
    And let thine eagle-glance my joy restore!
I can bear all, but seeing *thee* subdued –
Take to thee back thine own undaunted mood.   90

'Go forth beside the waters, and along
    The chamois-paths, and through the forests go;
And tell, in burning words, thy tale of wrong
    To the brave hearts that midst the hamlets glow.
God shall be with thee, my beloved, away!   95
Bless but thy child, and leave me – I can pray!'

He sprang up like a warrior-youth awaking
    To clarion-sounds upon the ringing air;
He caught her to his breast, while proud tears breaking
    From his dark eyes, fell o'er her braided hair,   100
And 'Worthy art thou' was his joyous cry,
'That man for thee should gird himself to die.

'My bride, my wife, the mother of my child!
    Now shall thy name be armour to my heart;
And this our land, by chains no more defiled,   105
    Be taught of thee to choose the better part!
I go – thy spirit on my words shall dwell,
Thy gentle voice shall stir the Alps – farewell!'

And thus they parted, by the quiet lake,
    In the clear starlight: he, the strength to rouse   110
Of the free hills; she, thoughtful for his sake,
    To rock her child beneath the whispering boughs,
Singing its blue, half-curtained eyes to sleep,
With a low hymn amidst the stillness deep.

PROPERZIA ROSSI

Properzia Rossi, a celebrated female sculptor of Bologna,[1] possessed also of talents for poetry and music, died in consequence of an unrequited attachment. A painting by Ducis[2] represents her showing her last work, a basso-relievo of Ariadne,[3] to a Roman knight, the object of her affection, who regards it with indifference.

PROPERZIA ROSSI
[1] Properzia Rossi (?1491–1530) specialized in bas-relief sculptures, usually in stone or wood.
[2] Louis Ducis (1775–1847), painter of historical subjects and portraits.

[3] An appropriate subject: Ariadne helped Theseus to escape the minotaur's labyrinth. Afterwards she married him and had his child, but he abandoned her at Naxos and married her sister, Phaedra.

Tell me no more, no more
Of my soul's lofty gifts! Are they not vain
To quench its haunting thirst for happiness?
Have I not loved, and striven, and failed to bind
One true heart unto me, whereon my own
Might find a resting-place, a home for all
Its burden of affections? I depart
Unknown, though Fame goes with me; I must leave
The earth unknown. Yet it may be that death
Shall give my name a power to win such tears
As would have made life precious.

I

One dream of passion and of beauty more,
And in its bright fulfilment let me pour
My soul away! Let earth retain a trace
Of that which lit my being, though its race
Might have been loftier far – yet one more dream!   5
From my deep spirit one victorious gleam
Ere I depart – for thee alone, for thee!
May this last work, this farewell triumph be –
Thou, loved so vainly! I would leave enshrined
Something immortal of my heart and mind   10
That yet may speak to thee when I am gone,
Shaking thine inmost bosom with a tone
Of lost affection – something that may prove
What she hath been whose melancholy love
On thee was lavished; silent pang and tear,   15
And fervent song that gushed when none were near,
And dream by night, and weary thought by day,
Stealing the brightness from her life away,
While thou – awake, not yet within me die
Under the burden and the agony   20
Of this vain tenderness; my spirit, wake!
Ev'n for thy sorrowful affection's sake,
Live! In thy work breathe out, that he may yet,
Feeling sad mastery there, perchance regret
Thine unrequited gift.

II
                    It comes – the power   25
Within me born flows back, my fruitless dower
That could not win me love. Yet once again
I greet it proudly, with its rushing train
Of glorious images: they throng, they press;
A sudden joy lights up my loneliness –   30
I shall not perish all!

The bright work grows
Beneath my hand, unfolding, as a rose,
Leaf after leaf, to beauty; line by line
I fix my thought, heart, soul, to burn, to shine
Through the pale marble's veins. It grows – and now   35
I give my own life's history to thy brow,
Forsaken Ariadne! Thou shalt wear
My form, my lineaments – but oh, more fair,
Touched into lovelier being by the glow
   Which in me dwells, as by the summer light   40
All things are glorified! From thee my woe
   Shall yet look beautiful to meet his sight
When I am passed away. Thou art the mould
Wherein I pour the fervent thoughts, th' untold,
The self-consuming! Speak to him of me,   45
Thou, the deserted by the lonely sea,
With the soft sadness of thine earnest eye;
Speak to him, lorn one, deeply, mournfully,
Of all my love and grief! Oh could I throw
Into thy frame a voice, a sweet and low   50
And thrilling voice of song – when he came nigh,
To send the passion of its melody
Through his pierced bosom – on its tones to bear
My life's deep feeling, as the southern air
Wafts the faint myrtle's breath – to rise, to swell,   55
To sink away in accents of farewell,
Winning but one, *one* gush of tears, whose flow
Surely my parted spirit yet might know,
If love be strong as death!

III

           Now fair thou art,
Thou form whose life is of my burning heart!   60
Yet all the vision that within me wrought,
   I cannot make thee! Oh, I might have given
Birth to creations of far nobler thought;
   I might have kindled, with the fire of heaven,
Things not of such as die! But I have been   65
Too much alone; a heart whereon to lean,
With all these deep affections that o'erflow
My aching soul, and find no shore below,
An eye to be my star, a voice to bring
Hope o'er my path, like sounds that breathe of spring,   70
These are denied me – dreamt of still in vain,
Therefore my brief aspirings from the chain
Are ever but as some wild fitful song,
Rising triumphantly to die erelong
In dirge-like echoes.

IV

Yet the world will see　75

Little of this, my parting work, in thee;
　Thou shalt have fame – oh mockery! Give the reed
From storms a shelter, give the drooping vine
Something round which its tendrils may entwine;
　Give the parched flower a raindrop, and the meed　80
Of love's kind words to woman! Worthless fame,
That in *his* bosom wins not for my name
Th' abiding place it asked! Yet how my heart,
In its own fairy world of song and art,
Once beat for praise! Are those high longings o'er?　85
That which I have been can I be no more?
Never, oh never more – though still thy sky
Be blue as then, my glorious Italy!
And though the music, whose rich breathings fill
Thine air with soul, be wandering past me still,　90
And though the mantle of thy sunlight streams
Unchanged on forms instinct with poet-dreams –
Never, oh never more! Where'er I move,
The shadow of this broken-hearted love　95
Is on me and around! Too well *they* know,
　Whose life is all within, too soon and well,
When there the blight hath settled – but I go
　Under the silent wings of peace to dwell;
From the slow wasting, from the lonely pain,　100
The inward burning of those words 'in vain'
　Seared on the heart – I go. 'Twill soon be past.
Sunshine, and song, and bright Italian heaven,
　And thou, oh thou on whom my spirit cast
Unvalued wealth, who know'st not what was given　105
In that devotedness – the sad and deep
And unrepaid, farewell! If I could weep
Once, only once, beloved one, on thy breast,
Pouring my heart forth ere I sink to rest!
But that were happiness, and unto me　110
Earth's gift is *fame*. Yet I was formed to be
So richly blessed! With thee to watch the sky,
Speaking not, feeling but that thou wert nigh;
With thee to listen, while the tones of song
Swept ev'n as part of our sweet air along,　115
To listen silently – with thee to gaze
On forms, the deified of olden days –
This had been joy enough, and hour by hour,
From its glad wellsprings drinking life and power,
How had my spirit soared, and made its fame　120
　A glory for thy brow. Dreams, dreams! The fire
Burns faint within me. Yet I leave my name –

As a deep thrill may linger on the lyre
When its full chords are hushed – awhile to live,
And one day haply in thy heart revive   125
Sad thoughts of me; I leave it with a sound,
A spell o'er memory, mournfully profound,
I leave it on my country's air to dwell –
Say proudly yet, ''Twas hers who loved me well!'

GERTRUDE, OR FIDELITY TILL DEATH

The Baron von der Wart, accused, though it is believed unjustly, as an accomplice in
the assassination of the Emperor Albert, was bound alive on the wheel, and attended
by his wife Gertrude throughout his last agonizing hours, with the most heroic
devotedness. Her own sufferings, with those of her unfortunate husband, are most
affectingly described in a letter which she afterwards addressed to a female friend, and
which was published some years ago, at Haarlem, in a book entitled *Gertrude von der
Wart, or Fidelity unto Death*.[1]

Dark lours our fate,
And terrible the storm that gathers o'er us;
But nothing, till that latest agony
Which severs thee from nature, shall unloose
This fixed and sacred hold. In thy dark prison-house,
In the terrific face of arméd law –
Yea, on the scaffold, if it needs must be,
I never will forsake thee.

Joanna Baillie[2]

Her hands were clasped, her dark eyes raised,
    The breeze threw back her hair;
Up to the fearful wheel she gazed –
    All that she loved was there.
The night was round her clear and cold,   5
    The holy heaven above,
Its pale stars watching to behold
    The might of earthly love.

'And bid me not depart', she cried,
    'My Rudolph, say not so!   10
This is no time to quit thy side –
    Peace, peace, I cannot go!
Hath the world aught for *me* to fear
    When death is on thy brow?

GERTRUDE
[1]   Johann Konrad Appenzeller, *Gertrude de Wart; or,
Fidelity unto Death* (London, 1826).

[2]   *De Monfort* V iv 66–73.

The world – what means it? *Mine* is *here* –   15
    I will not leave thee now.

'I have been with thee in thine hour
    Of glory and of bliss;
Doubt not its memory's living power
    To strengthen me through *this*!   20
And thou, mine honoured love and true,
    Bear on, bear nobly on!
We have the blessed heaven in view,
    Whose rest shall soon be won.'

And were not these high words to flow   25
    From woman's breaking heart?
Through all that night of bitterest woe
    She bore her lofty part;
But oh, with such a glazing eye,
    With such a curdling cheek –   30
Love, love, of mortal agony,
    Thou, only *thou* shouldst speak!

The wind rose high, but with it rose
    Her voice, that he might hear.
Perchance that dark hour brought repose   35
    To happy bosoms near,
While she sat striving with despair
    Beside his tortured form,
And pouring her deep soul in prayer
    Forth on the rushing storm.   40

She wiped the death-damps from his brow
    With her pale hands and soft,
Whose touch upon the lute-chords low
    Had stilled his heart so oft.
She spread her mantle o'er his breast,   45
    She bathed his lips with dew,
And on his cheek such kisses pressed
    As hope and joy ne'er knew.

Oh lovely are ye, love and faith
    Enduring to the last!   50
She had her meed – one smile in death –
    And his worn spirit passed,
While ev'n as o'er a martyr's grave
    She knelt on that sad spot,
And weeping blessed the God who gave   55
    Strength to forsake it not!

IMELDA

Sometimes
The young forgot the lessons they had learnt
And loved when they should hate – like thee, Imelda![1]

Italy, a Poem[2]

Passa la bella Donna, e par che dorma.[3]

Tasso

We have the myrtle's breath around us here,
　Amidst the fallen pillars; this hath been
Some naiad's fane[4] of old. How brightly clear,
　Flinging a vein of silver o'er the scene,
Up through the shadowy grass, the fountain wells,　　　　5
　And music with it, gushing from beneath
The ivied altar – that sweet murmur tells
　The rich wildflowers no tale of woe or death;
Yet once the wave was darkened, and a stain
Lay deep, and heavy drops (but not of rain)　　　　10
On the dim violets by its marble bed,
And the pale shining water-lily's head.

Sad is that legend's truth. A fair girl met
　One whom she loved by this lone temple's spring,
Just as the sun behind the pine-grove set,　　　　15
　And eve's low voice in whispers woke to bring
All wanderers home. They stood, that gentle pair,
　With the blue heaven of Italy above,
And citron-odours dying on the air,
　And light leaves trembling round, and early love　　　　20
Deep in each breast. What recked *their* souls of strife
Between their fathers? Unto them young life
Spread out the treasures of its vernal years,
And if they wept, they wept far other tears
Than the cold world wrings forth. They stood that hour　　　　25
Speaking of hope, while tree, and fount, and flower,
And star, just gleaming through the cypress[5] boughs,
Seemed holy things, as records of their vows.

IMELDA
[1] 'The tale of Imelda is related in Sismondi's *Historie des Republiques Italiennes*, vol. 3, p. 443' (Hemans's note). She refers to Jean Charles Léonard Simonde de Sismondi (1773–1842), *Histoire des républiques Italiennes du moyen âge* (16 vols, Paris, 1809–26). The story is essentially that of Romeo and Juliet. Imelda's brothers were of the Ghibelline party, her lover of the Guelphic party. Her lover's murder led to battle for forty days, and reconciliation did not come for another six years.

[2] Samuel Rogers (1763–1855), poet and banker, published *Italy* as a series of discrete poems in two parts in 1822 and 1828, before publishing the entire work in book form in 1830. It was one of the biggest best-sellers of its time. These lines are from *The Campagna of Florence* 228–30.
[3] 'The beautiful woman is dead, and she seems to sleep.'
[4] *naiad's fane* the temple of a water-nymph.
[5] *cypress* appropriately, a symbol of death.

But change came o'er the scene. A hurrying tread
   Broke on the whispery shades. Imelda knew   30
The footstep of her brother's wrath, and fled
   Up where the cedars make yon avenue
Dim with green twilight; pausing there, she caught –
Was it the clash of swords? A swift dark thought
   Struck down her lip's rich crimson as it passed,   35
And from her eye the sunny sparkle took
One moment with its fearfulness, and shook
   Her slight frame fiercely, as a stormy blast
Might rock the rose. Once more, and yet once more,
She stilled her heart to listen – all was o'er;   40
Sweet summer winds alone were heard to sigh,
Bearing the nightingale's deep spirit by.
That night Imelda's voice was in the song,
Lovely it floated through the festive throng,
Peopling her father's halls. That fatal night   45
Her eye looked starry in its dazzling light,
And her cheek glowed with beauty's flushing dyes,
Like a rich cloud of eve in southern skies –
A burning ruby cloud. There were[6] whose gaze
Followed her form beneath the clear lamp's blaze,   50
And marvelled at its radiance. But a few
Beheld the brightness of that feverish hue
With something of dim fear, and in that glance
   Found strange and sudden tokens of unrest,
Startling to meet amidst the mazy dance   55
   Where thought, if present, an unbidden guest,
Comes not unmasked. Howe'er this were, the time
Sped as it speeds with joy, and grief, and crime
Alike, and when the banquet's hall was left
Unto its garlands of their bloom bereft,   60
When trembling stars looked silvery in their wane,
And heavy flowers yet slumbered, once again
There stole a footstep, fleet and light and lone,
Through the dim cedar shade – the step of one
That started at a leaf, of one that fled,   65
Of one that panted with some secret dread:
What did Imelda there? She sought the scene
Where love so late with youth and hope had been;
Bodings were on her soul – a shuddering thrill
Ran through each vein, when first the naiad's rill   70
Met her with melody – sweet sounds and low;
We hear them yet – they live along its flow –
Her voice is music lost! The fountain-side
She gained – the wave flashed forth – 'twas darkly dyed

---

[6] *There were* i.e. there were [those] . . .

Ev'n as from warrior-hearts, and on its edge,   75
    Amidst the fern, and flowers, and moss-tufts deep,
There lay, as lulled by stream and rustling sedge,
    A youth, a graceful youth. 'Oh, dost thou sleep,
Azzo?' she cried, 'My Azzo, is this rest?'
But then her low tones faltered. 'On thy breast   80
Is the stain – yes, 'tis blood! And that cold cheek,
That moveless lip! Thou dost not slumber? Speak,
Speak, Azzo, my beloved! No sound – no breath –
What hath come thus between our spirits? Death!
Death? I but dream – I dream!' And there she stood,   85
A faint, frail trembler, gazing first on blood,
With her fair arm around yon cypress thrown,
Her form sustained by that dark stem alone,
And fading fast, like spell-struck maid of old,
Into white waves dissolving, clear and cold,   90
When from the grass her dimmed eye caught a gleam –
'Twas where a sword lay shivered[7] by the stream,
Her brother's sword! She knew it, and she knew
'Twas with a venomed point that weapon slew!
Woe for young love! But love is strong. There came   95
Strength upon woman's fragile heart and frame,
There came swift courage! On the dewy ground
She knelt, with all her dark hair floating round,
Like a long silken stole; she knelt and pressed
Her lips of glowing life tò Azzo's breast,   100
Drawing the poison forth – a strange, sad sight!
Pale death, and fearless love, and solemn night:
So the moon saw them last.
                    The morn came singing
    Through the green forests of the Apennines,
With all her joyous birds their free flight winging,   105
    And steps and voices out amongst the vines.
What found that dayspring *here*? Two fair forms laid
Like sculptured sleepers, from the myrtle shade
Casting a gleam of beauty o'er the wave –
Still, mournful, sweet. Were such things for the grave?   110
Could it be so indeed? That radiant girl,
Decked as for bridal hours – long braids of pearl
Amidst her shadowy locks were faintly shining,
    As tears might shine, with melancholy light;
And there was gold her slender waist entwining,   115
    And her pale graceful arms – how sadly bright!
And fiery gems upon her breast were lying,
And round her marble brow red roses dying.
But she died first! The violet's hue had spread

---

[7] *shivered* splintered.

O'er her sweet eyelids with repose oppressed,   120
She had bowed heavily her gentle head,
   And, on the youth's hushed bosom, sunk to rest.
So slept they well – the poison's work was done;
Love with true heart had striven, but Death had won.

EDITH, A TALE OF THE WOODS[1]

Du Heilige! rufe dein Kind zurück!
Ich habe genossen das irdische Glück,
Ich habe gelebt und geliebet.[2]

                                  Wallenstein[3]

The woods – oh, solemn are the boundless woods
   Of the great western world when day declines,
And louder sounds the roll of distant floods,
   More deep the rustling of the ancient pines;
When dimness gathers on the stilly air,   5
   And mystery seems o'er every leaf to brood,
Awful it is for human heart to bear
   The might and burden of the solitude!
Yet in that hour, midst those green wastes, there sate
One young and fair – and oh, how desolate   10
But undismayed; while sank the crimson light,
And the high cedars darkened with the night,
Alone she sate; though many lay around,
They, pale and silent on the bloody ground,
Were severed from her need and from her woe,   15
   Far as death severs life. O'er that wild spot
Combat had raged and brought the valiant low,
   And left them with the history of their lot
Unto the forest oaks. A fearful scene
For her whose home of other days had been   20
Midst the fair halls of England! But the love
   Which filled her soul was strong to cast out fear,
And by its might upborne all else above,
   She shrank not – marked not that the dead were near.
Of him alone she thought, whose languid head   25
   Faintly upon her wedded bosom fell;
Memory of aught but him on earth was fled,
   While heavily she felt his life-blood well
Fast o'er her garments forth, and vainly bound

EDITH, A TALE OF THE WOODS
[1] 'Founded on incidents related in an American work, *Sketches of Connecticut*' (Hemans's note). Lydia Howard Huntley, *Sketches of Connecticut, Forty Years Since* (Hartford, Conn., 1824), describes how Oriana Selden, a young English bride, was adopted by a Mohegan couple after her husband's death in battle.

[2] 'Thou holy one! Call thy child back! I have enjoyed earthly pleasure; I have lived and loved.'
[3] Johann Christoph Friedrich Schiller (1759–1805) composed *Wallenstein* in 1797–8; it was performed in 1799 and translated into English by Coleridge the following year. Hemans knew the play well both in the original and in Coleridge's rendering.

With her torn robe and hair the streaming wound,   30
Yet hoped, still hoped! Oh from such hope how long
   Affection woos the whispers that deceive,
Ev'n when the pressure of dismay grows strong,
   And we that weep, watch, tremble, ne'er believe
The blow indeed can fall! So bowed she there   35
Over the dying, while unconscious prayer
Filled all her soul. Now poured the moonlight down,
Veining the pine-stems through the foliage brown,
And fireflies, kindling up the leafy place,
Cast fitful radiance o'er the warrior's face   40
Whereby she caught its changes: to her eye
   The eye that faded looked through gathering haze
Whence love, o'ermastering mortal agony,
   Lifted a long, deep, melancholy gaze
When voice was not: that fond sad meaning passed –   45
She knew the fullness of her woe at last!
One shriek the forests heard, and mute she lay,
And cold, yet clasping still the precious clay
To her scarce-heaving breast. Oh love and death,
Ye have sad meetings on this changeful earth,   50
Many and sad! But airs of heavenly breath
Shall melt the links which bind you, for your birth
Is far apart.
       Now light of richer hue
Than the moon sheds came flushing mist and dew;
The pines grew red with morning; fresh winds played,   55
Bright-coloured birds with splendour crossed the shade,
Flitting on flower-like wings; glad murmurs broke
   From reed and spray and leaf, the living strings
Of Earth's Aeolian lyre,[4] whose music woke
   Into young life and joy all happy things.   60
And she too woke from that long dreamless trance
The widowed Edith: fearfully her glance
Fell, as in doubt, on faces dark and strange,
And dusky forms. A sudden sense of change
Flashed o'er her spirit, ev'n ere memory swept   65
The tide of anguish back with thoughts that slept;
Yet half instinctively she rose and spread
Her arms, as 'twere for something lost or fled,
Then faintly sank again. The forest bough,
With all its whispers waved not o'er her now –   70

---

[4] *reed and spray . . . lyre* reeds and spray and leaves are the strings of the Aeolian lyre of the earth. An Aeolian lyre is a stringed instrument placed in front of an open window, so that the outside breeze can 'play' across its strings (the equivalent of today's wind-chimes). This is almost certainly an allusion to Coleridge's great pantheist statement of faith, *The Eolian Harp*, in which he asks: 'And what if all of animated nature / Be but organic harps diversely framed . . . ?' (ll. 44–5).

Where was she? Midst the people of the wild,
  By the red hunter's fire: an aged chief
Whose home looked sad (for therein played no child)
  Had borne her, in the stillness of her grief,
To that lone cabin of the woods, and there,   75
Won by a form so desolately fair,
Or touched with thoughts from some past sorrow sprung,
O'er her low couch an Indian matron hung,
While in grave silence, yet with earnest eye,
The ancient warrior of the waste stood by,   80
Bending in watchfulness his proud grey head
  And leaning on his bow.
                   And life returned –
Life, but with all its memories of the dead,
  To Edith's heart; and well the sufferer learned
Her task of meek endurance, well she wore   85
The chastened grief that humbly can adore
Midst blinding tears. But unto that old pair,
Ev'n as a breath of spring's awakening air
Her presence was, or as a sweet wild tune
Bringing back tender thoughts, which all too soon   90
Depart with childhood. Sadly they had seen
  A daughter to the land of spirits go,
And ever from that time her fading mien
  And voice, like winds of summer, soft and low,
Had haunted their dim years; but Edith's face   95
Now looked in holy sweetness from her place,
And they again seemed parents. Oh the joy,
The rich, deep blessedness (though earth's alloy,
Fear that still bodes, be there) of pouring forth
The heart's whole power of love,[5] its wealth and worth   100
Of strong affection, in one healthful flow,
On something all its own! – that kindly glow,
Which to shut inward is consuming pain,
Gives the glad soul its flowering time again
When, like the sunshine, freed. And gentle cares   105
Th' adopted Edith meekly gave for theirs
Who loved her thus: her spirit dwelt the while
With the departed, and her patient smile
Spoke of farewells to earth – yet still she prayed,
Ev'n o'er her soldier's lowly grave, for aid   110
One purpose to fulfil, to leave one trace
Brightly recording that her dwelling-place
Had been among the wilds, for well she knew
The secret whisper of her bosom true,

---

5   *Oh the joy . . . power of love* the joy of loving a child
is mixed with fear for its safety.

Which warned her hence.

And now by many a word   115
Linked unto moments when the heart was stirred,
By the sweet mournfulness of many a hymn
Sung when the woods at eve grew hushed and dim,
By the persuasion of her fervent eye,
All eloquent with childlike piety,   120
By the still beauty of her life, she strove
To win for heaven, and heaven-born truth, the love
Poured out on her so freely. Nor in vain
Was that soft-breathing influence to enchain
The soul in gentle bonds: by slow degrees   125
Light followed on, as when a summer breeze
Parts the deep masses of the forest shade
And lets the sunbeam through. Her voice was made
Ev'n such a breeze, and she, a lowly guide,
By faith and sorrow raised and purified,   130
So to the Cross her Indian fosterers led,
Until their prayers were one. When morning spread
O'er the blue lake, and when the sunset's glow
Touched into golden bronze the cypress bough,
And when the quiet of the Sabbath time   135
Sank on her heart, though no melodious chime
Wakened the wilderness, their prayers were one.
Now might she pass in hope, her work was done.
And she *was* passing from the woods away;
The broken flower of England might not stay   140
Amidst those alien shades; her eye was bright
Ev'n yet with something of a starry light,
But her form wasted, and her fair young cheek
Wore oft and patiently a fatal streak,
A rose whose root was death. The parting sigh   145
Of autumn through the forests had gone by,
And the rich maple o'er her wanderings lone
Its crimson leaves in many a shower had strewn,
Flushing[6] the air; and winter's blast had been
Amidst the pines; and now a softer green   150
Fringed their dark boughs, for spring again had come,
The sunny spring! But Edith to her home
Was journeying fast. 'Alas, we think it sad
To part with life when all the earth looks glad
In her young lovely things, when voices break   155
Into sweet sounds, and leaves and blossoms wake.
Is it not brighter then, in that far clime
Where graves are not, nor blights of changeful time,[7]

---

[6]   *Flushing* reddening.   [7]   *blights of changeful time* disease that comes with the
passage of time.

If *here* such glory dwell with passing blooms,
Such golden sunshine rest around the tombs?'   160
So thought the dying one. 'Twas early day,
And sounds and odours with the breezes play,
Whispering of springtime, through the cabin-door
Unto her couch life's farewell sweetness bore;
Then with a look where all her hope awoke,   165
'My father!' – to the grey-haired chief she spoke –
'Know'st thou that I depart?' 'I know, I know',
He answered mournfully, 'that thou must go
To thy beloved, my daughter!' 'Sorrow not
  For me, kind mother!' With meek smiles once more   170
She murmured in low tones; 'one happy lot
  Awaits us, friends, upon the better shore;
For we have prayed together in one trust,
And lifted our frail spirits from the dust
To God who gave them. Lay me by mine own   175
Under the cedar-shade: where he is gone
Thither I go. There will my sisters be,
And the dead parents, lisping at whose knee
My childhood's prayer was learned – the Saviour's prayer
Which now *ye* know, and I shall meet you there,   180
Father and gentle mother! Ye have bound
The bruiséd reed, and mercy shall be found
By Mercy's children.' From the matron's eye
Dropped tears, her sole and passionate reply,
But Edith felt them not; for now a sleep,   185
Solemnly beautiful, a stillness deep,
Fell on her settled face. Then, sad and slow,
And mantling up his stately head in woe,
'Thou'rt passing hence', he sang, that warrior old,
In sounds like those by plaintive waters rolled.   190

Thou'rt passing from the lake's green side
  And the hunter's hearth away;
For the time of flowers, for the summer's pride,
  Daughter, thou canst not stay!

Thou'rt journeying to thy spirit's home,   195
  Where the skies are ever clear!
The corn-month's golden hours will come,
  But they shall not find thee here.

And we shall miss thy voice, my bird,
  Under our whispering pine!   200
Music shall midst the leaves be heard,
  But not a song like thine.

A breeze that roves o'er stream and hill
   Telling of winter gone
Hath such sweet falls – yet caught we still   205
   A farewell in its tone.

But thou, my bright one, thou shalt be
   Where farewell sounds are o'er;
Thou, in the eyes thou lov'st, shalt see
   No fear of parting more.   210

The mossy grave thy tears have wet,
   And the wind's wild moanings by,
Thou with thy kindred shalt forget,
   Midst flowers – not such as die.

The shadow from thy brow shall melt,   215
   The sorrow from thy strain,[8]
But where thine earthly smile hath dwelt,
   Our hearts shall thirst in vain.

Dim will our cabin be, and lone,
   When thou, its light, art fled;   220
Yet hath thy step the pathway shown
   Unto the happy dead.

And we will follow thee, our guide,
   And join that shining band;
Thou'rt passing from the lake's green side –   225
   Go to the better land!

The song had ceased – the listeners caught no breath;
That lovely sleep had melted into death.

THE INDIAN CITY[1]

What deep wounds ever closed without a scar?
The heart's bleed longest, and but heal to wear
That which disfigures it.

                                 Childe Harold[2]

I

Royal in splendour went down the day
On the plain where an Indian city lay,

---

[8] *strain* song.
THE INDIAN CITY
[1] 'From a tale in Forbes' *Oriental Memoirs*' (Hemans's
note). James Forbes (1749–1819) published his *Oriental
Memoirs* in 1813.

[2] Byron, *Childe Harold's Pilgrimage* iii 788–90.

With its crown of domes o'er the forest high,
Red as if fused in the burning sky,
And its deep groves pierced by the rays which made   5
A bright stream's way through each long arcade,
Till the pillared vaults of the banyan[3] stood
Like torch-lit aisles midst the solemn wood,
And the plantain glittered with leaves of gold,
As a tree midst the genii-gardens old,   10
And the cypress lifted a blazing spire,
And the stems of the cocoas were shafts of fire.
Many a white pagoda's gleam
Slept lovely round upon lake and stream,
Broken alone by the lotus-flowers,   15
As they caught the glow of the sun's last hours
Like rosy wine in their cups, and shed
Its glory forth on their crystal bed.
Many a graceful Hindu maid
With the water-vase from the palmy shade   20
Came gliding light as the desert's roe,
Down marble steps to the tanks below;
And a cool sweet plashing was ever heard,
As the molten glass of the wave was stirred;
And a murmur, thrilling the scented air,   25
Told where the Bramin[4] bowed in prayer.
   There wandered a noble Moslem boy
Through the scene of beauty in breathless joy;
He gazed where the stately city rose
Like a pageant of clouds in its red repose;   30
He turned where birds through the gorgeous gloom
Of the woods went glancing on starry plume;
He tracked the brink of the shining lake
By the tall canes feathered in tuft and brake,
Till the path he chose, in its mazes wound   35
To the very heart of the holy ground.
   And there lay the water, as if enshrined
In a rocky urn from the sun and wind,
Bearing the hues of the grove on high,
Far down through its dark still purity.   40
The flood beyond, to the fiery west
Spread out like a metal mirror's[5] breast,
But that lone bay, in its dimness deep,
Seemed made for the swimmer's joyous leap,
For the stag athirst from the noontide chase,   45
For all free things of the wildwood's race.
   Like a falcon's glance on the wide blue sky

---

[3] *banyan* East Indian fig tree.
[4] *Brahmin* highest priestly caste among the Hindus.

[5] *metal mirror* mirrors were at this time made of highly polished metal.

Was the kindling flash of the boy's glad eye,
Like a sea-bird's flight to the foaming wave
From the shadowy bank was the bound he gave;　　　　50
Dashing the spray-drops, cold and white,
O'er the glossy leaves in his young delight,
And bowing his locks to the waters clear –
Alas, he dreamt not that fate was near!
　　His mother looked from her tent the while　　　　55
O'er heaven and earth with a quiet smile;
She, on her way unto Mecca's fane,
Had stayed[6] the march of her pilgrim-train
Calmly to linger a few brief hours
In the Bramin city's glorious bowers,　　　　60
For the pomp of the forest, the wave's bright fall,
The red gold of sunset – she loved them all.

II

The moon rose clear in the splendour given
To the deep blue night of an Indian heaven;
The boy from the high-arched woods came back –　　　　65
Oh, what had he met in his lonely track?
The serpent's glance, through the long reeds bright?
The arrowy spring of the tiger's might?
No! Yet as one by a conflict worn,
With his graceful hair all soiled and torn,　　　　70
And a gloom on the lids of his darkened eye,
And a gash on his bosom – he came to die!
He looked for the face to his young heart sweet,
And found it, and sank at his mother's feet.
　　'Speak to me! Whence doth the swift blood run?　　　　75
What hath befall'n thee, my child, my son?'
The mist of death on his brow lay pale,
But his voice just lingered to breathe the tale,
Murmuring faintly of wrongs and scorn,
And wounds from the children of Brahma[7] born.　　　　80
This was the doom[8] for a Moslem found
With foot profane on their holy ground;
This was for sullying the pure waves free
Unto them alone – 'twas their God's decree.
　　A change came o'er his wandering look –　　　　85
The mother shrieked not then, nor shook;
Breathless she knelt in her son's young blood,
Rending her mantle to staunch its flood,
But it rushed like a river which none may stay,
Bearing a flower to the deep away.　　　　90

---

[6]　*stayed* halted.　　　　　　　　　　[8]　*doom* law.
[7]　*Brahma* God in Hindu myth.

That which our love to the earth would chain,
Fearfully striving with Heaven in vain,
That which fades from us while yet we hold,
Clasped to our bosoms, its mortal mould,
Was fleeting before her, afar and fast;   95
One moment – the soul from the face had passed!
    Are there no words for that common woe?
Ask of the thousands, its depths that know!
The boy had breathed, in his dreaming rest,
Like a low-voiced dove on her gentle breast;   100
He had stood, when she sorrowed, beside her knee,
Painfully stilling his quick heart's glee;
He had kissed from her cheek the widow's tears
With the loving lip of his infant years;
He had smiled o'er her path like a bright spring day –   105
Now in his blood on the earth he lay
Murdered! Alas, and we love so well
In a world where anguish like this can dwell!
    She bowed down mutely o'er her dead –
They that stood round her watched in dread;   110
They watched – she knew not they were by;
Her soul sat veiled in its agony.
On the silent lip she pressed no kiss,
Too stern was the grasp of her pangs for this;
She shed no tear as her face bent low   115
O'er the shining hair of the lifeless brow;
She looked but into the half-shut eye
With a gaze that found there no reply
And, shrieking, mantled her head from sight
And fell, struck down by her sorrow's might!   120
    And what deep change, what work of power,
Was wrought on her secret soul that hour?
How rose the lonely one? She rose
Like a prophetess from dark repose,
And proudly flung from her face the veil,   125
And shook the hair from her forehead pale,
And midst her wondering handmaids stood
With the sudden glance of a dauntless mood.
Aye, lifting up to the midnight sky
A brow in its regal passion high,   130
With a close and rigid grasp she pressed
The bloodstained robe to her heaving breast,
And said, 'Not yet, not yet I weep,
Not yet my spirit shall sink or sleep,
Not till yon city, in ruins rent,   135
Be piled for its victim's monument.
Cover his dust, bear it on before –
It shall visit those temple-gates once more!'

And away in the train of the dead she turned,
The strength of her step was the heart that burned;   140
And the Bramin groves in the starlight smiled
As the mother passed with her slaughtered child.

III

Hark, a wild sound of the desert's horn
Through the woods round the Indian city borne!
A peal of the cymbal and tambour afar –   145
War, 'tis the gathering of Moslem war!
The Bramin looked from the leaguered[9] towers –
He saw the wild archer amidst his bowers,
And the lake that flashed through the plantain shade
As the light of the lances along it played,   150
And the canes that shook as if winds were high
When the fiery steed of the waste swept by,
And the camp as it lay, like a billowy sea,
Wide round the sheltering banyan tree.
    There stood one tent from the rest apart –   155
That was the place of a wounded heart.
Oh, deep is a wounded heart, and strong
A voice that cries against mighty wrong,
And full of death as a hot wind's blight[10]
Doth the ire of a crushed affection light!   160
    Maimuna from realm to realm had passed,
And her tale had rung like a trumpet's blast;
There had been words from her pale lips poured,
Each one a spell to unsheath the sword.
The Tartar had sprung from his steed to hear,   165
And the dark chief of Araby grasped his spear
Till a chain of long lances begirt the wall,
And a vow was recorded that doomed its fall.
    Back with the dust of her son she came,
When her voice had kindled that lightning flame;   170
She came in the might of a queenly foe –
Banner, and javelin, and bended bow;
But a deeper power on her forehead sate –
There sought the warrior his star of fate;
Her eye's wild flash through the tented line   175
Was hailed as a spirit and a sign,
And the faintest tone from her lip was caught
As a sibyl's[11] breath of prophetic thought.
    Vain, bitter glory! The gift of grief
That lights up vengeance to find relief,   180

---

[9] *leaguered* beleaguered, besieged; as in Byron, *Siege of Corinth* 30–1: 'The tent is pitched, the crescent shines / Along the Moslem's leaguering lines'.

[10] *full of death as a hot wind's blight* winds were believed to be carriers of disease.

[11] *sibyl* female prophet.

Transient and faithless – it cannot fill
So the deep void of the heart, nor still
The yearning left by a broken tie,
That haunted fever of which we die!
    Sickening she turned from her sad renown,   185
As a king in death might reject his crown;
Slowly the strength of the walls gave way –
She withered faster from day to day.
All the proud sounds of that bannered plain
To stay the flight of her soul were vain;   190
Like an eagle caged, it had striven, and worn
The frail dust ne'er for such conflicts born,
Till the bars were rent, and the hour was come
For its fearful rushing through darkness home.
    The bright sun set in his pomp and pride,   195
As on that eve when the fair boy died;
She gazed from her couch, and a softness fell
O'er her weary heart with the day's farewell;
She spoke, and her voice in its dying tone
Had an echo of feelings that long seemed flown.   200
She murmured a low sweet cradle song,
Strange midst the din of a warrior throng,
A song of the time when her boy's young cheek
Had glowed on her breast in its slumber meek;
But something which breathed from that mournful strain   205
Sent a fiftul gust o'er her soul again,
And starting as if from a dream, she cried,
'Give him proud burial at my side!
There, by yon lake, where the palm-boughs wave,
When the temples are fallen, make there our grave.'   210
    And the temples fell, though the spirit passed
That stayed not for victory's voice at last,
When the day was won for the martyr-dead,
For the broken heart, and the bright blood shed.
    Through the gates of the vanquished the Tartar steed   215
Bore in the avenger with foaming speed;
Free swept the flame through the idol-fanes
And the streams flowed red, as from warrior-veins,
And the sword of the Moslem, let loose to slay,
Like the panther leapt on its flying prey,   220
Till a city of ruin begirt the shade
Where the boy and his mother at rest were laid.
    Palace and tower on that plain were left
Like fallen trees by the lightning cleft;
The wild vine mantled the stately square,   225
The Rajah's throne was the serpent's lair,
And the jungle grass o'er the altar sprung –
This was the work of one deep heart wrung!

THE PEASANT GIRL OF THE RHONE

There is but one place in the world –
Thither, where he lies buried! . . .
There, there is all that still remains of him,
That single spot is the whole earth to me.

Coleridge's *Wallenstein*[1]

Alas, our young affections run to waste,
Or water but the desert.

Childe Harold[2]

There went a warrior's funeral through the night,
A waving of tall plumes, a ruddy light
Of torches, fitfully and wildly thrown
From the high woods along the sweeping Rhone,
Far down the waters. Heavily and dead,   5
Under the moaning trees the horse-hoof's tread
In muffled sounds upon the greensward fell
As chieftains passed, and solemnly the swell
Of the deep requiem, o'er the gleaming river
Borne with the gale, and with the leaves' low shiver,   10
Floated and died. Proud mourners there, yet pale,
    Wore man's mute anguish sternly – but of *one*,
Oh who shall speak? What words *his* brow unveil?
    A father following to the grave his son –
That is no grief to picture! Sad and slow,   15
    Through the wood-shadows moved the knightly train
With youth's fair form upon the bier laid low,
    Fair even when found, amidst the bloody slain,
Stretched by its broken lance. They reached the lone
    Baronial chapel, where the forest gloom   20
Fell heaviest, for the massy boughs had grown
    Into thick archways, as to vault the tomb.
Stately they trod the hollow ringing aisle,
A strange deep echo shuddered through the pile
Till crested heads at last, in silence bent   25
Round the De Coucis' antique monument,
When dust to dust was given, and Aymer slept
    Beneath the drooping banners of his line,
Whose broidered folds the Syrian wind had swept
    Proudly and oft o'er fields of Palestine.   30
So the sad rite was closed. The sculptor gave
Trophies erelong, to deck that lordly grave,

THE PEASANT GIRL OF THE RHONE
[1] Coleridge, *The Death of Wallenstein* (1800), IV v 5–
6, 9–10. Coleridge translated both J. C. F. von Schiller's

The Piccolomini, or the First Part of Wallenstein and *The Death of Wallenstein* in 1800.
[2] Byron, *Childe Harold's Pilgrimage* iv 1072–3.

And the pale image of a youth arrayed
As warriors are for fight, but calmly laid
　In slumber on his shield. Then all was done, 35
All still around the dead. His name was heard
Perchance when wine-cups flowed, and hearts were stirred
　By some old song, or tale of battle won,
Told round the hearth; but in his father's breast
Manhood's high passions woke again, and pressed 40
On to their mark, and in his friend's clear eye
There dwelt no shadow of a dream gone by,[3]
And with the brethren of his fields, the feast
Was gay as when the voice whose sounds had ceased
Mingled with theirs. Ev'n thus life's rushing tide 45
Bears back affection from the grave's dark side;
Alas, to think of this! The heart's void place
　Filled up so soon – so like a summer-cloud,
All that we loved to pass and leave no trace!
　He lay forgotten in his early shroud. 50
Forgotten? Not of all! The sunny smile
Glancing in play o'er that proud lip erewhile,
And the dark locks whose breezy waving threw
A gladness round, whene'er their shade withdrew
From the bright brow, and all the sweetness lying 55
　Within that eagle-eye's jet radiance deep,
And all the music with that young voice dying,
　Whose joyous echoes made the quick heart leap
As at a hunter's bugle – these things lived
Still in one breast whose silent love survived 60
The pomps of kindred sorrow. Day by day
On Aymer's tomb fresh flowers in garlands lay,
Through the dim fane soft summer-odours breathing,
And all the pale sepulchral trophies wreathing,
And with a flush of deeper brilliance glowing 65
In the rich light, like molten rubies flowing
Through storied windows down. The violet there
Might speak of love, a secret love and lowly,
And the rose image all things fleet and fair,
And the faint passion-flower, the sad and holy, 70
Tell of diviner hopes. But whose light hand,
As for an altar, wove the radiant band?
Whose gentle nurture brought, from hidden dells
That gem-like wealth of blossoms and sweet bells,
To blush through every season? Blight and chill 75
Might touch the changing woods, but duly still
For years those gorgeous coronals renewed,

---

[3] *but in his father's breast ... dream gone by* Aymer's
father got over his grief and recovered his 'manly'
emotions, just as the clear (i.e. unweeping) eye of
Aymer's old friend saw no ghost of him.

And brightly clasping marble spear and helm,
Even through midwinter, filled the solitude
    With a strange smile, a glow of summer's realm.   80
Surely some fond and fervent heart was pouring
Its youth's vain worship on the dust, adoring
In lone devotedness!
                            One spring-morn rose,
    And found, within that tomb's proud shadow laid
(Oh, not as midst the vineyards, to repose   85
    From the fierce noon) a dark-haired peasant maid:
Who could reveal her story? That still face
    Had once been fair; for on the clear arched brow
And the curved lip, there lingered yet such grace
    As sculpture gives its dreams; and long and low   90
The deep black lashes o'er the half-shut eye
(For death was on its lids) fell mournfully.
But the cold cheek was sunk, the raven hair
Dimmed, the slight form all wasted as by care.
Whence came that early blight? *Her* kindred's place   95
Was not amidst the high De Couci race,
Yet there her shrine had been! She grasped a wreath,
The tomb's last garland – this was love in death!

INDIAN WOMAN'S DEATH SONG

An Indian woman, driven to despair by her husband's desertion of her for another wife, entered a canoe with her children, and rowed it down the Mississippi towards a cataract. Her voice was heard from the shore singing a mournful death-song until overpowered by the sound of the waters in which she perished. The tale is related in *Long's Expedition to the Source of St Peter's River*.[1]

> *Non, je ne puis vivre avec un coeur brisé. Il faut que je
> retrouve la joie, et que je m'unisse aux esprits libres de l'air.*[2]
>   *Bride of Messina*, translated by Madame de Staël[3]

> *Let not my child be a girl, for very sad is the life of a woman.*
>   *The Prairie*[4]

Down a broad river of the western wilds,
Piercing thick forest glooms, a light canoe

INDIAN WOMAN'S DEATH SONG
[1] William H. Keating, *Narrative of an Expedition to the source of the St Peter's River ... under the command of S. H. Long* was first published in two volumes in Philadelphia, 1824; it was published in London the following year.
[2] 'No, I can't live with a broken heart. I must retrieve my happiness, and be reunited with the free spirits of the air'.

[3] Schiller's *Die Braut von Messina* was first published in 1803, and not translated into English until 1837. Madame de Staël published her translation in chapter 19 of *Des Allemagnes*, in which she also gives a summary of the play. I am grateful to Susan Wolfson for this information.
[4] James Fenimore Cooper's popular book was first published in London, 1827.

Swept with the current: fearful was the speed
Of the frail bark, as by a tempest's wing
Borne leaf-like on to where the mist of spray   5
Rose with the cataract's thunder. Yet within,
Proudly, and dauntlessly, and all alone,
Save that a babe lay sleeping at her breast,
A woman stood. Upon her Indian brow
Sat a strange gladness, and her dark hair waved   10
As if triumphantly. She pressed her child,
In its bright slumber, to her beating heart,
And lifted her sweet voice that rose awhile
Above the sound of waters, high and clear,
Wafting a wild proud strain, her song of death.   15

Roll swiftly to the spirit's land, thou mighty stream and free!
Father of ancient waters, roll, and bear our lives with thee!
The weary bird that storms have tossed would seek the sunshine's calm,
And the deer that hath the arrow's hurt flies to the woods of balm.

Roll on! My warrior's eye hath looked upon another's face,   20
And mine hath faded from his soul, as fades a moonbeam's trace;
My shadow comes not o'er his path, my whisper to his dream,
He flings away the broken reed – roll swifter yet, thou stream!

The voice that spoke of other days is hushed within *his* breast,
But *mine* its lonely music haunts, and will not let me rest;   25
It sings a low and mournful song of gladness that is gone;
I cannot live without that light – father of waves, roll on!

Will he not miss the bounding step that met him from the chase?
The heart of love that made his home an ever-sunny place?
The hand that spread the hunter's board, and decked his couch of yore? 30
He will not! Roll, dark foaming stream, on to the better shore!

Some blessed fount amidst the woods of that bright land must flow
Whose waters from my soul may lave the memory of this woe;
Some gentle wind must whisper there, whose breath may waft away
The burden of the heavy night, the sadness of the day.   35

And thou, my babe, though born, like me, for woman's weary lot,
Smile – to that wasting of the heart, my own! I leave thee not;
Too bright a thing art *thou* to pine in aching love away,
Thy mother bears thee far, young fawn, from sorrow and decay.

She bears thee to the glorious bowers where none are heard to weep,   40
And where th' unkind one hath no power again to trouble sleep;
And where the soul shall find its youth, as wakening from a dream –
One moment, and that realm is ours: on, on, dark rolling stream!

JOAN OF ARC, IN RHEIMS

Jeanne d'Arc avait eu la joie de voir à Chalons quelques amis de son enfance. Une joie plus ineffable encore l'attendait à Rheims, au sein de son triomphe: Jacques d'Arc, son père, y se trouva, aussitot que les troupes de Charles VII y furent entrées; et comme les deux frères de notre Héroïne l'avaient accompagnés, elle se vit, pour un instant au milieu de sa famille, dans les bras d'un père vertueux.

Vie de Jeanne d'Arc[1]

> *Thou hast a charméd cup, oh fame,*
> *A draught that mantles high,*
> *And seems to lift this earth-born frame*
> *Above mortality;*
> *Away! To me, a woman, bring*
> *Sweet waters from affection's spring.*[2]

That was a joyous day in Rheims of old,
When peal on peal of mighty music rolled
Forth from her thronged cathedral, while around
A multitude whose billows[3] made no sound,
Chained to a hush of wonder, though elate   5
With victory, listened at their temple's gate.
And what was done within? Within, the light
   Through the rich gloom of pictured windows flowing,
Tinged with soft awfulness a stately sight –
   The chivalry of France, their proud heads bowing   10
In martial vassalage – while midst that ring,
And shadowed by ancestral tombs, a king
Received his birthright's crown. For this the hymn
   Swelled out like rushing waters, and the day
With the sweet censer's misty breath grew dim,   15
   As through long aisles it floated o'er th' array
Of arms and sweeping stoles. But who, alone
And unapproached, beside the altar-stone,
With the white banner, forth like sunshine streaming,
And the gold helm, through clouds of fragrance gleaming,   20
Silent and radiant stood? The helm was raised,
And the fair face revealed that upward gazed,
   Intensely worshipping – a still, clear face,
Youthful, but brightly solemn! Woman's cheek

JOAN OF ARC:

[1] 'Joan of Arc had had the pleasure of seeing some childhood friends at Châlons. A yet more sublime joy awaited her at Rheims, at the peak of her triumph. Jacques d'Arc, her father, had arrived there as soon as the troops of Charles VII had entered the city, and as our heroine's two brothers had accompanied him, she found herself momentarily amidst her family, and

in the arms of a virtuous father.' There were many lives of Joan of Arc in French; Hemans is probably using Jean Baptiste Prosper Jollois, *Histoire abrégée de la vie et des exploits de Jeanne d'Arc* (Paris, 1821).
[2] This epigraph is stanza 1 of Hemans's *Woman and Fame.*
[3] *billows* movements.

And brow were there, in deep devotion meek,   25
    Yet glorified with inspiration's trace
On its pure paleness, while, enthroned above,
The pictured Virgin with her smile of love
Seemed bending o'er her votaress – that slight form!
Was that the leader through the battle storm?   30
Had the soft light in that adoring eye
Guided the warrior where the swords flashed high?
'Twas so, even so, and thou, the shepherd's child,
Joanne, the lowly dreamer of the wild!
Never before, and never since that hour,   35
Hath woman, mantled with victorious power,
Stood forth as *thou* beside the shrine didst stand,
Holy amidst the knighthood of the land,
And beautiful with joy and with renown,
Lift thy white banner o'er the golden crown   40
Ransomed for France by thee!
                                    The rites are done.
Now let the dome with trumpet-notes be shaken,
And bid the echoes of the tombs awaken,
    And come thou forth, that Heaven's rejoicing sun
May give thee welcome from thine own blue skies,   45
    Daughter of Victory! A triumphant strain,
A proud rich stream of warlike melodies,
    Gushed through the portals of the antique fane
And forth she came. Then rose a nation's sound –
Oh, what a power to bid the quick heart bound   50
The wind bears onward with the stormy cheer
Man gives to glory on her high career!
Is there indeed such power? Far deeper dwells
In one kind household voice, to reach the cells
Whence happiness flows forth! The shouts that filled   55
The hollow heaven tempestuously were stilled
One moment, and in that brief pause the tone,
As of a breeze that o'er her home had blown,
Sank on the bright maid's heart – 'Joanne!'
                                    Who spoke
    Like those whose childhood with *her* childhood grew   60
Under one roof? 'Joanne!' – *that* murmur broke
    With sounds of weeping forth! She turned – she knew
Beside her, marked from all the thousands there,
In the calm beauty of his silver hair,
The stately shepherd; and the youth whose joy   65
From his dark eye flashed proudly; and the boy,
The youngest-born, that ever loved her best –
'Father! And ye, my brothers!' On the breast
Of that grey sire she sank – and swiftly back,
Ev'n in an instant, to their native track   70

Her free thoughts flowed. She saw the pomp no more –
The plumes, the banners; to her cabin-door,
And to the fairy's fountain in the glade,[4]
Where her young sisters by her side had played,
And to her hamlet's chapel, where it rose   75
Hallowing the forest unto deep repose,
Her spirit turned. The very woodnote sung
    In early springtime by the bird which dwelt
Where o'er her father's roof the beech-leaves hung
    Was in her heart; a music heard and felt,   80
Winning her back to nature. She unbound
    The helm of many battles from her head,
And, with her bright locks bowed to sweep the ground,
    Lifting her voice up, wept for joy, and said,
'Bless me, my father, bless me! And with thee,   85
To the still cabin and the beechen-tree,
Let me return!'
                    Oh, never did thine eye
Through the green haunts of happy infancy
Wander again, Joanne! Too much of fame
Had shed its radiance on thy peasant name,   90
And bought alone by gifts beyond all price,
The trusting heart's repose, the paradise
Of home with all its loves, doth fate allow
The crown of glory unto woman's brow.

PAULINE

To die for what we love! Oh there is power
In the true heart, and pride, and joy, for this;
It is to live *without the vanished light*
That strength is needed.

Così trapassa al trapassar d'un Giorno
Della vita mortal il fiore e'l verde.[1]

                                                    Tasso

Along the starlit Seine went music swelling,
    Till the air thrilled with its exulting mirth;
Proudly it floated, even as if no dwelling
    For cares or stricken hearts were found on earth;
And a glad sound the measure lightly beat,   5
A happy chime of many dancing feet.

---

[4] 'A beautiful fountain near Domremi, believed to be haunted by fairies, and a favourite resort of Jeanne d'Arc in her childhood' (Hemans's note). Domremy La Pucelle, a village in the department of Meuse, was Joan's birthplace.

PAULINE
[1] 'Thus the flower and the green of the mortal life fade as the day fades.'

For in a palace of the land that night,
   Lamps, and fresh roses, and green leaves were hung,
And from the painted walls a stream of light
   On flying forms beneath soft splendour flung;   10
But loveliest far amidst the revel's pride
Was one, the lady from the Danube side.[2]

Pauline, the meekly bright! Though now no more
   Her clear eye flashed with youth's all tameless glee,
Yet something holier than its dayspring wore,   15
   There in soft rest lay beautiful to see –
A charm with graver, tenderer sweetness fraught,
The blending of deep love and matron thought.[3]

Through the gay throng she moved, serenely fair,
   And such calm joy as fills a moonlight sky   20
Sate on her brow beneath its graceful hair,
   As her young daughter in the dance went by
With the fleet step of one that yet hath known
Smiles and kind voices in this world alone.

Lurked there no secret boding in her breast?   25
   Did no faint whisper warn of evil nigh?
Such oft awake when most the heart seems blessed
   Midst the light laughter of festivity –
Whence come those tones! Alas, enough we know,
To mingle fear with all triumphal show!   30

Who spoke of evil when young feet were flying
   In fairy-rings around· the echoing hall?
Soft airs through braided locks in perfume sighing,
   Glad pulses beating unto music's call?
Silence! The minstrels pause – and hark, a sound,   35
A strange quick rustling which their notes had drowned!

And lo, a light upon the dancers breaking –
   Not such their clear and silvery lamps had shed!
From the gay dream of revelry awaking,
   One moment holds them still in breathless dread;   40
The wild, fierce lustre grows – then bursts a cry –
Fire! Through the hall and round it gathering – fly![4]

---

2 'The Princess Pauline Schwartzenberg. The story of her fate is beautifully related in *L'Allemagne*, vol. 3, p. 336' (Hemans's note). Anne-Louise-Germaine Necker, Madame de Staël (1766–1817), published *De l'Allemagne*, her most celebrated non-fiction work, in 1807. It was immediately seized by Napoleon's chief of police, and she was ordered into exile. Hemans's reference is to the first English translation, published as *Germany*, by John Murray, in 1813. Pauline's story is told in vol. 3, pp. 337–9.

3 Hemans is very close to her source; de Staël says that Pauline 'still united the charm of perfect beauty to all the dignity of the maternal character' (*Germany* iii 337).

4 'On a sudden the numberless torches, which restored the splendour of the day, are about to be changed· into devouring flames' (*Germany* iii 337).

And forth they rush as chased by sword and spear –
   To the green coverts of the garden-bowers,
A gorgeous masque of pageantry and fear   45
   Startling the birds and trampling down the flowers,
While from the dome behind, red sparkles driven
Pierce the dark stillness of the midnight heaven.

And where is she, Pauline? The hurrying throng
   Have swept her onward, as a stormy blast   50
Might sweep some faint o'erwearied bird along –
   Till now the threshold of that death is passed,
And free she stands beneath the starry skies
Calling her child – but no sweet voice replies.

'Bertha, where art thou? Speak, oh speak, my own!'   55
   Alas, unconscious of her pangs the while,
The gentle girl, in fear's cold grasp alone,
   Powerless hath sunk within the blazing pile –
A young bright form, decked gloriously for death,
With flowers all shrinking from the flame's fierce breath!   60

But oh, thy strength, deep love! There is no power
   To stay the mother from that rolling grave,
Though fast on high the fiery volumes tower,
   And forth, like banners, from each lattice[5] wave.
Back, back she rushes through a host combined –   65
Mighty is anguish, with affection twined!

And what bold step may follow midst the roar
   Of the red billows, o'er their prey that rise?
None! Courage there stood still – and never more
   Did those fair forms emerge on human eyes!   70
Was one brief meeting theirs, one wild farewell?
And died they heart to heart? Oh, who can tell?

Freshly and cloudlessly the morning broke
   On that sad palace, midst its pleasure-shades;
Its painted roofs had sunk – yet black with smoke   75
   And lonely stood its marble colonnades;
But yestereve their shafts with wreaths[6] were bound –
Now lay the scene one shrivelled scroll around!

And bore the ruins no recording trace
   Of all that woman's heart had dared and done?   80
Yes, there were gems to mark its mortal place,
   That forth from dust and ashes dimly shone!

---

[5] *lattice* window.   [6] *wreaths* laurel wreaths, a sign of victory.

Those had the mother on her gentle breast
Worn round her child's fair image, there at rest.[7]

And they were all! The tender and the true   85
   Left this alone her sacrifice to prove,
Hallowing the spot where mirth once lightly flew
   To deep, lone, chastened thoughts of grief and love.
Oh, we have need of patient faith below,
To clear away the mysteries of such woe!   90

JUANA[1]

Juana, mother of the Emperor Charles V,[2] upon the death of her husband, Philip the
Handsome of Austria, who had treated her with uniform neglect, had his body laid
upon a bed of state in a magnificent dress and, being possessed with the idea that it
would revive, watched it for a length of time incessantly, waiting for the moment of
returning life.

> *It is but dust thou look'st upon. This love,*
> *This wild and passionate idolatry,*
> *What doth it in the shadow of the grave?*
> *Gather it back within thy lonely heart,*
> *So must it ever end: too much we give*
> *Unto the things that perish.*

The night-wind shook the tapestry round an ancient palace-room,
And torches, as it rose and fell, waved through the gorgeous gloom,
And o'er a shadowy regal couch threw fitful gleams and red,
Where a woman with long raven hair sat watching by the dead.

Pale shone the features of the dead, yet glorious still to see,   5
Like a hunter or a chief struck down while his heart and step were free;
No shroud he wore, no robe of death, but there majestic lay,
Proudly and sadly glittering in royalty's array.

But she that with the dark hair watched by the cold slumberer's side,
On *her* wan cheek no beauty dwelt, and in her garb no pride;   10
Only her full impassioned eyes as o'er that clay she bent,
A wildness and a tenderness in strange resplendence blent.

---

[7] 'A woman braved them; her hand seized that
of her daughter, her hand saved her daughter; and
although the fatal blow then struck her, her last act
was maternal; her last act preserved the object of her
affection; it was at this sublime instant that she
appeared before God; and it was impossible to recog-
nize what remained of her upon earth except by the
impression on a medal, given by her children, which
also marked the place where this angel perished'
(*Germany* iii 338–9).

JUANA
[1] Joan the Mad (1479–1555) was married to Philip
the Handsome as part of her father's policy in securing
allies against France. Philip was not only neglectful;
he was openly unfaithful to her. His death in Sep-
tember 1506, from a fever, intensified her depression,
and she refused to be separated from his embalmed
body.
[2] Charles V (1500–58), Holy Roman Emperor, 1519–
56.

And as the swift thoughts crossed her soul, like shadows of a cloud,
Amidst the silent room of death, the dreamer spoke aloud;
She spoke to him who could not hear, and cried, 'Thou yet wilt wake,   15
And learn my watchings and my tears, beloved one, for thy sake.

'They told me this was death, but well I knew it could not be;
Fairest and stateliest of the earth, who spoke of death for *thee*?
They would have wrapped the funeral shroud thy gallant form around,
But I forbade, and there thou art – a monarch, robed and crowned!   20

'With all thy bright locks gleaming still, their coronal beneath,
And thy brow so proudly beautiful – who said that this was death?
Silence hath been upon thy lips, and stillness round thee long,
But the hopeful spirit in my breast is all undimmed and strong.

'I know thou hast not loved me yet; I am not fair like thee,   25
The very glance of whose clear eye threw round a light of glee!
A frail and drooping form is mine – a cold unsmiling cheek,
Oh, I have but a woman's heart, wherewith *thy* heart to seek.

'But when thou wak'st, my prince, my lord, and hear'st how I have kept
A lonely vigil by thy side, and o'er thee prayed and wept;   30
How in one long, deep dream of thee my nights and days have passed,
Surely that humble, patient love *must* win back love at last!

'And thou wilt smile – my own, my own, shall be the sunny smile
Which brightly fell, and joyously, on all *but* me erewhile!
No more in vain affection's thirst my weary soul shall pine –   35
Oh, years of hope deferred were paid by one fond glance of thine!

'Thou'lt meet me with that radiant look when thou com'st from the chase,
For me, for me, in festal halls it shall kindle o'er thy face!
Thou'lt reck no more though beauty's gift mine aspect may not bless;
In thy kind eyes this deep, deep love shall give me loveliness.   40

'But wake! My heart within me burns yet once more to rejoice
In the sound to which it ever leaped – the music of thy voice;
Awake! I sit in solitude, that thy first look and tone,
And the gladness of thine opening eyes may all be mine alone.'

In the still chambers of the dust thus poured forth day by day   45
The passion of that loving dream from a troubled soul found way,
Until the shadows of the grave had swept o'er every grace
Left midst the awfulness of death on the princely form and face.

And slowly broke the fearful truth upon the watcher's breast,
And they bore away the royal dead with requiems to his rest,   50
With banners and with knightly plumes all waving in the wind –
But a woman's broken heart was left in its lone despair behind.

THE AMERICAN FOREST GIRL

A fearful gift upon thy heart is laid,
Woman − a power to suffer and to love,
Therefore thou so canst pity.

Wildly and mournfully the Indian drum
  On the deep hush of moonlight forests broke;
'Sing us a death-song, for thine hour is come',
  So the red warriors to their captive spoke.
Still, and amidst those dusky forms alone,   5
  A youth, a fair-haired youth of England stood
Like a king's son, though from his cheek had flown
  The mantling crimson of the island-blood,
And his pressed lips looked marble. Fiercely bright
And high around him blazed the fires of night,   10
Rocking beneath the cedars to and fro
As the wind passed, and with a fitful glow
Lighting the victim's face. But who could tell
Of what within his secret heart befell,
Known but to heaven that hour? Perchance a thought   15
Of his far home then so intensely wrought,
That its full image, pictured to his eye
On the dark ground of mortal agony,
Rose clear as day − and he might *see* the band,
Of his young sisters wandering hand in hand   20
Where the laburnums drooped, or haply binding
The jasmine, up the door's low pillars winding,
Or, as day closed upon their gentle mirth,
Gathering with braided hair around the hearth
Where sat their mother − and that mother's face,   25
Its grave sweet smile yet wearing in the place
Where so it ever smiled! Perchance the prayer
Learned at her knee came back on his despair,
The blessing from her voice, the very tone
Of her 'Goodnight!' might breathe from boyhood gone.   30
He started and looked up; thick cypress boughs,
  Full of strange sound, waved o'er him, darkly red
In the broad stormy firelight; savage brows
  With tall plumes crested and wild hues o'erspread,
Girt him like feverish phantoms, and pale stars   35
Looked through the branches as through dungeon bars,
Shedding no hope. He knew, he felt his doom −
Oh, what a tale to shadow with its gloom
That happy hall in England! Idle fear!
Would the winds tell it? Who might dream or hear   40
The secret of the forests? To the stake
  They bound him, and that proud young soldier strove

His father's spirit in his breast to wake,
   Trusting to die in silence! He, the love
Of many hearts, the fondly reared, the fair,   45
Gladdening all eyes to see! And fettered there
He stood beside his death-pyre, and the brand
Flamed up to light it in the chieftain's hand.
He thought upon his God. Hush, hark! A cry
Breaks on the stern and dread solemnity –   50
A step hath pierced the ring! Who dares intrude
On the dark hunters in their vengeful mood?
A girl, a young slight girl, a fawn-like child
Of green savannahs[1] and the leafy wild,
Springing unmarked till then, as some lone flower,   55
Happy because the sunshine is its dower,
Yet one that knew how early tears are shed,
For *hers* had mourned a playmate brother dead.

She had sat gazing on the victim long
Until the pity of her soul grew strong   60
And, by its passion's deep'ning fervour swayed,
Ev'n to the stake she rushed, and gently laid
His bright head on her bosom, and around
His form her slender arms to shield it wound
Like close lianes,[2] then raised her glittering eye   65
And clear-toned voice that said, 'He shall not die!'

'He shall not die!' – the gloomy forest thrilled
   To that sweet sound. A sudden wonder fell
On the fierce throng, and heart and hand were stilled,
   Struck down as by the whisper of a spell.   70
They gazed – their dark souls bowed before the maid,
She of the dancing step in wood and glade!
And as her cheek flushed through its olive hue,
As her black tresses to the night-wind flew,
Something o'ermastered them from that young mien,   75
Something of heaven, in silence felt and seen,
And seeming, to their childlike faith, a token
That the Great Spirit by her voice had spoken.

They loosed the bonds that held their captive's breath;
From his pale lips they took the cup of death;
They quenched the brand beneath the cypress tree;   80
'Away', they cried, 'young stranger, thou art free!'

THE AMERICAN FOREST GIRL   [2] *lianes* jungle creepers.
[1] *savannahs* treeless plains.

COSTANZA

Art thou then desolate?
Of friends, of hopes forsaken? Come to me,
I am thine own! Have trusted hearts proved false?
Flatterers deceived thee? Wanderer, come to me!
Why didst thou ever leave me? Know'st thou all
I would have borne, and called it joy to bear
For thy sake? Know'st thou that thy voice had power
To shake me with a thrill of happiness
By one kind tone, to fill mine eyes with tears
Of yearning love? And thou – oh, thou didst throw
That crushed affection back upon my heart –
Yet come to me! It died not.

She knelt in prayer. A stream of sunset fell
Through the stained window of her lonely cell,
And with its rich, deep, melancholy glow
Flushing her cheek and pale Madonna brow,
While o'er her long hair's flowing jet it threw   5
Bright waves of gold – the autumn forest's hue –
Seemed all a vision's mist of glory spread
By painting's touch around some holy head,
Virgin's or fairest martyr's. In her eye,
Which glanced as dark clear water to the sky,   10
What solemn fervour lived! And yet what woe
Lay like some buried thing, still seen below
The glassy tide! Oh, he that could reveal
What life had taught that chastened heart to feel
Might speak indeed of woman's blighted years,   15
And wasted love, and vainly bitter tears!
But she had told her griefs to heaven alone,
And of the gentle saint no more was known
Than that she fled the world's cold breath, and made
A temple of the pine and chestnut shade,   20
Filling its depths with soul, whene'er her hymn
Rose through each murmur of the green and dim
And ancient solitude; where hidden streams
Went moaning through the grass like sounds in dreams,
Music for weary hearts! Midst leaves and flowers   25
She dwelt, and knew all secrets of their powers,
All nature's balms, wherewith her gliding tread
To the sick peasant on his lowly bed
Came and brought hope; while scarce of mortal birth
He deemed the pale fair form, that held on earth   30
Communion but with grief.
                              Erelong a cell,

A rock-hewn chapel rose, a cross of stone
Gleamed through the dark trees o'er a sparkling well,
    And a sweet voice of rich yet mournful tone
Told the Calabrian wilds that duly there   35
Costanza lifted her sad heart in prayer.
And now 'twas prayer's own hour. That voice again
Through the dim foliage sent its heavenly strain
That made the cypress quiver where it stood
In day's last crimson soaring from the wood   40
Like spiry flame. But as the bright sun set,
Other and wilder sounds in tumult met
The floating song. Strange sounds! The trumpet's peal
Made hollow by the rocks, the clash of steel,
The rallying war-cry. In the mountain-pass   45
There had been combat; blood was on the grass;
Banners had strewn the waters; chiefs lay dying,
And the pine-branches crashed before the flying.
    And all was changed within the still retreat,
Costanza's home – there entered hurrying feet,   50
Dark looks of shame and sorrow; mail-clad men,
Stern fugitives from that wild battle-glen,
Scaring the ringdoves from the porch-roof, bore
A wounded warrior in. The rocky floor
Gave back deep echoes to his clanging sword   55
As there they laid their leader and implored
The sweet saint's prayers to heal him; then for flight,
Through the wide forest and the mantling night,
Sped breathlessly again. They passed – but he,
The stateliest of a host[1] – alas, to see   60
What mother's eyes have watched in rosy sleep
Till joy, for very fullness, turned to weep,
Thus changed – a fearful thing! His golden crest
Was shivered,[2] and the bright scarf on his breast
(Some costly love-gift) rent – but what of these?   65
There were the clustering raven-locks – the breeze
As it came in through lime and myrtle flowers
Might scarcely lift them – steeped in bloody showers
So heavily upon the pallid clay
Of the damp cheek they hung! The eyes' dark ray,   70
Where was it? And the lips – they gasped apart
With their light curve, as from the chisel's art,
Still proudly beautiful! But that white hue –
Was it not death's? That stillness, that cold dew
On the scarred forehead? No! His spirit broke   75
From its deep trance erelong, yet but awoke

COSTANZA
[1] *host* army.

[2] *shivered* broken in pieces.

To wander in wild dreams, and there he lay,
By the fierce fever as a green reed shaken,
The haughty chief of thousands, the forsaken
Of all save one! *She* fled not. Day by day   80
(Such hours are woman's birthright), she, unknown,
Kept watch beside him, fearless and alone,
Binding his wounds, and oft in silence laving
His brow with tears that mourned the strong man's raving.
He felt them not, nor marked the light veiled form   85
Still hovering nigh, yet sometimes when that storm
   Of frenzy sank, her voice, in tones as low
As a young mother's by the cradle singing,
Would soothe him with sweet *aves*, gently bringing
   Moments of slumber, when the fiery glow   90
Ebbed from his hollow cheek.
                              At last faint gleams
Of memory dawned upon the cloud of dreams,
And feebly lifting, as a child, his head,
And gazing round him from his leafy bed,
He murmured forth, 'Where am I? What soft strain   95
Passed like a breeze across my burning brain?
Back from my youth it floated, with a tone
Of life's first music, and a thought of one –
Where is she now? And where the gauds of pride[3]
Whose hollow splendour lured me from her side?   100
All lost – and this is death! I *cannot* die
Without forgiveness from that mournful eye!
Away – the earth hath lost her! Was *she* born
To brook abandonment, to strive with scorn?
My first, my holiest love! Her broken heart   105
Lies low, and I – unpardoned, I depart.'
   But then Costanza raised the shadowy veil
From her dark locks and features brightly pale,
And stood before him with a smile – oh, ne'er
Did aught that *smiled* so much of sadness wear –   110
And said, 'Cesario, look on me; I live
To say my heart hath bled, and can forgive.
I loved thee with such worship, such deep trust
As should be Heaven's alone – and Heaven is just!
I bless thee – be at peace!'
                             But o'er his frame   115
Too fast the strong tide rushed – the sudden shame,
The joy, th' amaze! He bowed his head – it fell
On the wronged bosom which had loved so well,
And love still perfect gave him refuge there –
His last faint breath just waved her floating hair.   120

---

[3] *gauds of pride* presumably medals.

MADELINE, A DOMESTIC TALE[1]

Who should it be? Where shouldst thou look for kindness?
When we are sick where can we turn for succour?
When we are wretched where can we complain?
And when the world looks cold and surly on us,
Where can we go to meet a warmer eye
With such sure confidence as to a mother?

Joanna Baillie[2]

'My child, my child, thou leav'st me! I shall hear
The gentle voice no more that blessed mine ear
With its first utterance; I shall miss the sound
Of thy light step amidst the flowers around,
And thy soft-breathing hymn at twilight's close,   5
And thy "Goodnight" at parting for repose.
Under the vine-leaves I shall sit alone,
And the low breeze will have a mournful tone
Amidst their tendrils, while I think of thee,
My child; and thou, along the moonlight sea,   10
With a soft sadness haply in thy glance,
Shalt watch thine own, thy pleasant land of France,
Fading to air. Yet blessings with thee go;
Love guard thee, gentlest, and the exile's woe
From thy young heart be far! And sorrow not   15
For me, sweet daughter; in my lonely lot
God shall be with me. Now farewell, farewell!
Thou that hast been what words may never tell
Unto thy mother's bosom, since the days
When thou wert pillowed there, and wont to raise   20
In sudden laughter thence thy loving eye
That still sought mine – those moments are gone by,
Thou too must go, my flower! Yet with thee dwell
The peace of God! One, one more gaze – farewell!'
     This was a mother's parting with her child,   25
A young meek bride on whom fair fortune smiled
And wooed her with a voice of love away
From childhood's home; yet there, with fond delay,
She lingered on the threshold, heard the note
Of her caged bird through trellised rose-leaves float,   30
And fell upon her mother's neck and wept,
Whilst old remembrances that long had slept
Gushed o'er her soul, and many a vanished day,
As in one picture traced, before her lay.

MADELINE, A DOMESTIC TALE   [2] *Rayner* IV ii 15–20.
[1] 'Originally published in the *Literary Souvenir* for
1826' (Hemans's note).

But the farewell was said, and on the deep,   35
When its breast heaved in sunset's golden sleep,
With a calmed heart young Madeline erelong
Poured forth her own sweet solemn vesper song,[3]
Breathing of home; through stillness heard afar,
And duly rising with the first pale star,   40
That voice was on the waters, till at last
The sounding ocean-solitudes were passed
And the bright land was reached, the youthful world
That glows along the west.[4] The sails were furled
In its clear sunshine, and the gentle bride   45
Looked on the home that promised hearts untried
A bower of bliss[5] to come. Alas, we trace
The map of our own paths, and long ere years
With their dull steps the briliant lines efface,
On sweeps the storm, and blots them out with tears.   50
That home was darkened soon: the summer breeze
Welcomed with death the wanderers from the seas,[6]
Death unto one, and anguish (how forlorn!)
To her that, widowed in her marriage-morn,
Sat in her voiceless dwelling, whence with him   55
   Her bosom's first beloved, her friend and guide,
Joy had gone forth, and left the green earth dim,
   As from the sun shut out on every side
By the close veil of misery! Oh, but ill,
   When with rich hopes o'erfraught, the young high heart   60
   Bears its first blow! It knows not yet the part
Which life will teach: to suffer and be still,
And with submissive love to count the flowers
Which yet are spared, and through the future hour
To send no busy dream! *She* had not learned   65
Of sorrow till that hour, and therefore turned
In weariness from life; then came th' unrest,
The heart-sick yearning of the exile's breast,
The haunting sounds of voices far away
And household steps, until at last she lay   70
On her lone couch of sickness, lost in dreams
Of the gay vineyards and blue-rushing streams
In her own sunny land, and murmuring oft
Familiar names in accents wild yet soft
To strangers round that bed, who knew not aught   75
Of the deep spells wherewith each word was fraught.

---

[3] *vesper song* evening song, a phrase used by Scott, *Lady of the Lake* iii stanza 23 7.
[4] *the youthful world / That glows along the west* America or, possibly, Canada. Hemans's brother had worked and died in Canada.

[5] *bower of bliss* the phrase is borrowed from Spenser, *Faerie Queene* II i stanza 51 9.
[6] *the summer breeze . . . the seas* the wind was believed to carry disease.

To strangers? Oh, could strangers raise the head
Gently as *hers* was raised? Did strangers shed
The kindly tears which bathed that feverish brow
And wasted cheek with half-unconscious flow? 80
Something was there that through the lingering night
Outwatches patiently the taper's light,
Something that faints not through the day's distress,
That fears not toil, that knows not weariness –
Love, true and perfect love! Whence came that power 85
Uprearing through the storm the drooping flower?
Whence? Who can ask? The wild delirium passed,
And from her eyes the spirit looked at last
Into her *mother's* face, and wakening knew
The brow's calm grace, the hair's dear silvery hue, 90
The kind sweet smile of old – and had *she* come,
Thus in life's evening, from her distant home,
To save her child? Ev'n so, nor yet in vain:
In that young heart a light sprung up again,
And lovely still, with so much love to give, 95
Seemed this fair world, though faded; still to live
Was not to pine forsaken. On the breast
That rocked her childhood, sinking in soft rest,
'Sweet mother, gentlest mother! Can it be?'
The lorn one cried, 'and do I look on thee? 100
Take back thy wanderer from this fatal shore,
Peace shall be ours beneath our vines once more.'

THE QUEEN OF PRUSSIA'S TOMB[1]

This tomb is in the garden of Charlottenburgh, near Berlin. It was not without surprise that I came suddenly, among trees, upon a fair white Doric temple. I might, and should have deemed it a mere adornment of the grounds, but the cypress and the willow declare it a habitation of the dead. Upon a sarcophagus of white marble lay a sheet, and the outline of the human form was plainly visible beneath its folds. The person with me reverently turned it back and displayed the statue of his Queen. It is a portrait-statue recumbent, said to be a perfect resemblance – not as in death, but when she lived to bless and be blessed. Nothing can be more calm and kind than the expression of her features. The hands are folded on the bosom, the limbs are sufficiently crossed to show the repose of life. Here the King brings her children annually to offer garlands at her grave.[2] These hang in withered mournfulness above this living image of their departed mother.

Sherer's *Notes and Reflections during a Ramble in Germany*[3]

THE QUEEN OF PRUSSIA'S TOMB

[1] The tomb is that of Queen Louise of Mecklenburg-Strelitz (1776–1810), who is buried in the mausoleum in the palace park of Charlottenburg, a district in Berlin, which also contains the grave of her husband, Frederick William III of Prussia (1770–1840). It was severely damaged in World War II but is still to be seen. Although in modern terms Hemans's sympathy for Prussia may seem odd, the Germans were at the time of writing recent allies of Britain in the fight against Napoleon.

[2] Louise had no less than ten children.

[3] Joseph Moyle Sherer (1789–1869), traveller, published his *Notes and Reflections during a Ramble in Germany* in 1826. The passage to which Hemans refers is on pp. 391–5.

In sweet pride upon that insult keen
She smiled; then drooping mute and broken-hearted,
To the cold comfort of the grave departed.

Milman[4]

It stands where northern willows weep,
  A temple fair and lone;
Soft shadows o'er its marble sweep,
  From cypress-branches thrown,
While silently around it spread,   5
Thou feel'st the presence of the dead.

And what within is richly shrined?
  A sculptured woman's form,
Lovely in perfect rest reclined
  As one beyond the storm –   10
Yet not of death but slumber lies
The solemn sweetness on those eyes.

The folded hands, the calm pure face,
  The mantle's quiet flow,
The gentle yet majestic grace   15
  Throned on the matron brow;
These, in that scene of tender gloom,
With a still glory robe the tomb.

There stands an eagle at the feet
  Of the fair image wrought;
A kingly emblem nor unmeet   20
  To wake yet deeper thought;
She whose high heart finds rest below
Was royal in her birth and woe.

There are pale garlands hung above   25
  Of dying scent and hue;
She was a mother – in her love
  How sorrowfully true!
Oh, hallowed long be every leaf,
The records of her children's grief!   30

She saw their birthright's warrior-crown
  Of olden glory spoiled,[5]
The standard of their sires borne down,
  The shield's bright blazon soiled;

---

[4] Henry Hart Milman (1791–1868), *Judicium Regale, An Ode* 74–6.
[5] Louise accompanied her husband to the battlefield in the Jena campaign, when Prussia and its ally, Russia, attempted to repulse Napoleon, October 1806. The result was defeat for the Prussians; Napoleon entered Berlin on 25 October, and ten days later the Prussian rear guard capitulated.

She met the tempest meekly brave,   35
    Then turned o'erwearied to the grave.[6]

She slumbered, but it came – it came,
    Her land's redeeming hour,[7]
With the glad shout and signal flame
    Sent on from tower to tower![8]   40
Fast through the realm a spirit moved –
'Twas hers, the lofty and the loved.

Then was her name a note that rung
    To rouse bold hearts from sleep,
Her memory as a banner flung   45
    Forth by the Baltic deep;
Her grief, a bitter vial poured
To sanctify th' avenger's sword.

And the crowned eagle[9] spread again
    His pinion to the sun,   50
And the strong land shook off its chain –
    So was the triumph won!
But woe for earth, where sorrow's tone
Still blends with victory's – *she* was gone![10]

THE MEMORIAL PILLAR

On the roadside between Penrith and Appleby stands a small pillar with this inscription:
'This pillar was erected in the year 1656 by Ann, Countess Dowager of Pembroke, for
a memorial of her last parting, in this place, with her good and pious mother, Margaret,
Countess Dowager of Cumberland, on 2 April 1616'. See notes to the *Pleasures of
Memory*.[1]

Hast thou, through Eden's wildwood vales, pursued
Each mountain-scene, magnificently rude,
Nor with attention's lifted eye, revered
That modest stone, by pious Pembroke reared,
Which still records, beyond the pencil's power,
The silent sorrows of a parting hour?

                                                                Rogers[2]

---

[6] Louise did not die immediately. She worked hard
to maintain the alliance with Russia, and damaged her
health in doing so; she died 18 July 1810.

[7] Prussia began the fight back against Napoleon in
1813, with their allies – Russia, Austria, and Britain.
Napoleon's defeat came with his abdication on 22
June 1815, after the battle of Waterloo.

[8] Before telephones or indeed telegraphs, the most
rapid means of communication was the chain of
beacons (or, as here, towers) that stretched across the
country, on hills, in which fires could be lit so as to
signal important events.

[9] *the crowned eagle* symbol of Prussian national identity.

[10] 'Originally published in the *Monthly Magazine*'
(Hemans's note).

THE MEMORIAL PILLAR

[1] Samuel Rogers (1763–1855), *The Pleasures of Memory*
(1792); most of Hemans's note is quoted from page
69 of Rogers's volume.

[2] *The Pleasures of Memory* ii 173–4, 177–80.

Mother and child, whose blending tears
   Have sanctified the place,
Where, to the love of many years,
   Was given one last embrace,
Oh ye have shrined[3] a spell of power,   5
Deep in your record of that hour!

A spell to waken solemn thought,
   A still small undertone[4]
That calls back days of childhood fraught[5]
   With many a treasure gone,   10
And smites, perchance, the hidden source
(Though long untroubled) of remorse.

For who that gazes on the stone
   Which marks your parting spot,
Who but a mother's love hath known,   15
   The *one* love changing not?
Alas, and haply learned its worth
First with the sound of 'earth to earth'?

But thou, high-hearted daughter, thou
   O'er whose bright honoured head   20
Blessings and tears of holiest flow
   Ev'n here were fondly shed –
Thou from the passion of thy grief,
In its full burst, couldst draw relief.

For oh, though painful be th' excess,   25
   The might wherewith it swells,
In nature's fount no bitterness
   Of nature's mingling dwells;
And thou hadst not, by wrong or pride,
Poisoned the free and healthful tide.   30

But didst thou meet the face no more
   Which thy young heart first knew?
And all – was all in this world o'er,
   With ties thus close and true?
It was! On earth no other eye   35
Could give thee back thine infancy.

No other voice could pierce the maze
   Where deep within thy breast

---

[3] *shrined* enshrined.
[4] *A still small undertone* an echo of I Kings 19:12:
'And after the earthquake a fire; but the Lord was

not in the fire: and after the fire a *still small voice*'
[my italics].
[5] *fraught* loaded, freighted.

The sounds and dreams of other days
   With memory lay at rest;   40
No other smile to thee could bring
A gladd'ning like the breath of spring.

Yet while thy place of weeping still
   Its lone memorial keeps,
While on thy name, midst wood and hill,   45
   The quiet sunshine sleeps
And touches in each graven line
Of reverential thought a sign,

Can I, while yet these tokens wear
   The impress of the dead,   50
Think of the love embodied there,
   As of a vision fled?
A perished thing, the joy and flower
And glory of one earthly hour?[6]

Not so; I will not bow me so   55
   To thoughts that breathe despair!
A loftier faith we need below,
   Life's farewell words to bear.
Mother and child, your tears are past –
Surely your hearts have met at last!   60

THE GRAVE OF A POETESS[1]

Ne me plaignez pas – si vous saviez
Combien de peines ce tombeau m'a epargnées![2]

---

[6] *joy and flower . . . hour* an echo of Wordsworth, *Ode* 180–1: 'Though nothing can bring back the hour / Of splendour in the grass, of glory in the flower'.

THE GRAVE OF A POETESS

[1] 'Extrinsic interest has lately attached to the fine scenery of Woodstock, near Kilkenny, on account of its having been the last residence of the author of *Psyche* [Mary Tighe]. Her grave is one of many in the churchyard of the village. The river runs smoothly by. The ruins of an ancient abbey that have been partially converted into a church reverently throw their mantle of tender shadow over it. (*Tales by the O'Hara Family*)' (Hemans's note). John Banim (1798–1842) and Michael Banim (1796–1874) published *Tales by the O'Hara Family* in 1825–7. Felicia managed to visit Mary Tighe's grave only in April 1831, when she described it as follows: 'We went to the tomb, "the grave of a poetess", where there is a monument by Flaxman. It consists of a recumbent female figure, with much of the repose, the mysterious sweetness of happy death, which is to me so affecting in monumental sculpture. There is, however, a very small Titania-looking sort of figure with wings, sitting at the head of the sleeper, which I thought interfered with the singleness of effect which the tomb would have produced. Unfortunately, too, the monument is carved in very rough stone, which allows no delicacy of touch. That place of rest made me very thoughtful; I could not but reflect on the many changes which had brought me to the spot I had commemorated three years since, without the slightest idea of ever visiting it; and, though surrounded by attention and the appearance of interest, my heart was envying the repose of her who slept there' (*The Works of Mrs Hemans*, i 238–9).

[2] 'Don't pity me; if only you knew how much suffering this tomb has spared me!'

I stood beside thy lowly grave,
   Spring odours breathed around,
And music in the river-wave
   Passed with a lulling sound.

All happy things that love the sun[3]   5
   In the bright air glanced by,
And a glad murmur seemed to run
   Through the soft azure sky.

Fresh leaves were on the ivy-bough
   That fringed the ruins near;   10
Young voices were abroad, but thou
   Their sweetness couldst not hear.

And mournful grew my heart for thee,
   Thou in whose woman's mind
The ray that brightens earth and sea,   15
   The light of song was shrined;[4]

Mournful that thou wert slumbering low
   With a dread curtain drawn
Between thee and the golden glow
   Of this world's vernal dawn.   20

Parted from all the song and bloom
   Thou wouldst have loved so well,
To thee the sunshine round thy tomb
   Was but a broken spell.

The bird, the insect on the wing,   25
   In their bright reckless play,
Might feel the flush and life of spring,
   And thou wert passed away!

But then, ev'n then, a nobler thought
   O'er my vain sadness came;   30
Th' immortal spirit woke, and wrought
   Within my thrilling[5] frame.

Surely on lovelier things, I said,
   Thou must have looked ere now,
Than all that round our pathway shed   35
   Odours and hues below,

---

[3] *All happy things that love the sun* an echo of
Wordsworth, *Resolution and Independence* 8: 'All things
that love the sun are out of doors'.

[4] *shrined* enshrined.

[5] *thrilling* her body ('frame') vibrates (thrills) at the
awakening within her of the 'immortal spirit'.

The shadows of the tomb are here,
  Yet beautiful is earth!
What seest thou then where no dim fear,
  No haunting dream hath birth?   40

Here a vain love to passing flowers
  Thou gav'st, but where thou art
The sway is not with changeful hours –
  There love and death must part.

Thou hast left sorrow in thy song,   45
  A voice not loud, but deep!
The glorious bowers of earth among,
  How often didst thou weep!

Where couldst thou fix on mortal ground
  Thy tender thoughts and high?   50
Now peace the woman's heart hath found,
  And joy the poet's eye.

Miscellaneous Poems[1]

THE HOMES OF ENGLAND

Where's the coward that would not dare
To fight for such a land?

                                        Marmion[2]

The stately homes of England,
  How beautiful they stand!
Amidst their tall ancestral trees,
  O'er all the pleasant land.
The deer across their greensward bound   5
  Through shade and sunny gleam,
And the swan glides past them with the sound
  Of some rejoicing stream.

The merry homes of England!
  Around their hearths by night,   10
What gladsome looks of household love
  Meet in the ruddy light!
There woman's voice flows forth in song
  Or childhood's tale is told,

THE HOMES OF ENGLAND
[1] These poems were published with *Records of Woman*
(1828) under the collective title *Miscellaneous Poems*.

[2] Walter Scott (1771–1832), *Marmion* (1808), iv stanza
30 34–5.

Or lips move tunefully along 15
   Some glorious page of old.

The blessed homes of England!
   How softly on their bowers
Is laid the holy quietness
   That breathes from Sabbath hours! 20
Solemn yet sweet, the church-bell's chime
   Floats through their woods at morn;
All other sounds, in that still time,
   Of breeze and leaf are born.

The cottage homes of England! 25
   By thousands on her plains,
They are smiling o'er the silvery brooks
   And round the hamlet fanes.[3]
Through glowing orchards forth they peep,
   Each from its nook of leaves, 30
And fearless there the lowly sleep,
   As the bird beneath their eaves.

The free, fair homes of England!
   Long, long, in hut and hall,
May hearts of native proof be reared 35
   To guard each hallowed wall!
And green for ever be the groves
   And bright the flowery sod,
Where first the child's glad spirit loves
   Its country and its God![4] 40

To Wordsworth

Thine is a strain[1] to read among the hills,
   The old and full of voices; by the source
Of some free stream, whose gladdening presence fills
   The solitude with sound, for in its course
Even such is thy deep song, that seems a part 5
Of those high scenes, a fountain from their heart.

Or its calm spirit fitly may be taken
   To the still breast in sunny garden bowers,
Where vernal winds each tree's low tones awaken,
   And bud and bell with changes mark the hours. 10
There let thy thoughts be with me, while the day
Sinks with a golden and serene decay.

---

[3] *fanes* churches.
[4] 'Originally published in *Blackwood's Magazine*'
(Hemans's note).

To Wordsworth
[1] *strain* i.e. poetry, verse.

Or by some hearth where happy faces meet,
　　When night hath hushed the woods with all their birds,
There, from some gentle voice, that lay were sweet   15
　　As antique music, linked with household words,
While, in pleased murmurs, woman's lip might move,
And the raised eye of childhood shine in love.

Or where the shadows of dark solemn yews
　　Brood silently o'er some lone burial-ground,   20
Thy verse hath power that brightly might diffuse
　　A breath, a kindling as of spring, around
From its own glow of hope and courage high,
And steadfast faith's victorious constancy.

True bard, and holy! Thou art ev'n as one   25
　　Who, by some secret gift of soul or eye,
In every spot beneath the smiling sun,
　　Sees where the springs of living waters lie;
Unseen awhile they sleep – till, touched by thee,
Bright healthful waves flow forth to each glad wanderer free.   30

THE SPIRIT'S MYSTERIES[1]

And slight, withal, may be the things which bring
Back on the heart the weight which it would fling
　Aside for ever; it may be a sound –
A tone of music – summer's breath, or spring –
　A flower – a leaf – the ocean – which may wound –
Striking th' electric chain wherewith we are darkly bound.

Childe Harold[2]

The power that dwelleth in sweet sounds to waken
　　Vague yearnings, like the sailor's for the shore,
And dim remembrances, whose hue seems taken
　　From some bright former state, our own no more –
Is not this all a mystery? Who shall say   5
Whence are those thoughts, and whither tends their way?

The sudden images of vanished things
　　That o'er the spirit flash, we know not why;
Tones from some broken harp's deserted strings,
　　Warm sunset hues of summers long gone by,   10
A rippling wave – the dashing of an oar –
A flower scent floating past our parents' door;

THE SPIRIT'S MYSTERIES
[1] The 1828 printed text has been collated with the
fair copy MS in Hemans's hand at the British Library,
and some variants are given in footnotes, where of
critical interest.
[2] Byron, *Childe Harold's Pilgrimage* iv 202–7.

A word scarce noted in its hour perchance,
    Yet back returning with a plaintive tone;
A smile – a sunny or a mournful glance,   15
    Full of sweet meanings now from this world flown –
Are not these mysteries when to life they start,
And press vain tears in gushes from the heart?

And the far wanderings of the soul in dreams,
    Calling up shrouded faces from the dead,   20
And with them bringing soft or solemn gleams,
    Familiar objects brightly to o'erspread,
And wakening buried love, or joy, or fear:
These are night's mysteries – who shall make them clear?

And the strange inborn sense of coming ill   25
    That ofttimes[3] whispers to the haunted breast
In a low tone which nought can drown or still,
    Midst feasts and melodies a secret guest;
Whence doth that murmur wake, that shadow fall?
Why shakes the spirit thus? 'Tis mystery all!   30

Darkly we move – we press upon the brink
    Haply of viewless[4] worlds, and know it not;
Yes, it may be that nearer than we think
    Are those whom death has parted from our lot!
Fearfully, wondrously, our souls are made –   35
Let us walk humbly on,[5] but undismayed!

Humbly – for knowledge strives in vain to feel[6]
    Her way amidst these marvels of the mind –
Yet undismayed; for do they not reveal
    Th' immortal being[7] with our dust entwined?   40
So let us deem, and e'en the tears they wake
Shall then be blessed, for that high nature's sake!

The Illuminated City

The hills all glowed with a festive light,
For the royal city rejoiced by night;
There were lamps hung forth upon tower and tree,
Banners were lifted and streaming free;
Every tall pillar was wreathed with fire,   5
Like a shooting meteor was every spire;
And the outline of many a dome on high
Was traced, as in stars, on the clear dark sky.

---

[3] *ofttimes* sometimes (MS).
[4] *viewless* unseen (MS).
[5] *Let us walk humbly on* an echo of Micah 6:8: 'what doeth the Lord require of thee, but to do justly, and to love mercy, and to walk humbly with thy God?'
[6] *strives in vain to feel* all in vain would feel (MS).
[7] *being* nature (MS).

I passed through the streets, there were throngs on throngs –
Like sounds of the deep were their mingled songs;   10
There was music forth from each palace borne –
A peal of the cymbal, the harp, and horn;
The forests heard it, the mountains rang,
The hamlets woke to its haughty clang;
Rich and victorious was every tone,   15
Telling the land of her foes o'erthrown.

Didst thou meet not a mourner for all the slain?
Thousands lie dead on their battle-plain!
Gallant and true were the hearts that fell –
Grief in the homes they have left must dwell;   20
Grief o'er the aspect of childhood spread,
And bowing the beauty of woman's head:
Didst thou hear, midst the songs, not one tender moan
For the many brave to their slumbers gone?

I saw not the face of a weeper there –   25
Too strong, perchance, was the bright lamp's glare!
I heard not a wail midst the joyous crowd –
The music of victory was all too loud!
Mighty it rolled on the winds afar,
Shaking the streets like a conqueror's car;   30
Through torches and streams its flood swept by –
How could I listen for moan or sigh?

Turn then away from life's pageants, turn,
If its deep story thy heart would learn!
Ever too bright is that outward show,   35
Dazzling the eyes till they see not woe.
But lift the proud mantle which hides from thy view
The things thou shouldst gaze on, the sad and true;
Nor fear to survey what its folds conceal –
So must thy spirit be taught to feel!   40

THE GRAVES OF A HOUSEHOLD

They grew in beauty, side by side,
    They filled one home with glee;
Their graves are severed far and wide,
    By mount and stream and sea.

The same fond mother bent at night   5
    O'er each fair sleeping brow;
She had each folded flower in sight –
    Where are those dreamers now?

One midst the forests of the west[1]
   By a dark stream is laid –   10
The Indian knows his place of rest
   Far in the cedar shade.

The sea, the blue lone sea hath one,
   He lies where pearls lie deep;
He was the loved of all, yet none   15
   O'er his low bed may weep.

One sleeps where southern vines are dressed
   Above the noble slain;
He wrapped his colours round his breast
   On a blood-red field of Spain.   20

And one – o'er *her* the myrtle showers
   Its leaves, by soft winds fanned;
She faded midst Italian flowers,
   The last of that bright band.

And parted thus they rest, who played   25
   Beneath the same green tree;
Whose voices mingled as they prayed
   Around one parent knee!

They that with smiles lit up the hall
   And cheered with song the hearth –   30
Alas, for love, if *thou* wert all,
   And nought beyond, oh earth!

From The Forest Sanctuary: With Other Poems (second edition, 1829)

CASABIANCA[1]

The boy stood on the burning deck
   Whence all but he had fled;
The flame that lit the battle's wreck
   Shone round him o'er the dead.

THE GRAVES OF A HOUSEHOLD
[1] Hemans was thinking in this stanza of her brother Claude, who was one year younger than she, and who died in Kingston, Canada, in 1821.
CASABIANCA
[1] 'Young Casabianca, a boy about thirteen years old, son to the Admiral of the Orient, remained at his post (in the Battle of the Nile) after the ship had taken fire, and all the guns had been abandoned, and perished in the explosion of the vessel, when the flames had reached the powder' (Hemans's note).

Yet beautiful and bright he stood,
  As born to rule the storm –
A creature of heroic blood,
  A proud though childlike form.   5

The flames rolled on, he would not go
  Without his father's word;   10
That father, faint in death below,
  His voice no longer heard.

He called aloud, 'Say, father, say
  If yet my task is done?'
He knew not that the chieftain lay   15
  Unconscious of his son.

'Speak, father!' once again he cried,
  'If I may yet be gone!
And –'. But the booming shots replied,
  And fast the flames rolled on.   20

Upon his brow he felt their breath
  And in his waving hair,
And looked from that lone post of death
  In still yet brave despair,

And shouted but once more aloud,   25
  'My father, must I stay?'
While o'er him fast, through sail and shroud,
  The wreathing fires made way.

They wrapped the ship in splendour wild,
  They caught the flag on high,   30
And streamed above the gallant child
  Like banners in the sky.

There came a burst of thunder sound;
  The boy – oh, where was he?
Ask of the winds that far around   35
  With fragments strewed the sea.

With mast, and helm, and pennon fair
  That well had borne their part,
But the noblest thing which perished there
  Was that young faithful heart!   40

From Songs of the Affections, with Other Poems (1830)

To a Departed Spirit

From the bright stars, or from the viewless air,
Or from some world unreached by human thought,
Spirit, sweet spirit! – if thy home be there,
And if thy visions with the past be fraught,
    Answer me, answer me!   5

Have we not communed here of life and death?
Have we not said that love, such love as ours,
Was not to perish as a rose's breath,
To melt away like song from festal bowers?
    Answer, oh answer me!   10

Thine eye's last light was mine – the soul that shone
Intensely, mournfully, through gathering haze –
Didst thou bear with thee to the shore unknown
Nought of what lived in that long, earnest gaze?
    Hear, hear, and answer me!   15

Thy voice – its low, soft, fervent, farewell tone
Thrilled through the tempest of the parting strife
Like a faint breeze; oh, from that music flown,
Send back *one* sound, if love's be quenchless life,
    But once, oh answer me!   20

In the still noontide, in the sunset's hush,
In the dead hour of night, when thought grows deep,
When the heart's phantoms from the darkness rush,
Fearfully beautiful, to strive with sleep –
    Spirit, then answer me!   25

By the remembrance of our blended prayer;
By all our tears, whose mingling made them sweet;
By our last hope, the victor o'er despair –
Speak, if our souls in deathless yearnings meet:
    Answer me, answer me!   30

The grave is silent, and the far-off sky,
And the deep midnight – silent all, and lone!
Oh, if thy buried love make no reply,
What voice has earth? Hear, pity, speak, mine own!
    Answer me, answer me!   35

THE CHAMOIS HUNTER'S LOVE

For all his wildness and proud fantasies,
I love him!

Croly[1]

Thy heart is in the upper world, where fleet the chamois bounds,
Thy heart is where the mountain-fir shakes to the torrent-sounds,
And where the snow-peaks gleam like stars, through the stillness of the air,
And where the Lauwine's[2] peal is heard – hunter, thy heart is there!

I know thou lov'st me well, dear friend, but better, better far   5
Thou lov'st that high and haughty[3] life, with rocks and storms at war;
In the green sunny vales with me, thy spirit would but pine,
And yet I will be thine, my love, and yet I will be thine!

And I will not seek to woo thee down from those thy native heights
With the sweet song, our land's own song, of pastoral delights;   10
For thou must live as eagles live, thy path is not as mine,
And yet I will be thine, my love, and yet I will be thine.

And I will leave my blessed home, my father's joyous hearth,
With all the voices meeting there in tenderness and mirth,
With all the kind and laughing eyes that in its firelight shine,   15
To sit forsaken in thy hut – yet know that thou art mine!

It is my youth, it is my bloom, it is my glad free heart
That I cast away for thee – for thee, all reckless as thou art!
With tremblings and with vigils lone, I bind myself to dwell,
Yet, yet I would not change that lot – oh no, I love too well!   20

A mournful thing is love which grows to one so wild as thou,
With that bright restlessness of eye, that tameless fire of brow!
Mournful – but dearer far I call its mingled fear and pride,
And the trouble of its happiness, than aught on earth beside.

To listen for thy step in vain, to start at every breath,   25
To watch through long long nights of storm, to sleep and dream of death,
To wake in doubt and loneliness – this doom I know is mine,
And yet I will be thine, my love, and yet I will be thine!

That I may greet thee from thine Alps, when thence thou com'st at last,
That I may hear thy thrilling voice tell o'er each danger past,   30
That I may kneel and pray for thee, and win thee aid divine,
For this I will be thine, my love, for this I will be thine!

THE CHAMOIS HUNTER'S LOVE
[1] George Croly (1780–1860), *Catiline: A Dramatic Poem in Five Acts* (1822), III i 253–4.
[2] '*Lauwine* the avalanche' (Hemans's note).
[3] *haughty* lofty, high up (in a literal sense).

THE RETURN

'Hast thou come with the heart of thy childhood back?
    The free, the pure, the kind?'
So murmured the trees in my homeward track,
    As they played to the mountain wind.

'Hath thy soul been true to its early love?'   5
    Whispered my native streams,
'Hath the spirit nursed amidst hill and grove,
    Still revered its first high dreams?

'Hast thou borne in thy bosom the holy prayer
    Of the child in his parent-halls?'   10
Thus breathed a voice on the thrilling air
    From the old ancestral walls.

'Hast thou kept thy faith with the faithful dead
    Whose place of rest is nigh?
With the father's blessing o'er thee shed,   15
    With the mother's trusting eye?'

Then my tears gushed forth in sudden rain
    As I answered, 'Oh ye shades,
I bring not my childhood's heart again
    To the freedom of your glades.   20

'I have turned from my first pure love aside,
    Oh bright and happy streams!
Light after light, in my soul have died
    The dayspring's glorious dreams.

'And the holy prayer from my thoughts hath passed,   25
    The prayer at my mother's knee;
Darkened and troubled I come at last,
    Home of my boyish glee!

'But I bear from my childhood a gift of tears
    To soften and atone,   30
And oh, ye scenes of those blessed years,
    They shall make me again your own.'

WOMAN ON THE FIELD OF BATTLE

Where hath not a woman stood,
Strong in affection's might? A reed, upborne
By an o'ermastering current!

Gentle and lovely form,
What didst thou hear
When the fierce battle-storm
Bore down the spear?

Banner and shivered[1] crest   5
Beside thee strewn
Tell that amidst the best
Thy work was done!

Yet strangely, sadly fair,
O'er the wild scene   10
Gleams, through its golden hair,
That brow serene.

Low lies the stately head,
Earthbound the free;
How gave those haughty dead   15
A place to thee?

Slumberer, *thine* early bier
Friends should have crowned,
Many a flower and tear
Shedding around.   20

Soft voices, clear and young,
Mingling their swell,
Should o'er thy dust have sung
Earth's last farewell.

Sisters, above the grave   25
Of thy repose,
Should have bid violets wave
With the white rose.

How must the trumpet's note,
Savage and shrill,   30
For requiem o'er thee float,
Thou fair and still!

And the swift charger sweep
In full career,
Trampling thy place of sleep –   35
Why camest thou here?

WOMAN ON THE FIELD OF BATTLE
[1] *shivered* broken in pieces.

Why? Ask the true heart why
   Woman hath been
Ever where brave men die,
   Unshrinking seen?   40

Unto this harvest ground
   Proud reapers came –
Some, for that stirring sound,
   A warrior's name;

Some for the stormy play   45
   And joy of strife;
And some, to fling away
   A weary life;

But thou, pale sleeper, thou,
   With the slight frame   50
And the rich locks whose glow
   Death cannot tame,

Only one thought, one power,
   Thee could have led,
So, through the tempest's hour,   55
   To lift thy head!

Only the true, the strong,
   The love whose trust
Woman's deep soul too long
   Pours on the dust!   60

THE BEINGS OF THE MIND

The beings of the mind are not of clay;
Essentially immortal, they create
And multiply in us a brighter ray,
And more beloved existence – that which Fate
Prohibits to dull life, in this our state
Of mortal bondage.

Byron[1]

Come to me with your triumphs and your woes,
   Ye forms to life by glorious poets brought!
I sit alone with flowers and vernal boughs,
   In the deep shadow of a voiceless thought,
Midst the glad music of the spring alone   5
And sorrowful for visions that are gone!

THE BEINGS OF THE MIND
[1] *Childe Harold's Pilgrimage* iv 37–42.

Come to me, make your thrilling whispers heard,
  Ye, by those masters of the soul endowed
With life, and love, and many a burning word
  That bursts from grief like lightning from a cloud,   10
And smites the heart till all its chords reply,
As leaves make answer when the wind sweeps by.

Come to me, visit my dim haunt! The sound
  Of hidden springs is in the grass beneath;
The stockdove's note above,[2] and all around,   15
  The poesy that with the violet's breath
Floats through the air in rich and sudden streams,
Mingling, like music, with the soul's deep dreams.

Friends, friends (for such to my lone heart ye are,
  Unchanging ones), from whose immortal eyes   20
The glory melts not as a waning star
  And the sweet kindness never, never dies –
Bright children of the bard, o'er this green dell
Pass once again, and light it with your spell!

Imogen! Fair Fidele![3] Meekly blending   25
  In patient grief, 'a smiling with a sigh',[4]
And thou, Cordelia, faithful daughter, tending
  That sire, an outcast to the bitter sky –
Thou of the soft low voice,[5] thou art not gone!
Still breathes for me its faint and flute-like tone.   30

And come to me, sing me thy willow-strain,[6]
  Sweet Desdemona! With the sad surprise
In thy beseeching glance, where still, though vain,
  Undimmed, unquenchable affection lies;
Come, bowing thy young head to wrong and scorn,   35
As a frail hyacinth by showers o'erborne.

And thou, too, fair Ophelia, flowers are here
  That well might win thy footstep to the spot –
Pale cowslips meet for maiden's early bier,
  And pansies for sad thoughts,[7] but needed not!   40
Come with thy wreaths, and all the love and light
In that wild eye still tremulously bright.

---

[2] *The stockdove's note above* probably an echo of
Wordsworth, *Resolution and Independence* 5, which was
one of Hemans's favourite lines of poetry: 'Over his
own sweet voice the stockdove broods'.
[3] Imogen and Fidele are characters from *Cymbeline*.
[4] '"Nobly he yokes / A smiling with a sigh." *Cymbeline*'
(Hemans's note). The quotation is from IV ii 51–2.

[5] *Thou of the soft low voice* Hemans is thinking of
Lear's lament for her: 'Her voice was ever soft, /
Gentle, and low, an excellent thing in woman' (*King
Lear* V iii 273–4).
[6] *sing me thy willow-strain* see *Othello* IV iii 40–52.
[7] '"Here's pansies for you – that's for thoughts." *Hamlet*'
(Hemans's note). The quotation is from IV v 176–7.

And Juliet, vision of the south,[8] enshrining
  All gifts that unto its rich heaven belong;
The glow, the sweetness, in its rose combining,   45
  The soul its nightingales pour forth in song!
Thou, making death deep joy – but *could'st* thou die?
No, thy young love hath immortality!

From earth's bright faces fades the light of morn,
  From earth's glad voices drops the joyous tone;   50
But ye, the children of the soul, were born
  Deathless and for undying love alone –
And oh, ye beautiful, 'tis well, how well,
In the soul's world, with you, where change is not, to dwell!

SECOND SIGHT

Ne'er erred the prophet heart that grief inspired,
Though joy's illusions mock their votarist.

                                    Maturin[1]

A mournful gift is mine, oh friends,
  A mournful gift is mine!
A murmur of the soul which blends
  With the flow of song and wine.

An eye that through the triumph's hour   5
  Beholds the coming woe,
And dwells upon the faded flower
  Midst the rich summer's glow.

Ye smile to view fair faces bloom
  Where the father's board is spread;   10
I see the stillness and the gloom
  Of a home whence all are fled.

I see the withered garlands lie
  Forsaken on the earth,
While the lamps yet burn and the dancers fly   15
  Through the ringing hall of mirth.

I see the blood-red future stain
  On the warrior's gorgeous crest,
And the bier amidst the bridal train
  When they come with roses dressed.   20

---

[8] *the south* Italy.

SECOND SIGHT
[1] Charles Robert Maturin (1782–1824), *Bertram* IV ii 144–5. Maturin's play was produced by Kean at Drury Lane in 1816, with great success.

I hear the still small moan of time[2]
    Through the ivy branches made,
Where the palace in its glory's prime
    With the sunshine stands arrayed.

The thunder of the seas I hear,   25
    The shriek along the wave,
When the bark sweeps forth, and song and cheer
    Salute the parting brave.

With every breeze a spirit sends
    To me some warning sign –   30
A mournful gift is mine, oh friends,
    A mournful gift is mine!

Oh, prophet heart, thy grief, thy power
    To all deep souls belong;
The shadow in the sunny hour,   35
    The wail in the mirthful song.

Their sight is all too sadly clear –
    For them a veil is riven;
Their piercing thoughts repose not here,
    Their home is but in heaven.   40

From Scenes and Hymns of Life, with other Religious Poems
(1834)

Thought from an Italian Poet

Where shall I find, in all this fleeting earth,
    This world of changes and farewells, a friend
That will not fail me in his love and worth,
    Tender, and firm, and faithful to the end?

Far hath my spirit sought a place of rest –   5
    Long on vain idols its devotion shed;
Some have forsaken whom I loved the best,
    And some deceived, and some are with the dead.

But *thou*, my Saviour, thou, my hope and trust,
    Faithful art thou when friends and joys depart;   10
Teach me to lift these yearnings from the dust,
    And fix on thee, th' unchanging one, my heart!

---

[2]   *the still small moan of time* an echo of I Kings 19:12:   not in the fire: and after the fire a *still small voice*'
'And after the earthquake a fire; but the Lord was   [my italics].

From The Works of Mrs Hemans (1839)

DESPONDENCY AND ASPIRATION

Per correr miglior acqua alza le vele,
Omai la navicella del mio Intelletto.[1]

Dante

My soul was mantled with dark shadows born
  Of lonely fear, disquieted in vain;
Its phantoms hung around the star of morn,
  A cloud-like weeping train;
Through the long day they dimmed the autumn gold[2]   5
On all the glistening leaves, and wildly rolled,
    When the last farewell flush of light was glowing
      Across the sunset sky,
    O'er its rich isles of vaporous glory throwing
      One melancholy dye.   10

    And when the solemn night
    Came rushing with her might
Of stormy oracles from caves unknown,
    Then with each fitful blast
    Prophetic murmurs passed,   15
Wakening or answering some deep sibyl tone[3]
Far buried in my breast, yet prompt to rise
With every gusty wail that o'er the wind-harp flies.

'Fold, fold thy wings', they cried, 'and strive no more,
Faint spirit, strive no more! For thee too strong   20
    Are outward ill and wrong,
And inward wasting fires! Thou canst not soar
    Free on a starry way
    Beyond their blighting sway,
At Heaven's high gate serenely to adore!   25
How shouldst *thou* hope earth's fetters to unbind?
Oh passionate yet weak, oh trembler to the wind!

'Never shall aught but broken music flow
From joy of thine, deep love, or tearful woe;
Such homeless notes as through the forest sigh,   30
    From the reeds hollow shaken
    When sudden breezes waken
      Their vague wild symphony:
No power is theirs, and no abiding-place

DESPONDENCY AND ASPIRATION
[1] 'This ship of my mind by now unfurls the sails to
navigate faster.'

[2] *autumn gold* this poem was composed in the
autumn of 1834, during Hemans's final illness.
[3] *sibyl tone* the voice of a female prophet.

In human hearts; their sweetness leaves no trace –   35
  Born only so to die!

'Never shall aught but perfume, faint and vain,
  On the fleet pinion of the changeful hour,
    From thy bruised life again
      A moment's essence breathe;   40
    Thy life, whose trampled flower
      Into the blessed wreath
Of household charities[4] no longer bound,
Lies pale and withering on the barren ground.

'So fade, fade on! Thy gift of love shall cling,   45
  A coiling sadness round thy heart and brain,
A silent, fruitless, yet undying thing
  All sensitive to pain!
And still the shadow of vain dreams shall fall
O'er thy mind's world, a daily darkening pall.   50
Fold, then, thy wounded wing, and sink subdued
In cold and unrepining quietude!'

Then my soul yielded; spells of numbing breath
Crept o'er it heavy with a dew of death,
Its powers, like leaves before the night rain, closing;   55
  And, as by conflict of wild sea-waves tossed
  On the chill bosom of some desert coast,
Mutely and hopelessly I lay reposing.

  When silently it seemed
  As if a soft mist gleamed   60
Before my passive sight, and, slowly curling,
  To many a shape and hue
  Of visioned beauty grew,
Like a wrought banner, fold by fold unfurling.
Oh, the rich scenes that o'er mine inward eye[5]   65
  Unrolling then swept by
With dreamy motion! Silvery seas were there
  Lit by large dazzling stars, and arched by skies
  Of southern midnight's most transparent dyes,
And gemmed with many an island, wildly fair,   70
Which floated past me into orient day
Still gathering lustre on th' illumined way,
Till its high groves of wondrous flowering trees
  Coloured the silvery seas.

And then a glorious mountain-chain uprose,   75
  Height above spiry height!

---

[4] *charities* affections; by this time Hemans's mother was dead.

[5] *inward eye* an echo of Wordsworth, *Daffodils* 15–16, where the memory of daffodils 'flash upon that inward eye / Which is the bliss of solitude'.

A soaring solitude of woods and snows
    All steeped in golden light!
While as it passed, those regal peaks unveiling,
    I heard, methought, a waving of dread wings   80
And mighty sounds, as if the vision hailing,
    From lyres that quivered through ten thousand strings;
Or as if waters forth to music leaping,
    From many a cave, the Alpine Echo's hall,
On their bold way victoriously were sweeping,   85
    Linked in majestic anthems, while through all
        That billowy swell and fall
Voices, like ringing crystal, filled the air
    With inarticulate melody that stirred
    My being's core, then, moulding into word   90
Their piercing sweetness, bade me rise and bear
    In that great choral strain my trembling part
Of tones, by love and faith struck from a human heart.

Return no more, vain bodings of the night!
    A happier oracle within my soul   95
Hath swelled to power – a clear unwavering light
    Mounts through the battling clouds that round me roll,
        And to a new control
Nature's full harp gives forth rejoicing tones,
    Wherein my glad sense owns   100
The accordant rush of elemental sound
To one consummate harmony profound,
        One grand creation hymn
        Whose notes the seraphim
Lift to the glorious height of music winged and crowned.   105

    Shall not those notes find echoes in my lyre,
Faithful though faint? Shall not my spirit's fire,
If slowly, yet unswervingly, ascend
        Now to its fount and end?
Shall not my earthly love, all purified,   110
        Shine forth a heavenward guide,
An angel of bright power, and strongly bear
My being upward into holier air,
    Where fiery passion-clouds have no abode,
And the sky's temple-arch o'erflows with God?   115

        The radiant hope new-born
        Expands like rising morn
In my life's life and, as a ripening rose,
The crimson shadow of its glory throws
More vivid, hour by hour, on some pure stream,   120
        So from that hope are spreading
        Rich hues, o'er nature shedding,
Each day, a clearer, spiritual gleam.

Let not those rays fade from me – once enjoyed,
    Father of spirits, let them not depart!   125
Leaving the chilled earth, without form and void,
    Darkened by mine own heart!
Lift, aid, sustain me! Thou by whom alone
    All lovely gifts and pure
    In the soul's grasp endure;   130
Thou, to the steps of whose eternal throne
All knowledge flows – a sea for evermore
Breaking its crested waves on that sole shore[6] –
Oh consecrate my life, that I may sing
Of Thee with joy that hath a living spring   135
In a full heart of music! Let my lays
Through the resounding mountains waft thy praise,
And with that theme the wood's green cloisters fill,
And make their quivering leafy dimness thrill
To the rich breeze of song! Oh let me wake   140
    The deep religion, which hath dwelt from yore,
Silently brooding by lone cliff and lake,
    And wildest river shore,
And let me summon all the voices dwelling
Where eagles build, and caverned rills are welling,   145
And where the cataract's organ-peal is swelling,
    In that one spirit gathered to adore!

Forgive, oh Father, if presumptuous thought
    Too daringly in aspiration rise!
Let not thy child all vainly have been taught   150
    By weakness, and by wanderings, and by sighs
Of sad confession! Lowly be my heart,
    And on its penitential altar spread
The offerings worthless, till Thy grace impart
    The fire from heaven, whose touch alone can shed   155
Life, radiance, virtue! Let that vital spark
Pierce my whole being, wildered else and dark!

Thine are all holy things – oh make *me* Thine,
So shall I, too, be pure – a living shrine
Unto that spirit which goes forth from Thee,   160
    Strong and divinely free,
Bearing thy gifts of wisdom on its flight,
And brooding o'er them with a dove-like wing,[7]

---

[6] *a sea for evermore . . . shore* a reminiscence of Wordsworth, *Ode* 169–70: 'And see the children sport upon the shore, / And hear the mighty waters rolling evermore.'

[7] *brooding o'er them with a dove-like wing* an allusion to *Paradise Lost* i 21–2, where the Holy Spirit 'Dove-like sat'st brooding on the vast abyss / And madest it pregnant'.

Till thought, word, song, to Thee in worship spring,
Immortally endowed for liberty and light.   165

Letitia Elizabeth Landon   (1802–1838)

Letitia was born on 14 August 1802 at 25 Hans Place, Chelsea. Catherine Jane Bishop, her mother, was of Welsh ancestry; her father, John Landon, had been an explorer in Africa, and had returned to London to become a partner in Adair's army agency in Pall Mall. Her education was fragmented and unsystematic; she was taught to read by an invalid neighbour, and at five sent to Miss Rowden's Chelsea school where Lady Caroline Lamb and Mary Russell Mitford had been pupils. But this was only for a few months. She was seven when her family moved to Coventry Farm, an ill-advised investment by her father at East Barnet, and the source of his later financial difficulties. Here she was educated by her cousin Elizabeth Landon, who by her own admission was less well-informed than her pupil: 'When I asked Letitia any question relating either to history, geography, grammar – to Plutarch's Lives, or to any book we had been reading, I was pretty certain her answers would be perfectly correct; still, not exactly recollecting, and unwilling she should find out just then that I was less learned than herself, I used thus to question her: "Are you quite certain?" . . . I never knew her to be wrong.'[1] She was a voracious reader, at an early age having memorized Scott's *Lady of the Lake*, and read between 100 and 150 volumes of Cooke's *Poets and Novelists*, in addition to 'Rollin's Ancient History, Hume and Smollett; then come Plutarch's Lives, the Fables of Gay and Aesop, Life of Josephus, Montesquieu's Spirit of the Laws, Dobson's Life of Petrarch, and many others, more or less adapted to the young reader.'[2] Also by this time she was composing poetry. 'I cannot remember the time when composition in some shape or other was not a habit', Letitia later told S. C. Hall. 'I used to invent long stories, which I was only too glad if I could get my mother to hear. These soon took a metrical form, and I used to walk about the grounds and lie awake half the night, reciting my verses aloud'.[3]

When she was thirteen the family moved back to Fulham and then to Old Brompton, largely because of her father's troubled finances. It was in Old Brompton, while still a teenager, that she first came to the notice of William Jerdan, editor of the *Literary Gazette*: 'My first recollection of the future poetess is that of a plump girl, grown enough to be almost mistaken for a woman, bowling a hoop round the walks, with the hoop-stick in one hand and a book in the other, reading as she ran, and as well as she could manage both exercise and instruction at the same time.'[4] At the age of eighteen she began contributing to the *Literary Gazette* under the initials 'L.E.L.', and quickly attracted a following of admirers. The curiosity aroused by the enigmatic initial letters of her name is evoked in a poem of February 1822 by the Quaker poet, Bernard Barton:

[1] Laman Blanchard, *Life and Literary Remains of L.E.L.* (2 vols, London, 1841), i 9.
[2] Ibid., i 10.
[3] S. C. Hall, *A Book of Memories of Great Men and Women of the Age, from Personal Acquaintance* (1871), p. 267.
[4] *The Autobiography of William Jerdan* (4 vols, London, 1853), iii 174.

> I know not who or what thou art,
>   Nor do I seek to know thee,
> Whilst thou, performing thus thy part,
>   Such banquets can bestow me.
> Then be, as long as thou shalt list,
>   My viewless, nameless, melodist.

At first she had great difficulty finding a publisher for a long poem she had written, *The Improvisatrice*; it was, she later recalled, rejected by every publisher in London. But the notoriety of her work for the *Literary Gazette* made it comparatively easy for her to find a publisher in 1824. She later told Alaric Watts that 'I wrote the *Improvisatrice* in less than five weeks, and during that time I often was for two or three days without touching it. I never saw the MS till in proof-sheets a year afterwards, and I made no additions, only verbal alterations.'[5] Her publishers paid her £300 for it, and it was an instant success, going through six editions within the year. Reviews were generally favourable, and among the first was an outrageous puff by Jerdan in the *Literary Gazette*; it began by describing Letitia as 'the English Sappho', and commenting: 'If true poetry consist in originality of conception, fineness of imagination, beautiful fitness and glow of expression, genuine feeling, and the outpourings of fresh and natural thoughts in all the force of fresh and natural language, it is pre-eminently conspicuous in the writings of L.E.L. Neither are her subjects nor mode of treating them, borrowed from others; but simplicity, gracefulness, fancy and pathos seem to gush forth in spontaneous and sweet union, whatever may be the theme.'[6] Jerdan was determined to present Letitia as an improvisatrice herself, gifted with spontaneous poetic utterance; he went on: 'What may spring from the continued cultivation of such promise, it is not easy to predicate; but if the author never excels what she has already done, we can confidently give her the assurance of what the possessor of such talents must most earnestly covet – *Immortality*.'[7] Jerdan was hardly a disinterested party, and the puff attracted the criticism of other reviewers. Alaric Watts in the *Literary Magnet* ridiculed him at length before reminding his readers of a recent hoax in which Jerdan was implicated: 'We remember that some time since, a report was spread of the premature death of this same interesting young lady, and the *Literary Gazette* joined in the solemn foolery, lamenting her timeless decease as if it really happened.'[8] Despite this, Watts contributed his share of praise to the new star on the literary horizon: 'We are no hermits, nor have we reached that sober decline of life, when the heyday of the blood attends upon the judgement; and, indeed, if we had, the verses of our "English Sappho" would go far in heating us again. Her descriptions are sufficiently warm and luxurious: she appears to be the very creature of passionate inspiration; and the wild and romantic being whom she describes as the Improvisatrice seems to be the very counterpart of her sentimental self. Her poetical breathing appears to proceed from a soul whose very essence is love; and seared hearts – withered hopes – broken lutes – blighted flowers – music and moonlight, sing their melancholy changes through all her verses.'[9] Jerdan's questionable marketing strategy also drew fire from the *Westminster Review*, which commented: 'If we are

---

[5] Alaric Alfred Watts, *Alaric Watts: A Narrative of his Life* (2 vols, London, 1884), ii 21.
[6] *Literary Gazette* 389–90 (3–10 July 1824) 417–20, 436–7, p. 417.
[7] Ibid., p. 420.
[8] *Literary Magnet* 2 (1824) 106–9, p. 108.
[9] Ibid., p. 106.

to trust the *Literary Gazette* and common gossip, authorities pretty much on a par on this subject, poets are as plenty as mushrooms, and start up, in the present day, as rapidly as they do after a shower. We cannot walk the streets of London without jostling a poet; and our provincial towns and country places equally abound in them.'[10] Although the reviewer had praise for the poem, it nonetheless contained 'much that is mere verbiage, and pages filled with puny and sickly thoughts clothed in glittering language that draws the eye off from their real character and value'.[11] Other reviewers had kinder words and fewer reservations: the *Gentleman's Magazine* claimed seldom to have 'seen a volume more conspicuous for vivid imagination, felicity of diction, vigorous condensation of language, and passionate intensity of sentiment'.[12] In rather a patronizing account of the work, *Blackwood's Edinburgh Magazine* conceded that 'Miss L. has a good command of language, and a fair store of poetical ideas, with a great deal of taste in arrangement, and an ear tuned to the varied melodies of the language'.[13] And the *New Monthly Magazine* commented: 'There is scarcely a line which does not glow with some ray of warm or bright feeling; scarcely an image which is not connected with the heart by some fine and secret association. . . . in ardent and impassioned feeling, clothed in language most befitting, *The Improvisatrice* and the poems which follow it have been seldom surpassed'.[14]

This was, of course, business. By 1824 women poets were not just acceptable to the literary marketplace – they were positively fashionable. Always hungry for new talent, publishers were willing to take anything saleable and feed it to the ever-open maw of the reading public. Felicia Hemans had colluded with the process because, as a single parent with five children, she had little choice; she burned herself out and died young. I doubt whether Letitia was fully aware of nature of the forces that were about to harness her talents, and Alaric Watts sounded an appropriately admonitory note when, in his review, he remarked that 'She possesses taste, sweetness, and a high poetical feeling; and we only regret she should have fallen into interested hands, by which her talents are prematurely thrust upon the world, and rated so far beyond their merits.'[15] His judgement is echoed by Germaine Greer who, in one of the most persuasive recent essays on Letitia, remarks: 'The reality of her life was daily work, endless deadlines, poor pay and no power whatsoever, even to express what she really believed. Grub Street destroyed her personal integrity, worked her to exhaustion and then turned on her.'[16] This judgement is, to some extent, corroborated by Letitia's own testimony to S. C. Hall, although she seems to have been grateful for the opportunity to make a living from her writing: 'I certainly am not one of the authors who complain of the booksellers. My whole life has been one of constant labour. My contributions to various periodicals – whether tales, poetry, or criticism – amount to far more than my published volumes. I have been urged to this by the necessity of aiding those nearly connected with me, whom my father's death left entirely destitute.'[17] William Jerdan calculated that Letitia earned £2,585 in total from her work, about £250 a year.[18] Besides *The Improvisatrice*, she published *The Troubadour* (1825), *The Golden Violet* (1827), and *The Venetian Bracelet* (1829), among other titles.

[10] *Westminster Review* 3 (1825) 537–9, p. 538.
[11] Ibid., p. 539.
[12] *Gentleman's Magazine* 94 (1824) 61–3, pp. 61–2.
[13] *Blackwood's Edinburgh Magazine* 16 (1824) 189–93, p. 191.
[14] *New Monthly Magazine* 12 (1824) 365–6, p. 365.
[15] *Literary Magnet* 2 (1824) 106–9, p. 109.
[16] *Slip-Shod Sibyls* (London, 1995), p. 259.
[17] S. C. Hall, *A Book of Memories of Great Men and Women of the Age, from Personal Acquaintance*, p. 268.
[18] *The Autobiography of William Jerdan*, iii 185.

But the real hardship in her literary life was her embroilment in scandal – first through her association with the dissolute William Maginn, and then through her friendship with Daniel Maclise, the artist. Despite the fuss that surrounded her private life, Germaine Greer is right to observe that 'There is no proof that L.E.L. ever had a lover by day or night, let alone several'.[19] All the same, rumours about her can only have intensified the desire for domestic stability, and on 7 June 1838 at St Mary's, Bryanston Square, she married George Maclean, Governor of Cape Coast Castle in Africa who, according to S. C. Hall, 'neither knew, felt, nor estimated her value. He wedded her, I am sure, only because he was vain of her celebrity'.[20] She sailed for Africa on 5 July, and arrived on 15 August. Life on the Gold Coast was not what she expected; she found herself cut off from the metropolitan society to which she was accustomed, and on 15 October wrote to Anna Maria Hall, 'I do not wish to form new friends, and never does a day pass without thinking most affectionately of my old ones.'[21] Later that day she was found dead, a bottle of prussic acid in her hand. She was only thirty-six. Suspicions about her husband, and the failure of the coroner to perform a post-mortem, led to much speculation about the causes and means of her death: 'The wildest rumours were immediately set afloat by the hapless lady's female friends in England – each pretending to have been in her confidence, and each affecting to know the facts of the case better than anybody else. One averred that a cup of coffee had been given her by a black boy, which had been drugged by a native woman who had lived with the Governor as his mistress; others denied that she had ever employed hydrocyanic acid, or taken any poison with her; and the rest accused Mr Maclean of cruelty and adultery, and even of being accessory to the murder of his wife.'[22]

It would be difficult, today, to claim Letitia as a neglected genius; she had talent and facility, and the best of her poems contain energy and charm, but her work was wildly variable, even within single works. *The Improvisatrice* remains her quintessential poem, featuring Lorenzo, its Byronic hero, and its thwarted, eponymous heroine, dark and passionate (like its author), doomed to be jilted for a vacuous blonde. But even her admirers tend to agree that she worked too rapidly for there to have been much polish to her work: 'The injury that resulted from the rule of rapidity – breathless and reckless rapidity – is shown throughout the various poems that compose the overwrought richness, the beautiful excess, the melodious confusion of the *Improvisatrice*. If the superfluities, amounting to at least one third of the poem had been cut away, all that is obscure would have been clear – all that is languid, strong – all that is incongruous, harmonised.'[23] It is easiest to value her verse for precisely the qualities Laman Blanchard singled out – its 'breathless rapidity', richness, and, indeed, confusion. Letitia had, as she rightly observed, 'a soul of romance', but if she represented in any sense the spirit of romanticism, it was of a transitional, even decadent, kind. True, she is capable of writing about Lake District beauty spots, such as Airey Force and Scale Force, in a decidedly Wordsworthian manner, and even her poem about Piccadilly Circus is reminiscent of *Composed upon Westminster Bridge, 3 September 1802*.[24] But the kind of subject-matter that appealed most to her was romantic not in the sense of the sublime set-pieces of *The Prelude*, but

[19] *Slip-Shod Sibyls*, p. 311.
[20] S. C. Hall, *A Book of Memories of Great Men and Women of the Age, from Personal Acquaintance*, p. 274.
[21] Anna Maria Hall, 'The Last Letters of L.E.L.', *Gentleman's Magazine* 11 (1839) 150–2, p. 152.

[22] The Hon. Grantley F. Berkeley, *My Life and Recollections* (4 vols, London, 1865–6), iii 192.
[23] Laman Blanchard, *Life and Literary Remains of L.E.L.*, i 42.
[24] See *Romanticism* 276.

in its melancholy preoccupation with thwarted or deceived love. *Sappho's Song* from *The Improvisatrice*, which many critics singled out for praise, is a good example. For Letitia, as for Mary Robinson, Sappho was the exemplar not just of the female poet, but of the jilted lover. Robinson had devoted over forty sonnets to an exploration of her heroine's inner world; Letitia's poem is no more than twenty lines long, but it is no less evocative of the compulsive intensity of love. That fascination is the distinctive preoccupation that drives Letitia's poetic vision. Even when writing about Airey Force, it is to imagine herself as a hermit no longer susceptible to such betrayals.[25]

In content, she is an inheritor of the romantic tradition of Hemans, Scott and Byron; in manner, she is one of the first Victorians: 'Her imaginary tableaux are dense and dramatic, all the space crowded like a pre-Raphaelite painting with flowers and luxury effects.'[26] Less pronounced in the poems and extracts selected here, the profusion of descriptive detail in the entirely imaginary account of Florence in *The Improvisatrice* is decadent by the standards of high romanticism. Her attitudes presaged those of the Victorian era in another sense: unlike most of those in this volume, she was one of the first truly urban poets. 'I have lived almost wholly in London', she told S. C. Hall, 'and though very susceptible to the impressions produced by the beauty of the country, certainly never felt at home but on the pavement'.[27] In a letter quoted by Laman Blanchard she is even more emphatic: 'I have such a horror of living in the country: hawthorn hedges and unhappy attachments always go together in my mind'.[28] She looks forward, quite literally, in *The Princess Victoria*, to the era that was about to dawn – one divorced from the depravity and indolence in which George IV had wallowed; the poem is a curious one, insofar as it features a heroine – the future Queen and Empress – who is not doomed in the manner of the heroines found throughout this volume (and certainly throughout the poems of Felicia Hemans). Instead, her 'fair young face' gazes fearlessly into a future in which her throne will be the source of 'knowledge, power, and liberty'. To describe such sentiments as conservative is to miss the point; for Letitia it is important that the next monarch is a woman whose status is such that she is not just preserved from the disappointment to which her other heroines are subject, but is capable of redeeming others. It is a form of transcendence – and if we are looking for some way of defining what is romantic in Letitia's poetry, that is as good a definition as any.

Her most impressive single work may be her lament, *Felicia Hemans*. Like much of her writing, it was composed to order, for *Fisher's Drawing Room Scrap-Book*. The idea behind this annual publication was that Letitia would compose verses to accompany engravings – the main reason for buying the volume. Three years before, she had composed her elegiac *Stanzas on the Death of Mrs Hemans* for the periodical to which both had contributed, the *New Monthly Magazine*.[29] In 1838, she still had much to say about her former colleague. 'Thy name was lovely and thy song was dear', she wrote:

> Was not this purchased all too dearly? – never
> Can fame atone for all that fame hath cost.
> We see the goal but know not the endeavour,

---

[25] See *Airey Force* 9–16.
[26] Germaine Greer, *Slip-Shod Sibyls*, pp. 264–5.
[27] S. C. Hall, *A Book of Memories of Great Men and Women of the Age, from Personal Acquaintance*, p. 268.
[28] Laman Blanchard, *Life and Literary Remains of L.E.L.*, i 269.
[29] See *Romanticism* 1092–5.

Nor what fond hopes have on the way been lost.
What do we know of the unquiet pillow
  By the worn cheek and tearful eyelid pressed,
When thoughts chase thoughts like the tumultuous billow
  Whose very light and foam reveals unrest?
We say the song is sorrowful, but know not
What may have left that sorrow on the song . . .

(ll. 33–42)

The verse is moving because Letitia identifies so strongly with her subject, and it indicates how drastically things had changed since Hannah More had first been admitted into the male-dominated world of letters back in the 1770s. By force of numbers, women had now won the right to be accepted as poets, providing they stuck to certain 'feminine' themes, but only at a price: in finding an audience for their work, they were sucked into an industry that exploited them mercilessly, before destroying them. 'Was not this purchased all too dearly?' Letitia poses the question she must already have been asking about her own career. Within months of publishing this tribute, she was dead.

Further Reading

Germaine Greer, *Slip-Shod Sibyls: Recognition, Rejection and the Woman Poet* (London, 1995), chapter 10

Letitia Elizabeth Landon, *The Improvisatrice, 1825* Introduction by Jonathan Wordsworth (Poole, 1996)

F. J. Sypher, 'The Magical Letters of L.E.L.', *Columbia Library Columns* 39 (1990) 3–9

Glennis Stephenson, 'Letitia Landon and the Victorian Improvisatrice: The Construction of L.E.L.', *Victorian Poetry* 30 (1992) 1–17

Virginia Blain, 'Letitia Elizabeth Landon, Eliza Mary Hamilton, and the Genealogy of the Victorian Poetess', *Victorian Poetry* 33 (1995) 31–52

From The Improvisatrice; and Other Poems. By L.E.L. (1824)

THE IMPROVISATRICE (EXTRACTS)

[INTRODUCTION]

I am a daughter of that land
Where the poet's lip and the painter's hand
Are most divine, where the earth and sky
Are picture both and poetry –
I am of Florence. Mid the chill   5
Of hope and feeling – oh, I still
Am proud to think to where I owe
My birth, though but the dawn of woe!
  My childhood passed mid radiant things,
Glorious as hope's imaginings;   10
Statues but known from shapes of the earth

By being too lovely for mortal birth;[1]
Paintings whose colours of life were caught
From the fairy tints in the rainbow wrought;
Music whose sighs had a spell like those   15
That float on the sea at the evening's close;
Language so silvery that every word
Was like the lute's awakening chord;
Skies half sunshine and half starlight,
Flowers whose lives were a breath of delight,   20
Leaves whose green pomp knew no withering,
Fountains bright as the skies of our spring,
And songs whose wild and passionate line
Suited a soul of romance like mine.

My power was but a woman's power,   25
Yet in that great and glorious dower
Which genius gives, I had my part;
I poured my full and burning heart
In song, and on the canvas made
My dreams of beauty visible;   30
I knew not which I loved the most –
Pencil or lute, both loved so well.

[SAPPHO'S SONG]

Farewell, my lute, and would that I
Had never waked thy burning chords!
Poison has been upon thy sigh,
And fever has breathed in thy words.

Yet wherefore, wherefore should I blame   145
Thy power, thy spell, my gentlest lute?
I should have been the wretch I am
Had every chord of thine been mute.

It was my evil star above,
Not my sweet lute that wrought me wrong;   150
It was not song that taught me love,
But it was love that taught me song.

If song be past, and hope undone,
And pulse, and head, and heart, are flame,
It is thy work, thou faithless one –   155
But no, I will not name thy name![1]

[INTRODUCTION]
[1] ll. 9–12 bear a general resemblance to Wordsworth's
Ode, including the use of the birth/earth rhyme from
Ode 16–18.

[SAPPHO'S SONG]
[1] *thou faithless one . . . thy name* Sappho's deepest pas-
sions were reserved for Phaon, who did not reciproc-
ate them, and for whom she committed suicide from
the Leucadian cliff. Cf. Mary Robinson's treatment of
this story in *Sappho to Phaon*, pp. 191–208.

Sun-god! lute, wreath are vowed to thee!
Long be their light upon my grave,
My glorious grave – yon deep blue sea;
I shall sleep calm beneath its wave!　　　　160

[LORENZO]

From many a lip came sounds of praise
　　Like music from sweet voices ringing,
For many a boat had gathered round
　　To list the song I had been singing.[1]　　415
There are some moments in our fate
　　That stamp the colour of our days,
As, till then, life had not been felt,
　　And mine was sealed in the slight gaze
Which fixed my eye and fired my brain,　　420
And bowed my heart beneath the chain.
'Twas a dark and flashing eye,
Shadows, too, that tenderly,
With almost female softness, came
O'er its mingled gloom and flame.　　425
His cheek was pale; or toil, or care,
Or midnight study had been there,
Making its young colours dull,
Yet leaving it most beautiful.
Raven curls their shadow threw　　430
Like the twilight's darkening hue
O'er the pure and mountain snow
Of his high and haughty brow,
Lighted by a smile whose spell
Words are powerless to tell.　　435
Such a lip! – oh, poured from thence,
Lava floods of eloquence
Would come with fiery energy
Like those words that cannot die;
Words the Grecian warrior spoke　　440
When the Persian's chain he broke,[2]
Or that low and honey tone
Making woman's heart his own,
Such as should be heard at night
In the dim and sweet starlight,　　445
Sounds that haunt a beauty's sleep,
Treasures for her heart to keep.
Like the pine of summer tall,

---

[1] The Improvisatrice has just sung a tale about thwarted love called *A Moorish Romance*.

[2] *Grecian warrior... broke* Alexander the Great twice defeated Darius III, King of Persia, in battle.

Apollo[3] on his pedestal
In our own gallery never bent   450
More graceful, more magnificent,
Ne'er looked the hero or the king
    More nobly than the youth who now,
As if soul-centred in my song,
    Was leaning on a galley's prow.   455
He spoke not when the others spoke,
    His heart was all too full for praise,
But his dark eyes kept fixed on mine
    Which sank beneath their burning gaze.
Mine sank, but yet I felt the thrill   460
Of that look burning on me still.
I heard no word that others said,
    Heard nothing save one low-breathed sigh.
My hand kept wandering on my lute
    In music, but unconsciously;   465
My pulses throbbed, my heart beat high,
A flush of dizzy ecstasy
    Crimsoned my cheek; I felt warm tears
Dimming my sight, yet was it sweet,
My wild heart's most bewildering beat,   470
    Consciousness without hopes or fears
Of a new power within me waking,
Like light before the morn's full breaking.
I left the boat, the crowd – my mood
Made my soul pant for solitude.   475

From The Golden Violet, with its Tales of Romance and Chivalry: and Other Poems (1827)

LOVE'S LAST LESSON

'Teach it me, if you can – forgetfulness!
I surely shall forget, if you can bid me;
I who have worshipped thee, my god on earth,
I who have bowed me at thy lightest word.
Your last command, "Forget me", will it not   5
Sink deeply down within my inmost soul?
Forget thee! Aye, forgetfulness will be
A mercy to me. By the many nights
When I have wept for that I dared not sleep,
A dream had made me live my woes again,   10

---

[3] *Apollo* son of Zeus, god of youth, poetry, music,
prophecy, archery, and healing.

Acting my wretchedness, without the hope
My foolish heart still clings to, though that hope
Is like the opiate which may lull awhile,
Then wake to double torture; by the days
Passed in lone watching and in anxious fears,   15
When a breath sent the crimson to my cheek
Like the red gushing of a sudden wound;
By all the careless looks and careless words
Which have to me been like the scorpion's stinging;
By happiness blighted, and by thee, for ever;   20
By thy eternal work of wretchedness;
By all my withered feelings, ruined health,
Crushed hopes, and rifled heart, I will forget thee!
Alas, my words are vanity. Forget thee!
Thy work of wasting is too surely done.   25
The April shower may pass and be forgotten,
The rose fall and one fresh spring in its place,
And thus it may be with light summer love.
It was not thus with mine: it did not spring,
Like the bright colour on an evening cloud,   30
Into a moment's life, brief, beautiful;
Not amid lighted halls, when flatteries
Steal on the ear like dew upon the rose,
As soft, as soon dispersed, as quickly passed;
But you first called my woman's feelings forth   35
And taught me love ere I had dreamed love's name.
I loved unconsciously: your name was all
That seemed in language, and to me the world
Was only made for you; in solitude,
When passions hold their interchange together,   40
Your image was the shadow of my thought;
Never did slave, before his eastern lord,
Tremble as I did when I met your eye,
And yet each look was counted as a prize;
I laid your words up in my heart like pearls   45
Hid in the ocean's treasure-cave. At last
I learned my heart's deep secret, for I hoped,
I dreamed, you loved me; wonder, fear, delight,
Swept my heart like a storm; my soul, my life
Seemed all too little for your happiness.   50
Had I been mistress of the starry worlds
That light the midnight, they had all been yours,
And I had deemed such boon but poverty.
As it was, I gave all I could – my love,
My deep, my true, my fervent, faithful love,   55
And now you bid me learn forgetfulness:
It is a lesson that I soon shall learn.
There is a home of quiet for the wretched,

A somewhat dark, and cold, and silent rest,
But still it is rest, for it is the grave.'   60
    She flung aside the scroll, as it had part
In her great misery. Why should she write?
What could she write? Her woman's pride forbade
To let him look upon her heart, and see
It was an utter ruin; and cold words,   65
And scorn and slight, that may repay his own,
Were as a foreign language to whose sound
She might not frame her utterance. Down she bent
Her head upon an arm so white that tears
Seemed but the natural melting of its snow,   70
Touched by the flushed cheek's crimson; yet life-blood
Less wrings[1] in shedding than such tears as those.
    And this then is love's ending! It is like
The history of some fair southern clime.
Hot fires are in the bosom of the earth,   75
And the warmed soil puts forth its thousand flowers,
Its fruits of gold, summer's regality,
And sleep and odours float upon the air.
At length the subterranean element
Breaks from its secret dwelling-place, and lays   80
All waste before it, the red lava stream.
Sweeps like the pestilence, and that which was
A garden in its colours and its breath,
Fit for the princess of a fairy-tale,
Is as a desert in whose burning sands   85
And ashy waters, who is there can trace
A sign, a memory of its former beauty?
It is thus with the heart; love lights it up
With hopes like young companions, and with joys
Dreaming deliciously of their sweet selves.   90
    This is at first – but what is the result?
Hopes that lie mute in their own sullenness,
For they have quarrelled even with themselves;
And joys indeed like birds of paradise.[2]
And in their stead despair coils scorpion-like,   95
Stinging itself, and the heart, burnt and crushed
With passion's earthquake, scorched and withered up,
Lies in its desolation: this is love.
    What is the tale that I would tell? Not one
Of strange adventure, but a common tale   100
Of woman's wretchedness; one to be read
Daily in many a young and blighted heart.
The lady whom I spake of rose again

LOVE'S LAST LESSON
[1] *wrings* strains, twists (the features of the face?).

[2] 'In eastern tales, the bird of paradise never rests on the earth' (Landon's note).

From the red fever's couch, to careless eyes
Perchance the same as she had ever been.   105
But oh, how altered to herself! She felt
That bird-like pining for some gentle home
To which affection might attach itself,
That weariness which hath but outward part
In what the world calls pleasure, and that chill   110
Which makes life taste the bitterness of death.
    And he she loved so well – what opiate
Lulled consciousness into its selfish sleep?
He said he loved her not, that never vow
Or passionate pleading won her soul for him,   115
And that he guessed not her deep tenderness.
    Are words, then, only false? Are there no looks,
Mute but most eloquent, no gentle cares
That win so much upon the fair weak things
They seem to guard? And had he not long read   120
Her heart's hushed secret in the soft dark eye
Lighted at his approach, and on the cheek
Colouring all crimson at his lightest look?
This is the truth; his spirit wholly turned
To stern ambition's dream, to that fierce strife   125
Which leads to life's high places, and recked not
What lovely flowers might perish in his path.
    And here at length is somewhat of revenge:
For man's most golden dreams of pride and power
Are vain as any woman's dreams of love;   130
Both end in weary brow and withered heart,
And the grave closes over those whose hopes
Have lain there long before.

From Fisher's Drawing Room Scrap-Book, 1838 (1838)[1]

FELICIA HEMANS

No more, no more, oh never more returning
    Will thy beloved presence gladden earth;
No more wilt thou with sad, yet anxious, yearning
    Cling to those hopes which have no mortal birth.
Thou art gone from us, and with thee departed   5
    How many lovely things have vanished too;
Deep thoughts[2] that at thy will to being started,

FELICIA HEMANS
[1] This poem appears opposite an engraving of Felicia Hemans taken from the portrait by W. E. West. Felicia died 16 May 1835, of tuberculosis.

[2] *Deep thoughts* possibly an echo of Wordsworth's 'Thoughts that do often lie too deep for tears' (*Ode* 206).

And feelings, teaching us our own were true.
Thou hast been round us like a viewless spirit
    Known only by the music on the air;   10
The leaf or flowers which thou hast named inherit
    A beauty known but from thy breathing there,
For thou didst on them fling thy strong emotion,
    The likeness from itself the fond heart gave,
As planets from afar look down on ocean   15
    And give their own sweet image to the wave.[3]
And thou didst bring from foreign lands their treasures,[4]
    As floats thy various melody along;
We know the softness of Italian measures,[5]
    And the grave cadence of Castilian song.   20
A general bond of union is the poet,
    By its immortal verse is language known,
And for the sake of song do others know it –
    One glorious poet makes the world his own.
And thou, how far thy gentle sway extended –   25
    The heart's sweet empire over land and sea;
Many a stranger and far flower was blended
    In the soft wreath that glory bound for thee.
The echoes of the Susquehanna's waters
    Paused in the pine-woods, words of thine to hear,[6]   30
And to the wide Atlantic's younger daughters[7]
    Thy name was lovely and thy song was dear.

Was not this purchased all too dearly? – never
    Can fame atone for all that fame hath cost.
We see the goal but know not the endeavour,[8]   35
    Nor what fond hopes have on the way been lost.
What do we know of the unquiet pillow
    By the worn cheek and tearful eyelid pressed,
When thoughts chase thoughts like the tumultuous billow
    Whose very light and foam reveals unrest?   40
We say the song is sorrowful, but know not
    What may have left that sorrow on the song;
However mournful words may be, they show not
    The whole extent of wretchedness and wrong.

---

[3] *The leaf or flowers ... to the wave* Felicia Hemans conferred beauty on the natural world through her emotional portrayal of them, just as the stars, by their reflection, beautify the sea.

[4] Hemans produced a volume of translations, *Translations from Camoens, and Other Poets, with Original Poetry* (1818), and experimented with foreign metres, subjects, and verse forms, in *Lays of Many Lands* (1826).

[5] *measures* metres.

[6] Landon alludes to the fact that Hemans's poems were especially popular in America. Collected editions of her poetry appeared in the USA in 1827–8, before appearing in England.

[7] *the wide Atlantic's younger daughters* American women.

[8] *endeavour* effort, pains.

They cannot paint the long sad hours passed only   45
    In vain regrets o'er what we feel we are.[9]
Alas, the kingdom of the lute is lonely –
    Cold is the worship coming from afar.

Yet what is mind in woman but revealing
    In sweet clear light the hidden world below,   50
By quicker fancies and a keener feeling
    Than those around, the cold and careless, know?
What is to feed such feeling, but to culture[10]
    A soil whence pain will never more depart?
The fable of Prometheus and the vulture[11]   55
    Reveals the poet's and the woman's heart.
Unkindly are they judged, unkindly treated
    By careless tongues and by ungenerous words,[12]
While cruel sneer and hard reproach repeated
    Jar the fine music of the spirit's chords.   60
Wert thou not weary, thou whose soothing numbers[13]
    Gave other lips the joy thine own had not?
Didst thou not welcome thankfully the slumbers
    Which closed around thy mourning human lot?

What on this earth could answer thy requiring,   65
    For earnest faith – for love, the deep and true,
The beautiful, which was thy soul's desiring,
    But only from thyself its being drew!
How is the warm and loving heart requited
    In this harsh world, where it awhile must dwell;   70
Its best affections wronged, betrayed and slighted –
    Such is the doom of those who love too well.
Better the weary dove should close its pinion,
    Fold up its golden wings and be at peace;
Enter, oh ladye, that serene dominion   75
    Where earthly cares and earthly sorrows cease.
Fame's troubled hour has cleared, and now replying,
    A thousand hearts their music ask of thine;
Sleep with a light, the lovely and undying,
    Around thy grave – a grave which is a shrine.   80

---

[9] *what we feel we are* perhaps an echo of Wordsworth, *Duddon Afterthought* 14: 'We feel that we are greater than we know'.

[10] *culture* cultivate.

[11] *The fable of Prometheus and the vulture* apparently a reference to the story of how Jupiter nailed Prometheus to a rock where, for 30,000 years, an eagle incessantly devoured his liver. Hercules finally freed him and killed the bird. Letitia means that woman's fate is, like Prometheus, forever to have her passions exposed and tormented.

[12] *By careless tongues and by ungenerous words* Letitia certainly experienced this in the wake of her scandalous associations with William Maginn and Daniel Maclise (see headnote).

[13] *numbers* poetry.

From The Works of L. E. Landon (Philadelphia, 1838)

AIREY FORCE[1]

Aye, underneath yon shadowy side
  I could be fain to fix my home,
Where dashes down the torrent's pride
  In sparkling wave, and silver foam.

No other sound is waking there   5
  But that perpetual voice which seems
Like spirit-music on the air,
  An echo from the world of dreams.

They were more wise in other days;
  Then turned the hermit to his cell   10
And left a world where all betrays,
  Apart with his own thoughts to dwell,

Content to curb the heart, to be
  Indifferent, quiet, mournful, cold
With hopes turned into memory,   15
  With feelings that had lost their hold.

Far better this than such vain life
  As is in crowded cities known,
Where care, repining, grief and strife
  Make every passing hour their own.   20

There by yon torrent's rushing wave
  I'd pass what yet of time remained,
And feel the quiet of the grave
  Long ere that grave itself were gained.

SCENES IN LONDON: PICCADILLY

The sun is on the crowded street,
  ·It kindles those old towers
Where England's noblest memories meet
  Of old historic hours.

Vast, shadowy, dark and indistinct,   5
  Tradition's giant fane

AIREY FORCE

[1] Aira Force, an impressive Lake District waterfall, is on the western shore of Ullswater, halfway between the head and foot of the lake. Landon probably did not know Wordsworth's famous *Airey-Force Valley*, composed September 1835, published 1842.

Whereto a thousand years are linked
  In one electric chain.

So stands it when the morning light
  First steals upon the skies,   10
And shadowed by the fallen night
  The sleeping city lies.

It stands with darkness round it cast,
  Touched by the first cold shine;
Vast, vague, and mighty as the past   15
  Of which it is the shrine.

'Tis lovely when the moonlight falls
  Around the sculptured stone,
Giving a softness to the walls
  Like love that mourns the gone.   20

Then comes the gentlest influence
  The human heart can know,
The mourning over those gone hence
  To the still dust below.

The smoke, the noise, the dust of day   25
  Have vanished from the scene;
The pale lamps[1] gleam with spirit ray
  O'er the park's sweeping green.

Sad shining on her lonely path,
  The moon's calm smile above   30
Seems as it lulled life's toil and wrath
  With universal love.

Past that still hour, and its pale moon,
  The city is alive;
It is the busy hour of noon   35
  When man must seek and strive.

The pressure of our actual life
  Is on the waking brow;
Labour and care, endurance, strife,
  These are around him now.   40

How wonderful the common street,
  Its tumult and its throng,

SCENES IN LONDON: PICCADILLY
[1] *lamps* oil lamps for illuminating London streets
were patented as early as 1685.

The hurrying of the thousand feet
That bear life's cares along.

How strongly is the present felt   45
With such a scene beside;
All sounds in one vast murmur melt
The thunder of the tide.

All hurry on – none pause to look
Upon another's face;   50
The present is an open book
None read, yet all must trace.

The poor man hurries on his race,
His daily bread to find;
The rich man has yet wearier chase,   55
For pleasure's hard to bind.[2]

All hurry, though it is to pass
For which they live so fast –
What doth the present but amass
The wealth that makes the past?   60

The past is round us, those old spires
That glimmer o'er our head;
Not from the present are their fires,
Their light is from the dead.

But for the past, the present's powers   65
Were waste of toil and mind,
But for those long and glorious hours
Which leave themselves behind.

THE PRINCESS VICTORIA[1]

A fair young face o'er which is only cast
The delicate hues of spring,
Though round her is the presence of the past,
And the stern future gathers darkly fast;
As yet no heavy shadow loads their wing.   5

A little while hast thou to be a child,
Thy lot is all too high;
Thy face is very fair, thine eyes are mild,

---

[2]   *bind* retain, keep.
THE PRINCESS VICTORIA
[1]   Princess Victoria (1819–1901) was Queen of the
United Kingdom of Great Britain and Ireland, 1837–

1901. By 1837 the monarchy had been brought into
disrepute; her reign was to restore its dignity, and
may even have saved the institution of the monarchy
from oblivion.

But duties on thine arduous path are piled –
A nation's hopes and fears blend with thy destiny.   10

Change is upon thy world – it may be thine
To soothe its troubled way,
To make thy throne a beacon and a shrine
Whence knowledge, power, and liberty may shine,
As yet they have not shone on mortal day.   15

There is much misery on this worn earth,
But much that may be spared;
Of great and generous thought there is no dearth,
And highest hopes of late have had their birth,
Hopes for the many, what the few have shared.   20

The wind that bears our flag[2] from soil to soil
Teaches us as it flies;
It carries in its breath a summer spoil,[3]
And seeds spring up to stimulate man's toil –
So should our mind spread round its rich supplies.   25

Thou royal child, the future is thine own,
May it be blessed in thee!
May peace that smiles on all be round thy throne,
And universal truth, whose light alone
Gives golden records unto history.   30

SCALE FORCE, CUMBERLAND

This cascade, distant about a mile and a half from the village of Buttermere, exceeds in extent of fall the renowned Niagara, yet, owing to a difficulty of access, it is frequently neglected by the tourist.

It sweeps, as sweeps an army
Adown the mountain-side,
With the voice of many thunders
Like the battle's sounding tide.

Yet the sky is blue above it,   5
And the dashing of the spray
Wears the colour of the rainbow
Upon an April day.

It rejoices in the sunshine
When after heavy rain   10

---

[2] *The wind that bears our flag* ships were the primary means of international trade.
[3] *spoil* reward, booty; Letitia is probably recalling *Paradise Lost* iv 156–8: '. . . now gentle gales dispense / Native perfumes, and whisper whence they stole / Those balmy spoils'.

It gathers the far waters
To dash upon the plain.

It is terrible yet lovely
Beneath the morning rays;
Like a dream of strength and beauty,   15
It haunted those who gaze.

We feel that it is glorious,
Its power is on the soul;
And lofty thoughts within us
Acknowledge its control.   20

A generous inspiration
Is on the outward world;
It waketh thoughts and feelings
In careless coldness furled.

To love and to admire   25
Seems natural to the heart;
Life's small and selfish interests
From such a scene depart.

From Laman Blanchard, Life and Literary Remains of L.E.L. (1841)

THE POET'S LOT

The poet's lovely faith creates
    The beauty he believes;
The light which on his footsteps waits,
    He from himself receives.

His lot may be a weary lot,   5
    His thrall a heavy thrall,
And cares and griefs the crowd know not,
    His heart may know them all.

But still he hath a mighty dower,
    The loveliness that throws   10
Over the common thought and hour
    The beauty of the rose.[1]

THE POET'S LOT
[1] There seems, in this stanza, to be a general reminiscence of Wordsworth's *Ode*, and perhaps an echo of ll. 10–11: 'The rainbow comes and goes / And lovely is the rose'.

DEATH IN THE FLOWER

'Tis a fair tree, the almond tree; there spring[1]
Shows the first promise of her rosy wreath,
Or ere the green leaves venture from the bud,
Those fragile blossoms light the winter bough
With delicate colours heralding the rose,   5
Whose own aurora[2] they might seem to be.
What lurks beneath their faint and lovely red?
What the dark spirit in those fairy flowers?
'Tis death!

EXPERIENCE TOO LATE

It is the past that maketh my despair;
The dark, the sad, the irrevocable past.
Alas, why should our lot in life be made
Before we know that life? Experience comes,
But comes too late. If I could now recall[1]   5
All that I now regret, how different
Would be my choice – at best a choice of ill,
But better than my miserable past.
Loathed yet despised, why must I think of it?

THE FAREWELL

Farewell,
Shadows and scenes that have, for many hours,
Been my companions; I part from ye like friends –
Dear and familiar ones – with deep sad thoughts,
And hopes, almost misgivings!   5

DEATH IN THE FLOWER
[1] The almond tree flowers in April.
[2] *aurora* dawn.

EXPERIENCE TOO LATE
[1] *recall* bring back, as at *Paradise Lost* ix 926: 'But
past who can recall, or done, undo?'

Index to Notes and Headnotes

Page numbers in **bold** denote author selections.

Index of Titles and First Lines

Romanticism: An Anthology Second Edition

Edited by *Duncan Wu*
University of Glasgow

In response to requests and suggestions from those who have adopted this anthology as a coursebook, the editor has redesigned it to make it even more useful to the teacher and student. Headnotes have been expanded and there are significantly more footnotes. Wordsworth's *Thirteen-Book Prelude* is replaced by the much shorter *Two-Part Prelude*, supplemented by well-chosen extracts from the thirteen-book poem. Several other key works, most notably by Byron, have also been added.

229 × 152 mm 1240 pages
0-631-20481-4   paperback   December 1997

Romantic Women Poets: An Anthology

Edited by *Duncan Wu*
University of Glasgow

Designed as a companion to *Romanticism: An Anthology*, this volume contains many complete and unabridged texts giving comprehensive coverage of the women poets of the period.

229 × 152 mm 672 pages
0-631-20329-X   hardback
0-631-20330-3   paperback   September 1997

A Companion to Romanticism

Edited by *Duncan Wu*
University of Glasgow

A Companion to Romanticism is a major introductory survey from an international assembly of scholars, writing new pieces specifically for a student readership, under the editorship of Duncan Wu. In a wide range of invitingly accessible chapters, it provides those new to the subject with key bearings and a foundation of study, while offering senior and graduate students a focus upon new developments and possible future directions.

246 × 171 mm 560 pages
0-631-19852-0   hardback   September 1997

Romanticism: The CD-ROM

Edited by *David S. Miall* and
Duncan Wu
University of Alberta; University of Glasgow

Teaching and research in Romanticism may now be revolutionized with *Romanticism: The CD-ROM*. This unique, easy-to-use electronic resource provides students and scholars of Romanticism with a huge range of fully linked texts and images from the Romantic period. Demonstration disc now available.

0-631-19944-6   September 1997

For further information on any of the above please contact: Louise Cashen, Blackwell Publishers, 108 Cowley Road, Oxford OX4 1JF. Fax: +44 (0)1865 791347.
E-mail: lcashen@blackwellpublishers.co.uk